Python GUI Programming with Tkinter

Second Edition

Design and build functional and user-friendly GUI applications

Alan D. Moore

BIRMINGHAM—MUMBAI

Python GUI Programming with Tkinter
Second Edition

Producer: Tushar Gupta

Acquisition Editor – Peer Reviews: Suresh Jain

Project Editor: Namrata Katare

Content Development Editor: Lucy Wan

Copy Editor: Safis Editing

Technical Editor: Karan Sonawane

Proofreader: Safis Editing

Indexer: Subalakshmi Govindhan

Presentation Designer: Ganesh Bhadwalkar

First published: May 2018
Second edition: October 2021

Production reference: 2281221

Published by Packt Publishing Ltd.
Livery Place
35 Livery Street
Birmingham
B3 2PB, UK.

ISBN 978-1-80181-592-5

www.packt.com

Contributors

About the author

Alan D. Moore has been coding in Python since 2005. He lives in Franklin, Tennessee, where he develops database apps for the local government. His technical interests include Python, JavaScript, Linux, and analog electronics. In his free time, he publishes coding videos on the YouTube channel *Alan D Moore Codes*, makes music, builds guitar effects, volunteers at his church and scout troop, and helps his wife raise their five children.

Profound thanks to Lucy and Alejandro, without whom this book would be riddled with errors; to Cara and the kids for their support and encouragement; and to the Python and Tcl/Tk communities for providing such great software. God bless you all!

About the reviewer

Alejandro Rodas de Paz is a computer engineer from Seville, Spain. He has developed several professional and academic Python projects, from artificial intelligence algorithms to DevOps scripting.

Prior to this publication, Alejandro wrote the Packt titles *Python Game Development by Example* and *Tkinter GUI Application Development Cookbook*. He also collaborated as a technical reviewer on the book *Tkinter GUI Application Development Hotshot*.

I would like to thank and dedicate this work to my sister Belen, whose next year will be the beginning of a long and joyful journey. Wish you all the best on this next chapter of life.

Table of Contents

Preface

Writing a book involves much more than the application of grammar and punctuation rules. In the same way, developing an application requires more than a knowledge of programming languages and library APIs. A mere mastery of syntax rules and function calls is not in itself sufficient for designing applications that empower users to perform work, safeguard valuable data, and produce flawless output. As programmers, we also need to be able to interpret user requests and expectations into effective interface designs and pick the best technologies to implement them. We need to be able to organize large code bases, test them, and maintain them in a way that keeps them manageable and free from careless errors.

This book aims to be much more than a reference manual for a particular GUI toolkit. As we walk through a fictitious workplace scenario, you will get a taste of what it's like to be an application programmer in a small office environment. In addition to learning Tkinter and a few other useful libraries, you will learn many of the skills you need to move from being a writer of short scripts to a writer of fully-featured graphical applications. By the time you've finished the book, you should feel confident that you can develop a simple but useful data-oriented application for a working environment.

Who this book is for

This book is for beginners who have learned the basics of Python but haven't written much beyond simple scripts. We'll walk you step-by-step through designing and creating a larger application, and we'll introduce you to skills that will help you advance as a programmer.

It's also aimed at those who have used Python for data science, web development, or system administration, but who now want to branch out into creating GUI applications. We'll go through the knowledge and skills required to create local GUI applications.

Finally, this book may also be useful for experienced Python programmers who just want to learn Tkinter, as much of the book details the finer points of using the Tkinter library.

What this book covers

Chapter 1, Introduction to Tkinter, introduces you to the basics of the Tkinter library and walks you through creating a basic Tkinter application. It will also introduce you to IDLE as an example of a Tkinter application.

Chapter 2, Designing GUI Applications, goes through the process of turning a set of user requirements into a design that we can implement.

Chapter 3, Creating Basic Forms with Tkinter and Ttk Widgets, shows you how to create a basic data entry application that appends entered data to a CSV file.

Chapter 4, Organizing Our Code with Classes, will introduce you to general object-oriented programming techniques as well as Tkinter-specific uses for classes that will make our GUI programs more maintainable and understandable.

Chapter 5, Reducing User Error with Validation and Automation, demonstrates how to automatically populate and validate data in our form's inputs.

Chapter 6, Planning for the Expansion of Our Application, familiarizes you with how to break a single-file script intelligently into multiple files, how to build a Python module that you can import, and how to separate the concerns of a large codebase to make it more manageable.

Chapter 7, Creating Menus with Menu and Tkinter Dialogs, outlines the creation of a main menu using Tkinter. It will also show the use of several built-in dialog types to implement common menu functionality.

Chapter 8, Navigating Records with Treeview and Notebook, details the construction of a data record navigation system using the Ttk Treeview and Notebook, as well as the conversion of our application from append-only to full read, write, and update capabilities.

Chapter 9, Improving the Look with Styles and Themes, informs you of how to change the colors, fonts, and widget styles of your application, and how to use them to make your application more usable and attractive.

Chapter 10, Maintaining Cross-Platform Compatibility, goes over Python and Tkinter techniques to keep your application running smoothly across Windows, macOS, and Linux systems.

Chapter 11, Creating Automated Tests with unittest, discusses how to verify your code with automated unit tests and integration tests.

Chapter 12, Improving Data Storage with SQL, takes you through the conversion of our application from CSV flat-file storage to SQL database storage. You'll learn all about SQL and relational data models as well.

Chapter 13, Connecting to the Cloud, covers how to work with network resources such as HTTP servers, REST services, and SFTP servers. You'll learn to interact with these services to download and upload data and files.

Chapter 14, Asynchronous Programming with Thread and Queue, explains how to use asynchronous and multithreaded programming to keep our application responsive during long-running processes.

Chapter 15, Visualizing Data Using the Canvas Widget, teaches you how to work with the Tkinter Canvas widget to create visualizations and animations. You'll also learn how to integrate Matplotlib charts and build a simple game.

Chapter 16, Packaging with setuptools and cxFreeze, explores preparing your Python application for distribution as a Python package or a standalone executable.

To get the most out of this book

This book expects that you know the basics of Python 3. You should know how to write and run simple scripts using built-in types and functions, how to define your own functions, and how to import modules from the standard library.

You can follow this book on a computer running a current version of Microsoft Windows, Apple macOS, or a distribution of GNU/Linux. Ensure that you have Python 3 and Tcl/Tk installed (*Chapter 1, Introduction to Tkinter,* contains instructions for Windows, macOS, and Linux) and that you have a code editing environment with which you are comfortable (we suggest IDLE since it comes with Python and uses Tkinter. We do not recommend the use of Jupyter, Spyder, or similar environments aimed at analytical Python rather than application development). In the later chapters, you'll need access to the internet so that you can install Python packages and the PostgreSQL database.

Download the example code files

The code bundle for the book is also hosted on GitHub at `https://github.com/ PacktPublishing/Python-GUI-Programming-with-Tkinter-2E`. We also have other code bundles from our rich catalog of books and videos available at `https://github. com/PacktPublishing/`. Check them out!

Download the color images

We also provide a PDF file that has color images of the screenshots/diagrams used in this book. You can download it here: https://static.packt-cdn.com/downloads/9781801815925_ColorImages.pdf.

Conventions used

There are a number of text conventions used throughout this book.

CodeInText: Indicates code words in text, database table names, folder names, filenames, file extensions, pathnames, dummy URLs, user input, and Twitter handles. For example: "Save the code in solve_the_worlds_problems.py and execute it by typing python solve_the_worlds_problems.py at a terminal prompt."

A block of code is set as follows:

```
import tkinter as tk

root = tk.TK()
def solve():
  raise NotImplemented("Sorry!")
tk.Button(
  root, text="Solve the world's problems", command=solve
).pack()
root.mainloop()
```

When we wish to draw your attention to a particular part of a code block, especially to indicate changes to existing code, the relevant lines or items are set in bold:

```
import tkinter as tk
from tkinter import messagebox

root = tk.TK()
def solve():
  messagebox.showinfo('The answer?', 'Bananas?')
tk.Button(
  root, text="Solve the world's problems", command=solve
).pack()
root.mainloop()
```

Note that all Python code in the book uses 2-space indents rather than the conventional 4-space indents.

Any command-line input or output is written with a $ indicating the prompt, as follows:

```
$ mkdir Bananas
$ cp plantains.txt Bananas/
```

Command line input intended for the Python shell or REPL is printed with a prompt of >>>, like so:

```
>>> print('This should be run in a Python shell')
'This should be run in a Python shell'
```

Expected output from the shell is printed on a line with no prompt.

Bold: Indicates a new term, an important word, or words that you see on the screen, for example, in menus or dialog boxes. For example: "Select **System info** from the **Administration** panel."

> Warnings or important notes appear like this.

> Tips and tricks appear like this.

Executing Python and pip

When we need to instruct the reader to execute a Python script in this book, we indicate a command line such as the following:

```
$ python myscript.py
```

Depending on your operating system or Python configuration, the python command may execute Python 2.x rather than Python 3.x. You can verify this by running the following command:

```
$ python --version
Python 3.9.7
```

If this command outputs Python 2 rather than 3 on your system, you will need to alter any `python` commands so that your code is executed in Python 3. Typically, that means using the `python3` command instead, like so:

```
$ python3 myscript.py
```

The same caveat applies to the `pip` command used to install libraries from the Python Package Index. You may need to use the `pip3` command instead to install libraries to your Python 3 environment, for example:

```
$ pip3 install --user requests
```

Get in touch

Feedback from our readers is always welcome.

General feedback: Email `feedback@packtpub.com`, and mention the book's title in the subject of your message. If you have questions about any aspect of this book, please email us at `questions@packtpub.com`.

Errata: Although we have taken every care to ensure the accuracy of our content, mistakes do happen. If you have found a mistake in this book, we would be grateful if you would report this to us. Please visit `http://www.packtpub.com/submit-errata`, selecting your book, clicking on the Errata Submission Form link, and entering the details.

Piracy: If you come across any illegal copies of our works in any form on the Internet, we would be grateful if you would provide us with the location address or website name. Please contact us at `copyright@packtpub.com` with a link to the material.

If you are interested in becoming an author: If there is a topic that you have expertise in and you are interested in either writing or contributing to a book, please visit `http://authors.packtpub.com`.

Reviews

Please leave a review. Once you have read and used this book, why not leave a review on the site that you purchased it from? Potential readers can then see and use your unbiased opinion to make purchase decisions, we at Packt can understand what you think about our products, and our authors can see your feedback on their book. Thank you!

For more information about Packt, please visit `packtpub.com`.

Share Your Thoughts

Once you've read *Python GUI Programming with Tkinter, Second Edition*, we'd love to hear your thoughts! Scan the QR code below to go straight to the Amazon review page for this book and share your feedback.

https://packt.link/r/1801815925

Your review is important to us and the tech community and will help us make sure we're delivering excellent quality content.

1

Introduction to Tkinter

Welcome, Python coder! If you've learned the basics of Python and want to start designing powerful GUI applications, this book is for you.

By now, you have no doubt experienced the power and simplicity of Python. Perhaps you've written web services, performed data analysis, or administered servers. Perhaps you've written a game, automated routine tasks, or simply played around with code. But now you're ready to tackle the GUI.

With so much emphasis on web, mobile, and server-side programming, the development of simple desktop GUI applications seems increasingly like a lost art; many otherwise experienced developers have never learned to create one. What a tragedy! Desktop computers still play a vital role in work and home computing, and the ability to build simple, functional applications for this ubiquitous platform should be a part of every software developer's toolbox. Fortunately, for Python coders, that ability is well within reach thanks to Tkinter.

In this chapter, you will cover the following topics:

- In *Introducing Tkinter and Tk*, you'll learn about Tkinter, a fast, fun, easy-to-learn GUI library built in to the Python Standard Library; and IDLE, an editor and development environment written in Tkinter.

- In *An overview of basic Tkinter*, you'll learn the basics of Tkinter with a "Hello World" program and create a Survey application.

Introducing Tkinter and Tk

The Tk widget library originates from the **Tool Command Language (Tcl)** programming language. Tcl and Tk were created by John Ousterhout while he was a professor at Berkeley in the late 1980s as an easier way to program the engineering tools being used at the university. Because of its speed and relative simplicity, Tcl/Tk rapidly grew in popularity among academic, engineering, and Unix programmers. Much like Python itself, Tcl/Tk originated on the Unix platform and only later migrated to macOS and Windows. Tk's practical intent and Unix roots still inform its design today, and its simplicity compared to other toolkits is still a major strength.

Tkinter is a Python interface to the Tk GUI library and has been a part of the Python standard library since 1994 with the release of Python version 1.1, making it the *de-facto* GUI library for Python. Documentation for Tkinter, along with links for further study, can be found in the standard library documentation at `https://docs.python.org/3/library/tkinter.html`.

Choosing Tkinter

Python coders who want to build a GUI have several toolkit options to choose from; unfortunately, Tkinter is often maligned or ignored as a legacy option. To be fair, it's not a glamorous technology that you can describe in trendy buzzwords and glowing hype. However, Tkinter is not only adequate for a wide variety of applications but also has some advantages that can't be ignored:

- **Tkinter is in the standard library**: With few exceptions, Tkinter is available wherever Python is available. There is no need to install pip, create virtual environments, compile binaries, or search the web for installation packages. For simple projects that need to be done quickly, this is a clear advantage.

- **Tkinter is stable**: While Tkinter development has not stopped, it is slow and evolutionary. The API has been stable for years, the changes mainly being additional functionality and bug fixes. Your Tkinter code will likely run unaltered for years or decades to come.

- **Tkinter is only a GUI toolkit**: Unlike some other GUI libraries, Tkinter doesn't have its own threading library, network stack, or filesystem API. It relies on regular Python libraries for such things, so it's perfect for applying a GUI to existing Python code.

- **Tkinter is simple and no-nonsense**: Tkinter is very basic and to-the-point; it can be used effectively in both procedural and object-oriented GUI designs. To use Tkinter, you don't have to learn hundreds of widget classes, a markup or templating language, a new programming paradigm, client-server technologies, or a different programming language.

Tkinter is not perfect, of course. It also has some disadvantages:

- **Tkinter's default look and feel is dated**: Tkinter's default appearance has long lagged behind current trends, and it still bears a few artifacts from the 1990s Unix world. While it lacks niceties like animated widgets, gradients, or scalable graphics, it has nevertheless improved a great deal in the last few years, thanks to updates in Tk itself and the addition of themed widget libraries. We'll learn how to fix or avoid some of Tkinter's more archaic defaults throughout the book.

- **Tkinter lacks more complex widgets**: Tkinter is missing advanced widgets like rich text editors, 3D graphics embedding, HTML viewers, or specialized input widgets. As we'll see later in this book, Tkinter gives us the ability to create complex widgets by customizing and combining its simple ones.

Tkinter might be the wrong choice for a game UI or slick commercial application; however, for data-driven applications, simple utilities, configuration dialogs, and other business logic applications, Tkinter offers all that is needed and more. In this book we're going to be working through the development of data entry application for a workplace environment, something that Tkinter can handle admirably.

Installing Tkinter

Tkinter is included in the Python standard library for the Windows and macOS distributions. So, if you have installed Python on these platforms using the official installers, you don't need to do anything to install Tkinter.

However, we're going to be exclusively focused on Python 3.9 for this book; so, you need to make sure that you have this version or later installed.

Installing Python 3.9 on Windows

You can obtain Python 3 installers for Windows from the python.org website by performing the following steps:

1. Go to https://www.python.org/downloads/windows.
2. Select the latest Python 3 release. At the time of writing, the latest version is 3.9.2.
3. Under the **Files** section, select the Windows executable installer appropriate to your system's architecture (x86 for 32-bit Windows, x86-64 for 64-bit Windows; if you're unsure, x86 will work on either).
4. Launch the downloaded installer.

5. Click on **Customize installation**. Make sure the **tcl/tk and IDLE** option is checked (it should be by default).

6. Continue through the installer with all defaults.

Installing Python 3 on macOS

As of this writing, macOS ships with Python 2.7 built in. However, Python 2 was officially deprecated in 2020, and the code in this book will not work with it, so macOS users will need to install Python 3 to follow this book.

Follow this procedure to install Python3 on macOS:

1. Go to `https://www.python.org/downloads/mac-osx/`.

2. Select the latest Python 3 release. At the time of writing, the latest version is 3.9.2.

3. Under the **Files** section, select and download the macOS 64-bit/32-bit installer.

4. Launch the `.pkg` file that you've downloaded and follow the steps of the install wizard, selecting defaults.

Installing Python 3 and Tkinter on Linux

Most Linux distributions include both Python 2 and Python 3; however, Tkinter is not always bundled with it or installed by default. To find out if Tkinter is installed, open a Terminal and try the following command:

```
$ python3 -m tkinter
```

This should open a simple window showing some information about Tkinter. If you get `ModuleNotFoundError` instead, you will need to use your package manager to install your distribution's Tkinter package for Python 3. In most major distributions, including Debian, Ubuntu, Fedora, and openSUSE, this package is called `python3-tk`.

Introducing IDLE

IDLE is an integrated development environment that is bundled with the official Python software distributions for Windows and macOS (it's readily available in most Linux distributions as well, usually as `idle` or `idle3`).

IDLE is written in Python using Tkinter, and it provides us with not only an editing environment for Python but also a great example of Tkinter in action. So, while IDLE's rudimentary feature set may not be considered professional grade by experienced Python coders, and while you may already have a preferred environment for writing Python code, I encourage you to spend some time using IDLE as you go through this book.

IDLE has two primary modes: shell mode and editor mode. We'll take a look at those in this section.

Using the shell mode of IDLE

When you launch IDLE, you begin in shell mode, which is simply a Python **Read-Evaluate-Print-Loop** (**REPL**) similar to what you get when you type python in a Terminal window.

You can see IDLE's shell mode in this screenshot:

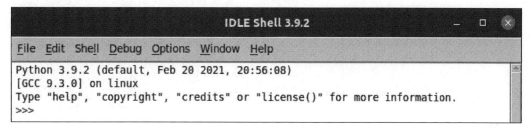

Figure 1.1: IDLE's shell mode

IDLE's shell has some nice features that you don't get from the command-line REPL, like syntax highlighting and tab completion. The REPL is essential to the Python development process, as it gives you the ability to test code in real time and inspect classes and APIs without having to write complete scripts. We'll use the shell mode in later chapters to explore the features and behaviors of modules. If you don't have a shell window open, you can open one by clicking on **Run | Python Shell** in the IDLE menu.

Using the editor mode of IDLE

Editor mode is for creating Python script files, which you can later run. When the book tells you to create a new file, this is the mode you'll use. To open a new file in the editor mode, simply navigate to **File | New File** in the menu or hit *Ctrl + N* on the keyboard.

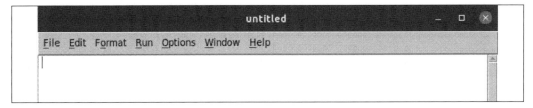

Figure 1.2: IDLE's file editor

You can run your script without leaving IDLE by hitting the *F5* key in the editor mode; IDLE will open a shell-mode window to execute the script and display the output.

IDLE as a Tkinter example

Before we start coding with Tkinter, let's take a quick look at what you can do with it by inspecting some of IDLE's UI. Navigate to **Options | Configure IDLE** from the main menu to open IDLE's configuration settings. Here you can change IDLE's fonts, colors and theme, keyboard shortcuts, and default behaviors, as shown in this screenshot:

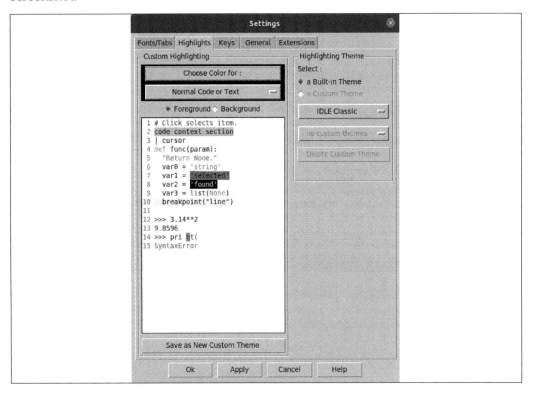

Figure 1.3: IDLE configuration settings

Consider some of the following components that make up this user interface:

- There are drop-down menus that allow you to select between large sets of options.
- There are checkable buttons that allow you to select between small sets of options.
- There are many push buttons that you can click on to execute actions.
- There is a text window that can display multi-colored text.
- There are labeled frames that contain groups of components.
- There are tabs across the top of the screen to select different sections of the configuration.

In Tkinter (as in most GUI libraries), each of these components is known as a **widget**; we're going to meet these widgets and more throughout this book and learn how to use them as they've been used here. We'll begin, however, with something much simpler.

Creating a Tkinter Hello World

One of the grand traditions in any programming language or library is to create a "Hello World" program: that is, a program that displays Hello World and exits. Let's walk through creating a "Hello World" application for Tkinter and talk about the pieces of it along the way.

First, create a new file called hello_tkinter.py in IDLE or your favorite editor, and enter the following code:

```
"""Hello World application for Tkinter"""
import tkinter as tk
```

The first line is called a **docstring**, and every Python script should start with one. At a minimum, it should give the name of the program but can also include details about how to use it, who wrote it, and what it requires.

The second line imports the tkinter module into our program. Although Tkinter is in the standard library, we have to import it before we can use any of its classes or functions.

Sometimes, you may see this import written as from tkinter import *. That approach is called a **wildcard import**, and it results in all the objects being brought into the global **namespace**. While popular in tutorials for its simplicity, it's a bad idea in actual code as there is a possibility of a collision between our own variable names and all names in the tkinter module, which can cause subtle bugs.

To avoid this, we're going to keep tkinter in its own **namespace**; however, to keep the code concise, we'll alias tkinter to tk. This convention will be used throughout the book.

Every Tkinter program must have exactly one **root window**, which represents both the top-level window of our application, and the application itself. Let's create our root window, like so:

```
root = tk.Tk()
```

The root window is an instance of the Tk class. We create it by calling Tk() as we've done here. This object must exist before we can create any other Tkinter objects, and when it is destroyed, the application quits.

Now, let's create a widget to put in our window:

```
label = tk.Label(root, text="Hello World")
```

This is a Label widget, which is just a panel that can display some text. The first argument to any Tkinter widget is always the **parent widget** (sometimes called **master widget**); in this case, we've passed in a reference to our root window. The parent widget is the widget on which our Label will be placed, so this Label will be directly on the root window of the application. Widgets in a Tkinter GUI are arranged in a hierarchy, each widget being contained by another all the way up to the root window.

We've also passed in a keyword argument, text. This argument, of course, defines the text that will be placed on the widget. For most Tkinter widgets, the majority of configuration is done using keyword arguments like this.

Now that we've created a widget, we need to actually place it on the GUI:

```
label.pack()
```

The pack() method of the Label widget is called a **geometry manager method**. Its job is to determine how the widget will be attached to its parent widget, and to draw it there. Without this call, your widget would exist but you wouldn't see it anywhere on the window. pack() is one of three geometry managers, which we'll learn more about in the next section.

The last line of our program looks like this:

```
root.mainloop()
```

This line starts our application's **event loop**. The event loop is an infinite loop that continually processes any **events** that happen during the execution of the program. Events can be things like keystrokes, mouse clicks, or other user-generated activity. This loop runs until the program exits, so any code after this line will not be run until the main window is closed. For this reason, this line is usually the last one in any Tkinter program.

Run the program in IDLE by hitting *F5*, or in your Terminal by typing the following command:

```
$ python hello_tkinter.py
```

You should see a very tiny window pop up with the text **Hello World** as shown here:

Figure 1.4: Our "Hello World" application

Feel free to play around with this script by adding more widgets before the `root.mainloop()` call. You can add more `Label` objects, or try some `Button` (which creates a clickable button) or `Entry` (which creates a text field) widgets. Just like `Label`, these widgets are initialized with a parent object (use `root`) and a `text` parameter. Don't forget to call `pack()` on each widget to place them on the root window.

> Example code for all chapters in this book can be downloaded from `https://github.com/PacktPublishing/Python-GUI-Programming-with-Tkinter-2E`. You may want to download these now so you can follow along.

When you're ready, move on to the next section where we'll create a more interesting application.

An overview of basic Tkinter

As exciting as it may be to see that first GUI window pop up on the screen, "Hello World" is not a terribly interesting application. Let's start again and dig a little deeper into Tkinter as we build a slightly larger program. Since the next chapter will see you landing a job at a fictitious agricultural laboratory studying fruit plants, let's create a little program to gauge your opinions about bananas.

Building a GUI with Tkinter widgets

Start a new file in your editor called banana_survey.py, and begin by importing tkinter like so:

```
# banana_survey.py
"""A banana preferences survey written in Python with Tkinter"""

import tkinter as tk
```

As with hello_tkinter.py, we need to create a root window before we can create any widgets or other Tkinter objects:

```
root = tk.Tk()
```

Once again, we've called this object root. The root window can be configured in various ways; for example, we can give it a window title or set its size like so:

```
# set the title
root.title('Banana interest survey')
# set the root window size
root.geometry('640x480+300+300')
root.resizable(False, False)
```

The title() method sets our window title (that is, the name that shows up in the task manager and in the window decorations), while geometry() sets the window size. In this case, we're telling the root window to be 640 by 480 pixels. The +300+300 sets the position of the window on the screen — in this case, 300 pixels from the top and 300 pixels from the left (the position portion is optional, if you only care about the size). Notice that the argument to geometry() is a string. In Tcl/Tk, every argument is treated as a string. Since Tkinter is just a wrapper that passes arguments on to Tcl/Tk, we'll often find that strings are used to configure Tkinter objects – even when we might expect to use integers or floats.

The resizable() method sets whether or not our window can be resized horizontally and vertically, respectively. True means the window can be resized in that direction, False means its dimension is fixed. In this case, we want to prevent the resizing of the window so that we don't have to worry about making the layout flexible to window size changes.

Now let's start adding widgets to our survey. We've already met the Label widget, so let's add one:

```
title = tk.Label(
    root,
```

```
    text='Please take the survey',
    font=('Arial 16 bold'),
    bg='brown',
    fg='#FF0'
)
```

As we saw in our "Hello World" example, the first argument passed to any Tkinter widget is the **parent** widget on which the new widget will be placed. In this case, we'll be placing this `Label` widget on the `root` window. The remaining arguments to a widget are specified as keyword arguments. Here, we've specified the following:

- `text`, which is the text the label will display.
- `font`, which specifies the family, size, and weight of the font used to display the text. Notice again that the font settings are specified as a simple string, just as our `geometry` settings were.
- `bg`, which sets the background color for the widget. We've used a color name here; Tkinter recognizes a great many color names, similar to those used by CSS or X11.
- `fg`, which sets the foreground (text) color for the widget. In this case, we've specified a short hexadecimal string, in which the three characters represent the red, green, and blue values respectively. We can also use a six-character hex string (for example, `#FFE812`) for finer-grained control over the color.

In *Chapter 9, Improving the Look with Styles and Themes*, we'll learn more sophisticated ways to set up fonts and colors, but this will work just fine for now.

Tkinter has many interactive widgets for data entry, of course, the simplest being the `Entry` widget:

```
name_label = tk.Label(root, text='What is your name?')
name_inp = tk.Entry(root)
```

The `Entry` widget is just a simple text-input box designed for a single line of text. Most input widgets in Tkinter do not include a label of any kind, so we've added one to make it clear to our user what the entry box is for.

One exception to that is the `Checkbutton` widget, which we'll create next:

```
eater_inp = tk.Checkbutton(
    root,
    text='Check this box if you eat bananas'
)
```

A `Checkbutton` creates a check box input; it includes a label that sits next to the box, and we can set its text using the `text` argument.

For entering numbers, Tkinter provides the `Spinbox` widget. Let's add one:

```
num_label = tk.Label(
  root,
  text='How many bananas do you eat per day?'
)
num_inp = tk.Spinbox(root, from_=0, to=1000, increment=1)
```

A `Spinbox` is like an `Entry`, but features arrow buttons that can increment and decrement the number in the box. We've used several arguments to configure it here:

- The `from_` and `to` arguments set the minimum and maximum values that the buttons will decrement or increment to, respectively. Notice that `from_` has an extra underscore at the end; this is not a typo! Since `from` is a Python keyword (used in importing modules), it can't be used as a variable name, so the Tkinter authors chose to use `from_` instead.

- The `increment` argument sets how much the arrow buttons will increase or decrease the number.

Tkinter has several widgets that allow you to choose from preset selection values; one of the simplest is `Listbox`, which looks like this:

```
color_label = tk.Label(
  root,
  text='What is the best color for a banana?'
)
color_inp = tk.Listbox(root, height=1)  # Only show selected item
# add choices
color_choices = (
  'Any', 'Green', 'Green-Yellow',
  'Yellow', 'Brown Spotted', 'Black'
  )
for choice in color_choices:
  color_inp.insert(tk.END, choice)
```

The `Listbox` takes a `height` argument that specifies how many lines are visible; by default the box is big enough to show all the options. We've changed that to 1 so that only the currently selected option is visible. The others can be accessed using the arrow keys.

To add options to the box, we need to call its `insert()` method and add each option one at a time. We've done that here using a `for` loop to save repetitive coding. The first argument to `insert` specifies where we want to insert the option; note that we've used a special **constant** provided by `tkinter`, `tk.END`. This is one of many special constants defined in Tkinter for certain configuration values. In this case, `tk.END` means the end of the widget, so that each choice that we insert will be placed at the end.

Another way to let a user select between a small number of options is the `Radiobutton` widget; these are like `Checkbutton` widgets, but, similar to the mechanical preset buttons in (very, very old) car radios, they only allow one to be checked at a time. Let's create a few `Radiobutton` widgets:

```python
plantain_label = tk.Label(root, text='Do you eat plantains?')
plantain_frame = tk.Frame(root)
plantain_yes_inp = tk.Radiobutton(plantain_frame, text='Yes')
plantain_no_inp = tk.Radiobutton(plantain_frame, text='Ewww, no!')
```

Notice what we've done here with `plantain_frame`: we've created a `Frame` object and used it as the parent widget for each of the `Radiobutton` widgets. A `Frame` is simply a blank panel with nothing on it, and it's useful for organizing our layout hierarchically. We'll use `Frame` widgets quite often in this book for keeping groups of widgets together.

`Entry` widgets work fine for single-line strings, but how about multi-line strings? For those, Tkinter offers us the `Text` widget, which we create like this:

```python
banana_haiku_label = tk.Label(
    root,
    text='Write a haiku about bananas'
)
banana_haiku_inp = tk.Text(root, height=3)
```

The `Text` widget is capable of much more than just multi-line text, and we'll explore a few of its more advanced capabilities in *Chapter 9, Improving the Look with Styles and Themes*. For now, though, we'll just use it for text.

Our GUI would not be complete without a submit button for our survey, which is provided by the `Button` class, like so:

```python
submit_btn = tk.Button(root, text='Submit Survey')
```

We'll use this button to submit the survey and display some output. What widget could we use to display that output? It turns out that `Label` objects are useful for more than just static messages; we can use them to display messages at runtime as well.

Let's add one for our program output:

```
output_line = tk.Label(root, text='', anchor='w', justify='left')
```

Here we've created the `Label` widget with no text (since we have no output yet). We're also using a couple of additional arguments for `Label`:

- `anchor` determines which side of the widget the text will be stuck to if the widget is wider than the text. Tkinter sometimes uses cardinal directions (North, South, East, and West) abbreviated to their first letter whenever it needs to specify a side of a widget; in this case, the string `'w'` indicates the West (or left) side of the widget.
- `justify` determines which side the text will align to when there are multiple lines of code. Unlike `anchor`, it uses conventional `'left'`, `'right'`, and `'center'` options.

`anchor` and `justify` may seem redundant, but they have slightly different behavior. In a multiline text situation, the text could be aligned to the center of each line, but the whole collection of lines could be anchored to the west side of the widget, for example. In other words, `anchor` affects the whole block of text with respect to the containing widget, while `justify` affects the individual lines of text with respect to the other lines.

Tkinter has many more widgets, and we'll meet many of them throughout the remainder of the book.

Arranging our widgets with geometry managers

If you were to add `root.mainloop()` to this script and execute it as-is, you would see… a blank window. Hmmm, what happened to all those widgets we just created? Well, you may remember from `hello_tkinter.py` that we need to use a geometry manager like `pack()` to actually place them somewhere on their parent widgets.

Tkinter has three geometry manager methods available:

- `pack()` is the oldest, and simply adds widgets to one of the four sides of a window sequentially.
- `grid()` is newer and preferred, and allows you to place widgets within a 2-dimensional grid table.

- `place()` is a third option, which allows you to put widgets at specific pixel coordinates. It is not recommended, as it responds poorly to changes in window sizes, font sizes, and screen resolution, so we won't be using it in this book.

While `pack()` is certainly fine for simple layouts involving a handful of widgets, it doesn't scale so well to more complex layouts without an inordinate amount of `Frame` widget nesting. For this reason, most Tkinter programmers rely on the more modern `grid()` geometry manager. As the name suggests, `grid()` allows you to lay out widgets on a 2-dimensional grid, much like a spreadsheet document or HTML table. In this book, we'll focus primarily on `grid()`.

Let's start laying out the widgets of our GUI using `grid()`, beginning with the `title` label:

```
title.grid()
```

By default, a call to `grid()` will place the widget in the *first column* (column 0) of the *next empty row*. Thus, if we were to simply call `grid()` on the next widget, it would end up directly under the first. However, we can also be explicit about this using the `row` and `column` arguments, like so:

```
name_label.grid(row=1, column=0)
```

Rows and columns count from the top-left corner of the widget, starting with 0. Thus, `row=1, column=0` places the widget in the second row at the first column. If we want an additional column, all we need to do is place a widget in it, like so:

```
name_inp.grid(row=1, column=1)
```

The grid automatically expands whenever we add a widget to a new row or column. If a widget is larger than the current width of the column, or height of the row, all the cells in that column or row are expanded to accommodate it. We can tell a widget to span multiple columns or multiple rows using the `columnspan` and `rowspan` arguments, respectively. For example, it might be nice to have our title span the width of the form, so let's amend it accordingly:

```
title.grid(columnspan=2)
```

As columns and rows expand, the widgets do not expand with them by default. If we want them to expand, we need to use the `sticky` argument, like this:

```
eater_inp.grid(row=2, columnspan=2, sticky='we')
```

sticky tells Tkinter to stick the sides of the widget to the sides of its containing cell so that the widget will stretch as the cell expands. Like the anchor argument we learned about above, sticky takes cardinal directions: n, s, e, and w. In this case we've specified West and East, which will cause the widget to stretch horizontally if the column expands further.

As an alternative to the strings, we can also use Tkinter's constants as arguments to sticky:

```
num_label.grid(row=3, sticky=tk.W)
num_inp.grid(row=3, column=1, sticky=(tk.W + tk.E))
```

There is no real difference between using constants and string literals as far as Tkinter is concerned; however, the advantage of using constants is that your editing software can more easily identify if you've used a constant that doesn't exist than an invalid string.

The grid() method allows us to add padding to our widgets as well, like so:

```
color_label.grid(row=4, columnspan=2, sticky=tk.W, pady=10)
color_inp.grid(row=5, columnspan=2, sticky=tk.W + tk.E, padx=25)
```

padx and pady indicate *external* padding – that is, they will expand the containing cell, but not the widget. ipadx and ipady, on the other hand, indicate *internal* padding. Specifying these arguments will expand the widget itself (and consequently the containing cell).

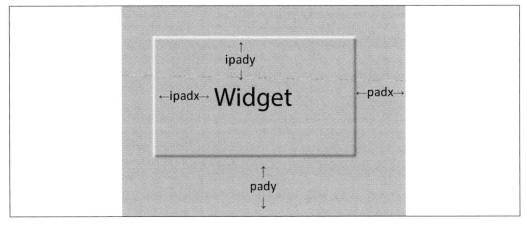

Figure 1.5: Internal padding (ipadx, ipady) versus external padding (padx, pady)

Tkinter does not allow us to mix geometry managers on the same parent widget; once we've called grid() on any child widget, a call to the pack() or place() method on a sibling widget will generate an error, and vice versa.

We can, however, use a different geometry manager on the sibling widget's children. For example, we can use `pack()` to place the child widgets on the `plantain_frame` widgets, as shown here:

```
plantain_yes_inp.pack(side='left', fill='x', ipadx=10, ipady=5)
plantain_no_inp.pack(side='left', fill='x', ipadx=10, ipady=5)
plantain_label.grid(row=6, columnspan=2, sticky=tk.W)
plantain_frame.grid(row=7, columnspan=2, stick=tk.W)
```

The `plantain_label` and `plantain_frame` widgets, as children of `root`, must be placed with `grid()`; `plantain_yes` and `plantain_no` are children of `plantain_frame`, though, so we can choose to use `pack()` (or `place()`) on them if we wish. The following diagram illustrates this:

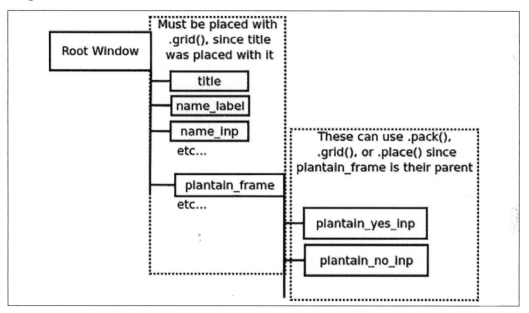

Figure 1.6: Each widget's children must use the same geometry manager method

This ability to choose the geometry manager for each container widget gives us enormous flexibility in how we lay out a GUI. While the `grid()` method is certainly capable of specifying most layouts, there are times when the semantics of `pack()` or `place()` make more sense for a piece of our interface.

 Although the `pack()` geometry manager shares some arguments with `grid()`, like `padx` and `pady`, most of the arguments are different. For example, the `side` argument used in the example determines which side widgets will be packed from, and the `fill` argument determines on which axis the widget will expand.

Let's add the last few widgets to our window:

```
banana_haiku_label.grid(row=8, sticky=tk.W)
banana_haiku_inp.grid(row=9, columnspan=2, sticky='NSEW')
submit_btn.grid(row=99)
output_line.grid(row=100, columnspan=2, sticky='NSEW')
```

Note that we've stuck the Text widget (banana_haiku_inp) to all four sides of its container. This will cause it to expand both vertically and horizontally as the grid is stretched. Also notice that we've skipped to rows 99 and 100 for the last two widgets. Remember that unused rows are collapsed into nothing, so by skipping rows or columns we can leave space for future expansion of our GUI.

By default, Tkinter will make our window just large enough to contain all the widgets we place on it; but what happens if our window (or containing frame) becomes larger than the space required by our widgets? By default, the widgets will remain as they are, stuck to the upper-left side of the application. If we want the GUI to expand and fill the space available, we have to tell the parent widget which columns and rows of the grid will expand. We do this by using the parent widget's columnconfigure() and rowconfigure() methods.

For example, if we want our second column (the one containing most of the input widgets) to expand into unused space, we can do this:

```
root.columnconfigure(1, weight=1)
```

The first argument specifies which column (counting from 0) we want to affect. The keyword argument weight takes an integer which will determine how much of the extra space the column will get. With only one column specified, any value greater than 0 will cause that column to expand into the leftover space.

The rowconfigure() method works the same way:

```
root.rowconfigure(99, weight=2)
root.rowconfigure(100, weight=1)
```

This time, we've given two rows a weight value, but note that row 99 is given a weight of 2 while 100 is given a weight of 1. In this configuration, any extra vertical space will be divided between rows 99 and 100, but row 99 will get twice as much of it as row 100.

As you can see, using a combination of grid(), pack() sub-frames, and some careful planning, we can achieve complex GUI layouts fairly easily in Tkinter.

Making the form actually do something

We've got a nice form all laid out now, complete with a submit button; so how do we make it actually do something? If you have only written procedural code in the past, you may be confused about how the flow of code works in a GUI application. Unlike a procedural script, the GUI cannot simply execute all the code from top to bottom. Instead, it has to respond to user actions, such as a button click or a keystroke, whenever and in whatever order they happen. Such actions are known as **events**. To make the program respond to an event, we need to **bind** the event to a function, which we call a **callback**.

There are a few ways to bind events to callback functions in Tkinter; for a button, the simplest is to configure its `command` attribute, like so:

```
submit_btn.configure(command=on_submit)
```

The `command` argument can be specified when creating a widget (for example, `submit_btn = Button(root, command=on_submit)`), or after creation of the widget using its `configure()` method. `configure()` allows you to change a widget's configuration after it's created, by passing in arguments just as you would when creating the widget.

In either case, `command` specifies a *reference* to a callback function to be called when the button is clicked. Note that we do not put parentheses after the function name here; doing so would cause the function to be called and its return value would be assigned to `command`. We only want a reference to the function here.

The callback function needs to exist before we can pass it to `command`. So, before the call to `submit_btn.configure()`, let's create the `on_submit()` function:

```python
def on_submit():
    """To be run when the user submits the form"""
    pass

submit_btn.configure(command=on_submit)
```

It is conventional to name callback functions in the format `on_<event_name>` when they are specifically created to respond to a particular event. However, it's not required, nor always appropriate (for example, if a function is a callback for many events).

A more powerful method of binding events is to use the widget's `bind()` method, which we will discuss in more detail in *Chapter 6, Planning for the Expansion of Our Application*.

Our on_submit() callback is rather boring at the moment, so let's make it better. Remove the pass statement and add in this code:

```python
def on_submit():
    """To be run when the user submits the form"""

    name = name_inp.get()
    number = num_inp.get()

    selected_idx = color_inp.curselection()
    if selected_idx:
        color = color_inp.get(selected_idx)
    else:
        color = ''
    haiku = banana_haiku_inp.get('1.0', tk.END)

    message = (
        f'Thanks for taking the survey, {name}.\n'
        f'Enjoy your {number} {color} bananas!'
    )
    output_line.configure(text=message)
    print(haiku)
```

The first thing we'll do in this function is retrieve values from some of the inputs. For many inputs, the get() method is used to retrieve the current value of the widget. Note that this value will be returned as a string, even in the case of our Spinbox.

For our list widget, color, things are more complicated. Its get() method requires an index number for a choice, and returns the text for that index number. We can use the widget's curselection() method to get the selected index. If there are no selections made, the selected index will be an empty tuple. In that case, we'll just set color to an empty string. If there is a selection, we can pass the value to get().

Getting data from the Text widget is again slightly different. Its get() method requires two values, one for a starting location and another for an ending location. These follow a special syntax (which we'll discuss in *Chapter 3, Creating Basic Forms with Tkinter and Ttk Widgets*), but basically 1.0 means the first character of the first line, and tk.END is a constant that represents the end of the Text widget.

 Retrieving data from our Checkbutton and Radiobutton is not possible without using Tkinter control variables, which we'll talk about in the section below, *Handling data with Tkinter control variables*.

Having gathered the data, our callback ends by updating the text property of the output Label widget with a string containing some of the entered data, then printing the user's haiku to the console.

To make this script runnable, finish with this line:

```
root.mainloop()
```

This executes the event loop of the script so that Tkinter can begin responding to events. Save your script and execute it, and you should see something like this:

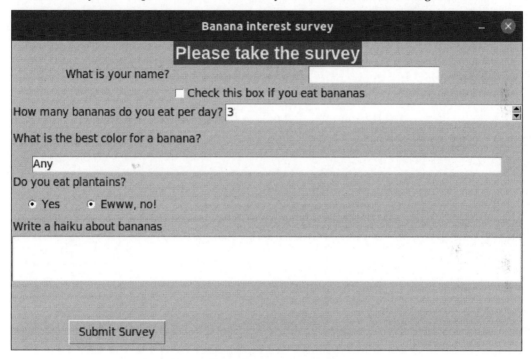

Figure 1.7: Our banana survey application

Congratulations, your banana survey works! Well, kind of. Let's see if we can get it fully working.

Handling data with Tkinter control variables

We've got the GUI layout well in hand, but our GUI has some problems. Retrieving data from our widgets is a bit of a mess, and we have no idea how to even get the values of the Checkbutton or Radiobutton widgets yet. In fact, if you try to operate the Radiobutton widgets, you'll see they are broken altogether. It seems we're missing a big piece of the puzzle.

What we're missing are Tkinter **control variables**. Control variables are special Tkinter objects that allow us to store data; there are four types of control variables:

- **StringVar**: Used to store strings of any length
- **IntVar**: Used to store integers
- **DoubleVar**: Used to store floating-point values
- **BooleanVar**: Used to store Boolean (True/False) values

But wait! Python already has variables that can store those types of data and much more. Why do we need these classes? Simply put, these variable classes have some special abilities that regular Python variables lack, for example:

- We can create a **two-way binding** between a control variable and a widget, so that if either the widget contents are changed or the variable contents are changed, both will be kept in sync.
- We can set up a **trace** on the variable. A trace binds a variable event (such as reading or updating the variable) to a callback function. (Traces will be discussed in *Chapter 4*, *Organizing Our Code with Classes*.)
- We can establish relationships between widgets. For example, we can tell our two Radiobutton widgets that they're connected.

Let's look at how control variables can help our survey application. Go back up to the top where the name input is defined and let's add a variable:

```
name_var = tk.StringVar(root)
name_label = tk.Label(root, text='What is your name?')
name_inp = tk.Entry(root, textvariable=name_var)
```

We can create a StringVar object by calling StringVar(); note that we've passed in the root window as the first argument. Control variables require a reference to a root window; however, in almost every case, they can work this out for themselves automatically, so it's rarely necessary to actually specify the root window here. It's important to understand, though, that *no control variable objects can be created until a Tk object exists*.

Once we have a StringVar object, we can bind it to our Entry widget by passing it to the textvariable argument. By doing this, the contents of the name_inp widget and the name_var variable are kept in sync. A call to the variable's get() method will return the current contents of the box, like so:

```
print(name_var.get())
```

For a checkbox, a `BooleanVar` is used:

```
eater_var = tk.BooleanVar()
eater_inp = tk.Checkbutton(
  root, variable=eater_var, text='Check this box if you eat bananas'
)
```

This time, we've passed the variable to the `Checkbutton` using the `variable` argument. Button widgets will use the keyword `variable` to bind a control variable, while widgets that you type into or that return string values typically use the keyword `textvariable`.

 Button widgets do take a `textvariable` argument as well, but it does not bind the value of the button; rather it binds to the text of the button's label. This feature allows you to dynamically update a button's text.

Variables can be initialized with a default value using the `value` argument, like this:

```
num_var = tk.IntVar(value=3)
num_label = tk.Label(text='How many bananas do you eat per day?')
num_inp = tk.Spinbox(
  root, textvariable=num_var, from_=0, to=1000, increment=1
)
```

Here, we've created an integer variable using `IntVar()` and set its value to 3; when we launch the form, the `num_inp` widget will be set to 3. Notice that, even though we think of the `Spinbox` as a number entry, it uses the `textvariable` argument to bind its control variable. A `Spinbox` widget can actually be used for more than just numbers, and as such its data is internally stored as text. However, by binding an `IntVar` or `DoubleVar` to it, the value retrieved will automatically be converted into an integer or float.

 The automatic conversion to integer or float done by `IntVar` and `DoubleVar` can be a problem if users are able to type letters, symbols, or other invalid characters into an entry. Calling `get()` on an integer or double variable bound to a widget containing an invalid number string (for example, `'1.1.2'` or `'I like plantains'`) will raise an exception, causing our application to crash. In *Chapter 5*, *Reducing User Error with Validation and Automation*, we'll learn how to address this problem.

Previously, we'd used `Listbox` to display a list of options to the user. Unfortunately, `Listbox` doesn't work well with control variables, but there is another widget, `OptionMenu`, that does.

Let's replace our `color_inp` with an `OptionMenu` widget:

```
color_var = tk.StringVar(value='Any')
color_label = tk.Label(
    root,
    text='What is the best color for a banana?'
)
color_choices = (
    'Any', 'Green', 'Green Yellow', 'Yellow', 'Brown Spotted', 'Black'
)
color_inp = tk.OptionMenu(
    root, color_var, *color_choices
)
```

The `OptionMenu` holds a list of options as strings, so we need to create a `StringVar` to bind to it. Note that, unlike the `ListBox` widget, the `OptionMenu` allows us to specify the options as we create it. The `OptionMenu` constructor is also a bit different from other Tkinter widget constructors in that it takes the control variable and options as positional arguments, like this:

```
# Example, don't add this to the program
menu = tk.OptionMenu(parent, ctrl_var, opt1, opt2, ..., optN)
```

In our survey code, we've added the options by using the unpack operator (*) to expand our `color_choices` list into positional arguments. We could also have just listed them explicitly, but doing it this way keeps our code a little neater.

We're going to learn about a better option for a drop-down list box when we discuss the Ttk widget set in *Chapter 3, Creating Basic Forms with Tkinter and Ttk Widgets*.

The `Radiobutton` widget handles variables slightly differently from other widgets as well. To use `Radiobutton` widgets effectively, we bind all the buttons that are grouped together to the same control variable, like this:

```
plantain_var = tk.BooleanVar()
plantain_yes_inp = tk.Radiobutton(
```

```
    plantain_frame, text='Yes', value=True, variable=plantain_var
)
plantain_no_inp = tk.Radiobutton(
    plantain_frame,
    text='Ewww, no!',
    value=False,
    variable=plantain_var
)
```

We can bind any kind of control variable to a `Radiobutton` widget, but we have to make sure to give each widget a `value` that matches the variable type. In this case, we're using the buttons for a `True`/`False` question, so `BooleanVar` is appropriate; we use the `value` argument to set one button to `True` and the other to `False`. When we call the variable's `get()` method, it will return the `value` argument of the selected button.

Unfortunately, not all Tkinter widgets work with control variables. Notably, our `Text` widget used for the `banana_haiku_inp` input cannot be bound to a variable, and (unlike `Listbox`) there is no alternative available. For the time being, we'll have to handle the `Text` entry widget as we have already done.

 The Tkinter `Text` box does not support variables because it is much more than just multi-line text; it can contain images, rich text, and other objects that can't be represented in a simple string. However, in *Chapter 4, Organizing Our Code with Classes*, we'll implement a workaround for this that will allow us to bind a variable to a multi-line string widget.

Control variables are not just for binding to input widgets; we can also use them to update strings in non-interactive widgets like `Label`. For example:

```
output_var = tk.StringVar(value='')
output_line = tk.Label(
    root, textvariable=output_var, anchor='w', justify='left'
)
```

With the `output_var` control variable bound to the `textvariable` argument of this `Label` widget, we can alter the text displayed by the label at runtime by updating `output_var`.

Using control variables in a callback function

Now that we've created all these variables and bound them to our widgets, what can we do with them? Skip down to the callback function, on_submit(), and delete the code that is in it. We will re-write it using our control variables.

Start with the name value:

```python
def on_submit():
    """To be run when the user submits the form"""
    name = name_var.get()
```

As mentioned earlier, the get() method is used to retrieve a variable's value. The data type returned by get() depends on the type of variable, as follows:

- StringVar returns a str
- IntVar returns an int
- DoubleVar returns a float
- BooleanVar returns a bool

Note that type conversion is performed whenever get() is called, so any incompatibility between what the widget contains and what the variable expects will raise an exception at this time. For example, if an IntVar is bound to an empty Spinbox, get() will raise an exception because an empty string cannot be cast to int.

For that reason, it is sometimes wise to put get() in a try/except block, like so:

```python
try:
    number = num_var.get()
except tk.TclError:
    number = 10000
```

Contrary to what an experienced Python programmer might expect, the exception raised for an invalid value is *not* ValueError. The conversion is actually done in Tcl/Tk, not in Python, so the exception raised is a tkinter.TclError. Here, we've caught the TclError and handled it by setting the number of bananas to 10,000.

 TclError exceptions are raised *any time* Tcl/Tk has difficulty executing our translated Python calls, so to properly handle them you may need to extract the actual error string from the exception. This is a bit ugly and un-Pythonic, but Tkinter doesn't leave us much choice.

Extracting the value of our `OptionMenu`, `Checkbutton`, and `Radiobutton` widgets is much cleaner now, as you can see here:

```
color = color_var.get()
banana_eater = eater_var.get()
plantain_eater = plantain_var.get()
```

For the `OptionMenu`, `get()` returns the selected string. For `Checkbutton`, it returns `True` if the button is checked, or `False` if it is not. For the `Radiobutton` widgets, `get()` returns the `value` of the selected widget. The nice thing about control variables is that we don't have to know or care what kind of widget they were bound to; simply calling `get()` is sufficient to retrieve the user's input.

The `Text` widget, as mentioned before, doesn't support control variables, so we have to get its content the old-fashioned way:

```
haiku = banana_haiku_inp.get('1.0', tk.END)
```

Now that we have all that data, let's build a message string for the survey taker:

```
    message = f'Thanks for taking the survey, {name}.\n'
if not banana_eater:
    message += "Sorry you don't like bananas!\n"
else:
    message += f'Enjoy your {number} {color} bananas!\n'
if plantain_eater:
    message += 'Enjoy your plantains!'
else:
    message += 'May you successfully avoid plantains!'
if haiku.strip():
    message += f'\n\nYour Haiku:\n{haiku}'
```

To display our message for the user, we need to update the `output_var` variable. This is done using its `set()` method, like so:

```
output_var.set(message)
```

The `set()` method will update the control variable, which in turn will update the `Label` widget to which it is bound. This way, we can dynamically update displayed messages, widget labels, and other text in our application.

Remember to use `set()` to change a control variable's value! Using the assignment operator (=) will just overwrite the control variable object with a different object and you won't be able to work with it anymore. For example, `output_var = message` would just reassign the name `output_var` to the string object `message`, and the control variable object currently bound to `output_line` would become nameless.

The importance of control variables

Hopefully, you see that control variables are a powerful and essential part of a Tkinter GUI. We will use them extensively in our applications to store and communicate data between Tkinter objects. In fact, once we've bound a variable to a widget, it's often unnecessary to keep a reference to our widget. For example, our survey code would work just fine if we defined the output section like this:

```
output_var = tk.StringVar(value='')
# remove the call to output_line.grid() in the layout section!
tk.Label(
    root, textvariable=output_var, anchor='w', justify='left'
).grid(row=100, columnspan=2, sticky="NSEW")
```

Since we don't need to interact directly with the output `Label`, we can just create it and place it all in one line, without bothering to save a reference. Since the widget's parent retains a reference to the object, Python won't destroy the object, and we can retrieve its contents at any time using the control variable. Of course, if we later want to manipulate the widget in some way (changing its `font` value, for example), we'll need to keep a reference to it.

Summary

In this chapter, you learned how to install Tkinter and IDLE, and you've gotten a taste of how easy it is to start building a GUI with Tkinter. You learned how to create widgets, how to arrange them in the main window with the `grid()` geometry manager, and how to bind their contents to control variables like `StringVar` and `BooleanVar`. You also learned how to bind events like button clicks to callback functions, and how to retrieve and process widget data.

In the next chapter, you'll start your new job at ABQ AgriLabs and be presented with a problem that will require your GUI programming skills. You will learn how to dissect this problem, develop a program specification, and design a user-friendly application that will be part of the solution.

2
Designing GUI Applications

Software applications are developed in three repeating phases: understanding a problem, designing a solution, and implementing the solution. These phases repeat throughout the life of an application as you add new features, refine functionality, and update your application until it is either optimal or obsolete. While many programmers want to jump right into the implementation phase, putting away your code editor and taking the time to work through the first two phases will give you a better chance to develop an application that solves the problem correctly.

In this chapter, we'll be introduced to a problem at your new workplace and begin designing a solution to that problem over the following topics:

- In *Analyzing a problem at ABQ AgriLabs*, we'll learn about an issue at your new job that you can help solve with your coding skills.

- In *Documenting specification requirements*, we'll create a program specification that lays out the requirements of our solution.

- In *Designing the application*, we'll develop a design for a GUI application that implements the solution.

- In *Evaluating technology options*, we'll consider which toolkit and language are most appropriate for our project.

Analyzing a problem at ABQ AgriLabs

Congratulations! Your Python skills have landed you a great job as a data analyst at ABQ AgriLabs. So far, your job is fairly simple: collating and doing simple data analysis on the CSV files sent to you daily by the lab's data entry staff.

There is a problem, though. You've noted with frustration that the quality of the CSV files from the lab is sadly inconsistent. Data is missing, typos abound, and often the files have to be re-entered in a time-consuming process. The lab director has noticed this as well and, knowing that you are a skilled Python programmer, she thinks you might be able to help. You've been enlisted to program a solution that will allow the data entry staff to enter lab data into a CSV file with fewer mistakes. Your application needs to be simple and allow as little room for error as possible.

Assessing the problem

Spreadsheets are often a first stop for computer users who need to keep track of data. Their table-like layouts and computational features seem to make them ideal for the task.

However, as a set of data grows and is added to by multiple users, the shortcomings of spreadsheets become apparent: they don't enforce data integrity, their table-like layout can be visually confusing when dealing with long rows of sparse or ambiguous data, and users can easily delete or overwrite data if they aren't being careful.

To improve this situation, you propose to implement a simple GUI data entry form that appends data to a CSV file in the format we need. Forms can help to improve data integrity in several ways:

- They can enforce the type of data to be entered (for example, numbers or dates).
- They can verify that entered data is within expected ranges, matches expected patterns, or is within a valid set of options.
- They can auto-fill information such as current dates, times, and usernames.
- They can ensure that required data fields have not been left empty.

By implementing a well-designed form, we can greatly reduce the amount of human error from the data entry staff. Where do we begin?

Gathering information about the problem

To build a truly effective data entry application, you need to do more than just throw some entry fields on a form. It's important to understand the data and the **workflow** around the data from all sides of the problem. It's also important to understand the human and technological limitations that you need to accommodate. To do that, we need to speak with a few different parties:

- The **originators** of the data for the application – in this case, the lab technicians who check the plots in each lab. They can help us understand the significance of the data, the possible values, and the possible outlier situations where the data might need special handling.

- The **users** of our application – in this case, the data entry staff. We need to understand what the data looks like when they receive it, what their workflow is like for entering the data, what practical or knowledge limitations they face, and ultimately how our software can make their job *easier* rather than harder.

- The **consumers** of the data from the application – that is, everyone who will use the CSV files (including you!). What are their expectations for the output of this application? How would they like outlier situations to be handled? What are their goals in keeping and analyzing the data?

- The **support staff** who are involved with the systems that will run or consume data from your application. What sort of technologies need to be supported? What technological limitations need to be accommodated? What security concerns need to be addressed?

Sometimes these groups overlap, of course. In any case, it's important to think through everyone whose job will be affected by the data and the software, and take their needs into consideration as you design your application. So, before we start coding away, we're going to put together some questions to help us gather these details.

Interviewing the interested parties

The first group you'll talk to are the lab technicians, from whom you'll try find out more detail about the data being recorded. This isn't always as easy as it sounds. Software needs absolute, black-and-white rules when dealing with data; people, on the other hand, tend to think in generalities about their data, and they often don't consider the exact details of limits or edge cases without some prompting. As an application designer, it's your job to come up with questions that will bring out the information you need.

Here are some questions we can ask the lab technicians to learn more about the data:

- What values are acceptable for character fields? Are any of them constrained to a discrete set of values?

- What units are represented by each of the numeric fields?

- Are numeric fields truly number-only fields? Would they ever need letters or symbols?

- What range of numbers is acceptable for each numeric field?
- How is unavailable data (such as from an equipment failure) notated?

Next, let's interview the users of the application. If we're making a program to help reduce user error, we have to understand those users and how they work. In the case of this application, our users will be the data entry staff. We need to ask them questions about their needs and workflow so that we can create an application that works well for them.

Here are some good questions we can ask the data entry staff:

- How is the data formatted when you receive it?
- When is the data received and how soon is it entered? When's the latest it might be entered?
- Are there fields that could be automatically populated? Should users be able to override the automatic values?
- What's the overall technical ability of the users? Are they strong typists, or would they prefer a mouse-driven interface?
- What do you like about the current solution? What do you dislike?
- Do any users have visual or manual impairments that should be accommodated?

 **Listen to your users!** When talking to users about an application design, they may often put forward requests or ideas that are impractical, that don't follow best practice, or that seem frivolous. For example, they may request that a button display an animation under certain conditions, that a particular field be yellow, or that a time field be represented as a set of dropdowns for hours and minutes. Rather than dismissing these ideas, try to understand the reasoning behind them, or the problem that prompted them. It will often uncover aspects of the data and the workflow you did not understand before, and lead to a better solution.

Once we have spoken with our users, it's time to talk to the consumers of our data. In this case, that's you! You already know a good deal about what you need and expect from the data, but even so, it's important to reflect and consider how you would ideally like to receive data from this application. For example:

- Is CSV really the best output format, or is that just what has always been used?

- Does the order of fields in the CSV matter? Are there constraints on the header values (no spaces, mixed case, and so on)?

- How should outlier cases be handled by the application? What should they look like in the data?

- How should different objects like Boolean or date values be represented in the data?

- Is there additional data that should be captured to help you accomplish your goals?

Finally, we need to understand the technology that our application will be working with; that is, the computers, networks, servers, and platforms available to accomplish the task. You come up with the following questions to ask the IT support staff:

- What kind of computer does data entry use? How fast or powerful is it?

- What operating system platform does it run?

- Is Python available on these systems? If so, are there any Python libraries installed?

- What other scripts or applications are involved in the current solution?

- How many users need to use the program at once?

Inevitably, more questions will come up about the data, workflow, and technologies as the development process continues. For that reason, be sure to keep in touch with all these groups and ask more questions as the need arises.

Analyzing what we've found out

You've done all your interviews with the interested parties, and now it's time to look over your notes. You begin by writing down the basic information about operations at ABQ that you already know:

- Your ABQ facility has three greenhouses, each operating with a different climate, marked A, B, and C

- Each greenhouse has 20 plots (labeled 1 through 20)

- There are currently four types of seed samples, each coded with a six-character label

- Each plot has 20 seeds of a given sample planted in it, as well as its own environmental sensor unit

Information from the data originators

Your talk with the lab technicians revealed a lot about the data. Four times a day, at 8:00, 12:00, 16:00, and 20:00, each technician checks the plots in his or her assigned lab. They use a paper form to record information about plants and environmental conditions at each plot, recording all numeric values to no more than two decimal places. This usually takes between 45 and 90 minutes, depending on how far along the plant growth has progressed.

Each plot has its own environmental sensor that detects the light, temperature, and humidity at the plot. Unfortunately, these devices are prone to temporary failure, indicated by an Equipment Fault light on the unit. Since a fault makes the environmental data suspect, they simply cross out the fields in those cases and don't record that data.

They provide you with an example copy of the paper form, which looks like this:

ABQ Agrilabs Data Entry Form										

Date: 10/3/21   Time (circle): (8:00) 12:00 16:00 20:00   Lab (circle): A (B) C   Tech: J. Simms

Plot	Seed	hum (g/m³)	light (klux)	temp (°C)	Plants	Bloss	Fruit	min ht (cm)	max ht (cm)	med ht (cm)	Notes
1	AX478	22.4	.72	29.21	10	29	7	41	63	58.2	
2		22.4	.73	29.2	12	34	12	45	68	59.3	
3		22.4	.51	29.24	12	37	14	47	72	62.9	
4		22.5	.62	29.28	14	42	17	42	88	65.0	
5					9	21	7	34	82	72.1	EQ Fault
6	AX479	23.1	.74	29.27	13	37	15	56	63	57.47	
7		23.0	.91	29.23	15	44	19	51	67	55.05	
8		22.75	.77	28.94	18	52	23	53	68	59.2	
9		22.6	.43	27.2	17	53	24	49	65	53.1	
10		23.25	.75	28.41	20	62	31	55	71	60.4	
11	AX480	28.15	.31	27.8	11	17	2	10	42	23.1	Seems more humid at these plots?
12		28.12	.43	28.17	12	15	0	23	47	25.0	Sickly leaves, Blight?
13		28.2	.51	28.05	10	8	1	17	51	28.7	
14		28.4	.54	28.21	9	10	0	9	31	25.1	
15		28.7	.51	27.95	7	6	0	10	29	17.2	
16	AX477	22.8	.78	29.37	14	43	21	31	63	37.4	
17		22.14	.71	29.5	18	56	24	43	67	52.9	
18		22.51	.69	30.15	15	54	31	51	65	55.0	
19		22.49	.77	29.71	16	59	29	37	62	42.1	
20		21.88	.72	29.42	16	62	25	44	68	54.2	

Figure 2.1: Paper form filled out by the lab technicians

Finally, the technicians tell you about the units and possible ranges of data for the fields, which you record in the following chart:

Field	Data type	Notes
Date	Date	The data collection date. Usually the current date.
Time	Time	The start of the period during which measurements were taken. One of 8:00, 12:00, 16:00, or 20:00.
Lab	Character	The lab ID, either A, B, or C.
Technician	Text	The name of the technician recording the data.
Plot	Integer	The plot ID, from 1 to 20.
Seed Sample	Text	ID string for the seed sample. Always a six-character code containing digits 0 to 9 and capital letters A to Z.
Fault	Boolean	True if environmental equipment registered a failure, otherwise False.
Humidity	Decimal	The absolute humidity in g/m³, roughly between 0.5 and 52.0.
Light	Decimal	The amount of sunlight at the plot center in kilolux, between 0 and 100.
Temperature	Decimal	The temperature at the plot, in degrees C; should be between 4 and 40.
Blossoms	Integer	The number of blossoms on the plants in a plot. No maximum, but unlikely to approach 1,000.
Fruit	Integer	The number of fruits on the plant. No maximum, but unlikely to ever approach 1,000.
Plants	Integer	The number of plants in the plot; should be no more than 20.
Max Height	Decimal	The height of the tallest plant in the plot, in cm. No maximum, but unlikely to approach 1,000.
Median Height	Decimal	The median height of the plants in the plot, in cm. No maximum, but unlikely to approach 1,000.
Min Height	Decimal	The height of the smallest plant in the plot, in cm. No maximum, but unlikely to approach 1,000.
Notes	Long Text	Additional observations about the plant, data, instruments, and so on.

Information from the users of the application

Your session with the data entry staff yielded good information about their workflow and practical concerns. You learn that the lab technicians drop off their paper forms as they're completed, from which the data is typically entered right away and usually on the same day as it's handed in.

The data entry staff are currently using a spreadsheet (LibreOffice Calc) to enter the data. They like that they can use copy and paste to bulk-fill fields with repeated data like the date, time, and technician name. They also note that the autocompletion feature of LibreOffice is often helpful in text fields, but sometimes causes accidental data errors in the number fields.

You take these notes about how they enter data from the forms:

- Dates are entered in month/day/year format, since this is how LibreOffice formats them by default with the system's locale setting.
- Time is entered as 24-hour time.
- Technicians are entered as first initial and last name.
- In the case of equipment faults, the environmental data is entered as N/A.
- The CSV file is generally created one lab at a time in plot order (from 1 to 20).

There are four data entry clerks in total, but only one working at any one time; while interviewing the clerks, you learn that one has red-green color blindness, and another has trouble using a mouse due to RSI issues. All are reasonably computer literate and prefer keyboard entry to mouse entry as it allows them to work faster.

One user in particular had some ideas about how your program should look. He suggested doing the labs as a set of checkboxes, and to have separate pop-up dialogs for plant data and environmental data.

Information from technical support

Speaking with IT personnel, you learn that the data entry staff have only a single PC workstation, which they share. It is an older system running Debian GNU/Linux, but it performs adequately. Python3 and Tkinter are already installed as part of the base system, though they are slightly older versions than you have on your workstation. The data entry staff save their CSV data for the current day to a file called abq_data_record.csv. When all the data is entered, the data entry staff have a script they can run to email you the file and build a new, empty file for the next day. The script also backs up the old file with a date-stamp so it can be pulled up later for corrections.

Information from the data consumer

As the main data consumer, it would be pretty easy for you to just stick with what you know already; nevertheless, you take the time to review a recent copy of abq_data_record.csv, which looks something like this:

	A	B	C	D	E	F	G	H	I	J	K	L	M	N	O	P	Q
1	date	time	lab	tchn	plt	ss	eqflt	klx	hum	tmp	blos	frt	plants	max ht	min ht	med ht	notes
2	09/01/21	08:00	A	J Simms	1	AXM477	N	50	34	31.2	2	0	16	102	24	57.2	
3	09/01/21	08:00	A	J Simms	2	AXM477	N	51	34	31.7	3	0	18	101	31	59.1	
4	09/01/21	08:00	A	J Simms	3	AXM477	Y	N/A	N/A	N/A	10	1	20	123	32.5	72.89	
5	09/01/21	08:00	A	J Simms	4	AXM477	N	42	37	29.8	0	0	8	56	2.3	24.77	Glass dirty
6																	

Figure 2.2: The abq_data_record.csv file

In reflecting on this, you realize there are a few changes to the status quo that could make life easier for you as you do your data analysis:

- It would be great to have the files date-stamped right away. Currently, you have an inbox full of files called abq_data_record.csv and no good way to tell them apart.

- It would be helpful if the data in the files were saved in a way that Python could more easily parse without ambiguity. For example, dates are currently saved with the local month/day/year formatting, but ISO-format would be less problematic.

- You'd like a field that indicates explicitly when there is an equipment fault, rather than just implying it with missing environmental data.

- The N/A is something you just have to filter out when you process the data. It would be nice if an equipment fault would just blank out the environmental data fields so that the file doesn't contain useless data like that.

- The current CSV headers are cryptic, and you're always having to translate them in your report scripts. It would be good to have readable headers.

These changes won't just make your job easier, they will also leave the data in a more usable state than it was before. Legacy data formats like these CSV files are often fraught with artifacts from obsolete software environments or outdated workflows. Improving the clarity and readability of the data will help anyone trying to use it in the future as the lab's usage of the data evolves.

Documenting specification requirements

Now that you've assembled your information about the data, people, and technologies affected by your application, it's time to write up a **software specification**. Software specifications can range from very formal, contractual documents that include time estimates and deadlines to a simple set of descriptions of what the programmer intends to build. The purpose of the specification is to give everyone involved in the project a point of reference for what the developer will create. It spells out the problem to be solved, the functionality required, and the scope of what the program should and shouldn't do.

Your scenario is rather informal and your application is simple, so you do not need a detailed formal specification in this case. However, a basic write-up of what you know will make sure that you, your employer, and the users all understand the essentials of the application you will be writing.

Contents of a simple specification

We'll start our specification with the following outline of the items we need to write:

- **Description**: This is one or two sentences that describe the primary purpose, function, and goals of the application. Think of it as the program's mission statement.

- **Requirements**: This section is a list of specific things the program must be able to do in order to be minimally functional. It can include both functional and non-functional requirements.

  - **Functional requirements** are concrete goals that the program must achieve; for example, the business logic that it must perform or the output format it must produce. Listing these helps us know when our program is ready for production use.

  - **Non-functional requirements** tend to be less specific and focus on user expectations and general goals, for example, usability, performance, or accessibility requirements. Although these aren't always measurable goals, they help to guide the focus of our development.

- **Functionality not required**: This section is a list of things the program does not need to do; it exists to clarify the scope of the software and make sure nobody expects unreasonable things from the application. We don't need to include every possible thing our application won't do; naturally, our program won't make toast or do the laundry. However, if there are features we are not implementing that users might reasonably expect, this is a good place to clarify what won't be done.

- **Limitations**: This is a list of constraints under which the program must operate, both technological and human.

- **Data dictionary**: This is a detailed list of the data fields in the application and their parameters. A data dictionary can get quite lengthy, and may be worthy of a document of its own. It will not only be useful during the development of our application but will become a critical reference to the data produced by the application as the application expands and the data gets utilized in other contexts.

Writing the ABQ data entry program specification

You could write a specification in your favorite word processor, but ideally the specification should be treated as a part of your code; it will need to be kept with the code and synchronized with any changes to the application. For that reason, we're going to write our specification in our code editor using the **reStructuredText** markup language.

 For Python documentation, reStructuredText, or reST, is the official markup language. The Python community encourages the use of reST to document Python projects, and many packaging and publication tools used in the Python community expect the reST format. For an in-depth coverage of reST, see *Appendix A, A Quick Primer on reStructuredText*, or see the official documentation at `https://docutils.sourceforge.io/rst.html`.

Let's start with the `Description` section of our documentation:

```
========================================
 ABQ Data Entry Program specification
========================================


Description
-----------
This program facilitates entry of laboratory observations
into a CSV file.
```

Now, let's list the `Requirements`. Remember that functional requirements are objectively attainable goals, like input and output requirements, calculations that must be done, or features that must be present. Non-functional requirements, on the other hand, are subjective or best-effort goals. Look through your findings from the last section, and consider which needs are which. You should come up with something like the following:

```
Requirements
--------------------

Functional Requirements:
```

```
   * Allow all relevant, valid data to be entered,
     as per the data dictionary.
   * Append entered data to a CSV file:
     - The CSV file must have a filename of
     abq_data_record_CURRENTDATE.csv, where CURRENTDATE is the date
     of the laboratory observations in ISO format (Year-month-day).
     - The CSV file must include all fields
     listed in the data dictionary.
     - The CSV headers will avoid cryptic abbreviations.
   * Enforce correct datatypes per field.

 Non-functional Requirements:

   * Enforce reasonable limits on data entered, per the data dict.
   * Auto-fill data to save time.
   * Suggest likely correct values.
   * Provide a smooth and efficient workflow.
   * Store data in a format easily understandable by Python.
```

Next, we'll reign in the scope of the program with the `Functionality Not Required` section. Remember that this is only an entry form for now; editing or deletion of data will be handled in the spreadsheet application. We'll clarify this as follows:

```
Functionality Not Required
--------------------------


The program does not need to:

   * Allow editing of data.
   * Allow deletion of data.


Users can perform both actions in LibreOffice if needed.
```

For the `Limitations` section, remember that we have some users with physical constraints, as well as hardware and operating system constraints. It should look something like this:

```
Limitations
-----------


The program must:

   * Be efficiently operable by keyboard-only users.
```

```
  * Be accessible to color blind users.
  * Run on Debian GNU/Linux.
  * Run acceptably on a low-end PC.
```

Finally, we will write the data dictionary. This is essentially the table we made previously, but we'll break out range, data types, and units for quick reference, as follows:

Field	Type	Unit	Valid Values	Description
Date	Date			Date of record
Time	Time		8:00, 12:00, 16:00, 20:00	Time period
Lab	String		A - C	Lab ID
Technician	String			Technician name
Plot	Int		1 - 20	Plot ID
Seed Sample	String		6-character string	Seed sample ID
Fault	Bool		True, False	Environmental sensor fault
Light	Decimal	klx	0 - 100	Light at plot blank on fault
Humidity	Decimal	g/m³	0.5 - 52.0	Abs humidity at plot blank on fault
Temperature	Decimal	°C	4 - 40	Temperature at plot blank on fault
Blossoms	Int		0 - 1000	No. blossoms in plot
Fruit	Int		0 - 1000	No. fruits in plot
Plants	Int		0 - 20	No. plants in plot

```
+-------------+--------+----+---------------+--------------------+
|Max Height   |Decimal |cm  | 0 - 1000      |Height of tallest   |
|             |        |    |               |plant in plot       |
+-------------+--------+----+---------------+--------------------+
|Min Height   |Decimal |cm  | 0 - 1000      |Height of shortest  |
|             |        |    |               |plant in plot       |
+-------------+--------+----+---------------+--------------------+
|Median       |Decimal |cm  | 0 - 1000      |Median height of    |
|Height       |        |    |               |plants in plot      |
+-------------+--------+----+---------------+--------------------+
|Notes        |String  |    |               |Miscellaneous notes |
+-------------+--------+----+---------------+--------------------+
```

That's our specification for now! The specification is very likely to grow, change, or evolve in complexity as we discover new needs, but it gives us a great starting point for designing the first version of our application.

Designing the application

With our specification in hand and our requirements clear, it's time to start designing our solution. The main focus of our application is the data entry form itself, so we'll begin with that GUI component.

We're going to create a basic design for our form in three steps:

1. Determine the appropriate input widget type for each data field
2. Group together related items to create a sense of organization
3. Lay out our widgets within their groups

Deciding on input widgets

Without committing ourselves to a particular GUI library or widget set, we can start our form design by deciding on an appropriate input widget type for each field. Most toolkits come with the same basic types of inputs for different types of data.

We've already seen some of these in our look at Tkinter, but let's see what sort of options are likely to be available:

Widget type	Tkinter example	Used for
Line entry	`Entry`	Single-line strings
Number entry	`Spinbox`	Integer or decimal values

Select list (drop-down)	`Listbox`, `OptionMenu`	Choice between many distinct values
Check box	`Checkbutton`	True/false value
Radio button	`Radiobutton`	Choice between a few distinct values
Text entry	`Text`	Multi-line text entry
Date entry	(None specific)	Dates

Looking at our data dictionary, what sort of widgets should we pick out for each of our fields? Let's consider:

- There are several decimal fields, many with clear boundary ranges, like Min Height, Max Height, Median Height, Humidity, Temperature, and Light. We'll need some kind of number entry, perhaps a Tkinter `Spinbox`, for these.

- There are also some integer fields, such as Plants, Blossoms, and Fruit. Again, a number entry like the `Spinbox` widget is the right choice.

- There are a couple of fields with a limited set of possible values: Time and Lab. For these we could go with radio buttons or a select list of some kind. It really depends on the number of options and how we want to lay it out: radio buttons take a lot of space with more than a few choices, but select list widgets take additional interaction and slow down a user. We'll choose a select/drop-down for the Time field, and radio buttons for the Lab field.

- The Plot field is a tricky case. At face value, it looks like an integer field, but think about it: the plots could just as well be identified by letters, or symbols, or names. Numbers just happen to be an easy set of values with which to assign arbitrary identifiers. The Plot ID, like the Lab ID, is actually a constrained set of values; so, it would make more sense to use a select list here.

- The Notes field is multiline text, so the Text widget is appropriate here.

- There is one Boolean field, Fault. A check box type widget is a good choice here, especially since this value is normally false and represents an exceptional circumstance.

- For the Date field, it would be nice to use a date entry of some sort. We don't know of one in Tkinter yet, but we'll see if we can solve that when we write our application.

- The remaining lines are simple, one-line character fields. We'll use a text entry-type widget for those fields.

Our final analysis comes to the following:

Field	Widget type
Date	Date entry
Time	Select list
Lab	Radio buttons
Technician	Text entry
Plot	Select list
Seed Sample	Text entry
Fault	Check box
Humidity	Number entry
Light	Number entry
Temperature	Number entry
Blossoms	Number entry
Fruit	Number entry
Plants	Number entry
Max Height	Number entry
Median Height	Number entry
Min Height	Number entry
Notes	Text entry

Bear in mind, this analysis is not set in stone; it will almost certainly be revised as we receive feedback from our users, as the application's use case evolves, or as we become more familiar with the capabilities and limitations of Python and Tkinter. This is simply a starting place from which we can create an initial design.

Grouping our fields

Humans tend to get confused when staring at a huge wall of inputs in no particular order. You can do your users a big favor by breaking up the input form into sets of related fields. Of course, that assumes that your data has related sets of fields, doesn't it? Does our data have groups?

Recall some of the information we gathered during our interviews:

- One of the employees requested separate forms for "environmental data" and "plant data"
- The layout of the paper form has Time, Date, Lab, and Technician, all together at the top; these things help identify the data recording session

Details like this tell you a lot about how your users *think* about their data, and that should inform how the application *presents* that data.

Considering all this, you identify the following related groups:

- The Date, Lab, Plot, Seed Sample, Technician, and Time fields are identifying data or metadata about the record itself. You could group these together under a heading calling *Record Information*.

- The Blossoms, Fruit, three Height fields, and Plants fields are all measurements that have to do with the plants in the Plot field. You could group these together under the heading *Plant Data*.

- The Humidity, Light, Temperature, and Equipment Fault fields are all information from the environmental sensor. You could group these as *Environmental Data*.

- The Notes field could be related to anything, so it's in a category of its own.

Most GUI libraries offer a variety of ways to group sections of a form together; think of some you have seen. A few are listed in this table:

Widget type	Description
Tabs (notebook)	Allows multiple tabbed pages that the user can switch between
Frames/boxes	Draws boxes around sections of a form, sometimes with a header
Accordion	Divides a form into sections that can be hidden or expanded one at a time

Framed boxes are the simplest way to break up a GUI. In cases where there are a lot of fields, a tabbed or accordion widget can help by hiding fields the user isn't working with. However, they require additional user interaction to switch between pages or sections. You decide, after some consideration, that framed boxes with headers will be perfectly adequate for this form. There are not really enough fields to justify separate pages, and switching between them would just add more overhead to the data entry process.

Laying out the form

So far, we know that we have 17 inputs, which are grouped as follows:

- Six fields under Record Information
- Four fields under Environmental Data
- Six fields under Plant Data
- One large Notes field

We want to group the preceding inputs using some kind of box or frame with a header label. Notice that two of the first three sections have widgets in multiples of three. That suggests that we could arrange them in a grid with three items across. How should we order the fields within each group?

Ordering of fields seems like a trivial item, but for the user it can make a significant difference in usability. Users who have to jump around a form haphazardly to match their workflow are more likely to make mistakes.

As you learned, the data is entered from paper forms filled out by the lab technicians. Refer back to the screenshot of the paper form shown in *Figure 2.1* in the previous section. It looks like items are mostly grouped the way our records are grouped, so we'll use the ordering on this form to order our fields. That way, data entry clerks can zip right through the form from top to bottom, left to right, without having to bounce around the screen.

 Remember, user workflow is important! When designing a new application to replace some part of an existing procedure, it's crucial to respect the established workflow. While improving the status quo may require adjusting the workflow, be careful that you aren't making someone else's job harder without a good reason.

One last consideration in our design is where to place field labels in relation to the fields. There is a good deal of debate in the UI design community over the best placement of labels, but the consensus is that one of the following two options is best:

- Labels above fields
- Labels to the left of fields

You might try sketching out both to see which you prefer, but for this application, labels above fields will probably work better for the following reasons:

- Since both fields and labels are rectangular in shape, our form will be more compact by stacking them
- It's a lot easier to make the layout work, since we don't have to find a label width that works for all the labels without distancing them too far from the fields

The one exception is the check button field; check buttons are typically labeled to the right of the widget.

Take a moment to make a mockup of your form, using paper and pencil, or a drawing program if you prefer. Your form should look something like this:

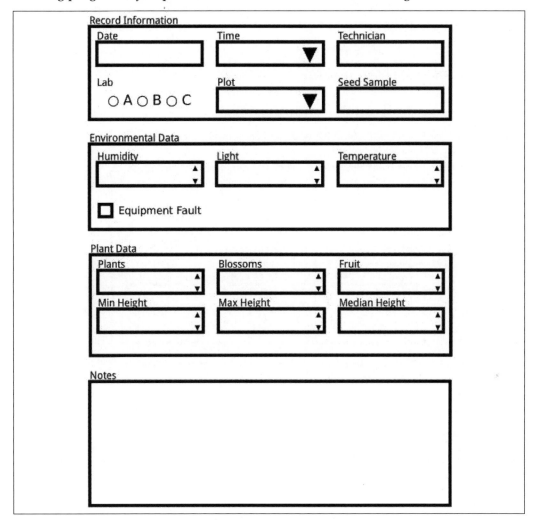

Figure 2.3: The form layout

Laying out the application

With your form designed, it's time to consider the rest of the application's GUI:

- You'll need a save button to trigger storage of the entered data.
- It's customary to include a button to reset the form, so the user can start over if needed.

- Sometimes, we might need to provide status information to the user. For example, we might want to let them know when a record was successfully saved, or if there is an error in a particular field. Applications typically have a **status bar** that displays these kinds of messages at the bottom of the window.

- Finally, it might be good to have a header indicating what the form is.

Adding the following things to our sketch, we have something like the following screenshot:

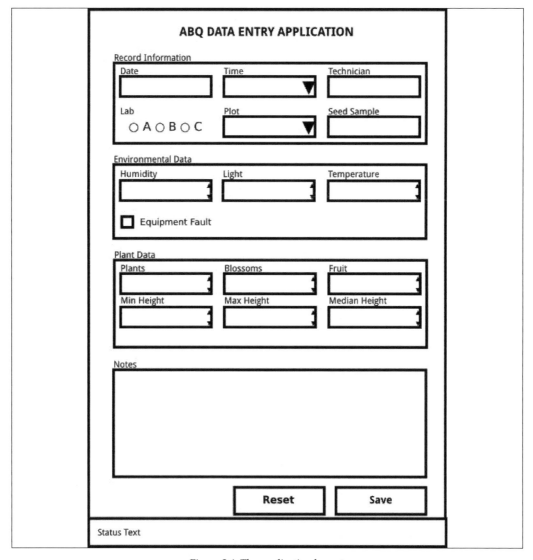

Figure 2.4: The application layout

Looks good! Your final step is to show these designs to your users and the director for any feedback or approval. Good luck!

 Keep stakeholders – your boss, users, and others who will be affected by your program – involved as much as possible in your application design process. This reduces the possibility that you'll have to go back and redesign your application later.

Evaluating technology options

Before we start coding, let's take a moment to evaluate the technology choices available to implement this design.

Naturally, we're going to build this form using Python and Tkinter, because that's what this book is about. However, in a real-world situation it's worth asking whether Tkinter is really a good choice of technology for the application. Many criteria come into play when making decisions about languages, libraries, and other technologies used in implementing an application, including performance, feature availability, cost and license, platform support, and developer knowledge and confidence.

Let's evaluate the situation with our ABQ application according to these criteria:

- **Performance**: This will not be a high-performance application. There are no computationally demanding tasks, and high speed is not critical. Python and Tkinter will work perfectly fine in terms of performance.

- **Feature availability**: Your application needs to be able to display basic form fields, validate the data entered, and write it to CSV. Tkinter can handle these front-end requirements, and Python can handle the CSV file easily. You are a little concerned about Tkinter's lack of a dedicated date entry field, but this may be something we can work around.

- **Cost and license**: This project isn't going to be distributed or sold, so licenses are not a big concern. There is no budget for the project, though, so whatever you use will need to be free from any financial cost. Both Python and Tkinter are free and liberally licensed, so in any case this is not a concern.

- **Platform support**: You will be developing the application on a Windows PC, but it will need to run on Debian Linux, so the choice of GUI should be cross-platform. The computer it will run on is old and slow, so your program needs to be frugal with resources. Python and Tkinter check both boxes here.

- **Developer knowledge and confidence**: Your expertise is in Python, but you have little experience in creating GUIs. For the fastest time to delivery, you need an option that works well with Python and isn't complicated to learn. You also want something established and stable, as you won't have time to keep up with new developments in the toolkit. Tkinter is a good fit here.

> Don't take your own skills, knowledge, and comfort level with the technology out of the equation here! While it's good to make objective choices and recognize your personal biases toward things you already know, it's equally important to recognize that your ability to confidently deliver and maintain a product is a critical factor in your evaluation.

Given the options available for Python, Tkinter is a good choice for this application. It's easy to learn, lightweight, free, readily available on both your development and target platforms, and provides the basic functionality necessary for our data entry form. Having settled this question, it's time to take a deeper look into Tkinter to find what we'll need to build this application.

> Python has other options for GUI development, including PyQt, Kivy, and wxPython. These have different strengths and weaknesses compared to Tkinter, but if you find Tkinter doesn't fit well for a project, one of these might be a better option.

Summary

In this chapter, you worked through the first two phases of application development: understanding the problem and designing a solution. You learned how to develop an application specification by interviewing users and examining the data and requirements, created an optimal form layout for your users, and learned about the different types of widgets available in GUI frameworks for dealing with different kinds of input data. After creating the specification, you evaluated Tkinter to see if it was an appropriate technology. Most importantly, you learned that developing an application doesn't begin with code, but with research and planning.

In the next chapter, you'll create a basic implementation of your designs with Tkinter and Python. You'll learn about a new widget set, Ttk, and use it along with some Tkinter widgets we've already met to create the form and the application.

3

Creating Basic Forms with Tkinter and Ttk Widgets

Good news! Your design has been reviewed and approved by the director. Now it's time to start implementing it! In this chapter, we'll be creating a very simple application that delivers the core functionality of the specification and little else. This is known as a **minimum viable product** or **MVP**. The MVP will not be production-ready, but it will give us something to show our users and help us better understand the problem and the technologies we're working with. We'll cover this in the following topics:

- In *The Ttk widget set*, we'll learn about a better widget set for Tkinter, Ttk.
- In *Implementing the application*, we'll build our form design using Python, Tkinter, and Ttk.

Let's get coding!

The Ttk widget set

In *Chapter 1*, *Introduction to Tkinter*, we created a survey application using the default Tkinter widgets. These widgets are perfectly functional and still used in many Tkinter applications, but modern Tkinter applications tend to prefer an improved set of widgets called **Ttk**. Ttk is a sub-module of Tkinter that provides themed versions of many (but not all) Tkinter widgets. These widgets are mostly identical to the traditional widgets but provide advanced styling options in an aim to look more modern and natural on Windows, macOS, and Linux.

On each platform, Ttk includes platform-specific themes that mimic the platform's native widgets. In addition, Ttk adds a few extra widgets that offer functionality not found in the default library.

 Although this chapter will cover the basic usage of Ttk widgets, full coverage of the fonts, colors, and other style customization for Ttk widgets can be found in *Chapter 9, Improving the Look with Styles and Themes.*

Ttk is already included as part of Tkinter, so we do not need to install anything extra. To use Ttk widgets in our Tkinter applications, we will need to import ttk like this:

```
from tkinter import ttk
```

In this section, we'll take a deeper look at the Ttk widgets that will be useful in our application. Remember from our design that we need the following types of widgets for our application:

- Labels
- Date entry
- Text entry
- Number entry
- Check boxes
- Radio buttons
- Select list
- Long text entry
- Buttons
- Boxed frames with headers

Let's look at the Ttk widgets that we can use to meet these needs.

The Label widget

We made good use of the Tkinter Label widget in *Chapter 1, Introduction to Tkinter*, and the Ttk version is essentially the same. We can create one like so:

```
mylabel = ttk.Label(root, text='This is a label')
```

This results in a label that looks like this:

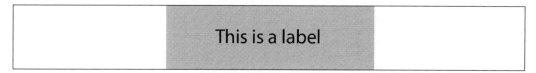

Figure 3.1: A Ttk Label widget

The Ttk `Label` widget shares most of the same options as the Tk version, the most common of which are listed here:

Argument	Values	Description
`text`	String	The text content of the label
`textvariable`	`StringVar`	The variable to bind to the contents of the label
`anchor`	Cardinal direction	The position of the text relative to the inner margins
`justify`	`left`, `right`, or `center`	The alignment of the lines of text relative to one another
`foreground`	Color string	The color of the text
`wraplength`	Integer	Number of pixels before the text is wrapped to the next line
`underline`	Integer	The index of a character in `text` to underline
`font`	Font string or tuple	The font to be used

Note that a label's text can either be specified directly using `text`, or bound to a `StringVar`, allowing for dynamic label text. The `underline` argument allows for underlining a single character in the label text; this is useful for indicating a keybinding for the user, for example, to activate a control widget labeled by the label. No keybinding is actually created by this argument; it's merely cosmetic. We'll learn to create keybindings in *Chapter 10*, *Maintaining Cross-Platform Compatibility*.

The Entry widget

The `ttk.Entry` widget is a simple one-line text entry, just like the Tkinter version. It looks like this:

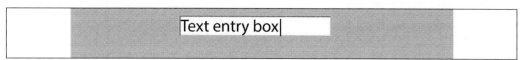

Figure 3.2: A Ttk Entry widget

We can create an `Entry` widget using this code:

```
myentry = ttk.Entry(root, textvariable=my_string_var, width=20)
```

The Ttk `Entry` is very similar to the Tkinter `Entry` widget we've already seen, and supports many of the same arguments. Here is a selection of the more common `Entry` options:

Argument	Values	Description
textvariable	StringVar	Tkinter control variable to bind.
show	String	Character or string to show when the user types. Useful for password fields, for example.
justify	left, right, or center	Alignment of the text in the entry. left is default.
foreground	Color string	Color of text.

We'll learn some more options for the `Entry` as we dig deeper into the capabilities of Ttk widgets in future chapters. The `Entry` will be used for all of our text entry fields, as well as our `Date` field. Ttk does not have a dedicated `date` widget, but we'll learn in *Chapter 5, Reducing User Error with Validation and Automation*, how to turn our `Entry` into a `date` field.

The Spinbox widget

Like the Tkinter version, the Ttk `Spinbox` adds increment and decrement buttons to the standard `Entry` widget, making it suitable for numerical data.

The Ttk `Spinbox` is shown here:

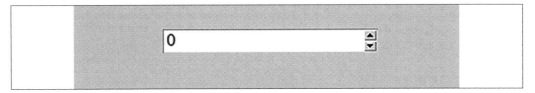

Figure 3.3: A Ttk Spinbox widget

We can create one like this:

```
myspinbox = ttk.Spinbox(
    root,
    from_=0, to=100, increment=.01,
```

```
    textvariable=my_int_var,
    command=my_callback
)
```

As this code shows, the Ttk `Spinbox` takes a number of arguments that control the behavior of its arrow buttons, listed in this table:

Argument	Values	Description
`from_`	Float or Int	Minimum value the arrows will decrement to.
`to`	Float or Int	Maximum value the arrows will increment to.
`increment`	Float or Int	Value that will be added or subtracted by the arrows.
`command`	Python function	Callback to be executed when either button is pushed.
`textvariable`	Control variable (any type)	Variable bound to the field value.
`values`	List of strings or numbers	Set of choices the buttons will scroll through. Overrides the `from_` and `to` values.

Note that these arguments do *not* restrict what is entered into the `Spinbox`; they only impact the behavior of the arrows. Also, be aware that if you specify only one of `from_` or `to`, the other defaults to 0 automatically. This can lead to unexpected behavior; for example, if you set `from_=1` without specifying `to`, then `to` will default to 0 and your arrows will only toggle between 1 and 0. To explicitly set no limit, you can use `from_='-infinity'` and `to='infinity'`.

The `Spinbox` widget is not merely for numbers, even though that's primarily how we'll be using it. As you can see, it can also take a `values` argument, which is a list of strings or numbers that can be scrolled through using the arrow buttons. Because of this, the `Spinbox` can be bound to any kind of control variable, not just `IntVar` or `DoubleVar` variables.

 Remember, none of these parameters actually limit what can be typed into a `Spinbox` widget. It's really nothing more than an `Entry` widget with buttons tacked on, and you can type not only numeric values outside the valid range but letters and symbols as well. Doing so can cause an exception if you've bound the widget to a non-string variable. In *Chapter 5, Reducing User Error with Validation and Automation*, we'll learn how to make the `Spinbox` widget limit entry to valid numeric characters only.

The Checkbutton widget

The Ttk Checkbutton widget is a labeled checkbox ideal for entering Boolean data. It can be created like so:

```
mycheckbutton = ttk.Checkbutton(
    root,
    variable=my_bool_var,
    textvariable=my_string_var,
    command=my_callback
)
```

Checkbutton widgets can take a number of arguments in addition to those listed above, as shown in this table:

Argument	Values	Description
variable	Control variable	The variable to which the checked/unchecked state of the box is bound
text	String	The label text
textvariable	StringVar	The variable to which the label text is bound
command	Python function	A callback to execute whenever the box is checked or unchecked
onvalue	Any	Value to set variable when the box is checked
offvalue	Any	Value to set variable when the box is unchecked
underline	Integer	Index of a character in text to underline

The label included in the Checkbutton can be set directly using the text argument, or it can be bound to a control variable using textvariable. This allows for dynamic labeling of the widget, which can be useful in many situations.

Although the Checkbutton is ideal for Boolean data and defaults to setting its bound variable to True or False, we can override this behavior with the onvalue and offvalue arguments, allowing it to be usable with any type of control variable.

For example, we can use it with a DoubleVar like so:

```
mycheckbutton2 = ttk.Checkbutton(
    root,
    variable=my_dbl_var,
    text='Would you like Pi?',
    onvalue=3.14159,
```

```
    offvalue=0,
    underline=15
)
```

The Ttk `Checkbutton` places the label to the right of the box, as shown in this screenshot:

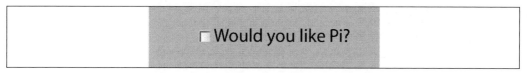

Figure 3.4: A Ttk Checkbutton widget with its built-in label

The Radiobutton widget

Like its Tkinter counterpart, the Ttk `Radiobutton` widget is used for selection among a set of mutually exclusive options. A single `Radiobutton` by itself is not a terribly useful widget; instead, they are usually created as a group, as shown here:

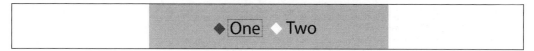

Figure 3.5: A pair of Ttk Radiobutton widgets

The following code shows how to create these buttons:

```
buttons = tk.Frame(root)
r1 = ttk.Radiobutton(
    buttons,
    variable=my_int_var,
    value=1,
    text='One'
)
r2 = ttk.Radiobutton(
    buttons,
    variable=my_int_var,
    value=2,
    text='Two'
)
```

To group `Radiobutton` widgets, you simply need to assign them all the same control variable, then add a distinct `value` to each button. In our example, we've also grouped them on the same parent widget, but this is merely for visual reasons and not strictly necessary.

This table shows some of the various arguments you can use with a `Radiobutton`:

Argument	Values	Description
variable	Control variable	A variable to be bound to the button's selected state
value	Any	A value to set the variable to when the button is selected
command	Python function	A callback to execute when the button is clicked
text	String	The label connected to the radio button
textvariable	StringVar	A variable bound to the button's label text
underline	Integer	Index of a character in text to underline

The Combobox widget

In *Chapter 1, Introduction to Tkinter*, we learned about a couple of options for providing a selection between distinct options: the `Listbox` and `OptionMenu` widgets. Ttk offers a new widget for this purpose, `Combobox`. The `Combobox` widget is an `Entry` widget that has a drop-down listbox added. It not only allows for mouse selection, but also keyboard entry. Although it may seem like `OptionMenu` is a better fit for our application in some ways, we're going to exploit the `Combobox` widget's keyboard functionality to build a superior drop-down widget.

We can create a `Combobox` widget like so:

```
mycombo = ttk.Combobox(
    root, textvariable=my_string_var,
    values=['This option', 'That option', 'Another option']
)
```

Running that code will give us a combo box that looks something like this:

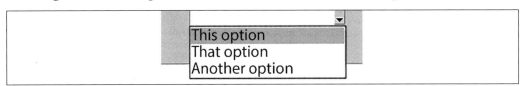

Figure 3.6: A Ttk Combobox widget

Note that while we can specify a list of possible values to populate the drop-down listbox, the `Combobox` widget is not limited to those values. Users can type any text they wish into the box and the bound variable will be updated accordingly. By default, the `Combobox` is not suited to a list of values that must remain constrained to a set list; however, in *Chapter 5, Reducing User Error with Validation and Automation*, we'll learn how to address this.

This table shows some of the common arguments used with a Combobox:

Argument	Values	Description
textvariable	StringVar	Variable bound to the contents of the Combobox
values	List of strings	Values to populate the drop-down listbox
postcommand	Python function	Callback to run just before the listbox is displayed
justify	left, right, or center	Alignment of text in the box

The Text widget

The Text widget, which we have already met in *Chapter 1, Introduction to Tkinter*, is the only widget we'll use that *does not* have a Ttk version. While this widget is most often used for multi-line text entry, it actually offers much more than that. The Text widget can be used to display or edit text that contains images, multicolored text, hyperlink-style clickable text, and much more.

We can add one to an application as follows:

```
mytext = tk.Text(
    root,
    undo=True, maxundo=100,
    spacing1=10, spacing2=2, spacing3=5,
    height=5, wrap='char'
)
```

The above code will produce something that looks like this:

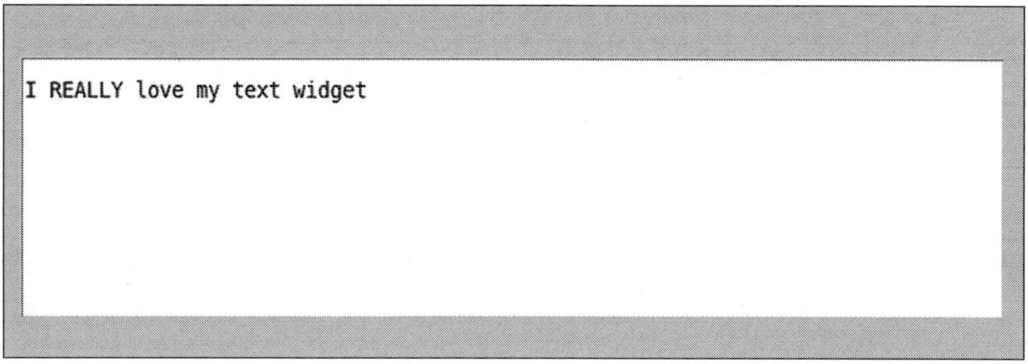

Figure 3.7: A Tk Text widget

The Text widget has a large number of arguments we can specify to control its appearance and behavior. Some of the more useful ones are listed in this table:

Argument	Values	Description
height	Integer	Height of the widget in lines of text.
width	Integer	Width of the widget in number of characters. For variable-width fonts, the width of a "0" character is used to calculate the width.
undo	Boolean	Activates or deactivates the undo functionality. Undo and redo actions are activated using the platform's default shortcuts.
maxundo	Integer	Maximum number of edits that will be stored for undo.
wrap	none, char, or word	Specifies how a line of text will be broken and wrapped when it exceeds the width of the widget.
spacing1	Integer	The number of pixels to pad above each complete line of text.
spacing2	Integer	The number of pixels to pad between displayed lines of wrapped text.
spacing3	Integer	The number of pixels to pad below each complete line of text.

More advanced visual configuration of the Text widget is implemented using **tags**. We'll discuss tags in *Chapter 9, Improving the Look with Styles and Themes*.

Text widget indices

Remember that a Text widget cannot be bound to a control variable; to access, set, or clear its contents, we need to use its get(), insert(), and delete() methods, respectively.

When reading or modifying with these methods, you are required to pass in one or two **index values** to select the character or range of characters that you're operating on. These index values are strings that can take any of the following formats:

- The line number and character number separated by a dot. Lines are numbered from 1 and characters from 0, so the first character on the first line is 1.0, while the twelfth character on the fourth line would be 4.11. Note that a *line* is determined by the presence of a newline character; a wrapped line of text is still only considered one line for index purposes.

- The string literal end, or the Tkinter constant END, indicating the end of the text.

- A numerical index plus one of the words linestart, lineend, wordstart, or wordend, indicating the start or end of the line or word relative to the numerical index. For example:
    - 6.2 wordstart would be the start of the word containing the third character on line 6
    - 2.0 lineend would be the end of line 2

- Any of the preceding, a plus or minus operator, and a number of characters or lines. For example:
    - 2.5 wordend - 1 chars would be the character before the end of the word containing the sixth character on line 2

The following example shows these indices in action:

```
# insert a string at the beginning
mytext.insert('1.0', "I love my text widget!")

# insert a string into the current text
mytext.insert('1.2', 'REALLY ')

# get the whole string
mytext.get('1.0', tk.END)

# delete the last character.
mytext.delete('end - 2 chars')
```

Note in the last example that we deleted two characters in order to delete the last character. The Text widget automatically appends a newline to the end of its text content, so we always need to remember to account for that extra character when dealing with indices or the extracted text.

 Remember, these indices should be *strings*, not float values! Float values will sometimes work due to implicit type casting, but don't rely on that behavior.

The Button widget

The Ttk `Button` is a simple clickable pushbutton that can activate a callback function. It appears something like this:

Figure 3.8: A Ttk Button widget

We can create one like so:

```
mybutton = ttk.Button(
    root,
    command=my_callback,
    text='Click Me!',
    default='active'
)
```

The button is a pretty straightforward widget, but it has a few options that can be used to configure it. These are shown in the table below:

Arguments	Values	Description
text	String	Label text on the button.
textvariable	StringVar	Variable bound to the label text of the button.
command	Python function	Callback to be executed when the button is clicked.
default	normal, active, disabled	If the button executes when Enter is pushed. active means it will execute in response to Enter, normal means it will only if selected first, and disabled means it will not respond to Enter.
underline	Integer	Index of a character in text to underline.

Buttons can also be configured to display images rather than text. We'll learn more about that in *Chapter 9, Improving the Look with Styles and Themes*.

The LabelFrame widget

In *Chapter 1, Introduction to Tkinter*, we used the `Frame` widget to group together our widgets. Ttk offers us a more powerful option in the `LabelFrame`, which provides a frame with a border and a label. This is a very useful widget to provide visual grouping for widgets in our GUI.

This code shows an example of a `LabelFrame`:

```
mylabelframe = ttk.LabelFrame(
    root,
    text='Button frame'
)

b1 = ttk.Button(
    mylabelframe,
    text='Button 1'
)
b2 = ttk.Button(
    mylabelframe,
    text='Button 2'
)
b1.pack()
b2.pack()
```

The resulting GUI would look like this:

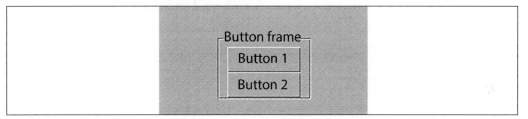

Figure 3.9: A Ttk LabelFrame widget

The `LabelFrame` widget offers us a few arguments for configuration, shown here:

Argument	Values	Description
text	String	The text of the label to display.
labelanchor	Cardinal direction	Where to anchor the text label.
labelwidget	ttk.Label object	A label widget to use for the label. Overrides `text`.
underline	Integer	The index of a character in `text` to underline.

As you can see, we can configure the label of the `LabelFrame` either by specifying the `text` argument, or by creating a `Label` widget and assigning it using the `labelwidget` argument. The latter case may be preferable if we want to take advantage of some of the `Label` widget's advanced features, such as binding a `textvariable` to it. If we use it, it will override the `text` argument.

Tkinter and Ttk contain many more widgets, some of which we'll encounter later in this book. Python also ships with a widget library called `tix`, which contains several dozen widgets. However, `tix` is very outdated, and we won't be covering it in this book. You should know that it exists, though.

Implementing the application

So far, we've learned some Tkinter basics, researched the user's needs, designed our application, and determined which Ttk widgets will be useful in our application. Now it's time to put all of this together and actually code the first version of the ABQ Data Entry application. Recall our design from *Chapter 2, Designing GUI Applications*, shown here:

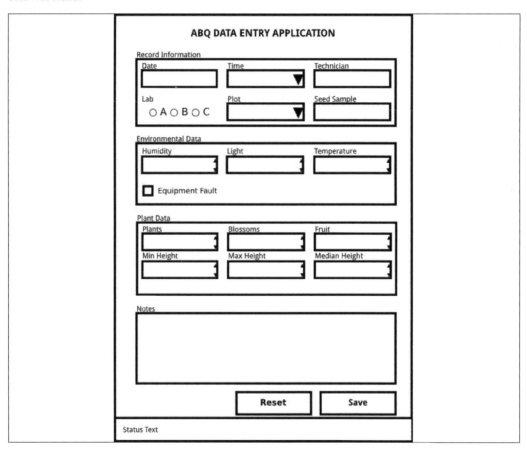

Figure 3.10: The ABQ Data Entry application layout

Take a moment to review the widgets we need to create, and we'll begin coding.

First steps

Open a new file in your editor called `data_entry_app.py`, and let's begin like this:

```python
# data_entry_app.py
"""The ABQ Data Entry application"""

import tkinter as tk
from tkinter import ttk
from datetime import datetime
from pathlib import Path
import csv
```

Our script starts with a **docstring**, as all Python scripts should. This string at a minimum should give the name of the application to which the file belongs, and may also include notes about usage, authorship, or other items a future maintainer would need to know.

Next, we're importing the Python modules that we'll need for this application; these are:

- `tkinter` and `ttk`, of course, for our GUI items
- The `datetime` class, from the `datetime` module, which we'll use to generate a datestring for the filename
- The `Path` class, from the `pathlib` module, which is used for some file operations in our save routine
- The `csv` module, which we'll use to interact with the CSV file

Next, let's create some global variables that the app will use to keep track of information:

```python
variables = dict()
records_saved = 0
```

The `variables` dictionary will hold all of the form's control variables. Keeping them in a dictionary will make it a little easier to manage them and will keep our global namespace lean and clean. The `records_saved` variable will store how many records the user has saved since opening the app.

Now it's time to create and configure the root window:

```python
root = tk.Tk()
root.title('ABQ Data Entry Application')
root.columnconfigure(0, weight=1)
```

We've set the window title for the application and also configured its layout grid so that the first column is allowed to expand. The root window will only have one column, but by setting this it will allow the form to remain centered on the application if the window is expanded. Without it, the form would be stuck to the left side of the window when the window is expanded.

Now we'll add a heading for the application:

```
ttk.Label(
    root, text="ABQ Data Entry Application",
    font=("TkDefaultFont", 16)
).grid()
```

Because we won't need to refer to this widget again, we won't bother assigning it to a variable. This also allows us to call `grid()` on the `Label` on the same line, keeping our code more concise and the namespace less cluttered. We'll do this for most of the widgets in the application, unless there is some reason we may need to interact with the widget elsewhere in the code.

> Note that we used `TkDefaultFont` as the font family value for this label widget. This is an alias defined in Tkinter that points to the default window font on your platform. We'll learn more about fonts in *Chapter 9, Improving the Look with Styles and Themes*.

Building the data record form

With the initial application window set up, let's start building the actual data entry form. We'll create a frame to contain the entire data record form, called `drf`:

```
drf = ttk.Frame(root)
drf.grid(padx=10, sticky=(tk.E + tk.W))
drf.columnconfigure(0, weight=1)
```

The `drf` frame is added to the main window with a bit of horizontal padding, and the `sticky` argument ensures that it will stretch when the containing column is stretched. We're also going to configure its grid to expand the first column.

> For windows or frames using a grid layout, if you want to make the child widgets stretch when the parent is stretched, you need to make sure both the container will expand (using `columnconfigure` and `rowconfigure` on the parent) *and* the child widget will expand with the container (using `sticky` when you call `grid()` on the child widget).

The Record Information section

The first section of our form is the Record Information section. Let's create and configure a LabelFrame to store that:

```
r_info = ttk.LabelFrame(drf, text='Record Information')
r_info.grid(sticky=(tk.W + tk.E))
for i in range(3):
  r_info.columnconfigure(i, weight=1)
```

We start by creating a Ttk LabelFrame widget with the data record form as its parent. We add it to the parent's grid, setting the sticky argument so that it will expand when the window is resized. Each frame of this form is going to have three columns of input widgets, and we want each column to expand evenly to fill the width of the frame. So, we have used a for loop to set the weight attribute of each column to 1.

Now we can begin creating the contents of the frame, starting with the first input widget, the Date field:

```
variables['Date'] = tk.StringVar()
ttk.Label(r_info, text='Date').grid(row=0, column=0)
ttk.Entry(
  r_info, textvariable=variables['Date']
).grid(row=1, column=0, sticky=(tk.W + tk.E))
```

First, we created a control variable and put it in the variables dictionary. Then we created our Label widget for the Date field and added it to the LabelFrame widget's grid. We're going to use explicit row and column values here, even when it's not strictly necessary, because we're going to be placing objects a little out of order. Without explicit coordinates, things could get confusing.

Finally, we create the Entry widget, passing in the control variable. Note that we aren't going to save any references to our widgets if we can use a variable to store the value. This will keep the code more concise. We've added our widget to the grid, placing it *below* its label by specifying the first column of the next row. For both the Entry and the Label, we've used the sticky argument to make sure the widget stretches when the GUI is expanded.

Now let's add the rest of the first line, the Time and Technician fields:

```
time_values = ['8:00', '12:00', '16:00', '20:00']
variables['Time'] = tk.StringVar()
ttk.Label(r_info, text='Time').grid(row=0, column=1)
ttk.Combobox(
  r_info, textvariable=variables['Time'], values=time_values
```

```
).grid(row=1, column=1, sticky=(tk.W + tk.E))

variables['Technician'] = tk.StringVar()
ttk.Label(r_info, text='Technician').grid(row=0, column=2)
ttk.Entry(
  r_info, textvariable=variables['Technician']
).grid(row=1, column=2, sticky=(tk.W + tk.E))
```

Once again, we create a variable, Label, and input widget for each item. Recall that the Combobox widget takes a list of strings for its values argument, which will populate the drop-down part of the widget. That takes care of the first row.

On the second row, we'll start with the Lab inputs:

```
variables['Lab'] = tk.StringVar()
ttk.Label(r_info, text='Lab').grid(row=2, column=0)
labframe = ttk.Frame(r_info)
for lab in ('A', 'B', 'C'):
  ttk.Radiobutton(
    labframe, value=lab, text=lab, variable=variables['Lab']
  ).pack(side=tk.LEFT, expand=True)
labframe.grid(row=3, column=0, sticky=(tk.W + tk.E))
```

Like before, we've created the control variable and Label, but for the input widget we've created a Frame to hold the three Radiobutton widgets. We're also creating our Radiobutton widgets using a for loop to keep the code more concise and consistent.

The pack() geometry manager comes in handy here because we can populate from left to right without having to explicitly manage column numbers. The expand argument causes the widget to use extra space when the window is resized; this will help our buttons to utilize available space and not be scrunched into the left side of the window.

Now let's do the remaining portion of line two, the Plot and Seed Sample fields:

```
variables['Plot'] = tk.IntVar()
ttk.Label(r_info, text='Plot').grid(row=2, column=1)
ttk.Combobox(
  r_info,
  textvariable=variables['Plot'],
  values=list(range(1, 21))
).grid(row=3, column=1, sticky=(tk.W + tk.E))

variables['Seed Sample'] = tk.StringVar()
```

```
ttk.Label(r_info, text='Seed Sample').grid(row=2, column=2)
ttk.Entry(
  r_info,
  textvariable=variables['Seed Sample']
).grid(row=3, column=2, sticky=(tk.W + tk.E))
```

We have the same thing going on here: create a variable, create a `Label`, create the input widget. Note that for the `Plot` values we're generating a list using `range()` to keep our code concise.

The Environment Data section

The next part of the form is the `Environment Data` frame. Let's begin that section as follows:

```
e_info = ttk.LabelFrame(drf, text="Environment Data")
e_info.grid(sticky=(tk.W + tk.E))
for i in range(3):
  e_info.columnconfigure(i, weight=1)
```

This is exactly what we did for the last `LabelFrame`, with only the names updated. Let's start populating it with the `Humidity`, `Light`, and `Temperature` widgets:

```
variables['Humidity'] = tk.DoubleVar()
ttk.Label(e_info, text="Humidity (g/m³)").grid(row=0, column=0)
ttk.Spinbox(
  e_info, textvariable=variables['Humidity'],
  from_=0.5, to=52.0, increment=0.01,
).grid(row=1, column=0, sticky=(tk.W + tk.E))

variables['Light'] = tk.DoubleVar()
ttk.Label(e_info, text='Light (klx)').grid(row=0, column=1)
ttk.Spinbox(
  e_info, textvariable=variables['Light'],
  from_=0, to=100, increment=0.01
).grid(row=1, column=1, sticky=(tk.W + tk.E))

variables['Temperature'] = tk.DoubleVar()
ttk.Label(e_info, text='Temperature (°C)').grid(row=0, column=2)
ttk.Spinbox(
  e_info, textvariable=variables['Temperature'],
  from_=4, to=40, increment=.01
).grid(row=1, column=2, sticky=(tk.W + tk.E))
```

Good! Now, for the second row of this section, we only need to add in the Equipment Fault check button:

```python
variables['Equipment Fault'] = tk.BooleanVar(value=False)
ttk.Checkbutton(
    e_info, variable=variables['Equipment Fault'],
    text='Equipment Fault'
).grid(row=2, column=0, sticky=tk.W, pady=5)
```

The first three values are all floating-point numbers, so we're using DoubleVar control variables and Spinbox widgets for entry. Don't forget to populate the from_, to, and increment values for the Spinbox widgets, so that the arrows behave properly. Our Checkbutton takes a BooleanVar control variable and doesn't need a Label widget due to its built-in label. Also, note that because we've started a new frame, our rows and columns for the grid start over. This is a benefit of breaking up the form into smaller frames: we don't have to keep track of ever-increasing row or column numbers.

The Plant Data section

We'll create the next frame, Plant Data, just like the other two:

```python
p_info = ttk.LabelFrame(drf, text="Plant Data")
p_info.grid(sticky=(tk.W + tk.E))
for i in range(3):
    p_info.columnconfigure(i, weight=1)
```

Now, having created and configured the frame, let's add in the first row of inputs, Plants, Blossoms, and Fruit:

```python
variables['Plants'] = tk.IntVar()
ttk.Label(p_info, text='Plants').grid(row=0, column=0)
ttk.Spinbox(
    p_info, textvariable=variables['Plants'],
    from_=0, to=20, increment=1
).grid(row=1, column=0, sticky=(tk.W + tk.E))

variables['Blossoms'] = tk.IntVar()
ttk.Label(p_info, text='Blossoms').grid(row=0, column=1)
ttk.Spinbox(
    p_info, textvariable=variables['Blossoms'],
    from_=0, to=1000, increment=1
).grid(row=1, column=1, sticky=(tk.W + tk.E))
```

```
variables['Fruit'] = tk.IntVar()
ttk.Label(p_info, text='Fruit').grid(row=0, column=2)
ttk.Spinbox(
  p_info, textvariable=variables['Fruit'],
  from_=0, to=1000, increment=1
).grid(row=1, column=2, sticky=(tk.W + tk.E))
```

There is nothing really new here, except that, since we're using `IntVar` control variables, we've set the `Spinbox` increment to 1. That won't really stop anyone from entering a decimal (or any arbitrary string for that matter), but at least the buttons won't steer the user wrong. In *Chapter 5, Reducing User Error with Validation and Automation*, we'll see how to enforce `increment` more thoroughly.

And now finally our last row of inputs, `Min Height`, `Max Height`, and `Med Height`:

```
variables['Min Height'] = tk.DoubleVar()
ttk.Label(p_info, text='Min Height (cm)').grid(row=2, column=0)
ttk.Spinbox(
  p_info, textvariable=variables['Min Height'],
  from_=0, to=1000, increment=0.01
).grid(row=3, column=0, sticky=(tk.W + tk.E))

variables['Max Height'] = tk.DoubleVar()
ttk.Label(p_info, text='Max Height (cm)').grid(row=2, column=1)
ttk.Spinbox(
  p_info, textvariable=variables['Max Height'],
  from_=0, to=1000, increment=0.01
).grid(row=3, column=1, sticky=(tk.W + tk.E))

variables['Med Height'] = tk.DoubleVar()
ttk.Label(p_info, text='Median Height (cm)').grid(row=2, column=2)
ttk.Spinbox(
  p_info, textvariable=variables['Med Height'],
  from_=0, to=1000, increment=0.01
).grid(row=3, column=2, sticky=(tk.W + tk.E))
```

We've made three more `DoubleVar` objects, three more labels, and three more `Spinbox` widgets. If this feels a little repetitive, don't be surprised; GUI code can tend to be quite repetitive. In *Chapter 4, Organizing Our Code with Classes*, we'll find ways to reduce this repetitiveness.

Finishing the GUI

That finishes our three info sections; now we need to add the Notes input. We'll add it directly to the drf frame with a label, like so:

```
ttk.Label(drf, text="Notes").grid()
notes_inp = tk.Text(drf, width=75, height=10)
notes_inp.grid(sticky=(tk.W + tk.E))
```

Since we cannot associate a control variable with the Text widget, we'll need to keep a regular variable reference to it.

> When you do need to save a reference to a widget, don't forget to call grid() in a separate statement! Since grid() (and other geometry manager methods) returns None, if you create and position the widget in one statement your saved widget reference will just be None.

We're almost finished with the form! We just need to add some buttons:

```
buttons = tk.Frame(drf)
buttons.grid(sticky=tk.E + tk.W)
save_button = ttk.Button(buttons, text='Save')
save_button.pack(side=tk.RIGHT)

reset_button = ttk.Button(buttons, text='Reset')
reset_button.pack(side=tk.RIGHT)
```

To keep the form's grid layout simpler, we've packed the two buttons into a sub-frame, using pack() with the side argument to keep them over on the right.

That finishes the data record form; to finish out the application GUI, we only need to add in a status bar with an associated variable, like so:

```
status_variable = tk.StringVar()
ttk.Label(
    root, textvariable=status_variable
).grid(sticky=tk.W + tk.E, row=99, padx=10)
```

The status bar is simply a Label widget, which we've placed on the root window's grid at row 99 to ensure that it stays at the bottom in case of any future additions to the application. Note that we have not added the status variable to the variables dictionary; that dictionary is reserved for variables that will hold user input. This variable is just going to be used to display messages to the user.

Writing the callback functions

Now that our layout is done, let's work on creating the functionality of our application. Our form has two buttons that need callback functions: Reset and Save.

The Reset function

The job of our reset function is to return the entire form to a blank state so the user can enter in more data. We'll need this function not only as a callback to the Reset button, but also to prepare the form for the next record after the user saves a record. Otherwise, the user would have to manually delete and overwrite the data in each field for every new record.

Since we'll need to call the reset callback from the save callback, we need to write the reset function first. At the end of data_entry_app.py, start a new function like so:

```
# data_entry_app.py
def on_reset():
  """Called when reset button is clicked, or after save"""
```

The function is called on_reset(). Recall from *Chapter 1, Introduction to Tkinter,* that, by convention, callback functions are typically named on_<eventname>, where eventname refers to the event that triggers it. Since this will be triggered by clicking the Reset button, we'll call it on_reset().

Inside the function, we need to reset all the widgets to an empty value. But wait! We didn't save references to any of the widgets, apart from the Notes input. What do we need to do?

Simple: we reset all the *variables* to a blank string, like this:

```
    for variable in variables.values():
      if isinstance(variable, tk.BooleanVar):
        variable.set(False)
      else:
        variable.set('')

    notes_inp.delete('1.0', tk.END)
```

StringVar, DoubleVar, and IntVar objects can be set to a blank string, which will cause any widgets bound to them to be blank. BooleanVar variables will raise an exception if we try to do that, so instead we'll check if our variable is a BooleanVar using Python's built-in isinstance() function. If it is, we simply set it to False.

For the Notes input, we can use the Text widget's delete() method to clear its contents. This method takes a start and end location, just like the get() method does. The values 1.0 and tk.END indicate the entire contents of the widget. Recall from our earlier discussion of the Text widget that this index is the *string* 1.0, *not* a float value.

That's all we need in our reset callback. To bind it to the button, use the button's configure() method:

```
reset_button.configure(command=on_reset)
```

 The configure() method can be called on any Tkinter widget to change its properties. It accepts the same keyword arguments as the widget's constructor.

The Save callback

Our last bit of functionality, and the most important, is the Save callback. Recall from our program specification that our application needs to append the entered data to a **CSV (comma-separated values)** file with the filename abq_data_record_CURRENTDATE.csv, where CURRENTDATE is the date in ISO format (year-month-day). The CSV should be created if it doesn't exist, and have the column headers written to the first row. Therefore, this function needs to do the following:

- Determine the current date and generate the filename
- Determine if the file exists, and if not create it and write a header row
- Extract the data from the form and do any clean-up necessary
- Append the row of data to the file
- Increment records_saved and alert the user that the record was saved
- Reset the form for the next record

Let's start the function out this way:

```
def on_save():
    """Handle save button clicks"""

    global records_saved
```

Once again, we're using the on_<eventname> naming convention. The first thing we've done is declared records_saved as a global variable. If we don't do this, Python will interpret the name records_saved as a local variable and we won't be able to update it.

Modifying global variables is generally bad form, but Tkinter doesn't really give us many options here: we can't use a return value to update the variable, because this is a callback function that is called in response to an event, not at any place in our code where we have direct access to `records_saved`. In *Chapter 4*, *Organizing Our Code with Classes*, we'll learn a better way to implement this functionality without global variables; for now, though, we're stuck with it.

Next, let's figure out the details of the filename and whether it exists or not:

```python
datestring = datetime.today().strftime("%Y-%m-%d")
filename = f"abq_data_record_{datestring}.csv"
newfile = not Path(filename).exists()
```

The `datetime.today()` function returns a `Date` object for the current day, and its `strftime()` method allows us to format that date into a string in any way we specify. The syntax for `strftime()` has its roots in C programming, so it's rather cryptic in some cases; but hopefully it is clear that `%Y` means year, `%m` means month, and `%d` means day. This will return the date in ISO format; for example, 2021-10-31 for October 31, 2021.

With the `datestring` in hand, we can use it to build the filename for the day's CSV file. In the next line, `Path(filename).exists()` tells us whether the file exists in the current working directory. It does this by constructing a `Path` object using the filename, then calling its `exists()` method to see if the file is already on the filesystem. We'll save this information to a variable called `newfile`.

Now it's time to get the data from the form:

```python
data = dict()
fault = variables['Equipment Fault'].get()
for key, variable in variables.items():
  if fault and key in ('Light', 'Humidity', 'Temperature'):
    data[key] = ''
  else:
    try:
      data[key] = variable.get()
    except tk.TclError:
      status_variable.set(
        f'Error in field: {key}.  Data was not saved!'
      )
      return
# get the Text widget contents separately
data['Notes'] = notes_inp.get('1.0', tk.END)
```

We're going to store the data in a new dictionary object called data. To do this, we'll iterate through our variables dictionary, calling get() on each variable. Of course, if there is an equipment fault, we want to skip the values for Light, Humidity, and Temperature, so we're first getting the value of Equipment Fault and checking it before those field values are being retrieved. If we do need to retrieve a value from the variable, we'll do this in a try block. Remember that variables will raise a TclError if the get() method is called when there is an invalid value in them, so we need to handle that exception. In this case, we'll let the user know that there was a problem with that particular field and exit the function immediately.

Finally, we need to get the data from the Notes field using get().

Now that we have the data, we need to write it to a CSV. Add the following code next:

```
with open(filename, 'a', newline='') as fh:
    csvwriter = csv.DictWriter(fh, fieldnames=data.keys())
    if newfile:
        csvwriter.writeheader()
    csvwriter.writerow(data)
```

First, we're opening the file using a context manager (the with keyword). Doing it this way ensures that the file will be closed when we exit the indented block. We're opening in *append* mode (indicated by the a argument to open), which means any data we write will simply be added to the end of whatever is already there. Note the newline argument, which we've set to an empty string. This is to work around a bug in the CSV module on Windows that causes an extra empty line to appear between each record. It does no harm on other platforms.

Inside the block, we need to create something called a **CSV Writer object**. The standard library csv module contains a few different types of objects that can write data into a CSV file. The DictWriter class is handy in that it can take a dictionary of values in any order and write them to the proper fields of the CSV, provided the first row contains the names of the columns. We can tell the DictWriter what those header values should be by passing it data.keys(), which is all the names of our data values.

Append mode will create the file if it does not exist, but it won't write the header row automatically. Therefore, we need to check if the file is a new file (using the newfile value we found earlier), and if it is, we'll write the header row. The DictWriter object has a method for this, which causes it to just write a single row containing all the field names.

Finally, we can use the DictWriter object's writerow() method to pass in our dictionary of data to be written to the file. As we exit the indented block, Python closes the file and saves it to disk.

That leaves us with just a few final lines in the on_save() function:

```python
records_saved += 1
status_variable.set(
    f"{records_saved} records saved this session"
)
on_reset()
```

First, we'll increment the records_saved variable, then alert the user in the status bar how many records have been saved so far. This is good feedback that helps the user know their actions were successful. Finally, we call on_reset() to prepare the form for the next record to be entered.

With the save method implemented, let's go ahead and bind it to our button:

```python
save_button.configure(command=on_save)
```

Last of all, let's reset the form and launch the main event loop:

```python
on_reset()
root.mainloop()
```

That's it, your first application for ABQ is finished and ready to go!

Finishing up and testing

Before we send our application out into the world, let's fire it up and give it a test:

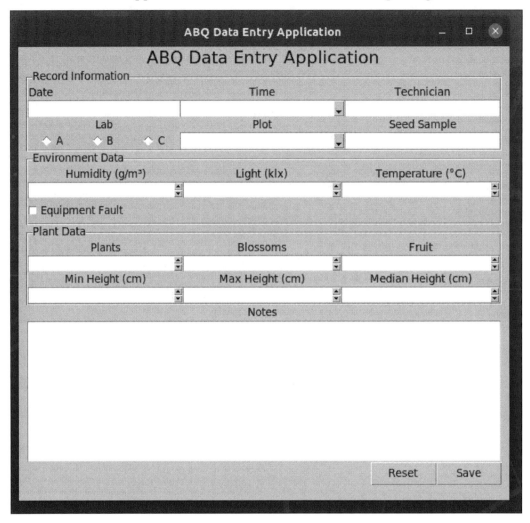

Figure 3.11: Our first ABQ Data Entry application

Looking good! And it works, too. Go ahead and enter some test data and save it. Of course, this isn't the end – we haven't quite addressed everything on the program specification, and once users get their hands on the application, the feature requests will undoubtedly begin. But for now, we can celebrate the victory of a working MVP.

Summary

Well, we've come a long way in this chapter! You took your design from a specification and some drawings to a running MVP of the application that already covers the basic functionality you need. You learned about basic Ttk widgets, such as Entry, Spinbox, Combobox, Radiobutton, and Checkbutton, as well as the Tkinter Text widget. You learned how to assemble these widgets into a complex but organized GUI using nested LabelFrame widgets, and how to save a file using a callback method.

In the next chapter, we're going to utilize classes and object-oriented programming techniques to clean up our code and expand the capabilities of our widgets.

4

Organizing Our Code with Classes

Things are going great with your data entry form! Your boss and coworkers and excited to see the progress you've made and are already coming up with some ideas of what other features could be added. This makes you a little nervous, to be honest! While they see a professional-looking form, you know that the code underneath is getting bulky and repetitive. You've got some warts in there too, like a global variable and a very cluttered global namespace. Before you start adding more features, you'd like to get a handle on this code and start breaking it down into some manageable chunks. For this, you'll need to create **classes**.

In this chapter, we'll cover the following topics:

- In *A primer on Python classes*, we'll review how to create Python classes and subclasses.

- In *Using classes with Tkinter*, we'll discover ways to utilize classes effectively in Tkinter code.

- In *Rewriting our application using classes*, we'll apply these techniques to the ABQ Data Entry application.

A primer on Python classes

While the concept of a class is simple enough on the surface, classes bring with them a number of terms and concepts that confuse many beginners. In this section, we'll discuss the advantages of using classes, explore the different features of classes, and review the syntax for creating classes in Python.

The advantages of using classes

Many beginners and even intermediate Python coders avoid or dismiss the use of classes in Python; unlike functions or variables, classes do not have obvious uses in short, simple scripts. As our application code grows, however, classes become an indispensable tool for organizing our code into manageable units. Let's look at some ways classes can help us build cleaner code.

Classes are an integral part of Python

A class is essentially a blueprint for creating an **object**. What is an object? In Python, *everything* is an object: integers, strings, floats, lists, dictionaries, Tkinter widgets, and even functions are all objects. Each of these types of objects is defined by a class. You can see this easily at a Python prompt if you use the type command, like so:

```
>>> type('hello world')
<class 'str'>
>>> type(1)
<class 'int'>
>>> type(print)
<class 'builtin_function_or_method'>
```

The type function shows you what class was used to construct the object in question. When an object is built from a particular class, we say it is an **instance** of that class.

> *Instance* and *object* are often used interchangeably, because every object is an instance of some class.

Because everything in Python is a class, creating our own classes allows us to work with custom objects using the same syntax we use with built-in objects.

Classes make relationships between data and functions explicit

Often, in code, we have a set of data that all relates to the same thing. For example, in a multiplayer game, you might have variables for each player's score, health, or progress. Functions that operate on these variables would need to be sure to operate on the variables that refer to the same player. Classes would allow us to create an explicit relationship between these variables and the functions that operate on them, so that we can more easily keep them organized as a unit.

Classes help create reusable code

Classes are a great tool for reducing code redundancy. Suppose we have a set of forms that have similar behavior on submission, but different input fields. Using class inheritance, we can create a base form with the desired common behaviors; then, we can derive the individual form classes from that, only having to implement what is unique in each form.

Syntax of class creation

Creating a class is very similar to creating a function, except that we use the `class` keyword, like so:

```python
class Banana:
  """A tasty tropical fruit"""
  pass
```

Note that we've also included a **docstring**, which is used by Python tools (such as the built-in `help` function) to generate documentation about the class. Class names in Python traditionally use **Pascal Case**, meaning the first letter of each word is capitalized; sometimes, third-party libraries will use other conventions, however.

Once we have defined a class, we can create instances of the class by calling it, just like a function:

```python
my_banana = Banana()
```

In this case, `my_banana` is an object that is an instance of the `Banana` class. Of course, a more useful class will have some things defined inside the class body; specifically, we can define **attributes** and **methods**, which are collectively known as **members**.

Attributes and methods

Attributes are simply variables, and they can be either **class attributes** or **instance attributes**. A class attribute is defined in the top scope of the class body, like this:

```python
class Banana:
  """A tasty tropical fruit"""
  food_group = 'fruit'
  colors = [
    'green', 'green-yellow', 'yellow',
    'brown spotted', 'black'
  ]
```

Class attributes are shared by all instances of the class, and are usually used for setting defaults, constants, and other read-only values.

 Note that unlike class names, member names, by convention, use **snake case**, where lowercase words are separated by underscores.

Instance attributes store values specific to a single instance of the class; to create one, we need access to an instance. We could do it like this:

```
my_banana = Banana()
my_banana.color = 'yellow'
```

However, it would be more ideal if we could define some instance attributes inside our class definition, instead of doing it externally like that. In order to do so, we need a reference to the instance of the class inside the class definition. This can be done with an **instance method**.

Methods are simply functions attached to the class. An instance method is a method that automatically receives a reference to the instance as its first argument. We can define one like this:

```
class Banana:

  def peel(self):
    self.peeled = True
```

As you can see, defining an instance method is simply defining a function inside the class body. The first argument that this function will receive is a reference to the instance of the class; it can be called anything you like, but by long-standing Python convention, we name it self. Inside the function, self can be used to do operations on the instance, such as assigning an instance attribute.

Note that the instance (self) also has access to class attributes (for example, self.colors), as shown here:

```
def set_color(self, color):
  """Set the color of the banana"""
  if color in self.colors:
    self.color = color
  else:
    raise ValueError(f'A banana cannot be {color}!')
```

When we use an instance method, we do not explicitly pass `self`; it's passed implicitly, like so:

```
my_banana = Banana()
my_banana.set_color('green')
my_banana.peel()
```

 The implicit passing of `self` often leads to confusing error messages when you pass the wrong number of arguments. For example, if you called `my_banana.peel(True)`, you'd get an exception saying that one argument was expected but two were passed. From your point of view, you only passed one argument, but the method got two because the instance reference was automatically added.

In addition to instance methods, classes can have **class methods** and **static methods**. Unlike instance methods, these methods do not have access to the instance of the class and cannot read or write instance attributes.

Class methods are created using a **decorator** just before the method definition, like this:

```
@classmethod
def check_color(cls, color):
    """Test a color string to see if it is valid."""
    return color in cls.colors


@classmethod
def make_greenie(cls):
    """Create a green banana object"""
    banana = cls()
    banana.set_color('green')
    return banana
```

Just as an instance method is implicitly passed a reference to the instance, a class method is implicitly passed a reference to the class as the first argument. Once again, you can call that argument anything you like, but conventionally it is called `cls`. Class methods are usually used for interaction with class variables. For example, in the `check_color()` method above, the method needs a reference to the class variable `colors`. Class methods are also used as convenience functions for geneating specifically configured instances of the class; for example, the `make_greenie()` method above uses its class reference to create instances of `Banana` with the color preset to green.

A **static method** is also a function that's attached to the class, but it does not get any implicit arguments, and the code within the method has no access to the class or instance. Just like the class methods, we use a decorator to define a static method, as follows:

```
@staticmethod
def estimate_calories(num_bananas):
    """Given `num_bananas`, estimate the number of calories"""
    return num_bananas * 105
```

Static methods are often used for defining algorithms or utility functions used internally by the class.

 Class and static methods can be called on the class itself; for example, we could call `Banana.estimate_calories()` or `Banana.check_color()` without actually creating an instance of Banana. Instance methods, however, *must* be called on an instance of the class. It would make no sense to call `Banana.set_color()` or `Banana.peel()`, since these methods are meant to operate on an instance. Instead, we should create an instance and call those methods on it (for example, `my_banana.peel()`).

Magic attributes and methods

All Python objects automatically get a set of attributes called **magic attributes** and a set of methods called **magic methods**, also called special methods or *dunder methods*, because they are indicated by double underscores around the attribute or method name ("dunder" is a portmanteau of "double under").

Magic attributes generally store metadata about the object. For example, the `__class__` attribute of any object stores a reference to the object's class:

```
>>> print(my_banana.__class__)
<class '__main__.Banana'>
```

Magic methods define how a Python object responds to operators (like +, %, or []) or built-in functions (like `dir()` or `setattr()`). For example, the `__str__()` method defines what an object returns when passed to the `str()` function (either explicitly or implicitly, by being passed to `print()`, for example):

```
class Banana:

    # ....
```

```
def __str__(self):
    # "Magic Attributes" contain metadata about the object
    return f'A {self.color} {self.__class__.__name__}'
```

Here, we're not only accessing the instance's `color` attribute, but using the `__class__` attribute to retrieve its class, and then using the class object's `__name__` attribute to get the class name.

 As confusing as it is, the *class* is also an *object*. It's an instance of the `type` class. Remember, everything in Python is an object, and all objects are instances of some class.

Thus, when a `Banana` object is printed, it looks like this:

```
>>> my_banana = Banana()
>>> my_banana.set_color('yellow')
>>> print(my_banana)
A yellow Banana
```

By far the most important magic method is the **initializer** method, `__init__()`. This method is executed whenever we call the class object to create an instance, and the arguments we define for it become the arguments we can pass in when creating the instance. For example:

```
def __init__(self, color='green'):

    if not self.check_color(color):
        raise ValueError(
            f'A {self.__class__.__name__} cannot be {color}'
        )
    self.color = color
```

Here, we've created the initializer with an optional argument called `color`, allowing us to set the `Banana` object's color value when creating the object. Thus, we can create a new `Banana` like so:

```
>>> my_new_banana = Banana('green')
>>> print(my_new_banana)
A green Banana
```

Ideally, any instance attributes used in the class should be created within __init__(), so that we can ensure they exist for all instances of the class. For example, we should create our peeled attribute like so:

```python
def __init__(self, color='green'):

    # ...

    self.peeled = False
```

If we didn't define this attribute here, it would not exist until the peel() method is called. Code looking for the value of my_banana.peel before that method was called would raise an exception.

Ultimately, the initializer should leave the object in a state where it is ready to be used by the program.

> In other object-oriented languages, the method that sets up a class object is known as the **constructor**, which not only initializes the new object but returns it as well. Sometimes, Python developers will casually refer to __init__() as a constructor. However, the actual constructor method for Python objects is __new__(), which we generally leave untouched in Python classes.

Public, private, and protected members

Classes are a powerful tool for *abstraction* – that is, taking a complicated object or process and providing a simple, high-level interface to the rest of the application. To help them do that, Python programmers use some naming conventions to distinguish between public, private, and protected members:

- **Public members** are those intended to be read or called by code outside the class. They use ordinary member names.

- **Protected members** are meant only for use inside the class or its subclasses. They are prefixed with a single underscore.

- **Private members** are meant only for use within the class. They're prefixed with double underscores.

Python does not actually enforce any distinction between public, protected, and private members; these are merely conventions that are understood by other programmers to indicate which parts of the class can be accessed externally, and which ones are part of the internal implementation and not meant for use outside the class.

Python *will* assist in enforcing private members by automatically changing their names to _classname__member_name.

For example, let's add this code to the Banana class:

```
__ripe_colors = ['yellow', 'brown spotted']

def _is_ripe(self):
  """Protected method to see if the banana is ripe."""
  return self.color in self.__ripe_colors


def can_eat(self, must_be_ripe=False):
  """Check if I can eat the banana."""
  if must_be_ripe and not self._is_ripe():
    return False
  return True
```

Here, __ripe_colors is a private attribute. If you tried to access my_banana.__ripe_colors, Python would raise an AttributeError exception because it has implicitly renamed this property to my_banana._Banana__ripe_colors. The method _is_ripe() is a protected member but, unlike the private member, Python does not alter its name. It could be executed as my_banana._is_ripe(), but programmers using your class would understand that this method is meant for internal use and not to be relied upon in external code. Instead, the can_eat() method, which is public, should be called.

There are a variety of reasons why you'd want to indicate a member as private or protected, but in general, it's because the member is part of some internal process and would be either meaningless, unreliable, or lacking in context for use in outside code.

Although the words *private* and *protected* seem to indicate a security feature, that is not their intention, and using them does not provide any security to the class. The intention is simply to distinguish the public interface of the class (which outside code should use) from the internal machinery of the class (which should be left alone).

Inheritance and subclasses

Building our own classes is a powerful tool indeed, but since everything in Python is an object built from a class, wouldn't it be nice if we could take one of those existing classes and simply alter it to fit our needs? That way, we wouldn't have to start from scratch every time.

Fortunately, we can! When we create a class, Python allows us to derive it from an existing class, like so:

```python
class RedBanana(Banana):
  """Bananas of the red variety"""
  pass
```

We've created the class `RedBanana` as a **child class** or **subclass** of Banana. Banana is known as the **parent class** or **superclass** in this case. Initially, `RedBanana` is an exact copy of Banana and will behave identically, but we can modify it by simply defining members, like so:

```python
class RedBanana(Banana):

  colors = ['green', 'orange', 'red', 'brown', 'black']
  botanical_name = 'red dacca'

  def set_color(self, color):
    if color not in self.colors:
      raise ValueError(f'A Red Banana cannot be {color}!')
```

Specifying existing members, like `colors` and `set_color`, will mask the superclass versions of those members. Thus, calling `set_color()` on a `RedBanana` instance will call the `RedBanana` version of the method, which, in turn, will consult the `RedBanana` version of `colors` when `self.colors` is referenced. We can also add new members, such as the `botanical_name` a ttribute, which will only exist in the subclass.

In some cases, we might want our subclass method to add to the superclass method, but still execute the code in the superclass version of the method. We could copy the superclass code into our subclass code, but there's a better way: using `super()`.

Inside an instance method, `super()` gives us a reference to the superclass version of our instance, like so:

```python
def peel(self):
  super().peel()
  print('It looks like a regular banana inside!')
```

In this case, calling `super().peel()` causes the code in `Banana.peel()` to be executed on our `RedBanana` instance. Then, we can add additional code to our subclass version of `peel()`.

> As you'll see in the next section, `super()` is often used in the `__init__()` method to run the superclass's initializer. This is especially true for Tkinter GUI classes, which do a lot of critical external setup in their initializer methods.

There is much more to Python classes than we have discussed here, including the concept of **multiple inheritance**, which we will learn about in *Chapter 5, Reducing User Error with Validation and Automation*. What we've learned so far, however, is more than enough to apply to our Tkinter code. Let's see how classes can help us in a GUI context.

Using classes with Tkinter

GUI frameworks and object-oriented code go hand in hand. While Tkinter, more than most frameworks, allows you to create GUIs using procedural programming, we miss out on a great deal of organizational power in doing so. Although we'll find many ways to use classes in our Tkinter code throughout this book, we'll look at three primary ways of using them here:

- Improving or expanding Tkinter classes for more power
- Creating **compound widgets** to save repetitive typing
- Organizing our application into self-contained **components**

Improving Tkinter classes

Let's face it: some Tkinter objects are a little lacking in functionality. We can fix that by subclassing Tkinter classes and making our own improved versions. For instance, while we've seen that Tkinter control variable classes are useful, hey are limited to string, integer, double, and Boolean types. What if we wanted the functionality of these variables, but for more complex objects like dictionaries or lists? We can, with subclassing and some help from JSON.

> **JavaScript Object Notation (JSON)** is a standardized format for representing lists, dictionaries, and other compound objects as strings. The Python standard library comes with a `json` library, which allows us to convert such objects to string format and back again. We'll use JSON more in *Chapter 7, Creating Menus with Menu and Tkinter Dialogs*.

Open a new script called `tkinter_classes_demo.py`, and let's begin with some imports, like this:

```
# tkinter_classes_demo.py
import tkinter as tk
import json
```

In addition to Tkinter, we've imported the standard library `json` module. This module contains two functions that we'll use to implement our variable:

- `json.dumps()` takes a Python object like a list, dictionary, string, int, or float, and returns a string in JSON format.
- `json.loads()` takes a JSON string and returns a Python object like a list, dict, or string, depending on what was stored in the JSON string.

Begin the new variable class by creating a subclass of `tk.StringVar` called `JSONVar`:

```
class JSONVar(tk.StringVar):
  """A Tk variable that can hold dicts and lists"""
```

To make our `JSONVar` work, we need to intercept the `value` argument wherever it is passed to the object and convert it into a JSON string using the `json.dumps()` method. The first such place is in `__init__()`, which we'll override like so:

```
  def __init__(self, *args, **kwargs):
    kwargs['value'] = json.dumps(kwargs.get('value')
    super().__init__(*args, **kwargs)
```

Here, we're simply retrieving the `value` argument from the keywords and converting it into a string using `json.dumps()`. The converted string will overwrite the `value` argument, which will then be passed to the superclass initializer. In the event that a `value` argument isn't provided (remember, it is an optional argument), `kwargs.get()` will return `None`, which will be converted into a JSON `null` value.

> When overriding methods in a class you didn't write, it's always a good idea to include `*args` and `**kwargs` to catch any arguments that you don't explicitly list. That way, the method will continue to allow all the arguments that the superclass version did, but you won't have to explicitly enumerate them all.

The next place we need to intercept the value is in the `set()` method, like this:

```
  def set(self, value, *args, **kwargs):
    string = json.dumps(value)
    super().set(string, *args, **kwargs)
```

Once again, we've intercepted the value argument and converted it into a JSON string before passing it to the superclass version of set().

Last of all, let's fix get():

```
def get(self, *args, **kwargs):
  string = super().get(*args, **kwargs)
  return json.loads(string)
```

Here, we've done the opposite of the other two methods: first, we got the string from the superclass, and then converted it back into an object using json.loads(). With that done, we're ready! What we now have is a variable that can store and retrieve a list or dictionary, just like any other Tkinter variable.

Let's test it out:

```
root = tk.Tk()
var1 = JSONVar(root)
var1.set([1, 2, 3])
var2 = JSONVar(root, value={'a': 10, 'b': 15})

print("Var1: ", var1.get()[1])
# Should print 2

print("Var2: ", var2.get()['b'])
# Should print 15
```

As you can see, subclassing Tkinter objects opens up a whole new range of possibilities for our code. We'll apply this same concept to widget classes both later in this chapter and more extensively in *Chapter 5, Reducing User Error with Validation and Automation*. First, though, let's look at two more ways we can use classes with Tkinter code.

Creating compound widgets

Many GUIs (particularly data entry forms) contain patterns that require a lot of repetitive boilerplate code. For example, input widgets usually have an accompanying label to tell the user what they need to enter. This often requires several lines of code to create and configure each object and add them to the form. We can not only save time, but ensure better consistency of output by creating a reusable **compound widget** that combines both into a single class.

Let's combine an input widget and label by creating a `LabelInput` class, starting with this:

```python
# tkinter_classes_demo.py
class LabelInput(tk.Frame):
  """A label and input combined together"""
```

The `tk.Frame` widget, a bare widget with nothing on it, is an ideal class to subclass for a compound widget. After starting our class definition, the next thing we need to do is think through all the pieces of data our widget will need, and make sure those can be passed into the __init__() method.

For a basic widget, the minimal set of arguments might look like this:

- The parent widget
- The text for the label
- The type of input widget to use
- A dictionary of arguments to pass to the input widget

Let's implement that in our `LabelInput` class:

```python
def __init__(
    self, parent, label, inp_cls,
    inp_args, *args, **kwargs
):
    super().__init__(parent, *args, **kwargs)

    self.label = tk.Label(self, text=label, anchor='w')
    self.input = inp_cls(self, **inp_args)
```

The first thing we do here is call the superclass initializer so that the `Frame` widget can be constructed. Note that we pass along the `parent` argument, since that will be the parent widget of the `Frame` itself; the parent widget for the `Label` and input widget is `self` – that is, the `LabelInput` object itself.

Don't confuse "parent class" and "parent widget." "Parent class" refers to the superclass from which our subclass inherits its members. "Parent widget" refers to the widget (of a probably unrelated class) to which our widget is attached. To help avoid confusion, we'll stick to the super/subclass terminology in this book when speaking of class inheritance.

After creating our `label` and `input` widgets, we can arrange them on the `Frame` however we wish; for example, we might want labels next to the input, like so:

```
self.columnconfigure(1, weight=1)
self.label.grid(sticky=tk.E + tk.W)
self.input.grid(row=0, column=1, sticky=tk.E + tk.W)
```

Or, we might prefer labels above our input widgets, as implemented here:

```
self.columnconfigure(0, weight=1)
self.label.grid(sticky=tk.E + tk.W)
self.input.grid(sticky=tk.E + tk.W)
```

In either case, if we create all the inputs on our form using a `LabelInput`, we have the power to change the layout of *the entire form* using only three lines of code. We could conceivably add an initializer argument to configure the layout individually for each instance as well.

Let's see this class in action. Since our `inp_args` argument is going to be expanded directly into our call to the `inp_cls` initializer, we can populate it with any arguments we'd like our input widget to receive, like so:

```
# tkinter_classes_demo.py
li1 = LabelInput(root, 'Name', tk.Entry, {'bg': 'red'})
li1.grid()
```

We can even pass in a variable to bind to the widget:

```
age_var = tk.IntVar(root, value=21)
li2 = LabelInput(
  root, 'Age', tk.Spinbox,
  {'textvariable': age_var, 'from_': 10, 'to': 150}
)
li2.grid()
```

The compound widget saves us a few lines of code, but more importantly, it raises our input form code to a higher-level description of what's going on. Instead of being full of details about how each label is placed in relation to each widget, we can think about the form in terms of these larger components.

Building encapsulated components

Creating compound widgets is useful for structures we plan to reuse in our application, but the same concept can be applied beneficially to larger pieces of our application, even if they only appear once.

Doing so allows us to attach methods to the components of our application to build self-contained units of functionality that are more easily managed.

For example, let's create a `MyForm` class to hold a simple form:

```
# tkinter_classes_demo.py
class MyForm(tk.Frame):

  def __init__(self, parent, data_var, *args, **kwargs):
    super().__init__(parent, *args, **kwargs)
    self.data_var = data_var
```

Just as we did with the compound wiget, we've subclassed `tk.Frame` and defined a new initializer method. The `parent`, `*args`, and `**kwargs` arguments will get passed on to the superclass's initializer, but we'll also take a `data_var` argument, which will be an instance of our new `JSONVar` type. We'll use this argument to communicate the form data back out of the form.

Next, we'll create some internal control variables to bind to our form widgets:

```
self._vars = {
  'name': tk.StringVar(self),
  'age': tk.IntVar(self, value=2)
}
```

As we've already seen in our data entry application, keeping our form data variables in a dictionary will make it simple to extract data from them later. Rather than using a global variable, however, we've created the dictionary as a protected instance variable by adding it to `self` and prefixing it with an underscore. That's because this dictionary is meant for our form's internal use only.

Now, let's put our `LabelInput` class to work to create the actual widgets for our form:

```
LabelInput(
  self, 'Name', tk.Entry,
  {'textvariable': self._vars['name']}
).grid(sticky=tk.E + tk.W)
LabelInput(
  self, 'Age', tk.Spinbox,
  {'textvariable': self._vars['age'], 'from_': 10, 'to': 150}
).grid(sticky=tk.E + tk.W)
```

You can see that `LabelInput` has trimmed our GUI-building code considerably! Now, let's add a submit button for our form:

```
tk.Button(self, text='Submit', command=self._on_submit).grid()
```

The submit button is configured to call a protected instance method named
_on_submit. This shows us a powerful feature of using classes for our GUI
components: by binding our button to an instance method, that method will have
access to all the other instance members. For example, it can access our _vars
dictionary:

```
def _on_submit(self):
  data = { key: var.get() for key, var in self._vars.items() }
  self.data_var.set(data)
```

Without using a class, we would have had to rely on global variables, such as we
did in the data_entry_app.py application we wrote in *Chapter 3, Creating Basic Forms
with Tkinter and Ttk Widgets*. Instead, our callback method needs only the implicitly
passed self object to have access to all the objects that it needs. In this case, we're
using a **dictionary comprehension** to extract all the data frm our widgets and, then
storing the resulting dictionary in our JSONVar object.

> A dictionary comprehension is similar to a list comprehension, but
> creates a dictionary instead; the syntax is
> { key: value for expression in iterator }. For example,
> if you wanted to create a dictionary of numbers with their squares,
> you could write { n: n**2 for n in range(100) }.

Thus, whenever the submit button is clicked, the data_var object will be updated
with the current contents of the input widgets.

Subclassing Tk

We can extend this concept of component building all the way up to our top
window, the Tk object. By subclassing Tk and building our other application
components in their own classes, we can compose our application's layout and
behavior in a high-level way.

Let's try this with our current demo script:

```
# tkinter_classes_demo.py

class Application(tk.Tk):
  """A simple form application"""

  def __init__(self, *args, **kwargs):
    super().__init__(*args, **kwargs)
```

Remember that the Tk object is not just our top-level window, but also represents the core of our application itself. Therefore we've named our subclass Application to indicate that it represents the foundation of our entire application. Our initializer method begins with the obligatory call to super().__init__(), passing along any arguments to the Application.__init__() method.

Next, we'll create some variables to keep track of the data in our application:

```
self.jsonvar = JSONVar(self)
self.output_var = tk.StringVar(self)
```

The JSONVar, as you might expect, will be passed into our MyForm object to handle its data. The output_var is just a StringVar we'll use to display some output. Let's next add some widgets to our window:

```
tk.Label(self, text='Please fill the form').grid(sticky='ew')
MyForm(self, self.jsonvar).grid(sticky='nsew')
tk.Label(self, textvariable=self.output_var).grid(sticky='ew')
self.columnconfigure(0, weight=1)
self.rowconfigure(1, weight=1)
```

Here, we've added a simple header label for the form, a MyForm object, and another label to display the output. We've also configured the frame so that the first (and only) column expands into the extra space, and the second row (the one containing the form) expands into extra vertical space.

Since a submission of MyForm updates the JSONVar object we passed to it, we'll need a way to execute a submission-handling callback whenever the variable contents are changed. We can do this by setting a **trace** on jsonvar, like this:

```
self.jsonvar.trace_add('write', self._on_data_change)
```

The trace_add() method can be used on any Tkinter vaiable (or variable subclass) to execute a callback function whenever a variable-related event occurs. Let's take a moment to examine it in more detail

The first argument to trace_add() specifies the event that the trace will trigger on; it can be one of the following:

- read: The variable value is read (by a get() call, for example).
- write: The variable value is modified (by a set() call, for example).
- unset: The variable is deleted.
- array: This is an artifact of Tcl/Tk, not really meaningful in Python, but still valid syntax. You will likely never use it.

The second argument specifies a callback for the event, which, in this case, is the instance method _on_data_change(), which will be triggered whenever jsonvar is updated. We'll handle it like this:

```python
def _on_data_change(self, *args, **kwargs):
    data = self.jsonvar.get()
    output = ''.join([
    f'{key} = {value}\n'
    for key, value in data.items()
    ])
    self.output_var.set(output)
```

This method simply iterates through the values in the dictionary retrieved from jsonvar, and then joins them together into a single formatted string. Finally, the formatted string is passed into output_var, which will update the label at the bottom of the main window to display our values from the form. In a real application, you might save the retrieved data to a file or use them as parameters to a batch operation, for example.

> When should you use an instance variable (for example, self.jsonvar), and when should you use regular variables (for example, data), in an instance method? Regular variables in a method are **local** in their scope, meaning they are destroyed as soon as the method returns. In addition, they cannot be referenced by other methods in the class. Instance variables stay in scope for the lifetime of the instance itself, and are available for any other instance method to read or write. In the case of the Application class, the data variable was only needed inside the _on_data_change() method, whereas jsonvar needed to be accessed in both __init__() and _on_datachange().

Since we've subclassed Tk, we should no longer start our script with the line root = tk.Tk(). Make sure to delete that line, and also to delete the previous lines of the code that reference root. Instead, we'll execute our application like this:

```python
if __name__ == "__main__":
    app = Application()
    app.mainloop()
```

Note that these lines, our class definitions, and our imports are the only top-level code we're executing. That cleans up our global scope considerably, isolating the finer details of our code to a more limited scope.

In Python, `if __name__ == "__main__":` is a common idiom to check if a script is being run directly, such as when we type `python3 tkinter_classes_demo.py` at a command prompt. If we were to import this file as a module into another Python script, this check would be false and the code inside the block would not be run. It's a good practice to put your program's main execution code below this check so that you can safely reuse your classes and functions in larger applications.

Rewriting our application using classes

Now that we've learned these techniques for using classes in our code, let's apply it to our ABQ Data Entry application. We'll start with a fresh file called data_entry_app.py and add in our import statements, like so:

```
# data_entry_app.py
from datetime import datetime
from pathlib import Path
import csv
import tkinter as tk
from tkinter import ttk
```

Now, let's see how we can apply some class-based techniques to rewrite a cleaner version of our application code.

Adding a StringVar to the Text widget

One annoyance we discovered in creating our application was that the `Text` widget does not allow the use of a `StringVar` to store its content, requiring us to treat it differently than all our other widgets. There *is* a good reason for this: the Tkinter `Text` widget is far more than just a multi-line `Entry` widget, capable of containing rich text, images, and other things that a lowly `StringVar` cannot store. That said, we're not using any of those features, so it would be better for us to have a more limited `Text` widget that can be bound to a variable.

Let's create a subclass called `BoundText` to solve this problem; start with this code:

```
class BoundText(tk.Text):
  """A Text widget with a bound variable."""
```

Our class needs to add three things to the Text class:

- It needs to allow us to pass in a StringVar, which it will be bound to.
- It needs to update the widget contents whenever the variable is updated; for example, if it were loaded in from a file or changed by another widget.
- It needs to update the variable contents whenever the widget is updated; for example, when the user types or pastes content into the widget.

Passing in a variable

We'll begin by overriding the initializer to allow a control variable to be passed in:

```python
def __init__(self, *args, textvariable=None, **kwargs):
    super().__init__(*args, **kwargs)
    self._variable = textvariable
```

In keeping with Tkinter convention, we'll use the textvariable argument to pass in the StringVar object. Having passed the remaining arguments to super().__init__(), we store the variable as a protected member of the class.

Next, if the user has provided a variable, we'll go ahead and insert its contents into the widget (this takes care of any default value assigned to the variable):

```python
if self._variable:
    self.insert('1.0', self._variable.get())
```

Note that, if a variable was not passed in, textvariable (and consequently self._variable) will be None.

Synchronizing the widget to the variable

The next thing we need to do is bind modifications of the control variable to an instance method that will update the widget.

Still working in the __init__() method, let's add a trace inside the if block we just created, like so:

```python
if self._variable:
    self.insert('1.0', self._variable.get())
    self._variable.trace_add('write', self._set_content)
```

The callback for our trace is a protected member function called _set_content(), which will update the content of the widget with the contents of the variable. Let's go ahead and create that callback:

```python
def _set_content(self, *_):
    """Set the text contents to the variable"""
    self.delete('1.0', tk.END)
    self.insert('1.0', self._variable.get())
```

First, note that the argument list of our callback includes *_. This notation simply wraps up any positional arguments passed to the function in a variable called _ (underscore). A single underscore, or series of underscores, is a conventional way of naming Python variables that we need to provide but don't intend to use. In this case, we're using it to consume any additional arguments that Tkinter will pass to this function when it calls it in response to an event. You'll see this same technique used in other callback methods whenever we intend to bind them to Tkinter events.

Inside the method, we'll simply modify the widget contents using its delete() and insert() methods.

Synchronizing the variable to the widget

Updating the variable when the widget is modified is slightly more involved. We need to find an event that will fire whenever the Text widget is edited to bind to our callback. We could use the <Key> event, which fires whenever a key is pressed, but it won't capture mouse-based edits such as a paste operation. The Text widget does, however, have a <<Modified>> event that is emitted when it is first modified.

We can start with that; add another line to the end of our if statement in __init__(), as shown here:

```python
if self._variable:
    self.insert('1.0', self._variable.get())
    self._variable.trace_add('write', self._set_content)
    self.bind('<<Modified>>', self._set_var)
```

Rather unintuitively, though, <<Modified>> only fires the first time the widget is modified. After that, we'll need to reset the event by changing the widget's modified flag. We can do this using the Text widget's edit_modified() method, which also allows us to retrieve the state of the modified flag.

To see how this will work, let's write the _set_var() callback:

```python
def _set_var(self, *_):
    """Set the variable to the text contents"""
```

```
if self.edit_modified():
    content = self.get('1.0', 'end-1chars')
    self._variable.set(content)
    self.edit_modified(False)
```

In this method, we begin by checking if the widget has been modified by calling `edit_modified()`. If it has, we'll retrieve the content using the widget's `get()` method. Notice that the ending index for get is `end-1chars`. This means "one character before the end of the content." Recall that the `Text` widget's `get()` method automatically appends a newline to the end of the content, so by using this index, we can eliminate the extra newline.

After retrieving the contents of the widget, we need to reset the modified flag by passing `False` into the `edit_modified()` method. That way, it is ready to fire the `<<Modified>>` event the next time the user interacts with the widget.

Creating a more advanced LabelInput()

The `LabelInput` class we created earlier under *Creating compound widgets* seems useful, but if we want to use it in our program, it's going to require some more fleshing out.

Let's start, once again, with our class definition and initializer method:

```python
# data_entry_app.py
class LabelInput(tk.Frame):
    """A widget containing a label and input together."""

    def __init__(
        self, parent, label, var, input_class=ttk.Entry,
        input_args=None, label_args=None, **kwargs
    ):
        super().__init__(parent, **kwargs)
        input_args = input_args or {}
        label_args = label_args or {}
        self.variable = var
        self.variable.label_widget = self
```

As before, we've got arguments for the parent widget, label text, input class, and input arguments. Since every widget we want to use can now have a variable bound to it, we'll also go ahead and accept that as a required argument, and we'll add an optional argument for a dictionary of arguments to pass to the label widget, should we need that. We're defaulting `input_class` to `ttk.Entry`, since we have several of those.

 Note that the default values for the input_args and label_args arguments are None, and that we make them dictionaries inside the method if they are None. Why not just use empty dictionaries as default arguments? In Python, default arguments are evaluated when the function definition is first run. This means that a dictionary object created in the function signature will be the same object every time the function is run, rather than a fresh, empty dictionary each time. Since we want a fresh, empty dictionary each time, we create the dictionaries inside the function body rather than the argument list. The same holds for lists and other mutable objects.

Inside the method, we call super().__init__() as usual, and then ensure that input_args and label_args are dictionaries. Finally, we'll save the input_var to an instance variable, and save the label widget itself as a property of the variable object. Doing this means we won't have to store references to our LabelInput objects; we can just access them through the variable object if we need to.

Next, it's time to set up the label, like this:

```
if input_class in (ttk.Checkbutton, ttk.Button):
    input_args["text"] = label
else:
    self.label = ttk.Label(self, text=label, **label_args)
    self.label.grid(row=0, column=0, sticky=(tk.W + tk.E))
```

Checkbutton and Button widgets have a label built into them, so we don't want to have a separate label hanging around. Instead, we'll just set the text argument of the widget to whatever is passed in. (Radiobutton objects also have a label built in, but we'll handle those slightly differently, as you'll see in a moment). For all other widgets, we'll add a Label widget to the first row and column of the LabelInput.

Next, we need to set up the input arguments so that the input's control variable will be passed in with the correct argument name:

```
if input_class in (
    ttk.Checkbutton, ttk.Button, ttk.Radiobutton
):
    input_args["variable"] = self.variable
else:
    input_args["textvariable"] = self.variable
```

Recall that button classes use variable as the argument name, while all others use textvariable. By handling this inside the class, we won't need to worry about that distinction when building our form.

Now, let's set up the input widget. Most widgets will be simple to set up, but for Radiobutton, we need to do something different. We need to create a Radiobutton widget for each possible value that's passed in (using the values key in input_args). Remember that we link the buttons by having them share the same variable, which we'll do here.

We'll add it like this:

```
if input_class == ttk.Radiobutton:
  self.input = tk.Frame(self)
  for v in input_args.pop('values', []):
    button = ttk.Radiobutton(
      self.input, value=v, text=v, **input_args
    )
    button.pack(
      side=tk.LEFT, ipadx=10, ipady=2, expand=True, fill='x'
    )
```

First, we create a Frame object to hold the buttons; then, for each value passed into values, we add a Radiobutton widget to the Frame layout. Note that we call the pop() method to get the values item from the input_args dict. dict.pop() is nearly identical to dict.get(), returning the value of the given key if it exists, or the second argument if it does not. The difference is that pop() also deletes the retrieved item from the dictionary. We're doing this because values isn't a valid argument for Radiobutton, so we need to remove it before passing input_args to the Radiobutton initializer. The remaining items in input_args should be valid keyword arguments to the widget.

In the case of non-Radiobutton widgets, it's pretty straightforward:

```
else:
  self.input = input_class(self, **input_args)
```

We simply call whatever input_class class has been passed in with the input_args. Now that we have self.input created, we just need to add it to the LabelInput layout:

```
self.input.grid(row=1, column=0, sticky=(tk.W + tk.E))
self.columnconfigure(0, weight=1)
```

The final call to columnconfigure tells the LabelWidget widget to fill its entire width with column 0.

One convenient thing we can do when creating our own widgets (either a custom subclass or compound widget) is to set some reasonable defaults for the geometry layout. For example, we're going to want all our `LabelInput` widgets to stick to the left- and right-hand sides of their container so that they fill the maximum width available. Rather than having to pass in `sticky=(tk.E + tk.W)` every single time we position a `LabelInput` widget, let's make it the default, like this:

```python
def grid(self, sticky=(tk.E + tk.W), **kwargs):
    """Override grid to add default sticky values"""
    super().grid(sticky=sticky, **kwargs)
```

We've overridden `grid` and simply passed on the arguments to the superclass version but added a default for `sticky`. We can still override it if needed, but it will save us a lot of clutter to make that default.

Our `LabelInput` is fairly robust now; time to put it to work!

Creating a form class

Now that our building blocks are ready, it's time to build the major components of our application. Breaking the application into sensible components requires some thinking about what might constitute a reasonable division of responsibilities. Initially, it seems like our application could be broken into two components: the data entry form and the root application itself. But which features go where?

One reasonable assessment might be as follows:

- The data entry form itself should contain all the widgets, of course. It should also hold the Save and Reset buttons, since these make no sense being separate from the form.
- The application title and status bar belong at a universal level, since they will apply to all parts of the application. File saving could go with the form, but it also has to interact with some application-level items like the status bar or `records_saved` variable. It's a tricky call, but we'll put it with the application object for now.

Let's begin by building our data entry form class, `DataRecordForm`:

```python
# data_entry_app.py
class DataRecordForm(ttk.Frame):
    """The input form for our widgets"""

    def __init__(self, *args, **kwargs):
        super().__init__(*args, **kwargs)
```

As always, we begin by subclassing `Frame` and calling the superclass's initializer method. We don't really need to add any custom arguments at this point.

Now, let's create a dictionary to hold all our variable objects:

```python
self._vars = {
    'Date': tk.StringVar(),
    'Time': tk.StringVar(),
    'Technician': tk.StringVar(),
    'Lab': tk.StringVar(),
    'Plot': tk.IntVar(),
    'Seed Sample': tk.StringVar(),
    'Humidity': tk.DoubleVar(),
    'Light': tk.DoubleVar(),
    'Temperature': tk.DoubleVar(),
    'Equipment Fault': tk.BooleanVar(),
    'Plants': tk.IntVar(),
    'Blossoms': tk.IntVar(),
    'Fruit': tk.IntVar(),
    'Min Height': tk.DoubleVar(),
    'Max Height': tk.DoubleVar(),
    'Med Height': tk.DoubleVar(),
    'Notes': tk.StringVar()
}
```

This is just straight out of our data dictionary. Note that, thanks to our `BoundText` class, we can assign a `StringVar` object to Notes. Now, we're ready to start adding widgets to our GUI. In the current version of our application, we added a `LabelFrame` widget for each section of the application using a chunk of code like this:

```python
r_info = ttk.LabelFrame(drf, text='Record Information')
r_info.grid(sticky=(tk.W + tk.E))
for i in range(3):
    r_info.columnconfigure(i, weight=1 )
```

This code was repeated for each frame, with only a change to the variable name and label text. To avoid this repetition, we can abstract this process into an instance method. Let's create a method that can add a new label frame for us; add this code just above the __init__() definition:

```python
def _add_frame(self, label, cols=3):
    """Add a LabelFrame to the form"""

    frame = ttk.LabelFrame(self, text=label)
```

```
        frame.grid(sticky=tk.W + tk.E)
        for i in range(cols):
            frame.columnconfigure(i, weight=1)
        return frame
```

This method simply redefines the earlier code in a generic way, so we can just pass in the label text and, optionally, a number of columns. Scroll back down to where we were in the DataRecordForm.__init__() method, and let's put this method to use by making a Record Information section, like so:

```
    r_info = self._add_frame("Record Information")
```

Now that we have our frame, let's give LabelInput a try and start building the first section of the form, like this:

```
LabelInput(
    r_info, "Date", var=self._vars['Date']
).grid(row=0, column=0)
LabelInput(
    r_info, "Time", input_class=ttk.Combobox,
    var=self._vars['Time'],
    input_args={"values": ["8:00", "12:00", "16:00", "20:00"]}
).grid(row=0, column=1)
LabelInput(
    r_info, "Technician",  var=self._vars['Technician']
).grid(row=0, column=2)
```

As you can see, LabelInput has saved us a lot of redundant clutter already!

Let's continue with the second line:

```
LabelInput(
    r_info, "Lab", input_class=ttk.Radiobutton,
    var=self._vars['Lab'],
    input_args={"values": ["A", "B", "C"]}
).grid(row=1, column=0)
LabelInput(
    r_info, "Plot", input_class=ttk.Combobox,
    var=self._vars['Plot'],
    input_args={"values": list(range(1, 21))}
).grid(row=1, column=1)
LabelInput(
    r_info, "Seed Sample",  var=self._vars['Seed Sample']
).grid(row=1, column=2)
```

Remember that to use `RadioButton` widgets with `LabelInput`, we need to pass in a list of values to the input arguments, just as we do for `Combobox`. Having finished the `Record Information` section, let's continue with the next section, `Environmental Data`:

```
e_info = self._add_frame("Environment Data")

LabelInput(
  e_info, "Humidity (g/m³)",
  input_class=ttk.Spinbox,  var=self._vars['Humidity'],
  input_args={"from_": 0.5, "to": 52.0, "increment": .01}
).grid(row=0, column=0)
LabelInput(
  e_info, "Light (klx)", input_class=ttk.Spinbox,
  var=self._vars['Light'],
  input_args={"from_": 0, "to": 100, "increment": .01}
).grid(row=0, column=1)
LabelInput(
  e_info, "Temperature (°C)",
  input_class=ttk.Spinbox,  var=self._vars['Temperature'],
  input_args={"from_": 4, "to": 40, "increment": .01}
).grid(row=0, column=2)
LabelInput(
  e_info, "Equipment Fault",
  input_class=ttk.Checkbutton,
  var=self._vars['Equipment Fault']
).grid(row=1, column=0, columnspan=3)
```

Again, we have added and configured a `LabelFrame` using our `_add_frame()` method, populating it with the four `LabelInput` widgets.

Now, let's add the `Plant Data` sections:

```
p_info = self._add_frame("Plant Data")

LabelInput(
  p_info, "Plants", input_class=ttk.Spinbox,
  var=self._vars['Plants'],
  input_args={"from_": 0, "to": 20}
).grid(row=0, column=0)
LabelInput(
  p_info, "Blossoms", input_class=ttk.Spinbox,
  var=self._vars['Blossoms'],
  input_args={"from_": 0, "to": 1000}
```

```
  ).grid(row=0, column=1)
  LabelInput(
    p_info, "Fruit", input_class=ttk.Spinbox,
    var=self._vars['Fruit'],
    input_args={"from_": 0, "to": 1000}
  ).grid(row=0, column=2)
  LabelInput(
    p_info, "Min Height (cm)",
    input_class=ttk.Spinbox,  var=self._vars['Min Height'],
    input_args={"from_": 0, "to": 1000, "increment": .01}
  ).grid(row=1, column=0)
  LabelInput(
    p_info, "Max Height (cm)",
    input_class=ttk.Spinbox,  var=self._vars['Max Height'],
    input_args={"from_": 0, "to": 1000, "increment": .01}
  ).grid(row=1, column=1)
  LabelInput(
    p_info, "Median Height (cm)",
    input_class=ttk.Spinbox,  var=self._vars['Med Height'],
    input_args={"from_": 0, "to": 1000, "increment": .01}
  ).grid(row=1, column=2)
```

We're almost done; let's add our `Notes` section next:

```
  LabelInput(
    self, "Notes",
    input_class=BoundText,  var=self._vars['Notes'],
    input_args={"width": 75, "height": 10}
  ).grid(sticky=tk.W, row=3, column=0)
```

Here, we're taking advantage of our `BoundText` object so we can attach a variable. Otherwise, this looks like all the other calls to `LabelInput`.

Now, it's time for the buttons:

```
  buttons = tk.Frame(self)
  buttons.grid(sticky=tk.W + tk.E, row=4)
  self.savebutton = ttk.Button(
    buttons, text="Save", command=self.master._on_save)
  self.savebutton.pack(side=tk.RIGHT)

  self.resetbutton = ttk.Button(
    buttons, text="Reset", command=self.reset)
  self.resetbutton.pack(side=tk.RIGHT)
```

As before, we've added our button widgets on a `Frame`. This time, though, we're going to pass in some instance methods as callback commands for the buttons. The `Reset` button will get an instance method we'll define in this class, but since we decided that saving a file was the application object's responsibility, we're binding the `Save` button to an instance method on the parent object (accessed through this object's `master` attribute).

 Binding GUI objects directly to commands on other objects is not a good way to approach the problem of inter-object communication, but for now it will do the job. In *Chapter 6, Planning for the Expansion of Our Application*, we'll learn a more elegant way to accomplish this.

That wraps up our `__init__()` method, but we're going to need a couple more methods on this class before we're done. First, we need to implement the `reset()` method that handles our form reset; it will look like this:

```python
def reset(self):
    """Resets the form entries"""

    for var in self._vars.values():
        if isinstance(var, tk.BooleanVar):
            var.set(False)
        else:
            var.set('')
```

Essentially, we just need to set all our variables to an empty string. In the case of `BooleanVar` objects, though, this will raise an exception, so we need to set it to `False` to uncheck our checkbox.

Finally, we need a method that will allow the application object to retrieve data from the form so that it can save the data. In keeping with Tkinter convention, we'll call this method `get()`:

```python
def get(self):
    data = dict()
    fault = self._vars['Equipment Fault'].get()
    for key, variable in self._vars.items():
        if fault and key in ('Light', 'Humidity', 'Temperature'):
            data[key] = ''
        else:
            try:
                data[key] = variable.get()
```

```
        except tk.TclError:
            message = f'Error in field: {key}.  Data was not saved!'
            raise ValueError(message)

    return data
```

The code here is very similar to the data retrieval code in the on_save() function of our previous version of the application, with a couple of differences. First, we're retrieving data from self._vars rather than a global variables dictionary. Secondly, in the event of an error, we're creating an error message and re-raising a ValueError rather than directly updating the GUI. We'll have to make sure that code that calls this method is written to handle a ValueError exception. Finally, rather than saving the data as we did in the previous version of the application, we're merely returning it.

That completes the form class! Now all that remains is to code an application to keep it in.

Creating an application class

Our application class is going to handle application-level functionality as well as being our top-level window. GUI-wise, it needs to contain:

- A title label
- An instance of our DataRecordForm class
- A status bar

It will also need a method to save the data in the form to a CSV.

Let's begin our class:

```
class Application(tk.Tk):
  """Application root window"""

  def __init__(self, *args, **kwargs):
    super().__init__(*args, **kwargs)
```

Nothing new here, except that now we're subclassing Tk instead of Frame.

Let's set up some window parameters:

```
    self.title("ABQ Data Entry Application")
    self.columnconfigure(0, weight=1)
```

As with the procedural version of the program, we've set the window title and configured the first column of the grid to expand. Now, we'll create the title label:

```
ttk.Label(
    self, text="ABQ Data Entry Application",
    font=("TkDefaultFont", 16)
).grid(row=0)
```

Nothing is really different here, except note that the parent object is now `self` – there isn't going to be a `root` object anymore; `self` is our `Tk` instance inside this class.

Let's create a record form:

```
self.recordform = DataRecordForm(self)
self.recordform.grid(row=1, padx=10, sticky=(tk.W + tk.E))
```

Despite the size and complexity of `DataRecordForm`, adding it to the application is just like adding any other widget.

Now, for the status bar:

```
self.status = tk.StringVar()
ttk.Label(
    self, textvariable=self.status
).grid(sticky=(tk.W + tk.E), row=2, padx=10)
```

Again, this is just like the procedural version, except that our `status` variable is an instance variable. This means it will be accessible to any of the methods in our class.

Finally, let's create a protected instance variable to hold the number of records saved:

```
self._records_saved = 0
```

With `__init__()` finished up, we can now write the last method: `_on_save()`. This method will be very close to the procedural function we wrote previously:

```
def _on_save(self):
    """Handles save button clicks"""

    datestring = datetime.today().strftime("%Y-%m-%d")
    filename = "abq_data_record_{}.csv".format(datestring)
    newfile = not Path(filename).exists()

    try:
        data = self.recordform.get()
```

```
    except ValueError as e:
      self.status.set(str(e))
      return

    with open(filename, 'a', newline='') as fh:
      csvwriter = csv.DictWriter(fh, fieldnames=data.keys())
      if newfile:
        csvwriter.writeheader()
      csvwriter.writerow(data)

    self._records_saved += 1
    self.status.set(
      "{} records saved this session".format(self._records_saved))
    self.recordform.reset()
```

Once again, this function generates the filename using the current date, and then opens the file in append mode. This time, though, we can get our data by simply calling self.recordform.get(), which abstracts the process of getting data from its variables. Remember that we do have to handle ValueError exceptions in case there is bad data in the form, which we've done here. In the case of bad data, we simply display the error in the status bar and exit before the method attempts to save the data. If there is no exception, the data is saved, so we increment the _records_saved attribute and update the status.

The final thing we need to make this application run is to create an instance of our Application object and start its mainloop:

```
  if __name__ == "__main__":
    app = Application()
    app.mainloop()
```

Note that, other than our class definitions and module imports, these two lines are the only ones being executed in the top-level scope. Also, because Application takes care of building the GUI and other objects, we can execute it and the mainloop() call together at the end of the application using the if __name__ == "__main__" guard.

Summary

In this chapter, you learned to take advantage of the power of Python classes. You learned to create your own classes, to define attributes and methods, and the function of magic methods. You also learned how to extend the functionality of existing classes with subclassing.

We explored how these techniques can be applied powerfully to Tkinter classes, to extend their functionality, build compound widgets, and organize our application into components.

In the next chapter, we'll learn about Tkinter's validation features, and further employ subclassing to make our widgets more intuitive and robust. We'll also learn how to automate input to save users time and ensure consistent data entry.

5

Reducing User Error with Validation and Automation

Things are going well for our project: the data entry form works well, the code is better organized, and the users are excited at the prospect of using the application. We're not ready for production yet, though! Our form doesn't yet perform the promised task of preventing or discouraging user errors: number boxes still allow letters, combo boxes aren't limited to the choices given, and dates are just text fields that have to be filled in by hand. In this chapter, we're going to set things right as we work through the following topics:

- In *Validating user input*, we'll talk about some strategies for enforcing correct values in our widgets and how to implement them in Tkinter.
- In *Creating validated widget classes*, we'll super-charge Tkinter's widget classes with some custom validation logic.
- In *Implementing validated widgets in our GUI*, we'll use our new widgets to improve ABQ Data Entry.
- In *Automating input*, we'll implement auto-population of data in our widgets to save users time and effort.

Let's get started!

Validating user input

At first glance, Tkinter's selection of input widgets seems a little disappointing.

It gives us neither a true number entry that only allows digits, nor a truly keyboard-friendly, modern drop-down selector. We have no date inputs, email inputs, or other specially formatted input widgets.

Nevertheless, these weaknesses can become strengths. Because these widgets assume nothing, we can make them behave in a way that's appropriate to our specific needs. For example, alphabetical characters may seem inappropriate in a number entry, but are they? In Python, strings such as NaN and Infinity are valid float values; having a box that could increment numerals but also handle those string values may be very useful in some applications.

Of course, before we can tailor our widgets to our needs, we'll need to think about what exactly we want them to do. Let's do some analysis.

Strategies to prevent data errors

There is no universal answer to how a widget should react to a user trying to enter bad data. The validation logic found in various GUI toolkits can differ greatly; when bad data is entered, an input widget might validate the user input in any of the following ways:

- Prevent the invalid keystrokes from registering at all
- Accept the input, but return an error or list of errors when the form is submitted
- Show an error when the user leaves the entry field, perhaps disabling form submission until it's corrected
- Lock the user in the entry field until valid data is entered
- Silently correct the bad data using a best-guess algorithm

The correct behavior in a data entry form (which is filled out hundreds of times a day by the same users, who may not even be looking at it) may be different from an instrument control panel (where values absolutely must be correct to avoid a disaster) or an online user registration form (which is filled out once by a user who has never seen it before). We need to ask ourselves – and our users – which behavior will best minimize errors.

After discussing this with your users on the data entry staff, you come to the following set of guidelines:

- Whenever possible, meaningless keystrokes should be ignored (for example, letters in a number field).

- Fields containing bad data should be marked in some visible way at focus-out (when the user exits the field) with an error describing the problem.

- A required field left empty at focus-out should be marked with an error.

- Form submission should be disabled if there are fields with outstanding errors.

Let's add the following requirements to our specification before moving on. Under the Requirements section, update the `Functional Requirements` as follows:

```
Functional Requirements:
  (...)
  * have inputs that:
    - ignore meaningless keystrokes
    - display an error if the value is invalid on focusout
    - display an error if a required field is empty on focusout
  * prevent saving the record when errors are present
```

So far so good, but how do we implement this?

Validation in Tkinter

Tkinter's validation system is one of those parts of the toolkit that is less than intuitive. It relies on three configuration arguments that we can pass into any input widget:

- `validate`: This option determines which type of event will trigger the validation callback.

- `validatecommand`: This option takes the command that will determine if the data is valid.

- `invalidcommand`: This option takes a command that will run if `validatecommand` returns `False`.

This all seems pretty straightforward, but there are some unexpected curves. Let's look in depth at each argument.

The validate argument

The `validate` argument specifies what kind of event triggers the validation. It can be one of the following string values:

Value	Trigger event
none	Never. This option turns off validation.
focusin	The user selects or enters the widget.
focusout	The user leaves the widget.
focus	Both focusin and focusout.
key	The user presses a key while in the widget.
all	Any of the focusin, focusout, or key events.

Only one `validate` argument can be specified, and all matching events will trigger the same validation callback. Most of the time, you will want to use key and focusout (validating on focusin is rarely useful), but since there isn't a value that combines those two events, it's often best to use all and let the callback switch its validation logic based on the event type if necessary.

The validatecommand argument

The `validatecommand` argument specifies the callback function that will be run when the `validate` event is triggered. This is where things get a little tricky. You might think this argument takes the name of a Python function or method, but that's not quite it. Instead, we need to give it a tuple containing a string reference to a Tcl/Tk function, and (optionally) some **substitution codes** that specify information about the triggering event that we want to pass into the function.

How do we get a reference to a Tcl/Tk function? Fortunately, this isn't too hard; we just need to pass a Python callable to the `register()` method of any Tkinter widget. This returns string reference that we can use with `validatecommand`.

For example, we can create a (somewhat pointless) validation command like this:

```
# validate_demo.py
import tkinter as tk
root = tk.Tk()

entry = tk.Entry(root)
entry.grid()

def always_good():
  return True
```

```
validate_ref = root.register(always_good)

entry.configure(
  validate='all',
  validatecommand=(validate_ref,)
)


root.mainloop()
```

In this example, we've retrieved our function reference by passing the always_good function to root.register(). Then we can pass this reference in a tuple to validatecommand. The validation callback that we register must return a Boolean value indicating whether the data in the field is valid or invalid.

A validatecommand callback *must* return a Boolean value. If it returns anything else (including the implicit None value when there is no return statement), Tkinter will turn off validation on the widget (that is, it will set validate to none). Remember that its purpose is *only* to indicate whether the data is acceptable or not. The handling of invalid data will be done by our invalidcommand callback.

Of course, it's not easy to validate the data unless we provide the function with some data to be validated. To make Tkinter pass information to our validation callback, we can add one or more substitution codes to our validatecommand tuple. These codes are as follows:

Code	Value passed
%d	A code indicating the action being attempted: 0 for delete, 1 for insert, and -1 for other events. Note that this is passed as a string, and not as an integer.
%P	The proposed value that the field would have after the change (key events only).
%s	The value currently in the field (key events only).
%i	The index (from 0) of the text being inserted or deleted on key events, or -1 on non-key events. Note that this is passed as a string, not an integer.
%S	For insertion or deletion, the text that is being inserted or deleted (key events only).
%v	The widget's validate value.
%V	The event type that triggered validation, one of focusin, focusout, key, or forced (indicating the widget's variable was changed).
%W	The widget's name in Tcl/Tk, as a string.

We can use these codes to create a slightly more useful validated Entry, like so:

```
# validate_demo.py
# Place just before root.mainloop()
entry2 = tk.Entry(root)
entry2.grid(pady=10)

def no_t_for_me(proposed):
  return 't' not in proposed

validate2_ref = root.register(no_t_for_me)
entry2.configure(
  validate='all',
  validatecommand=(validate2_ref, '%P')
)
```

Here, we're passing the %P substitution code into our validatecommand tuple so that our callback function will be passed the proposed new value for the widget (that is, the value of the widget if the keystroke is accepted). In this case, we're going to return False if the proposed value contains the t character.

Note that the behavior of the widget when the validatecommand callback returns changes depending on the type of event that triggered validation. If a validation callback is triggered by a key event and it returns False, Tkinter's built-in behavior is to reject the keystroke and leave the contents as they are. In the event of a focus event triggering validation, a False return value will simply flag the widget as invalid. In both cases, the invalidcommand callback will also be executed. If we haven't specified a callback, Tkinter will simply do nothing further.

For example, run the above script; you'll find you cannot type a t in the Entry widget. That's because the key validation returned False, so Tkinter rejected the keystroke.

The invalidcommand argument

The invalidcommand argument works exactly the same as the validatecommand argument, requiring the use of the register() method and the same substitution codes. It specifies a callback function to be run when validatecommand returns False. It could be used to show an error or possibly correct the input.

To see what this looks like together, consider the following code for an Entry widget that only accepts five characters:

```
entry3 = tk.Entry(root)
entry3.grid()
```

```
entry3_error = tk.Label(root, fg='red')
entry3_error.grid()

def only_five_chars(proposed):
    return len(proposed) < 6

def only_five_chars_error(proposed):
    entry3_error.configure(
    text=f'{proposed} is too long, only 5 chars allowed.'
    )

validate3_ref = root.register(only_five_chars)
invalid3_ref = root.register(only_five_chars_error)

entry3.configure(
    validate='all',
    validatecommand=(validate3_ref, '%P'),
    invalidcommand=(invalid3_ref, '%P')
)
```

Here, we've created a simple GUI with an `Entry` widget and a `Label` widget. We've also created two functions, one that returns whether or not the length of a string is less than six characters, and another that configures the `Label` widget to show an error. We then register the two functions with Tk using the `root.register()` method, passing them to the `Entry` widget's `validatecommand` and `invalidcommand` arguments. We also include the `%P` substitution code so that the proposed value of the widget is passed into each function. Note that you can pass in as many substitution codes as you wish, and in any order, as long as your callback function is written to accept those arguments.

Run this example and test its behavior; note that not only can you *not* type more than five characters in the box, but you also receive a warning in the label that your attempted edit was too long.

Creating validated widget classes

As you can see, adding even very simple validation to Tkinter widgets involves several steps with some less-than-intuitive logic. Adding validation to even a fraction of our widgets could get quite verbose and ugly. However, we learned in the previous chapter that we can improve on Tkinter widgets by subclassing them to add new configuration and functionality. Let's see if we can apply this technique to widget validation by creating validated versions of Tkinter's widget classes.

For example, let's implement our five-character entry again, this time as a subclass of ttk.Entry, like so:

```python
# five_char_entry_class.py
class FiveCharEntry(ttk.Entry):
  """An Entry that truncates to five characters on exit."""

  def __init__(self, parent, *args, **kwargs):
    super().__init__(parent, *args, **kwargs)
    self.error = tk.StringVar()
    self.configure(
      validate='all',
      validatecommand=(self.register(self._validate), '%P'),
      invalidcommand=(self.register(self._on_invalid), '%P')
    )

  def _validate(self, proposed):
    return len(proposed) <= 5

  def _on_invalid(self, proposed):
    self.error.set(
      f'{proposed} is too long, only 5 chars allowed!'
    )
```

This time, we've implemented validation by subclassing Entry and defining our validation logic in a method rather than an external function. This simplifies access to the widget in our validation methods, should we need it, and also allows us to refer to the methods in __init__() before they are actually defined. We've also added a StringVar called error as an instance variable. We can use this variable to hold an error message should our validation fail.

Note that we've registered these functions using self.register() rather than root. register(). The register() method does not have to be run on the root window object; it can be run on any Tkinter widget. Since we don't know for sure that the code using our class will call the root window root, or if it will be in scope when the __init__() method runs, it makes sense to use the FiveCharEntry widget itself to register the functions. However, this must be done *after* we call super().__init__ (), since the underlying Tcl/Tk object doesn't actually exist (and cannot register functions) until that method is run. That is why we're using configure() to set these values rather than passing them into super().__init__().

We can then use this class like so:

```
root = tk.Tk()
entry = FiveCharEntry(root)
error_label = ttk.Label(
    root, textvariable=entry.error, foreground='red'
)
entry.grid()
error_label.grid()
root.mainloop()
```

Here, we've created an instance of the FiveCharEntry widget as well as a Label widget to display errors. Note that we pass the widget's built-in error variable, entry.error, to the label's textvariable argument. When you execute this, you should see the label displaying an error when you try to type more than five characters, like so:

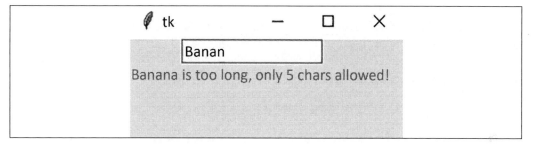

Figure 5.1: The five-character entry refusing to accept "Banana"

Creating a Date field

Let's try something a little more useful now: creating a validating DateEntry widget to use for our Date field. Our widget will prevent any keystrokes that aren't valid for a date string, and check for validity of the date on focusout. If the date is invalid, we'll mark the field in some way and set an error message in a StringVar, which some other widget could use to display the error.

First, open a new file called DateEntry.py and begin with the following code:

```
# DateEntry.py
import tkinter as tk
from tkinter import ttk
from datetime import datetime
```

```
class DateEntry(ttk.Entry):
  """An Entry for ISO-style dates (Year-month-day)"""

  def __init__(self, parent, *args, **kwargs):
    super().__init__(parent, *args, **kwargs)
    self.configure(
      validate='all',
      validatecommand=(
        self.register(self._validate),
        '%S', '%i', '%V', '%d'
      ),
      invalidcommand=(self.register(self._on_invalid), '%V')
    )
    self.error = tk.StringVar()
```

After importing `tkinter` and `ttk`, we also import `datetime`, which we'll need for validating the date strings entered. As with our previous class, we've overridden `__init__()` to set up validation and add an error variable. This time, however, we're going to be passing several more arguments into our `validatecommand` method: the character being inserted (`%S`), the index where it's being inserted (`%i`), the event type triggering validation (`%V`), and the action type (`%d`). `invalidcommand` is receiving only the event type (`%V`). Since we're triggering validation on all events, we'll need this value to decide how to handle the invalid data appropriately.

Next, let's create a method called `_toggle_error()` to turn an error state on or off in the widget:

```
  def _toggle_error(self, error=''):
    self.error.set(error)
    self.config(foreground='red' if error else 'black')
```

We'll use this method to handle how our widget behaves when an error occurs or is corrected. It starts by setting our error variable to the string provided. If the string is not blank, we set a visual error indicator (in this case, turning the text red); if it's blank, we turn off the visual indicator.

Now that we have that, we can create our `_validate()` method, as follows:

```
  def _validate(self, char, index, event, action):

    # reset error state
    self._toggle_error()
    valid = True
```

```
# ISO dates only need digits and hyphens
if event == 'key':
  if action == '0':
    valid = True
  elif index in ('0', '1', '2', '3', '5', '6', '8', '9'):
    valid = char.isdigit()
  elif index in ('4', '7'):
    valid = char == '-'
  else:
    valid = False
```

This method will take an "innocent until proven guilty" approach to validating the user input, so we begin by toggling off any error state and setting a `valid` flag to `True`. Then, we'll start looking at keystroke events. The line `if action == '0':` tells us if the user is trying to delete characters. We always want to allow this so that the user can edit the field, so that should always return `True`.

The basic format of an ISO date is four digits, a dash, two digits, a dash, and two digits. We can test whether the user is following this format by checking whether the inserted characters match our expectations at the inserted index. For example, the line `index in ('0','1', '2', '3', '5', '6', '8', '9')` will tell us if the character is being inserted at one of the positions that requires a digit, and if so we check that the character is a digit. The characters at indexes 4 and 7 should be a dash. Any other keystroke is invalid.

 Although you might expect them to be integers, Tkinter passes both action codes and character indexes as strings. Keep this in mind when writing your comparisons.

While this is a hopelessly naive heuristic for a correct date, since it allows for complete nonsense dates like `0000-97-46`, or right-looking-but-still-wrong dates like `2000-02-29`, it at least enforces the basic format and removes a large number of invalid keystrokes. A completely accurate partial date analyzer is a project unto itself, but for now, this will do.

Checking our date for correctness on focus-out is simpler and much more foolproof, as you can see here:

```
# still in DateEntry._validate()
    elif event == 'focusout':
      try:
        datetime.strptime(self.get(), '%Y-%m-%d')
```

```
        except ValueError:
            valid = False
    return valid
```

Since we have access to the final value the user meant to enter at this point, we can use `datetime.strptime()` to try to convert the string to a Python `datetime` object using the format `%Y-%m-%d`. If this fails, we know the date is invalid.

Finally, at the end of the method, we return our `valid` flag. As you saw previously, it's sufficient to return `False` for keystroke events to prevent the character from being inserted; but for errors on focus events, we'll need to respond in some user-visible way.

This will be handled in our `_on_invalid()` method as follows:

```
def _on_invalid(self, event):
    if event != 'key':
        self._toggle_error('Not a valid date')
```

We have configured this method to receive only the event type, which we'll use to ignore keystroke events (they're already adequately handled by the default behavior). For any other event type, we'll use our `_toggle_error()` method to set our visual indicator and the error string.

Let's test the `DateEntry` class with a small test script at the end of the file:

```
if __name__ == '__main__':
    root = tk.Tk()
    entry = DateEntry(root)
    entry.pack()
    ttk.Label(
        textvariable=entry.error, foreground='red'
    ).pack()

    # add this so we can unfocus the DateEntry
    ttk.Entry(root).pack()
    root.mainloop()
```

Save the file and run it to try the new `DateEntry` class. Try entering various bad dates or invalid keystrokes, and then click the second `Entry` widget to unfocus the `DateEntry` and note what happens.

You should see something like this:

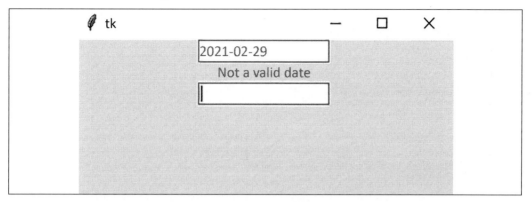

Figure 5.2: A validating DateEntry widget warning us about a bad date string

Implementing validated widgets in our GUI

Now that you know how to validate your widgets, you have your work cut out for you! We have 17 input widgets, and you'll have to write validation code like that shown in the previous section for all of them to get the behavior we need. Along the way, you'll need to make sure the widgets respond consistently to errors and present a consistent API to the application.

If that sounds like something you'd like to put off indefinitely, I can't blame you. Maybe there's a way we can cut down the amount of repetitive code we need to write.

Introducing the power of multiple inheritance

So far, we have learned that Python allows us to create new classes by subclassing, inheriting features from the superclass, and only adding or changing what's different about our new class. Python also supports building classes using **multiple inheritance**, in which a subclass can inherit from multiple superclasses. We can exploit this feature to our advantage by creating what's called a **mixin class**.

Mixin classes contain only a specific set of functionalities that we want to be able to "mix in" with other classes to compose a new class.

Take a look at the following example code:

```python
class Fruit():

    _taste = 'sweet'

    def taste(self):
        print(f'It tastes {self._taste}')

class PeelableMixin():

    def __init__(self, *args, **kwargs):
        super().__init__(*args, **kwargs)
        self._peeled = False

    def peel(self):
        self._peeled = True

    def taste(self):
        if not self._peeled:
            print('I will peel it first')
            self.peel()
        super().taste()
```

In this example, we have a class called `Fruit` with a `_taste` class attribute and a `taste()` method that prints a message indicating how the fruit tastes. We then have a mixin class called `PeelableMixin`. The mixin class adds an instance attribute called `_peeled` to indicate if the fruit has been peeled, as well as a `peel()` method to update the `_peeled` attribute. It also overrides the `taste()` method to check if the fruit is peeled before tasting. Note that the mixin class's `__init__()` method also calls the superclass initializer, even though it doesn't inherit from another class. We'll see why this is in a moment.

Now, let's use multiple inheritance to create a new class, like so:

```python
class Plantain(PeelableMixin, Fruit):
    _taste = 'starchy'

    def peel(self):
        print('It has a tough peel!')
        super().peel()
```

The `Plantain` class is created from the combination of the `PeelableMixin` and the `Fruit` class. When we create a class using multiple inheritance, the rightmost class we specify is called the **base class**, and mixin classes should be specified before it (that is, to the left of the base class). Thus, `Fruit` is the base class in this case.

Let's create an instance of our class and call `taste()`, like so:

```
plantain = Plantain()
plantain.taste()
```

As you can see, the resulting subclass has both a `taste()` and a `peel()` method, but note that there are two versions of each method defined between all the classes. When we call one of these methods, which version is used?

In a multiple inheritance situation, `super()` does something a little more complex than just standing in for the superclass. It looks up the chain of inheritance using something called the **method resolution order** (**MRO**) and determines the nearest class that defines the method we're calling. The resolution order starts with the current class, and then follows the chain of superclasses from the leftmost to the base class.

Thus, when we call `plantain.taste()`, a series of method resolutions occurs, as follows:

- `plantain.taste()` is resolved to `PeelableMixin.taste()`.
- `PeelableMixin.taste()` then calls `self.peel()`. Since `self` is a `Plantain` object, `self.peel()` is resolved to `Plantain.peel()`.
- `Plantain.peel()` prints a message and calls `super().peel()`. Python resolves this call to the leftmost class with a `peel()` method, `PeelableMixin.peel()`.
- When that's returned, `PeelableMixin.taste()` then calls `super().taste()`. The next leftmost class from `PeelableMixin` is `Fruit`, so this is resolved to `Fruit.taste()`.
- `Fruit.taste()` refers to the class variable `_taste`. Even though the method being run is in the `Fruit` class, the class of our object is `Plantain`, so `Plantain._taste` is used here.

If this seems confusing, just remember that `self.method()` or `self.attribute` will always look for `method()` or `attribute` in the current class first, and then follow the list of inherited classes from left to right until the method or attribute is found. The `super()` object will do the same, except that it skips the current class.

This is the reason why we called `super().__init__()` inside the mixin class's initializer in the example.

Without this call, only the mixin class initializer would be called. By calling super().__init__(), Python will also continue up the MRO chain and call the base class initializer. This is particularly important to remember when creating mixins for Tkinter classes, since the Tkinter class's initializer creates the actual Tcl/Tk object.

> The method resolution order of a class is stored in its __mro__ property; you can inspect this method in a Python shell or debugger if you're having trouble with inherited methods or attributes.

Note that PeelableMixin is not usable on its own: it only works when combined with a class that has a taste() method. This is why it's a mixin class: it is meant to be mixed in to enhance other classes, not used on its own.

> Unfortunately, Python does not give us a way to explicitly annotate in code that a class is a mixin or what classes it must be mixed with, so be sure to document your mixin classes well.

Building a validating mixin class

Let's apply our knowledge of multiple inheritance to build a mixin class that will help us create validated widget classes with less boilerplate code. Open data_entry_app.py and add the new class just above your Application class definition:

```python
# data_entry_app.py
class ValidatedMixin:
    """Adds a validation functionality to an input widget"""

    def __init__(self, *args, error_var=None, **kwargs):
        self.error = error_var or tk.StringVar()
        super().__init__(*args, **kwargs)
```

We've started this class as usual, though we're not subclassing anything this time because this is a mixin class. The constructor also has an extra argument called error_var. This will allow us to pass in a variable to use for the error message; if we don't, the class creates its own. Remember that the call to super().__init__() will ensure that the base class initializer will be executed as well.

Next, we set up validation, as follows:

```
vcmd = self.register(self._validate)
invcmd = self.register(self._invalid)

self.configure(
  validate='all',
  validatecommand=(vcmd, '%P', '%s', '%S', '%V', '%i', '%d'),
  invalidcommand=(invcmd, '%P', '%s', '%S', '%V', '%i', '%d')
)
```

As we've done before, we're registering instance methods for validation and invalid data handling, and then using `configure` to set them up with the widget. We'll go ahead and pass in all the substitution codes (except `%w`, the widget name, since it's fairly useless inside a class context). We're running validation on `all` conditions, so we can capture both `focus` and `key` events.

Now, we'll define our error condition handler:

```
def _toggle_error(self, on=False):
  self.configure(foreground=('red' if on else 'black'))
```

This will just change the text color to red if there's an error, or black otherwise. Unlike our previous validated widget classes, we won't set the error string in this function; instead, we'll do that in the validation callback since we'll have a better idea of what the error is in that context.

Our validation callback will look like this:

```
def _validate(self, proposed, current, char, event, index, action):
  self.error.set('')
  self._toggle_error()
  valid = True
  # if the widget is disabled, don't validate
  state = str(self.configure('state')[-1])
  if state == tk.DISABLED:
    return valid

  if event == 'focusout':
    valid = self._focusout_validate(event=event)
  elif event == 'key':
```

```
        valid = self._key_validate(
        proposed=proposed,
        current=current,
        char=char,
        event=event,
        index=index,
        action=action
    )
    return valid
```

Since this is a mixin, our _validate() method doesn't actually contain any validation logic. Rather, it's going to start by handling a few setup chores, like toggling off the error and clearing the error message. It then checks to see if the widget is disabled by retrieving the last item in the widget's state value. If it is disabled, the value of the widget is immaterial, so validation should always pass.

After that, the method calls an event-specific callback method, depending on the event type passed in. We only care about the key and focusout events right now, so any other event just returns True. Those event-specific methods will be defined in our subclasses to determine the actual validation logic used.

> Notice that we call the individual methods using keyword arguments; when we create our subclasses, we'll be overriding these methods. By using keyword arguments, our overridden functions can just specify the needed keywords or extract individual arguments from **kwargs, rather than having to get all the arguments in the right order. Also, notice that all the arguments are passed into _key_validate(), but only event is passed into _focusout_validate(). Focus events don't pass anything useful for any of the other arguments, so there's no point in passing them along.

Next, we'll put in placeholders for the event-specific validation methods:

```
def _focusout_validate(self, **kwargs):
    return True


def _key_validate(self, **kwargs):
    return True
```

The ultimate idea here is that our subclasses only need to override one or both of _focusout_validate() or _key_validate(), depending on what we care about for that widget. If we don't override them, they just return True, so validation passes.

Now, let's do something similar for our invalid input handler:

```python
def _invalid(self, proposed, current, char, event, index, action):
    if event == 'focusout':
        self._focusout_invalid(event=event)
    elif event == 'key':
        self._key_invalid(
            proposed=proposed,
            current=current,
            char=char,
            event=event,
            index=index,
            action=action
        )

def _focusout_invalid(self, **kwargs):
    """Handle invalid data on a focus event"""
    self._toggle_error(True)

def _key_invalid(self, **kwargs):
    """Handle invalid data on a key event.
    By default we want to do nothing"""
    pass
```

We take an identical approach to these methods. Unlike the validate methods, though, our invalid data handlers don't need to return anything. For invalid key events, we do nothing by default, and for invalid input on focusout events, we toggle on our error status.

The last thing we want to add is a way to manually execute validation on the widget. Keystroke validation only really makes sense in the context of entering keys, but there may be times when we want to manually run the focus-out checks since they effectively check the complete entered value. Let's implement that with the following public method:

```python
def trigger_focusout_validation(self):
    valid = self._validate('', '', '', 'focusout', '', '')
    if not valid:
        self._focusout_invalid(event='focusout')
    return valid
```

In this method, we're just duplicating the logic that occurs when a focus-out event happens: run the validation function, and if it fails, run the invalid handler. This completes the ValidatedMixin. Now let's see how it works by applying it to some of our widgets.

Building validating input widgets with ValidatedMixin

To begin, let's think through what classes we need to implement with our new `ValidatedMixin` class:

- All our fields except the Notes field are required (when not disabled), so we'll need a basic `Entry` widget that registers an error if there's no input.

- We have one Date field, so we need an `Entry` widget that enforces a valid date string.

- We have a number of `Spinbox` widgets for decimal or integer input. We'll need to make sure these only accept valid number strings.

- We have a few `Combobox` widgets that don't behave quite the way we want them to.

Let's get started!

Requiring data

Let's start with a basic `Entry` widget that requires data. We can use these for the Technician and Seed Sample fields.

Add a new class just after the `ValidatedMixin` class:

```
# data_entry_app.py
class RequiredEntry(ValidatedMixin, ttk.Entry):
  """An Entry that requires a value"""

  def _focusout_validate(self, event):
    valid = True
    if not self.get():
      valid = False
      self.error.set('A value is required')
    return valid
```

There's no keystroke validation to do here, so we just need to create `_focusout_validate()`. All we need to do in that method is check whether the entered value is empty. If so, we just set an `error` string and return `False`.

That's all there is to it!

Creating a Date widget

Next, let's apply the mixin class to the `DateEntry` class we made before, keeping the same validation algorithm. Add the following code just under the `RequiredEntry` class:

```python
class DateEntry(ValidatedMixin, ttk.Entry):
  """An Entry that only accepts ISO Date strings"""

  def _key_validate(self, action, index, char, **kwargs):
    valid = True

    if action == '0':  # This is a delete action
      valid = True
    elif index in ('0', '1', '2', '3', '5', '6', '8', '9'):
      valid = char.isdigit()
    elif index in ('4', '7'):
      valid = char == '-'
    else:
      valid = False
    return valid

  def _focusout_validate(self, event):
    valid = True
    if not self.get():
      self.error.set('A value is required')
      valid = False
    try:
      datetime.strptime(self.get(), '%Y-%m-%d')
    except ValueError:
      self.error.set('Invalid date')
      valid = False
    return valid
```

In this class, we've once again simply overridden the key and focus validation methods, this time copying in the validation logic we used in our `DateEntry` widget from the previous section. The `_focusout_validate()` method also includes the logic from our `RequiredEntry` class too, since the `Date` value is required.

Those classes were both pretty easy to create; let's move on to something a bit more intricate.

A better Combobox widget

The drop-down widgets in different toolkits or widget sets behave fairly consistently when it comes to mouse operation, but the response to keystrokes varies; for example:

- Some do nothing, such as the Tkinter OptionMenu
- Some require the use of arrow keys to select items, such as the Tkinter ListBox
- Some move to the first entry that begins with any key pressed and cycle through entries beginning with that letter on subsequent presses
- Some narrow down the list to entries that match what's typed

We need to think about what behavior our Combobox widget should have. Since our users are accustomed to doing data entry with the keyboard, and some have difficulty with the mouse, the widget needs to work well with the keyboard. Making them use repeated keystrokes to select options is not very intuitive, either. After talking with the data entry staff, you decide on this behavior:

- If the proposed text matches no entries, the keystroke will be ignored
- When the proposed text matches a single entry, the widget is set to that value
- A delete or backspace clears the entire box

Let's see if we can implement this with validation. Add another class after the DateEntry definition:

```
class ValidatedCombobox(ValidatedMixin, ttk.Combobox):
  """A combobox that only takes values from its string list"""

  def _key_validate(self, proposed, action, **kwargs):
    valid = True
    if action == '0':
      self.set('')
      return True
```

The _key_validate() method starts out by setting up a valid flag and doing a quick check to see if this is a delete action. If it is, we set the value to a blank string and return True. That takes care of the last requirement.

Now, we'll add the logic to match the proposed text to our values:

```
    values = self.cget('values')
    # Do a case-insensitive match against the entered text
    matching = [
```

```
    x for x in values
    if x.lower().startswith(proposed.lower())
  ]
  if len(matching) == 0:
    valid = False
  elif len(matching) == 1:
    self.set(matching[0])
    self.icursor(tk.END)
    valid = False
  return valid
```

A copy of the widget's list of values is retrieved using its `cget()` method. Then, we use a list comprehension to reduce this list to only the entries that begin with the proposed text. To make matching case-insensitive, we're calling `lower()` on both the values in the list item and the proposed text before comparing them.

> Every Tkinter widget supports the `cget()` method. It can be used to retrieve any of the widget's configuration values by name.

If the length of the matching list is `0`, nothing starts with the typed value and we reject the keystroke. If it's `1`, we've found our match, so we'll set the variable to that value. This is done by calling the widget's `set()` method and passing in the matching value. As a final touch, we'll send the cursor to the end of the field using the combo box's `.icursor()`. This isn't strictly necessary, but it looks better than leaving the cursor in the middle of the text. Note that we set `valid` to `False` even though the value matched successfully; since we are setting the value ourselves to the matching item, we want to stop any further input to the widget. Otherwise, the proposed keystroke would be appended to the end of the value we set, creating an invalid input.

Also note that if our matching list contains more than one value, the method will just return `True`, allowing the user to continue typing and filtering the list.

Next, let's add the `focusout` validator:

```
def _focusout_validate(self, **kwargs):
  valid = True
  if not self.get():
    valid = False
    self.error.set('A value is required')
  return valid
```

We don't have to do much here, because the key validation method ensures that the only possible values are a blank field or an item from the `values` list, but since all fields require a value, we'll copy in the validation logic from `RequiredEntry`.

That takes care of our `Combobox` widget. Next, we'll deal with the `Spinbox` widget.

A range-limited Spinbox widget

A number entry seems like it shouldn't be too complicated to deal with, but there are several subtleties to work through to make it bulletproof. In addition to limiting the field to valid number strings, you'll want to enforce the `from_`, `to`, and `increment` arguments as the minimum, maximum, and precision of the input, respectively.

The algorithm needs to implement the following rules:

- Deletion is always allowed
- Digits are always allowed
- If `from_` is less than 0, a minus is allowed as the first character
- If `increment` has a decimal component, one (and only one) dot is allowed
- If the proposed value is greater than the to value, ignore the keystroke
- If the proposed value requires more precision than `increment`, ignore the keystroke
- On `focusout`, make sure the value is a valid number string
- Also on `focusout`, make sure the value is greater than the `from_` value

This is a lot of rules, so let's proceed slowly as we try to implement them. The first thing we'll want to do is import the `Decimal` class from the standard library. At the top of the file, add the following to the end of the import list:

```
from decimal import Decimal, InvalidOperation
```

The `Decimal` class helps our decimal values be a bit more precise than the built-in `float` class, and also makes converting between numbers and strings a bit easier. `InvalidOperation` is a decimal-specific exception we can use in our validation logic.

Now, let's add a new `ValidatedSpinbox` class under the `ValidatedCombobox` class, like so:

```
class ValidatedSpinbox(ValidatedMixin, ttk.Spinbox):
  def __init__(
    self, *args, from_='-Infinity', to='Infinity', **kwargs
  ):
```

```
        super().__init__(*args, from_=from_, to=to, **kwargs)
        increment = Decimal(str(kwargs.get('increment', '1.0')))
        self.precision = increment.normalize().as_tuple().exponent
```

We start by overriding the __init__() method so that we can specify some defaults and grab the from_, to, and increment values from the initializer arguments for use in establishing our validation rules. Note that we have set defaults for to and from_: -Infinity and Infinity. Both float and Decimal will happily accept these values and treat them as you'd expect them to do. Recall that if we specify one limit, we must also specify the other. Adding these defaults allows us to only specify the one we need, and our Spinbox will act as we expect it to.

Once we have run the superclass's initializer method, we're going to figure out the precision value; that is, the number of digits we want to the right of the decimal.

To do this, we're first going to retrieve the increment value from the keyword arguments, using 1.0 if it's not specified. We then convert this value to a Decimal object. Why do this? The Spinbox widget's arguments can be passed in as floats, integers, or strings. Regardless of how you pass them in, Tkinter converts them to floats when the Spinbox initializer is run. Determining the precision of a float is problematic because of floating-point error, so we want to convert it to a Python Decimal before it becomes a float.

 What is a floating-point error? Floats attempt to represent decimal numbers in binary form. Open a Python shell and enter 1.2 / 0.2. You might be surprised to find the answer is 5.99999999999999 rather than 6. This is a result of calculations being done on binary numbers rather than decimal numbers, and it's a source of computation error in nearly every programming language. Python offers us the Decimal class, which takes a numeric string and stores it in a way that makes mathematical operations safe from floating-point errors.

Notice that we cast increment to str before passing it to Decimal. Ideally, we should pass increment to our widget as a string to ensure it will be interpreted correctly, but if we need to pass in a float for some reason, str will do some sensible rounding first.

Having converted increment to a Decimal object, we can extract its precision value by taking the exponent of the smallest valid decimal place. We'll use this value in the validation method to make sure our entered data doesn't have too many decimal places.

Our constructor is now settled, so let's write the validation methods. The _key_validate() method is a bit tricky, so we'll walk through it chunk by chunk.

First, we start the method:

```
def _key_validate(
    self, char, index, current, proposed, action, **kwargs
):
    if action == '0':
        return True
    valid = True
    min_val = self.cget('from')
    max_val = self.cget('to')
    no_negative = min_val >= 0
    no_decimal = self.precision >= 0
```

First, because deletion should always work, we'll return True immediately if the action is a deletion. After that, we retrieve the from_ and to values using cget() and declare some flag variables to indicate if negatives and decimals should be allowed.

Next, we need to test if the proposed keystroke is a valid character:

```
if any([
    (char not in '-1234567890.'),
    (char == '-' and (no_negative or index != '0')),
    (char == '.' and (no_decimal or '.' in current))
]):
    return False
```

Valid characters are digits, the - symbol, and the decimal (.). The minus sign is only valid at index 0, and only when negative numbers are allowed. The decimal can only appear once, and only if our precision is less than 1. We've put all these conditions in a list and passed it to the built-in any() function.

 The built-in any() function takes a list of expressions and returns True if any one of the expressions in the list is true. There's also an all() function that returns True only if every expression in the list is true. These functions allow you to condense a long chain of Boolean expressions.

We're almost guaranteed at this point to have a valid Decimal string, but not quite; we might have just the -, ., or -. characters.

Those are not valid `Decimal` strings, but they are valid *partial* entries, so we should allow them. This code will check for those combinations and allow them:

```
if proposed in '-.':
  return True
```

If we have not yet returned at this point, the proposed text can only be a valid `Decimal` string, so we'll make a `Decimal` from it and do some final tests:

```
proposed = Decimal(proposed)
proposed_precision = proposed.as_tuple().exponent

if any([
  (proposed > max_val),
  (proposed_precision < self.precision)
]):
  return False


return valid
```

Our last two tests check to see whether the proposed text is either greater than our maximum value or has more precision than the increment that we specified (the reason we use a < operator here is because precision is given as a negative value for decimal places). Finally, in case nothing has been returned yet, we return the `valid` value.

That takes care of key validation; our focus-out validator is much simpler, as you can see:

```
def _focusout_validate(self, **kwargs):
  valid = True
  value = self.get()
  min_val = self.cget('from')
  max_val = self.cget('to')

  try:
    d_value = Decimal(value)
  except InvalidOperation:
    self.error.set(f'Invalid number string: {value}')
    return False

  if d_value < min_val:
```

```
        self.error.set(f'Value is too low (min {min_val})')
        valid = False
    if d_value > max_val:
        self.error.set(f'Value is too high (max {max_val})')
        valid = False
    return valid
```

With the entire intended value at our disposal, we only need to make sure it's a valid `Decimal` string and within the specified value range. In theory, our key validation should have prevented an invalid decimal string or high value from being entered, but it doesn't hurt to check regardless.

With that method completed, our `ValidatedSpinbox` is ready to go.

Validating Radiobutton widgets

Validating `Radiobutton` widgets may seem initially pointless since the widget itself can only be on or off; however, validating a *group* of buttons can be quite useful in some situations. For example, in our ABQ data form, the Lab field is required to have a value, but currently the user can submit a record without clicking on one of the options.

To fix this, we're going to create a new class that will represent a group of buttons and add validation code to this compound widget.

Unfortunately, our mixin class cannot help us here as neither our compound widget nor Ttk `Radiobutton` widgets can support the `validate`, `validatecommand`, or `invalidcommand` arguments. Therefore, we'll have to implement validation of the button group without help from Tkinter's validation system.

To begin, we'll subclass `ttk.Frame` to build the compound widget on:

```
# data_entry_app.py

class ValidatedRadioGroup(ttk.Frame):
  """A validated radio button group"""

  def __init__(
    self, *args, variable=None, error_var=None,
    values=None, button_args=None, **kwargs
  ):
    super().__init__(*args, **kwargs)
```

```
self.variable = variable or tk.StringVar()
self.error = error_var or tk.StringVar()
self.values = values or list()
self.button_args = button_args or dict()
```

The initializer for this class takes a number of keyword values:

- `variable` will be the control variable for the group's value. If not passed in, it will be created by the class.

- `error_var` is a control variable for the error string. Just as with our other validated classes, we have allowed the possibility of accepting a `StringVar` control variable to hold the error string, or we just create one if one wasn't passed in, saving it as `self.error`.

- `values` will be a list containing the string values that each button in the group represents.

- `button_args` will be a dictionary of keyword arguments that we can pass to the individual `Radiobutton` widgets. This will allow us to pass arguments to the buttons separately from the `Frame` container.

The remaining positional and keyword arguments are passed to the superclass initializer. After saving the keyword values to instance variables, we'll next create the buttons like so:

```
for v in self.values:
  button = ttk.Radiobutton(
    self, value=v, text=v,
    variable=self.variable, **self.button_args
  )
  button.pack(
    side=tk.LEFT, ipadx=10, ipady=2, expand=True, fill='x'
  )
```

Just as we did in the `LabelInput` initializer, we are iterating through the `values` list, creating a `Radiobutton` widget for each value, and binding it to the common control variable. Each one is packed onto the `Frame` from the left side of the widget.

To finish the initializer, we need to trigger a validation callback whenever the `Frame` widget loses focus. To do that, we can just use `bind()`, like so:

```
self.bind('<FocusOut>', self.trigger_focusout_validation)
```

Now, whenever the widget loses focus, the validation callback will be called. Let's write that callback next:

```python
def trigger_focusout_validation(self, *_):
    self.error.set('')
    if not self.variable.get():
        self.error.set('A value is required')
```

This method will begin by setting the error variable to an empty string and then simply check if our bound variable contains a value. If it's empty, the error string is populated.

Before we can use this compound widget with our application, we'll need to make one minor change to the `LabelInput` class. Remember that `LabelInput` makes sure that the correct control variable keyword argument gets passed into the widget initializer. We need to make sure our new compound widget class is getting the correct keyword (`variable`, in this case).

Update the `LabelInput` initializer like so:

```python
# data_entry_app, in LabelInput.__init__()
    if input_class in (
      ttk.Checkbutton, ttk.Button,
      ttk.Radiobutton, ValidatedRadioGroup
    ):
      input_args["variable"] = self.variable
    else:
      input_args["textvariable"] = self.variable
```

With that, the `ValidatedRadio` widget should be ready to use!

Updating our form with validated widgets

Now that our widgets are all made, it's time to make use of them in our form GUI. In `data_entry_app.py`, scroll down to the `DataRecordForm` class's `__init__()` method, and we'll start updating our widgets one row at a time. Line 1 is fairly straightforward:

```python
LabelInput(
    r_info, "Date", var=self._vars['Date'], input_class=DateEntry
).grid(row=0, column=0)
LabelInput(
```

```
    r_info, "Time", input_class=ValidatedCombobox,
    var=self._vars['Time'],
    input_args={"values": ["8:00", "12:00", "16:00", "20:00"]}
).grid(row=0, column=1)
LabelInput(
    r_info, "Technician",  var=self._vars['Technician'],
    input_class=RequiredEntry
).grid(row=0, column=2)
```

It's as simple as swapping out the input_class value in each LabelInput call with one of our new classes. Go ahead and run your application and try out the widgets. Try some different valid and invalid dates in the DateEntry, and see how the ValidatedCombobox widget works (RequiredEntry won't do much at this point since the only visible indication is red text, and there's no text to mark red if it's empty; we'll address that in the next section).

Now let's work on line 2, which includes the Lab, Plot, and Seed Sample inputs:

```
LabelInput(
    r_info, "Lab", input_class=ValidatedRadioGroup,
    var=self._vars['Lab'], input_args={"values": ["A", "B", "C"]}
).grid(row=1, column=0)
LabelInput(
    r_info, "Plot", input_class=ValidatedCombobox,
    var=self._vars['Plot'],
    input_args={"values": list(range(1, 21))}
).grid(row=1, column=1)
LabelInput(
    r_info, "Seed Sample",  var=self._vars['Seed Sample'],
    input_class=RequiredEntry
).grid(row=1, column=2)
```

 An astute reader might note that this shouldn't work, since our list of values contains integers, and the ValidatedCombobox widget's validation callback assumes the values are strings (for example, we run lower() on each item in the list, and compare the item to the proposed string). It turns out that Tkinter converts the items in the value list to strings implicitly as it converts the call to Tcl/Tk. This is good to be aware of as you're writing validation methods on fields containing numbers.

Great! Let's move on now to the Environmental Data. We only need to update the number entries to ValidatedSpinbox widgets here:

```
LabelInput(
  e_info, "Humidity (g/m³)",
  input_class=ValidatedSpinbox,  var=self._vars['Humidity'],
  input_args={"from_": 0.5, "to": 52.0, "increment": .01}
).grid(row=0, column=0)
LabelInput(
  e_info, "Light (klx)", input_class=ValidatedSpinbox,
  var=self._vars['Light'],
  input_args={"from_": 0, "to": 100, "increment": .01}
).grid(row=0, column=1)
LabelInput(
  e_info, "Temperature (°C)",
  input_class=ValidatedSpinbox,  var=self._vars['Temperature'],
  input_args={"from_": 4, "to": 40, "increment": .01}
).grid(row=0, column=2)
```

Save and execute the script at this point and give the ValidatedSpinbox widget a try. You should find it impossible to enter values greater than the maximum or with more than two decimal places, and should also find the text turns red if you leave it less than the minimum.

Next, we'll update the first row of Plant Data with more ValidatedSpinbox widgets:

```
LabelInput(
  p_info, "Plants", input_class=ValidatedSpinbox,
  var=self._vars['Plants'], input_args={"from_": 0, "to": 20}
).grid(row=0, column=0)
LabelInput(
  p_info, "Blossoms", input_class=ValidatedSpinbox,
  var=self._vars['Blossoms'], input_args={"from_": 0, "to": 1000}
).grid(row=0, column=1)
LabelInput(
  p_info, "Fruit", input_class=ValidatedSpinbox,
  var=self._vars['Fruit'], input_args={"from_": 0, "to": 1000}
).grid(row=0, column=2)
```

Save and run the form again; you should find that these widgets will not allow you to type a decimal place, since the increment is at the default (1.0).

All that remains is our last row of number inputs. Before we do those, however, let's address some issues of form widget interaction.

Implementing validation interaction between form widgets

So far, we've used validation to create widgets that can validate based on the user's input to that widget. However, sometimes widgets might need to validate based on the state of another widget on the form. We have two such examples on our form:

- Our Height fields (Min Height, Med Height, and Max Height) should not allow a user to enter a Min Height that is greater than the other two fields, a Max Height that is less than the other two fields, nor a Med Height that is not between the other fields.

- Our Equipment Fault checkbox should disable entry of Environmental Data, since we do not want to record data suspected of being faulty.

Dynamically updating the Spinbox range

To solve the problem with our Height fields, we're going to update our ValidatedSpinbox widget so that its ranges can be dynamically updated. To do this, we can use the variable tracing feature we learned about in *Chapter 4*, *Organizing Our Code with Classes*.

Our strategy will be to allow optional min_var and max_var arguments to be passed into the ValidatedSpinbox class, and then set a trace on these variables to update the ValidatedSpinbox object's minimum or maximum values whenever the corresponding variable is changed. We'll also have a focus_update_var variable that will be updated with the Spinbox widget's value at focus-out time. This variable can then be passed in as the min_var or max_var variable to a second ValidatedSpinbox so that the first widget's value can alter the second's valid range.

Let's make these changes to our ValidatedSpinbox. To start, update the ValidatedSpinbox.__init__() method with our new keyword arguments as follows:

```
def __init__(self, *args, min_var=None, max_var=None,
  focus_update_var=None, from_='-Infinity', to='Infinity', **kwargs
):
```

Some of our code for this feature is going to require that the Spinbox has a variable bound to it, so the next thing we're going to do is make sure that happens; put this code at the end of __init__():

```
self.variable = kwargs.get('textvariable')
if not self.variable:
  self.variable = tk.DoubleVar()
  self.configure(textvariable=self.variable)
```

We start by retrieving the `textvariable` from the keyword arguments; if it's not set to anything, we'll just create a `DoubleVar` and make it our variable. We're storing a reference to the variable so we can use it easily in our instance methods.

> Note that this arrangement could cause problems if a variable is assigned later using `configure()`. This won't be a problem in our code, but if you're using this class in your own Tkinter programs, you may want to override `configure()` to make sure the variable reference is kept in sync.

Next, still in `__init__()`, let's set up our minimum and maximum variables:

```
if min_var:
    self.min_var = min_var
    self.min_var.trace_add('write', self._set_minimum)
if max_var:
    self.max_var = max_var
    self.max_var.trace_add('write', self._set_maximum)
```

If we pass in either a `min_var` or `max_var` argument, the value is stored and a trace is configured. The callback for the trace points to an appropriately named private method.

We'll also need to store a reference to the `focus_update_var` argument and bind focus-out events to a method that will be used to update it. To do that, add the following code to `__init__()`:

```
self.focus_update_var = focus_update_var
self.bind('<FocusOut>', self._set_focus_update_var)
```

> The `bind()` method can be called on any Tkinter widget, and it's used to connect widget events to a Python callable. Events can be keystrokes, mouse movements or clicks, focus events, window management events, and more.

Now, we need to add the callback methods for our `trace()` and `bind()` commands. We'll start with the one that updates the `focus_update_var`, which we'll call `_set_focus_update_var()`. Add it as follows:

```
def _set_focus_update_var(self, event):
    value = self.get()
    if self.focus_update_var and not self.error.get():
        self.focus_update_var.set(value)
```

This method simply gets the widget's current value and, if there is a focus_update_var argument present in the instance, sets it to the same value. Note that we don't set the value if there's an error currently present on the widget, since it wouldn't make sense to update the value to something invalid.

Also notice that the method takes an event argument. We don't use this argument, but it is necessary since this is a callback for a bind. When Tkinter calls a bind callback, it passes in an event object that contains information about the event that triggered the callback. Even if you aren't going to use this information, your function or method needs to be able to take this argument.

Now, let's create the callback for setting the minimum, starting with this:

```
def _set_minimum(self, *_):
  current = self.get()
```

The first thing this method does is retrieve the current value of the widget using self.get(). The reason we're doing this is because the Spinbox widget has the slightly annoying default behavior of correcting its value when the to or from_ values are changed, moving too-low values to the from_ value and too-high values to the to value. This kind of silent auto-correction might slip past the attention of our user and cause bad data to be saved.

What we would prefer is to leave the out-of-range value as-is and mark it as an error; so to work around the Spinbox widget, we're going to save the current value, change the configuration, and then put the original value back in the field.

After storing the current value in current, we attempt to get the value of the min_var and set our widget's from_ value from it, like so:

```
try:
    new_min = self.min_var.get()
    self.config(from_=new_min)
except (tk.TclError, ValueError):
    pass
```

There are several things that could go wrong here, such as a blank or invalid value in min_var, all of which should raise either a tk.TclError or a ValueError. In any case, we'll just do nothing, leaving the current minimum in place.

> It's generally a bad idea to just silence exceptions; however, in this case, there's nothing we can reasonably do if the variable is bad except ignore it.

Now, we just need to write the current value that we saved back into the field, like so:

```
if not current:
  self.delete(0, tk.END)
else:
  self.variable.set(current)
```

If current is empty, we just delete the contents of the field; otherwise, we set the input's variable to current.

Finally, we'll want to trigger the widget's focus-out validation to see if the current value is acceptable in the new range; we can do that by calling our trigger_focusout_validation() method, like this:

```
self.trigger_focusout_validation()
```

The _set_maximum() method will be identical to this method, except that it will update the to value using max_var instead. It is shown here:

```
def _set_maximum(self, *_):
  current = self.get()
  try:
    new_max = self.max_var.get()
    self.config(to=new_max)
  except (tk.TclError, ValueError):
    pass
  if not current:
    self.delete(0, tk.END)
  else:
    self.variable.set(current)
  self.trigger_focusout_validation()
```

That finishes our ValidatedSpinbox changes. Now we can implement the last line of our Plant Data with this new capability.

First, we'll need to set up variables to store the minimum and maximum height, as follows:

```
min_height_var = tk.DoubleVar(value='-infinity')
max_height_var = tk.DoubleVar(value='infinity')
```

Each variable is a DoubleVar, set to -infinity or infinity, effectively defaulting to no minimum or maximum. Our widgets won't be affected by the values of these variables until they're actually changed (triggering the trace callback), so they won't initially override the to or from_ values entered into the widgets.

Note that these need not be instance variables, as our widgets will store references to them.

Now, we'll create the Min Height widget, as follows:

```
LabelInput(
    p_info, "Min Height (cm)",
    input_class=ValidatedSpinbox,  var=self._vars['Min Height'],
    input_args={
        "from_": 0, "to": 1000, "increment": .01,
        "max_var": max_height_var, "focus_update_var": min_height_var
    }
).grid(row=1, column=0)
```

We'll use `max_height_var` to update the maximum here, and set the `focus_update_var` to `min_height_var` so that entry into the Min Height widget will update the minimum height variable. We do not want to set a `min_var` on this field because its value represents the minimum for other fields.

Next, let's update the Max Height widget:

```
LabelInput(
    p_info, "Max Height (cm)",
    input_class=ValidatedSpinbox,  var=self._vars['Max Height'],
    input_args={
        "from_": 0, "to": 1000, "increment": .01,
        "min_var": min_height_var, "focus_update_var": max_height_var
    }
).grid(row=1, column=1)
```

This time, we use our `min_height_var` variable to set the widget's minimum value and set the `max_height_var` to be updated with the widget's current value on focus-out. We do not set a `max_var` on this field since its value will represent the maximum and shouldn't be constrained beyond its initial limits.

Finally, the Median Height field should be updated like so:

```
LabelInput(
    p_info, "Median Height (cm)",
    input_class=ValidatedSpinbox,  var=self._vars['Med Height'],
    input_args={
        "from_": 0, "to": 1000, "increment": .01,
        "min_var": min_height_var, "max_var": max_height_var
    }
).grid(row=1, column=2)
```

Here, we're setting the minimum and maximum values for the field from the `min_height_var` and `max_height_var` variables, respectively. We're not updating any variables from the Median Height field, although we could add additional variables and code here to make sure that Min Height couldn't go above it or Max Height below it. In most cases, it won't matter as long as the user is entering data in order since Median Height is last.

You might wonder why we don't just use the bound variables from Min Height and Max Height to hold these values instead. If you try this, you'll discover the reason: the bound variable updates as you type, which means your partial value instantly becomes the new maximum or minimum value. We'd rather wait until the user has committed to the value to update the ranges, and thus we created a separate variable that is only updated on focus-out.

Dynamic disabling of fields

To implement the disabling of our Environment Data fields when the Equipment Fault checkbox is activated, we'll once again use control variable tracing. This time, however, instead of implementing it at the widget class level, we'll implement it in our compound widget, the `LabelInput`.

Locate the `LabelInput` class in your code, and let's add a new keyword argument to its `__init__()` method:

```
class LabelInput(tk.Frame):
  """A widget containing a label and input together."""

  def __init__(
    self, parent, label, var, input_class=ttk.Entry,
      input_args=None, label_args=None, disable_var=None,
      **kwargs
  ):
```

The `disable_var` argument will allow us to pass in a Boolean control variable that will be monitored to determine if our field should be disabled. To make use of it, we'll need to store it in the `LabelInput` instance and configure a trace. Add this code to the end of `LabelInput.__init__()`:

```
    if disable_var:
      self.disable_var = disable_var
      self.disable_var.trace_add('write', self._check_disable)
```

The trace is linked to an instance method called `_check_disable()`. This method will need to check the value of `disable_var` and take appropriate action with the `LabelInput` widget's input.

Let's implement the method in our `LabelInput` class like this:

```
def _check_disable(self, *_):
  if not hasattr(self, 'disable_var'):
    return

  if self.disable_var.get():
    self.input.configure(state=tk.DISABLED)
    self.variable.set('')
  else:
    self.input.configure(state=tk.NORMAL)
```

First, our method uses `hasattr` to see if this `LabelInput` even has a `disable_var`. In theory, the method shouldn't even get called if it doesn't, since there would be no trace, but just to be sure, we'll check and simply return if the instance variable doesn't exist.

If we have a `disable_var`, we'll check its value to see if it's `True`. If it is, we disable the input widget. To disable an input widget, we need to configure its `state` property. The `state` property determines the current disposition of the widget. In this case, we want to disable it, so we can set `state` to the `tk.DISABLED` constant. That will have the effect of "graying out" our field and making it read-only. We also want to clear out any information in the disabled fields, to make sure the user understands no data will be recorded for these fields. So, we'll set the variable to an empty string.

If the `disable_var` is false, we need to re-enable the widget. To do that, we can just set its state to `tk.NORMAL`.

 The `state` property will be covered in more detail in *Chapter 9, Improving the Look with Styles and Themes.*

With that method written, we just need to update our Environmental Data fields with a `disable_var` variable. Scroll back to your `DataRecordForm.__init__()` method and find where we've created those fields. We'll update them like so:

```
LabelInput(
  e_info, "Humidity (g/m³)",
  input_class=ValidatedSpinbox,  var=self._vars['Humidity'],
  input_args={"from_": 0.5, "to": 52.0, "increment": .01},
  disable_var=self._vars['Equipment Fault']
).grid(row=0, column=0)
```

```
LabelInput(
  e_info, "Light (klx)", input_class=ValidatedSpinbox,
  var=self._vars['Light'],
  input_args={"from_": 0, "to": 100, "increment": .01},
  disable_var=self._vars['Equipment Fault']
).grid(row=0, column=1)
LabelInput(
  e_info, "Temperature (°C)",
  input_class=ValidatedSpinbox, var=self._vars['Temperature'],
  input_args={"from_": 4, "to": 40, "increment": .01},
  disable_var=self._vars['Equipment Fault']
).grid(row=0, column=2)
```

In each case, we've added the disable_var argument and set it to self._vars['Equipment Fault']. If you run the script now, you should find that checking the Equipment Fault box disables and clears these three fields, and unchecking it re-enables them.

Our form is now much better at enforcing correct data and catching potential errors during data entry, but it's not quite user-friendly yet. Let's see what can be done about that in the next section.

Displaying errors

If you run the application, you may notice that while fields with the focus-out errors turn red, we don't get to see the actual error. This is a bit of a problem for user-friendliness, so let's see if we can fix it. Our plan will be to update the LabelInput compound widget with another Label that can display an error string in the event of an error.

To implement this, first locate your LabelInput class. Add this code to the end of the __init__() method:

```
self.error = getattr(self.input, 'error', tk.StringVar())
ttk.Label(self, textvariable=self.error, **label_args).grid(
  row=2, column=0, sticky=(tk.W + tk.E)
)
```

Here, we check to see if our input has an error variable, and if not, we create one. Our validated widgets should already have such a variable, but unvalidated widgets such as the BoundText widget used for the Notes field do not, so we need this check to make sure.

Next, we're creating and placing a Label widget and binding the error variable to its textvariable argument. This will update the Label contents with whatever our widget's error variable contains as it is updated by the validation logic.

Save the application, run it, and try entering some bad data in the fields (for example, a low value in one of the Spinbox widgets). You should see an error pop up under the field when you focus the next field. Success!

There is one small issue to fix, though. If you happen to be focused on an Environment Data field like Humidity when you click the Equipment Fault checkbox, an error will be left under the field. The reason is that clicking the checkbox causes the field to lose focus, triggering its validation. Meanwhile, the _check_disable() method sets its value to an invalid blank string, which the validation logic rejects.

The solution is for us to clear the error string when we disable the field. In the LabelInput._check_disable() method, update the code like so:

```
if self.disable_var.get():
    self.input.configure(state=tk.DISABLED)
    self.variable.set('')
    self.error.set('')
```

Run the application again and you should see the errors disappear when the checkbox is checked.

Preventing form submission on error

The final step in preventing errors from getting into our CSV file is to stop the application from saving the record if the form has known errors.

Record saving happens in our Application object, so we need a way for that object to determine the error state of the form before it saves the data. That means our DataRecordForm will need a public method. We'll call that method get_errors().

At the end of the DataRecordForm class, add the following method:

```
def get_errors(self):
    """Get a list of field errors in the form"""

    errors = {}
    for key, var in self._vars.items():
        inp = var.label_widget.input
        error = var.label_widget.error
```

```
      if hasattr(inp, 'trigger_focusout_validation'):
        inp.trigger_focusout_validation()
      if error.get():
        errors[key] = error.get()

    return errors
```

We begin by defining an empty `dict` object to store the errors. We'll store our errors in the dictionary as `field: error_string` so that the calling code can be specific about the fields that have errors.

Recall that our `LabelInput` class attaches a reference to itself to the control variable passed into its __init__() method. We can use this reference now as we loop through our dictionary of variables. For each variable, we've done the following:

- We retrieve its input widget and the associated `error` variable from the `LabelWidget` reference
- If the input defines a `trigger_focusout_validation()` method, we call it, just to be sure that its value has been validated
- If the value is invalid, that should populate the error variable; so, if `error` is not empty, we add it to the `errors` dictionary
- After we've gone through all the fields, we can return the `errors` dictionary

Now that we have a way to retrieve the form's errors, we need to utilize it in the `Application` class's `on_save()` method. Locate that method, and then add the following code to the beginning of the method:

```
    errors = self.recordform.get_errors()
    if errors:
      self.status.set(
        "Cannot save, error in fields: {}"
        .format(', '.join(errors.keys())))
      )
    return
```

Recall that our `Application` object stores a reference to the form in `self.recordform`. We can now retrieve its dictionary of errors by calling its `get_errors()` method. If the dictionary is not empty, we'll construct an error string by joining all its keys (that is, the field names) and appending them to an error message. This is then passed to the `status` control variable, causing it to be displayed in the status bar. Finally, we return from the method so that the remaining logic in `on_save()` is not executed.

Start the application and try it out by trying to save a blank form. You should get error messages in all fields and a message at the bottom telling you which fields have errors, as shown here:

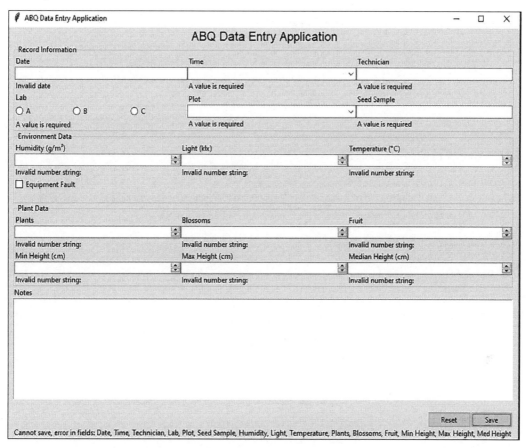

Figure 5.3: The application with all errors showing

Automating input

Preventing users from entering bad data is one way to improve the quality of their output; another approach is to automate the entry of data wherever the values are predictable. Using our understanding of how the forms are likely to be filled out, we can insert values that are very likely to be correct for certain fields.

Remember from *Chapter 2, Designing GUI Applications*, that the forms are nearly always recorded the same day that they're filled out, starting with Plot 1 and going to Plot 20 in order for each paper form.

Also remember that the Date, Time, Lab, and Technician values remain the same for each form that is filled in. That gives us the possibility of implementing some helpful automation, specifically:

- The current date can automatically be inserted in the Date field
- If the previous Plot was not the last plot in the lab, we can increment its value and leave the Time, Technician, and Lab values the same

Let's see how we can implement these changes for the users.

Date automation

Inserting the current date is an easy place to start. The place to do this is in the `DataRecordForm.reset()` method, which is called when the form is initialized and every time a record is saved to set up the form for a new record.

Update that method as follows:

```
def reset(self):
    """Resets the form entries"""

    for var in self._vars.values():
        if isinstance(var, tk.BooleanVar):
            var.set(False)
        else:
            var.set('')

    current_date = datetime.today().strftime('%Y-%m-%d')
    self._vars['Date'].set(current_date)
    self._vars['Time'].label_widget.input.focus()
```

After clearing the values of all the variables, we're going to get the current date in ISO format using `datetime.today().strftime()`, just as we do for the datestamp in `Application.on_save()`. Once we have that value, it's simply a matter of setting the `Date` variable to it.

As a final touch, we should update the focus of the form to the next input that needs entry, in this case, the Time field. Otherwise, the user would have to manually tab through the Date field, which is already filled in. To do this, we have accessed the input widget associated with the `Time` variable by way of its `label_widget` member and called the widget's `focus()` method. This method gives the widget keyboard focus.

Automating Plot, Lab, Time, and Technician

Handling Plot, Lab, Time, and Technician is a bit more complex. Our strategy will go something like this:

- Before clearing the data, store the Plot, Lab, Time, and Technician values.
- Clear all the values.
- If the stored Plot value is less than the last value (20), we'll put the Lab, Time, and Technician values back in the fields. We'll also increment the Plot value.
- If the stored Plot value *is* the last value (or no value), leave those fields blank.

Let's begin to add this logic to the reset() method, as follows:

```python
def reset(self):
  """Resets the form entries"""

  lab = self._vars['Lab'].get()
  time = self._vars['Time'].get()
  technician = self._vars['Technician'].get()
  try:
    plot = self._vars['Plot'].get()
  except tk.TclError:
    plot = ''
  plot_values = (
    self._vars['Plot'].label_widget.input.cget('values')
  )
```

Before anything else in reset(), we're going to get the values of the affected fields and save them. Note that we have put plot in a try/except block. In the event that the Plot input is blank, it will throw a TclError, since a blank string is an invalid integer string. In that case, we'll assign the plot to be a blank string and carry on.

We're also retrieving the list of possible plot values by accessing the Plot widget by way of the Plot variable's label_widget member. Since we know there are 20 plots in each lab, we could just hardcode a list of 1 to 20 here, but that kind of hardcoding of information is bad form; if plots are added or eliminated from the lab, we would have to scour our code for the number 20 to fix all the places where we'd made this assumption. It's far better to query the widget itself to find out its possible values.

Next, at the end of this method (after clearing the fields and setting the date), let's add this code to update the fields:

```python
if plot not in ('', 0, plot_values[-1]):
  self._vars['Lab'].set(lab)
```

```
        self._vars['Time'].set(time)
        self._vars['Technician'].set(technician)
        next_plot_index = plot_values.index(str(plot)) + 1
        self._vars['Plot'].set(plot_values[next_plot_index])
        self._vars['Seed Sample'].label_widget.input.focus()
```

This code checks to see if the plot value is a blank string, 0, or the last value in the list of plot values. If it's not, we start populating the automated fields. First Lab, Time, and Technician are populated with our stored values. Then we need to increment the Plot value.

Plot *should* be an integer at this point, but because of Tkinter's habit of implicitly casting things to string, it's better to work with it as though it were not. So, instead of merely incrementing the value of Plot, we're instead going to retrieve its index from `plot_values` and increment that instead. Then we can set the value of the Plot variable to the incremented index.

As a final touch, we will set the focus of the form to the Seed Sample input, just as we did previously with the Time input.

Our validation and automation code is complete, and the form is now ready for a trial run with our users. It's definitely an improvement over the CSV entry at this point and will help data entry to make quick work of those forms. Great work!

Summary

The application has really come a long way. In this chapter, we learned about Tkinter validation, created a validation mixin class, and used it to create validated versions of the `Entry`, `Combobox`, and `Spinbox` widgets. We also learned how to validate widgets like `Radiobutton`, which don't support the built-in validation framework. We validated different kinds of data on keystrokes and focus events, and created fields that dynamically change state or update their constraints based on the values of related fields. Finally, we automated input on several fields to reduce the amount of manual data entry required by the user.

In the next chapter, we're going to prepare our code base for expansion by learning how to organize a large application for easier maintenance. More specifically, we'll learn about the MVC pattern and how to structure our code in multiple files for simpler maintenance. We'll also learn about version control software and how it can help us keep track of changes.

6

Planning for the Expansion of Our Application

The application is a real hit! After some initial testing and orientation, the data entry staff have been utilizing your new form for a few weeks now. The reduction in errors and data entry time is dramatic, and there's a lot of excited talk about what other problems this program might solve. With even the director joining in on the brainstorming, you have a strong suspicion that you'll be asked to add some new features soon.

There's a problem, though: the application is already a script of several hundred lines, and you're worried about its manageability as it grows. You need to take some time to organize your code base in preparation for future expansion.

In this chapter, we'll learn about the following topics:

- In *Separating concerns*, you'll learn about using the **model-view-controller (MVC)** pattern.
- In *Structuring our application directory*, you'll learn how to organize your code into a Python package.
- In *Splitting our application into multiple files*, you'll reorganize the data entry application into an MVC Python package.
- In *Using version control software*, you'll discover how to use the Git version control system to track your changes.

Separating concerns

Proper architectural design is essential for any project that needs to scale. Anyone can prop up some studs and build a garden shed, but a house or skyscraper takes careful planning and engineering. Software is no different; simple scripts can get away with shortcuts such as global variables or manipulating class properties directly, but as the program grows, our code needs to isolate and encapsulate different functionalities in a way that limits the amount of complexity we need to understand at any given moment.

We call this concept **separation of concerns**, and it's accomplished through the use of architectural patterns that describe different application components and how they interact.

The MVC pattern

Probably the most enduring of these architectural patterns is the **model-view-controller** (**MVC**) pattern, which was introduced in the 1970s. While this pattern has evolved and spun off variations over the years, the basic gist remains: keep the data, the presentation of the data, and the application logic in separate, independent components.

The roles and relationships of the MVC components are shown in this diagram:

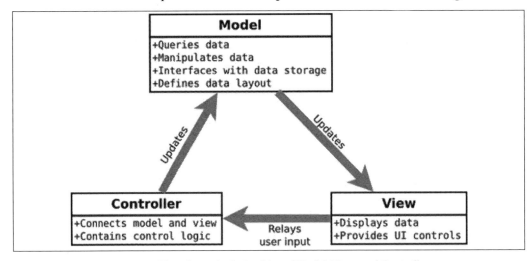

Figure 6.1: The roles and relationships of Model, View, and Controller

Let's take a deeper look at each of these components and understand them in the context of our current application.

What is a model?

The **model** in MVC represents the data. This includes the storage of the data, but also the various ways data can be queried or manipulated. Ideally, the model is not concerned with or affected by how the data will be presented (that is, what GUI widgets will be used, how the fields will be ordered, and so on), but rather presents a high-level interface that only minimally concerns other components with its inner workings. In theory, if you decided to completely change the user interface of the program (say, from a Tkinter application to a web application), the model should be totally unaffected.

Some examples of functionality or information you find in the model include:

- Preparation and saving of program data to a persistent medium (data file, database, and so on)
- Retrieval of data from a file or database into a format useful to the program
- An authoritative list of the fields in a set of data, along with their data types and limits
- Validation of data against the data types and limits defined
- Calculations on stored data

We don't have a model class in our application currently; the data layout is defined in the form class, and the `Application.onsave()` method is the only code concerned with data persistence so far. To implement MVC in our application, we're going to need to split this logic off into a separate object that will define the data layout and handle all the CSV operations.

What is a view?

A **view** is an interface for presenting data and controls to the user. Applications may have many views, often on the same data. Views may or may not have direct access to the model; if they do, they generally have read-only access, sending write requests through the controller.

Some examples of code you find in a view include:

- GUI layout and widget definitions
- Form automations, such as auto-completion of fields, dynamic toggling of widgets, or display of error dialogs
- Formatting of raw data for presentation

Our DataRecordForm class is an example of a view: it contains most of the code for our application's user interface. It also contains the _vars dictionary, which currently defines the structure of our data records. This dictionary can stay in the view, because the view does need a way to store the data temporarily before handing it off to the model, but _vars shouldn't be defining our data record from here on out — that's the model's job. To implement MVC, we'll need to make the view's concept of the data dependent on the model, not on its own definitions.

What is a controller?

The **controller** is the "Grand Central Station" for the application. It handles requests from the user and takes care of routing data between the views and the model. Most variations of MVC change the role (and sometimes the name) of the controller, but the important thing is that it acts as the intermediary between the view and the model. Our controller object will need to hold references to the views and models used by our application and be responsible for managing interactions between them.

Examples of code you find in the controller include:

- Startup and shutdown logic for the application
- Callbacks for user interface events
- Creation of model and view instances

Our Application object is currently acting as the controller for our application, though it has some view and model logic in it as well. Unfortunately, the Tk object in Tkinter combines both the central point of control and the root window, so it's not entirely possible to separate the controller from the application's main view. Our Application object will therefore contain a little of both, but in the interest of implementing a more MVC design, we'll need to move some of its presentation logic into the views and some of its data logic into the models. Ideally, though, we want the Application object focused mainly on connecting code between the models and views.

Why complicate our design?

Initially, it may seem like a lot of needless overhead to split up the application this way. We'll have to shuttle data around between different objects and ultimately write more code to do exactly the same thing. Why would we do this?

Put simply, we're doing it to make expansion manageable. As the application grows, the complexity will also grow. Isolating our components from one another limits the amount of complexity that any one component has to manage; for example, if we wanted to restructure the layout of the Data Record Form, we should not have to worry if doing so will change the structure of the data in the output file.

Those two aspects of the program should be independent of one another.

It also helps us to be consistent about where we put certain types of logic. For example, having a discrete model object helps us to avoid littering our UI code with ad hoc data queries or file access attempts.

The bottom line is, without some guiding architectural strategy, our program is in danger of becoming a hopeless tangle of spaghetti logic. Even without adhering to a strict definition of MVC design, consistently following even a loose MVC pattern will save a lot of headaches as the application becomes more complex.

Structuring our application directory

Just as logically breaking our program into separate concerns helps us manage the logical complexity of each component, physically breaking the code into multiple files helps us keep the complexity of each file manageable. It also reinforces more isolation between components; for example, you can't share global variables between files, and you know that if your `models.py` file imports `tkinter`, you're doing something wrong.

Basic directory structure

There is no official standard for laying out a Python application directory, but there are some common conventions that will help us keep things tidy and make it easier to package our software later on. Let's set up our directory structure.

To begin, create a directory called `ABQ_Data_Entry`. This is the root directory of our application, so whenever we refer to the **application root**, this is it.

Under the application root, create another directory called `abq_data_entry`. Notice it's in lowercase. This is going to be a Python package that will contain all the code for the application; it should always be given a fairly unique and descriptive name so that it won't be confused with existing Python packages. Normally, you wouldn't have a different casing between the application root and this main module, but it doesn't hurt anything either; we're doing it here to avoid confusion.

 Python packages and modules should always be named using all lowercase letters and underscores to separate words. This convention is spelled out in PEP 8, Python's official style guide. See `https://www.python.org/dev/peps/pep-0008` for more information about PEP 8.

Next, create a docs folder under the application root. This folder will be for documentation files about the application.

Finally, create two empty files in the application root: README.rst and abq_data_entry.py. Your directory structure should look as follows:

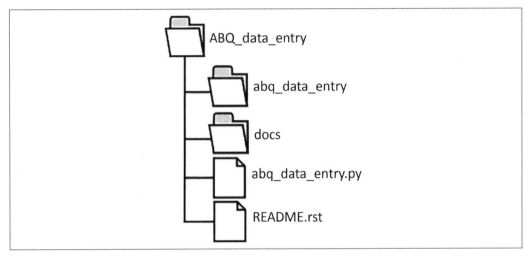

Figure 6.2: Directory structure of our application root directory

Now, let's put some code in these files.

The abq_data_entry.py file

The abq_data_entry.py file is going to be the main file that gets executed to start the program. However, it won't contain the bulk of our program. In fact, it will contain only the following code:

```
from abq_data_entry.application import Application

app = Application()
app.mainloop()
```

Add that code to the file and save it. The only purpose of this file is to import our Application class, make an instance of it, and run it. The remainder of the work will happen inside the abq_data_entry package. We haven't created that yet, so this file won't run just yet. Before we do anything about the application package, let's deal with our documentation.

The README.rst file

Since as far back as the 1970s, programs have included a short text file called README, containing a condensed summary of the program's documentation. For small programs, it may be the only documentation; for larger programs, it usually contains essential pre-flight instructions for users or administrators.

There's no prescribed set of contents for a README file, but as a basic guideline, consider the following sections:

- **Description**: A brief description of the program and its function. We can reuse the description from our specification, or something like it. This might also contain a brief list of the main features.

- **Author information**: The names of the authors and copyright date. This is especially important if you plan to share your software, but even for something in-house, it's useful for future maintainers to know who created the software and when.

- **Requirements**: A list of the software and hardware requirements for the software, if any.

- **Installation**: Instructions for installing the software, its prerequisites, dependencies, and basic setup.

- **Configuration**: How to configure the application and what options are available. This is generally aimed at the command-line or configuration file options, not options set interactively in the program.

- **Usage**: A description of how to launch the application, command-line arguments, and other notes a user would need to know to use the basic functionality of the application.

- **General notes**: A catch-all for notes or critical information users should be aware of.

- **Bugs**: A list of known bugs or limitations in the application.

Not all of these sections will apply to every program; for example, ABQ Data Entry doesn't currently have any configuration options, so there's no reason to have a configuration section. You might add other sections as well, depending on the situation; for example, publicly distributed software may have an FAQ section for common questions, or open source software might have a Contributing section with instructions on how to submit patches.

The README file is written in plain ASCII or Unicode text, either free-form or using a markup language. Since we're doing a Python project, we'll use **reStructuredText**, the official markup for Python documentation (which is why our file uses an rst file extension).

For more information on reStructuredText, see the *Appendix A, A Quick Primer on reStructuredText*.

A sample README.rst file is included in the example code in the GitHub repo. Take a moment to look it over; then, we can move on to the docs folder.

Populating the docs folder

The docs folder is where documentation goes. This can be any kind of documentation: user manuals, program specifications, API references, diagrams, and so on.

For now, let's just copy in these things:

- The program specification we wrote in the previous chapters
- Your interface mockups
- A copy of the form used by the technicians

At some point, you might need to write a user manual, but for now, the program is simple enough not to need it.

Making a Python package

Creating your own Python package is surprisingly easy. A Python package consists of the following three things:

- A directory
- A file called __init__.py in the directory
- Optionally, one or more Python files in that directory

Once you've done this, you can import your package in whole or in part, just like you would import standard library packages, provided your script is in the same parent directory as the package directory.

Note that the __init__.py file in a module is somewhat analogous to what the initializer method is for a class. Code inside it will run whenever the package is imported, and any names created or imported into it are available directly under the package namespace. The Python community generally discourages putting too much code in this file, though; and since no code is actually required, we'll leave this file empty.

Let's start building our application's package. Create the following six empty files under abq_data_entry:

- __init__.py
- widgets.py
- views.py
- models.py
- application.py
- constants.py

Each of those Python files is called a **module**. A module is nothing more than a Python file inside a package directory. Your directory structure should now look like this:

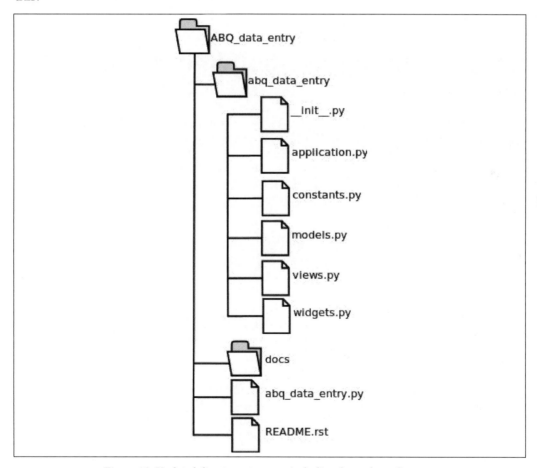

Figure 6.3: Updated directory structure, including the package directory

At this point, you have a working package, albeit with no actual code in it. To test this, open a Terminal or command-line window, change to your ABQ_Data_Entry directory, and start a Python shell.

Now, type the following command:

```
from abq_data_entry import application
```

This should execute without error. Of course, it doesn't do anything, but we'll get to that next.

Don't confuse the term *package* here with the actual distributable Python packages, such as those you download using pip. We will learn how to make distributable Python packages in *Chapter 16, Packaging with setuptools and cxFreeze*. In this context, a package is just a collection of Python modules.

Splitting our application into multiple files

Now that our directory structure is in order, we need to start dissecting our application script and splitting it up into our module files. We'll also need to create our model class.

Open up your data_entry_app.py file from *Chapter 5, Reducing User Error with Validation and Automation*, and let's begin!

Creating the models module

When your application is all about data, it's good to begin with the model. Remember that the job of a model is to manage the storage, retrieval, and processing of our application's data, usually with respect to its persistent storage format (in this case, CSV). To accomplish this, our model should contain all the knowledge about our data.

Currently, our application has nothing like a model; knowledge about the application's data is scattered the form fields, and the Application object simply takes whatever data the form contains and stuffs it directly into a CSV file when a save operation is requested. Since we aren't yet retrieving or updating information, our application has no actual knowledge about what's inside the CSV file.

To move our application to an MVC architecture, we'll need to create a model class that both manages data storage and retrieval, and represents the authoritative source of knowledge about our data. In other words, we have to encode the knowledge contained in our data dictionary here in our model. We don't really know what we'll do with this knowledge yet, but this is where it belongs.

There are a few ways we could store this data, such as creating a custom field class or a namedtuple object, but we'll keep it simple for now and just use a dictionary, mapping field names to field metadata.

The field metadata will likewise be stored as a dictionary of attributes about the field, which will include:

- The type of data stored in the field
- Whether or not the field is required
- The list of possible values, if applicable
- The minimum, maximum, and increment of values, if applicable

To store the data type for each field, we're going to define a set of constants that will let us refer to the different field types in a consistent and explicit way. We'll place this in the constants.py file, so open that file in your editor and add the following code:

```
# abq_data_entry/constants.py

from enum import Enum, auto

class FieldTypes(Enum):
    string = auto()
    string_list = auto()
    short_string_list = auto()
    iso_date_string = auto()
    long_string = auto()
    decimal = auto()
    integer = auto()
    boolean = auto()
```

We've created a class called FieldTypes that simply stores some named integer values, which will describe the different types of data we're going to store. This class is based on Python's Enum class, which is a useful class for defining collections of constants like this. The values of these variables are not at all important, so long as each one is unique; in an Enum, we're really just interested in having a set of variable names that are not equal to one another.

We could set them to strings or sequential integers by hand, but the enum module provides the auto() function, which gives each constant of the class a unique integer value automatically. Using this approach better communicates that the values themselves are not significant; only the names matter.

Now that we have these constants, let's open models.py and begin creating our model class:

```
# abq_data_entry/models.py, at the top
import csv
from pathlib import Path
from datetime import datetime
import os

from .constants import FieldTypes as FT

class CSVModel:
  """CSV file storage"""
```

We begin by importing the libraries we will need for our model: csv, pathlib, datetime, os, and our new FieldTypes constants. The first three were the libraries we needed for our on_save() method in Application. Now, the model class will be handling most of this functionality. The os module will be used to check file permissions, and the FieldTypes constants will be used to define our model's data dictionary.

Notice the way we import FieldTypes: from .constants import FieldTypes. The dot in front of constants makes this a **relative import**. Relative imports can be used inside a Python package to locate other modules in the same package. In this case, we're in the models module, and we need to access the constants module inside the abq_data_entry package. The single dot represents our current parent module (abq_data_entry), and thus .constants within this file means the constants module of the abq_data_entry package.

Relative imports distinguish our custom modules from modules in PYTHONPATH. By using them, we don't have to worry about any third-party or standard library packages conflicting with our module names.

Next, we're going to need to create a class member variable that contains a dictionary of all the fields in our model. Each item in the dictionary will contain details about the field: its data type, if it's required, and valid values, ranges, and increments.

In addition to field attributes, we're also documenting the order of fields for the CSV here. In Python 3.6 and later, dictionaries retain the order they were defined by; if you're using an older version of Python 3, you need to use the `OrderedDict` class from the `collections` standard library module to preserve the field order.

Add this dictionary like this:

```
fields = {
  "Date": {'req': True, 'type': FT.iso_date_string},
  "Time": {'req': True, 'type': FT.string_list,
    'values': ['8:00', '12:00', '16:00', '20:00']},
  "Technician": {'req': True, 'type':  FT.string},
  "Lab": {'req': True, 'type': FT.short_string_list,
    'values': ['A', 'B', 'C']},
  "Plot": {'req': True, 'type': FT.string_list,
    'values': [str(x) for x in range(1, 21)]},
  "Seed Sample":  {'req': True, 'type': FT.string},
  "Humidity": {'req': True, 'type': FT.decimal,
    'min': 0.5, 'max': 52.0, 'inc': .01},
  "Light": {'req': True, 'type': FT.decimal,
    'min': 0, 'max': 100.0, 'inc': .01},
  "Temperature": {'req': True, 'type': FT.decimal,
    'min': 4, 'max': 40, 'inc': .01},
  "Equipment Fault": {'req': False, 'type': FT.boolean},
  "Plants": {'req': True, 'type': FT.integer,
    'min': 0, 'max': 20},
  "Blossoms": {
    'req': True, 'type': FT.integer, 'min': 0, 'max': 1000},
  "Fruit": {'req': True, 'type': FT.integer,
    'min': 0, 'max': 1000},
  "Min Height": {'req': True, 'type': FT.decimal,
    'min': 0, 'max': 1000, 'inc': .01},
  "Max Height": {'req': True, 'type': FT.decimal,
    'min': 0, 'max': 1000, 'inc': .01},
  "Med Height": {'req': True, 'type': FT.decimal,
    'min': 0, 'max': 1000, 'inc': .01},
  "Notes": {'req': False, 'type': FT.long_string}
}
```

This list is straight from our data dictionary, and we've seen these same values already in our `DataRecordForm` class; but from now on, this dictionary is going to be the authoritative source of this information. Any other class that needs information about a model field will have to retrieve it from this dictionary.

Before we start designing our model class's methods, let's take a moment to look at the existing file-save logic in our application and consider which parts belong to the model. The code in our current script looks like this:

```python
def _on_save(self):
    errors = self.recordform.get_errors()
    if errors:
        self.status.set(
            "Cannot save, error in fields: {}"
            .format(', '.join(errors.keys()))
        )
        return

    datestring = datetime.today().strftime("%Y-%m-%d")
    filename = f"abq_data_record_{datestring}.csv"
    newfile = not Path(filename).exists()

    data = self.recordform.get()

    with open(filename, 'a') as fh:
        csvwriter = csv.DictWriter(fh, fieldnames=data.keys())
        if newfile:
            csvwriter.writeheader()
        csvwriter.writerow(data)

    self._records_saved += 1
    self.status.set(
        f"{self._records_saved} records saved this session"
    )
    self.recordform.reset()
```

Let's go through this code and determine what goes into the model and what stays in the `Application` class:

- The first block pulls errors from the `DataRecordForm` class. Since the model will have no knowledge of the form, this should stay in `Application`. In fact, the model doesn't even need to know about form errors, since the only action taken is UI-related (that is, displaying the errors).

- The next set of lines define the filename we're going to use. Since this is a detail of the file storage, it is clearly the model's concern.

- The `newfile` assignment line determines whether the file exists or not. As an implementation detail of the data storage medium, this is clearly the model's problem, not the application's.

- The line `data = self.recordform.get()` pulls data from the form. Since our model has no knowledge of the form's existence, this needs to stay in `Application`.

- The next block opens the file, creates a `csv.DictWriter` object, and appends the data. This is definitely the model's concern.

- The final block communicates the results of the file-save operation to the user and resets the form. This is all user interface-related, so it does not belong in the model.

So, our model will need to determine the filename and take care of writing the data received from the `Application` object to it, while the application will be responsible for checking the form for errors, retrieving the data from the form, and communicating the results of the save operation to the user.

Let's create the initializer method for our model class. Because the `CSVModel` represents an interface to a specific CSV file, we're going to determine the filename in `__init__()` and keep it for the lifespan of the model object. The method begins like this:

```
# models.py, in the CSVModel class

  def __init__(self):

    datestring = datetime.today().strftime("%Y-%m-%d")
    filename = "abq_data_record_{}.csv".format(datestring)
    self.file = Path(filename)
```

The `__init__()` method begins by determining the `filename` from the current date and converting it into a `Path` object, which it stores as an instance variable.

Since the instance of the model is tied to the filename and represents our access to that file, it would be a relatively useless model if we did not have permission to append data to the file. Therefore, we will want the initializer to check access to the file and alert us if there is any problem with it before we start entering data into our form.

To do that, we need to use the `os.access()` function, like so:

```
# models.py, in CSVModel.__init__()

    file_exists = os.access(self.file, os.F_OK)
    parent_writeable = os.access(self.file.parent, os.W_OK)
    file_writeable = os.access(self.file, os.W_OK)
    if (
      (not file_exists and not parent_writeable) or
      (file_exists and not file_writeable)
    ):
        msg = f'Permission denied accessing file: {filename}'
        raise PermissionError(msg)
```

The `os.access()` function takes two arguments: a file path string or `Path` object, and a constant indicating the mode we want to check. The two constants we'll be using are `os.F_OK`, which checks if the file exists, and `os.W_OK`, which checks that we have write permission to it. Note that checking for `W_OK` will return `False` if the file doesn't exist (which is a distinct possibility if no data has been saved yet), so we need to check for two possible scenarios:

- The file exists, but we cannot write to it
- The file does not exist, and we cannot write to its parent directory

In either of these cases, we won't be able to write to the file and should raise an exception. You might wonder why we're raising an exception and not displaying some kind of error (such as in the status bar or by printing to the console). Remember that the model class should not assume anything about the UI or contain any UI code. The appropriate way to handle an error situation in a model is to pass a message back to the controller using an exception, so that the controller can take actions appropriate to our user interface.

 The idea of raising an exception on purpose often seems strange to beginners; after all, exceptions are something we're trying to avoid, right? This is true in the case of small scripts where we are essentially consumers of existing modules; when writing your own module, however, exceptions are the correct way for your module to communicate problems to the code using its classes and functions. Trying to handle – or worse, silence – bad behavior on the part of external code will, at best, break the modularization of our code; at worst, it will create subtle bugs that are difficult to track down.

Now that we have our model initialized with a writable filename, we need to create a method to save the data. In the CSVModel class, let's create a public method to store data. Add the following code for the save_record() method:

```
# models.py, in the CSVModel class

def save_record(self, data):
  """Save a dict of data to the CSV file"""
  newfile = not self.file.exists()

  with open(self.file, 'a', newline='') as fh:
    csvwriter = csv.DictWriter(fh, fieldnames=self.fields.keys())
    if newfile:
      csvwriter.writeheader()

    csvwriter.writerow(data)
```

Since the model does not need to know about form errors and already has a filename established in its initializer, the only argument this method requires is a dictionary of the form data. What remains is to determine if we are dealing with a new file and to write the data to the CSV.

Note that, when writing the field names to a new CSV file, we use the keys of our fields dictionary, rather than relying on the keys in the incoming data. Remember that CSVModel.fields is now the authoritative source of information about application data, so it should determine the headers that are used.

Our model class is now complete. Let's get to work on the user interface!

Moving the widgets

While we could put all of our UI-related code in one views module, we have a lot of custom widget classes. It would make sense to put them in their own separate module to limit the complexity of the views module. So, instead, we're going to move all of the code for our widget classes into a widgets.py file. The widget classes we'll move include all the classes that implement reusable GUI components, including compound widgets like LabelInput. If we develop more custom widgets, we'll add them to this file as well.

Open widgets.py and copy in all of the code for ValidatedMixin, DateEntry, RequiredEntry, ValidatedCombobox, ValidatedSpinbox, ValidatedRadioGroup, BoundText, and LabelInput. These are all the widget classes we've created so far.

The `widgets.py` file will, of course, need to import any module dependencies used by the code being copied in. We'll need to look through our code and find what libraries we use and import them. Add the following to the top of the file:

```
# top of widgets.py
import tkinter as tk
from tkinter import ttk
from datetime import datetime
from decimal import Decimal, InvalidOperation
```

Obviously, we need `tkinter` and `ttk`; our `DateEntry` class uses the `datetime` class from the `datetime` library, and our `ValidatedSpinbox` class makes use of the `Decimal` class and `InvalidOperation` exception from the `decimal` library. This is all we need in `widgets.py`.

Moving the views

Next, we'll work on the `views.py` file. Recall that views are larger GUI components, like our `DataRecordForm` class. Currently, in fact, it is our only view, but as we create more large GUI components, they will be added here.

Open the `views.py` file and copy in the `DataRecordForm` class; then, go back to the top to deal with the module imports. Again, we'll need `tkinter` and `ttk`, as well as `datetime`, since our auto-fill logic requires it.

Add them to the top of the file, as follows:

```
# abq_data_entry/views.py, at the top
import tkinter as tk
from tkinter import ttk
from datetime import datetime
```

We aren't done, though; our actual widgets aren't here anymore, so we'll need to import them, like so:

```
from . import widgets as w
```

Just as we did with the `FieldTypes` in our `models.py` file, we've imported our `widgets` module using a relative import. We've kept the widgets in their own namespace to keep our global namespace clean, but given it a short alias, `w`, so that our code won't get overly cluttered.

This means, though, that we'll need to go through the code and prepend `w.` to all instances of `LabelInput`, `RequiredEntry`, `DateEntry`, `ValidatedCombobox`, `ValidatedRadioGroup`, `BoundText`, and `ValidatedSpinbox`. This should be easy enough to do in IDLE or any other text editor using a series of search and replace actions.

For example, line 1 of the form should be as follows:

```
w.LabelInput(
  r_info, "Date", var=self._vars['Date'],
  input_class=w.DateEntry
).grid(row=0, column=0)
w.LabelInput(
  r_info, "Time", input_class=w.ValidatedCombobox,
  var=self._vars['Time'],
  input_args={"values": ["8:00", "12:00", "16:00", "20:00"]}
).grid(row=0, column=1)
w.LabelInput(
  r_info, "Technician",  var=self._vars['Technician'],
  input_class=w.RequiredEntry
).grid(row=0, column=2)
```

Before you go through and change that everywhere, though, let's stop and take a moment to refactor some of the redundancy out of this code.

Removing redundancy in our view logic

Consider the arguments we're passing into the `LabelInput` widgets: they contain a lot of information that is also in our model. Minimums, maximums, increments, and possible values are defined both here and in our model code. Even the type of the input widget we're choosing is related directly to the type of data being stored: numbers get a `ValidatedSpinbox` widget, dates get a `DateEntry` widget, and so on. Ideally, our source for information about each field should only be defined in one place, and that place should be the model. If we need to update the model for some reason, our form should synchronize with those changes.

Rather than redundantly define these options in the view, we need to give our view access to the field specifications from our model so that the widgets' details can be determined from it. Since our widget instances are being defined inside the `LabelInput` class, we're going to enhance that class with the ability to automatically work out the input class and arguments from our model's field specification format.

To do that, open up the `widgets.py` file. We'll begin by importing the `FieldTypes` class, like so:

```
# at the top of widgets.py
from .constants import FieldTypes as FT
```

Next, we need to tell the `LabelInput` class how to translate a field type into a widget class. To do that, locate the `LabelInput` class and add the following `field_types` class attribute just above the `__init__()` method:

```
# widgets.py, inside LabelInput
    field_types = {
        FT.string: RequiredEntry,
        FT.string_list: ValidatedCombobox,
        FT.short_string_list: ValidatedRadioGroup,
        FT.iso_date_string: DateEntry,
        FT.long_string: BoundText,
        FT.decimal: ValidatedSpinbox,
        FT.integer: ValidatedSpinbox,
        FT.boolean: ttk.Checkbutton
    }
```

This dictionary will act as a key to translate our model's field types into an appropriate widget type.

 Note that all of these widgets need to exist before we can create this dictionary, so be sure to place the `LabelInput` class definition at the *end* of `widgets.py`, if it's not already there.

Now, we need to update `LabelInput.__init__()` to take a `field_spec` argument and, if given, use it to define the parameters of the input widget. To begin with, update the argument list of the initializer as follows:

```
# widgets.py, inside LabelInput
    def __init__(
        self, parent, label, var, input_class=None,
        input_args=None, label_args=None, field_spec=None,
        disable_var=None, **kwargs
    ):
```

Although `field_spec` will largely remove the requirement for the `input_class` and `input_args` arguments, we're going to retain them in case we should later need to build a form that is not tied to a model.

Inside the initializer method, we'll need to read the field spec and apply the information. Add the following code after the variable setup and before the label setup:

```
# widgets.py, inside LabelInput.__init__():
    if field_spec:
        field_type = field_spec.get('type', FT.string)
        input_class = input_class or self.field_types.get(field_type)
        if 'min' in field_spec and 'from_' not in input_args:
            input_args['from_'] = field_spec.get('min')
        if 'max' in field_spec and 'to' not in input_args:
            input_args['to'] = field_spec.get('max')
        if 'inc' in field_spec and 'increment' not in input_args:
            input_args['increment'] = field_spec.get('inc')
        if 'values' in field_spec and 'values' not in input_args:
            input_args['values'] = field_spec.get('values')
```

The first thing we'll do with the `field_spec`, if it is supplied, is retrieve the field type. This will be used to look up an appropriate widget using the `field_types` dictionary. If we want to override this for a particular `LabelInput` instance, an explicitly passed `input_class` argument will override the lookup value.

Next, we need to set up the field parameters, `min`, `max`, `inc`, and `values`. For each of these, we check if the key exists in the field specification and make sure the corresponding `from_`, `to`, `increment`, or `values` argument has not been passed in explicitly using `input_args`. If so, we'll set up the `input_args` with the appropriate value. Now that `input_class` and `input_args` have been determined from the field specification, the remainder of the initializer method can continue as previously defined.

With `LabelInput` refactored to accept a `field_spec` argument, we can update our view code to take advantage of this new capability. To do this, our `DataRecordForm` class will first need access to the `model` object from which it can obtain the field specifications for the data model.

Back in the `views.py` file, edit the initializer method for `DataRecordForm` so that we can pass in a copy of the `model`:

```
# views.py, in DataRecordForm class

  def __init__(self, parent, model, *args, **kwargs):
    super().__init__(parent, *args, **kwargs)

    self.model= model
    fields = self.model.fields
```

We've stored the `model` itself in an instance variable, and also extracted the `fields` dictionary into a local variable to cut down the code verbosity as we use this dictionary in the initializer method. Now, we can go through our `LabelInput` calls and replace the `input_args` and `input_class` arguments with a single `field_spec` argument.

With these changes, the first line looks like this:

```python
# views.py, in DataRecordForm.__init__()
    w.LabelInput(
        r_info, "Date",
        field_spec=fields['Date'],
        var=self._vars['Date'],
    ).grid(row=0, column=0)
    w.LabelInput(
        r_info, "Time",
        field_spec=fields['Time'],
        var=self._vars['Time'],
    ).grid(row=0, column=1)
    w.LabelInput(
        r_info, "Technician",
        field_spec=fields['Technician'],
        var=self._vars['Technician']
    ).grid(row=0, column=2)
```

Go ahead and update the rest of the widgets in the same way, replacing `input_class` and `input_args` with the `field_spec` argument. Note that when you get to the height fields, you'll still need to pass in an `input_args` dictionary to define the `min_var`, `max_var`, and `focus_update_var` arguments.

For example, the following is the Min Height input definition:

```python
    w.LabelInput(
        p_info, "Min Height (cm)",
        field_spec=fields['Min Height'],
        var=self._vars['Min Height'],
        input_args={
            "max_var": max_height_var,
            "focus_update_var": min_height_var
        })
```

That does it. Now, any changes to a given field specification can be made solely in the model, and the form will simply do the correct thing.

Using custom events to remove tight coupling

Before we leave the `DataRecordForm` class, there is one fix we should make to improve the separation of concerns in our application. Currently, the `savebutton` widget on our form is bound to `self.master._on_save()`, which refers to the `_on_save()` method of the `Application` class. However, the way we have bound this command makes the assumption that `self.master` (that is, the parent widget of the `DataRecordForm`) is `Application`. What would happen if we decided to put our `DataRecordForm` widget inside a `Notebook` or `Frame` widget, rather than directly under the `Application` object? In that case, `self.master` would change and the code would break. Since the parent widget is really a layout concern, we would not expect that a change to it would impact the save button callback.

A situation like this, where a class depends too much on the architecture of the application outside the class, is known as **tight coupling**, and is something we should work to avoid in our code. Instead, we want **loose coupling** in our code so that changes to one class will not cause unexpected bugs in another.

There are a few ways we could address this issue. We could pass a reference to the callback or the `Application` class to the view so that it could more explicitly reference the method in question. This would work, but it would still be tighter coupling than we'd ideally like to have.

A better approach is to utilize **events**. As you know, Tkinter generates an event whenever the user interacts with the GUI in some way, like clicking a button or making a keystroke. These events can be explicitly bound to a callback function using the `bind()` method of any Tkinter widget. Tkinter also allows us to generate our own custom events that we can bind just like the built-in ones.

Let's implement a callback method in `DataRecordForm` that will generate a custom event, as follows:

```
def _on_save(self):
    self.event_generate('<<SaveRecord>>')
```

The `event_generate()` method can be called on any Tkinter widget to cause it to emit the event specified. In this case, we're calling our event `<<SaveRecord>>`. All custom event sequences must use double angle brackets to differentiate them from built-in event types. Apart from that, you can call them whatever you wish.

Back in the `DataRecordForm.__init__()` method, we'll update our save button definition to use this method as a callback, like so:

```
# views.py, in DataRecordForm.__init__()
    self.savebutton = ttk.Button(
        buttons, text="Save", command=self._on_save)
```

Now, rather than directly executing the Application object's _on_save() method, the button will simply cause DataRecordForm to emit a message that the record-save operation was requested by the user. It will be the Application object's responsibility to deal with that message.

 We'll be utilizing custom events more extensively in *Chapter 7, Creating Menus with Menu and Tkinter Dialogs,* when we build our application menu.

Creating the application file

The last piece we need to create is our controller and root window class, Application. Open the application.py file and copy in the Application class definition from the old data_entry_app.py file.

As before, we need to add the module imports required for this code. At the top of the file, add the following:

```
# abq_data_entry/application.py, at the top
import tkinter as tk
from tkinter import ttk
from . import views as v
from . import models as m
```

Once again, we need tkinter and ttk, of course; we also need the views module for our DataRecordForm and the models module for our CSVModel.

Now, we're going to need to make several changes to the Application.__init__() method. To begin with, we'll need to create a model instance that we can pass to the DataRecordForm and to save our data. Create this object near the top of the initializer method:

```
# application.py, inside the Application class
  def __init__(self, *args, **kwargs):
    super().__init__(*args, **kwargs)

    self.model = m.CSVModel()
```

Next, we need to update the call to DataRecordForm, both to add the namespace and make sure we pass in the model instance, as follows:

```
# application.py, inside Application.__init__()
```

```
self.recordform = v.DataRecordForm(self, self.model)
```

We will also need to bind our custom event, <<SaveRecord>>, to the Application object's record-save callback. Add the bind command like so:

```
# application.py, inside Application.__init__()
    self.recordform = v.DataRecordForm(self, self.model)
    self.recordform.grid(row=1, padx=10, sticky=(tk.W + tk.E))
    self.recordform.bind('<<SaveRecord>>', self._on_save)
```

Finally, we need to update the code in Application._on_save() to use the model. The new method should look like this:

```
def _on_save(self, *_):
    """Handles file-save requests"""
    errors = self.recordform.get_errors()
    if errors:
        self.status.set(
            "Cannot save, error in fields: {}"
            .format(', '.join(errors.keys()))
        )
        return

    data = self.recordform.get()
    self.model.save_record(data)
    self._records_saved += 1
    self.status.set(
        f"{self._records_saved} records saved this session"
    )
    self.recordform.reset()
```

As you can see, using our model is pretty seamless; once we have checked for errors and retrieved the data from the form, we just pass it to self.model.save_record(). The Application doesn't have to know any details about how the data is saved.

Note that we've added an argument of *_ to the method definition. When we use bind to bind an event to a callback, the callback will receive an event object. We aren't going to be using this event argument, so by Python convention, we'll just roll up any positional arguments into a variable called _ (underscore). This way, our callback can handle receiving arguments, but we've indicated we aren't going to use them.

Running the application

The application is now completely migrated to the new data format. To test it, navigate to the application root folder, ABQ_Data_Entry, and execute the following command:

```
$ python3 abq_data_entry.py
```

It should look and act just like the single script from *Chapter 5, Reducing User Error with Validation and Automation,* and run without errors, as shown in the following screenshot:

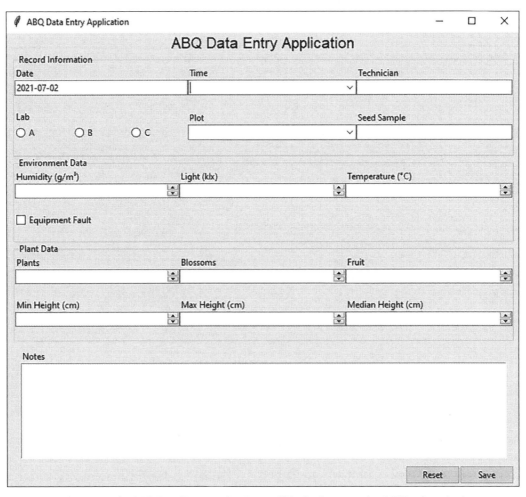

Figure 6.4: The ABQ Data Entry application – still looks the same after MVC refactoring!

Success!

Using version control software

Our code is nicely structured for expansion, but there's one more critical item we should address: **version control**. You may already be familiar with a **version control system** (**VCS**), sometimes called **revision control** or **source code management**, but if not, it's an indispensable tool for dealing with a large and changing code base.

When working on an application, we sometimes think we know what needs to be changed, but it turns out we're wrong. Sometimes, we don't know exactly how to code something, and it takes several attempts to find the correct approach. Sometimes, we need to revert to code that was changed a long time ago. Sometimes, we have multiple people working on the same piece of code, and we need to merge their changes together. Version control systems were created to address these issues and more.

There are dozens of different version control systems, but most of them follow essentially the same workflow:

- You have a **working copy** of the code to which you make changes
- You periodically select changes and **commit** them to a **master copy**
- You can **checkout** (that is, retrieve into your working copy) older versions of the code at any point, then later revert back to the master copy
- You can create **branches** of the code to experiment with different approaches, new features, or large refactors
- You can later **merge** these branches back into the master copy

VCS provides a safety net that gives you the freedom to change your code without the fear that you'll hopelessly ruin it: reverting to a known working state is just a few quick commands away. It also helps us to document changes to our code and collaborate with others if the opportunity arises.

There are dozens of version control systems available, but by far the most popular for many years now is **Git**. Let's take a look at how to use Git to track changes to our application.

A super-quick guide to using Git

Git was created by Linus Torvalds to be the version control software for the Linux kernel project, and has since grown to be the most popular VC software in the world. It is utilized by source sharing sites like GitHub, Bitbucket, SourceForge, and GitLab. Git is extremely powerful, and mastering it can take months or years; fortunately, the basics can be grasped in a few minutes.

First, you'll need to install Git; visit `https://git-scm.com/downloads` for instructions on how to install Git on macOS, Windows, Linux, or other Unix operating systems.

Initializing and configuring a Git repository

Once Git is installed, we need to initialize and configure our project directory as a Git repository. To do this, open a command terminal, navigate to the application's root directory (`ABQ_Data_Entry`), and run the following command:

```
$ git init
```

This command creates a hidden directory under our project root called `.git` and initializes it with the basic files that make up the repository. The `.git` directory will contain all the data and metadata about our saved revisions.

Before we add any files to the repository, we need to instruct Git to ignore certain kinds of files. For example, Python creates bytecode (`.pyc`) files whenever it executes a file, and we don't want to save these as part of our code. To do this, create a file in your project root called `.gitignore` and put the following lines in it:

```
*.pyc
__pycache__/
```

You can add more directory names, filenames, or wildcard patterns to ignore various file types you don't want to save (for example, some editors create temporary files or backup copies by adding particular characters to a filename).

Adding and committing code

Now that our repository has been initialized, we can add files and directories to our Git repository using the `git add` command, like so:

```
$ git add abq_data_entry
$ git add abq_data_entry.py
$ git add docs
$ git add README.rst
```

At this point, our files have been **staged**, but not yet committed to the repository. Because a single change to an application may require altering several files, Git allows you to stage as many files as you wish to be part of a single commit. Note that we can specify directories rather than individual files; in this case, all the files currently inside the directory will be staged for our next commit.

You can check the status of your repository and the files in it at any time by entering the command `git status`. Try this now and you should get the following output:

```
On branch master
No commits yet
Changes to be committed:
(use "git rm --cached <file>..." to unstage)
new file: README.rst
new file: abq_data_entry.py
new file: abq_data_entry/~__init__.py~
new file: abq_data_entry/application.py
new file: abq_data_entry/models.py
new file: abq_data_entry/views.py
new file: abq_data_entry/widgets.py
new file: docs/Application_layout.png
new file: docs/abq_data_entry_spec.rst
new file: docs/lab-tech-paper-form.png
Untracked files:
(use "git add <file>..." to include in what will be committed)
.gitignore
```

This shows you that all the files under `abq_data_entry/` and `docs/`, as well as the files you specified directly, are staged to be committed to the repository.

Let's go ahead and commit the changes with the following command:

```
$ git commit -m "Initial commit"
```

The `-m` flag here allows you to specify a **commit message**, which is stored with the commit. Each time you commit code to the repository, you will be required to write a message. You should always make these messages as meaningful as possible, detailing what changes you made and the rationale behind them.

Viewing and using our commits

To view your repository's history, run the `git log` command, like so:

```
$ git log
commit df48707422875ff545dc30f4395f82ad2d25f103 (HEAD -> master)
Author: Alan Moore <alan@example.com>
Date: Thu Dec 21 18:12:17 2017 -0600
Initial commit
```

As you can see, the Author, Date, and commit message is displayed for our last commit. If we had more commits, they would be listed here as well, from newest to oldest. The long hexadecimal value you see in the first line of output is the **commit hash**, a unique value that identifies the commit. This value can be used to refer to the commit in other operations.

For example, we can use it to reset our repository to a past state. Try this out by following these steps:

1. Delete the README.rst file, and verify that it's completely gone.
2. Run git log to get the hash of your last commit.
3. Now, enter the command git reset --hard df48707, replacing df48707 with the first seven characters of your last commit's hash.
4. Check your file listing again: the README.rst file should be back.

What happened here is that we altered our repository, then told Git to **hard reset** the state of the repository to the last commit. If you don't want to reset your repository, you can also use git checkout to switch to an old commit temporarily, or use git branch to create a new branch using a particular commit as the base. As you can see already, this gives us a powerful safety net for experimentation; no matter how much you tinker with the code, any commit is just a command away!

Git has many more features that are beyond the scope of this book. If you'd like to learn more, the Git project provides a free online manual at https://git-scm.com/book, where you can learn about advanced features like branching and setting up remote repositories. For now, the important thing is to commit changes as you go, so that you maintain your safety net and document the history of changes.

Summary

In this chapter, you learned to prepare your simple script for some serious expansion. You learned how to divide your application's areas of responsibility into separate components using the model-view-controller model. You reimplemented the ABQ application as a Python package, splitting the code into multiple modules to further enforce separation of concerns and provide an organized framework for later expansion. Finally, you set up a Git repository for your code so that you can track all your changes with version control.

In the next chapter, we're going to put the convenience of our new project layout to the test by implementing file opening and saving, informational popups, and a main menu. You'll also learn how to provide configurable settings for your application and save them to disk.

7
Creating Menus with Menu and Tkinter Dialogs

As an application grows in functionality, it becomes increasingly counterproductive to cram all its functions and inputs into a single form. Instead, we will need to organize access to features, information, and controls in a way that keeps them available without cluttering up the visual presentation. GUI toolkits like Tkinter offer us a couple of tools to help deal with this. First, the **menu system**, typically located at the top of the application window (or, on some platforms, in a global desktop menu), can be used to organize application functions in a condensed hierarchy. Second, **dialog windows**, often referred to as **dialog boxes**, provide a quick means of displaying temporary windows containing information, errors, or basic forms.

In this chapter, we're going to explore the use and best practices of menus and dialog boxes in Tkinter through the following topics:

- In *Solving problems in our application*, we'll analyze some reported problems with our application and design a solution involving menus and dialog boxes.

- In *Implementing Tkinter dialogs*, we'll explore Tkinter's dialog classes and how to use them to implement common application functionality.

- In *Designing the application menu*, we'll organize our application's features into a main menu system using Tkinter's Menu widget.

Let's begin by seeing what improvements our application needs.

Solving problems in our application

Although everyone is happy with your application so far, your boss, after discussion with the staff, has brought you this set of problems that need to be addressed:

- The hard-coded filename is a problem. Occasionally the data entry staff aren't able to get to a form until the following day; in this situation, they need to be able to manually enter the filename that they'd like to append the data to.

- Also, the data entry staff have mixed feelings about the auto-filling features in the form. Some find it very helpful, but others would like auto-fill to be partially or completely disabled.

- Some users have a hard time noticing the status bar text at the bottom, and would like the application to be more assertive when it fails to save a data record due to field errors.

- Finally, the lab is bringing in some interns to work in the labs, and the issue of data security has been raised. IT has suggested a simple login requirement would be advisable. It doesn't have to have high security, just enough to "keep the honest person honest."

Planning solutions to the issues

It's clear you need to implement a way to enter login credentials, select a save file name, and toggle the auto-populate features of the form. You also need to make the status text more noticeable. First, you consider just adding controls to the main application for these features and increasing the size of the status text. You make a quick mock-up that looks like this:

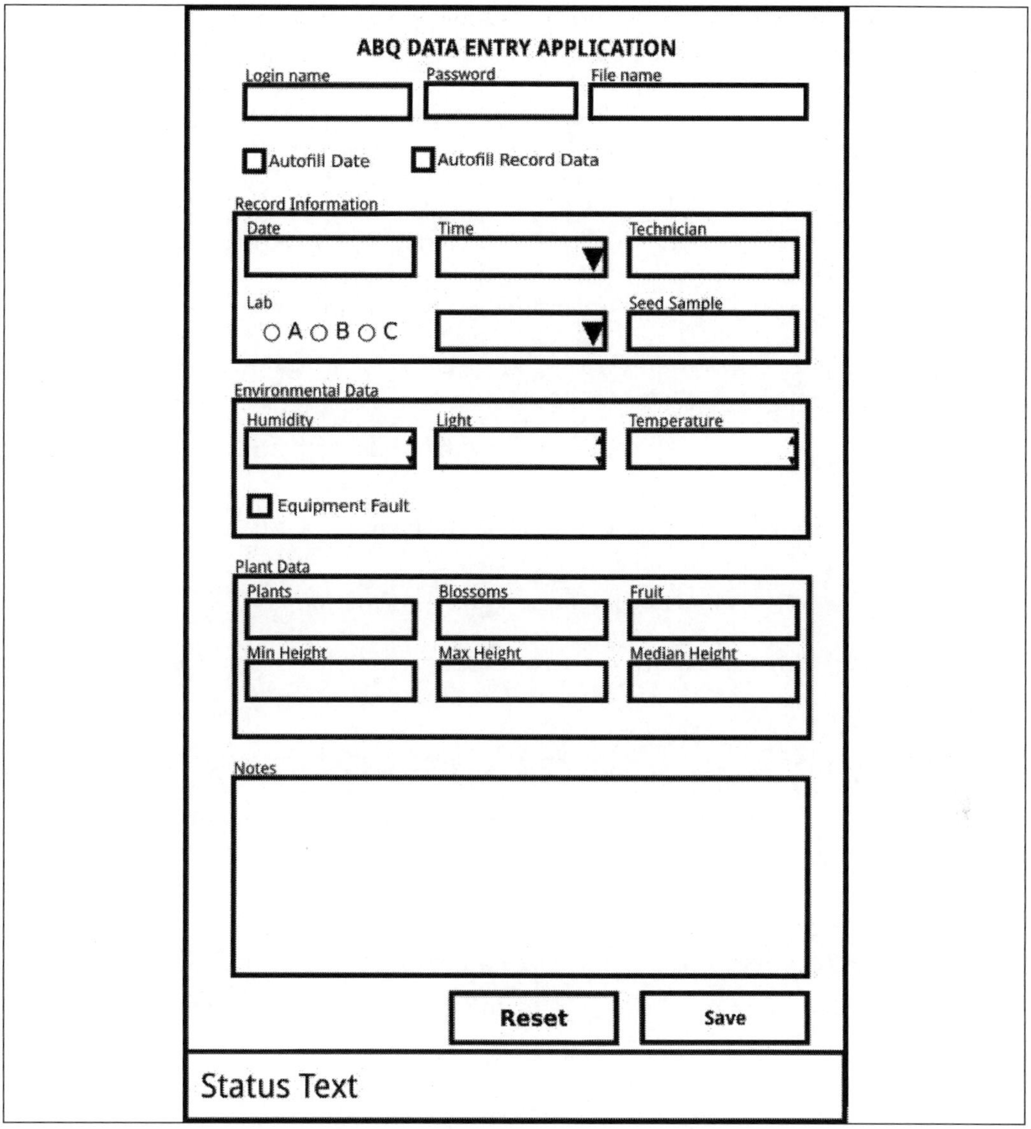

Figure 7.1: Our first attempt at adding the new features: three Entry widgets for login data and filename, and two Checkbutton widgets for the settings

It's immediately evident that this is not a great design, and certainly not one that will accommodate growth. Your users don't want to have to type a file path and filename blindly into the box, nor do they need the extra login fields and check boxes cluttering up the user interface. Making the status font larger seems like a good idea, until you realize that the form is now so long it will likely just get pushed off the bottom of the screen.

Thinking through other GUI applications, you realize that these features are typically handled by dialog windows, usually activated from menu options. Taking menus and dialogs into consideration, you plan the following solutions to the problems:

- A **file dialog**, activated from a menu system, can be used to select the file that the data will be saved to.
- A **settings menu** in our menu system will handle activating or disabling auto-fill.
- An **error dialog** will be used to display problematic status messages more assertively.
- A **login dialog** can be used to enter login information.

Before we can code this solution, we'll need to learn more about dialogs in Tkinter.

Implementing Tkinter dialogs

Tkinter contains a number of submodules that provide ready-made dialog windows for different situations. These include:

- `messagebox`, for displaying simple messages and warnings
- `filedialog`, for prompting the user for a file or folder path
- `simpledialog`, for requesting string, integer, or float values from a user

In this section, we're going to explore these dialogs and use them to solve some of the problems with our application.

Error dialogs with the Tkinter messagebox

The best way to display simple dialog boxes in Tkinter is by using the `tkinter.messagebox` module, which provides a variety of information-display dialog types.

Since it is a submodule, we need to explicitly import it before we can use it, like so:

```
from tkinter import messagebox
```

Rather than having a lot of widget classes that we create instances of, the `messagebox` module provides a selection of **convenience functions** for making use of its various dialog types. When executed, each function displays a different combination of buttons and a preset icon, along with a message and detail text that you specify. When the user clicks a button in the dialog or closes it, the function will return a Boolean or string value depending on which button was clicked.

The following table shows some of the `messagebox` module's functions with their icons and return values:

Function	Icon	Button text/Return value
askokcancel()	Question	OK (True), Cancel (False)
askretrycancel()	Warning	Retry (True), Cancel (False)
askyesno()	Question	Yes (True), No (False)
askyesnocancel()	Question	Yes (True), No (False), Cancel (None)
showerror()	Error	OK (ok)
showinfo()	Information	OK (ok)
showwarning()	Warning	OK (ok)

Each `messagebox` function accepts this same set of arguments:

- `title` sets the title of the window, which is displayed in the title bar and/or task bar in your desktop environment.
- `message` sets the main message of the dialog. It's usually in a heading font and should be kept fairly short.
- `detail` sets the body text of the dialog, which is usually displayed in the standard window font.

A basic call to `messagebox.showinfo()` would look something like this:

```
messagebox.showinfo(
    title='This is the title',
    message='This is the message',
    detail='This is the detail'
)
```

In Windows 10, it results in a dialog box that looks like this:

Figure 7.2: A showinfo() message box on Windows 10

On macOS, you'd see something like this:

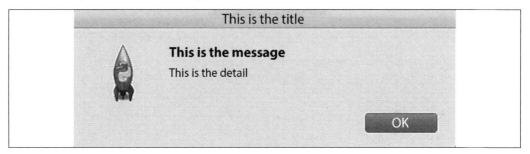

Figure 7.3: A showinfo() message box on macOS

On Ubuntu Linux, the dialog looks like this:

Figure 7.4: A showinfo() message box on Ubuntu Linux

Note that Tkinter `messagebox` dialog boxes are **modal**, which means that the program execution pauses and the rest of the UI is unresponsive while the dialog box is open. There is no way to change this, so only use them in situations where it's acceptable for the program to pause execution while the box is open.

Let's create a small example script to show the use of the `messagebox` functions:

```python
# messagebox_demo.py
import tkinter as tk
from tkinter import messagebox

see_more = messagebox.askyesno(
  title='See more?',
  message='Would you like to see another box?',
  detail='Click NO to quit'
)

if not see_more:
  exit()

messagebox.showinfo(
  title='You got it',
  message="Ok, here's another dialog.",
  detail='Hope you like it!'
)
```

This creates a dialog with **Yes** and **No** buttons. If the user clicks **No**, the function returns `False` and the application exits. In the case our user wants to see more boxes, the program continues and displays an information box.

Showing error dialogs in ABQ Data Entry

Now that you understand how to use `messagebox`, error dialogs should be easy to implement in our application. The `Application._on_save()` method already displays errors in the status bar; we just need to make the same text display in an error dialog as well.

First, open `application.py`, and let's import `messagebox` like so:

```python
# application.py at the top of the file

from tkinter import messagebox
```

Now, locate the line in the `Application._on_save()` method that updates the application status with any errors (inside the `if errors:` block). Just after that line, let's add some code to display the error dialog, like so:

```python
# application.py, inside Application._on_save()

    if errors:
```

```
# ... after setting the status:
message = "Cannot save record"
detail = (
  "The following fields have errors: "
  "\n  * {}".format(
    '\n  * '.join(errors.keys())
))
messagebox.showerror(
  title='Error',
  message=message,
  detail=detail
)
return False
```

The first thing we've done is build the message and detail strings for the dialog, making a bullet list of the fields that have errors by joining them with \n * (that is, a newline, space, and asterisk). Unfortunately, messagebox dialogs don't support any sort of markup or rich text, so constructs like bullet lists need to be built manually using regular characters.

After building the messages, we call messagebox.showerror() to display them. Remember that the application will freeze at this point until the user clicks **OK** and the showerror() function returns.

Open the program and hit **Save**; you'll see a dialog box alerting you to the errors in the application, as shown in the following screenshot:

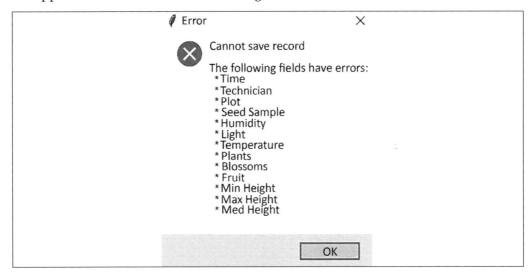

Figure 7.5: The error message on Windows 10 when we try to save with no data

This error should be hard for anyone to miss!

 One shortcoming of the messagebox module's dialogs is that they don't scroll; a long error message will create a dialog that may fill (or extend beyond) the screen. If this is a potential problem, you'll want to create a custom dialog containing a scrollable widget. We'll make a custom dialog later in this section.

Using filedialog

When a user needs to enter a file or directory path, the preferred way to do this is to display a dialog containing a miniature file browser, commonly called a **file dialog**. Like most toolkits, Tkinter provides us with dialogs for opening files, saving files, and selecting a directory. These are all part of the filedialog module.

Just like messagebox, filedialog is a Tkinter submodule that needs to be explicitly imported to be used. Also like messagebox, it contains a set of convenience functions that create file dialogs appropriate to different scenarios.

The following table lists the functions, what they return, and what can be selected in the dialog shown:

Function	Return value	Allows selection of
askdirectory()	Directory path as string	Directories only
askopenfile()	File handle object	Existing file only
askopenfilename()	File path as string	Existing file only
askopenfilenames()	Multiple file paths as a list of strings	Multiple existing files
asksaveasfile()	File handle object	New or existing file
asksaveasfilename()	File path as string	New or existing file

As you can see, each file selection dialog comes in two versions: one that returns a path as a string, and one that returns an open file object.

Each function can take the following arguments:

- title specifies the dialog window title.
- parent specifies the (optional) parent widget. The file dialog will appear over this widget.
- initialdir sets the directory in which the file browser should start.

- `filetypes` is a list of tuples, each with a label and matching pattern, which will be used to build the "Format" or "files of type" drop-down typically seen under the filename entry. This is used to filter the visible files to only those supported by the application. For example, a value of `[('Text', '*.txt'), ('Python', '*.py')]` would provide the ability to see only `.txt` or `.py` files.

The `asksaveasfile()` and `asksaveasfilename()` functions take the following two additional arguments:

- `initialfile`: This argument is a default file path to select
- `defaultextension`: This argument is a file extension string that will be automatically appended to the filename if the user doesn't include one

Finally, the methods that return a file object take a `mode` argument that specifies the mode to use when opening the file; these are the same one- or two-character strings used by Python's built-in `open()` function (for example, `r` for read-only, `w` for write, and so on).

 Be aware that `asksaveasfile()` automatically opens the selected file in write mode by default. This immediately empties the contents of the selected file, *even if you do not subsequently write anything to the file or close the file handle!* For that reason, this function should be avoided unless you're absolutely certain the selected file should be overwritten.

On macOS and Windows, `filedialog` uses the operating system's built-in file dialogs, which you are likely familiar with. On Linux, it will use its own dialog, which looks something like this:

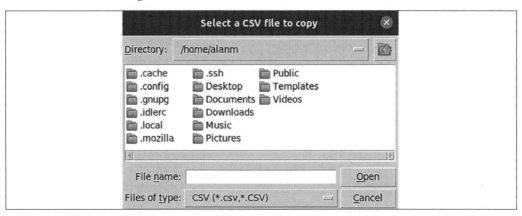

Figure 7.6: File dialog on Ubuntu Linux

Which dialog do we need to use in our application? Let's consider our needs:

- We need a dialog that allows us to select an existing file.
- We also need to be able to create a new file.
- Since opening the file is the responsibility of the model, we don't want Tkinter to open it for us, so we'll just want to get a filename to pass to the model.

These requirements clearly point to the `asksaveasfilename()` function. Let's create a method on our `Application` object that will use this dialog to get a filename and build a new model.

Open `abq_data_entry/application.py` and start a new method on the `Application` class called `_on_file_select()`:

```
# abq_data_entry/application.py, in the Application class

def _on_file_select(self, *_):
    """Handle the file->select action"""

    filename = filedialog.asksaveasfilename(
        title='Select the target file for saving records',
        defaultextension='.csv',
        filetypes=[('CSV', '*.csv *.CSV')]
    )
```

The method first launches an `asksaveasfilename` file dialog; using the `filetypes` argument, the selection of existing files will be limited to those ending in `.csv` or `.CSV`. When the dialog exits, the function will return the path to the selected file as a string to `filename`. Somehow, we have to get this path to our model.

Currently, the filename used by the model is generated in the model's initializer method. To create a new model with a user-provided filename, we'll need to update the initializer so that it can accept a filename as an argument instead.

Open `abq_data_entry/model.py` and let's edit the `CSVModel.__init__()` method, like so:

```
# abq_data_entry/models.py, in CSVModel

def __init__(self, filename=None):

    if not filename:
        datestring = datetime.today().strftime("%Y-%m-%d")
        filename = "abq_data_record_{}.csv".format(datestring)
    self.file = Path(filename)
```

As you can see, we've added `filename` as a keyword argument with a default value of `None`. If `filename` does happen to be empty, we'll use our generated filename as before. This way, we don't have to alter any existing code using `CSVModel`, but we have the option to pass in a filename.

Now, go back to the `Application` class and let's finish out the `_on_file_select()` method, like so:

```
# abq_data_entry/application.py, in CSVModel._on_file_select()

    if filename:
        self.model = m.CSVModel(filename=filename)
```

This is all that we need to change to use a different file. Currently there's no way for us to run this callback; we'll address that in the next section, *Designing the application menu*. First, though, let's talk about the last dialog module, `simpledialog`.

Using simpledialog and creating a custom dialog

Quite often in a GUI application, you will need to stop everything and ask the user for a value before the program can continue with an operation. For this purpose, Tkinter provides the `simpledialog` module. Like `messagebox`, it provides us with some convenience functions that display a modal dialog and return a value based on the user's interaction. However, with `simpledialog`, the dialog box contains an `Entry` widget that allows the user to provide a value.

As with the other dialog libraries, we have to import `simpledialog` to use it, like so:

```
from tkinter import simpledialog as sd
```

There are three convenience functions available: `askstring()`, `askinteger()`, and `askfloat()`. Each one takes a `title` and `prompt` argument, for providing the window title and the text prompt for the entry, respectively.

For example, let's ask the user for a word:

```
word = sd.askstring('Word', 'What is the word?')
```

This will display a box like this:

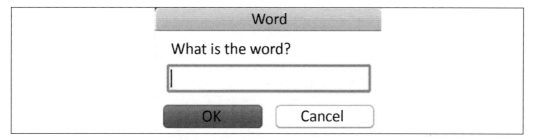

Figure 7.7: The askstring dialog box on macOS

When the user clicks **OK**, the function will return whatever was typed into the Entry widget as a string. askinteger() and askfloat() work exactly the same, except that they will try to convert the entered value into an integer or float before returning it. The Entry widget itself is not validated using validation callbacks, but Tkinter will display an error box when the dialog is submitted if there is a problem converting the entered value, as shown here:

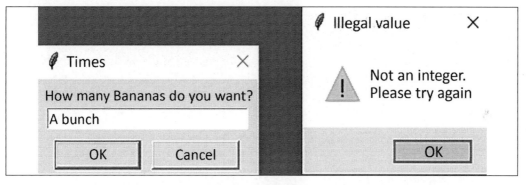

Figure 7.8: Error generated from askinteger() when a non-integer value is submitted

Creating a Login dialog using simpledialog

One of the tasks we've been given for this chapter is adding a Login dialog to our application. It seems like something simpledialog can help us with, but none of the built-in convenience functions really work well for this purpose: askstring() could be used, but it only asks for one string at a time, and it would be nice if we could mask the password entry for user security.

Fortunately we can create our own custom simpledialog class with any set of fields we wish. To do that, we'll subclass the simpledialog.Dialog class.

Since this is a GUI form, let's add it to our abq_data_entry/views.py file. Open that file and start with importing Dialog:

```
# abq_data_entry/views.py at the top

from tkinter.simpledialog import Dialog
```

Now, at the end of the file, let's start a new class called LoginDialog, like this:

```
# abq_data_entry/views.py at the bottom

class LoginDialog(Dialog):
    """A dialog that asks for username and password"""

    def __init__(self, parent, title, error=''):

        self._pw = tk.StringVar()
        self._user = tk.StringVar()
        self._error = tk.StringVar(value=error)
        super().__init__(parent, title=title)
```

The Dialog initializer expects a parent argument specifying the widget over which it will appear, as well as a title argument for the window title of the box. We've also added a keyword argument, error, that will allow us to pass an error message to the dialog box when we display it.

Inside the initializer, we're setting up private control variables for the user, password, and error strings, then calling the superclass initializer. To actually build the GUI for the Dialog class, we need to override a method called body(). This method is expected to build the main body of the GUI and return an instance of an input widget, which should receive focus when the dialog is displayed.

Our body() method will look like this:

```
    def body(self, frame):
        ttk.Label(frame, text='Login to ABQ').grid(row=0)

        if self._error.get():
            ttk.Label(frame, textvariable=self._error).grid(row=1)
        user_inp = w.LabelInput(
            frame, 'User name:', input_class=w.RequiredEntry,
            var=self._user
        )
        user_inp.grid()
```

```
w.LabelInput(
  frame, 'Password:', input_class=w.RequiredEntry,
  input_args={'show': '*'}, var=self._pw
).grid()
return user_inp.input
```

The frame argument to this method is a tkinter.Frame object created by the super-class initializer on which the body of the dialog can be built. Our method needs to build the form on this frame. Here, we've added a Label widget for the top of the form, then made use of our LabelInput class to add User name and Password fields. For our password input, we're using the show argument to mask password entry with asterisks. Also note that we've saved a local reference to the user input class; remember that body() needs to return a reference to a widget that will have focus when the dialog is shown.

Notice there are no buttons defined by our body() method. By default, Dialog creates an **OK** button and **Cancel** button, which are connected to the Dialog.ok() and Dialog.cancel() callbacks, respectively. This is fine for many situations, but we might prefer for our dialog to show **Login** and **Cancel** instead. To do that, we need to override the buttonbox() method. This method is responsible for putting the buttons on the form and connecting them to their callbacks.

Let's override that method like so:

```
def buttonbox(self):
  box = ttk.Frame(self)
  ttk.Button(
    box, text="Login", command=self.ok, default=tk.ACTIVE
  ).grid(padx=5, pady=5)
  ttk.Button(
    box, text="Cancel", command=self.cancel
  ).grid(row=0, column=1, padx=5, pady=5)
  self.bind("<Return>", self.ok)
  self.bind("<Escape>", self.cancel)
  box.pack()
```

In this method, we've created a Frame widget, then added Login and Cancel buttons. Each button is connected to the appropriate callback and added to the frame. Next, we've bound the same callbacks to the Return and Escape keys, respectively. This isn't strictly necessary, but it's a nice touch for keyboard-only users, and it's what the superclass version of the method does.

To make the entered data easily available to the code calling the dialog, we'll create a tuple with the entered username and password and make it available as a class member when the user clicks **Login**.

We could override the ok() method to do this, but that method takes care of some other logic (like closing the dialog) that we don't want to have to re-implement. Instead, Dialog features an apply() method that we are meant to override with our custom logic.

Ours will simply look like this:

```
def apply(self):
    self.result = (self._user.get(), self._pw.get())
```

This function builds a tuple containing the entered data and stores it as a public member, result. Code using our LoginDialog class can access this attribute to retrieve the username and password.

Incorporating the LoginDialog in our class

The convenience functions, askstring(), askfloat(), and askinteger(), essentially create an instance of their associated dialog class and return its result attribute. To use our custom dialog class, we'll essentially do the same thing. When we get the result, however, we'll pass it to an authentication method that will decide if the credentials are valid or not. If they're not, we'll re-display the dialog with an error until either the credentials are correct, or the user cancels the dialog.

To begin, let's write an authentication method. We'll be adding this to the Application class, so open application.py and add this _simple_login() method to the end of the class:

```
# application.py, at the end of the Application class

@staticmethod
def _simple_login(username, password):
    return username == 'abq' and password == 'Flowers'
```

Notice we've implemented this as a static method, since it does not need access to the instance or class. It will simply take the username and password given and see if they match hard-coded values. It returns True or False accordingly.

This is quite possibly the worst way you can do password security in an application; *do not* ever use this approach in a real application. We are using it here for the sake of illustration, since the point is to understand dialogs. In *Chapter 12, Improving Data Storage with SQL*, we'll implement an authentication backend that's actually production-worthy.

Now, let's create a second method that will display the login dialog and test the entered credentials for validity, like so:

```
# application.py, at the end of the Application class

def _show_login(self):
  error = ''
  title = "Login to ABQ Data Entry"
  while True:
    login = v.LoginDialog(self, title, error)
    if not login.result:  # User canceled
      return False
    username, password = login.result
    if self._simple_login(username, password):
      return True
    error = 'Login Failed' # Loop and redisplay
```

In this method, we begin by creating error and title variables, then entering an infinite loop. Inside the loop, we create our LoginDialog instance using the title and error strings. This will display the dialog, and execution will halt here until the user either cancels or submits the dialog. When that happens, login is assigned to the instance of the dialog (*not* to the results!). Now we can check login.result to see what the user entered.

If result is empty, the user canceled, so we can return False from the method. If the user entered something, we'll extract result into its username and password values, then pass those to our _simple_login() method. If the credentials check out, we will return True; if not, we'll update the error string and let the loop iterate again, re-displaying the dialog. The net result is that this method will return either False if the dialog was canceled, or True if the authentication succeeded.

Now, we need to call this method during the startup of our application. We'll do this in the application's initializer. Since dialogs cannot be created until a root window has been created, we'll have to do this just after the call to super().__init__() (remember that Application is a subclass of Tk, so calling super().__init__() is what creates our Tk instance).

Add the following code to Application.__init__(), just under the call to super().__init__():

```
# application.py, inside Application.__init__()

    self.withdraw()
    if not self._show_login():
```

```
        self.destroy()
        return
    self.deiconify()
```

The first line calls the `withdraw()` method, which hides our main window. We don't strictly have to do this, but without it we'll have a blank `Application` window hanging around while the login dialog is being presented.

After hiding the blank window, we'll call `_show_login()` and test its `return` value. Remember it will return `True` if the user successfully authenticates, or `False` if the user cancels the dialog. In the latter case, we'll call `self.destroy()`, which deletes our `Tk` instance, and return from the method. Effectively, this quits the application.

Normally you would call `Application.quit()` to exit a Tkinter program; this method of the `Tk` object causes the main loop to exit and thus the program ends. However, at this point in the program, we haven't started the main loop yet, so `quit()` won't do anything. If we destroy the window and return without adding anything else, the main loop will see that the root window is destroyed and exit after its first iteration.

If the user is successful in authenticating, we'll call the application's `deiconify()` method, which restores its visibility. Then we continue with the remainder of the initializer.

Go ahead and launch the application to give your `LoginDialog` class a test run. It should look something like this:

Figure 7.9: The login dialog

Great job!

Designing the application menu

Most applications organize functionality into a hierarchical menu system, typically displayed at the top of the application or screen (depending on the operating system). While the organization of this menu varies between operating systems, certain items are fairly common across platforms.

Of these common items, our application will need the following:

- A **File menu** containing file operations such as **Open/Save/Export**, and often an option to quit the application. Our users will need this menu to select a file to save to, and to quit the program.

- An **Options menu** where users can configure the application. We'll need this menu for our toggle settings; sometimes a menu like this is called Preferences or Settings, but we'll go with Options for now.

- A **Help menu**, which contains links to help documentation, or, at the very least, an About message giving the basic information about the application. We'll implement this menu for the About dialog.

 Apple, Microsoft, and the GNOME Project publish guidelines for macOS, Windows, and the GNOME desktop environment (used on Linux and BSD), respectively; each set of guidelines addresses the layout of menu items specific to that platform. We'll explore this in more detail in *Chapter 10, Maintaining Cross-Platform Compatibility.*

Before we can implement our menu, we'll need to understand how menus work in Tkinter.

The Tkinter Menu widget

The `tkinter.Menu` widget is the building block used to implement menus in Tkinter applications; it's a fairly simple widget that acts as a container for any number of menu items.

The menu items can be one of the following five types:

Item type	Description
`command`	A labeled item that executes a command when clicked
`checkbutton`	A labeled checkbutton that can be tied to a Boolean control variable
`radiobutton`	A labeled radio button that can be tied to a control variable
`separator`	A system-appropriate visual separator, usually a black line
`cascade`	A submenu, implemented as a second `Menu` instance

To explore how the Menu class works, let's start a simple example script, like so:

```
# menu_demo.py
import tkinter as tk
root = tk.Tk()
root.geometry('200x150')
main_text = tk.StringVar(value='Hi')
label = tk.Label(root, textvariable=main_text)
label.pack(side='bottom')
```

This application sets up a 200-by-150-pixel main window with a Label widget, whose text is controlled by a string variable, main_text. Now, let's start adding the menu components, like so:

```
main_menu = tk.Menu(root)
root.config(menu=main_menu)
```

This creates a Menu instance and then sets it as the main menu of our application by assigning it to the root window's menu argument.

Currently, the menu is empty, so let's add an item; add this code to the script:

```
main_menu.add('command', label='Quit', command=root.quit)
```

Here, we've added a command item to quit the application. The Menu.add() method allows us to specify an item type and any number of keyword arguments to create a new menu item. In the case of a command item, we need to at least have a label argument specifying the text that will show in the menu and a command argument pointing to a Python callback.

 Some platforms, such as macOS, don't allow a command in the top-level menu. We'll cover the differences between menus on different platforms in more detail in *Chapter 10, Maintaining Cross-Platform Compatibility.*

Next, let's try creating a submenu, like so:

```
text_menu = tk.Menu(main_menu, tearoff=False)
```

Creating a submenu is just like creating a menu, except that we specify the parent menu as the widget's parent. Notice the tearoff argument; by default, submenus in Tkinter are **tearable**, which means they can be pulled off and moved around as independent windows.

You don't have to disable this option, but it is a rather archaic UI feature that is rarely used on modern platforms. Our users will likely just find it confusing, so we're going to disable it whenever we create submenus.

Now that we have a submenu object, let's add some commands, like so:

```
text_menu.add_command(
    label='Set to "Hi"',
    command=lambda: main_text.set('Hi')
)
text_menu.add_command(
    label='Set to "There"',
    command=lambda: main_text.set('There')
)
```

The `add_command()` method used here is simply a shortcut for `add('command')`, and it can be used on any `Menu` object. There are analogous methods for adding other items as well (`add_cascade()`, `add_separator()`, and so on).

Now that we've populated the `text_menu`, let's use the `add_cascade()` method to add our menu back to its parent widget as follows:

```
main_menu.add_cascade(label="Text", menu=text_menu)
```

When adding a submenu to its parent menu, we simply have to provide the label for the menu and the menu object itself.

Using Checkbutton and Radiobutton items

In addition to commands and submenus, we can also add `Checkbutton` and `Radiobutton` widgets to the menu. To demonstrate this, let's create another submenu with options to alter the label's appearance.

First, we'll need to add the following setup code:

```
font_bold = tk.BooleanVar(value=False)
font_size = tk.IntVar(value=10)

def set_font(*args):
    size = font_size.get()
    bold = 'bold' if font_bold.get() else ''
    font_spec = f'TkDefaultFont {size} {bold}'
    label.config(font=font_spec)
```

```
font_bold.trace_add('write', set_font)
font_size.trace_add('write', set_font)
set_font()
```

To use checkbutton and radiobutton items in a menu, we need to first create control variables to bind to them. Here, we're just creating a Boolean variable for the bold font toggle, and an integer variable for the font size. Next, we've created a callback function that reads the variables and sets the Label widget's font property from them when called. Finally, we've set up a trace on both variables to call the callback whenever the values are changed, and called the callback to initialize the font settings.

Now, we just need to create the menu options to change the variables; add this code next:

```
appearance_menu = tk.Menu(main_menu, tearoff=False)
main_menu.add_cascade(label="Appearance", menu=appearance_menu)
appearance_menu.add_checkbutton(label="Bold", variable=font_bold)
```

Here we've created the submenu for the appearance options and added the checkbutton for bold text. Like a regular Checkbutton widget, the add_checkbutton() method uses a variable argument to assign its control variable. Unlike a regular Checkbutton widget, though, it uses the label argument, rather than the text argument, to assign the label text.

 The checkbutton item works with a BooleanVar by default; however, just like a Checkbutton widget, you can use it with different control variable types by passing in onvalue and offvalue arguments.

To demonstrate radiobutton items, let's add a submenu to our Appearance submenu, like so:

```
size_menu = tk.Menu(appearance_menu, tearoff=False)
appearance_menu.add_cascade(label='Font size', menu=size_menu)
for size in range(8, 24, 2):
  size_menu.add_radiobutton(
    label="{} px".format(size),
    value=size, variable=font_size
  )
```

Just as we added a submenu to our main menu, we can add submenus to submenus. In theory, you could nest submenus indefinitely, but most UI guidelines discourage more than two levels.

To create the items for our size menu, we're just iterating a generated list of even numbers between 8 and 24; for each one, we call add_radiobutton(), adding an item with a value equal to that size. Just as with regular Radiobutton widgets, the control variable passed to the variable argument will be updated with the value stored in the value argument when the button is selected.

Finally, let's add a call to mainloop():

```
root.mainloop()
```

Launch the application and try it out. You should get something like this:

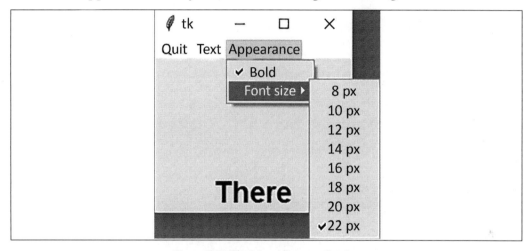

Figure 7.10: The Menu demo application

Now that we understand how to work with the Menu widget, let's design and implement a menu for our application.

Implementing the ABQ application menu

As a major component of the GUI, our main menu code would be right at home in the views.py file. However, because it's going to be expanded considerably as our application grows, we'll put it in its own module file. Create a new file the abq_data_entry directory called mainmenu.py. Then begin the file with a docstring and our imports:

```
# mainmenu.py
"""The Main Menu class for ABQ Data Entry"""

import tkinter as tk
from tkinter import messagebox
```

Next, let's subclass `tkinter.Menu` to create our own main menu class, like so:

```python
class MainMenu(tk.Menu):
  """The Application's main menu"""

  def __init__(self, parent, **kwargs):
    super().__init__(parent, **kwargs)
```

We will be building the rest of the menu inside the initializer, though for the moment this doesn't do anything extra. Before we start building the menu, let's drop back into our `application.py` module and set up this class as the application's main menu.

First, import the class at the top of the file, like this:

```python
# application.py, at the top after the import statements
from .mainmenu import MainMenu
```

Next, inside `Application.__init__()`, we need to create an instance of our `MainMenu` class and make it the application's menu. Update the method as follows:

```python
# application.py, inside Application.__init__()

    self.title("ABQ Data Entry Application")
    self.columnconfigure(0, weight=1)

    menu = MainMenu(self)
    self.config(menu=menu)
```

Now let's head back to `mainmenu.py` and start building the components of our menu.

Adding a Help menu

Let's begin with something simple. We'll just add an About dialog to display some information about our program. This is typically located in a Help menu.

Add the following code to `MainMenu.__init__()`:

```python
# mainmenu.py, inside MainMenu.__init__()

    help_menu = tk.Menu(self, tearoff=False)
    help_menu.add_command(label='About...', command=self.show_about)
```

Here, we've added a Help menu and a command for About.

The command specifies an instance method, show_about(), as its callback; so, we'll need to add that method to the class, as follows:

```
# mainmenu.py, inside the MainMenu class

def show_about(self):
    """Show the about dialog"""

    about_message = 'ABQ Data Entry'
    about_detail = (
        'by Alan D Moore\n'
        'For assistance please contact the author.'
    )
    messagebox.showinfo(
        title='About', message=about_message, detail=about_detail
    )
```

This method just specifies some basic information about the application and displays it in a messagebox dialog. You can, of course, update the about_detail variable with your own information, or a much longer (and hopefully more helpful) message.

Adding a File menu

The next menu we'll create is a File menu. This will have two commands, one for selecting a file and another for quitting the application. Unlike the About dialog, though, we can't really implement the callback logic for either command in the menu class itself. File selection will need to call the Application._on_file_select() method we created earlier in the chapter, and the quit command will need to call Application.quit().

Since the menu's parent widget will be the Application object, we could just bind these commands to parent._on_file_select and parent.quit, but that would create a tight coupling situation as we discussed in *Chapter 6, Planning for the Expansion of Our Application*. As we did in that chapter, we'll instead use generated events to communicate back to the controller class.

One possible way to implement our File menu commands is to use a lambda function, like so:

```
file_menu.add_command(
    label="Select file…",
    command=lambda: self.event_generate('<<FileSelect>>')
)
```

The `lambda` keyword creates an anonymous inline function that contains a single expression. It is often used in situations where we need a reference to a function (such as a widget's `command` argument) but don't need the overhead of defining a named function. In this case, we're creating an anonymous function that generates a custom `<<FileSelect>>` event on the `MainMenu` object using `event_generate()`.

 You can find out more about Lambda expressions in *Section 6.14* of the Python official documentation, available at `https://docs.python.org/3/reference/expressions.html`.

However, there are two problems with this approach.

First, using `lambda` every time is rather verbose and ugly, and since our menu is going to be generating a lot of custom events as the application grows, we'd like to avoid a lot of repetitive boilerplate code.

Second, binding events on a `Menu` object doesn't work on all platforms (particularly, it doesn't work on Microsoft Windows). This has to do with the fact that the `Menu` is built around the native menu system of each platform. To work around this, we'll need to get a reference to our `root` window and bind our events to that.

Since this makes our code even uglier, it makes sense to create a simple wrapper function that will keep our menu definitions nice and clean.

Add the following `_event()` method to the `MainMenu` class above the initializer:

```
# mainmenu.py, inside MainMenu

def _event(self, sequence):
  def callback(*_):
    root = self.master.winfo_toplevel()
    root.event_generate(sequence)
  return callback
```

This simple method creates a function that causes the `root` window instance to generate the provided `sequence` string, then returns a reference to the newly defined function. To get a reference to the `root` window, we call `winfo_toplevel()` on the menu's parent widget (`self.master`), which returns the top-level window of the menu's parent widget. You might wonder why we don't just use `self.master`, or just call `winfo_toplevel()` on the `Menu` object itself. In the first case, we can't be sure what the menu's parent widget will be until we create an instance of it, especially as our program evolves in the future. While we can't be sure exactly what the parent widget will be, we can be sure it will be a widget on a window; by calling `winfo_toplevel()` we should get the `root` window.

In the second case, the `winfo_toplevel()` method, when called on a `Menu` object, actually returns the top level of the *menu*. In other words, `self.winfo_toplevel()` in this context would just return our `MainMenu` object.

Now we can update our menu items to use this wrapper method, like so:

```
# mainmenu.py, inside MainMenu.__init__()
    file_menu = tk.Menu(self, tearoff=False)
    file_menu.add_command(
      label="Select file…",
      command=self._event('<<FileSelect>>')
    )

    file_menu.add_separator()
    file_menu.add_command(
      label="Quit",
      command=self._event('<<FileQuit>>')
    )
```

> Note the use of the ellipsis character (…) after `"Select file"`. This is a convention in menus to indicate when a command will open another window or dialog to get information from the user rather than just running a command directly.

Now our code looks much cleaner. To make these commands work, we'll need to tell our `Application` class to listen for these events and take appropriate action when they're generated.

Back in the `application.py` file, let's add the following lines to `Application.__init__()`, just after the menu object setup:

```
# application.py, inside Application.__init__()

    event_callbacks = {
      '<<FileSelect>>': self._on_file_select,
      '<<FileQuit>>': lambda _: self.quit(),
    }
    for sequence, callback in event_callbacks.items():
      self.bind(sequence, callback)
```

Here, we've created an `event_callbacks` dictionary, matching event sequences to callback methods. Then, we're iterating through the dictionary, binding each sequence to its event.

As we add more items to our menu, we'll just need to update the dictionary with the additional bindings. Note that we cannot bind the <<FileQuit>> action directly to self.quit(). That's because callbacks bound using the bind() method pass arguments when the callback is called, and self.quit() takes no arguments. We're using a lambda call here just to filter out the added argument from the callback.

Adding a settings menu

The next thing we need to add is our Options menu, which will allow the user to specify whether they want the Date and Sheet data auto-filled in the form or not. We've already seen that adding checkbutton options to a menu is fairly easy, but actually making these options work is going to take some additional plumbing work. Somehow, we need to connect these menu options to the DataRecordForm instance so that it can disable the automation appropriately.

To do this, let's begin by creating a dictionary in the Application class that will store some control variables:

```python
# application.py, inside Application.__init__()
# before the menu setup

self.settings = {
    'autofill date': tk.BooleanVar(),
    'autofill sheet data': tk.BooleanVar()
}
```

Next, we will need to make sure both our DataRecordForm and MainMenu objects have access to these settings; we will do this by passing the settings dictionary to their initializer methods and storing it as an instance variable on each class.

First, in views.py, let's update the DataRecordForm.__init__() method, like so:

```python
# views.py, inside DataRecordForm class

def __init__(self, parent, model, settings, *args, **kwargs):
    super().__init__(parent, *args, **kwargs)

    self.model = model
    self.settings = settings
```

Next, in mainmenu.py, let's update the MainMenu.__init__() method, like so:

```python
# mainmenu.py, inside MainMenu class
def __init__(self, parent, settings, **kwargs):
```

```
        super().__init__(parent, **kwargs)
        self.settings = settings
```

Now, back in the Application class, we have to update the code that creates instances of these classes to pass in the settings dictionary to each one. Update the code in Application.__init__() as follows:

```
# application.py, in Application.__init__()

    # update the menu creation Line:
    menu = MainMenu(self, self.settings)

    #...
    # update the data record form creation Line:
    self.recordform = v.DataRecordForm(
        self,
        self.model,
        self.settings
    )
```

Each class now has access to the settings dictionary, so let's put it to use. To begin with, let's add our Options menu to the main menu.

In the MainMenu file, add this code to the initializer method to build the menu:

```
# mainmenu.py, in MainMenu.__init__()

    options_menu = tk.Menu(self, tearoff=False)
    options_menu.add_checkbutton(
        label='Autofill Date',
        variable=self.settings['autofill date']
    )
    options_menu.add_checkbutton(
        label='Autofill Sheet data',
        variable=self.settings['autofill sheet data']
    )
```

Very simply, we've created a Menu widget called options_menu with two checkbutton items that are bound to our settings variable. That's all the configuration our MainMenu needs for the settings.

The last thing we need to do is make these settings work with the DataRecordForm class's reset() method, which handles the auto-filling of these fields.

In the `views.py` file, locate the `DataRecordForm.reset()` method, and find the code that sets the date variable. Update it as follows:

```
# views.py, in DataRecordForm.reset()

if self.settings['autofill date'].get():
    current_date = datetime.today().strftime('%Y-%m-%d')
    self._vars['Date'].set(current_date)
    self._vars['Time'].label_widget.input.focus()
```

All we've done here is put this date-setting logic below an `if` statement that checks the `settings` value. We need to do the same for our sheet data section, as follows:

```
if (
    self.settings['autofill sheet data'].get() and
    plot not in ('', 0, plot_values[-1])
):
    self._vars['Lab'].set(lab)
    self._vars['Time'].set(time)
    # etc...
```

Since this logic was already under an `if` statement, we've just added another condition to the check. This should now give us functioning options.

Finishing the menu

The last thing we need to do in our main menu is add the submenus we've created to the main menu. At the end of `MainMenu.__init__()`, add the following lines:

```
# mainmenu.py, at the end of MainMenu.__init__()

self.add_cascade(label='File', menu=file_menu)
self.add_cascade(label='Options', menu=options_menu)
self.add_cascade(label='Help', menu=help_menu)
```

The submenus will be arranged from left to right in the order we add them. Typically the File menu is first and the Help menu is last, with the other menus arranged in between. We'll learn more about how to arrange menus with respect to platform in *Chapter 10, Maintaining Cross-Platform Compatibility*.

Run the application, and you should see a nice main menu like this:

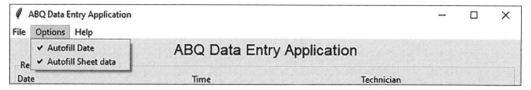

Figure 7.11: The ABQ application sporting a fancy main menu

Give the settings a try by un-checking them and entering some records. They should disable the auto-fill functionality when disabled.

Persisting settings

Our settings work, but there's a major annoyance: they don't persist between sessions. Shut down the application and start it up again, and you'll see that the settings are back to their defaults. It's not a major problem, but it's a rough edge we shouldn't leave for our users. Ideally, their personal settings should load up each time they launch the application.

Python gives us a variety of ways to persist data in files. We've already experienced CSV, which is designed for tabular data; there are other formats designed with different capabilities in mind. The following table shows just a few of the options for storing data available in the Python standard library:

Module	File type	Suitable for	Benefits	Drawbacks
pickle	Binary	Any Python object	Fast, easy, small files	Not safe, files not human-readable, whole file must be read
configparser	Text	Key -> value pairs	Human-readable files	Can't handle sequences or complex objects, limited hierarchy
json	Text	Simple values and sequences	Widely used, easy, human-readable	Can't handle dates, complex objects without modification
xml	Text	Any kind of Python object	Powerful, flexible, human-readable files	Not safe, complex to use, verbose syntax
sqlite	Binary	Relational data	Fast, powerful, can represent complex relationships	Requires SQL knowledge, objects must be translated to tables

Table 7.3:

If this weren't enough, there are even more options available in the third-party libraries. Almost any of them would be suitable for storing a couple of Boolean values, so how do we choose? Let's consider the options:

- SQL and XML are powerful, but far too complex for our simple needs here.
- We'd like to stick to a text format in case we need to debug a corrupt settings file, so pickle is out.
- configparser would work for now, but its inability to handle lists, tuples, and dictionaries may be limiting in the future.

That leaves json, which is a good option. While it can't handle every kind of Python object, it can handle strings, numbers, and Boolean values, as well as lists and dictionaries. It can even be extended to handle other kinds of data. It should cover our current configuration needs just fine, and most likely our future needs as well.

What does it mean when we say that a library is "not safe"? Some data formats are designed with powerful capabilities, such as extensibility, linking, or aliasing, which parser libraries must implement. Unfortunately, those capabilities can be exploited for malicious purposes. For example, the "billion laughs" XML vulnerability combines three XML capabilities to craft a file that, when parsed, expands to a massive size (usually causing the program or, in some cases, the operating system, to crash).

Building a model for settings persistence

As with any kind of data persistence, we need to start by implementing a model. As with our CSVModel class, the settings model needs to save and load the data, as well as authoritatively defining the layout of the settings data. Since we're using json, we need to import it. Add this to the top of models.py:

```
import json
```

Now, down at the end of models.py, let's start a new SettingsModel class as follows:

```
# models.py, at the bottom

class SettingsModel:
  """A model for saving settings"""

  fields = {
    'autofill date': {'type': 'bool', 'value': True},
```

```
    'autofill sheet data': {'type': 'bool', 'value': True}
  }
```

As we did with the CSVModel, we've begun our class with a class variable that defines the fields included in the settings file. Currently, it only contains our two Boolean values. Each field in the dictionary defines a data type and default value for the field. Note that we're using strings here rather than Python type objects; doing this will allow us to persist both the type and the value to a text file.

Next, let's create the initializer method, as follows:

```
# models.py, in SettingsModel

def __init__(self):
  filename = 'abq_settings.json'
  self.filepath = Path.home() / filename
```

The initializer will determine the file path to which our settings will be saved; for now, we've hard-coded the name abq_settings.json and stored it in the user's home directory. Path.home() is a class method of the Path class that provides us with a Path object pointed to the user's home directory. In this way, each user on the system can have their own settings file.

As soon as the model is created, we'll want to load the user's saved options from disk, so let's add a call to an instance method we'll call load():

```
# models.py, at the end of SettingsModel.__init__()
    self.load()
```

Now we need to implement the load() method. A simplistic implementation may look like this:

```
def load(self):
  with open(self.filepath, 'r') as fh:
    self.fields = json.load(fh)
```

This simply opens the file stored in our self.filepath location and overwrites the fields variable with whatever contents are extracted by json.load(). This is the gist of what we need to do, but there are two problems with this approach:

- What happens if the file doesn't exist? (For example, if the user has never run the program before.)
- What happens if the JSON data in the model doesn't match with the keys expected by our application? (For example, if it was tampered with, or created by an older version of the application.)

Let's create a more robust callback that addresses these issues, as follows:

```python
# models.py, inside the SettingsModel class
  def load(self):
    if not self.filepath.exists():
      return

    with open(self.filepath, 'r') as fh:
      raw_values = json.load(fh)

    for key in self.fields:
      if key in raw_values and 'value' in raw_values[key]:
        raw_value = raw_values[key]['value']
        self.fields[key]['value'] = raw_value
```

In this version, we address the first issue by checking to see if the file exists. If the file doesn't exist, the method simply returns and does nothing. It's perfectly reasonable for the file not to exist, especially if the user has never run the program or edited any of the settings. In this case, the method would leave `self.fields` alone and the user would end up with the defaults.

To address the second problem, we've pulled the JSON data into a local variable called `raw_values`; then, we update `fields` by retrieving from `raw_values` only those keys that are defined by our class. If the JSON data lacks a particular key, we skip it, leaving `fields` with its default value.

In addition to loading settings, our model will of course need to save its data. Let's write a `save()` method to write our values to the file:

```python
# models.py, inside the SettingsModel class

  def save(self):
    with open(self.filepath, 'w') as fh:
      json.dump(self.fields, fh)
```

The `json.dump()` function is the inverse of `json.load()`: it takes a Python object and a file handle, converts the object to a JSON string, and writes it to the file. Saving our settings data is as simple as converting the `fields` dictionary to a JSON string and writing it to the specified text file.

The final method our model needs is a way for external code to set values; we could just allow external code to manipulate the `fields` dictionary directly, but in the interest of protecting our data integrity, we'll do it through a method call.

Keeping with Tkinter convention, we'll call this method `set()`.

A basic implementation of the `set()` method is as follows:

```
def set(self, key, value):
  self.fields[key]['value'] = value
```

This simple method just takes `key` and `value` arguments and writes them to the `fields` dictionary. This opens up some potential problems, though:

- What if the value provided isn't valid for the data type?
- What if the key isn't in our `fields` dictionary? Should we allow outside code to just add new keys?

These situations could create problems in the application that would be hard to debug, so our `set()` method should safeguard against these scenarios.

Let's create a more robust version, as follows:

```
# models.py, inside the SettingsModel class

def set(self, key, value):
  if (
    key in self.fields and
    type(value).__name__ == self.fields[key]['type']
  ):
    self.fields[key]['value'] = value
  else:
    raise ValueError("Bad key or wrong variable type")
```

In this version, we check if the given key argument exists in `fields`, and if the `type` of the data matches the type defined for that field. To match the `value` variable's object type to the `field` dictionary's type strings, we have extracted the variable's data type as a string using `type(value).__name__`. This returns a string like `bool` for Boolean variables, or `str` for strings. With these checks protecting our value assignment, an attempt to write an unknown key or incorrect variable type will fail.

However, we don't let it fail silently; if there is bad data, we immediately raise a `ValueError` exception. Why raise an exception? If the test fails, it can only mean a bug in the calling code. With an exception, we'll know immediately if the calling code is sending bad requests to our model. Without it, requests would fail silently, leaving a hard-to-find bug.

Using the settings model in our application

Our application needs to load in the settings when it starts, then save them automatically whenever they are changed. Currently, the application's `settings` dictionary is created manually, but our model, as the authority on the settings data structure, should really be telling it what kind of variables to create.

Back in the `Application.__init__()` method, locate the line that creates our `settings` dictionary, and replace it with the following code:

```
# application.py, inside Application.__init__()
    self.settings_model = m.SettingsModel()
    self._load_settings()
```

First, we've created a `SettingsModel` instance, storing it as an instance variable. Then, we're running an instance method called `_load_settings()`. This method will be responsible for querying the `settings_model` to create the `Application.settings` dictionary.

At the end of the class definition, let's create the `_load_settings()` method:

```
# application.py, inside the Application class

    def _load_settings(self):
        """Load settings into our self.settings dict."""

        vartypes = {
            'bool': tk.BooleanVar,
            'str': tk.StringVar,
            'int': tk.IntVar,
            'float': tk.DoubleVar
        }
        self.settings = dict()
        for key, data in self.settings_model.fields.items():
            vartype = vartypes.get(data['type'], tk.StringVar)
            self.settings[key] = vartype(value=data['value'])
```

Our model stores the type and value for each variable, but our application needs Tkinter control variables. We need to translate the model's representation of the data into a structure that `Application` can use. So the first thing this function does is create a `vartypes` dictionary to translate our `type` strings to control variable types.

Although we currently only have Boolean variables in our settings, we're going to anticipate more settings in the future and create a function capable of handling strings, floats, and integers as well.

After defining the `vartypes` dictionary and creating an empty dictionary for `settings`, we just need to iterate through `self.settings_model.fields`, creating a matching control variable for each field. Note that `vartypes.get(data['type'], tk.StringVar)` ensures that, if we get a variable type not listed in `vartypes`, we'll just create a `StringVar` for it.

The main reason for using Tkinter variables here is so that we can trace any changes the user makes to the values via the UI and respond immediately. Specifically, we want to save our settings whenever the user makes a change. To implement this, add the last two lines to the method:

```
# application.py, inside Application._load_settings()

    for var in self.settings.values():
      var.trace_add('write', self._save_settings)
```

This adds a trace that calls `_save_settings` whenever a settings variable is changed. Of course, this means we need to write a method called `Application._save_settings()`, which will save the settings to disk.

Add this code to the end of `Application`:

```
    def _save_settings(self, *_):
      for key, variable in self.settings.items():
        self.settings_model.set(key, variable.get())
      self.settings_model.save()
```

The `save_settings()` method just needs to get the data back from `Application.settings` to the model and then save it. It's as simple as iterating through `self.settings` and calling our model's `set()` method to pull in the values one at a time. Once we've updated the values, we call the model's `save()` method.

This completes our settings persistence; you should be able to run the program and observe that the settings are saved, even when you close and re-open the application. You'll also find a file in your home directory called `abq_settings.json` (this isn't the ideal place to keep a settings file, but we'll address that in *Chapter 10, Maintaining Cross-Platform Compatibility*).

Summary

In this chapter, our simple form has taken a big step forward toward being a full-blown application. We've implemented a main menu, option settings that are persisted between executions, and an About dialog. We've added the ability to select a file where records are saved, and improved the visibility of form errors with an error dialog. Along the way, you learned about Tkinter menus, file dialogs, message boxes, and custom dialogs, as well as the various options for persisting data in the standard library.

In the next chapter, we're going to be asked to make the program read data as well as write it. We'll learn about Ttk's `Treeview` and `Notebook` widgets, and how to make our `CSVModel` and `DataRecordForm` classes capable of reading and updating existing data.

8

Navigating Records with Treeview and Notebook

You've received another request for features in the application. Now that your users can open arbitrary files for appending, they'd like to be able to see what's in those files and correct old records using the data entry form they've grown accustomed to, rather than having to switch over to a spreadsheet. In a nutshell, it's finally time to implement read and update capabilities in our application.

In this chapter, we're going to cover the following topics:

- In *Implementing read and update in the model*, we'll modify our CSV model for read and update capabilities.

- In *The Ttk Treeview*, we'll explore the Ttk Treeview widget.

- In *Implementing a record list with Treeview*, we'll use our knowledge of the Treeview widget to create an interactive display of records in the CSV file.

- In *Adding the record list to the application*, we'll incorporate our new record list view into our application using the Ttk Notebook widget.

Implementing read and update in the model

Our entire design up to this point has been centered around a form that only appends data to a file; adding read and update capabilities is a fundamental change that will touch nearly every portion of the application.

It may seem like a daunting task, but by taking it one component at a time, we'll see that the changes are not so overwhelming.

The first thing we should do is update our documentation. Open the abq_data_entry_spec.rst file in the docs folder, and let's start with the Requirements section:

```
Functional Requirements:

  * Provide a UI for reading, updating, and appending

    data to the CSV file

  * ...
```

And, of course, we should also update the part that is not required, like so:

```
The program does not need to:

  * Allow deletion of data.
```

Now, it's a simple matter of making the code match with the documentation. Let's get started!

Adding read and update to the CSVModel class

Take a moment to consider what's missing from the CSVModel class that we'll need to add for read and update functionality:

- We'll need a method that can retrieve all records in a file so we can display them. We'll call it get_all_records().
- We'll need a method to fetch individual records from the file by row number. We can call this one get_record().
- We'll need to save records in a way that can not only append new records but update existing records as well. We can update our save_record() method to accommodate this.

Open up models.py in your editor, and let's work through making these changes.

Implementing get_all_records()

Let's start a new method in CSVModel called get_all_records():

```
# models.py, in the CSVModel class

def get_all_records(self):
    """Read in all records from the CSV and return a list"""
    if not self.file.exists():
        return []
```

The first thing we've done is check if the model's file exists yet (recall that self. file is a Path object, so we can just call exists() to see if it exists). When our users start the program each morning, the CSVModel generates a default filename pointing to a file that likely doesn't exist yet, so get_all_records() will need to handle this situation gracefully. It makes sense to return an empty list in this case, since there's no data if the file doesn't exist.

If the file does exist, we will open it in read-only mode and get all the records. We could do that like this:

```
with open(self.file, 'r') as fh:
    csvreader = csv.DictReader(fh)
    records = list(csvreader)
```

While not terribly efficient, pulling the entire file into memory and converting it into a list is acceptable in our case, since we know that our largest files should be limited to a mere 241 rows: 20 plots times 3 labs times 4 check sessions, plus a header row. That amount of data is easy work for Python, even on an old workstation. This method is just a little too trusting, however. We should at least do some sanity checks to make sure that the user has actually opened a CSV file containing the proper fields and not some other arbitrary file, which would likely crash the program.

Let's revise the method so that it will check the file for the correct field structure:

```
# models.py, inside CSVModel.get_all_records()

    with open(self.file, 'r', encoding='utf-8') as fh:
        csvreader = csv.DictReader(fh.readlines())
        missing_fields = (
            set(self.fields.keys()) - set(csvreader.fieldnames)
        )
        if len(missing_fields) > 0:
            fields_string = ', '.join(missing_fields)
            raise Exception(
```

```
              f"File is missing fields: {fields_string}"
        )
        records = list(csvreader)
```

In this version, we first find any missing fields by comparing the `CSVModel.fields` dictionary keys to the `fieldnames` list in the CSV file. To find the missing fields, we're using a simple trick involving the Python `set` type: if we convert both lists to `set` objects, we can subtract one from the other, leaving us with a `set` object containing the fields from the first list (our `fields` keys) that were missing from the second list (the CSV field names).

If `missing_fields` has any items, those are missing fields from the CSV file. We'll raise an exception in this case, detailing which fields are absent. Otherwise, we convert the CSV data to a list, as we did in our simpler version of the method.

Python `set` objects are very useful for comparing the content of the list, tuple, and other sequence objects. They provide an easy way to get information such as the difference (items in *x* that are not in *y*) or intersection (items in both *x* and *y*) between two sets and allow you to compare sequences without respect to order.

Before we can return the `records` list from the method, we need to correct one issue; all data in a CSV file is stored as text, and read by Python as a string. Most of this is not a problem, since Tkinter will take care of converting strings to `float` or `int` as necessary. Boolean values, however, are stored in the CSV file as the strings `True` and `False`, and coercing these values directly back to `bool` doesn't work. The string `False` is a non-empty string, and all non-empty strings evaluate to `True` in Python.

To fix this, let's first define a list of strings that should be interpreted as `True`:

```
# models.py, inside CSVModel.get_all_records()
    trues = ('true', 'yes', '1')
```

Any values not in this list will be considered `False`. We'll do a case-insensitive comparison, so there are only lowercase values in our list.

Next, we create a list of model fields that are Boolean using a list comprehension, like so:

```
        bool_fields = [
            key for key, meta
            in self.fields.items()
            if meta['type'] == FT.boolean
        ]
```

Technically, we know that Equipment Fault is our only Boolean field, so in reality, we could just hard-code the method to correct that field. However, it's wiser to design the model so that any changes to the schema will be automatically handled appropriately by the logic portions. If fields are added or altered, we should ideally only need to alter the field specification and the rest of the model code should behave correctly.

Now, let's iterate through the records and correct all the Boolean fields in each row:

```
for record in records:
    for key in bool_fields:
        record[key] = record[key].lower() in trues
```

For every record, we iterate through our list of the Boolean fields and check the field's value against our list of truthy strings, setting the value of the item accordingly.

With the Boolean values fixed, we can finish our function by returning the list of records, like so:

```
return records
```

Note that the rows returned by this method are dictionaries in the same format expected by the `save_record()` method when saving data. It's good practice for the model to be consistent about the way it represents data. In a more robust model, you might even make a class to represent a row of data, though for simpler applications a dictionary usually serves as well.

Implementing get_record()

The `get_record()` method needs to take a row number and return a single dictionary containing the data for that row. Given that we are dealing in very small amounts of data, we can simply leverage the `get_all_records()` method we just wrote and take care of this in just a few lines, like so:

```
# models.py, inside the CSVModel class
    def get_record(self, rownum):
        return self.get_all_records()[rownum]
```

Keep in mind, however, that it's possible to pass a `rownum` value that doesn't exist in our records list; in this case, Python would raise an `IndexError` exception.

Since there's no meaningful way for us to handle that situation inside the model, we'll need to remember to have our controller catch this exception and deal with it appropriately when using this method.

Adding update capability to save_record()

To convert our `save_record()` method so that we can update records, the first thing we'll need to do is provide the ability to pass in a row number to update. The default will be `None`, which will indicate that the data is a new row that should be appended to the file.

The updated method signature looks like this:

```
# models.py, in the CSVModel class

def save_record(self, data, rownum=None):
    """Save a dict of data to the CSV file"""
```

Our existing record-saving logic doesn't need to change, but it should only be run if `rownum` is `None`.

So, the first thing to do in the method is check `rownum`:

```
if rownum is None:
    # This is a new record
    newfile = not self.file.exists()
    with open(self.file, 'a') as fh:
        csvwriter = csv.DictWriter(fh, fieldnames=self.fields.keys())
        if newfile:
            csvwriter.writeheader()
        csvwriter.writerow(data)
```

If `rownum` is `None`, we're just running our existing code: writing a header if the file doesn't exist, and then appending the row to the end of the file.

In the case that the `rownum` is *not* `None`, we'll need to update the given row and save the file. There are several approaches to this task, but for relatively small files, the simplest way to update a single row is:

1. Load the entire file into a list

2. Change the row in the list

3. Write the entire list back to a clean file

That may seem inefficient, but again, we're dealing with very small amounts of data. A more surgical approach would only be required with much larger sets of data (more than should be stored in a CSV file, for sure!).

So, let's add the following code that does this:

```
# models.py, inside CSVModel.save_record()

    else:
      # This is an update
      records = self.get_all_records()
      records[rownum] = data
      with open(self.file, 'w', encoding='utf-8') as fh:
        csvwriter = csv.DictWriter(fh, fieldnames=self.fields.keys())
        csvwriter.writeheader()
        csvwriter.writerows(records)
```

Once again, we leverage our `get_all_records()` method to fetch the CSV file's content into a list. We then replace the dictionary in the requested row with the data dictionary provided. Finally, we open the file in write mode (w), which will clear its content and replace it with whatever content we write to the file. We then write the header and all records back to the empty file.

 Note that the approach we're taking makes it unsafe for two users to work in the same CSV file simultaneously. Creating software that allows multiple users to edit a single file at the same time is notoriously difficult, and many programs simply opt to prevent it in the first place using lock files or other protection mechanisms. In *Chapter 12, Improving Data Storage with SQL*, we'll update our program so that multiple users can use it simultaneously.

This method is finished, and that's all we need to change in our model to enable the updating and viewing of data. Now, it's time to add the necessary features to our GUI.

The Ttk Treeview

For users to be able to view the contents of a CSV file and select records to edit, we'll need to implement a new view in the application capable of displaying tabular data. This record list view will allow our users to browse the content of the file and open records for viewing or editing.

Our users are accustomed to seeing this data in a spreadsheet, laid out in a table-like format, so it makes sense to design our view in a similar fashion.

For building table-like views with selectable rows, Tkinter gives us the **Ttk Treeview** widget. To build our record list view, we'll need to learn about `Treeview`.

Anatomy of a Treeview

To help us explore the treeview, let's go through a few basic terms and concepts related to the widget. A treeview is designed to display **hierarchical data**; that is, data that is organized into **nodes**, where each node can have exactly one parent node and zero or more child nodes. The following diagram shows an example of hierarchical data:

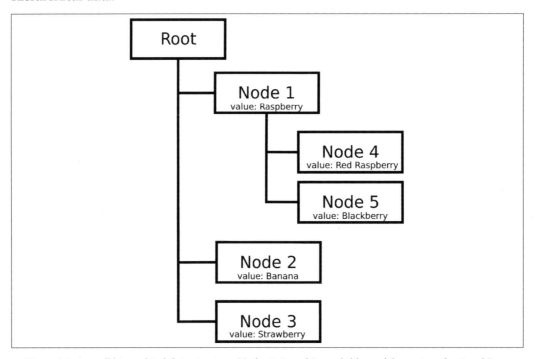

Figure 8.1: A small hierarchical data structure. Nodes 1, 2, and 3 are children of the root, nodes 4 and 5 are children of node 1; "value" is an attribute of each node.

The `Treeview` widget displays hierarchical data in a table format; each row of the table represents a single node, which it calls an **item**. Each column of the table represents some attribute of the node. When a node has child nodes, those rows are displayed under their parent and can be hidden or shown by clicking the parent row.

For example, the hierarchy pictured above in a `Treeview` would look like this:

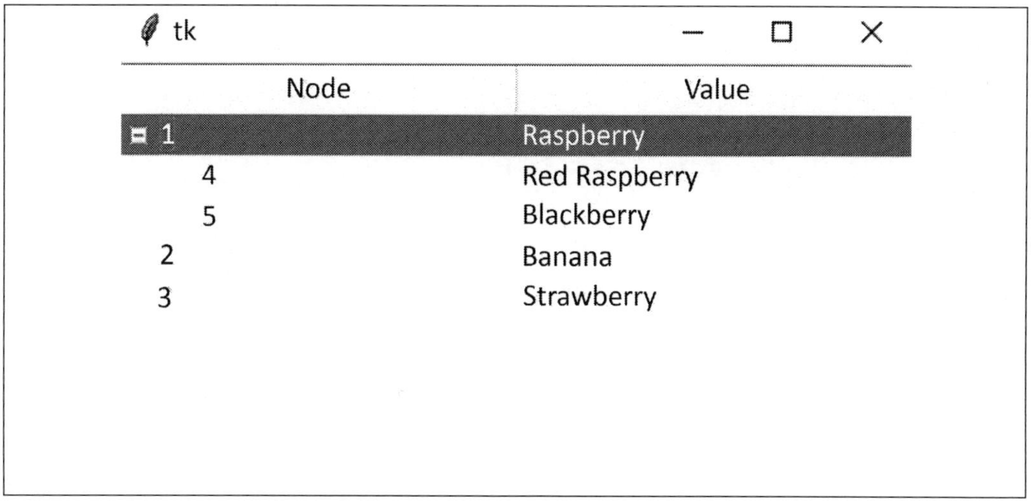

Node	Value
⊟ 1	Raspberry
4	Red Raspberry
5	Blackberry
2	Banana
3	Strawberry

Figure 8.2: The berry hierarchy displayed in a Treeview widget

Each item in a treeview is identified by a unique **item identifier (IID)**, and each column by a **column identifier (CID)**. These values are strings, and you can either assign them manually or let the widget choose them automatically.

At the top of the treeview's columns are **header widgets**. These are buttons that can display the name of each column, and optionally run a callback when clicked.

The first column of the `Treeview` widget is known as the **icon column** and has a CID of `#0`. It cannot be removed, nor can its CID be altered. Typically it contains identifying information about the item.

Building a file browser

Perhaps the best example of the kind of data we can represent in a treeview is a filesystem tree:

- Each row can represent a file or directory
- Each directory can contain additional files or directories
- Each row can have additional data properties, such as permissions, size, or ownership information

To better understand how a `Treeview` widget works, let's create a simple file browser.

Open a new file called `treeview_demo.py` and start with this template:

```
# treeview_demo.py

import tkinter as tk
from tkinter import ttk
from pathlib import Path
root = tk.Tk()
# Code will go here

root.mainloop()
```

We'll start by getting a list of all the file paths under the current working directory. `Path` has a method called `glob()` that will give us such a list. Add this line just below the `root = tk.Tk()` line:

```
paths = Path('.').glob('**/*')
```

`glob()` searches a file path for files or directories matching a filesystem-matching expression. The expression can contain wildcard characters like * (which means "zero or more characters") and ? (which means "a single character"). The name "glob" goes back to a very early Unix command, though this same wildcard syntax is now used across most modern operating systems' command-line interfaces.

`Path('.')` creates a path object referencing the current working directory, and `**/*` is a special wildcard syntax that recursively grabs all objects under the path. Given that wildcard expression, the `glob()` method returns a list of the `Path` objects that include every directory and file under our current directory.

Creating and configuring a Treeview

Now that we have some data to display, let's create a `Treeview` widget to display it, like so:

```
tv = ttk.Treeview(
    root, columns=['size', 'modified'], selectmode='none'
)
```

Like any Tkinter widget, the first argument to `Treeview` is its parent widget. Next, we've passed in a list of strings to the `column` argument. These are the CID values for our columns. Note that these columns are *in addition to* the default icon column, so this `Treeview` widget will have 3 total columns: #0, `size`, and `modified`.

The `selectmode` argument determines how users can select items in the tree. The different options for `selectmode` are shown here:

Value	Behavior
`"none"`	No selections can be made
`"browse"`	User can select one item only
`"extended"`	User can select multiple items

In this case, we're preventing selection, so we set it to none (note that this is the string none, not a `None` object).

While Tkinter will add a column for each CID value, it will not automatically give those columns a header label. We need to do that ourselves using the `Treeview.heading()` method, like this:

```
tv.heading('#0', text='Name')
tv.heading('size', text='Size', anchor='center')
tv.heading('modified', text='Modified', anchor='e')
```

The treeview's `heading()` method allows us to configure the column heading widget; it takes the CID of the column we wish to operate on, followed by any number of keyword arguments to configure the header widget.

Those attributes can include:

- `text`: The text displayed for the heading. By default, it's blank.
- `anchor`: The alignment of the text; it can be any of eight cardinal directions or center, specified as strings or Tkinter constants.
- `command`: A callback to run when the heading is clicked. This might be used to order the rows by that column, or select all the values in the column, for example.
- `image`: An image to display in the heading.

In addition to configuring the headers, we can configure some attributes that affect the entire column using the `Treeview.column()` method.

For example:

```
tv.column('#0', stretch=True)
tv.column('size', width=200)
```

In this code, we've set `stretch=True` in the first column, which will cause it to expand to fill any available space. Then we've set the `width` value on the `size` column to `200` pixels.

The column parameters that can be set include:

- `stretch`: Whether or not to expand this column to fill the available space.
- `width`: The width of the column in pixels.
- `minwidth`: The minimum width to which the column can be resized, in pixels.
- `anchor`: The alignment of the text in the column. Can be any of eight cardinal directions or `center`, specified as strings or Tkinter constants.

With the treeview configured, let's add it into the GUI, like so:

```
tv.pack(expand=True, fill='both')
```

Populating a Treeview with data

Now that we've finished the GUI portion, our view needs to be filled with data. Populating a `Treeview` widget with data is done one row at a time using its `insert()` method.

A basic call to the `insert()` method looks like this:

```
mytreeview.insert(
    parent, 'end', iid='item1',
    text='My Item 1', values=['12', '42']
)
```

The first argument specifies the **parent item** for the inserted row. This is *not* the parent widget, but rather the IID of the parent node under which the inserted node belongs in the hierarchical structure. For top-level items, this value should be an empty string.

The next argument specifies where the item should be inserted under its parent node with respect to its sibling nodes. It can be either a numerical index or the string end, which places the item at the end of the list.

After those positional arguments, `insert()` takes a number of keyword arguments, which can include:

- `text`: This is the value to be shown in the icon column (CID #0).

- values: This is a list of values for the remaining columns. Note that we need to specify them in order.

- image: This is an image object to display in the far left of the icon column.

- iid: The row's IID string. This will be automatically assigned if you don't specify it.

- open: For nodes with children, this sets if the row is initially open (displaying child items) or not.

- tags: A list of tag strings. We'll learn more about tags when we discuss styling in *Chapter 9, Improving the Look with Styles and Themes*.

To insert our file paths into the treeview, let's iterate the paths list as follows:

```
for path in paths:
  meta = path.stat()
  parent = str(path.parent)
  if parent == '.':
    parent = ''
```

Before calling insert(), we need to extract and prepare some data from the path object. The path.stat() method will give us an object containing various file information, from which we'll extract the size and modified time. path.parent provides us with the containing path; however, we need to change the name of the root path (currently a single dot) to an empty string, which is how Treeview represents the root node.

Now, still in the for loop, we add the insert() method call as follows:

```
tv.insert(
  parent,
  'end',
  iid=str(path),
  text=str(path.name),
  values=[meta.st_size, meta.st_mtime]
)
```

By using the path string as the IID, we can then specify it as a parent for its child objects. We use only the path name (that is, the file or directory name without the containing path) as our display value, then retrieve st_size and st_mtime from the stat() data for populating the size and modification time columns.

Run this script and you should see a simple file tree browser that looks something like this:

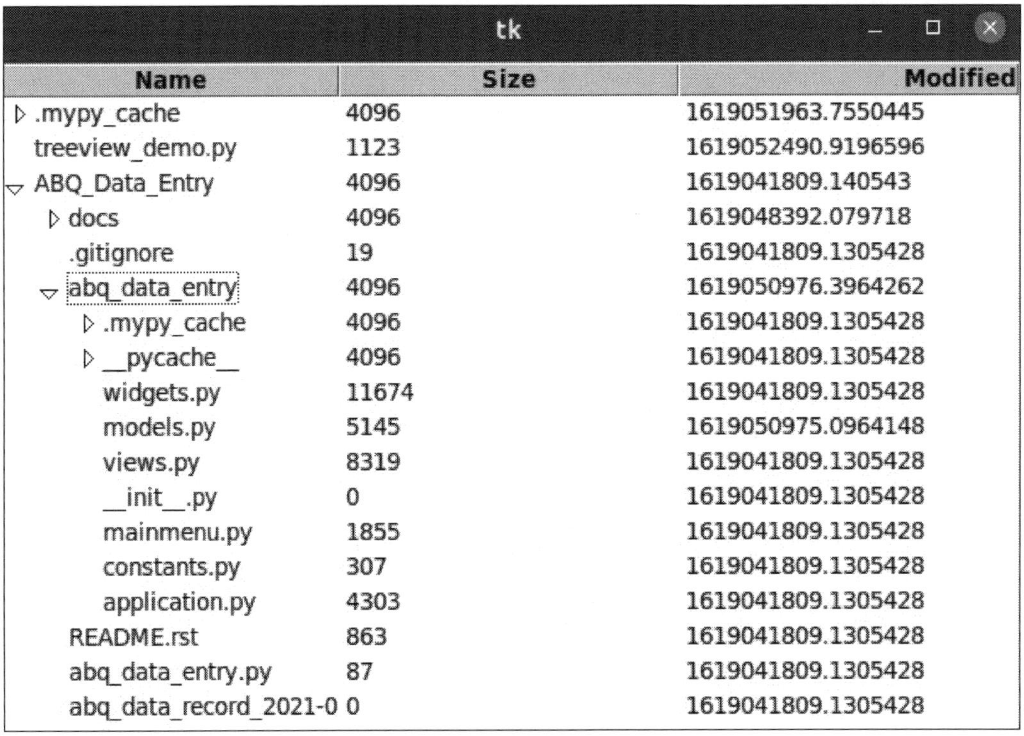

Name	Size	Modified
▷ .mypy_cache	4096	1619051963.7550445
treeview_demo.py	1123	1619052490.9196596
▽ ABQ_Data_Entry	4096	1619041809.140543
▷ docs	4096	1619048392.079718
.gitignore	19	1619041809.1305428
▽ abq_data_entry	4096	1619050976.3964262
▷ .mypy_cache	4096	1619041809.1305428
▷ __pycache__	4096	1619041809.1305428
widgets.py	11674	1619041809.1305428
models.py	5145	1619050975.0964148
views.py	8319	1619041809.1305428
__init__.py	0	1619041809.1305428
mainmenu.py	1855	1619041809.1305428
constants.py	307	1619041809.1305428
application.py	4303	1619041809.1305428
README.rst	863	1619041809.1305428
abq_data_entry.py	87	1619041809.1305428
abq_data_record_2021-0	0	1619041809.1305428

Figure 8.3: Our Treeview widget file browser running on Ubuntu Linux

Sorting Treeview records

The `Treeview` widget doesn't offer any kind of sorting functionality by default, but we can implement sorting by adding a callback function to the column headers.

Sorting through hierarchical data of an unknown depth is a bit tricky; to do it, we're going to write a **recursive function**. A recursive function is a function that calls itself, and they are most commonly employed when dealing with hierarchical data of unknown depth.

Let's start by defining our function signature, like so:

```
def sort(tv, col, parent='', reverse=False):
```

This `sort()` function takes a `Treeview` widget, a CID string of the column we want to sort on, an optional parent node IID, and a Boolean value indicating if the sort should be reversed. The default value for `parent` is an empty string, indicating the root of the hierarchy.

The first thing we're going to do is build a list of tuples, each containing the value we want to sort on and the IID of the row containing that value, like so:

```
sort_index = list()
for iid in tv.get_children(parent):
    sort_value = tv.set(iid, col) if col != '#0' else iid
    sort_index.append((sort_value, iid))
```

The `Treeview.get_children()` method retrieves a list of IID strings that are immediate children of the given `parent` IID. For example, in our file browser, calling `tv.get_children('')` would return a list of all the IID values for the files and folders in the current directory (not in any sub-directories).

Once we have this list, we iterate through it and start building a list we can sort on. To do this, we need to retrieve the contents of the sort column for each IID. Rather confusingly, this is done using the `Treeview.set()` method. `Treeview.set()` can be called with either two or three arguments, the first two always being the IID and CID of the cell we want to reference. If the third argument is present, `set()` will write that value to the cell. If it is omitted, `set()` will return the current value of that cell. There is no `Treeview.get()` method, so this is how we retrieve the value of a particular cell.

However, `set()` cannot be called on CID `#0`, even if we only want to retrieve the value. So we have added a check in case the user is sorting on that column, and return the IID instead. After obtaining the contents of the table cell, we add it with its IID to the `sort_index` list.

Now, we can sort the index:

```
sort_index.sort(reverse=reverse)
```

Because our table cell value is first in each tuple, the tuples will be sorted on it by default. Note that we've passed in the `reverse` value, to indicate which direction the list will be sorted in.

Now that we have a sorted list, we'll need to move each node accordingly. Add this code next:

```
for index, (_, iid) in enumerate(sort_index):
    tv.move(iid, parent, index)
```

The `enumerate()` function returns a tuple containing each item in the list with an integer indicating its index in the list. Since each item in our list is already a tuple, we're expanding that as well, giving us three variables: `index`, the index number of the list item; `_`, the sort value (which we no longer need, so we're naming it with an underscore); and `iid`.

For each item in the list, we call `Treeview.move()`, which takes three arguments: the IID of the row we want to move, the parent node to which we want to move it, and the index under that node into which it should be inserted. This will effectively sort the rows according to the order of the `sort_index` list.

So far, though, this has only sorted the immediate children of our root node. Now it is time to employ recursion so that we can sort all the child nodes; this takes only one additional line of code:

```
for index, (_, iid) in enumerate(sort_index):
    tv.move(iid, parent, index)
    sort(tv, col, parent=iid, reverse=reverse)
```

The last line of the `for` loop calls the `sort()` function again, this time passing in the child IID as the parent, and all other arguments the same. `sort()` will continue to call itself recursively until it reaches a node that has no children. In the case where a node has no children, that call to `sort()` will return without doing anything. In this way, all sub-directories containing files will be individually sorted by their own call to `sort()`.

To use our `sort()` function, we need to bind it to our column headers; we can do that once again by calling the `Treeview.heading()` method, like so:

```
for cid in ['#0', 'size', 'modified']:
    tv.heading(cid, command=lambda col=cid: sort(tv, col))
```

Here we're looping through each of our CID values, calling the `heading()` method to add a `command` argument to the heading. We're doing this in the form of a `lambda` function with a default argument for the CID.

Why use a default argument to pass in the CID? The body of a `lambda` function is evaluated using **late binding**, meaning that the value of the variables isn't established until the moment the body is run. By that point, `cid` will be the last value in the list (`'modified'`) no matter which column is calling the callback. The signature of the `lambda` function, however, is evaluated immediately, meaning the default value of `col` will be whatever `cid` is when we create the function.

One last fix to make to this function; typically, a sort will reverse with a second click of the header. We can implement this with a second set of calls to the `heading()` method inside the `sort()` function that will replace the `lambda` function with a reversed version.

Inside the `sort()` function, add this code:

```
if parent == '':
  tv.heading(
    col,
    command=lambda col=col: sort(tv, col, reverse=not reverse)
  )
```

Since the function is called recursively, we do not want to call this more than once per sorting; so, we'll only run this code for the root node, indicated by the `parent` value being a blank string. Inside that block, we reset the `lambda` function on the column being sorted, this time setting `reverse` to be the opposite of its current value.

Now when you run the application, you should be able to sort in both directions by clicking the headers of each column.

 Note that even though two of the columns contain numbers, they are sorted in **lexical order** – that is, as though they were strings, not numerical values. This is because the values put into a `Treeview` widget are implicitly converted to strings, so the sort value returned by `Treeview.set()` is a string. To sort these using a numerical sort, you would need to cast them back to integer or float values before sorting.

Using Treeview virtual events

To make it possible to respond to user interaction with the `Treeview` widget's items, the widget includes three virtual events, shown in this table:

Event	Generated
`<<TreeviewSelect>>`	When the user selects an item
`<<TreeviewOpen>>`	When a parent item is expanded to display child items
`<<TreeviewClose>>`	When an open parent item is closed again

For example, we can use these events to display some directory information in a status bar when the user opens a directory. First, let's add a status bar to the application:

```
# treeview_demo.py
status = tk.StringVar()
tk.Label(root, textvariable=status).pack(side=tk.BOTTOM)
```

Next, we'll create a callback for the event that will get some information about the opened directory and display it:

```
def show_directory_stats(*_):
  clicked_path = Path(tv.focus())
  num_children = len(list(clicked_path.iterdir()))
  status.set(
    f'Directory: {clicked_path.name}, {num_children} children'
  )
```

When a user clicks on an item to open it, that item gains focus, so we can use the treeview's focus() method to get the IID of the item that was clicked on. We've converted that to a Path and calculated the number of child objects in the directory using the Path object's iterdir() method. Then, we update the status variable with that information.

Now, we can bind this callback to the appropriate virtual events, like so:

```
tv.bind('<<TreeviewOpen>>', show_directory_stats)
tv.bind('<<TreeviewClose>>', lambda _: status.set(''))
```

In addition to binding the open event to our callback, we've bound the close event to a lambda function that clears the status control variable. Now, run the demo script and click on a directory. You should see some information show up in the status bar. Click it again and the information goes away.

Implementing a record list with Treeview

Now that we understand how to use the Treeview widget, it's time to implement a GUI that will allow us to browse the records in the CSV file and open them for editing. Let's take a moment to plan out what it is that we need to create:

- We want to lay out the CSV data in a table structure, similar to how it would look in a spreadsheet. This will be a flat table, not a hierarchy.

- Each table row will represent a record in the file. When a user double-clicks the row, or highlights it and presses *Enter*, we want the record form to open with the selected record.

- We don't really need to show every field in the table, since its purpose is merely to locate records for editing. Instead, we'll show only the rows that uniquely identify a record to the user. Namely, those are Date, Time, Lab, and Plot. We can also show the CSV row number.

- There isn't really a need to sort the data, so we won't implement sorting. The point is to visualize the CSV file, and its order shouldn't change.

To make all of this work, we'll first implement a widget, using a treeview, to display all the records and allow the selection of a record. Then, we'll go through the rest of the application components and integrate the new functionality. Let's get started!

Creating the RecordList class

We'll begin building our `RecordList` class by subclassing `tkinter.Frame`, just as we did with our record form:

```
# views.py, at the end of the file
class RecordList(tk.Frame):
  """Display for CSV file contents"""
```

To save ourselves from some repetitious code, we'll define our treeview's column properties and defaults as class attributes. This will also make it easier to tweak them later to suit our evolving needs. Add these properties to the class:

```
# views.py, inside the RecordList class

  column_defs = {
    '#0': {'label': 'Row', 'anchor': tk.W},
    'Date': {'label': 'Date', 'width': 150, 'stretch': True},
    'Time': {'label': 'Time'},
    'Lab': {'label': 'Lab', 'width': 40},
    'Plot': {'label': 'Plot', 'width': 80}
  }
  default_width = 100
  default_minwidth = 10
  default_anchor = tk.CENTER
```

Recall that we're going to be displaying `Date`, `Time`, `Lab`, and `Plot`. For the `#0` column, we'll show the CSV row number. We've also set the `width` and `anchor` values for some columns and configured the `Date` field to `stretch`. We'll use these values when configuring the `Treeview` widget in the `RecordList` class's initializer.

Moving on to the initializer method, let's begin it as follows:

```
# views.py, inside the RecordList class

def __init__(self, parent, *args, **kwargs):
  super().__init__(parent, *args, **kwargs)
  self.columnconfigure(0, weight=1)
  self.rowconfigure(0, weight=1)
```

Here, after running the superclass initializer, we've configured the grid layout to expand the first row and first column. This is where our Treeview widget will be placed, so we want it to take up any available space on the frame.

Configuring a Treeview widget

Now we're ready to create our Treeview widget, as follows:

```
# views.py, inside the RecordList.__init__() method

self.treeview = ttk.Treeview(
  self,
  columns=list(self.column_defs.keys())[1:],
  selectmode='browse'
)
self.treeview.grid(row=0, column=0, sticky='NSEW')
```

Here, we've created a Treeview widget and added it to the frame's layout. We've generated the columns list by retrieving the keys from the column_defs dictionary and excluding the first entry (#0). Remember that #0 is automatically created and should not be included in the columns list. We're also choosing the browse selection mode so that users can select only individual rows of the CSV file. This will be important in the way we communicate back to the controller.

Next, we'll configure the columns and headings of the Treeview widget by iterating through the column_defs dictionary:

```
for name, definition in self.column_defs.items():
  label = definition.get('label', '')
  anchor = definition.get('anchor', self.default_anchor)
  minwidth = definition.get('minwidth', self.default_minwidth)
  width = definition.get('width', self.default_width)
  stretch = definition.get('stretch', False)
  self.treeview.heading(name, text=label, anchor=anchor)
  self.treeview.column(
    name, anchor=anchor, minwidth=minwidth,
    width=width, stretch=stretch
  )
```

For each entry in column_defs, we're extracting the configuration values specified, then passing them to Treeview.heading() or Treeview.column() as appropriate. If the values aren't specified in the dictionary, the class default values will be used.

Finally, we're going to set up some bindings so that double-clicking or hitting *Enter* on a record will cause a record to be opened, like so:

```
# views.py, in RecordList.__init__()

    self.treeview.bind('<Double-1>', self._on_open_record)
    self.treeview.bind('<Return>', self._on_open_record)
```

The event `<Double-1>` refers to double-clicking mouse button 1 (that is, the left mouse button), while the `<Return>` event signifies striking the *Return* or *Enter* key (depending on how it's labeled on your hardware). These are both bound to an instance method called `_on_open_record()`. Let's go ahead and implement that method, like so:

```
# views.py, in the RecordList class

def _on_open_record(self, *args):
    self.event_generate('<<OpenRecord>>')
```

Since opening a record is something that happens outside the `RecordList` class, we're simply going to generate a custom event called `<<OpenRecord>>` that our `Application` class can listen for. Of course, `Application` will need to know which record to switch to, so we'll need a way for it to retrieve the currently selected row from the table. We'll do this using a feature of Python classes called a **property**. A class property appears to outside code to be a regular attribute, but runs a method to determine its value whenever it is evaluated. We could use a method here, of course, but using a property simplifies access for code outside the class. To create a property, we need to write a method that takes only `self` as an argument and returns a value, then use the `@property` decorator on it. We'll call our property `selected_id`; add it to the `RecordList` class like so:

```
@property
def selected_id(self):
    selection = self.treeview.selection()
    return int(selection[0]) if selection else None
```

In this method, we first retrieve a list of selected items using the `selection()` method. This method always returns a list, even when only one item is selected (and even when only one item *can* be selected). Since we only want to return one IID, we retrieve item 0 from the list if it exists, or `None` if nothing is selected. Remember that the IID of each row in our treeview is the CSV row number *as a string*. We'll want to convert that to an integer so that the controller can easily use it to locate the CSV record from the model.

Adding a scrollbar for the Treeview

Since the CSV files are going to get several hundred records long, the record list is bound to overflow the height of the application window, even if the application is maximized. If this should happen, it would be helpful for users to have a scroll bar to navigate the list vertically.

The Treeview widget does not have a scrollbar by default; it can be scrolled using the keyboard or mouse-wheel controls, but users would reasonably expect a scrollbar on a scrollable area like the Treeview to help them visualize the size of the list and their current position in it.

Fortunately, Ttk provides us with a Scrollbar widget that can be connected to our Treeview widget. Back in the initializer, let's add one:

```
# views.py , in RecordList.__init__()

    self.scrollbar = ttk.Scrollbar(
      self,
      orient=tk.VERTICAL,
      command=self.treeview.yview
    )
```

The Scrollbar class takes two important keyword arguments:

- orient: This argument determines whether it is a horizontal or vertical scroll. The strings horizontal or vertical can be used, or the Tkinter constants tk.HORIZONTAL and tk.VERTICAL.
- command: This argument provides a callback for scrollbar move events. The callback will be passed arguments describing the scroll movement that happened.

In this case, we set the callback to the treeview's yview() method, which is used to make the treeview scroll up and down. (The other option would be xview(), which would be used for horizontal scrolling.) The result is that when the scrollbar is moved, the position data is sent to Treeview.yview(), causing the treeview to scroll up and down.

We also need to connect our Treeview back to the scrollbar:

```
    self.treeview.configure(yscrollcommand=self.scrollbar.set)
```

This tells the Treeview to send its current vertical position to the Scrollbar widget's set() method whenever it is scrolled. If we don't do this, our scrollbar won't know how far down the list we've scrolled or how long the list is, and won't be able to set the size or location of the bar widget appropriately.

With our `Scrollbar` widget configured, we need to place it on the frame. By convention, it should be just to the right of the widget being scrolled, like so:

```
self.scrollbar.grid(row=0, column=1, sticky='NSW')
```

Notice we set `sticky` to north, south, and west. North and south make sure the scrollbar stretches the entire height of the widget, and west makes sure it's snug against the `Treeview` widget to the left of it.

Populating the Treeview

Now that we have created and configured our `Treeview` widget, we'll need a way to fill it with data. Let's create a `populate()` method to do this:

```
# views.py, in the RecordList class

def populate(self, rows):
    """Clear the treeview and write the supplied data rows to it."""
```

The `rows` argument will take a list of dictionaries, such as what is returned from the model's `get_all_records()` method. The idea is that the controller will fetch a list from the model and then pass it to the `RecordList` via this method.

Before refilling `Treeview`, we need to empty it:

```
# views.py, in RecordList.populate()

for row in self.treeview.get_children():
    self.treeview.delete(row)
```

To delete records from the treeview, we just need to call its `delete()` method with the IID of the row we want to delete. Here, we've retrieved all row IIDs using `get_children()`, then passed them one by one to `delete()`.

Now that the treeview is cleared, we can iterate through the `rows` list and populate the table:

```
cids = self.treeview.cget('columns')
for rownum, rowdata in enumerate(rows):
    values = [rowdata[cid] for cid in cids]
    self.treeview.insert('', 'end', iid=str(rownum),
        text=str(rownum), values=values)
```

The first thing we do here is create a list of all the CIDs we actually want to fetch from each row by retrieving the treeview's `columns` value.

Next, we iterate through the provided data rows using the `enumerate()` function to generate a row number. For each row, we'll create a list of values in the proper order using a list comprehension, then insert the list at the end of the `Treeview` widget with the `insert()` method. Notice that we're just using the row number (converted to a string) as both the IID and text for the first column of the row.

The last thing we need to do in this function is a small usability tweak. To make our record list keyboard-friendly, we need to initially focus the first item so that keyboard users can immediately start to navigate it via the arrow keys.

Doing this in a `Treeview` widget actually takes three method calls:

```
if len(rows) > 0:
    self.treeview.focus_set()
    self.treeview.selection_set('0')
    self.treeview.focus('0')
```

First, the `focus_set()` method moves focus to the `Treeview` widget. Next, `selection_set('0')` selects the first record in the list (note that the string 0 is the IID of the first record). Finally, `focus('0')` focuses the row with an IID of 0. And, of course, we only do this if there are any rows at all; if we called these methods on an empty `Treeview`, we would cause an exception.

The `RecordList` class is now complete. Now it's time to update the rest of the application to make use of it.

Adding the record list to the application

Now that we have a model capable of reading and updating data, and a `RecordList` widget capable of displaying the contents of a file, we need to make changes to the rest of the application to enable everything to work together. Specifically, we'll have to do the following:

- We'll need to update the `DataRecordForm` to be suitable for updating existing records as well as adding new ones.
- We'll need to update the layout of the `Application` window to accommodate the new record list.
- We'll need to create new `Application` callbacks to handle loading records and navigating the application.
- Finally, we'll need to update the main menu with new options for the added functionality.

Let's get started!

Modifying the record form for read and update

As long as we're still in `views.py`, let's scroll up to look at our `DataRecordForm` class and adjust it to make it capable of loading and updating existing records.

Take a moment and consider the following changes we'll need to make:

- The form will need to keep track of what record it's editing, or if it's a new record.
- The user will need some visual indication of what record is being edited.
- The form will need some way to load in a record provided by the controller.

Let's implement these changes.

Adding a current record property

To keep track of the current record being edited, we'll just use an instance property. In the `__init__()` method, just above where the first `LabelFrame` widget is created, add this code:

```
# views.py, in DataRecordForm.__init__()

    self.current_record = None
```

The `current_record` instance attribute is initially set to `None`, which we'll use to indicate that no record is loaded and the form is being used to create a new record. When we edit a record, we'll update this value to an integer referencing a row in the CSV data. We could use a Tkinter variable here, but there's no real advantage in this case, and we wouldn't be able to use `None` as a value.

Adding a label to show what is being edited

Since the form might now be editing an existing record or a new one, it would be helpful to the user to be able to see what is going on at a glance. To do that, let's add a `Label` to the top of the form to display the current record being edited, like so:

```
# views.py, in DataRecordForm.__init__()
    self.record_label = ttk.Label(self)
    self.record_label.grid(row=0, column=0)
```

We're placing the new `Label` widget in row `0`, column `0`, which is going to cause the other widgets to bump down one row. This won't affect our `Frame` widgets generated by `_add_frame()`, since they use implicit row numbers, but our Notes input and buttons will need to be moved. Let's update those widgets with a new position:

```
# views.py, in DataRecordForm.__init__()

    w.LabelInput(
        self, "Notes", field_spec=fields['Notes'],
        var=self._vars['Notes'], input_args={"width": 85, "height": 10}
    ).grid(sticky="nsew", row=4, column=0, padx=10, pady=10)

    buttons = tk.Frame(self)
    buttons.grid(sticky=tk.W + tk.E, row=5)
```

 Feel free to adjust the height of the Notes field if this change pushes the bottom of the form off-screen on your system!

Adding a load_record() method

The last thing to add to the `DataRecordForm` class is a method for loading in a new record. This method will need to accept a row number and dictionary of data from the controller and use them to update the `current_record`, the data in the form, and the label at the top. This will be a public method, since it will be called from the controller, and it will begin like this:

```
    def load_record(self, rownum, data=None):
        self.current_record = rownum
        if rownum is None:
            self.reset()
            self.record_label.config(text='New Record')
```

After updating the `current_record` attribute, we check to see if `rownum` is `None`. Recall that this indicates we're requesting a blank form to enter a new record. In that case, we'll call the `reset()` method and configure the label to show **New Record**.

Note that our `if` condition here checks specifically whether `rownum` is `None`; we can't just check the truth value of `rownum`, since 0 is a valid `rownum` for updating!

If we do have a valid `rownum`, we'll need it to act differently:

```
else:
    self.record_label.config(text=f'Record #{rownum}')
    for key, var in self._vars.items():
        var.set(data.get(key, ''))
        try:
            var.label_widget.input.trigger_focusout_validation()
        except AttributeError:
            pass
```

In this block, we first set the label appropriately with the row number we're editing. Then, we iterate over the form's _vars dictionary, retrieving matching values from the data dictionary that was passed to the function. Finally, we attempt to call the `trigger_focusout_validation()` method on each variable's input widget, since it's possible that the CSV file contains invalid data. If the input has no such method (that is, if we used a regular Tkinter widget rather than one of our validated widgets), we just do nothing.

Our form is now ready to load data records!

Updating the application layout

We have the form ready for loading records, and we have the record list ready to display them. We now need to incorporate all of this into the main application. First, though, we need to consider how we can accommodate both forms into our GUI layout.

Back in *Chapter 2, Designing GUI Applications*, we listed a few options for widgets that can help us group GUI components and cut down on the clutter of the GUI. We chose to use framed boxes to organize our data entry form; could we do the same again?

A quick mockup of the idea might look something like this:

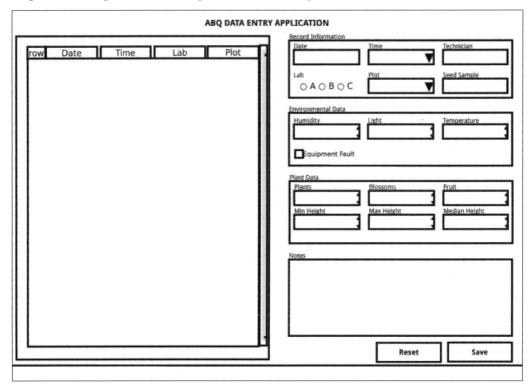

Figure 8.4: A layout of our application using side-by-side frames

This could work, but it's a lot of information on the screen at once, and the user doesn't really need to see all of this at the same time. The Record List is primarily for navigating, and the Data Entry form is for editing or entering data. It would probably be better if we showed only one component at a time.

Another option for organizing these two large components into the same GUI is the **notebook**. This type of widget can switch between multiple pages in a GUI by using tabs. Ttk offers us a Notebook widget that implements this feature; you've seen it before, back in *Chapter 1, Introduction to Tkinter*, when we looked at the IDLE configuration dialog. It can be seen here:

Figure 8.5: Ttk Notebook tabs in IDLE's config dialog

Let's take a quick look at the Ttk Notebook to see how it can be used in an application.

The Ttk Notebook widget

The Notebook widget is part of the ttk module, so we don't need to add any additional imports to use it. Creating one is fairly simple, as shown here:

```
# notebook_demo.py

import tkinter as tk
from tkinter import ttk

root = tk.Tk()
notebook = ttk.Notebook(root)
notebook.grid()
```

To add pages to the widgets, we need to create some child widgets. Let's create a couple of Label widgets with some informative content:

```
banana_facts = [
    'Banana trees are of the genus Musa.',
    'Bananas are technically berries.',
    'All bananas contain small amounts of radioactive potassium.'
    'Bananas are used in paper and textile manufacturing.'
]

plantain_facts = [
    'Plantains are also of genus Musa.',
    'Plantains are starchier and less sweet than bananas',
    'Plantains are called "Cooking Bananas" since they are'
    ' rarely eaten raw.'
]

b_label = ttk.Label(notebook, text='\n\n'.join(banana_facts))
p_label = ttk.Label(notebook, text='\n\n'.join(plantain_facts))
```

Here, we've created a couple of labels to be pages in our notebook. Typically your notebook page widgets would probably be Frame objects or subclasses like our RecordList or DataRecordForm components, but any widget can be used.

Rather than use a geometry manager to place these components in the notebook, we instead use the widget's add() method, like so:

```
notebook.add(b_label, text='Bananas', padding=20)
notebook.add(p_label, text='Plantains', padding=20)
```

The add() method creates a new page containing the given widget at the end of the notebook. If we wanted to insert the page somewhere other than the end, we could also use the insert() method, like so:

```
notebook.insert(1, p_label, text='Plantains', padding=20)
```

This method is identical, except that it takes an index number as the first argument. The page will be inserted at that index.

Both methods take a number of keyword arguments to configure the page and its tab, shown here:

Argument	Values	Description
text	String	The text shown on the label. By default, tabs are blank.
padding	Integer	Padding in pixels to add around the widget on the page.
sticky	Cardinal values (N, S, E, W)	Where to stick the widget on the notebook page. NSEW by default.
underline	Integer	Index of a letter in the text to bind for keyboard traversal.
image	Tkinter Photoimage	An image to display on the tab. See *Chapter 9, Improving the Look with Styles and Themes.*
compound	LEFT, RIGHT, CENTER, TOP, BOTTOM	If both text and image are specified, where to display the image in relation to the text.

The underline option is one we've seen before on other widgets (see *Chapter 3, Creating Basic Forms with Tkinter and Ttk Widgets*); however, in the ttk.Notebook widget, the option actually sets up a keyboard binding when we use it.

Let's try that out on our example notebook:

```
notebook.tab(0, underline=0)
notebook.tab(1, underline=0)
```

The tab() method, similar to a widget's config() method, allows us to change configuration options on the tab after we've already added it.

In this case, we're specifying underline=0 for both tabs, meaning the first letter of each tab's text string will be underlined. In addition, a keybinding will be created so that the key combination of *Alt* plus the underlined letter will switch to the matching tab. For example, in our application, we underlined letter 0 in the tab labeled **Banana**, so *Alt-B* will switch to that tab; we also underlined letter 0 in the tab labeled **Plantain**, so *Alt-P* will switch to the **Plantain** tab.

In addition to these bindings, we can enable general keyboard traversal of the notebook by calling its enable_traversal() method, like so:

```
notebook.enable_traversal()
```

If this method is called, *Control-Tab* will cycle through the tabs from left to right, and *Shift-Control-Tab* will cycle through them right to left.

Our code may sometimes need to select a tab; for this, we can use the select() method, like so:

```
notebook.select(0)
```

In this case, we're passing in the integer 0, which indicates the first tab. We could also pass in the name of the widget contained by the tab, like this:

```
notebook.select(p_label)
```

This works for the tab() method as well, and any method that requires a tab ID.

 The Notebook widget has a <<NotebookTabChanged>> virtual signal that is generated whenever the user changes tabs. You might use this to refresh pages or display help messages, for example.

Now that we're familiar with the notebook, let's incorporate one into our application.

Adding a notebook to our application

To add a Notebook widget to our layout, we'll need to create one in Application.__init__() before we create the DataRecordForm and RecordList widgets. Open the application.py file and locate the lines that currently create the DataRecordForm object, and let's create a notebook just above them, like so:

```
# application.py, in Application.__init__()

    self.notebook = ttk.Notebook(self)
```

```
self.notebook.enable_traversal()
self.notebook.grid(row=1, padx=10, sticky='NSEW')
```

Note that we're enabling keyboard traversal for our keyboard-only users, and sticking the widget to all sides of the grid. Now, update the lines that create the record form as follows:

```
self.recordform = v.DataRecordForm(
    self,
    self.model,
    self.settings
)
self.recordform.bind('<<SaveRecord>>', self._on_save)
self.notebook.add(self.recordform, text='Entry Form')
```

Here, we've simply removed the call to `self.recordform.grid()` and replaced it with `self.notebook.add()`. Next, let's create an instance of the `RecordList` class and add it to the notebook:

```
self.recordlist = v.RecordList(self)
self.notebook.insert(0, self.recordlist, text='Records')
```

Although we're adding the `RecordList` widget second, we'd like it to display first; so, we're using `insert()` to add it to the beginning of the tab list. That completes adding our pages, but let's start adding the necessary callbacks to make them work.

Adding and updating application callbacks

To bring all of these new widgets together in a functional way, we need to create a few callback methods on the `Application` object that will allow the application to get the user and the data to appropriate areas of the GUI when required. Specifically, we need to create four methods:

- A `_show_recordlist()` method we can use to display the record list when required
- A `_populate_recordlist()` method we can call to repopulate the record list from file data
- A `_new_record()` method that we can use to switch to a new, empty record
- An `_open_record()` method we can call to load a particular record into the form from the record list

We also need to fix the `Application._on_save()` method to make sure it's passing the model all the information necessary for both updating existing records and creating new records.

Let's go through each method, creating or updating the method and binding or calling it where appropriate.

The _show_recordlist() method

The first method we'll write is `_show_recordlist()`. This method is fairly simple, as you can see:

```python
# application.py, in the Application class

    def _show_recordlist(self, *_):
        self.notebook.select(self.recordlist)
```

It's almost not worth writing such a simple method, but by having this as a method we can easily bind it as a callback without resorting to a `lambda` function. Note that we could have written this as `self.notebook.select(0)`, but passing the widget reference is more explicit about our intentions. Should we decide to switch the order of the tabs, this method will continue to work without alteration.

One place we'll want to bind this callback is in our main menu. Back in the initializer for `Application`, let's add this method to our dictionary of callback functions, like so:

```python
# application.py, in Application.__init__()

    event_callbacks = {
      #...
      '<<ShowRecordlist>>': self._show_recordlist
    }
```

We'll add the necessary code for the menu itself in the next section. One other place we ought to call this method is at the end of `__init__()`, to ensure that the record list is displayed when the user opens the program. Add this at the end of `Application.__init__()`:

```python
# application.py, at the end of Application.__init__()

    self._show_recordlist()
```

The _populate_recordlist() method

The _populate_recordlist() method needs to retrieve data from the model and hand it to the record list's populate() method. We could write it like so:

```
def _populate_recordlist(self):
    rows = self.model.get_all_records()
    self.recordlist.populate(rows)
```

However, remember that CSVModel.get_all_records() can potentially raise an Exception if there are problems with the data in the file. It's the controller's responsibility to catch that exception and take appropriate action, so we'll write the method like this instead:

```
# application.py, in the Application class
def _populate_recordlist(self):
    try:
        rows = self.model.get_all_records()
    except Exception as e:
        messagebox.showerror(
            title='Error',
            message='Problem reading file',
            detail=str(e)
        )
    else:
        self.recordlist.populate(rows)
```

In this version, if we get an exception from get_all_records(), we'll display its message in an error dialog. It will then be up to the user to deal with that issue.

Now that we have this method, when should it be called? To begin with, it should be called whenever we select a new file to work with; so, let's add a call to it at the end of _on_file_select(), like so:

```
def _on_file_select(self, *_):
    # ...
    if filename:
        self.model = m.CSVModel(filename=filename)
        self._populate_recordlist()
```

In addition, we need to populate the list whenever we open the program, since it will automatically load the default file. Let's add a call to this method in the initializer just after creating the record list widget, as follows:

```
# application.py, in Application.__init__()
```

```
self.recordlist = v.RecordList(self)
self.notebook.insert(0, self.recordlist, text='Records')
self._populate_recordlist()
```

Finally, whenever we save a record, this should also update the record list, since the new record will have been added to the file. We need to add a call to the method in _on_save(), like this:

```
# application.py, in Application._on_save()

def _on_save(self, *_):

    #...
    self.recordform.reset()
    self._populate_recordlist()
```

Now our record list should stay in sync with the state of the file we're working on.

The _new_record() method

Next, we need a method that can open the data record form for the entry of a new record. Remember that our DataRecordForm.load_record() method can take None as arguments for the record number and data, indicating that we want to work on a new record, so we just need to write a callback that will do this.

Add this method to Application:

```
# application.py, in the Application class
def _new_record(self, *_):
    self.recordform.load_record(None)
    self.notebook.select(self.recordform)
```

After calling load_record() to prepare the form for a new record entry, we switch the notebook to the record form using notebook.select(). To enable users to call this method, we'll create a menu entry, so we'll need to add another entry to the event_callbacks dictionary.

In Application.__init__(), update the dictionary as follows:

```
# application.py, in Application.__init__()
    event_callbacks = {
        #...
        '<<NewRecord>>': self._new_record
    }
```

We'll add the necessary code to the menu in the next section.

The _open_record() method

Next, we need to write a callback method that will open an existing record when the user selects one from the record list. Add this method to the Application class:

```
# application.py, in the Application class
  def _open_record(self, *_):
    """Open the selected id from recordlist in the recordform"""
    rowkey = self.recordlist.selected_id
    try:
      record = self.model.get_record(rowkey)
    except Exception as e:
      messagebox.showerror(
        title='Error', message='Problem reading file', detail=str(e)
      )
    else:
      self.recordform.load_record(rowkey, record)
      self.notebook.select(self.recordform)
```

Remember that the RecordList object updates its selected_id property whenever a record is double-clicked or activated with the *Enter* key. We're retrieving this ID number and passing it to the model's get_record() method. Because get_record() calls get_all_records(), it can also potentially raise an exception if there is a problem with the file. Therefore, just as we did in _populate_recordlist(), we're catching the exception and displaying its message to the user in the case of problem.

If there's no problem, we've retrieved the data, and we need only pass the row number and dictionary of data to the form's load_record() method. Last of all, we call notebook.select() to switch to the record form view.

This callback needs to be called whenever the user chooses a file from the record list. Remember that we have written our RecordList objects to generate an <<OpenRecord>> event whenever this happens. Back in the application's initializer method, we need to set up a binding to this event.

Back in Application.__init__(), add this binding just after creating the RecordList widget, like so:

```
# application.py, inside Application.__init__()
    self.notebook.insert(0, self.recordlist, text='Records')
    self._populate_recordlist()
```

```
self.recordlist.bind('<<OpenRecord>>', self._open_record)
```

Now a double-click or *Enter* keypress will open the selected record in the form.

The _on_save() method

Finally, now that our model can handle updating existing records, we need to alter the call that we make to the model's `save_record()` method to make sure we're passing in all the information it needs to either update an existing record or insert a new one. Recall that we updated `save_record()` to take a `rownum` argument. When this value is `None`, a new record is added; when it is an integer, the indicated row number is updated.

In `Application._on_save()`, update the code as follows:

```python
# application.py, inside Application._on_save()
    data = self.recordform.get()
    rownum = self.recordform.current_record
    self.model.save_record(data, rownum)
```

Recall that the record form object's `current_record` holds the value of the current row being edited, or `None` if it is a new record. We can pass that value directly on to the model's `save()` method, ensuring that the data is saved to the proper place.

Main menu changes

The last change we need to make to our application is updating the main menu with the new options for navigating the application; specifically, we need to add a command for adding a new file, and a command for going back to the record list. Remember that the `Application` object has bound callbacks for these operations to the `<<ShowRecordlist>>` and `<<NewRecord>>` events, respectively.

There isn't really a standard location for commands that navigate around the application, so we'll create a new sub-menu called Go. Open the `mainmenu.py` file, and let's add a new sub-menu in the initializer method:

```python
# mainmenu.py, inside MainMenu.__init__()

    go_menu = tk.Menu(self, tearoff=False)
    go_menu.add_command(
      label="Record List",
      command=self._event('<<ShowRecordlist>>')
    )
```

```
go_menu.add_command(
    label="New Record",
    command=self._event('<<NewRecord>>')
)
```

Here, we've added a new sub-menu widget and added our two navigation commands, once again taking advantage of the _event() method, which gives us a reference to a method that generates the given event. Now add the Go menu between the File and Options menus, like so:

```
# mainmenu.py, at the end of MainMenu.__init__()

self.add_cascade(label='File', menu=file_menu)
self.add_cascade(label='Go', menu=go_menu)
self.add_cascade(label='Options', menu=options_menu)
```

Testing our program

At this point, you should be able to run the application and load in a sample CSV file as shown in the following screenshot:

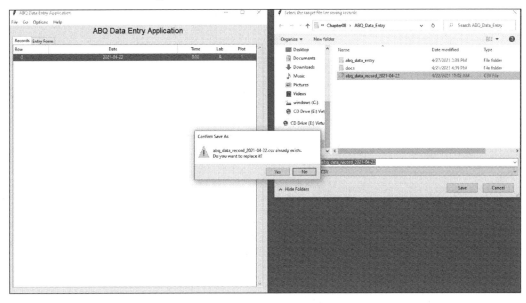

Figure 8.6: Selecting an existing file for writing with our new menu and record list

Make sure to try opening a record, editing and saving it, as well as inserting new records and opening different files. You should also test the following error conditions:

- Try opening a file that isn't a CSV file, or a CSV with incorrect fields. What happens?
- Open a valid CSV file, select a record for editing, then, before clicking **Save**, select a different or empty file. What happens?
- Open two copies of the program and point them to the saved CSV file. Try alternating edit or update actions between the programs. Note what happens.

Consider how you might address some of these issues; in some cases it may not be possible, and users will just have to be informed of the limitations. Also, if possible, try the last test on different operating systems. Are the results different?

Summary

We have changed our program from being an append-only data entry form to an application capable of loading, viewing, and updating data from existing files. In the process, you learned how to update our model so that it could read and update CSV files. You also explored the Treeview widget, including its basic use, virtual events, and column callbacks. You explored using the Treeview widget with hierarchical data structures by creating a file-browsing tool. You learned how to organize multi-form applications using a Notebook widget, and how to create scrolling interfaces using the Scrollbar widget. Finally, you integrated these concepts into the ABQ Data Entry application to address user needs.

In our next chapter, we'll be learning how to modify the look and feel of our application. We'll learn about using widget attributes, styles, and themes, as well as working with bitmapped graphics.

9
Improving the Look with Styles and Themes

While programs can be perfectly functional with plain text in shades of black, white, and gray, the subtle use of colors, fonts, and images can enhance the visual appeal and usability of even the most utilitarian applications. Your data entry application is no exception, and the current round of requests brought to you by your coworkers seems to require some retooling of the application's look and feel.

Specifically, you've been asked to address these points:

- Your manager has informed you that ABQ's corporate policy requires the company logo to be displayed on all in-house software. You've been provided with a corporate logo image to include in the application.
- The data entry staff have some readability issues with the form. They want more visual distinction between the sections of the form and more visibility for error messages.
- The data entry staff have also requested that you highlight records they've added or updated during a session to help them keep track of their work.

In addition to the user's requests, you'd like to make your application look more professional by adding some icons to your buttons and menu.

In this chapter, we're going to learn about some features of Tkinter that will help us to solve these issues:

- In *Working with images in Tkinter*, we'll learn how to add pictures and icons to our Tkinter GUI.

- In *Styling Tkinter widgets*, we'll learn how to adjust the colors and visual style of Tkinter widgets, both directly and using tags.
- In *Working with fonts in Tkinter*, we'll learn the ins and outs of using fonts in Tkinter.
- In *Styling Ttk widgets*, we'll learn how to adjust the look of Ttk widgets using styles and themes.

Working with images in Tkinter

To solve the corporate logo issue and spruce up our application with some icons, we're going to need to understand how to work with images in Tkinter. Tkinter provides access to image files through two classes: the `PhotoImage` class and the `BitmapImage` class. Let's see how these classes can help us add graphics to our application.

Tkinter PhotoImage

Many Tkinter widgets, including `Label` and `Button`, accept an `image` argument that allows us to display an image on the widget. This argument requires that we create and pass in a `PhotoImage` (or `BitmapImage`) object.

Making a `PhotoImage` object is fairly simple:

```
myimage = tk.PhotoImage(file='my_image.png')
```

`PhotoImage` is typically called with the keyword argument `file`, which is pointed to a file path. Alternatively, you can use the `data` argument to point to a `bytes` object containing image data. In either case, the resulting object can now be used wherever an `image` argument is accepted, such as in a `Label` widget:

```
mylabel = tk.Label(root, image=myimage)
```

Note that if we pass both an `image` and `text` argument to the `Label` initializer, only the image will be displayed by default. To display both, we need to also provide a value for the `compound` argument, which determines how the image and text will be arranged with respect to one another. For example:

```
mylabel_1 = tk.Label(root, text='Banana', image=myimage)
mylabel_2 = tk.Label(
    root,
    text='Plantain',
    image=myimage,
    compound=tk.LEFT
)
```

In this situation, the first label would only show the image; the text will not be displayed. In the second, since we have specified a compound value of tk.LEFT, the image will be displayed to the left of the text. compound can be any of LEFT, RIGHT, BOTTOM, or TOP (either lowercase strings or the Tkinter constants), and indicates where the image will be placed in relation to the text.

PhotoImage and variable scope

When using a PhotoImage object, it is critical to remember that your application must retain a reference to the object that will stay in scope for as long as the image is shown; otherwise, the image will not appear. To understand what this means, consider the following example:

```python
# image_scope_demo.py
import tkinter as tk

class App(tk.Tk):

    def __init__(self):
        super().__init__()
        smile = tk.PhotoImage(file='smile.gif')
        tk.Label(self, image=smile).pack()

App().mainloop()
```

If you run this example, you'll notice that no image gets displayed. That's because the variable holding the PhotoImage object, smile, is a local variable, and therefore destroyed as soon as the initializer returns. With no reference remaining to the PhotoImage object, it is discarded and the image vanishes, even though we've packed it into the layout.

Let's fix our script by making a simple change:

```python
    def __init__(self):
        super().__init__()
        self.smile = tk.PhotoImage(file='smile.gif')
        tk.Label(self, image=self.smile).pack()
```

In this case, we've stored the PhotoImage object in an instance variable, self.smile. Instance variables continue to exist until the object itself is destroyed, so the picture remains on the screen.

Using Pillow for extended image support

Image support in Tkinter is limited to GIF, PGM, PPM, and PNG files. If you're merely adding logos and icons to a GUI, these formats are probably sufficient, but for more graphics-heavy scenarios, the absence of such common formats as JPEG, SVG, and WebP becomes quite limiting. If you need support for any of these formats, you can use the `Pillow` library.

`Pillow` is not part of the standard library, nor shipped with most Python distributions. To install it, follow the instructions at `https://python-pillow.org`; though in most cases, you can simply enter the following at a terminal:

```
$ pip install -U pillow
```

This will install `Pillow` from the **Python Package Index** (**PyPI**). Pillow provides us with a class called `ImageTk`, which we can use to create `PhotoImage` objects from a wide range of image file formats. To see how it works, let's build a small Tkinter-based image viewer with filters.

Open a new file called `image_viewer_demo.py` and start with the following code:

```python
# image_viewer_demo.py

import tkinter as tk
from tkinter import ttk
from tkinter import filedialog
from PIL import Image, ImageTk, ImageFilter
```

Note that `Pillow` is imported as `PIL`. Pillow is actually a fork of a discontinued project called `PIL` (Python Imaging Library). For backward compatibility, it continues to use the `PIL` module name. From `PIL` we're importing the `Image` class, which is used to load images; the `ImageTk` class, which is used to convert Pillow `Image` objects for use in Tkinter; and `ImageFilter`, which will provide some filters for transforming our images.

Next, let's create our main application class for this app, `PictureViewer`:

```python
class PictureViewer(tk.Tk):

  def __init__(self, *args, **kwargs):
    super().__init__(*args, **kwargs)
    self.title('My Image Viewer')
    self.geometry('800x600')
    self.rowconfigure(0, weight=1)
    self.columnconfigure(0, weight=1)
```

This class begins by subclassing `Tk`, just as we did in our ABQ application, and the initializer starts with some basic window and grid layout configuration. Next, we'll create the GUI elements, like so:

```
self.image_display = ttk.Label(self)
self.image_display.grid(columnspan=3)
ttk.Button(
  self, text='Select image', command=self._choose_file
).grid(row=1, column=0, sticky='w')
```

So far, we just have a `Label` widget for displaying the image and a `Button` widget bound to an instance method, `self._choose_file()`. Let's create that method, like so:

```
def _choose_file(self):
  filename = filedialog.askopenfilename(
    filetypes=(
      ('JPEG files', '*.jpg *.jpeg *.JPG *.JPEG'),
      ('PNG files', '*.png *.PNG'),
      ('All files', '*.*')
    ))
  if filename:
    self.image = Image.open(filename)
    self.photoimage = ImageTk.PhotoImage(self.image)
    self.image_display.config(image=self.photoimage)
```

This method starts by asking the user for the filename with the `filedialog.askopenfilename()` method we learned about in *Chapter 7, Creating Menus with Menu and Tkinter Dialogs*. If the user selects a file, we call the `Image.open()` method to create a Pillow `Image` object from the file. `Image.open()` is a convenience method that simply takes a filename or path and returns an `Image` object containing that file's image data. Next, we create a Tkinter `PhotoImage` object by passing the `Image` object to `ImageTk.PhotoImage()`. Finally, we update our `image_display` widget with the new `PhotoImage` object.

Using this approach, you can display a much wider variety of image formats in Tkinter — Pillow has full read support for over 40 different formats! However, Pillow offers far more than just image format conversions. We can also use it to edit or transform our images in a variety of ways. For example, we can apply filtering to our Pillow `Image` objects. Let's add this feature to the demo application.

Back up in `PictureViewer.__init__()`, add the following GUI code:

```
self.filtervar = tk.StringVar()
filters =[
```

```
        'None', 'BLUR', 'CONTOUR', 'DETAIL', 'EDGE_ENHANCE',
        'EDGE_ENHANCE_MORE', 'EMBOSS', 'FIND_EDGES',
        'SHARPEN', 'SMOOTH', 'SMOOTH_MORE'
    ]
    ttk.Label(self, text='Filter: ').grid(
        row=1, column=1, sticky='e'
    )
    ttk.OptionMenu(
        self, self.filtervar, 'None', *filters
    ).grid(row=1, column=2)
    self.filtervar.trace_add('write', self._apply_filter)
```

The `filters` list contains the names of all the filter objects Pillow provides that we can apply to an `Image` object (these can be found in the `Pillow` documentation). We've added all these to an `OptionMenu` along with the string `None`. The `OptionMenu` widget is then bound to the `filtervar` control variable, on which we've added a trace that calls the `_apply_filter()` method.

The `_apply_filter()` method looks like this:

```
    def _apply_filter(self, *_):
        filter_name = self.filtervar.get()
        if filter_name == 'None':
            self.filtered_image = self.image
        else:
            filter_object = getattr(ImageFilter, filter_name)
            self.filtered_image = self.image.filter(filter_object)
        self.photoimage = ImageTk.PhotoImage(self.filtered_image)
        self.image_display.config(image=self.photoimage)
```

First, this method retrieves the filter name from the control variable. If it's `None`, we set `self.filtered_image` to the current `self.image` object. Otherwise, we retrieve the filter object from the `ImageFilter` module using `getattr()` and apply the filter to our Pillow `Image` object using its `filter()` method.

Finally, we update the displayed image in the application by creating a new `PhotoImage` object and updating the configuration of the `Label` widget.

To see this program in action, add the last two lines to the script:

```
app = PictureViewer()
app.mainloop()
```

You should see something that looks like this:

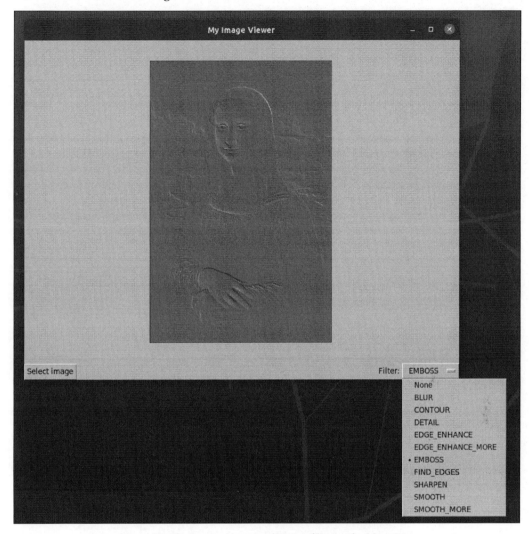

Figure 9.1: The image viewer application, filtering the Mona Lisa

Now that we have a handle on using images in Tkinter, let's apply this knowledge to the ABQ Data Entry application.

Adding the company logo to ABQ Data Entry

With our knowledge of `PhotoImage`, adding the company logo to our program should be simple. We've been provided with several PNG files of the company logo in different sizes.

You could simply copy one into the application root directory and add something like this to the `Application` class's initializer:

```
# application.py, in Application.__init__()

    self.logo = tk.PhotoImage(file='abq_logo_32x20.png')
    ttk.Label(
      self, text="ABQ Data Entry Application",
      font=("TkDefaultFont", 16),
      image=self.logo, compound=tk.LEFT
    ).grid(row=0)
```

In this snippet, we've created a `PhotoImage` object from a file path, storing it as an instance variable so it does not go out of scope. Then, we've assigned this object to the `image` argument of the application's title label, also adding the `compound` argument so that the image is displayed to the left of the text.

If you run the application from a terminal inside the application root directory, this approach works fine. However, if you run it from any other directory, the image won't appear. For example, try this from the command line in the directory containing your root:

```
$ cd ABQ_Data_Entry
$ python3 abq_data_entry.py
# the image will show when you run it this way.
$ cd ..
$ python3 ABQ_Data_Entry/abq_data_entry.py
# the image will not show this way.
```

Why is this, and what can we do about it?

Dealing with the image path problem

When you give Python only a filename (with no path) to open, it assumes the file is in the **current working directory**. This is the directory the user was in when running the application. In the example above, when we ran the program the first time, our working directory was the application's root directory. The image was in that directory, so Python found it. The second time we ran it, our working directory was the parent directory of the application root. Python looked for the image in *that* directory, and it wasn't found.

If you know where your file is on the system, you can provide an absolute path; for example, if you're on Windows 10 and the application root is on your home directory, you could do this:

```
self.logo = tk.PhotoImage(
    file=r'C:\Users\myuser\ABQ_Data_Entry\abq_logo_32x20.png'
)
```

The problem, though, is that this reference would break if we put the code anywhere else on the system. Remember, as well, that our application needs to run on Linux and Windows, so providing an absolute path like this won't work across different platforms.

The r in front of the path string above makes it a raw string. When a string is marked as raw, Python does not interpret backslash escape sequences in the string. This makes raw strings useful for file paths on Windows, which uses the backslash for a path separator. See *Chapter 10, Maintaining Cross-Platform Compatibility,* for more details on solving cross-platform path issues.

A more robust approach is to provide a relative path from some known point. Every Python script has access to a variable called __file__, which is a string containing the path to the script file. We can use this variable in conjunction with the pathlib module to locate files inside our application root directory.

For example, we could rewrite our PhotoImage object's configuration like this:

```
self.logo = tk.PhotoImage(
    Path(__file__).parent.parent / 'abq_logo_32x20.png'
)
```

Since we are in application.py, __file__ points to ABQ_Data_Entry/abq_data_entry/ application.py. We can use this reference point to find the parent of the parent directory, where the image files are located. This will enable Python to successfully find the images no matter what the current working directory is.

This approach is functionally acceptable, but it's rather cluttered and clumsy to do these kinds of path manipulation every time we need to access an image file. Let's employ some of our organizational skills from *Chapter 6, Planning for the Expansion of Our Application,* to put the images in their own module.

Under the abq_data_entry directory, create a new directory called images, and place within it an appropriately sized PNG file that we can use in our application (the image in the example code has an 8x5 aspect ratio, so in this case, we're using 32x20).

Next, create an __init__.py file inside the images folder, in which we'll add the following code:

```
# images/__init__.py
from pathlib import Path

IMAGE_DIRECTORY = Path(__file__).parent

ABQ_LOGO_16 = IMAGE_DIRECTORY / 'abq_logo-16x10.png'
ABQ_LOGO_32 = IMAGE_DIRECTORY / 'abq_logo-32x20.png'
ABQ_LOGO_64 = IMAGE_DIRECTORY / 'abq_logo-64x40.png'
```

In this case, __file__ points to ABQ_Data_Entry/abq_data_entry/images/__init__.py, so we can use that point of reference to get paths to all the image files we put in ABQ_Data_Entry/abq_data_entry/images/.

Now, our application.py module can import the images module like this:

```
# application.py, at the top

from . import images
```

Once imported, we can reference the image paths for our PhotoImage object easily:

```
# application.py, inside Application.__init__()

    self.logo = tk.PhotoImage(file=images.ABQ_LOGO_32)
    ttk.Label(
      self, text="ABQ Data Entry Application",
      font=("TkDefaultFont", 16),
      image=self.logo, compound=tk.LEFT
    ).grid(row=0)
```

Now, regardless of what working directory you run the script from, you should see the title looking something like this:

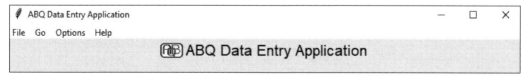

Figure 9.2: The ABQ Data Entry application sporting a company logo

Setting a window icon

Currently, our application's window icon (the icon that shows up in both the window decorations and in the operating system's taskbar) is the Tkinter logo, which is the default for any Tkinter application. It would make more sense for us to use the company logo image for this icon. How can we make this happen?

As a subclass of `Tk`, our `Application` object has a method called `iconphoto()` which should, given a path to an icon file, set the window icon appropriately. Unfortunately, this method is a bit inconsistent in its results across platforms. Let's go ahead and add it to our initializer as follows and see what happens. Add this code just after the call to `super().__init__()`:

```
# application.py, inside Application.__init__()
    self.taskbar_icon = tk.PhotoImage(file=images.ABQ_LOGO_64)
    self.iconphoto(True, self.taskbar_icon)
```

The first line creates another `PhotoImage` object, referencing a larger version of the logo. Next, we execute `self.iconphoto()`. The first argument indicates whether we want this icon to be the default across all new windows, or whether it's only for this window. Passing `True` here makes it the default for all. The second argument is our `PhotoImage` object.

Now, when you run the application, you should see an ABQ icon being used as the window icon; how it is used depends on the platform. For example, on Windows, it shows up in the window decorations, as seen here:

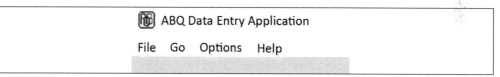

Figure 9.3: The ABQ logo as a taskbar icon

Here's a summary of how the `iconphoto` is used on different platforms:

- On Linux, it will depend on your desktop environment, but typically, it will show up in both the taskbar or dock and on the window decorations
- On macOS, it will show up as the icon in the dock, but not in the global menu or on the window itself
- On Windows 10, it will appear on the window decorations, but not on the taskbar

Part of the reason for this inconsistency is that our application is a script being executed by Python, so from the operating system's point of view, the program we're running isn't ABQ Data Entry, but rather Python. For that reason, you may see the Python logo appearing instead of the ABQ logo on your platform. We'll address this further when we package our application in *Chapter 16, Packaging with setuptools and cxFreeze* .

Adding icons to buttons and menus

While not required by the users or company, you feel your application would look a little more impressive with some simple icons accompanying the text on your buttons and menu items. Unfortunately, Tkinter does not ship with any icon themes, nor is it able to access the operating system's built-in icon themes. So, in order to use icons, we'll have to first acquire some PNG or GIF images to use. These can be acquired from a number of sources online or, of course, you can create your own.

 The example code comes with some icons taken from the **Open-Iconic** project, which features a large selection of standard application icons released under an MIT license. You can find this project at `https://useiconic.com/open`.

Assuming you have obtained some icon files, let's add them to the `images` folder and then update `images/__init__.py` as follows:

```
SAVE_ICON = IMAGE_DIRECTORY / 'file-2x.png'
RESET_ICON = IMAGE_DIRECTORY / 'reload-2x.png'
LIST_ICON = IMAGE_DIRECTORY / 'list-2x.png'
FORM_ICON = IMAGE_DIRECTORY / 'browser-2x.png'
```

Here, we've added images for the **Save** and **Reset** buttons, as well as images to represent the Record List and Data Entry Form portions of the GUI. We can now begin adding these to our application; for example, let's add them to the buttons in the `DataRecordForm` frame. Start by importing `images` into `views.py`, like so:

```
# views.py, at the top


from . import images
```

Now, in the initializer, let's update the buttons in the `DataRecordForm` with image icons:

```
# views.py, inside DataRecordForm.__init__()
```

```python
self.save_button_logo = tk.PhotoImage(file=images.SAVE_ICON)
self.savebutton = ttk.Button(
  buttons, text="Save", command=self._on_save,
  image=self.save_button_logo, compound=tk.LEFT
)
#...
self.reset_button_logo = tk.PhotoImage(file=images.RESET_ICON)
self.resetbutton = ttk.Button(
  buttons, text="Reset", command=self.reset,
  image=self.reset_button_logo, compound=tk.LEFT
)
```

Now, the form should look something like this:

Figure 9.4: The buttons in the Data Record Form, now with icons

Remember that we can also add images to the Notebook widget's tabs. Back in application.py, locate the code in __init__() that creates the notebook tabs and let's update it as follows:

```python
# application.py, inside Application.__init__()

  self.recordform_icon = tk.PhotoImage(file=images.FORM_ICON)
  self.recordform = v.DataRecordForm(
    self, self.model, self.settings
  )
  self.notebook.add(
    self.recordform, text='Entry Form',
    image=self.recordform_icon, compound=tk.LEFT
  )
  #...
  self.recordlist_icon = tk.PhotoImage(file=images.LIST_ICON)
  self.recordlist = v.RecordList(self)
  self.notebook.insert(
    0, self.recordlist, text='Records',
    image=self.recordlist_icon, compound=tk.LEFT
  )
```

It's as simple as adding an image argument to the notebook's add() and insert() method calls. As with buttons and labels, be sure to include the compound argument, or else only the icon will be displayed. Now, when we run the application, the tabs should look like this:

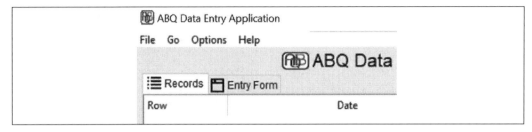

Figure 9.5: The notebook tabs with icons

As you can see, the workflow for using the icons is fairly consistent:

1. Create a PhotoImage object, making sure a reference to it will stay in scope.
2. Pass the object to the image argument of the widget you want it to appear on.
3. Pass the widget's compound argument to specify the layout for widgets that will display both text and the image.

Rather than creating an individual class attribute for every icon, you may find it more efficient to store them in a dictionary object. For example, we should do this in the MainMenu class, where we'll need a lot of icons. Import images into mainmenu.py, just as you did in the other two files, and let's create a new _create_icons() instance method in MainMenu, as follows:

```
# mainmenu.py, in the MainMenu class

def _create_icons(self):

    self.icons = {
        'file_open': tk.PhotoImage(file=images.SAVE_ICON),
        'record_list': tk.PhotoImage(file=images.LIST_ICON),
        'new_record': tk.PhotoImage(file=images.FORM_ICON),
    }
```

Here, we're using an instance method to create a dictionary of PhotoImage objects and storing it as an instance attribute, self.icons. You might wonder why we don't create MainMenu.icons as a class attribute, similar to the fields dictionaries we created for our models.

The reason is that `PhotoImage` objects, like all Tkinter objects, cannot be created until an instance of `Tk` has been created (in our case, the `Application` object).

Class definitions, and therefore class attributes, are executed by Python before the main thread of execution begins, so there would be no `Application` object when this class is defined.

We can call this method inside the initializer to make sure `self.icons` is populated before we define the menu; add that code like so:

```python
# mainmenu.py, inside the MainMenu class
  def __init__(self, parent, settings, **kwargs):
    super().__init__(parent, **kwargs)
    self.settings = settings
    self._create_icons()
```

Now, each menu item can access its `PhotoImage` object via the dictionary, as follows:

```python
# mainmenu.py, inside MainMenu.__init__()

    file_menu.add_command(
      label="Select file…", command=self._event('<<FileSelect>>'),
      image=self.icons['file_open'], compound=tk.LEFT
    )
    #...
    go_menu.add_command(
      label="Record List", command=self._event('<<ShowRecordlist>>'),
      image=self.icons['record_list'], compound=tk.LEFT
    )
    go_menu.add_command(
      label="New Record", command=self._event('<<NewRecord>>'),
      image=self.icons['new_record'], compound=tk.LEFT
    )
```

Now our menu boasts some professional-looking icons, as shown here:

Figure 9.6: The Go menu, with some nice icons

Using BitmapImage

Using `PhotoImage` with PNG files is more than sufficient for our application, but there is one other option for images in Tkinter that bears mentioning: `BitmapImage`. The `BitmapImage` object is similar to `PhotoImage`, but works exclusively with **XBM** (X11 Bitmap) files. This is a very old image format that only allows for monochromatic images. Despite being monochromatic, XBM images are not compressed, and therefore not smaller than PNG files of equivalent size. The only real advantage to a `BitmapImage` object is that we can tell Tkinter to render it with any colors we wish.

To see how this works, let's add a few XBM files to our `images` module; copy in some XBM files and then add them to __init__.py, like so:

```
QUIT_BMP = IMAGE_DIRECTORY / 'x-2x.xbm'
ABOUT_BMP = IMAGE_DIRECTORY / 'question-mark-2x.xbm'
```

 Some XBM files are included in the sample code; alternatively, you can convert your own image files to XBM using image editing software like the GNU Image Manipulation Program from `https://www.gimp.org`.

Now, back in `mainmenu.py`, let's add them to our `icons` dictionary, as follows:

```
# mainmenu.py, in MainMenu._create_icons()

    self.icons = {
      #...
      'quit': tk.BitmapImage(
        file=images.QUIT_BMP, foreground='red'
      ),
      'about': tk.BitmapImage(
        file=images.ABOUT_BMP,
        foreground='#CC0', background='#A09'
      )
    }
```

As you can see, creating a `BitmapImage` is identical to creating a `PhotoImage` object, but with the possibility of specifying `foreground` and `background` colors for the image. Once created, adding them to the menu item is identical to using `PhotoImage`, as shown here:

```
# mainmenu.py, inside MainMenu.__init__()
```

```
help_menu.add_command(
    label='About…', command=self.show_about,
    image=self.icons['about'], compound=tk.LEFT
)
#...
file_menu.add_command(
    label="Quit", command=self._event('<<FileQuit>>'),
    image=self.icons['quit'], compound=tk.LEFT
)
```

Now the **Help** menu should have a colorful icon, as shown here:

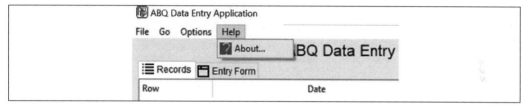

Figure 9.7: The now colorful About icon

You may find `BitmapImage` objects useful if you want to reuse a single file with different colors, or perhaps dynamically change the color scheme of your icons to fit with a theme or indicate some kind of state. Most of the time, though, using `PhotoImage` objects will be preferable.

These images have dramatically changed the look of our application, but the rest of it is still a rather drab gray. In the next sections, we'll work on updating its colors.

Styling Tkinter widgets

Tkinter has essentially two styling systems: the old Tkinter widgets system, and the newer Ttk system. Although we are using Ttk widgets wherever possible, there are still situations where regular Tkinter widgets are required, so it's good to know both systems. Let's take a look first at the older Tkinter system and apply some styling to the Tkinter widgets in our application.

Widget color properties

As you saw in *Chapter 1, Introduction to Tkinter*, basic Tkinter widgets allow you to change two color values: the foreground color, meaning mainly the color of text and borders, and the background color, meaning the rest of the widget. These can be set using the `foreground` and `background` arguments, or their aliases, `fg` and `bg`.

For example, we can set the colors of a label like so:

```python
# tkinter_color_demo.py
import tkinter as tk


l = tk.Label(text='Hot Dog Stand!', fg='yellow', bg='red')
```

The values for the colors can be color name strings or CSS-style RGB hex strings.

For example, this code produces the same effect:

```python
l2 = tk.Label(
  text='Also Hot Dog Stand!',
  foreground='#FFFF00',
  background='#FF0000'
)
```

 There are over 700 named colors recognized by Tkinter, roughly corresponding to those recognized by the X11 display server used on Linux and Unix, or the CSS named colors used by web designers. For a complete list, see `https://www.tcl.tk/man/tcl8.6/TkCmd/colors.htm`.

Using widget properties on the MainMenu

We aren't using many Tkinter widgets in our views, preferring Ttk as much as possible. One place where we *are* using a Tkinter widget is our application's main menu. We can use the main menu to demonstrate how Tkinter widget colors can be configured.

 Note that setting colors and other appearance options on the menu system *only* works consistently on Linux or BSD. The effect on Windows or macOS is incomplete, so readers on those platforms may see incomplete results. In *Chapter 10, Maintaining Cross-Platform Compatibility*, we'll redesign our menu so that these differences in compatibility are accounted for.

The `tk.Menu` widget accepts the following appearance-related arguments:

Argument	Values	Description
background	Color string	The color of the background under normal conditions
foreground	Color string	The color of the foreground (text) under normal conditions
borderwidth	Integer	The width of the widget border, in pixels, under normal conditions
activebackground	Color string	The background color when the widget is active (being hovered over or selected via the keyboard)
activeforeground	Color string	The foreground (text) color when the widget is active
activeborderwidth	Integer	The border width, in pixels, of the widget when active
disabledforeground	Color string	The foreground (text) color when the widget is disabled
relief	One of the Tkinter constants RAISED, SUNKEN, FLAT, RIDGE, SOLID, or GROOVE	The style of the border drawn around the widget

Note that there are versions of background, foreground, and borderwidth for both the normal and active states, and a version of foreground for the disabled state. Depending on what is applicable to the widget, many Tkinter widgets support additional arguments for certain states, conditions, or features; for example, widgets with selectable text like the Entry widget support highlightbackground and highlightforeground arguments to specify the colors used when text is selected.

 The Tcl/Tk documentation at https://www.tcl.tk/man/ provides the most complete reference for widget-specific options, including styling options.

Open up the `mainmenu.py` file and let's add some styles to our menu inside the initializer method:

```
# mainmenu.py, inside MainMenu.__init__()

    self.configure(
      background='#333',
      foreground='white',
      activebackground='#777',
      activeforeground='white',
      'relief'=tk.GROOVE
    )
```

Execute the application, and note the menu's appearance. On Linux or BSD, it should look something like this:

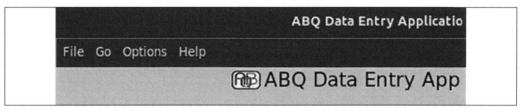

Figure 9.8: A styled Tkinter menu on Ubuntu Linux

Note that the styling does not go past the main menu; the sub-menus are still the default black-on-gray. To make the menu consistent, we'll need to apply these styles to all the sub-menus as well. To avoid a lot of repetition, let's change our code so that the styles are stored in a dictionary, which we can then unpack in each call to `tk.Menu`. Update the code like so:

```
# mainmenu.py, inside MainMenu.__init__()

    self.styles = {
      'background': '#333',
      'foreground': 'white',
      'activebackground': '#777',
      'activeforeground': 'white',
      'relief': tk.GROOVE
    }
    self.configure(**self.styles)
```

Now, to add the styling to each sub-menu, we just need to add **self.styles to each sub-menu initialization, like so:

```python
# mainmenu.py, inside MainMenu.__init__()

    help_menu = tk.Menu(self, tearoff=False, **self.styles)
    #...
    file_menu = tk.Menu(self, tearoff=False, **self.styles)
    #...
    options_menu = tk.Menu(self, tearoff=False, **self.styles)
    #...
    go_menu = tk.Menu(self, tearoff=False, **self.styles)
```

Assuming your platform supports menu styling, you should now see the styles applied to the sub-menus as well.

Styling widget content with tags

Foreground and background colors are sufficient for simple widgets such as buttons and labels, but more complex Tkinter widgets like the Text widget or the Ttk Treeview widget rely on a **tag**-based system for more detailed styling. A **tag** in Tkinter is a named region of a widget's content to which color and font settings can be applied. To see how this works, let's build a crude, but pretty, Python terminal emulator.

Open a new file called tags_demo.py, and we'll start by creating a Text widget to store the terminal input and output:

```python
# tags_demo.py
import tkinter as tk

text = tk.Text(width=50, height=20, bg='black', fg='lightgreen')
text.pack()
```

Here, we've used the fg and bg arguments to set up a green-on-black terminal theme, a classic combination popular with programmers. Rather than having only green text, though, let's configure different colors for our prompt and our interpreter output.

To do this, we'll define some tags:

```python
text.tag_configure('prompt', foreground='magenta')
text.tag_configure('output', foreground='yellow')
```

The `tag_configure()` method allows us to declare and configure tags on the `Text` widget. We've created one called `prompt` with magenta text for the shell prompt, and another called `output` with yellow text for the Python output. Note that we aren't restricted to a single configuration argument here; we could conceivably pass a `font` or `background` argument as well, if we wished.

To insert text with a given tag applied, we do the following:

```
text.insert('end', '>>> ', ('prompt',))
```

As you may remember, the `Text.insert()` method takes an index and string as its first two arguments. Notice the third argument: this is a tuple of the tags with which we want to mark the inserted text. This value must be a tuple, even if you're only using one tag; naturally, you can include as many tags as you wish.

If you add `text.mainloop()` to the end of the code and run it, you'll see that we have a black text entry window with a magenta prompt; however, if you type anything, your text will show up in green (the widget's default foreground color). So far so good; now, let's make it execute some Python.

Create a function just before the `mainloop()` call:

```
def on_return(*args):
    cmd = text.get('prompt.last', 'end').strip()
```

Recall that, when retrieving text from a `Text` widget, we're required to supply start and end indices for the text we want to retrieve. We can utilize tag names in our index values, as we've done here: `prompt.last` tells Tkinter to fetch the text starting *after* the end of the region tagged `prompt`.

Next, let's execute the entered command:

```
if cmd:
    try:
        output = str(eval(cmd))
    except Exception as e:
        output = str(e)
```

If the `cmd` variable actually contains anything, we'll try to execute it with `eval()`, and then store a string of the response value as output. If it raises an exception, we'll cast our exception to a string and set that as the output.

 Note that `eval()` only works on expressions, so our "shell" won't be able to handle loops, conditionals, or other statements.

Then, we'll just show our output, like so:

```
# (still in the if block)
text.insert('end', '\n' + output, ('output',))
```

Here, we've inserted our output string, prefixed with a newline and tagged as output.

We'll finish off the function by giving the user back a prompt:

```
text.insert('end', '\n>>> ', ('prompt',))
return 'break'
```

Note that we also return the string break here. This tells Tkinter to ignore the original event that triggered the callback. Since we're going to trigger this from a *Return/Enter* keystroke, we want to ignore that keystroke after we're finished. If we don't, the keystroke will be executed *after* our function returns, inserting the newline after the display of the prompt and leaving the user on the line under the prompt.

Finally, we need to bind our function to the *Return* key:

```
text.bind('<Return>', on_return)
```

 Note that the event for the *Enter/Return* key is always <Return>, even on non-Apple hardware (where the key is more commonly labeled "Enter").

Make sure to add a call to text.mainloop() at the end of the script, and then launch the application. You should get something like this:

```
tk                                    —  □  ⊗
>>> 2 + 5
7
>>> 'B' + 'n'.join('aaa')
Banana
>>>
```

Figure 9.9: The colorful Python shell

While this shell won't be supplanting IDLE any time soon, it does look rather nice, don't you think?

Styling our record list with tags

Although Treeview is a Ttk widget, it uses tags to control the styling of individual rows. We can use this capability to address another of the requests you've gotten from the data entry staff – specifically, that they'd like the record list to highlight the records updated and inserted during the current session.

The first thing we'll need to do is have our RecordList object keep track of which rows have been updated or inserted during the session.

We'll start in RecordList.__init__() by creating a couple of instance variables to store the updated or inserted rows:

```
# views.py, inside RecordList.__init__()
    super().__init__(parent, *args, **kwargs)
    self._inserted = list()
    self._updated = list()
```

When a record is inserted or updated, we'll need to append its row number to the appropriate list. Since RecordList doesn't know when a record is updated or inserted, we'll have to create some public methods that the Application object can call to append to the lists. Create these two methods in the RecordList class:

```
# views.py, inside RecordList
  def add_updated_row(self, row):
    if row not in self._updated:
      self._updated.append(row)

  def add_inserted_row(self, row):
    if row not in self._inserted:
      self._inserted.append(row)
```

Each method takes a row number and appends it to the corresponding list. To avoid duplicates, we only do so if the row is not in the list. Now, to use these methods, we'll have to update the Application._on_save() method so that it calls the appropriate update method *after* the record is saved, but *before* we repopulate the record list.

In _on_save(), right after calling self.model.save_record(), add these lines:

```
# application.py, in Application._on_save()

    if rownum is not None:
      self.recordlist.add_updated_row(rownum)
```

Updates have a `rownum` value that is not `None`, but could be 0, so we explicitly test for `None` here rather than just using `if rownum:`. If `rownum` is not `None`, we'll append it to the updated list.

Now, we need to deal with inserts:

```
else:
    rownum = len(self.model.get_all_records()) -1
    self.recordlist.add_inserted_row(rownum)
```

Inserted records are a little more troublesome in that we don't have a row number readily available to record. We do know that an insert is always appended to the end of the file, though, so its row number should be one smaller than the number of rows in the file.

Our inserted and updated records will be kept until the end of the program session (when the user exits the program) or until the user selects a new file to work on. If the user selects a new file, we will need to clear out the lists since we're working with a completely new set of records.

Once again, since `RecordList` doesn't know when this happens, we'll need to create a public method that clears the lists. Add the following `clear_tags()` method to the `RecordList` class:

```
# views.py, inside RecordList
  def clear_tags(self):
    self._inserted.clear()
    self._updated.clear()
```

Now we need the `Application` class to call this whenever a new file is selected for saving, which happens in `Application._on_file_select()`. Add a call to the method just before repopulating the record list:

```
# application.py inside Application._on_file_select()

    if filename:
      self.model = m.CSVModel(filename=filename)
      self.recordlist.clear_tags()
      self._populate_recordlist()
```

Now that we have these lists updating correctly, we need to use them to color-code the list items.

To do this, we first need to configure tags with appropriate colors. Our data entry staff feel that light green would be a sensible color for inserted records, and light blue for updated.

Add the following code at the end of RecordList.__init__():

```
# views.py, inside RecordList.__init__()
    self.treeview.tag_configure(
        'inserted', background='lightgreen'


    self.treeview.tag_configure('updated', background='lightblue')
```

Just as we did with the Text widget earlier, we call the TreeView object's tag_configure() method to connect background color settings with our tag names. To add the tags to our TreeView rows, we'll need to update the populate() method so that as rows are inserted, the appropriate tag (if any) is added.

Inside the populate() method's for loop, just before inserting the row, we'll add this code:

```
# views.py, inside RecordList.populate()


    for rownum, rowdata in enumerate(rows):
        values = [rowdata[cid] for cid in cids]
        if rownum in self._inserted:
          tag = 'inserted'
        elif rownum in self._updated:
          tag = 'updated'
        else:
          tag = ''
```

Now, our treeview.insert() call just needs to be amended with this tag value:

```
        self.treeview.insert(
            '', 'end', iid=str(rownum),
            text=str(rownum), values=values, tag=tag
        )
```

Run the application and try to insert and update some records.

You should get something like this:

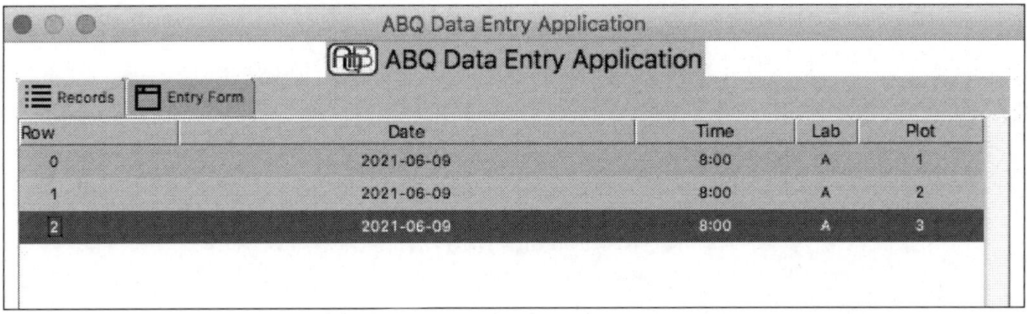

Figure 9.10: The treeview with styled rows. The light blue corresponds to updated rows (row 0) and the light green to inserted rows (row 1). Note that the dark blue row is just the selected row (row 2).

> In addition to the Text and Treeview widgets, tags are also used with the Tkinter Canvas widget, which we'll learn more about in *Chapter 15, Visualizing Data Using the Canvas Widget.*

Working with fonts in Tkinter

Some of our data entry users have complained that the font of the application is just a little too small to read easily, but others dislike the idea of you increasing it because it makes the application too big for the screen. To accommodate all the users, we can add a configuration option that allows them to set a preferred font size and family.

Configuring Tkinter fonts

Any widget in Tkinter that displays text allows us to specify a font, typically through its font configuration property. For widgets that support tags, we can also specify font settings for each tag. We've been using the font argument as far back as *Chapter 1, Introduction to Tkinter,* but now it's time to take a deeper look into what Tkinter allows us to do with fonts.

There are three ways of specifying a widget's font in Tkinter: using a string, using a tuple, and using a Font object. Let's take a look at each one.

Configuring fonts with strings and tuples

The simplest way to configure a font in Tkinter is to just use a font specification string:

```
tk.Label(text="Format with a string", font="Times 20 italic bold")
```

The string takes the format `font-family size styles`, where:

- `font-family` is the name of the font family. It can only be a single word; no spaces are allowed.
- `size` is an integer describing the size. A positive integer indicates a size in *points*, a negative indicates a size in *pixels*. Float values are not supported.
- `styles` can be any valid combination of text style keywords.

Everything but the font family is optional, though you need to specify a size if you want to specify any of the styling keywords. The keywords that can be used for styles include:

- `bold` for boldface text, or `normal` for normal weight
- `italic` for italicized text, or `roman` for regular slant
- `underline` for underlined text
- `overstrike` for struck-out text

The ordering of style keywords doesn't matter, but the weight and slant keywords are mutually exclusive (that is, you can't have `bold normal` or `italic roman`).

While quick and simple, the string approach has its shortcomings; for one, it can't handle fonts with spaces in the name, something that is fairly common on modern systems.

To handle fonts like that, you can use the tuple format:

```
tk.Label(
    text="Tuple font format",
    font=('Noto sans', 15, 'overstrike')
)
```

This format is exactly like the string format, except that the different components are written as items in a tuple.

The size component can be an integer or a string containing digits, which provides some flexibility depending on where the value comes from.

The font module

The string or tuple approach works fine for setting up a handful of font changes at launch time, but for situations where we need to dynamically manipulate font settings, Tkinter offers the `font` module. This module offers us a few font-related functions as well as a `Font` class, whose instances can be assigned to widgets and dynamically changed.

To use the `font` module, it must first be imported:

```
from tkinter import font
```

Now, we can create a custom `Font` object and assign it to some widgets:

```
labelfont = font.Font(
    family='Courier', size=30,
    weight='bold', slant='roman',
    underline=False, overstrike=False
)
tk.Label(text='Using the Font class', font=labelfont).pack()
```

As you can see, the values passed to the `Font` initializer arguments correlate with the weight and slant values used in string and tuple font specifications. The `weight` argument also supports the use of the constants `font.NORMAL` or `font.BOLD`, while `slant` supports the use of `font.ITALIC` or `font.ROMAN`.

Once we've created a `Font` object and assigned it to one or more widgets, we can dynamically alter aspects of it at runtime. For example, we could create a button that will toggle the `overstrike` property of our font:

```
def toggle_overstrike():
    labelfont['overstrike'] = not labelfont['overstrike']

tk.Button(text='Toggle Overstrike', command=toggle_overstrike).pack()
```

The `Font` object is a Python interface to a Tcl/Tk feature called **named fonts**. In Tcl/Tk, a named font is just a collection of font properties associated with a name.

Tk comes with several named fonts already configured, as shown in the following table:

Font name	Defaults to	Used for
TkCaptionFont	System title font	Window and dialog caption bars
TkDefaultFont	System default font	Items not otherwise specified
TkFixedFont	System fixed-width font	Text widget
TkHeadingFont	System heading font	Column headings in lists and tables
TkIconFont	System icon font	Icon captions
TkMenuFont	System menu font	Menu labels
TkSmallCaptionFont	System title	Subwindows, tool dialogs
TkTextFont	System input font	Input widgets: Entry, Spinbox, and so on
TkTooltipFont	System tooltip font	Tooltips

The font module includes a function called names() that returns a list of the current named fonts on the system, including those that you create yourself (by creating Font objects). We can use the font.nametofont() function to generate a Font object from a given name.

For example, we can create a small program to demonstrate all the named fonts included with Tkinter, as follows:

```
# named_font_demo.py

import tkinter as tk
from tkinter import font
root = tk.Tk()

for name in font.names():
  font_obj = font.nametofont(name)
  tk.Label(root, text=name, font=font_obj).pack()

root.mainloop()
```

In this script, we retrieve a list of all the named fonts using font.names() and iterate through it. For each name, we create a Font object using font.nametofont(), and then create a label showing the named font name and using the Font object as its font.

This script will show what all the built-in named fonts look like on your system.

For example, on Ubuntu Linux, they look like this:

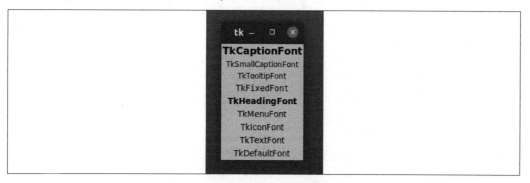

Figure 9.11: The Tkinter named fonts on Ubuntu Linux

Since Tkinter uses its built-in named fonts by default, we can change the overall look of the whole application by creating Font objects for these default named fonts and overriding their properties. The changes we make will get applied across all widgets that don't otherwise have an explicit font configuration.

For example, we could add some code to the preceding script, just before root. mainloop(), to allow us to customize the built-in fonts:

```python
# named_font_demo.py

namedfont = tk.StringVar()
family = tk.StringVar()
size = tk.IntVar()

tk.OptionMenu(root, namedfont, *font.names()).pack()
tk.OptionMenu(root, family, *font.families()).pack()
tk.Spinbox(root, textvariable=size, from_=6, to=128).pack()

def setFont():
  font_obj = font.nametofont(namedfont.get())
  font_obj.configure(family=family.get(), size=size.get())

tk.Button(root, text='Change', command=setFont).pack()
```

In this code, we set up three control variables to hold the named font name, family, and size values, and then set up three widgets to select them. The first OptionMenu widget uses font.names() to retrieve a list of all the named fonts, and the second uses the font.families() function to retrieve a list of the available font families on the operating system (this is likely to be a very long list on most modern systems). Then we have a Spinbox for selecting a font size.

The callback function, setFont(), creates a font object from the selected named font and then configures it with the selected family and size. This function is then bound to a button.

If you run the script now, you should be able to select any named font and edit its family and size. When you click **Change**, you should see the associated label change according to your selections. You may also note that changing certain named fonts affects your OptionMenu, Spinbox, and Button widgets as well.

For example, on Ubuntu Linux, it looks like this:

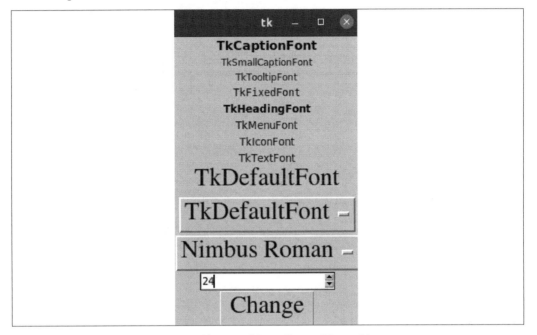

Figure 9.12: The named font editor on Ubuntu Linux

Giving users font options in ABQ Data Entry

Now that we understand how to work with fonts in Tkinter, let's add the ability for our users to configure fonts in the application. We'll allow them to choose a size and a font family that will be used for all the widgets and data displayed in the application.

Since users will want to persist this value between sessions, we should begin by adding keys for font size and font family to our settings model. Open models.py and append these to the fields dictionary, like so:

```
# models.py, inside SettingsModel
```

```
fields = {
  # ...
  'font size': {'type': 'int', 'value': 9},
  'font family': {'type': 'str', 'value': ''}
}
```

We have set the size default to 9 points, but the family default to a blank string. Configuring a font with a blank family value will cause Tkinter to use its own default font family.

Recall that the `Application` object will read the `fields` dictionary and set up a control variable for each setting, and that a dictionary of these control variables will be passed to our `MainMenu` object. So, our next task will be to create menu items for setting the size and family values of these variables.

Open `mainmenu.py` and let's begin by importing the `font` module:

```
# mainmenu.py, at the top

from tkinter import font
```

Now, inside the `MainMenu` initializer method, let's create some sub-menus for the `options_menu` cascade:

```
# mainmenu.py, inside MainMenu.__init__(),
# after creating options_menu

    size_menu = tk.Menu(
      options_menu, tearoff=False, **self.styles
    )
    options_menu.add_cascade(label='Font Size', menu=size_menu)
    for size in range(6, 17, 1):
      size_menu.add_radiobutton(
        label=size, value=size,
        variable=self.settings['font size']
      )
    family_menu = tk.Menu(
      options_menu, tearoff=False, **self.styles
    )
    options_menu.add_cascade(
      label='Font Family', menu=family_menu
    )
```

```
for family in font.families():
  family_menu.add_radiobutton(
    label=family, value=family,
    variable=self.settings['font family']
  )
```

This should look familiar, since we created a nearly identical font size menu when learning about the Tkinter Menu widget in *Chapter 7, Creating Menus with Menu and Tkinter Dialogs*. We're allowing font sizes from 6 to 16, which should provide plenty of range for our users.

The font family menu is nearly identical, except we're pulling the list of possible values from font.families(), just as we did in our demonstration script earlier in this chapter.

Now that the user can select fonts and store their selection, let's actually make those settings change the fonts in the application. To do that, we'll first need to add a method to the Application class that will read the values and alter the appropriate named fonts accordingly.

Open application.py; add an import statement for font at the top, and then let's add this new _set_font() method to the Application class:

```
# application.py, inside the Application class

def _set_font(self, *_):
  """Set the application's font"""
  font_size = self.settings['font size'].get()
  font_family = self.settings['font family'].get()
  font_names = (
    'TkDefaultFont', 'TkMenuFont', 'TkTextFont', 'TkFixedFont'
  )
  for font_name in font_names:
    tk_font = font.nametofont(font_name)
    tk_font.config(size=font_size, family=font_family)
```

This method begins by retrieving the size and family settings from their respective control variables. Next, we're going to loop through a tuple of built-in named fonts that we want to change. TkDefaultFont will change most of the widgets, TkMenuFont will affect the main menu, TkTextFont will change the text-input widgets, and TkFixedFont will set the default for our Text widget.

For each one, we retrieve a Font object using nametofont() and reconfigure it with the values retrieved from settings.

This method needs to be called after the settings are initially loaded, and whenever the size or family values are changed. So, let's add the following lines to the end of Application._load_settings():

```
# application.py, in Application._load_settings()

    self._set_font()
    self.settings['font size'].trace_add('write', self._set_font)
    self.settings['font family'].trace_add(
      'write', self._set_font
    )
```

Now, whenever Application() creates new settings control variables, it will set up the font and add a trace to reconfigure the application fonts whenever these values are changed.

Run the application and try out the font menu. It should look something like this:

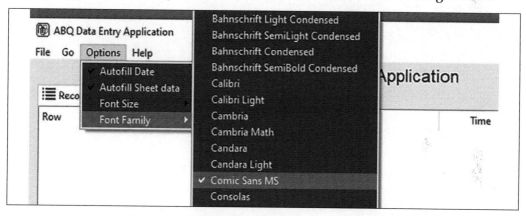

Figure 9.13: Switching our ABQ Data Entry to Comic Sans

Styling Ttk widgets

The final user requests we need to address involve the styles and colors of our Ttk widgets; users have asked for more visual distinction between the form sections, and more visibility for error messages.

After some thought and discussion, you decide to color-code the sections of the form as follows:

- The Record Information section will use khaki, suggesting the classic manila folders used for paper records

- The Environment Data section will use light blue, symbolic of water and air
- The Plant Data will have a light green background, symbolic of plants
- The Notes input is distinctive enough, so it will remain the same default gray

To improve the visibility of error messages, we'd like to make the background of the fields turn red when they have errors, and the error text itself display in a dark red color. To accomplish this, we're going to need to understand how to style Ttk widgets.

TTk styling breakdown

Ttk widgets represent a major improvement over standard Tkinter widgets in terms of the power and flexibility with which they can be styled. This flexibility is what gives Ttk widgets the ability to mimic native UI controls across platforms, but it comes at a cost: Ttk styling is confusing, complicated, poorly documented, and occasionally inconsistent.

To understand Ttk styling, let's start with some vocabulary, from the most basic parts to the most complex:

- Ttk starts with **elements**. An element is one piece of a widget, such as a border, an arrow, or a field where text can be typed.

- Each element has a set of **options** that define properties such as color, size, and font.

- Elements are composed using **layouts** into a complete widget (a Combobox or Treeview, for example).

- **Styles** are collections of element option settings that are applied to widgets. A style is identified by its name. Usually, the name is "T" plus the name of the widget, such as TButton or TEntry, although there are some exceptions to this.

- Widgets also have a number of **states**, which are flags that can be turned on or off:

  - Styles can be configured with a **map** that associates element option values with states or combinations of states.

- A collection of layouts and their associated styles is called a **theme**. Ttk comes with a different set of themes on different platforms, and each platform has a default that aims to match the look of its native widget set. Because each theme may contain elements with different style options, not every option is available, nor has the same effect, in every theme. For example, a ttk.Button on the default macOS theme may contain a different set of elements, applying style settings differently compared to a ttk.Button using the default theme in Windows.

If you're confused at this point, that's understandable. To make things clearer, let's take a deep dive into the anatomy of a `ttk.Combobox`.

Exploring a Ttk widget

To get a better picture of how a Ttk widget is built, open a shell in IDLE and import `tkinter`, `ttk`, and `pprint`:

```
>>> import tkinter as tk
>>> from tkinter import ttk
>>> from pprint import pprint
```

Now, create a root window, `Combobox`, and `Style` object:

```
>>> root = tk.Tk()
>>> cb = ttk.Combobox(root)
>>> cb.pack()
>>> style = ttk.Style()
```

The `Style` object is, perhaps, slightly misnamed; it doesn't point to a single *style*, but rather gives us a point of access to examine and alter the styles, layouts, and maps for the current *theme*.

In order to examine our `Combobox`, we'll first get its style name using the `winfo_class()` method:

```
>>> cb_stylename = cb.winfo_class()
>>> print(cb_stylename)
TCombobox
```

As expected, the name is `TCombobox`, which is just `T` plus the widget name. We can use this name to find out more about this `Combobox` widget.

For example, we can examine its layout by passing the name to the `Style.layout()` method, as follows:

```
>>> cb_layout = style.layout(cb_stylename)
>>> pprint(cb_layout)
[(
  'Combobox.field',
  {
    'children': [
      (
        'Combobox.downarrow',
```

```
          {'side': 'right', 'sticky': 'ns'}
        ),
        (
          'Combobox.padding',
          {
          'children': [
            ('Combobox.textarea', {'sticky': 'nswe'})
          ],
          'expand': '1',
          'sticky': 'nswe'
          }
          )
      ],
      'sticky': 'nswe'
      }
  )]
```

> Note that the output of `layout()` may be different on your system, as the layout contents depend on the theme. Different operating systems use a different default theme.

The returned layout specification shows the hierarchy of elements used to construct this widget. The elements, in this case, are "Combobox.field", "Combobox.downarrow", "Combobox.padding", and "Combobox.textarea". As you can see, each element has associated positioning properties similar to what you'd pass into a geometry manager method.

> The `layout()` method can also be used to replace a style's layout by passing in a new specification as a second argument. Unfortunately, since styles are built using immutable tuples, this requires replacing the *entire* layout specification – you can't just adjust or replace a single element in place.

To see what options are available for the elements in this layout, we can use the `style.element_options()` method. This method takes an element name and returns a list of options that can be used to alter it.

For example:

```
>>> pprint(style.element_options('Combobox.downarrow'))
('background', 'relief', 'borderwidth', 'arrowcolor', 'arrowsize')
```

Once again, this list may be different (or even empty) depending on your operating system and theme settings.

This tells us that the downarrow element of the Combobox widget offers the background, relief, borderwidth, arrowcolor, and arrowsize style properties to adjust its appearance. To change these properties, we can use the style.configure() method.

For instance, let's change the color of the arrow to red:

```
>>> style.configure('TCombobox', arrowcolor='red')
```

If your operating system doesn't support the arrowcolor option, feel free to try a different option or switch to the alt theme. See the next section on how to switch themes.

You should see that the arrow's color has changed to red. This is all we need to know to configure widgets for static changes, but what about dynamic changes, such as when an input is disabled or invalid?

To make dynamic changes, we'll need to work with our widget's state and map. We can inspect or alter the state of our Combobox using the state() method, like so:

```
>>> print(cb.state())
()
```

state() with no arguments will return a tuple with the currently set state flags; as you can see, the Combobox widget had no state flags by default. We can also set the state by passing in a sequence of strings, like so:

```
>>> cb.state(['active', 'invalid'])
('!active', '!invalid')
>>> print(cb.state())
('active', 'invalid')
>>> cb.state(['!invalid'])
('invalid',)
>>> print(cb.state())
('active',)
```

Notice that in order to turn off a state flag, we prefix the flag name with a !. When you call state() with an argument to change the value, the return value is a tuple containing a set of states (or negated states) that would, if applied, *undo the state change you just set.* So, in this case, when we passed in the list that turned on active and invalid, the method returned a tuple that would turn these states off again. Likewise, when we passed in the negated invalid state, we got back a tuple containing invalid. This might be useful in a situation where you want to temporarily set a widget's state and then return it to its previous (possibly unknown) state.

You can't just use any arbitrary strings for state(); they must be one of the supported values, listed here in this table:

State	Indicates
active	Widget element is being hovered on by the mouse
disabled	Interaction with the widget is turned off
focus	Widget will receive keyboard events
pressed	Widget is currently being clicked on
selected	Widget has been selected by the user (for example, a radio button)
background	Widget is on a window that is not the foreground window
readonly	Widget will not allow modification
alternate	Different things, depending on the widget
invalid	Widget contains invalid data (that is, the validate command has returned False)
hover	Like active, but referring to the whole widget rather than an element

Exactly how different widgets use each of these states depends on the widget and the theme; not every state is configured by default to have an effect on every widget. For example, readonly has no effect on a Label widget, since it is not editable to begin with.

Widget states interact with the theme's widget style through the use of a **style map**. We can use the style.map() method to inspect or set the map for each style.

Take a look at the default map for TCombobox:

```
>>> pprint(style.map(cb_stylename))
{
    'arrowcolor': [
        ('disabled', '#a3a3a3')
    ],
    'fieldbackground': [
        ('readonly', '#d9d9d9'),
```

```
    ('disabled', '#d9d9d9')
  ]
}
```

As you can see, `TCombobox` has style maps for the `arrowcolor` and `fieldbackground` options by default. Each style map is a list of tuples, and each tuple is one or more state flags followed by a value for the element option. When all of the state flags match the current state of the widget, the value (that is, the last string in the tuple) takes effect.

The default map turns the arrow color to a light gray color when the `disabled` flag is set, and turns the field background to a different light gray color when either the `disabled` or `readonly` flags are set.

We can set our own style mapping using the same method:

```
>>> style.map(
  'TCombobox',
  arrowcolor=[('!invalid', 'blue'), ('invalid', 'focus', 'red')]
)
{}
>>> pprint(style.map('TCombobox'))
{
  'arrowcolor': [
    ('!invalid', 'blue'), ('invalid', 'focus', 'red')
  ],
  'fieldbackground': [
    ('readonly', '#d9d9d9'), ('disabled', '#d9d9d9')
  ]
}
```

Here, we've configured the `arrowcolor` property to be `blue` when the `invalid` flag is not set, and `red` when both the `invalid` and `focus` flags are set. Notice that while our call to `map()` completely overwrote the `arrowcolor` style map, the `fieldbackground` map was unaffected. You can replace style mappings individually for each option without affecting other options, though whatever mapping you do specify for the option overwrites the whole mapping for that option.

So far, we've been operating on the `TCombobox` style, which is the default style for all `Combobox` widgets. Any changes we made would impact every `Combobox` widget in the application. What if we only want to change a particular widget, or a particular set of widgets? We can do this by creating **custom styles**. Custom styles must be derived from the existing style by prefixing a name and a dot to an existing style name.

For example:

```
>>> style.configure('Blue.TCombobox', fieldbackground='blue')
>>> cb.configure(style='Blue.TCombobox')
```

Blue.TCombobox inherits all of the properties of TCombobox (including the dynamically colored down arrow we previously configured), but can add or override them with settings of its own that won't affect TCombobox. This allows you to create custom styles for some widgets without affecting other widgets of the same type.

 We can even customize our custom styles by adding more prefixes; for example, the style MyCB.Blue.TCombobox would inherit all the styles of TCombobox and Blue.TCombobox, along with whatever additional settings we wanted to add or override in it.

Using themes

We can alter the look of all the Ttk widgets in our application at once by changing the theme. Remember that a theme is a collection of styles *and layouts*; so changing a theme doesn't just change the appearance, it may also change the available styling options as well.

Ttk comes with a different set of themes on each OS platform; to see the themes available on your platform, use the Style.theme_names() method:

```
>>> style.theme_names()
('clam', 'alt', 'default', 'classic')
```

(These are the themes available on Debian Linux; yours may differ.)

To query the current theme, or to set a new theme, use the Style.theme_use() method:

```
>>> style.theme_use()
'default'
>>> style.theme_use('alt')
```

With no arguments, the method returns the name of the current theme. With an argument, it sets the theme to the given theme name. Notice how the previous styling is gone when you change the theme. If you switch back to the default, however, you'll see that your changes were retained. That's because any changes we make using Style.configure() *only affect the currently running theme*.

Adding some color to ABQ Data Entry

Now that you have a firmer grasp of Ttk themes and styling, let's add some color to our data entry form. To begin, we will set a different background color for each `LabelFrame` widget in the data record form. Since we want to configure three widgets of the same type differently, we'll need to use custom styles. For each frame, we will create a custom style, configure it with the proper color, and then assign it to the frame.

Start by opening `views.py` and let's add the following code to the `DataRecordForm` initializer method:

```
# views.py, inside DataRecordForm.__init__()

style = ttk.Style()

# Frame styles
style.configure(
  'RecordInfo.TLabelframe',
  background='khaki', padx=10, pady=10
)
style.configure(
  'EnvironmentInfo.TLabelframe', background='lightblue',
  padx=10, pady=10
)
style.configure(
  'PlantInfo.TLabelframe',
  background='lightgreen', padx=10, pady=10
)
```

We begin by creating a `Style` object, which we can use to access and modify the widget styles. We then use the `style.configure()` method to set up three custom styles based on `TLabelframe`, the default style for Ttk `Labelframe` widgets. We've set the colors according to our plan, and also added some padding to the style.

Now, we need to assign these styles to each frame. Remember that our `LabelFrame` widgets are being created in an instance method called `_add_frame()`. We'll need to update this method to take a `style` argument that we can pass to the widget. Update the method as follows:

```
# views.py, inside the DataRecordForm class

def _add_frame(self, label, style='', cols=3):
  """Add a labelframe to the form"""
```

```
frame = ttk.LabelFrame(self, text=label)
if style:
  frame.configure(style=style)
frame.grid(sticky=tk.W + tk.E)
for i in range(cols):
  frame.columnconfigure(i, weight=1)
return frame
```

In this version, we take a string for the style, and if one is passed, we'll configure our LabelFrame widget to use it. Now, let's update our calls to _add_frame() in the initializer to pass in the custom styles we've created, like so:

```
# views.py, in DataRecordForm.__init__()
    r_info = self._add_frame(
      "Record Information", 'RecordInfo.TLabelframe'
    )
    #...
    e_info = self._add_frame(
      "Environment Data", 'EnvironmentInfo.TLabelframe'
    )
    #...
    p_info = self._add_frame("Plant Data", 'PlantInfo.TLabelframe')
```

Now, execute the application and let's take a look at the form. It should look something like this:

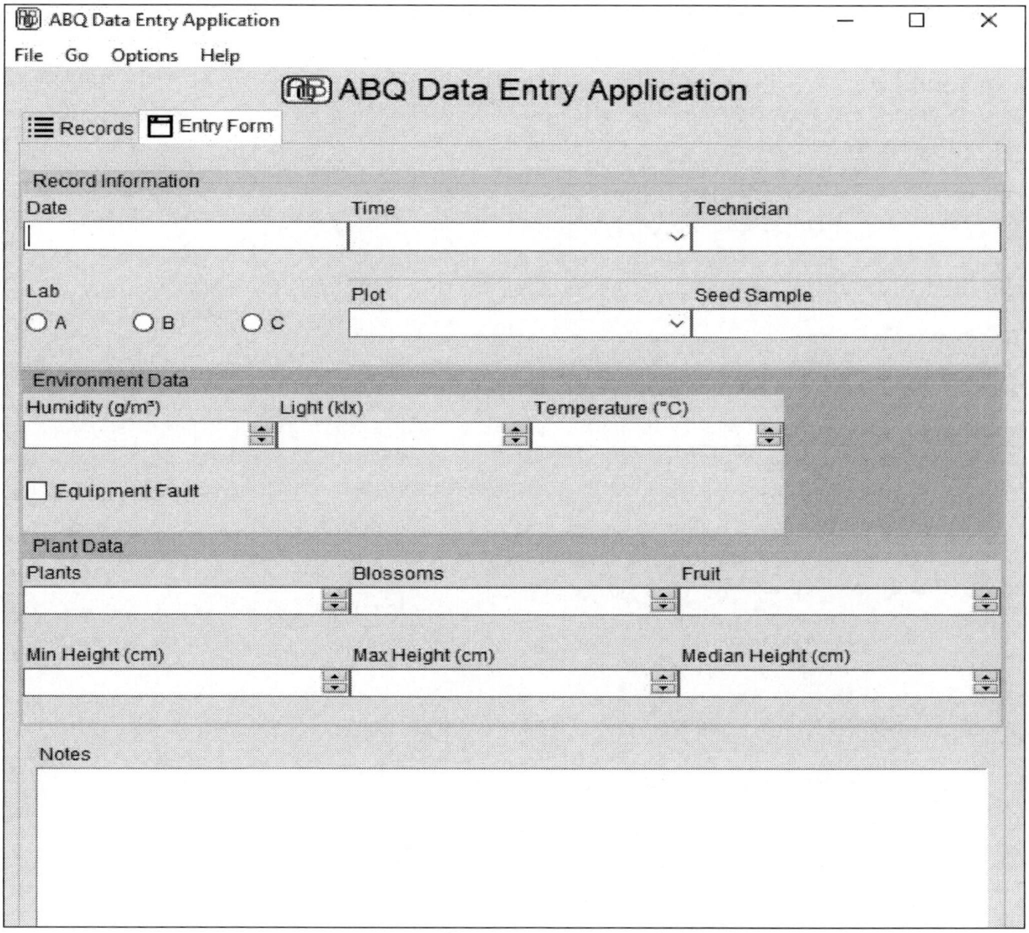

Figure 9.14: Our first attempt at coloring our record form frames

As you can see, that's far from ideal. While there is a small amount of color peeking out from behind the widgets, the widgets in each section are still the default drab color, and even the label portion of the LabelFrame widgets is still gray. Styles do *not* propagate to child widgets, so we're going to have to set each widget individually to get the full effect.

Adding styles to individual form widgets

The first thing we can quickly fix is the label portion of each LabelFrame widget. Although each widget has been assigned to the custom style, the label element of the widget needs to be explicitly styled. We can do that merely by adding the following code to the DataRecordForm initializer:

```python
# views.py, inside DataRecordForm.__init__()

    style.configure(
        'RecordInfo.TLabelframe.Label', background='khaki',
        padx=10, pady=10
    )
    style.configure(
        'EnvironmentInfo.TLabelframe.Label',
        background='lightblue', padx=10, pady=10
    )
    style.configure(
        'PlantInfo.TLabelframe.Label',
        background='lightgreen', padx=10, pady=10
    )
```

This is exactly the same thing we did to create the custom TLabelframe styles, except that we have added the name of the individual element we want to style (in this case, Label). If you run the program again, you'll see now that each frame's label also shares the background color of the frame. We're still not finished though, because we need all our widget labels to show the background color of the frame.

Let's consider which widgets we need to create a custom style for:

- We need a style for the Label widgets for each section, since we'll need different colors for these widgets in Record Information, Environment Data, and Plant Data.

- We'll need to style our Checkbutton, since it uses its own built-in label rather than a separate label widget. Since there's only one right now, we only need one style for it.

- We'll need to style the `Radiobutton` widgets, since they also use a built-in label. We only need one style, though, since they also appear in only one form section.

Let's create those styles:

```
# views.py, inside DataRecordForm.__init__()

    style.configure('RecordInfo.TLabel', background='khaki')
    style.configure('RecordInfo.TRadiobutton', background='khaki')
    style.configure('EnvironmentInfo.TLabel', background='lightblue')
    style.configure(
      'EnvironmentInfo.TCheckbutton',
      background='lightblue'
    )
    style.configure('PlantInfo.TLabel', background='lightgreen')
```

Now that we've created the styles, we need to add them to each widget in the form. Remember that the `LabelInput` initializer takes a `label_args` dictionary for keywords that need to be passed to its `Label` widget, so we'll need to add the label styles there.

For example, here's what the first line should look like:

```
    w.LabelInput(
      r_info, "Date",
      field_spec=fields['Date'],
      var=self._vars['Date'],
      label_args={'style': 'RecordInfo.TLabel'}
    ).grid(row=0, column=0)
    w.LabelInput(
      r_info, "Time",
      field_spec=fields['Time'],
      var=self._vars['Time'],
      label_args={'style': 'RecordInfo.TLabel'}
    ).grid(row=0, column=1)
    w.LabelInput(
      r_info, "Technician",
      field_spec=fields['Technician'],
      var=self._vars['Technician'],
      label_args={'style': 'RecordInfo.TLabel'}
    ).grid(row=0, column=2)
```

For the Lab input, remember that we're using our `ValidatedRadioGroup` widget, which takes a `button_args` dictionary for arguments that need to be passed to the radio buttons. We will have to specify both a `label_args` argument and an `input_args` argument to get our styles set on these widgets, like so:

```python
w.LabelInput(
    r_info, "Lab",
    field_spec=fields['Lab'],
    var=self._vars['Lab'],
    label_args={'style': 'RecordInfo.TLabel'},
    input_args={
        'button_args':{'style': 'RecordInfo.TRadiobutton'}
    }
).grid(row=1, column=0)
```

Continue adding these styles to the rest of the `LabelInput` widgets; if you get stuck, refer to the code example included with the book. When you're finished, the application should look like this:

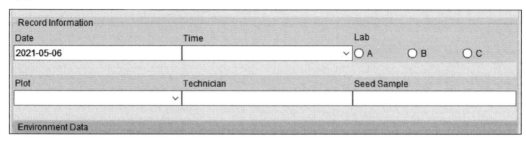

Figure 9.15: The application with colored labels

This is a marked improvement, but it's not quite there yet; the error labels are still the old, default color. Let's address that next.

Fixing the error colors

To fix the error labels, we need to edit our `LabelInput` widget so that, when it creates the `Label` widget for the error, it uses the style value passed in with the `label_args` dictionary. However, we have a complication: we want to make our error text dark red. How can we honor the background color of the style passed in, but also customize the foreground just for this widget?

The answer is that we can further prefix our custom style to create a new style that inherits all the traits of the custom, while adding or overriding its own. In other words, if we were to create a style called `Error.RecordInfo.TLabel`, it would inherit all the properties of `RecordInfo.TLabel` but allow us to make additional changes.

Open the `widgets.py` file, and let's see if we can implement this in the `LabelInput` initializer method:

```
# widgets.py, inside LabelInput.__init__()

    error_style = 'Error.' + label_args.get('style', 'TLabel')
    ttk.Style().configure(error_style, foreground='darkred')
    self.error = getattr(self.input, 'error', tk.StringVar())
    ttk.Label(
      self, textvariable=self.error, style=error_style
    ).grid(row=2, column=0, sticky=(tk.W + tk.E))
```

In this code, we've extracted the `style` value from the `label_args` dictionary, defaulting to `TLabel` if no style was passed. Then, we create a new style name by prefixing the given style with `Error.` (note the dot, that's important!). Then, we call `Style.configure()` to set the text color of our new style to a dark red. Note that we don't give the `Style` object a name here; since we're only making one change, it's OK to just call `configure()` directly on the created object and then let the object get thrown away.

Now, you should see that the error display widgets match the color of your background, but also display in dark red.

Styling input widgets on error

Setting the error text to dark red is a minor improvement on the error visibility issue, but for our color-blind users in particular, the improvement is subtle at best, if it's even noticeable. We can use our knowledge of styling to take things a bit farther, though. Rather than just changing the color of the text, let's invert the colors of the input so that we have light text on a dark background.

To do this, we will want to update the `ValidatedMixin` class. Recall that we previously implemented a `_toggle_error()` method that sets the foreground color to red when the widget is invalid on focus-out. We could update that command to apply a different style to the widget instead, so that the background color would change as well. However, there's a better way.

Earlier in this chapter, we learned that widgets get flagged with an `invalid` state when validation fails, and that Ttk styles can have colors and other properties tied to different widget states by means of a style map. Rather than explicitly changing styles or colors when validation fails, we can create a style map that changes colors automatically in response to a failed validation.

To begin, go ahead and remove any calls to self._toggle_error() in the ValidatedMixin class, which can be found in the _validate() method and the _focusout_invalid() method. That will leave the _focusout_invalid() method empty, so replace it with pass, like so:

```python
# widget.py, inside the ValidatedMixin class

def _focusout_invalid(self, **kwargs):
    """Handle invalid data on a focus event"""
    pass
```

Although the method now does nothing, we're leaving it in place because it's part of the mixin class's API that child classes can override. You can actually delete the _toggle_error() method, however, since its functionality will be handled by a style map.

Now, in the initializer, let's configure a style and style map for our widget:

```python
# widget.py, inside ValidatedMixin.__init__()

    style = ttk.Style()
    widget_class = self.winfo_class()
    validated_style = 'ValidatedInput.' + widget_class
    style.map(
      validated_style,
      foreground=[('invalid', 'white'), ('!invalid', 'black')],
      fieldbackground=[
        ('invalid', 'darkred'),
        ('!invalid', 'white')
      ]
    )
    self.configure(style=validated_style)
```

Since this is a mixin class, we don't know the original style name of the widget we're mixing with, so we've fetched that using the winfo_class() method. After getting the widget class, we're creating a custom style by prefixing the class with ValidatedInput. Then, we call style.map() to configure the foreground and background colors of this style in both invalid and not-invalid states: an invalid state will cause the widget to have white text on dark red background, and a !invalid state (that is, if the widget doesn't have an invalid flag) black on white. Finally, we apply the style to the widget using self.configure().

If you try the application now, you might see that fields with errors now turn a dark red color with white text:

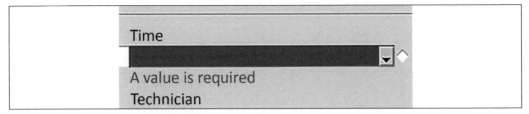

Figure 9.16: Our new validation styles at work

That is to say, you will see this on Linux or macOS; on Microsoft Windows, the field background will remain unchanged. What's going on here?

Remember that from our earlier discussion in *Exploring a Ttk widget*, each platform comes with its own set of distinct themes, and each theme defines a unique layout for its widgets. These layouts define the individual elements of each widget and what properties can be defined for them. That means that some style properties might work on one theme, but not on another.

In this case, the default Ttk theme for Windows (the vista theme) does not allow the background color of our input widgets to be altered. Our target users for ABQ Data Entry are on Debian Linux, so this won't impact them. But it would be nice if we could see this feature working on other platforms.

Setting themes

Generally speaking, the default Ttk theme on any given platform is probably the best one to use on that platform, but looks are subjective and sometimes we might feel that Tkinter gets it wrong. And sometimes, as we saw in the previous section, features we require for an application may not work in the default theme. Having a way to switch the theme might help to smooth out some rough edges and make some users feel more comfortable with the look of the application.

As we've already seen, querying available themes and setting a new theme is fairly simple. Let's create a configuration option to change the theme of our application.

Building a theme selector

Themes aren't something users are going to need to change often, and as we've seen, changing the theme can undo style changes we've made to our widgets. In light of this, we'll play it safe by designing our theme changer in such a way that it requires a restart of the program to make the actual change.

We'll start by adding a theme option to our `SettingsModel` class's `fields` dictionary:

```
# models.py, inside the SettingsModel class

fields = {
  #...
  'theme': {'type': 'str', 'value': 'default'}
  }
```

Every platform has a theme aliased to `default`, so this is a safe and sensible default value.

Next, our `Application` object will need to check this value when the settings are loaded and apply it. Add this code to the end of the `Application._load_settings()` method:

```
# application.py, in Application._load_settings()
style = ttk.Style()
theme = self.settings.get('theme').get()
if theme in style.theme_names():
  style.theme_use(theme)
```

This code will create a `Style` object, retrieve the theme, and then set the theme using the `theme_use()` method. If we should happen to give Tkinter a theme that doesn't exist, it will raise a `TCLError` exception; to avoid this, we have added an `if` statement to make sure the given theme is in the list returned by `theme_names()`.

What remains now is to create the UI elements required. As we did with our font options, we will add a sub-menu to our `Options` menu for selecting a theme.

To do this, open `mainmenu.py` and add an import statement for `ttk` at the top. Then, add the following code to the initializer method just after the font menus:

```
# mainmenu.py, inside MainMenu.__init__()

    style = ttk.Style()
    themes_menu = tk.Menu(self, tearoff=False, **self.styles)
    for theme in style.theme_names():
      themes_menu.add_radiobutton(
        label=theme, value=theme,
        variable=self.settings['theme']
      )
    options_menu.add_cascade(label='Theme', menu=themes_menu)
```

Here, as we did with our font settings, we simply loop through the available themes retrieved from theme_names() and add a Radiobutton item for each theme, tying it to our settings['theme'] variable.

It may not be obvious to users that changing the theme requires a restart, so let's make sure to let them know.

We can do that using a variable trace, like so:

```
self.settings['theme'].trace_add(
  'write', self._on_theme_change
)
```

Whenever the theme is changed, this trace will call the self._on_theme_change() method; let's add this method to the end of the MainMenu class:

```
# mainmenu.py, inside MainMenu

@staticmethod
def _on_theme_change(*_):
  message = "Change requires restart"
  detail = (
    "Theme changes do not take effect"
    " until application restart"
  )
  messagebox.showwarning(
    title='Warning',
    message=message,
    detail=detail
  )
```

Note that we don't actually take any action here to change the theme; this method simply displays the warning message box and nothing else. The actual change to the setting is handled by the control variable bound to the menu checkboxes, so we don't really need to explicitly do anything. Also, because this method doesn't require access to the instance or class, we've made it a static method.

Now, you can run the application and try changing the theme, and then restart the application. You should notice a change in the application's appearance. For example, here's the application using the "clam" theme:

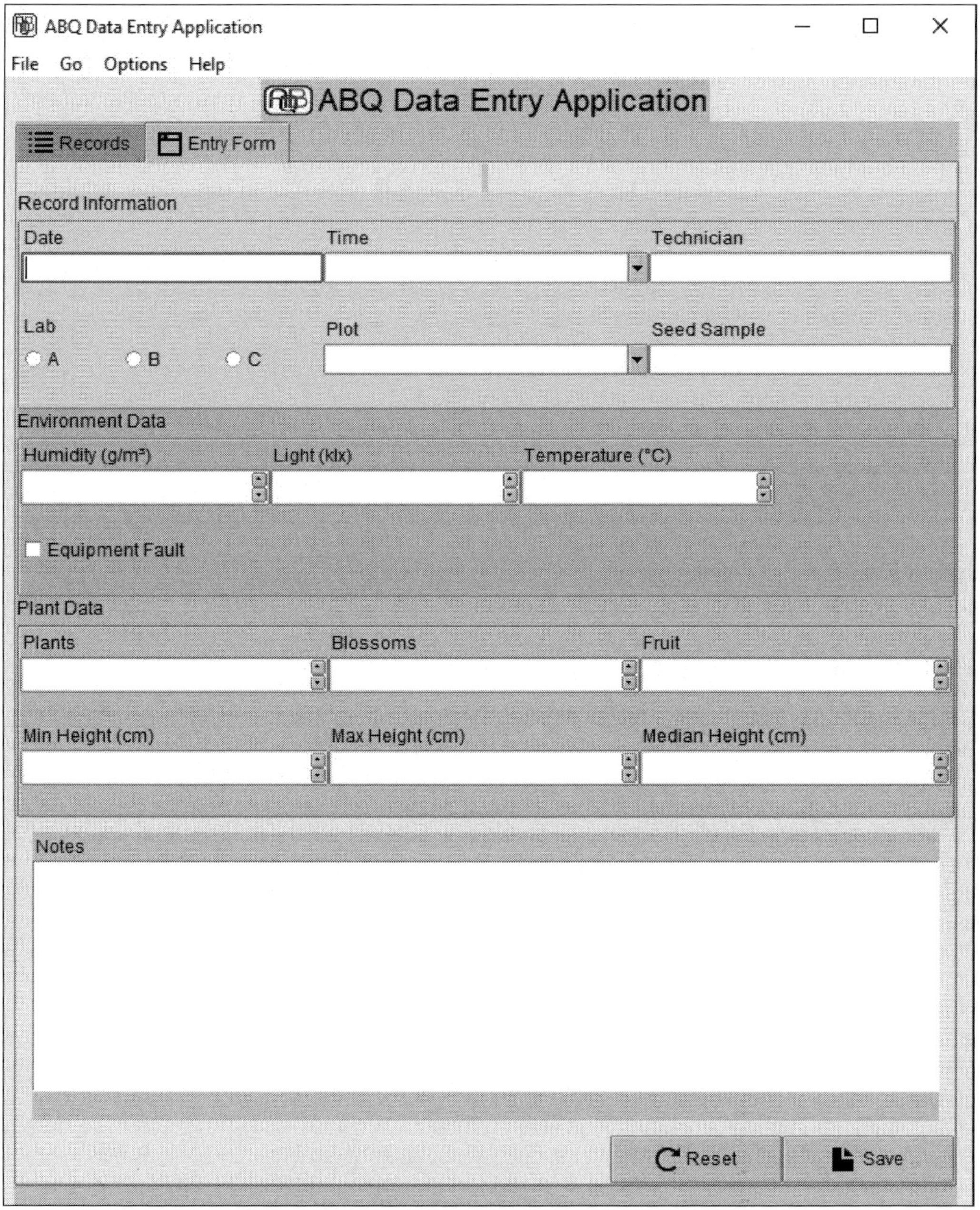

Figure 9.17: ABQ Data Entry using the "clam" theme on Windows

As you can see, not every theme looks so good with our changes. Try the different themes available on your platform. Which theme looks best on your platform? Which ones work best with our style changes? Try them all out and see.

Summary

In this chapter, we overhauled the look and feel of our application for both aesthetic and usability improvements. You learned how to use images and icons in your application using PhotoImage and BitmapImage, and how to extend image format support using Pillow. You learned to assign fonts to widgets, and to change the settings for built-in fonts. You learned how to work with color and font settings for default Tkinter widgets and how to use tags to style individual Treeview items and Text widget contents. We explored the intricate world of Ttk styles and learned to create custom styles based on the built-in defaults. Finally, we applied our knowledge of styling to the ABQ Data Entry application to make it more aesthetically pleasing and user-friendly.

In the next chapter, we'll take steps to make sure our program runs effectively across major desktop platforms. You'll learn strategies to avoid cross-platform pitfalls in both general Python programming and Tkinter programming in particular. We'll also explore the various guidelines platform vendors offer to developers targeting their platforms.

10
Maintaining Cross-Platform Compatibility

Word has spread throughout ABQ AgriLabs about your application, and it is being requested as a way to visualize and work on experimental data files. As a result, it now needs to run on Windows, macOS, and Linux systems equally well. Fortunately for you, Python and Tkinter are supported on these three operating systems, and you'll be pleasantly surprised to find that your application already runs unaltered on all three. However, there are some small issues that you need to address and remain aware of in order for your application to be a good citizen on each platform.

In this chapter, we'll learn more about cross-platform compatibility as we cover the following topics:

- In *Writing cross-platform Python*, you'll learn how to keep basic Python code functional across multiple platforms.

- In *Writing cross-platform Tkinter*, you'll learn about cross-platform issues that affect Tkinter code specifically.

- In *Improving our application's cross-platform compatibility*, we'll update our ABQ Data Entry application for better cross-platform support.

Writing cross-platform Python

At the time of writing, Python is supported on nearly a dozen operating system platforms, covering everything from common desktop systems like Windows to high-end commercial Unixes like AIX and obscure OS projects such as Haiku OS.

Across all these platforms, most Python code works without any significant alteration, as Python has been designed to translate high-level functionality into appropriate low-level operations on each system. Even so, there are situations where OS differences cannot be (or simply have not been) abstracted away, and careful handling is required to avoid platform-specific failures.

In this section, we'll look at some of the larger issues that impact cross-platform Python.

Filenames and file paths across platforms

Filesystems are probably the biggest source of pitfalls for cross-platform development. Although most platforms share the concept of files and directories arranged in a hierarchy, there are some crucial differences that can trip up developers who are unfamiliar with a variety of operating systems.

Path separators and drives

When it comes to identifying locations on a filesystem, operating systems generally use one of the following two models:

- Windows/DOS: In this model, each partition or storage device is assigned a volume label (usually a single letter), and each volume has its own filesystem tree. Paths are separated by a backslash (\) character. This system is used by Windows, DOS, and VMS.

- Unix: In this model, there is one filesystem tree, into which devices and partitions are mounted at arbitrary points. Paths are separated by a forward slash (/). This model is used by macOS, Linux, BSD, iOS, Android, and other Unix-like operating systems.

Thus, a path like `E:\Server\Files\python` is meaningless on Linux or macOS, while a path like `/mnt/disk1/files/python` is equally meaningless on Windows. This could make it quite difficult to write code that accesses files in a cross-platform way, but Python gives us a few tools to deal with the differences.

Path separator translation

If you use the Unix-style forward slash path separators on a Windows system, Python will automatically translate them into backslashes. This is quite useful for cross-platform purposes because using backslashes in strings can be problematic. For example, if you try to create the string `C:\Users` in Python, you'll get an exception, because `\u` is an escape sequence for specifying Unicode sequences, and `sers` (the rest of the string after `\U`) is not a valid Unicode sequence.

To use backslashes in a string, you must either escape them by entering a double-backslash (\\) or you must use a raw string (by prefixing the string literal with an r).

Note that there is no Windows-to-Unix path separator translation: Python will not translate backslashes into Unix-style forward slashes. Thus, a path like r'\usr\bin\python' will simply not work on macOS or Linux.

The os.path module

Even with automatic path-separator interpolation, building or hardcoding paths as strings is a messy business. Python's powerful string manipulation methods make it tempting to try to work with paths as strings, and many programmers attempt to do so.

The result is often ugly, non-portable code like this:

```
script_dir = '/'.join(some_path.split('/')[:-1])
```

While this approach might work most of the time (even on Windows), it's prone to breaking on some edge cases (for example, if some_path is /script.sh). For this reason, the Python standard library includes the os.path module for working with filesystem paths.

The path module appears to be a collection of functions and constants that help abstract common filenames and directory operations, though it's actually a wrapper around the low-level modules posixpath for Unix-like systems and ntpath for Windows. When you import path, Python simply detects your operating system and loads the appropriate low-level library.

The following table shows some common os.path functions that are useful for cross-platform developers:

Function	Purpose
join()	Joins two or more path segments in a platform-appropriate way
expanduser()	Expands the ~ or username shortcuts to the user's home directory or user name, respectively
expandvars()	Expands any shell variables present in a path string
dirname()	Extracts the parent directory of the path
isfile()	Determines whether the path points to a file
isdir()	Determines whether the path points to a directory
exists()	Determines whether the given path exists

Using these functions rather than directly manipulating path strings guarantees that your code will work across platforms consistently.

The pathlib module

A more recent addition to the Python standard library is the pathlib module. The pathlib module is a more object-oriented and somewhat higher-level take on filesystem paths, which we have been using throughout this book. Unlike os.path, which is just a collection of functions and constants, pathlib offers the Path object, which represents a filesystem location and provides a variety of methods for modifying the path and obtaining information about it.

We typically use pathlib by importing the Path class from it. For example:

```
>>> from pathlib import Path
>>> p = Path()
>>> print(p)
.
>>> print(p.absolute())
'/home/alanm'
```

Path defaults to the current working directory, but you can also provide it with an absolute or relative path string. Relative paths will be calculated against the current working directory.

Path objects have a variety of useful properties and methods:

```
# Create a Path object for the current working directory
p = Path()

# Find the parent directory
parent = p.parent

# Check if the path /var/log exists
has_var_log = Path('/var/log').exists()

# Join Paths together, using the division operator
image_path = Path(__file__) / 'images' / 'png'
```

Refer to the pathlib module's documentation at https://docs.python.org/3/library/pathlib.html for more information on this powerful library.

Should you use `os.path` or `pathlib.Path`? Generally speaking, `pathlib` is the better choice and results in much cleaner code overall. However, there are a few edge cases where you might need `os.path`. For example, `pathlib` has no equivalent to `expandvars()`; also, the `os.path` module's function-oriented approach may be more useful in functional programming situations.

Case sensitivity

Platforms also differ in terms of filesystem case sensitivity. On Linux, BSD, and Unix, for example, the files `log.txt`, `LOG.txt`, and `LoG.TxT` are all different files that can coexist in the same directory. On Windows or macOS (depending on your settings), all three names would refer to the same file, and three files with these names could not exist in the same directory.

The following table breaks down the case sensitivity of major operating systems:

System	Case-sensitive
Windows	No
macOS	Not by default (configurable)
Linux	Yes
BSD, most other Unix systems	Yes

Problems with case (in)sensitivity usually depend on which system you're accustomed to:

- Programmers used to a case-insensitive system tend to run into problems with inconsistent use of cases when referencing files and paths. For instance, you might save a file as `UserSettings.json` but try to retrieve it as `usersettings.JSON`.

- Programmers used to a case-sensitive system can have problems when depending on a case to differentiate between file or directory names. For example, you might have the files `ImportIngest.txt` and `ImportingEst.txt` in the same directory.

Avoiding these issues is fairly simple with the following few basic rules:

- Use all-lowercase names for file and path names unless there is a good reason not to.

- If you do mix cases, follow consistent rules, so that you don't need to remember arbitrary case usage.

- Avoid CamelCase or similar naming schemes that rely on case to denote word breaks. Use underscores, hyphens, or spaces (they're valid in all modern filesystems!).

To put it another way: treat all paths and filenames as if you had a case-sensitive system, but don't rely on the system being case-sensitive.

Symbolic links

A symbolic link is a special filesystem-level construct that appears to be a file or directory but is actually just a pointer to another file or directory on the system. They're often used to provide aliases to files or directories, or to make it appear as though the same file exists in multiple places without using additional disk space. Although they exist on Windows, they're far more commonly used on Linux, macOS, and other Unix-like systems; thus, they can be a point of confusion for programmers coming from a Windows environment.

 Symbolic links are not to be confused with desktop shortcuts, which also exist on all three major platforms. Shortcuts are just metadata files implemented at the desktop environment level, whereas symbolic links are implemented at the filesystem level.

File and path operations sometimes need to clarify if they're working with the symbolic link itself or the file that the link points to.

For example, suppose we had a symbolic link in our current directory, `secret_stuff.txt`, that points to the nonexistent file `/tmp/secret_stuff.txt`. Look at how `os.path()` responds to such a file:

```
>>> from os import path
>>> path.exists('secret_stuff.txt')
False
>>> path.lexists('secret_stuff.txt')
True
```

The regular `path.exists()` function will follow the link and discover that the actual file in question does not exist. `os.path` also includes a `lexists()` function that will tell us if the *link* exists, even if the *file* does not. This situation could be a problem; for example, your program might be attempting to create a directory with the same name as a broken symbolic link. In this case, `os.path.exists()` or `Path.exists()` would both return `False`, but the name conflict would still exist, and directory creation would fail. Checking `os.path.lexists()` or `Path.is_symlink()` as well would be a good idea in this case.

The following table shows some of the os.path functions that help deal with symbolic links:

Method	Description
islink()	Returns True if a path is a symbolic link
lexists()	Returns True if a path exists, even if it's a broken symbolic link
realpath()	Returns the actual path, resolving any symbolic links to real files and directories

pathlib.Path objects also feature these link-related methods:

Method	Description
is_symlink()	Returns True if the path is a symbolic link
resolve()	Returns a path with all symbolic links resolved to real files and directories
lchmod()	Changes permissions on a symbolic link, rather than the file it is pointed to
lstat()	Returns filesystem information on a symbolic link, rather than the file it is pointed to

In summary, our code should be mindful of symbolic links in situations where they might cause it to behave unexpectedly.

Path variables

Most platforms, including Windows, macOS, and Linux, support some kind of shell variables, which are often automatically set up by the system to point to common filesystem locations. The os.path module provides the expandvars() function to expand these variables into their actual values (pathlib has no equivalent method). While these variables can be useful in locating common path locations, the cross-platform developer should understand that they are not consistent across platforms.

Some commonly used variables across different systems include the following:

Description	Windows	macOS	Linux
Current user home directory	%HOME%, %USERPROFILE%	$HOME	$HOME
Temporary directory	%TMP%, %TEMP%	$TMPDIR	None
Path to default shell	N/A	$SHELL	$SHELL
Current working directory	None	$PWD	$PWD
Configuration directory	%APPDATA%, %LOCALAPPDATA%	None	$XDG_CONFIG_HOME (often not set)
OS directory	%WINDIR%, %SYSTEMROOT%	N/A	N/A
Program files directory	%PROGRAMFILES%, %PROGRAMW6432%	N/A	N/A

Note that Windows variables can be spelled using the native %VARIABLENAME% format or the Unix-style $VARIABLENAME format; macOS and Linux only accept the Unix-style format.

Using these variables is not necessarily a bad idea (they can help abstract differences between versions or configurations of an OS), but be aware that they are not consistently available, or even meaningful, across platforms.

Inconsistent library and feature support

While it's understandable that many third-party Python libraries only support a limited number of platforms, you might be surprised to learn that the standard library contains a slightly different set of modules depending on the platform. Even those that do exist across platforms might behave slightly differently, or have inconsistent contents, depending on the platform.

Naturally, these have to be handled carefully in cross-platform applications. Let's look at a few examples of these libraries and features.

Python's platform-limited libraries

In sections 34 and 35 of Python's standard library documentation (https://docs. python.org/3/library/index.html), you'll find a list of libraries available only on Windows or Unix-like systems, respectively. Careful reading of the documentation shows that there are a couple more platform-limited libraries listed in other sections as well.

This is a list of the more common platform-limited libraries you may encounter:

Library	Description	Availability
ossaudiodev	Open Sound System (OSS) audio server interface	Linux, FreeBSD
winsound	Windows audio interface	Windows
msilib	Windows software packaging tools	Windows
winreg	Windows registry tools	Windows
syslog	Unix system log interface	Linux, macOS, BSD
pwd, spwd	Unix password database interface	Linux, macOS, BSD
resource	System resource limits	Linux, macOS, BSD
curses	Terminal-based UI library	Linux, macOS, BSD

In some cases, there are higher-level, cross-platform libraries that you can use to replace these (for example, use `logging` instead of `syslog`), but in other cases the functionality is so platform-specific that you may have no choice (`winreg`, for example). In this case, you'll need to do a platform check before importing these libraries, as you'll get an `ImportError` exception on unsupported platforms.

Checking low-level function compatibility

Even in universally available libraries, there are sometimes functions or methods that are unavailable or exhibit different behaviors depending on the platform. The `os` module is perhaps the most notable case.

The `os` module is a relatively thin wrapper around system calls or commands, and while it attempts to abstract some roughly analogous calls across platforms, many of its functions are too platform-specific to make available universally.

The `os` module documentation at `https://docs.python.org/3/library/os.html` contains complete details on platform support, but some examples are listed here:

Library	Description	Availability
`getuid, getgid, getgroups, geteuid`	Get user or group information for the current process	Unix-like
`setuid, setgid, setgroups, seteuid`	Set user or group information for the current process	Unix-like
`getpriority, setpriority`	Get or set the priority of the current process	Unix-like
`chown, lchown`	Change the owner of a file or its symbolic link	Unix-like
`startfile`	Open a file as if it were double-clicked	Windows

Attempting to use an unavailable function will cause an exception, so none of these functions should be in a cross-platform application without appropriate checks or exception handling. By far, most of the platform-limited functions in `os` are limited to Unix-like systems (Linux, macOS, BSD, and so on), and most of the analogous functions for Windows will be found in the third-party `pywin32` package (which is only available for Windows, of course).

In general, you need to check the documentation of the libraries you use to make sure they're available on all the platforms you intend to support. Caution is especially warranted when using libraries that interact with operating system functions (such as window management, filesystems, user authentication, and so on) or with services that are only available on certain platforms (Microsoft SQL Server, for example).

The dangers of the subprocess module

The subprocess module provides tools to launch and manage other programs and commands from within your Python application. For programmers already familiar with their operating system's command-line interface, it often provides a fast and convenient way to accomplish filesystem operations or other administrative tasks. It's also highly effective at sabotaging cross-platform compatibility!

For example, a programmer on Linux or macOS might be tempted to copy files as follows:

```python
import subprocess
subprocess.call(['cp', 'file1.txt', 'file2.txt'])
```

This would work on Unix-like operating systems but fail on Windows, as cp is not a valid Windows shell command. The better option in this case is to use the shutil library, which contains high-level functions for copying files.

To avoid problems here, follow these guidelines:

1. Look for high-level libraries before resorting to subprocess to solve a problem.
2. If you must use subprocess, carefully study the called command on each supported platform, making sure the syntax, output, and behavior are identical.
3. If they're not, make sure to create different cases for each platform (see the section *Writing code that changes according to the platform*, below).

Naturally, all this advice applies equally to any third-party modules that allow you to execute operating system commands from within Python.

Text file encodings and formats

Plaintext files on different platforms use different character encodings and end-of-line characters by default. Although most operating systems can handle a wide variety of encodings, each system has a default (often determined by language or localization settings) that will be used if none is specified. Text files on different platforms also use different character codes for end-of-line characters.

Modern versions of Linux and macOS use UTF-8 as a default encoding and the line feed character (\n) as a line terminator. Windows 10, however, uses cp1252 as its default encoding and the combination of the carriage return and line feed (\r\n) characters as a line terminator. Most of the time, these differences do not represent a problem, especially if you are only reading and writing files in Python and working with standard English characters.

Consider, however, a scenario where you attempt to append a Unicode character to a text file, like so:

```
with open('testfile.test', 'a') as fh:
    fh.write('\U0001F34C')
```

On Windows, or other systems with a non-Unicode default encoding, the preceding code will raise an exception, like so:

```
UnicodeEncodeError: 'charmap' codec can't encode character '\U0001f34c'
in position 0: character maps to <undefined>
```

To avoid this problem, you can manually specify a character encoding when opening a file, as follows:

```
with open('testfile.test', 'a', encoding='utf-8') as fh:
    fh.write('\U0001F34C')
```

The line-terminator character can also be specified when opening a file using the `newline` argument, like so:

```
with open('testfile.test', 'w', newline='\n') as fh:
    fh.write('banana')
```

We've already been doing this in ABQ Data Entry to work around a bug in Windows with the `csv` module. In a cross-platform situation, it's a good idea to specify both the `encoding` and `newline` arguments whenever saving data you don't control (such as user-entered data).

Graphical and console modes

On Windows, programs are launched in either GUI mode or console mode, as determined by metadata in the executable. The Python distribution for Windows includes a utility called Python launcher, which is associated with Python files during installation. Python launcher will launch your application in either GUI or console mode depending on its file extension, as follows:

- Files ending in the `.py` extension will be launched in console mode using `python.exe`. This will cause a command-line window to open in the background, which must stay open while the program runs.

- Files ending in `.pyw` will be launched in GUI mode using `pythonw.exe`. No command-line window will be launched, and if run from a command line the program will not block the console (that is, the prompt will return immediately, while the program is still running); however, `print()` will have no effect and `sys.stderr` and `sys.stdout` will not exist. Trying to access them will raise an exception.

This distinction often causes confusion for developers coming from Linux or macOS, where it is common to have graphical applications that output errors and debugging information to the terminal. Even for Windows programmers who are new to GUI applications, the lack of command-line output for GUI applications can be problematic.

To avoid issues, simply remember the following:

1. Remove any `sys.stdout()` or `sys.stderr()` calls from the code if deploying to Windows.

2. Rely on logging rather than `print()` or `sys.stderr()` calls to record debugging information.

3. Create a copy of the main executable script with a `.pyw` extension so that Windows users can launch it without a command-line window.

While macOS does not distinguish between GUI and console applications (apart from the obvious presence of a GUI), its desktop launches regular `.py` files by launching a Terminal window, just like Windows. While macOS Python includes a `pythonw.exe` file that launches without the Terminal, there are two problems with it. First, it is not associated with the `.pyw` extension by default; you'd need to do that manually if you wanted that behavior. Second, depending on how you installed Python 3 (for instance, if you installed it using `homebrew`), your installation may not have `pythonw`.

> There is a way to set up Python programs on macOS so that they behave like proper GUI applications, which we'll cover in *Chapter 16, Packaging with setuptools and cxFreeze*.

Writing code that changes according to the platform

As you've seen so far, there are certain situations where you simply can't avoid writing platform-specific code, either because a high-level library is unavailable or because the actions that need to be performed are fundamentally different on a particular platform.

In this case, it becomes necessary to detect the platform. There are a few ways of doing this in Python, including the `os.system()` function and the `sys.platform` attribute, but the standard library `platform` module contains the best set of functionality for determining the OS details most useful in making decisions. When called, the `platform.system()` function returns a string identifying the operating system: `Windows`, `Linux`, `freebsd7`, or `Darwin` (for macOS).

Some other useful functions in the platform module include release(), which returns the version string of the OS (for example, "10" on Windows 10, "17.3.0" on macOS High Sierra, or the running kernel version on Linux); and architecture(), which tells us if the system is 64 bit or 32 bit.

For simple differences in code, using this information in a nested if / else chain usually suffices:

```python
# simple_cross_platform_demo.py

import platform
import subprocess

os_name = platform.system()
if os_name in ('Darwin', 'freebsd7'):
    cmd = ['ps', '-e', '-o', "comm=''", '-c']
elif os_name == 'Linux':
    cmd = ['ps', '-e', '--format', 'comm', '--no-heading']
elif os_name == 'Windows':
    cmd = ['tasklist', '/nh', '/fo', 'CSV']
else:
    raise NotImplemented("Command unknown for OS")

processes = subprocess.check_output(cmd, text=True)
print(processes)
```

This example defines a platform-appropriate list of command tokens based on the value returned by platform.system(). The correct list is saved as cmd, which is then passed to subprocess.check_output() to run the command and obtain its output.

This works acceptably for the occasional call, but for more complex situations, it makes sense to bundle platform-specific code into backend classes that we can then select on the basis of our platform string. For example, we could re-implement the above code as follows:

```python
# complex_cross_platform_demo/backend.py
import subprocess
import platform

class GenericProcessGetter():
  cmd = []

  def get_process_list(self):
```

```
    if self.cmd:
      return subprocess.check_output(self.cmd)
    else:
      raise NotImplementedError

class LinuxProcessGetter(GenericProcessGetter):
  cmd = ['ps', '-e', '--format', 'comm', '--no-heading']

class MacBsdProcessGetter(GenericProcessGetter):
  cmd = ['ps', '-e', '-o', "comm=''", '-c']

class WindowsProcessGetter(GenericProcessGetter):
  cmd = ['tasklist', '/nh', '/fo', 'CSV']
```

In this approach, we have created a generic class to handle the common logic for getting processes, then subclassed it to override the cmd attribute specifically for each platform.

Now, we can create a selector function to return an appropriate backend class when given an OS name:

```
# complex_cross_platform_demo/backend.py

def get_process_getter_class(os_name):
  process_getters = {
    'Linux': LinuxProcessGetter,
    'Darwin': MacBsdProcessGetter,
    'Windows': WindowsProcessGetter,
    'freebsd7': MacBsdProcessGetter
  }
  try:
    return process_getters[os_name]
  except KeyError:
    raise NotImplementedError("No backend for OS")
```

Now, code that needs to use this class can utilize this function to retrieve a platform-appropriate version. For example:

```
# complex_cross_platform_demo/main.py

os_name = platform.system()
process_getter = get_process_getter_class(os_name)()
print(process_getter.get_process_list())
```

This script can now be run on Linux, Windows, macOS, or BSD to print a process list. Other platforms can be easily added by creating more `GenericProcessGetter` subclasses and updating `get_process_getter_class()`.

For even more complex situations, where multiple classes or functions need to be implemented differently between platforms, we can take an approach similar to the standard library's `os.path` module: implement completely separate modules for each platform, then import them with a common alias depending on the platform. For example:

```python
import platform
os_name = platform.system()

if os_name == 'Linux':
    import linux_backend as backend
elif os_name == 'Windows':
    import windows_backend as backend
elif os_name in ('Darwin', 'freebsd7'):
    import macos_bsd_backend as backend
else:
    raise NotImplementedError(f'No backend for {os_name}')
```

Bear in mind that each backend module should ideally contain identical class and function names and produce similar output. That way `backend` can be used by the code without concern for the platform in question.

Writing cross-platform Tkinter

As you've seen so far, Tkinter mostly works identically across platforms, and even has the capability to do the right thing on each platform with minimal effort. However, there are some minor issues to be aware of as you support a Tkinter application across multiple operating systems. In this section, we'll explore the more significant differences.

Tkinter version differences across platforms

As of 2021, the official Python 3 distributions for major platforms ship at least Tcl/Tk 8.6; this is the latest major release of Tcl/Tk and includes all the functionality discussed in this book. However, not every platform includes the latest minor version, which may impact bug fixes and minor features. At the time of writing, the latest version of Tcl/Tk is 8.6.11.

Historically, some platforms (notably macOS) have lagged behind in shipping the latest version of Tcl/Tk. While platform support at the time of writing is fairly consistent, it's possible that differences may arise again in the future.

To discover the exact version of Tcl/Tk installed on your system, you can execute the following commands at a Python prompt:

```
>>> import tkinter as tk
>>> tk.Tcl().call('info', 'patchlevel')
```

This code uses the `Tcl()` function to create a new Tcl interpreter, then calls the `info patchlevel` command. Here's what this command returns on several platforms using the most commonly used Python 3 distribution for each platform:

Platform	Python version	Tcl/Tk version
Windows 10	3.9 (from python.org)	8.6.9
macOS High Sierra	3.9 (from python.org)	8.6.8
Ubuntu 20.04	3.8 (from the repositories)	8.6.10
Debian 10	3.7 (from the repositories)	8.6.9

As you can see, none of these platforms offer the latest version of Tcl/Tk, and even those with newer versions of Python may have older versions of Tcl/Tk. Ultimately, if you intend to write cross-platform Tkinter code, make sure you are not relying on features from the very latest version of Tcl/Tk.

Application menus across platforms

The application menu is probably one of the most visible areas where both capabilities and conventions vary between platforms. As mentioned in *Chapter 7, Creating Menus with Menu and Tkinter Dialogs*, we should be aware of both the limitations and the expectations on major operating systems when designing our menus.

Menu widget capabilities

The `Menu` widget, which we learned about in *Chapter 7*, is different from most other Tkinter widgets in that it relies on the menu facilities of the underlying platform. This allows your application to have a menu that behaves natively; for example, on macOS, the menu appears in the global menu area at the top of the screen, while on Windows it appears in the application window under the taskbar.

Because of this design, there are some limitations when working with cross-platform Menu widgets. To demonstrate this, let's build an extremely non-cross-platform menu.

We'll begin by creating a simple Tk window with a menu, like so:

```python
# non_cross_platform_menu.py

import tkinter as tk
from tkinter.messagebox import showinfo
root = tk.Tk()
root.geometry("300x200")
menu = tk.Menu(root)
```

Now, we'll create a cascade menu:

```python
smile = tk.PhotoImage(file='smile.gif')
smile_menu = tk.Menu(menu, tearoff=False)
smile_menu.add_command(
  image=smile,
  command=lambda: showinfo(message="Smile!")
)
smile_menu.add_command(label='test')
menu.add_cascade(image=smile, menu=smile_menu)
```

The smile_menu contains two commands, one with a text label and the other with only an image. We've also used the image when adding the cascade to the menu, so that it shouldn't have a text label, just an image.

While we're at it, let's add some colors; in *Chapter 9, Improving the Look with Styles and Themes*, we customized the color of the application menu, mentioning that it only worked in Linux. Let's see what it does on other platforms; add in the following code:

```python
menu.configure(foreground='white', background='navy')
smile_menu.configure(foreground='yellow', background='red')
```

That should make our main menu white text on a black background, and the cascade yellow on red.

Next, let's add a separator and a command directly to the main menu, after the smile_menu:

```python
menu.add_separator()
menu.add_command(
  label='Top level command',
  command=lambda: showinfo(message='By your command!')
)
```

Last of all, we'll create a Checkbutton widget directly on the main menu, and finish with the usual boilerplate to configure root and run the mainloop() method:

```
boolvar = tk.BooleanVar()
menu.add_checkbutton(label="It is true", variable=boolvar)

root.config(menu=menu)
root.mainloop()
```

Save this file and execute the code. Depending on your operating system, you'll see some different things.

If you are on Linux (in this case, Ubuntu 20.04), it seems to work mostly as expected:

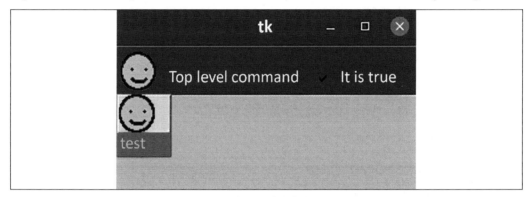

Figure 10.1: The menu experiment on Ubuntu 20.04

We have our first cascade labeled with the smiley face GIF, our top-level menu command, and our top-level Checkbutton (which we've checked, because it is true that our menu works!). The colors also seem to be correct, although the background of the GIF is the default grey rather than the red we would expect (the GIF itself has a transparent background).

If you're using Windows 10, you should see something more like this:

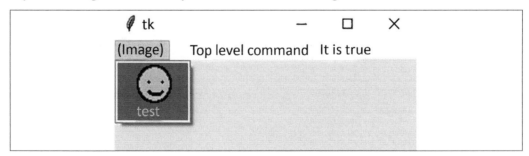

Figure 10.2: The menu experiment on Windows 10

Instead of our smiling icon in the top menu, we only have the text **(Image)**. Even if we specify a label, this text shows up where the image should be. Fortunately, the image does appear when we use it in the cascade menu. As for the colors, they work as expected in the cascade menu, but the top-level menu ignores them completely. The command in the main menu appears and works just fine, but the Checkbutton widget does not. Its label appears and can be clicked on, but the check mark itself does not appear.

Finally, let's try this menu on macOS. It should look something like this:

Figure 10.3: The menu experiment on macOS

On macOS, our menu shows up not in the program window, but in the global menu at the top of the screen, as macOS users would expect it to. However, there are some obvious problems.

First, while our smiling icon appears, it's cut off. Since the top bar is a fixed height and Tkinter will not resize our icon for us, images larger than the top bar height get truncated. There are bigger problems too: neither the top-level command nor the Checkbutton widget are anywhere to be seen. Only our cascade menu shows up. Color-wise, the top-level menu ignored our colors, while the cascades only honored the foreground color (resulting in a fairly unreadable yellow-on-gray combination). Also note that we have a "Python" cascade menu that we did not create.

On each platform, we're limited by the capabilities of the menu system, and while it appears that anything goes for menus on Linux, the other two operating systems require more care when constructing menus.

To avoid any issues with menus, follow these guidelines:

- Avoid command, Checkbutton, and Radiobutton items in the main menu; stick to cascade menus only.
- Don't use images in the top-level main menu.
- Don't use colors to style the menu, at least not on Windows or macOS.
- If you must do any of the preceding points, create separate menus for each platform.

If you take the approach of building separate menus for each platform, of course, you can implement whatever features are supported on the platform in question. However, just because you *can* use a feature on a platform doesn't necessarily mean you *should*. In the next section, we'll look at the guidelines and standards that can help you decide how to implement a menu on each platform.

Menu guidelines and standards

Each of our major platforms offers standards to direct developers in making user interfaces that meet the expectations of that system's users. While these standards should be taken into consideration for the whole application, one of the most visible areas affected by them is the layout of the application menu (or menu bar, to use the standard terminology).

Let's look at the standards available for each platform, which we'll refer to later in the chapter when we create a cross-platform main menu.

Windows user experience interaction guidelines

Microsoft's *Windows user experience interaction guidelines*, available at `https://docs.microsoft.com/en-us/windows/win32/uxguide/guidelines`, offer developers a wealth of information for designing applications that fit right in to the Windows desktop. Among many guidelines offered for menu bar design is a description of the standard menu items and how they should be arranged.

> At the time of writing, Microsoft has just released newer guidelines aimed at Windows 11 and the Universal Windows Platform, available at `https://docs.microsoft.com/en-us/windows/apps/design/basics/`. However, these newer guidelines do not offer specific guidance on menu structure, so we have used the older guidelines instead.

Apple's human interface guidelines

Apple's human interface guidelines are available at `https://developer.apple.com/macos/human-interface-guidelines/` and offer a detailed set of rules for creating macOS-friendly interfaces.

While much of the basic advice for menu bar design is similar to that offered by Microsoft, the layout recommendations are quite different and much more specific. For example, the first cascade on a macOS application should be the App menu, a menu named after the application, which contains items like **About** and **Preferences**.

Linux and BSD human interface guidelines

In sharp contrast to Windows and macOS, Linux, BSD, and other X11 systems have no blessed default desktop environments or controlling entities to dictate UI standards. There are well over a dozen full desktop environments available for these platforms, each with its own goals and ideas about user interaction. While there are multiple projects working to create **human interface guidelines (HIG)** for these platforms, we'll be following the Gnome HIG from the Gnome project. This set of guidelines is used by the Gnome, MATE, and XFCE desktops and is available at `https://developer.gnome.org/hig/`. The Gnome desktop is the default desktop environment on many Linux distributions, including Red Hat, Ubuntu, and notably Debian, which is our target Linux environment at ABQ.

Menus and accelerator keys

Accelerator keys are keyboard shortcuts assigned to common application actions, particularly menu items. Thus far, we've added no accelerator keys, which is bad for keyboard-only users.

In Tkinter, accelerator keys can be assigned to a widget using the `bind()` method. We can also use the `bind_all()` method, which can be called on any widget and effectively binds an event globally (that is, even if the widget that called `bind_all()` is not focused). Our menu items also take an `accelerator` argument, which can be used to specify a string that will be shown in the menu as an accelerator key hint.

The UI guidelines on each platform define standard accelerator keys for common actions, most of which are the same across platforms since they descend from the IBM **Common User Access (CUA)** standard established in the 1980s. The most notable difference is the use of the command (⌘) key on macOS in place of the control (*Ctrl*) key used by Windows and Linux.

As we rewrite our application menus for cross-platform compatibility, we'll also add platform-appropriate accelerator keys.

Cross-platform fonts

In *Chapter 9*, *Improving the Look with Styles and Themes*, we learned how easy it is to customize Tkinter's fonts to change the look and feel of your application. Doing so, however, can cause inconsistencies across platforms.

There are around 18 fonts that are shared between macOS and Windows, but not all of them look identical on both platforms. As for Linux, most distributions ship with none of those 18 fonts due to license issues.

Unless you can guarantee that a particular font is available on all supported platforms, it's best to avoid naming specific font families in your styles. Fortunately, if you do happen to specify a nonexistent font, Tkinter will just use the default, but even that could cause layout or readability issues in certain cases.

To be safe, stick with Tkinter's named fonts, which are automatically set to the same defaults on each platform.

Cross-platform theme support

As we saw in *Chapter 9, Improving the Look with Styles and Themes*, Ttk provides a number of themes that differ from platform to platform. Each platform contains an alias called "default", which points to the most sensible theme for that platform. Attempting to set a theme that doesn't exist results in an exception, so avoid hardcoding a theme setting in your application, and make sure theme choices are checked against the output of `Style.theme_names()`.

Window zoomed state

In addition to maximized and minimized windows, many windowing environments have the concept of a "zoomed" window, which takes over the screen completely. On Windows or macOS, it can be activated for a Tkinter application using the root window's `state()` method, as follows:

```
from tkinter import *
root = Tk()
root.state('zoomed')
root.mainloop()
```

On Windows or macOS, this creates a window that takes over the screen; on Linux or BSD, however, it raises an exception because X11 does not provide anything for setting a zoomed state.

On X11, this is accomplished by turning on the root window's `-zoomed` attribute as follows:

```
root.attributes('-zoomed', True)
```

Unfortunately, the preceding code raises an exception on Windows and macOS. If you need to be able to set this state in a program, you'll need to use some platform-specific code.

Now that we've walked through a variety of cross-platform issues, let's take a look at ABQ Data Entry and see what we can do to improve its behavior across different operating systems.

Improving our application's cross-platform compatibility

Our application does pretty well across platforms, but there are some things we can do to improve it:

- First, our application stores its preferences in the user's home folder, which is not ideal on any platform. Most desktop platforms define specific locations where configuration files should be placed, so we will fix our application to use those for the abq_settings.json file.

- Second, we're creating our CSV files without specifying any encoding; if a user inserted a Unicode character (say, in the Notes field), file saving would raise an exception and fail on non-Unicode platforms.

- Finally, the current menu structure does not really come close to following any of the human interface guidelines we've discussed. We'll implement separate menus for each platform to ensure users have a UI that is consistent with their platform.

Let's get started!

Storing preferences correctly

Each platform defines a proper location for storing user configuration files:

- Linux and other X11 systems store configuration files in a location defined in the $XDG_CONFIG_HOME environment variable, which defaults to $HOME/.config if it's not defined.

- macOS user configuration files are stored in $HOME/Library/Application Support/.

- Windows user configuration files are stored in %USERPROFILE%\AppData\ Local. Though if your environment uses **Active Directory** (**AD**) with roaming profiles, you might prefer to use %HOME%\AppData\Roaming instead.

To realize this in our application, we'll need to update the SettingsModel class. Remember that our SettingsModel class's initializer method currently places the configuration file in Path.home(), which returns the user's home directory on each platform. Let's update this with some platform-specific code.

To begin, open models.py and import the platform module, like so:

```
# models.py, at the top
import platform
```

To figure out the directories required, we're going to need to get the name of the platform, as well as some environment variables. The os.environ variable is a dictionary containing the environment variables set on the system. Since we've already imported os into the models.py file, we can use os.environ to retrieve the variables we need.

In the SettingsModel class, we'll create a dictionary for looking up the correct configuration directories, like so:

```
config_dirs = {
  "Linux": Path(
    os.environ.get('$XDG_CONFIG_HOME', Path.home() / '.config')
  ),
  "freebsd7": Path(
    os.environ.get('$XDG_CONFIG_HOME', Path.home() / '.config')
  ),
  'Darwin': Path.home() / 'Library' / 'Application Support',
  'Windows': Path.home() / 'AppData' / 'Local'
}
```

In each case, we've matched a platform name with a pathlib.Path object pointing to the default configuration directory for each platform. Now, inside the SettingsModel initializer, we just need to look up the correct directory using the value of platform.system().

Update the __init__() method as follows:

```
def __init__(self):
  filename = 'abq_settings.json'
  filedir = self.config_dirs.get(platform.system(), Path.home())
  self.filepath = filedir / filename
  self.load()
```

If the platform is not in our list, we simply default to Path.home() to place the configuration file in the user's home directory. Otherwise, the file should be placed correctly for the platform.

Now when you run the application, you should find that any previous preferences are reset to the default (since we're now looking for the configuration file in a different location), and that if you save new preferences, the file abq_settings.json shows up in your platform's configuration directory.

Specifying an encoding for our CSV file

Our application is currently saving CSV files using the system's default encoding. This could be a problem for Windows users if they try to use Unicode characters.

In `models.py`, we need to locate the three instances of `open()` in our `CSVModel` class and specify an encoding, as in this example:

```
# models.py, in CSVModel.save_record()

    with open(
      self.filename, 'a', encoding='utf-8', newline=''
    ) as fh:
```

Make sure to update all the `open()` calls in `models.py`, including those in `SettingsModel`. With this change, the Unicode characters should no longer be a problem.

Making platform-appropriate menus

Creating platform-specific menus is going to be a bit more involved than the previous fixes. Our basic approach will be to create multiple menu classes and use a selector function to return an appropriate class as explained in the previous section.

Before we can do this, we'll need to prepare our `MainMenu` class so that it's easier to subclass.

Preparing our MainMenu class

Currently, the bulk of the configuration of our `MainMenu` class takes place in `__init__()`. For each platform, though, we're going to need to build the menu with a different structure, and with some different details for certain commands. To make this simpler, we're going to take a compositional approach, in which we'll break the menu creation into many discrete methods that we can then compose in each subclass as needed.

The first thing we'll do is change its name to explain its role more clearly:

```
class GenericMainMenu(tk.Menu):

  styles = dict()
```

We've also created an empty `styles` dictionary as a class attribute. Since menu styles are not supported across all platforms well, this empty dictionary can act as a placeholder so that we can apply styles when desired by simply overriding this attribute.

Next, we're going to create individual methods for creating each menu item. Because these items may be added to different menus depending on the platform, each method will take a `menu` argument that will be used to specify which `Menu` object it will be added to.

Let's begin with methods for creating our **Select file** and **Quit** command entries:

```python
def _add_file_open(self, menu):

  menu.add_command(
     label='Select file…', command=self._event('<<FileSelect>>'),
     image=self.icons.get('file'), compound=tk.LEFT
)

def _add_quit(self, menu):
  menu.add_command(
     label='Quit', command=self._event('<<FileQuit>>'),
     image=self.icons.get('quit'), compound=tk.LEFT
  )
```

Next, create the methods to add the auto-fill settings options:

```python
def _add_autofill_date(self, menu):
  menu.add_checkbutton(
     label='Autofill Date', variable=self.settings['autofill date']
  )

def _add_autofill_sheet(self, menu):
  menu.add_checkbutton(
     label='Autofill Sheet data',
     variable=self.settings['autofill sheet data']
  )
```

For our font options that have their own sub-menus, we'll create methods that create the whole sub-menu, like so:

```python
def _add_font_size_menu(self, menu):
  font_size_menu = tk.Menu(self, tearoff=False, **self.styles)
  for size in range(6, 17, 1):
```

```
      font_size_menu.add_radiobutton(
        label=size, value=size,
        variable=self.settings['font size']
      )
    menu.add_cascade(label='Font size', menu=font_size_menu)

  def _add_font_family_menu(self, menu):
    font_family_menu = tk.Menu(self, tearoff=False, **self.styles)
    for family in font.families():
      font_family_menu.add_radiobutton(
        label=family, value=family,
        variable=self.settings['font family']
      )
    menu.add_cascade(label='Font family', menu=font_family_menu)
```

Note that we've used the self.styles dict in defining our cascade menus; although it's empty in this class, we want the styles to apply to all menus if we define them.

For the themes menu, we'll do the same, and also set up the trace that displays the warning message, as follows:

```
  def _add_themes_menu(self, menu):
    style = ttk.Style()
    themes_menu = tk.Menu(self, tearoff=False, **self.styles)
    for theme in style.theme_names():
      themes_menu.add_radiobutton(
        label=theme, value=theme,
        variable=self.settings['theme']
      )
    menu.add_cascade(label='Theme', menu=themes_menu)
    self.settings['theme'].trace_add('write', self._on_theme_change)
```

Finally, let's add the last three methods for our navigation and About commands:

```
  def _add_go_record_list(self, menu):
    menu.add_command(
      label="Record List", command=self._event('<<ShowRecordlist>>'),
      image=self.icons.get('record_list'), compound=tk.LEFT
    )

  def _add_go_new_record(self, menu):
    menu.add_command(
      label="New Record", command=self._event('<<NewRecord>>'),
      image=self.icons.get('new_record'), compound=tk.LEFT
```

```
  )

def _add_about(self, menu):
  menu.add_command(
    label='About…', command=self.show_about,
    image=self.icons.get('about'), compound=tk.LEFT
  )
```

Now, to compose these methods into a menu, we'll create a new method called
_build_menu(). This method can be overridden by our subclasses, leaving __init__
() to take care of the common setup tasks.

To see how this will work, let's create a version of this method that will recreate our
generic menu:

```
def _build_menu(self):
  # The file menu
  self._menus['File'] = tk.Menu(self, tearoff=False, **self.styles)
  self._add_file_open(self._menus['File'])
  self._menus['File'].add_separator()
  self._add_quit(self._menus['File'])

  # The options menu
  self._menus['Options'] =
    tk.Menu(
      self, tearoff=False, **self.styles
    )
  self._add_autofill_date(self._menus['Options'])
  self._add_autofill_sheet(self._menus['Options'])
  self._add_font_size_menu(self._menus['Options'])
  self._add_font_family_menu(self._menus['Options'])
  self._add_themes_menu(self._menus['Options'])

  # switch from recordlist to recordform
  self._menus['Go'] = tk.Menu(self, tearoff=False, **self.styles)
  self._add_go_record_list(self._menus['Go'])
  self._add_go_new_record(self._menus['Go'])

  # The help menu
  self._menus['Help'] = tk.Menu(self, tearoff=False, **self.styles)
  self.add_cascade(label='Help', menu=self._menus['Help'])
  self._add_about(self._menus['Help'])

  for label, menu in self._menus.items():
    self.add_cascade(label=label, menu=menu)
```

Here, we're creating our File, Options, Go, and Help cascade menus, and passing each one to the appropriate item-adding methods to set up its items. We're storing these in a dictionary, self._menus, rather than as local variables. At the end of the method, we iterate through the dictionary to add each cascade to the main menu.

Now, we can reduce the initializer of this class to a bare skeleton of method calls, like so:

```
def __init__(self, parent, settings, **kwargs):
    super().__init__(parent, **kwargs)
    self.settings = settings
    self._create_icons()
    self._menus = dict()
    self._build_menu()
    self.configure(**self.styles)
```

After calling the superclass initializer, this method just saves the settings, creates the icons and the _menus dictionary, then calls _build_menu(). If any styles are set, those are applied to the main menu by self.configure().

Adding accelerators

Before we start building subclasses of GenericMainMenu, let's make it possible to add platform-specific accelerator keys to each menu. These are simply keyboard shortcuts that can activate our menu items. We don't need these for every menu item, just a few commands that will be commonly used.

To create a key binding to menu items, there are two steps:

1. Bind the keyboard event to the callback using the bind_all() method.
2. Label the menu item with the keyboard sequence using the menu entry's accelerator argument.

It's important to understand that we need to do both; the accelerator argument does not automatically set up the key binding, it just determines how the menu item will be labeled. Likewise, the bind_all() method will not cause menu items to be labeled, it will just create the event binding.

To accomplish both, we'll create two class attribute dictionaries, one for the accelerators and one for the key bindings, like so:

```
class GenericMainMenu(tk.Menu):

    accelerators = {
```

```
    'file_open': 'Ctrl+O',
    'quit': 'Ctrl+Q',
    'record_list': 'Ctrl+L',
    'new_record': 'Ctrl+R',
}

keybinds = {
    '<Control-o>': '<<FileSelect>>',
    '<Control-q>': '<<FileQuit>>',
    '<Control-n>': '<<NewRecord>>',
    '<Control-l>': '<<ShowRecordlist>>'
}
```

The first dictionary simply matches accelerator strings with keys that we can use in our menu definition methods. To use this dictionary, we just need to update those methods to include the accelerator; for example, update the _add_file_open() method like so:

```
# mainmenu.py, inside the GenericMainMenu class

def _add_file_open(self, menu):

    menu.add_command(
        label='Select file…',
        command=self._event('<<FileSelect>>'),
        accelerator=self.accelerators.get('file_open'),
        image=self.icons.get('file'),
        compound=tk.LEFT
    )
```

Go ahead and add the `accelerator` argument to the `add_command()` calls in `_add_quit()`, `_add_go_record_list()`, and `_add_go_new_record()` as well.

To handle the key bindings, we just need to create a method that will make the key bindings. Add this `_bind_accelerators()` method to the class:

```
# mainmenu.py, inside the GenericMainMenu class
def _bind_accelerators(self):

    for key, sequence in self.keybinds.items():
        self.bind_all(key, self._event(sequence))
```

The _bind_accelerators() method iterates the keybinds dictionary and binds each key sequence to a function created by the _event() method that will generate the given event. Note that we've used bind_all() here; unlike the bind() method, which only responds to events on the widget, the bind_all() method will cause the callback to be executed when the event is generated on *any* widget. Thus, regardless of what widget is selected or in focus, a *Control + Q* keystroke will quit the program, for example.

The final piece is to call this new method from our initializer. Add this to the end of GenericMainMenu.__init__():

```
    self._bind_accelerators()
```

Now the GenericMainMenu class is ready for subclassing. Let's go through one platform at a time and figure out what needs to be updated.

Building the Windows menu

After studying the *Windows user experience interaction guidelines*, you deem the following changes are necessary to make our menu Windows-friendly:

- **File | Quit** should be changed to **File | Exit**, and there should be no accelerator for it. Windows uses *Alt + F4* to close programs, and this is handled by Windows automatically.

- Windows can handle commands in the menu bar just fine, and the guidelines encourage this for frequently used functionality. We'll move our Record List and New Record commands directly to the main menu. We'll have to remove the icons, though, since it can't handle icons in the main menu.

- Configuration option items are supposed to go under a Tools menu, separated from the rest of the items in tools (if there are any). We'll need to create a Tools menu and move our options there.

Let's implement these changes and create our Windows menu class. Start by subclassing the GenericMainMenu class like so:

```
class WindowsMainMenu(GenericMainMenu):
```

The first thing we'll do is override the initializer so we can remove the keybinding for **File | Exit**:

```
# mainmenu.py, inside WindowsMainMenu
  def __init__(self, *args, **kwargs):
    del(self.keybinds['<Control-q>'])
    super().__init__(*args, **kwargs)
```

Next, we'll need to override the _add_quit() method to relabel it and remove the accelerator:

```python
def _add_quit(self, menu):
  menu.add_command(
    label='Exit', command=self._event('<<FileQuit>>'),
    image=self.icons.get('quit'), compound=tk.LEFT
  )
```

We need to remove the icons for the two navigation commands, so that we don't have the **(Image)** string showing up in our menu. To do that, we'll next override the _create_icons() method, as follows:

```python
# mainmenu.py, inside WindowsMainMenu

def _create_icons(self):
  super()._create_icons()
  del(self.icons['new_record'])
  del(self.icons['record_list'])
```

The superclass version of the method creates self.icons, so we just need to run it and delete the icons we don't want.

Now that those are fixed, we can create the _build_menu() method to compose our menu, starting with the three cascades like so:

```python
def _build_menu(self):
  # The File menu
  self._menus['File'] = tk.Menu(self, tearoff=False)
  self._add_file_open(self._menus['File'])
  self._menus['File'].add_separator()
  self._add_quit(self._menus['File'])

  # The Tools menu
  self._menus['Tools'] = tk.Menu(self, tearoff=False)
  self._add_autofill_date(self._menus['Tools'])
  self._add_autofill_sheet(self._menus['Tools'])
  self._add_font_size_menu(self._menus['Tools'])
  self._add_font_family_menu(self._menus['Tools'])
  self._add_themes_menu(self._menus['Tools'])

  # The Help menu
  self._menus['Help'] = tk.Menu(self, tearoff=False)
  self._add_about(self._menus['Help'])
```

Since we'd like to add our navigation command entries for Record List and New Record directly to the main menu rather than to a cascade menu, we can't just iterate over the _menus dictionary to add the cascades. Instead, we'll have to manually add the entries to the top-level menu, like so:

```
self.add_cascade(label='File', menu=self._menus['File'])
self.add_cascade(label='Tools', menu=self._menus['Tools'])
self._add_go_record_list(self)
self._add_go_new_record(self)
self.add_cascade(label='Help', menu=self._menus['Help'])
```

The Windows menu is now complete and ready to use. Let's move on to the next platform!

Building the Linux menu

Our GenericMainMenu class is pretty close to the Gnome HIG, but there is one change to be made: our Options menu doesn't really belong; rather, we need to split its items into two categories:

- The autofill options, since they change the way data is entered in the form, belong in an Edit menu.
- The font and theme options, since they only change the appearance of the application and not the actual data, belong in a View menu.

Since Linux also fully supports menu colors, we'll add our color styles back to this version of the menu.

Let's start by subclassing GenericMainMenu and defining some styles:

```
# mainmenu.py

class LinuxMainMenu(GenericMainMenu):

  styles = {
    'background': '#333',
    'foreground': 'white',
    'activebackground': '#777',
    'activeforeground': 'white',
    'relief': tk.GROOVE
  }
```

These menu styles aren't strictly necessary, but if we're going to make a separate menu for Linux, we may as well take advantage of some of its features!

Now let's begin the _build_menu() method with the File and Edit menus:

```python
def _build_menu(self):
    self._menus['File'] = tk.Menu(self, tearoff=False, **self.styles)
    self._add_file_open(self._menus['File'])
    self._menus['File'].add_separator()
    self._add_quit(self._menus['File'])
    self._menus['Edit'] = tk.Menu(self, tearoff=False, **self.styles)
    self._add_autofill_date(self._menus['Edit'])
    self._add_autofill_sheet(self._menus['Edit'])
```

Note that we've added back **self.styles to each Menu() call to apply the styles. We'll do the same building the next three cascades, as follows:

```python
    self._menus['View'] = tk.Menu(self, tearoff=False, **self.styles)
    self._add_font_size_menu(self._menus['View'])
    self._add_font_family_menu(self._menus['View'])
    self._add_themes_menu(self._menus['View'])
    self._menus['Go'] = tk.Menu(self, tearoff=False, **self.styles)
    self._add_go_record_list(self._menus['Go'])
    self._add_go_new_record(self._menus['Go'])
    self._menus['Help'] = tk.Menu(self, tearoff=False, **self.styles)
    self._add_about(self._menus['Help'])
```

Finally, we'll iterate over the _menus dictionary and add all the cascades:

```python
    for label, menu in self._menus.items():
        self.add_cascade(label=label, menu=menu)
```

We don't need to change anything else; our accelerators and the rest of the menu line up pretty well with the Gnome HIG.

Building the macOS menu

Of the three platform-specific menus, the macOS menu will need the most extensive changes. Unlike the Windows and Gnome guidelines, which mostly suggest categories, the Apple guidelines are very specific about which menus should be created and which items belong in them. Furthermore, macOS also creates and pre-populates some of these menus with default commands, so we'll need to use special arguments to hook into those menus and add our own items.

The changes we need to make to comply with Apple's HIG are as follows:

- We need to create an **App menu**. This is the first menu macOS creates, just to the right of the Apple icon on the menu bar. It's created by default, but we'll need to hook into it to add some custom items.

- The About command belongs in the App menu; we'll move it there and remove the unused Help menu.

- Since macOS will provide a Quit command for us, we'll remove ours.

- As we did with the Linux menu, our options will be split between the Edit and View menus.

- We need to add a Window menu; this is another autogenerated menu that macOS fills with window management and navigation functions. Our navigation items will be moved from the Go menu to this menu.

- Finally, macOS uses the *command* key rather than the *Control* key to activate accelerators. We need to update both our key bindings and accelerator dictionaries accordingly.

As before, we'll start by creating a subclass of `GenericMainMenu`:

```python
class MacOsMainMenu(GenericMainMenu):

  keybinds = {
    '<Command-o>': '<<FileSelect>>',
    '<Command-n>': '<<NewRecord>>',
    '<Command-l>': '<<ShowRecordlist>>'
  }
  accelerators = {
    'file_open': 'Cmd-O',
    'record_list': 'Cmd-L',
    'new_record': 'Cmd-R',
  }
```

The first thing we've done is redefine the `keybinds` and `accelerators` dictionaries to remove the Quit entries and change `"Control"` to `"Command"`. Note that, when the menu displays, Tkinter will automatically replace the strings `Command` or `Cmd` with the symbol for the command key (⌘), so make sure to use one or the other when specifying accelerators.

Now, let's start working on the `_build_menu()` method, as follows:

```python
def _build_menu(self):
  self._menus['ABQ Data Entry'] = tk.Menu(
    self, tearoff=False,
    name='apple'
  )
  self._add_about(self._menus['ABQ Data Entry'])
  self._menus['ABQ Data Entry'].add_separator()
```

The first order of business is the App menu. To access this built-in menu, all we need to do is pass in a `name` argument set to `apple` when we create the `Menu` object. The App menu should contain both our About option and our Quit option, but we only need to add the former since macOS automatically adds a Quit action. Note that we've also added a separator, which should always be added after the About command.

> The App menu should *always* be the first menu you add to the main menu on macOS. If you add anything else first, your customized app menu items will be added in their own menu rather than in the generated App menu.

Before moving on, we need to make one correction to our About command. Apple's HIG specifies that this command should read *About <program name>* rather than just *About*. So, we'll need to override `_add_about()` to correct this, like so:

```
# mainmenu.py, inside MacOSMainMenu

def _add_about(self, menu):
  menu.add_command(
    label='About ABQ Data Entry', command=self.show_about,
    image=self.icons.get('about'), compound=tk.LEFT
  )
```

> Your App menu will currently read "Python" rather than "ABQ Data Entry". We'll address this when we package our application in *Chapter 16, Packaging with setuptools and cxFreeze*.

After the App menu is created, let's create our File, Edit, and View menus, like so:

```
# mainmenu.py, inside MacOSMainMenu._build_menu()
    self._menus['File'] = tk.Menu(self, tearoff=False)
    self.add_cascade(label='File', menu=self._menus['File'])
    self._add_file_open(self._menus['File'])

    self._menus['Edit'] = tk.Menu(self, tearoff=False)
    self._add_autofill_date(self._menus['Edit'])
    self._add_autofill_sheet(self._menus['Edit'])

    self._menus['View'] = tk.Menu(self, tearoff=False)
    self._add_font_size_menu(self._menus['View'])
    self._add_font_family_menu(self._menus['View'])
    self._add_themes_menu(self._menus['View'])
```

We don't really need to do anything different there; however, the `Window` menu is another automatically generated menu created by macOS, so we will once again need to use the `name` argument when creating it:

```python
self._menus['Window'] = tk.Menu(
    self, name='window', tearoff=False
)
self._add_go_record_list(self._menus['Window'])
self._add_go_new_record(self._menus['Window'])
```

Finally, let's iterate over the _menus dictionary and add all the cascades:

```python
for label, menu in self._menus.items():
    self.add_cascade(label=label, menu=menu)
```

 Even though macOS automatically creates the App and Window menus, you still need to explicitly add the `Menu` objects to the main menu using `add_cascade()`, or your added items will not appear on the automatically created menu.

That completes our macOS menu class.

Creating and using our selector function

With our classes created, let's add a simple selector function to return the appropriate class for each platform; add this code to `mainmenu.py`:

```python
# mainmenu.py, at the end
def get_main_menu_for_os(os_name):
  menus = {
    'Linux': LinuxMainMenu,
    'Darwin': MacOsMainMenu,
    'freebsd7': LinuxMainMenu,
    'Windows': WindowsMainMenu
  }

  return menus.get(os_name, GenericMainMenu)
```

The keys in this dictionary are the output strings from `platform.system()`, which we have pointed to a platform-appropriate menu class. In the event we're running on some new, unknown system, we default to the `GenericMainMenu` class.

Now, back in `application.py`, we'll change our import statement from `mainmenu` to only import this function, like so:

```
# application.py, at the top

from .mainmenu import get_main_menu_for_os
import platform
```

Note that we've also imported `platform`, which we'll use to determine the running operating system.

Now, instead of calling `v.MainMenu()` (which no longer exists), we use the following function:

```
# application.py, inside Application.__init__()

    # menu = MainMenu(self, self.settings)
    menu_class = get_main_menu_for_os(platform.system())
    menu = menu_class(self, self.settings)
    self.config(menu=menu)
```

Now when you run the application, your menu appearance will change according to the platform. On Windows, you should see something like this:

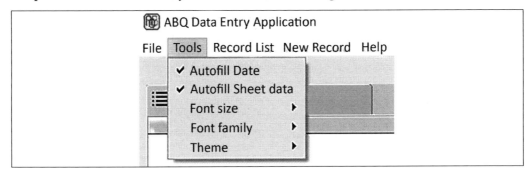

Figure 10.4: The menu system on a Windows computer

On macOS, you'll see something like this:

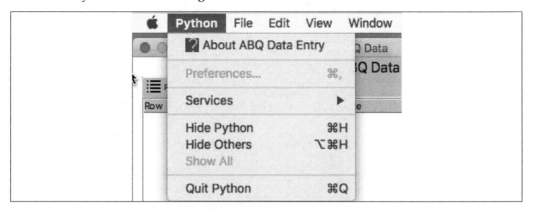

Figure 10.5: The menu system on macOS

On Linux or BSD, you'll see a menu as shown in the following screenshot:

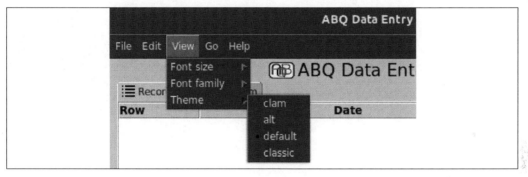

Figure 10.6: The menu system on Ubuntu Linux

Summary

In this chapter, you learned how to write Python software that works well across multiple platforms. You learned how to avoid common platform pitfalls in Python code such as filesystem differences and library support, and how to write software that intelligently adapts to the needs of different operating systems. You also learned about published guidelines that help developers write software that meets platform users' expectations, and you used these guidelines to create platform-specific menus for ABQ Data Entry.

In the next chapter, we're going to learn about automated testing. You'll learn to write tests that ensure your code works correctly, both for regular Python code and specifically for Tkinter code, and to take advantage of the testing framework included in the Python standard library.

11
Creating Automated Tests with unittest

With the size and complexity of your application rapidly expanding, you've become nervous about making changes. What if you break something? How will you know? You can, of course, run through all the features of the program manually with various input and watch for errors, but this approach gets harder and more time consuming as you add more features. What you really need is a fast and reliable way to make sure your program is working properly whenever you make a code change.

Fortunately, there is a way: automated testing. In this chapter, you'll learn about automated testing in the following topics:

- In *Automated testing basics*, you'll discover the fundamentals of automated testing in Python using unittest.
- In *Testing Tkinter code*, we'll discuss specific strategies for testing Tkinter applications.
- In *Writing tests for our application*, we'll apply this knowledge to the ABQ Data Entry application.

Automated testing basics

Up until now, testing our application has been a process of launching it, running it through a few basic procedures, and verifying that it did what we expected it to do. This approach works acceptably on a very small script, but, as our application grows, it becomes an increasingly time-consuming and error-prone process to verify the application's behavior.

Using automated testing, we can consistently verify our application logic within seconds. There are several forms of automated testing, but the two most common are **unit testing** and **integration testing**. Unit tests work with discrete pieces of code in isolation, allowing us to quickly verify the behavior of specific sections. Integration tests verify the interactions of multiple units of code. We'll be writing both kinds of tests to verify the behavior of our application.

A simple unit test

At its most basic, a unit test is just a short program that runs a unit of code under different conditions and compares its output against expected results.

Consider the following calculation class:

```python
# unittest_demo/mycalc.py

import random

class MyCalc:
    def __init__(self, a, b):
        self.a = a
        self.b = b

    def add(self):
        return self.a + self.b

    def mod_divide(self):
        if self.b == 0:
            raise ValueError("Cannot divide by zero")
        return (int(self.a / self.b), self.a % self.b)

    def rand_between(self):
        return (
            (random.random() * abs(self.a - self.b))
            + min(self.a, self.b)
        )
```

This class is initialized with two numbers on which it can subsequently perform a variety of mathematical operations.

Suppose we want to write some code to test if this class works as it should. A naive approach might look like this:

```
# unittest_demo/test_mycalc_no_unittest.py

from mycalc import MyCalc
mc1 = MyCalc(1, 100)
mc2 = MyCalc(10, 4)
try:
    assert mc1.add() == 101, "Test of add() failed."
    assert mc2.mod_divide() == (2, 2), "Test of mod_divide() failed."
except AssertionError as e:
    print("Test failed: ", e)
else:
    print("Tests succeeded!")
```

This test code creates a `MyCalc` object and then uses `assert` statements to check the output of `add()` and `mod_divide()` against expected values. The `assert` keyword in Python is a special statement that raises an `AssertionError` exception if the expression that follows it evaluates to `False`. The message string after the comma is the error string that will be passed to the `AssertionError` exception's initializer.

In other words, the statement `assert expression, "message"` is equivalent to:

```
if not expression:
    raise AssertionError("message")
```

Currently, all tests pass if you run the test script for `MyCalc`. Let's try changing the `add()` method to make it fail:

```
def add(self):
    return self.a - self.b
```

Now, running the test gives this error:

```
Test failed: Test of add() failed.
```

What is the value of such tests? With such a simple function, it seems pointless. But suppose someone decides to refactor our `mod_divide()` method as follows:

```
def mod_divide(self):
    #...
    return (self.a // self.b, self.a % self.b)
```

This method is a little more complex, and you may or may not be familiar with all the operators involved. However, since this passes our tests, we have some evidence that this algorithm is correct, even if we didn't completely understand the code. If there were a problem with the refactor, our tests could help us identify the problem quickly.

Testing pure mathematical functions is fairly simple; unfortunately, testing real application code presents us with some challenges that demand a more sophisticated approach.

Consider these issues:

- Code units often rely on a pre-existing state that must be set up before the test and cleared up afterward.
- Code may have side effects that change objects outside the code unit.
- Code may interact with resources that are slow, unreliable, or unpredictable.
- Real applications contain many functions and classes that require testing, and ideally we'd like to be alerted to all problems at once. Our test script, as written, would stop on the first failed assertion, so we'd only get alerted to one problem at a time.

To address these issues and others, programmers rely on **testing frameworks** to make writing and executing automated tests as simple, efficient, and reliable as possible.

The unittest module

The unittest module is the Python standard library's automated testing framework. It provides us with some powerful tools to make testing our code reasonably easy, and is based on some standard unit testing concepts found in many test frameworks. These concepts include:

- **Test**: A test is a single method that will either finish or raise an exception. Tests generally focus on one unit of code, such as a function, method, or process. A test can either pass, meaning the test was successful; fail, meaning the code failed the test; or error, meaning the test itself encountered a problem.
- **Test case**: A test case is a collection of tests that should be run together and contain similar setup and tear-down requirements, typically corresponding to a class or module. Test cases can have **fixtures**, which are items that need to be set up before each test and torn down after each test to provide a clean, predictable environment in which the test can run.

- **Test suite**: A test suite is a collection of test cases that cover all the code for an application or module.
- **Mock**: A mock is an object that stands in for another object. Typically, they're used to replace an external resource, such as a file, database, or library module. Mocks are patched over those resources during the test to provide a fast and predictable stand-in with no side effects.

To explore these concepts in depth, let's test our MyCalc class using unittest.

Writing a test case

Let's create a test case for the MyCalc class. Create a new file called test_mycalc.py, and enter this code:

```python
# unittest_demo/test_mycalc.py

import mycalc
import unittest

class TestMyCalc(unittest.TestCase):

    def test_add(self):
        mc = mycalc.MyCalc(1, 10)
        assert mc.add() == 11

if __name__ == '__main__':
    unittest.main()
```

 The names of both your test modules and your test methods should be prefixed with test_. Doing so allows the unittest runner to automatically find test modules and distinguish test methods from other methods in your test case classes.

As you probably guessed, the TestCase class represents a test case. To make our test case for MyCalc, we have subclassed TestCase and added a test_ method that will test some aspect of our class. Inside the test_add() method, we created a MyCalc object, then made an assertion about the output of add().

At the end of the file, we've added a call to unittest.main(), which will cause all test cases in the file to be executed.

If you run your test file at the command line, you should get the following output:

```
.
-----------------------------------------------------------------------
Ran 1 test in 0.000s
OK
```

The single dot on the first line represents our one test (test_add()). For each test method, unittest.main() will output one of the following:

- A dot, which means the test passed
- F, which means it failed
- E, meaning the test caused an error

At the end, we get a summary of what happened, including the number of tests run and how long it took. The OK indicates that all tests passed successfully.

To see what happens when a test fails, let's alter our test so that it intentionally fails:

```
def test_add(self):
    mc = mycalc.MyCalc(1, 10)
    assert mc.add() == 12
```

Now when you run the test module, you should see output like this:

```
F
=======================================================================
FAIL: test_add (__main__.TestMyCalc)
-----------------------------------------------------------------------
Traceback (most recent call last):
File "test_mycalc.py", line 8, in test_add
assert mc.add() == 12
AssertionError

-----------------------------------------------------------------------
Ran 1 test in 0.000s
FAILED (failures=1)
```

Note the single F at the top, representing our failed test. After all the tests have run, we get the full traceback of any failed tests, so that we can easily locate the failing code and correct it.

This traceback output isn't very ideal, though; we can see that mc.add() didn't return 12, but we don't know what it *did* return. We could add a comment string to our assert call, but unittest provides a nicer approach: TestCase assertion methods.

TestCase assertion methods

TestCase objects have a number of assertion methods that provide a cleaner and more robust way to run various tests on our code output.

For example, there is the TestCase.assertEqual() method to test equality, which we can use as follows:

```
def test_add(self):
    mc = mycalc.MyCalc(1, 10)
    self.assertEqual(mc.add(), 12)
```

When we run our test case with this code, you can see that the traceback is improved:

```
Traceback (most recent call last):
File "test_mycalc.py", line 11, in test_add
self.assertEqual(mc.add(), 12)
AssertionError: 11 != 12
```

Now, we can see the value that mc.add() returned, which is much more helpful for debugging. TestCase contains more than 20 assertion methods that can simplify testing for a variety of conditions such as class inheritance, raised exceptions, and sequence membership.

Some more commonly used ones are listed in the following table:

Method	Tests
assertEqual(a, b)	a == b
assertTrue(a)	a is True
assertFalse(a)	a is False
assertIn(item, sequence)	item in sequence
assertRaises(exception, callable, *args)	callable raises exception when called with args
assertGreater(a, b)	a is greater than b
assertLess(a, b)	a is less than b

 A full list of the available assertion methods can be found in the unittest documentation at https://docs.python.org/3/library/unittest.html#unittest.TestCase.

Let's use an assertion method to test that mod_divide() raises a ValueError exception when b is 0:

```
def test_mod_divide(self):
    mc = mycalc.MyCalc(1, 0)
    self.assertRaises(ValueError, mc.mod_divide)
```

assertRaises() *passes* if the function raises the given exception when called. If we need to pass any arguments into the tested function, they can be specified as additional arguments to assertRaises().

assertRaises() can also be used as a context manager like so:

```
def test_mod_divide(self):
    mc = mycalc.MyCalc(1, 0)
    with self.assertRaises(ValueError):
        mc.mod_divide()
```

This code accomplishes the exact same thing, but is a little clearer and more flexible, since it allows us to put multiple lines of code in the block.

 You can easily add your own custom assertion methods to your test case as well; it's simply a matter of creating a method that raises an AssertionError exception under some condition.

Fixtures

It should be clear that each test in our test case is going to need access to a MyCalc object. It would be nice if we didn't have to do this manually in each test method. To help us avoid this tedious task, the TestCase object offers a setUp() method. This method is run before every test case is run, and by overriding it we can take care of any setup that needs to be done for each test.

For example, we can use it to create MyCalc objects, like so:

```
def setUp(self):
    self.mycalc1_0 = mycalc.MyCalc(1, 0)
    self.mycalc36_12 = mycalc.MyCalc(36, 12)
```

Now, every test case can use these objects to run its tests rather than creating their own. Understand that the setUp() method will be rerun before *every* test, so these objects will always be reset between test methods. If we have items that need to be cleaned up after each test, we can override the tearDown() method as well, which is run after each test (in this case, it's not necessary).

Now that we have a `setUp()` method, our `test_add()` method can be much simpler:

```
def test_add(self):
  self.assertEqual(self.mycalc1_0.add(), 1)
  self.assertEqual(self.mycalc36_12.add(), 48)
```

In addition to the instance methods `setUp()` and `tearDown()`, `TestCase` also has class methods for setup and tear-down of the object itself as well; these are `setUpClass()` and `tearDownClass()`. These two methods can be used for slower operations that can be run when the test case is created and destroyed, rather than needing to be refreshed between each test; for example, you might use them to create complex objects that are required for your tests, but won't be altered by any of them.

Using Mock and patch

The `MyCalc.rand_between()` method generates a random number between a and b. Because we can't possibly predict its output, we can't provide a fixed value to test it against. How can we test this method?

A naive approach might look something like this:

```
def test_rand_between(self):
  rv = self.mycalc1_0.rand_between()
  self.assertLessEqual(rv, 1)
  self.assertGreaterEqual(rv, 0)
```

This test passes if our code is correct, but it doesn't necessarily fail if the code is wrong; in fact, if the code is wrong, it may pass or fail unpredictably since the return value of `rand_between()` is random. For example, if `MyCalc(1,10).rand_between()` was incorrectly returning values between 2 and 11, the test would pass if it returned 2 through 10, and only fail if it returned 11. Thus, even though the code is wrong, there would be only a 10% chance that the test would fail on each run of the test suite.

For the purposes of our tests, we can safely assume that a standard library function such as `random()` works correctly; so our unit test should really test whether *our* method correctly handles the number provided to it by `random()`. If we could temporarily replace `random()` with a function that returns a predictable fixed value, it would be simple to test the correctness of our subsequent calculations.

The `unittest.mock` module provides us with the `Mock` class for this purpose. `Mock` objects can be used to predictably simulate the behavior of another class, method, or library. We can give our `Mock` objects return values, side effects, properties, methods, and other features needed to fake the behavior of another class, object, function, or module, then drop them in place before running our tests.

To see this in action, let's create a fake `random()` function using `Mock`, like so:

```
from unittest.mock import Mock

#... inside TestMyCalc
def test_rand_between(self):
    fakerandom = Mock(return_value=.5)
```

The `Mock` object's `return_value` argument allows us to hard-code a value to be returned whenever it's called as a function. Here, our mock object `fakerandom` will behave like a function that always returns `0.5`.

Now we can put `fakerandom` in place of `random()` as follows:

```
#...
orig_random = mycalc.random.random
mycalc.random.random = fakerandom
rv = self.mycalc1_0.rand_between()
self.assertEqual(rv, 0.5)
mycalc.random.random = orig_random
```

We start by saving a reference to `mycalc.random.random` before replacing it. Note that we're specifically replacing *only* the version of `random` being used in `mycalc.py` so that we don't affect calls to `random()` anywhere else. It's a best practice to be as specific as possible when patching libraries to avoid unforeseen side effects.

With `fakerandom` in place, we can call `rand_between()` and test the output. Because `fakerandom()` will always return `0.5`, we know that the answer when a is 1 and b is 0 should be (`0.5 × 1 + 0`) = `0.5`. Any other value would indicate an error in our algorithm. At the end of the test code, we revert `random` to the original standard library function so that other tests (or the classes or functions they call) don't accidentally use the mock.

Having to store or revert the original library each time is an annoyance we can do without, so `unittest.mock` provides a cleaner approach using `patch()`. The `patch()` function can be used as either a context manager or a decorator, and either approach makes patching a `Mock` object into our code much cleaner.

Swapping in `fakerandom()` using `patch()` as a context manager looks like this:

```
# test_mycalc.py

from unittest.mock import patch

#... inside TestMyCalc
  def test_rand_between(self):
```

```
    with patch('mycalc.random.random') as fakerandom:
        fakerandom.return_value = 0.5
        rv = self.mycalc1_0.rand_between()
        self.assertEqual(rv, 0.5)
```

The `patch()` command takes an import path string and provides us with a new `Mock` object that it has patched in place of the object at that path. Inside the context manager block, we can set methods and properties on the `Mock` object, then run our actual tests. The patched function will be reverted to its original version when the block ends.

Using `patch()` as a decorator is similar:

```
    @patch('mycalc.random.random')
    def test_rand_between2(self, fakerandom):
        fakerandom.return_value = 0.5
        rv = self.mycalc1_0.rand_between()
        self.assertEqual(rv, 0.5)
```

In this case, the `Mock` object created by `patch()` is passed as an argument to our test method and will remain patched for the duration of the decorated function. This approach works well if we plan to use the mock multiple times in a test method.

Running multiple unit tests

While we can run our unit tests by including a call to `unittest.main()` at the end of the file, that approach doesn't scale well. As our application grows, we're going to write many test files, which we'll want to run in groups or all at once.

Fortunately, `unittest` can discover and run all tests in a project with one command:

```
$ python -m unittest
```

So long as you have followed the recommended naming scheme of prefixing your test modules with `test_`, running this command in your project's root directory should run all your test scripts.

Testing Tkinter code

Testing Tkinter code presents us with a few particular challenges. First, Tkinter handles many callbacks and methods asynchronously, meaning that we can't count on the results of some code to be apparent immediately. Also, testing GUI behaviors often relies on external factors such as window management or visual cues that our tests cannot detect.

In this section, we're going to learn some tools and strategies to address these issues and help you craft tests for your Tkinter code.

Managing asynchronous code

Whenever you interact with a Tkinter UI – whether it's clicking a button, typing in a field, or raising a window, for example – the response is not executed immediately in place.

Instead, these actions are placed in a sort of to-do list, called an **event queue**, to be handled later while code execution continues. While these actions seem instant to users, test code cannot count on a requested action being completed before the next line of code is run.

To solve this problem, Tkinter widgets have some methods that allow us to manage the event queue:

- `wait_visibility()`: This method causes the code to wait until a widget is fully drawn on-screen before executing the next line of code.
- `update_idletasks()`: This method forces Tkinter to process any idle tasks currently outstanding on the widget. Idle tasks are low-priority tasks such as drawing and rendering.
- `update()`: This method forces Tkinter to process all events that are outstanding on a widget, including calling callbacks, redraws, and geometry management. It includes everything that `update_idletasks()` does and more.

 The event queue will be discussed in more detail in *Chapter 14, Asynchronous Programming with Thread and Queue*.

Simulating user actions

When automating GUI tests, we may wish to know what happens when a user clicks on a certain widget, or types a certain keystroke. When these actions happen in the GUI, Tkinter generates an Event object for the widget and passes it to the event queue. We can do the same thing in code, using a widget's `event_generate()` method.

Specifying an event sequence

As we learned in *Chapter 6, Planning for the Expansion of Our Application*, we can cause an event to be registered on a widget by passing an event **sequence string** to event_generate() in the format `<EventModifier-EventType-EventDetail>`. Let's look at sequence strings in more detail.

The core part of a sequence string is the **event type**. It specifies the kind of event we're sending, such as a keystroke, mouse click, windowing event, and so on.

Tkinter has around 30 event types, but you will typically only need to work with the following:

Event types	Action represented
ButtonPress or Button	Mouse-button click
ButtonRelease	Lifting off a mouse button
KeyPress or Key	Pressing a keyboard key
KeyRelease	Lifting off a keyboard key
FocusIn	Giving focus to a widget, such as a button or input widget
FocusOut	Exiting a focused widget
Enter	The mouse cursor entering a widget
Leave	The mouse cursor moving off a widget
Configure	A change in the widget's configuration, for example, a config() call, or the user resizing the window, and so on

Event modifiers are optional words that can alter the event type; for example, Control, Alt, and Shift can be used to indicate that one of those modifier keys is held down; Double or Triple can be used with Button to indicate a double- or triple-click of the described button. Multiple modifiers can be strung together if required.

Event detail, only valid for keyboard or mouse events, describes which key or button was pressed. For example, `<Button-1>` refers to the left mouse button, while `<Button-3>` refers to the right. For letter and number keys, the literal letter or number can be used, such as `<Control-KeyPress-a>`; most symbols, however, are described by a word (minus, colon, semicolon, and so on) to avoid syntactic clashes.

For button presses and keypresses, the event type is technically optional; for example, you could use `<Control-a>` instead of `<Control-KeyPress-a>`. However, it's probably a good idea to leave it in for the sake of clarity. For example, `<1>` is a valid event, but does it refer to pressing the left mouse button or the 1 key? You may be surprised to find that it's the mouse button.

The following table shows some examples of valid event sequences:

Sequence	Meaning
`<Double-Button-3>`	Double-clicking the right mouse button
`<Alt-KeyPress-exclam>`	Holding *Alt* and typing an exclamation point
`<Control-Alt-Key-m>`	Holding *Control* and *Alt* and pressing the *M* key
`<KeyRelease-minus>`	Lifting off a pressed minus key

In addition to the sequence, we can pass other arguments to `event_generate()` that describe various aspects of the event. Many of these are redundant, but, in some cases, we need to provide extra information for the event to have any meaning; for example, mouse button events need to include an x and a y argument that specify the coordinates of the click.

Single brackets around a sequence indicate a built-in event type. Double brackets are used for custom events, such as those we have been using in our main menu and elsewhere.

Managing focus and grab

Focus refers to the widget or window that is currently receiving keyboard input. Widgets can also **grab focus**, preventing mouse movements or keystrokes outside their bounds.

Tkinter gives us these widget methods for managing focus and grab, some of which are useful for running tests:

Method	Description
`focus_set()`	Focuses the widget whenever its window next gains focus
`focus_force()`	Focuses a widget and the window it's in, immediately
`grab_set()`	The widget grabs all events for the application
`grab_set_global()`	The widget grabs all screen events
`grab_release()`	The widget relinquishes its grab

In a test environment, we can use these methods to make sure that our generated keyboard and mouse events are going to the correct widget or window.

Most of the time the focus_set() method will be adequate, but depending on the behavior of your application and your operating system's windowing environment, you may need the more extreme enforcement of focus_force() or grab_set().

Getting widget information

Tkinter widgets have a set of winfo_ methods that give us access to information about the widget. While the available functionality leaves much to be desired, these methods include some information we can use in tests to provide feedback about the state of a given widget.

The following are a few winfo_ methods that we will find useful:

Method	Description
winfo_height(), winfo_width()	Get the height and width of the widget
winfo_children()	Get a list of child widgets
winfo_geometry()	Get the size and location of the widget
winfo_ismapped()	Determine whether the widget is mapped (that is, it's been added to a layout using a geometry manager)
winfo_viewable()	Determine whether a widget is viewable (that is, it and all its parents have been mapped)
winfo_x(), winfo_y()	Get the x or y coordinate of the widget's top-left corner

Writing tests for our application

Let's put our knowledge of unittest and Tkinter to work and write some automated tests for our application. To get started, we need to create a test module. Make a directory called test inside the abq_data_entry package, and create the customary empty __init__.py file inside. We'll create all of our test modules inside this directory.

Testing the data model

Our CSVModel class is fairly self-contained apart from its need to read and write files. We'll need to mock out this functionality so that the tests don't disturb the filesystem. Since file operations are one of the more common things that need to be mocked out in a test, the mock module provides mock_open(), a Mock subclass ready-made to replace Python's open() method. When called, a mock_open object returns a mock file handle object, complete with support for the read(), write(), and readlines() methods.

Create a new file in the `test` directory called `test_models.py`. This will be our test module for our data model classes. Begin it with some module imports:

```python
# test_models.py
from .. import models
from unittest import TestCase
from unittest import mock
from pathlib import Path
```

In addition to the `models` module, we'll need `TestCase` and `mock`, of course, as well as the `Path` class since our `CSVModel` works with `Path` objects internally.

Now, we'll begin a test case for the `CSVModel` class, like so:

```python
class TestCSVModel(TestCase):

  def setUp(self):

    self.file1_open = mock.mock_open(
      read_data=(
        "Date,Time,Technician,Lab,Plot,Seed Sample,"
        "Humidity,Light,Temperature,Equipment Fault,"
        "Plants,Blossoms,Fruit,Min Height,Max Height,"
        "Med Height,Notes\r\n"
        "2021-06-01,8:00,J Simms,A,2,AX478,24.47,1.01,21.44,"
        "False,14,27,1,2.35,9.2,5.09,\r\n"
        "2021-06-01,8:00,J Simms,A,3,AX479,24.15,1,20.82,"
        "False,18,49,6,2.47,14.2,11.83,\r\n"
      )
    )
    self.file2_open = mock.mock_open(read_data='')

    self.model1 = models.CSVModel('file1')
    self.model2 = models.CSVModel('file2')
```

In the `setUp()` method for this case, we've created two mocked data files. The first contains a CSV header and two rows of CSV data, while the second is empty. The `mock_open` object's `read_data` argument allows us to specify a string that will be returned when code attempts to read data from it.

We've also created two `CSVModel` objects, one with a filename of `file1` and the other with a filename of `file2`. It's worth mentioning that there's no actual connection between our models and our `mock_open` objects; the filenames given are arbitrary, since we won't actually be opening a file, and the choice of which `mock_open` object we use will be made in our test methods using `patch()`.

Testing file reading in get_all_records()

To see how we use these, let's start a test for the get_all_records() method as follows:

```
# test_models.py, inside TestCSVModel

@mock.patch('abq_data_entry.models.Path.exists')
def test_get_all_records(self, mock_path_exists):
  mock_path_exists.return_value = True
```

Since our filenames don't actually exist, we're using the decorator version of patch() to replace Path.exists() with a mock function that always returns True. We can later change the return_value value property of this object if we want to test a scenario where the file doesn't exist.

To run the get_all_records() method against one of our mock_open objects, we'll use the context manager form of patch() as follows:

```
with mock.patch(
    'abq_data_entry.models.open',
    self.file1_open
):
    records = self.model1.get_all_records()
```

Any call to open() in models.py initiated by code inside this context manager block will be replaced by our mock_open object, and the file handle returned will contain the read_data string we specified.

Now we can start making assertions about the records that have been returned:

```
# test_models.py, inside TestCSVModel.test_get_all_records()

    self.assertEqual(len(records), 2)
    self.assertIsInstance(records, list)
    self.assertIsInstance(records[0], dict)
```

Here, we're checking that records contains two lines (since our read data contained two CSV records), that it's a list object, and that its first member is a dict object (or a subclass of dict).

Next, let's make sure all our fields made it through and that our Boolean conversion worked:

```
    fields = (
```

```
    'Date', 'Time', 'Technician', 'Lab', 'Plot',
    'Seed Sample', 'Humidity', 'Light',
    'Temperature', 'Equipment Fault', 'Plants',
    'Blossoms', 'Fruit', 'Min Height', 'Max Height',
    'Med Height', 'Notes')

for field in fields:
  self.assertIn(field, records[0].keys())


self.assertFalse(records[0]['Equipment Fault'])
```

By iterating over a tuple of all our field names, we can check that all our fields are present in the record output. Don't be afraid to use loops in a test this way to check a large amount of content quickly.

A `Mock` object can do more than just stand in for another class or function; it also has its own assertion methods that can tell us if it's been called, how many times, and with what arguments.

For example, we can check our `mock_open` object to make sure it was called with the expected arguments:

```
self.file1_open.assert_called_with(
  Path('file1'), 'r', encoding='utf-8', newline=''
)
```

`assert_called_with()` takes any number of positional and keyword arguments and checks if the last call to the mock object included those exact arguments. We expected `file1_open()` to be called with a `Path` object containing the filename `file1`, a mode of `r`, a `newline` set to a blank string, and an `encoding` value of `utf-8`. By confirming that a mocked function was called with the correct arguments, and assuming the correctness of the real function (the built-in `open()` function, in this case), we can avoid having to test the actual outcome.

 Note that the order in which the keyword arguments are passed does not matter for this method.

Testing file saving in save_record()

To demonstrate how to test file-writing with `mock_open`, let's test `save_record()`. Begin by creating a test method that defines some data:

```python
@mock.patch('abq_data_entry.models.Path.exists')
def test_save_record(self, mock_path_exists):

  record = {
    "Date": '2021-07-01', "Time": '12:00',
    "Technician": 'Test Technician', "Lab": 'C',
    "Plot": '17', "Seed Sample": 'test sample',
    "Humidity": '10', "Light": '99',
    "Temperature": '20', "Equipment Fault": False,
    "Plants": '10', "Blossoms": '200',
    "Fruit": '250', "Min Height": '40',
    "Max Height": '50', "Med Height": '55',
    "Notes": 'Test Note\r\nTest Note\r\n'
  }
  record_as_csv = (
    '2021-07-01,12:00,Test Technician,C,17,test sample,10,99,'
    '20,False,10,200,250,40,50,55,"Test Note\r\nTest Note\r\n"'
    '\r\n')
```

This method begins by once again mocking `Path.exists` and creating a dictionary of data, and the same data represented as a row of CSV data.

 You may be tempted to generate either the record or its expected CSV output using code, but it's always better to stick to literal values in tests; doing so makes the expectations of the test explicit and avoids logic errors in your tests.

Now, for our first test scenario, let's simulate writing to an empty but existing file by using `file2_open` and `model2` as follows:

```python
mock_path_exists.return_value = True
with mock.patch('abq_data_entry.models.open', self.file2_open):
  self.model2.save_record(record, None)
```

Setting our `mock_path_exists.return_value` to `True` to tell our method that the file already exists, we then patch over `open()` with our second `mock_open` object (the one representing an empty file) and call the `CSVModel.save_record()` method. Since we passed in a record with no row number (which indicates a record insert), this should result in our code trying to open `file2` in append mode and writing in the CSV-formatted record.

`assert_called_with()` will test that assumption as follows:

```
self.file2_open.assert_called_with(
  Path('file2'), 'a', encoding='utf-8', newline=''
)
```

While this method can tell us that `file2_open` was called with the expected parameters, how do we access its actual file handler so that we can see what was written to it?

It turns out we can just call our `mock_open` object and retrieve the mock file handle object, like so:

```
file2_handle = self.file2_open()
file2_handle.write.assert_called_with(record_as_csv)
```

Once we have the mock file handle (which is itself a `Mock` object), we can run test methods on its `write()` member to find out if it was called with the CSV data as expected. In this case, the file handle's `write()` method should have been called with the CSV-format record string.

Let's do a similar set of tests, passing in a row number to simulate a record update:

```
with mock.patch('abq_data_entry.models.open', self.file1_open):
    self.model1.save_record(record, 1)
    self.file1_open.assert_called_with(
      Path('file1'), 'w', encoding='utf-8'
    )
```

Checking that our update was done correctly presents a problem: `assert_called_with()` only checks the *last* call made to the mock function. When we update our CSV file, the entire CSV file is updated, with one `write()` call per row. We can't just check that the last call was correct; we need to make sure the `write()` calls for *all* the rows were correct. To accomplish this, `Mock` contains a method called `assert_has_calls()`, which we can use to test the history of calls made to the object.

To use it, we need to create a list of `Call` objects. Each `Call` object represents a call to the mock object. We create `Call` objects using the `mock.call()` function as follows:

```
file1_handle = self.file1_open()
file1_handle.write.assert_has_calls([
  mock.call(
     'Date,Time,Technician,Lab,Plot,Seed Sample,'
     'Humidity,Light,Temperature,Equipment Fault,Plants,'
     'Blossoms,Fruit,Min Height,Max Height,Med Height,Notes'
     '\r\n'),
  mock.call(
     '2021-06-01,8:00,J Simms,A,2,AX478,24.47,1.01,21.44,'
     'False,14,27,1,2.35,9.2,5.09,\r\n'),
  mock.call(
     '2021-07-01,12:00,Test Technician,C,17,test sample,'
     '10,99,20,False,10,200,250,40,50,55,'
     '"Test Note\r\nTest Note\r\n"\r\n')
])
```

The arguments to `mock.call()` represent the arguments that should have been passed to the function call, which in our cases should just be single strings of CSV row data. The list of `Call` objects we pass to `assert_has_calls()` represents each call that should have been made to the mocked file handle's `write()` method, *in order*. The `assert_has_calls()` method's `in_order` argument can also be set to `False`, in which case the order won't need to match. In our case, order matters, since a wrong order would result in a corrupt CSV file.

More tests on the models

Testing the remainder of the `CSVModel` class and the `SettingsModel` class methods should be essentially along the same lines as these two methods. A few more tests are included in the sample code, but see if you can come up with some of your own as well.

Testing our Application object

We've implemented our application as a Tk object that acts not only as a main window but also as a controller, patching together models and views defined elsewhere in the application. As you may expect, then, `patch()` is going to figure heavily into our testing code as we mock out all of those other components to isolate the `Application` object.

Open a new file under the `test` directory called `test_application.py`, and we'll begin with our imports:

```
# test_application.py

from unittest import TestCase
from unittest.mock import patch
from .. import application
```

Now, let's begin our test case class like so:

```
class TestApplication(TestCase):
  records = [
    {'Date': '2018-06-01', 'Time': '8:00', 'Technician': 'J Simms',
     'Lab': 'A', 'Plot': '1', 'Seed Sample': 'AX477',
     'Humidity': '24.09', 'Light': '1.03', 'Temperature': '22.01',
     'Equipment Fault': False,  'Plants': '9', 'Blossoms': '21',
     'Fruit': '3', 'Max Height': '8.7', 'Med Height': '2.73',
     'Min Height': '1.67', 'Notes': '\n\n',
    },
    {'Date': '2018-06-01', 'Time': '8:00', 'Technician': 'J Simms',
     'Lab': 'A', 'Plot': '2', 'Seed Sample': 'AX478',
     'Humidity': '24.47', 'Light': '1.01', 'Temperature': '21.44',
     'Equipment Fault': False, 'Plants': '14', 'Blossoms': '27',
     'Fruit': '1', 'Max Height': '9.2', 'Med Height': '5.09',
     'Min Height': '2.35', 'Notes': ''
    }
  ]

  settings = {
    'autofill date': {'type': 'bool', 'value': True},
    'autofill sheet data': {'type': 'bool', 'value': True},
    'font size': {'type': 'int', 'value': 9},
    'font family': {'type': 'str', 'value': ''},
    'theme': {'type': 'str', 'value': 'default'}
  }
```

As our `TestApplication` class will be using mocks in place of our data and settings models, we've created some class properties here to store samples of the data that `Application` expects to retrieve from those models. The `setUp()` method is going to patch out all the external classes with mocks, configure the mocked models to return our sample data, and then create an `Application` instance that our tests can use.

Note that while the Boolean values in the test records are `bool` objects, the numeric values are strings. This is actually how `CSVModel` returns the data, since no actual data type conversion is done at this point in the model.

Now, let's create our `setUp()` method, which looks like this:

```
# test_application.py, inside TestApplication class
  def setUp(self):
    with \
      patch(
        'abq_data_entry.application.m.CSVModel'
      ) as csvmodel,\
      patch(
        'abq_data_entry.application.m.SettingsModel'
      ) as settingsmodel,\
      patch(
        'abq_data_entry.application.Application._show_login'
      ) as show_login,\
      patch('abq_data_entry.application.v.DataRecordForm'),\
      patch('abq_data_entry.application.v.RecordList'),\
      patch('abq_data_entry.application.ttk.Notebook'),\
      patch('abq_data_entry.application.get_main_menu_for_os')\
    :
      show_login.return_value = True
      settingsmodel().fields = self.settings
      csvmodel().get_all_records.return_value = self.records
      self.app = application.Application()
```

Here, we've created a `with` block using seven `patch()` context managers, one for each class, method, or function that we're mocking out, including:

- The CSV and Settings models. These have been patched out with aliases, so that we can configure them to return the appropriate data.

- The `show_login()` method, whose return value we hard-code to `True` so login will always succeed. Note that if we were going to write full test coverage of this class, we'd want to test this function too, but for now we'll just mock it out.

- The record form and record list classes, since we don't want issues in those classes to cause errors in our `Application` test code. Those classes will have their own test cases, so we aren't interested in testing them in this case. We don't need to configure anything about them, so we have not aliased these mock objects.

- The `Notebook` class. Without mocking this, we'd be passing `Mock` objects to its `add()` method, causing an unnecessary error. We can assume Tkinter classes work correctly, so we mock this out.

- The `get_main_menu_for_os` class, since we don't want to deal with an actual menu object. Like the record form and record list, our menu classes will have their own test cases, so we are better off just taking them out of the equation here.

> Since Python 3.2, you can create a block with multiple context managers by separating each context manager call with a comma. Unfortunately, in Python 3.9 or lower, you can't put them in parentheses, so we're using the comparatively ugly escaped-newline method of breaking this gigantic call into multiple lines. If you're using Python 3.10 or later, you can use parentheses around your list of context managers for a cleaner layout.

Notice that we're creating instances of our `settingsmodel` and `csvmodel` objects and configuring methods on the *return values* from the mock objects rather than the mocks themselves. Remember that our mocks are replacing the *classes*, not the *objects*, and it is the objects that will contain the methods our `Application` object will be calling. Therefore, we need to call the mocked classes to access the actual `Mock` object that will be used by `Application` as the data or settings model.

Unlike the actual class that it stands in for, a `Mock` object called as a function will return the same object every time it's called. Thus, we don't have to save a reference to the object created by calling a mocked class; we can just call the mocked class repeatedly to access that object. Note, however, that a unique `Mock` object is created by the `Mock` *class* itself each time.

Because `Application` is a subclass of Tk, it's a good idea for us to safely dispose of it after each use; even though we're reassigning its variable name, the Tcl/Tk object will go on existing and cause problems with our tests. To solve this, create a `tearDown()` method in `TestApplication`:

```
def tearDown(self):
    self.app.update()
    self.app.destroy()
```

Notice the call to `app.update()`. If we don't call this before destroying app, there may be tasks in the event queue that will try to access it after it's gone. This won't break our code, but it will clutter up our test output with error messages.

Now that our fixtures are taken care of, let's write a test:

```
def test_show_recordlist(self):
  self.app._show_recordlist()
  self.app.notebook.select.assert_called_with(self.app.recordlist)
```

`Application._show_recordlist()` contains one line of code, which is merely a call to `self.notebook.select()`. Because we made `recordlist` a mock object, all of its members (including `select`) are also mock objects. Thus we can use the mock assertion methods to check that `select()` was called and with what arguments.

We can use a similar technique to check `_populate_recordlist()` as follows:

```
def test_populate_recordlist(self):
  self.app._populate_recordlist()
  self.app.model.get_all_records.assert_called()
  self.app.recordlist.populate.assert_called_with(self.records)
```

In this case, we're also using the `assert_called()` method to see if `CSVModel.get_all_records()` was called, which it should have been as part of populating the recordlist. Unlike `assert_called_with()`, `assert_called()` merely checks to see if a function was called, and as such is useful for functions that take no arguments.

Under some circumstances, `get_all_records()` can raise an exception, in which case we're supposed to show an error message box. But since we've mocked out our data model, how can we get the `Mock` object to raise an exception? The solution is to use mock's `side_effect` property as follows:

```
self.app.model.get_all_records.side_effect = Exception(
  'Test message'
)
```

`side_effect` can be used to simulate more complex functionality in a mocked function or method. It can be set to a function, in which case the mock will run that function and return the results when called; it can be set to an iterable, in which case the mock will return the next item in the iterable each time it's called; or, as in this case, it can be set to an exception, which will be raised when the mock is called.

Before we can use this, we'll need to patch out `messagebox` as follows:

```
with patch('abq_data_entry.application.messagebox'):
  self.app._populate_recordlist()
  application.messagebox.showerror.assert_called_with(
    title='Error', message='Problem reading file',
    detail='Test message'
  )
```

This time when we call _populate_recordlist(), our mocked CSVModel object raises an exception, which should result in the method calling messagebox.showerror(). Since we've mocked showerror(), we can assert that it was called with the expected arguments using assert_called_with().

Clearly, the hardest part of testing our Application object is patching in all the mocked components and making sure they behave enough like the real thing to satisfy Application. Once we've done that, writing the actual tests is fairly straightforward.

Testing our widgets

So far, we've done well testing our components with patch(), Mock, and the default TestCase class, but testing our widgets module is going to present some new challenges. To begin with, our widgets will need a Tk instance to be their root window. We can create this in each case's setUp() method, but this will slow down the tests considerably, and it isn't really necessary to do it over and over again: our tests aren't going to modify the root window, so one root window will suffice for each test case. To keep things running at a reasonable pace, we can take advantage of the setUpClass() method to create a single instance of Tk just once when the test case instance is created.

Secondly, we have a large number of widgets to test, each of which will need its own TestCase class. As a result, we'll need to create a large number of test cases requiring this same Tk setup and tear down. To address this, we'll create a custom TestCase base class to handle the root window setup and tear-down, then subclass it for each of our widget test cases. Open a new file under the test directory called test_widgets.py, and begin with this code:

```
# test_widgets.py
from .. import widgets
from unittest import TestCase
from unittest.mock import Mock
import tkinter as tk
from tkinter import ttk

class TkTestCase(TestCase):
  """A test case designed for Tkinter widgets and views"""

  @classmethod
  def setUpClass(cls):
    cls.root = tk.Tk()
    cls.root.wait_visibility()
```

```
@classmethod
def tearDownClass(cls):
  cls.root.update()
  cls.root.destroy()
```

The `setUpClass()` method creates the Tk object and calls `wait_visibility()` just to make sure the root window is visible and completely drawn before our tests start working with it. We've also supplied a complementary tear-down method that updates the Tk instance (to finish out any events in the queue) and destroys it.

Now, for each widget test case, we will subclass `TkTestCase` to ensure we have a proper testing environment for the widget.

Unit testing the ValidatedSpinbox widget

`ValidatedSpinbox` is one of the more complicated widgets we created for our application, so it's a good place to start writing tests.

Subclass the `TkTestCase` class to create a test case for `ValidatedSpinbox` as follows:

```
class TestValidatedSpinbox(TkTestCase):

  def setUp(self):
    self.value = tk.DoubleVar()
    self.vsb = widgets.ValidatedSpinbox(
      self.root,
      textvariable=self.value,
      from_=-10, to=10, increment=1
    )
    self.vsb.pack()
    self.vsb.wait_visibility()

  def tearDown(self):
    self.vsb.destroy()
```

Our `setUp()` method creates a control variable in which to store the widget's value, then creates an instance of the `ValidatedSpinbox` widget with some basic settings: a minimum value of `-10`, a maximum of `10`, and an increment of `1`. After creating it, we pack it and wait for it to become visible. For our tear-down method, we simply destroy the widget.

Now, let's begin writing tests. We'll start with a unit test of the _key_validate() method:

```
def test_key_validate(self):
  for x in range(10):
    x = str(x)
    p_valid = self.vsb._key_validate(x, 'end', '', x, '1')
    n_valid = self.vsb._key_validate(x, 'end', '-', '-' + x, '1')
    self.assertTrue(p_valid)
    self.assertTrue(n_valid)
```

In this test, we're simply iterating from 0 to 9 and testing both the positive and negative of the number against _key_validate(), which should return True for all of these values.

Note that the _key_validate() method takes a lot of positional arguments, and most of them are redundant; it might be nice to have a wrapper method that makes it easier to call, since a proper test of this function will likely need to call it dozens of times.

Let's call that method key_validate() and add it to our TestValidatedSpinbox class as follows:

```
def key_validate(self, new, current=''):
  return self.vsb._key_validate(
    new,  # inserted char
    'end',  # position to insert
    current,  # current value
    current + new,  # proposed value
    '1'  # action code (1 == insert)
  )
```

This will make future calls to the method shorter and less error-prone. Let's use this method now to test some invalid input, like so:

```
def test_key_validate_letters(self):
  valid = self.key_validate('a')
  self.assertFalse(valid)

def test_key_validate_increment(self):
  valid = self.key_validate('1', '0.')
  self.assertFalse(valid)

def test_key_validate_high(self):
```

```
valid = self.key_validate('0', '10')
self.assertFalse(valid))
```

In the first example, we're entering the letter a; in the second, a 1 character when 0. is already in the box (resulting in a proposed value of 0.1); in the third, a 0 character when 10 is in the box (resulting in a proposed value of 100). All of these scenarios should fail the validation method, causing it to return False.

Integration testing the ValidatedSpinbox widget

In the preceding tests, we weren't actually entering any data into the widget; we were simply calling the key validation method directly and evaluating its output. This is good unit testing, but as a test of our widget's functionality it isn't very satisfying, is it? Since our custom widget is so deeply interactive with Tkinter's validation API, we'd like to test that we've actually interfaced with this API correctly. After all, *that* aspect of the code was more challenging than the actual logic in our validation methods.

We can accomplish this by creating some integration tests that simulate actual user actions and then check the results of those actions. To do this cleanly, we'll first need to create some supporting methods.

First of all, we'll need a way to simulate typing text into the widget. Let's start a new type_in_widget() method in the TkTestCase class that will do this:

```
# test_widgets.py, in TkTestCase

def type_in_widget(self, widget, string):
  widget.focus_force()
```

The first thing this method does is force the focus to the widget; recall that focus_force() gives the widget focus even if the containing window is not in focus; we need to use this because our test Tk window is unlikely to be in focus when the test is being run.

Once we have focus, we'll need to iterate through the characters in the string and translate the raw character into the appropriate key symbols for our event sequence. Recall that some characters, particularly symbols, must be represented as name strings, such as minus or colon. To make this work, we'll need a way to translate between characters and their key symbols. We can do this with a dictionary added as a class property, like so:

```
# test_widgets.py, in TkTestCase
```

```
keysyms = {
  '-': 'minus',
  ' ': 'space',
  ':': 'colon',
}
```

More key symbols can be found at `http://www.tcl.tk/man/tcl8.4/TkCmd/keysyms.htm`, but these should do for now. Let's finish the `type_in_widget()` method like so:

```
# test_widgets.py, in TkTestCase.type_in_widget()

    for char in string:
        char = self.keysyms.get(char, char)
        widget.event_generate(f'<KeyPress-{char}>')
        self.root.update_idletasks()
```

In this loop, we start by checking to see if our `char` value has a name string in `keysyms`. Then we generate a `KeyPress` event on the widget with the given character or key symbol. Note that we call `self.root.update_idletasks()` after generating the keypress event. This ensures that the typed characters register after being generated.

In addition to simulating keyboard input, we'll need to be able to simulate mouse clicks. We can create a similar method, `click_on_widget()`, for simulating mouse button clicks as follows:

```
    def click_on_widget(self, widget, x, y, button=1):
        widget.focus_force()
        widget.event_generate(f'<ButtonPress-{button}>', x=x, y=y)
        self.root.update_idletasks()
```

This method takes a widget, an x and y coordinate for the click, and optionally a mouse button that will be clicked (defaulting to 1, which is the left mouse button). Just as we did with our keystroke method, we first force focus, generate our events, then update the application. The x and y coordinates for the mouse click specify where the widget is clicked, relative to its upper-left corner.

With these methods in place, return to the `TestValidatedSpinbox` class and write a new test:

```
# test_widgets.py, in TestValidatedSpinbox

    def test__key_validate_integration(self):
        self.vsb.delete(0, 'end')
        self.type_in_widget(self.vsb, '10')
        self.assertEqual(self.vsb.get(), '10')
```

This method starts by clearing the widget, then simulates some valid input with `type_in_widget()`. Then we retrieve the value from the widget using `get()`, checking that it matches the expected value. Note that in these integration tests we'll need to clear the widget each time because we are simulating keystrokes in an actual widget and triggering all the side effects of that action.

Next, let's test some invalid input; add the following to the test method:

```
        self.vsb.delete(0, 'end')
        self.type_in_widget(self.vsb, 'abcdef')
        self.assertEqual(self.vsb.get(), '')
        self.vsb.delete(0, 'end')
        self.type_in_widget(self.vsb, '200')
        self.assertEqual(self.vsb.get(), '2')
```

This time, we've simulated typing non-numeric or out-of-range values into the widget and check the widget to make sure it has properly rejected the invalid keystrokes. In the first example, the `ValidatedSpinbox` should reject all the keystrokes since they are letters; in the second, only the initial 2 should be accepted since the subsequent 0 keystrokes would put the number out of range.

We can use our mouse click method to test the functionality of the `ValidatedSpinbox` widget's arrow buttons as well. To make this simpler, we could create a helper method in our test case class to click on the arrow we want. Of course, to click a particular arrow, we have to figure out how to locate that element within the widget.

One approach would be to just estimate a hard-coded number of pixels. In most default themes, the arrows are on the right side of the box, and the box is about 20 pixels high. So, something like this method could work:

```
# test_widgets.py, inside TestValidatedSpinbox

  def click_arrow_naive(self, arrow='inc', times=1):
    x = self.vsb.winfo_width() - 5
    y = 5 if arrow == 'inc' else 15
    for _ in range(times):
      self.click_on_widget(self.vsb, x=x, y=y)
```

This approach actually works fairly well and may be sufficient for your needs. However, it's a little brittle as it makes assumptions about your theme and screen resolution. For more complex custom widgets, you may have a hard time locating elements this way. What would be better is a way to find the actual coordinates of widget elements.

Unfortunately, Tkinter widgets don't offer us a way to locate the x and y coordinates of elements within a widget; Ttk elements, however, do offer us a way to see which element is at a given set of coordinates, using the identify() method. Using this, we can write a method that scans through a widget looking for a particular element and returns the first set of x and y coordinates where it can be found.

Let's add this as a static method to the TkTestCase class, like so:

```
# test_widgets.py, inside TkTestCase

@staticmethod
def find_element(widget, element):
  widget.update_idletasks()
  x_coords = range(widget.winfo_width())
  y_coords = range(widget.winfo_height())
  for x in x_coords:
    for y in y_coords:
      if widget.identify(x, y) == element:
        return (x + 1, y + 1)
  raise Exception(f'{element} was not found in widget')
```

The method begins by updating the widget's idle tasks. Without this call, it's possible that all the elements are not yet drawn, and identify() will return an empty string. Next, we get a list of all the x and y coordinates in the widget by passing its width and height into the range() function. We iterate through these lists, calling widget.identify() on each pixel coordinate in the widget. If the returned element name matches the element name we're looking for, we return the current coordinates as a tuple. If we make it all the way through the widget without returning, we raise an exception stating that the element was not found.

Note that we add 1 to each of the x and y coordinates; that's because this element returns the upper-left corner coordinate of the widget. In some cases, clicking on these corner coordinates doesn't register as a click on the widget. To be sure we're actually clicking *in* the widget, we return coordinates 1 pixel right and down from the corner.

Of course, there's a snag here: what is the name of the element we're looking for? Recall from *Chapter 9, Improving the Look with Styles and Themes*, that the elements that compose a widget are determined by the theme, and that different themes may have completely different elements. For example, if you're looking for the increment arrow element, the default theme on Windows calls it Spinbox.uparrow. The default theme on Linux, however, calls it simply uparrow, and the default theme on macOS doesn't even have a separate element for it (both arrows are a single element called Spinbox. spinbutton)!

To address this, we need to force our test window to a specific theme so that we can rely on the names being consistent. In the TestValidatedSpinbox.setUp() method, we'll add some code to force an explicit theme:

```
# test_widgets.py, inside TestValidatedSpinbox.setUp()


    ttk.Style().theme_use('classic')
    self.vsb.update_idletasks()
```

The classic theme should be available on all platforms, and it uses the simple element names uparrow and downarrow for the Spinbox arrow elements. We've added a call to update_idletasks() to make sure the theme changes have taken effect in the widget before our tests start.

Now, we can write a better click_arrow() method for TestValidatedSpinbox that relies on element names instead of hard-coded pixel values. Add this method to the class:

```
# test_widgets.py, inside TestValidatedSpinbox

  def click_arrow(self, arrow, times=1):
    element = f'{arrow}arrow'
    x, y = self.find_element(self.vsb, element)
    for _ in range(times):
      self.click_on_widget(self.vsb, x=x, y=y)
```

Just as with our naive version, this method takes an arrow direction and a number of times. We use the arrow direction to build an element name, then use our find_element() method to locate the appropriate arrow inside the ValidatedSpinbox widget. Once we have the coordinates, we can use the click_on_widget() method we wrote to click on it.

Let's put this method to work and test our arrow key functionality in a new test method:

```
# test_widgets.py, inside TestValidatedSpinbox

  def test_arrows(self):
    self.value.set(0)
    self.click_arrow('up', times=1)
    self.assertEqual(self.vsb.get(), '1')

    self.click_arrow('up', times=5)
    self.assertEqual(self.vsb.get(), '6')
```

```
        self.click_arrow(arrow='down', times=1)
        self.assertEqual(self.vsb.get(), '5')
```

By setting the value of the widget, then clicking the appropriate arrow a specified number of times, we can test that the arrows did their jobs according to the rules we created in our widget class.

Testing our mixin class

One additional challenge we haven't approached yet is testing our mixin class. Unlike our other widget classes, our mixin cannot really exist on its own: it depends on methods and properties found in the Ttk widget with which it's combined.

One approach to testing this class would be to mix it with a Mock object that mocks out any inherited methods. This approach has merit, but a simpler (if less theoretically pure) approach is to subclass it with the simplest possible Ttk widget and test the resulting child class.

We'll create a test case that uses the latter approach. Start it in test_widgets.py, like so:

```
# test_widgets.py

class TestValidatedMixin(TkTestCase):

  def setUp(self):
    class TestClass(widgets.ValidatedMixin, ttk.Entry):
      pass
    self.vw1 = TestClass(self.root)
```

Here, the setUp() method creates just a basic child class of ValidatedMixin and ttk.Entry with no other modifications, then creates an instance of it.

Now let's write a test case for the _validate() method, like so:

```
  def test__validate(self):

    args = {
      'proposed': 'abc',
      'current': 'ab',
```

```
        'char': 'c',
        'event': 'key',
        'index': '2',
        'action': '1'
    }
    self.assertTrue(
      self.vw1._validate(**args)
    )
```

Because we're sending a key event to _validate(), it routes the request to _key_validate(), which simply returns True by default. We'll need to verify that _validate() does what is needed when _key_validate() returns False as well.

We'll employ Mock to do this:

```
    fake_key_val = Mock(return_value=False)
    self.vw1._key_validate = fake_key_val
    self.assertFalse(
      self.vw1._validate(**args)
    )
    fake_key_val.assert_called_with(**args)
```

By testing that False is returned and that _key_validate() was called with the correct arguments, we've demonstrated that _validate() is properly routing events to the right validation methods.

By updating the event value in args, we can check that focus-out events also work:

```
    args['event'] = 'focusout'
    self.assertTrue(self.vw1._validate(**args))
    fake_focusout_val = Mock(return_value=False)
    self.vw1._focusout_validate = fake_focusout_val
    self.assertFalse(self.vw1._validate(**args))
    fake_focusout_val.assert_called_with(event='focusout')
```

We've taken an identical approach here, just mocking out _focusout_validate() to make it return False.

As you can see, once we've created our test class, testing ValidatedMixin is like testing any other widget class. There are other test method examples in the included source code; these should be enough to get you started with creating a complete test suite.

Summary

In this chapter, you learned about the benefits of automated testing and the capabilities provided by Python's unittest library. You learned how to isolate units of code by using Mock and patch() to replace external modules, classes, and functions. You learned strategies for controlling Tkinter's event queue and simulating user input to automate tests of our GUI components, and wrote both unit tests and integration tests against sections of the ABQ application.

In the next chapter, we'll upgrade our backend to use a relational database. In the process, you'll learn about relational database design and data normalization. You'll also learn to work with the PostgreSQL database server and Python's psycopg2 PostgreSQL interface library.

12
Improving Data Storage with SQL

As weeks have passed by, there is a growing problem at the lab: CSV files are everywhere! Conflicting copies, missing files, records getting changed by non-data entry staff, and other CSV-related frustrations are plaguing the project. Unfortunately, the password protection in the application does nothing meaningful to prevent anyone from editing the files and corrupting data. It's clear that the current data storage solution is not working out. Something better is needed!

The facility has an older Linux server with a PostgreSQL database installed. You've been asked to update your program so that it stores data in the PostgreSQL database rather than in the CSV files, and authenticates users against the database. This way there can be one authoritative source of data to which the support staff can easily manage access. In addition, the SQL database will help enforce correct data types and allow for more complex data relationships than the simple flat file. This promises to be a major update to your application!

In this chapter, you'll learn the following topics:

- In *PostgreSQL*, we'll install and configure the PostgreSQL database system.
- In *Modeling relational data*, we'll discuss the art of structuring data in a database for good performance and reliability.
- In *Creating the ABQ database*, we'll build a SQL database for the ABQ Data Entry application.
- In *Connecting to PostgreSQL with psycopg2*, we'll use the psycopg2 library to connect our program to PostgreSQL.

- Finally, in *Integrating SQL into our application*, we'll update ABQ Data Entry to utilize the new SQL database.

 This chapter assumes you have a basic knowledge of SQL. If you don't, please see *Appendix B, A Quick SQL Tutorial*.

PostgreSQL

Python can interact with a wide variety of relational databases, including Microsoft SQL Server, Oracle, MariaDB, MySQL, and SQLite; in this book, we're going to focus on a very popular choice in the Python world, PostgreSQL. PostgreSQL (usually pronounced post-gress, with the "QL" silent) is a free, open source, cross-platform relational database system. It runs as a network service with which you can communicate using client programs or software libraries. At the time of writing, version 13 is the current stable.

Although ABQ has provided a PostgreSQL server that is already installed and configured, you'll need to download and install the software on your workstation for development purposes. Let's take a look at how we can get our workstation ready for PostgreSQL development.

 Shared production resources such as databases and web services should never be used for testing or development. Always set up a separate development copy of these resources on your own workstation or a separate server machine.

Installing and configuring PostgreSQL

To download PostgreSQL, visit https://www.postgresql.org/download and download an installation package for your operating system. Installation packages are provided for Windows, macOS, Linux, BSD, and Solaris by EnterpriseDB, a commercial entity that provides paid support for PostgreSQL. These installers include the server, command-line client, and **pgAdmin** graphical client all in one package. To install the software, launch the installer using an account with administrative rights and follow the screens in the installation wizard. During installation, you'll be asked to set a password for the postgres superuser account; make sure to take note of this password.

Configuring PostgreSQL using the GUI utility

Once installed, you can configure and interact with PostgreSQL using the **pgAdmin** graphical utility. Go ahead and launch pgAdmin from your application menu and follow these steps to create a new admin user for yourself:

1. Select **Servers** from the **Browser** pane on the left. You'll be prompted for your superuser password.
2. Once authenticated, select **Object | Create | Login/Group Role**. Enter a username to use for database access on the **General** tab. Then visit the **Privileges** tab to check **Superuser** and **Can Login**, and the **Definition** tab to set a password.
3. Click the **Save** button at the bottom of the window.

Next, we need to create a database. To do that, follow these steps:

1. Select **Object | Create | Database** from the menu.
2. Name the database abq, and set your new user account as the owner.
3. Click the **Save** button at the bottom of the window.

Your database is now ready to work with. You can begin entering SQL to run against your database by selecting the database in the **Browser** pane and clicking on **Tools | Query Tool** in the menu.

Configuring PostgreSQL using the command line

If you prefer to work directly in the command line, PostgreSQL includes several command-line utilities, including the following:

Command	Description
createuser	Create PostgreSQL user accounts
dropuser	Delete PostgreSQL user accounts
createdb	Create PostgreSQL databases
dropdb	Delete PostgreSQL databases
psql	Command-line SQL shell

For example, on macOS or Linux, we can complete the configuration of our database with the following commands:

```
$ sudo -u postgres createuser -sP myusername
$ sudo -u postgres createdb -O myusername abq
$ psql -d abq -U myusername
```

These three commands create the user, create the database, and open a SQL shell where queries can be entered. Note that we use the sudo command to run these as the postgres user. Remember that this is the superuser account you set up during installation.

 Although EnterpriseDB provides binary installers for Linux, most Linux users will prefer to use packages supplied by their distribution. You may end up with a slightly older version of PostgreSQL, but that won't matter for most basic use cases. Be aware that pgAdmin is usually part of a separate package, and also may be at a slightly older version. Regardless, you should have no trouble following this chapter with the older version.

Modeling relational data

Our application currently stores data in a single CSV file; a file like this is often called a **flat file**, because the data has been flattened to two dimensions. While this format works acceptably for our application and could be translated directly to a SQL table, a more accurate and useful data model requires more complexity. In this section, we're going to go through some concepts of data modeling that will help us convert our CSV data into effective relational tables.

Primary keys

Every table in a relational database should have something called a **primary key**. The primary key is a value, or set of values, that uniquely identifies a record in the table; as such, it should be a value or set of values that is unique and non-null for every row in a table. Other tables in the database can use this field to reference particular rows of the table. This is called a **foreign key** relationship.

How do we figure out what the primary key is for a set of data? Consider this table:

Fruit	Classification
Banana	Berry
Kiwi	Berry
Orange	Citrus
Lemon	Citrus

In this table, each row represents a type of fruit. It would make no sense for the Fruit column to be empty in this table, or for two rows to have the same value for Fruit. This makes the column a perfect candidate for a primary key.

Now consider a different table:

Fruit	Variety	Quantity
Banana	Cavendish	452
Banana	Red	72
Orange	Navel	1023
Orange	Red	875

In this table, each row represents a subvariety of fruit; however, there is no one field that uniquely defines a single variety of a single fruit. Instead, it requires both the Fruit and Variety fields. When we need multiple fields to determine the primary key, we call this a **composite primary key**. In this case, our composite primary key uses both the Fruit and Variety fields.

Using surrogate primary keys

Consider this table of employees:

First	Last	Title
Bob	Smith	Manager
Alice	Jones	Analyst
Pat	Thompson	Developer

Suppose this table were to use First and Last as a composite primary key, and suppose that other tables in the database reference rows using the primary keys. Leaving aside the obvious problem that two people can have the same first and last name, what would happen if Bob Smith decided he would prefer to be called Robert, or if Alice Jones married and took a new last name? Remember that other tables use the primary key value to reference rows in the table; if we change the contents of the primary key field, all the tables referencing these employees would either have to be updated as well or they would be unable to locate the record in the employees table.

While using actual data fields to build a primary key value is arguably the most theoretically pure approach, there are two big downsides that come up when you start relating tables using foreign keys:

- You have to duplicate the data in every table that needs to reference your table. This can particularly become onerous if you have a composite key of many fields.
- You can't change the values in the original table without breaking foreign key references.

For this reason, database engineers may opt for using **surrogate keys**. These are typically integer or **globally unique identifier (GUID)** values stored in an **identity column** that are automatically added to a record when it is inserted into a table. In the case of the employees table, we could simply add an ID field containing an auto-incrementing integer value, like so:

ID	First	Last	Title
1	Bob	Smith	Manager
2	Alice	Jones	Analyst
3	Pat	Thompson	Developer

Now other tables can simply refer to employees.ID=1, or employees.ID=2, leaving Bob and Alice free to change their names without consequence.

The use of surrogate keys arguably breaks the theoretical purity of a database; it also may require us to manually specify uniqueness or non-null constraints on columns that are implicit when they are used as a primary key. Sometimes, though, the practical advantages of surrogate keys outweigh these concerns. You will need to evaluate which option works best with your application and its data.

One rule of thumb in making this determination is to consider whether the data you propose to use as a key **describes** or **defines** the item represented by the row. For example, a name does not define a person: a person can change their name and still be the same person. On the other hand, the plot checks stored in our CSV files are defined by the date, time, lab, and plot values. Change any one of those values and you are referring to a different plot check.

Normalization

The process of breaking out a flat data file into multiple tables is called **normalization**. The normalization process is broken into a series of levels called **normal forms**, which progressively remove duplication and create a more precise model of the data we're storing. Although there are many normal forms, most issues encountered in common business data can be handled by conforming to the first three.

The purpose of conforming data to these forms is to eliminate the potential for redundant, conflicting, or undefined data situations. Let's briefly look at each of the first three normal forms, and what kind of issues it prevents.

First normal form

The **first normal form** requires that each field contains only one value, and that repeating columns must be eliminated. For example, suppose we have a flat file that looks like this:

Fruit	Varieties
Banana	Cavendish, Red, Apple
Orange	Navel, Valencia, Blood, Cara Cara

The `Varieties` field in this table has multiple values in a single column, so this table is not in the first normal form. We might try to fix it like so:

Fruit	Variety_1	Variety_2	Variety_3	Variety_4
Banana	Cavendish	Red	Apple	
Orange	Navel	Valencia	Blood	Cara Cara

This is an improvement, but it's still not in the first normal form, because we have **repeating columns**. All of the `Variety_` columns represent the same attribute (the variety of fruit), but have been arbitrarily broken out into distinct columns. One way to tell if you have repeating columns is if the data is equally valid whether it goes in one column or the other; for example, `Cavendish` could just as well go in the `Variety_2`, `Variety_3`, or `Variety_4` columns.

Consider some of the problems with this format:

- What would it mean if we had the same data in multiple `Variety` fields; for example, if the `Banana` row had `Cavendish` for `Variety_1` and `Variety_4`? Or what would it indicate for `Variety_1` to be blank, but `Variety_2` to have a value? These ambiguous situations are known as **anomalies** and can lead to conflicting or confusing data in the database.

- How complex would it be to query the table to see if two fruits share a variety name? We would have to check each `Variety_` field against every other `Variety_` field. What if we needed more than four varieties for a particular fruit? We would have to add columns, meaning our query would get exponentially more complex.

To bring this table to the first normal form, we would need to create one `Fruit` and one `Variety` column, something like this:

Fruit	Variety
Banana	Cavendish
Banana	Red
Banana	Apple
Orange	Navel
Orange	Valencia
Orange	Blood
Orange	Cara Cara

Note that this changes the nature of our table, as it's no longer one row per `Fruit`, but rather one row per `Fruit-Variety` combination. In other words, the primary key has changed from `Fruit` to `Fruit` + `Variety`. What if there are additional fields in the table that relate specifically to the `Fruit` type without respect to `Variety`? We'll address that as we look at the second normal form.

Second normal form

The **second normal form** requires the first normal form, and additionally that *every value must be dependent on the entire primary key*. In other words, if a table has primary key fields A, B, and C, and the value of column X depends solely on the value of column A without respect to B or C, the table violates the second normal form. For example, suppose we added a `Classification` field to our table, like so:

Fruit	Variety	Classification
Banana	Cavendish	Berry
Banana	Red	Berry
Orange	Navel	Citrus
Orange	Valencia	Citrus

In this table, `Fruit` and `Variety` comprise the primary key of each row. `Classification` only depends on `Fruit`, though, since all bananas are berries, and all oranges are citrus. Consider the problems with this format:

- First, we have a data redundancy, since every `Fruit` type is going to have its `Classification` listed multiple times (once each time the `Fruit` value is repeated).

- The redundancy creates the potential for an anomaly where the same `Fruit` value has a different `Classification` value in different rows. This would make no sense.

To address this, we'd need to break our table into two tables; one containing `Fruit` and `Classification`, with a primary key of `Fruit`, and one containing `Fruit` and `Variety`, with both fields comprising the primary key.

Third normal form

The **third normal form** requires the second normal form, and additionally that *every value in the table is dependent only on the primary key*. In other words, given a table with primary key A, and data fields X and Y, the value of Y can't depend on the value of X. It can only depend on A.

For example, consider this table:

Fruit	Leading Export Country	Leading Export Continent
Banana	Ecuador	South America
Orange	Brazil	South America
Apples	China	Asia

This table complies with the second normal form, because both columns are distinct to the primary key – each fruit can only have one leading export country, and one leading export continent. However, the `Leading Export Continent` value depends on the `Leading Export Country` value (a non-primary key field), because a country is on a continent without any respect to its fruit exports. The problems with this format are:

- There is data redundancy, as any country appearing multiple times would result in its continent appearing multiple times.

- Once again, the redundancy creates the potential for an anomaly, where the same country could have two different continents listed. That makes no sense.

To bring this to the third normal form, we would need to create a separate table of countries that could contain the continent column and any other column that depended on the country.

More normalization forms

Database theorists propose other higher normalization forms that can help further eliminate ambiguities and redundancies in data, but for this book the first three should suffice to organize our data. Be aware that it is possible to **over-normalize** data for an application. Deciding what constitutes over-normalization really depends on the data and the users.

For example, if you have a contacts database that contains the columns `telephone_1` and `telephone_2`, the first normal form would dictate that you put telephone numbers in their own table to eliminate the repeating field. But if your users never need more than two fields, rarely use the second one, and never do complex queries on the data, it may not be worth complicating your database and application to conform to a theoretically pure model.

Entity-relationship diagrams

One effective way to help normalize our data and prepare it for a relational database is to create an **entity-relationship diagram**, or **ERD**. An ERD is a way of diagramming the things that our database is storing information about and the relationships between those things.

Those "things" are called **entities**. An entity is a uniquely identifiable object; it corresponds to a single row of a single table. Entities have **attributes**, which correspond to the columns of a table. Entities also have **relationships** with other entities, which correspond to the foreign key relationships we define in SQL.

Let's consider the entities in our lab scenario with their attributes and relationships:

- There are **labs**. Each lab has a name.
- There are **plots**. Each plot belongs to a lab and has a number. A single seed sample is planted in each plot.
- There are **lab technicians**, who each have a name.
- There are **lab checks**, which are performed by a lab tech at a given lab. Each lab check has a date and time.
- There are **plot checks**, which are the data gathered at a single plot during a lab check. Each plot check has various plant and environmental data recorded on it.

The following diagram shows these entities and their relationships:

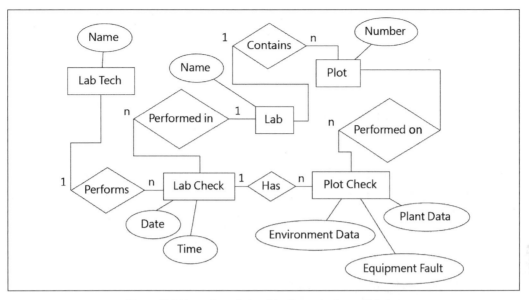

Figure 12.1: An entity-relationship diagram of our ABQ data

In this diagram, the entities are represented by rectangles. We have five entities: Lab, Plot, Lab Tech, Lab Check, and Plot Check. Each entity has attributes, represented by the ovals. The relationships between entities are represented by diamonds, with the words describing the left-to-right relationship. For example, a Lab Tech performs a Lab Check, and a Lab Check is performed in a Lab. Note the small *1* and *n* characters around the relationship: these show the **cardinality** of the relationship. There are three types of cardinality commonly seen in a database:

- A **one-to-many** (1 to n) relationship, where one row in the left table is related to many rows in the right table. For example, one Lab Tech performs many Lab Checks.

- A **many-to-one** (n to 1) relationship, where many rows in the left table are related to the same row in the right. For example, multiple Lab Checks are performed in the same Lab.

- A **many-to-many** (n to n) relationship, where many rows in the left table are related to many rows in the right. For example, if we needed to update our database to allow more than one tech to work on the same lab check, then one lab tech would still perform many checks, but one check would have multiple techs (fortunately, we don't need to implement this!).

This diagram represents a reasonably normalized structure for our data. To implement it in SQL, we'd just make a table for each entity, a column for each attribute, and a foreign key relationship for each relationship. Before we can do that, though, let's consider one more thing: SQL data types.

Assigning data types

Standard SQL defines 16 data types, including types for integers and floating-point numbers of various sizes, ASCII or Unicode strings of either fixed or variable sizes, date and time types, and single-bit types. In addition to implementing standard types, nearly every SQL engine extends this list with yet more types to accommodate things like binary data, JSON data, currency values, network addresses, and other special types of strings or numbers. Many data types seem a little redundant, and several have aliases that may be different between implementations. Choosing data types for your columns can be surprisingly confusing!

For PostgreSQL, the following chart provides some reasonable choices:

Data being stored	Recommended type	Notes
Fixed-length strings	CHAR	Requires a length, for example, CHAR(256).
Short-to-medium strings	VARCHAR	Requires a max length argument, for example, VARCHAR(256).
Long, freeform text	TEXT	Unlimited length, slower performance.
Smaller integers	SMALLINT	Up to ±32,767.
Most integers	INT	Up to around ±2.1 billion.
Larger integers	BIGINT	Up to around ±922 quadrillion.
Decimal numbers	NUMERIC	Takes optional length and precision arguments.
Integer primary key	SERIAL, BIGSERIAL	Auto-incrementing integers or big integers.
Boolean	BOOLEAN	Can be TRUE, FALSE, or NULL.
Date and time	TIMESTAMP WITH TIMEZONE	Stores date, time, and timezone. Accurate to 1 μs.
Date without time	DATE	Stores date.
Time without date	TIME	Can be with or without time zone.

These types will probably meet the vast majority of your needs in most applications, and we'll be using a subset of these for our ABQ database. As we create our tables, we'll refer to our data dictionary and choose appropriate data types for our columns.

> Be careful not to choose overly specific or restrictive data types. Any data can ultimately be stored in a TEXT field; the purpose of choosing more specific types is mainly to enable the use of operators, functions, or sorting specific to that type of data. If those aren't required, consider a more generic type. For example, phone numbers and U.S. social security numbers can be represented purely with digits, but that's no reason to make them INTEGER or NUMERIC fields; after all, you wouldn't do arithmetic with them!

Creating the ABQ database

Now that we've modeled our data and gotten a feel for the data types available, it's time to build our database. Make sure you've installed PostgreSQL and created the abq database as described in the first section of this chapter, and let's begin writing SQL to create our database structure.

Under your project root folder, create a new directory called sql. Inside the sql folder, create a file called create_db.sql. We'll start writing our table definition queries in this file.

Creating our tables

The order in which we create our tables is significant. Any table referred to in a foreign key relationship will need to exist before the relationship is defined. Because of this, it's best to start with your lookup tables and follow the chain of one-to-many relationships until all the tables are created. In our ERD, that takes us from roughly the upper left to the lower right.

Creating the lookup tables

We need to create the following three lookup tables:

- labs: This lookup table will contain the ID strings for our laboratories. Since the names of the labs aren't going to change, we'll just use the single-letter names as the primary key values.
- lab_techs: This lookup table will have the names of the lab technicians. Since we don't want to use employee names for primary keys, we'll create a column for the employee ID number and use it for the primary key.

- **plots**: This lookup table will have one row for each physical plot, identified by lab and plot numbers. It will also keep track of the current seed sample planted in the plot.

Add the SQL query for creating these tables to `create_db.sql`, as follows:

```
# create_db.sql
CREATE TABLE labs (id CHAR(1) PRIMARY KEY);
CREATE TABLE lab_techs (
  id SMALLINT PRIMARY KEY,
  name VARCHAR(512) UNIQUE NOT NULL
);

CREATE TABLE plots (
  lab_id CHAR(1) NOT NULL REFERENCES labs(id),
  plot SMALLINT NOT NULL,
  current_seed_sample CHAR(6),
  PRIMARY KEY(lab_id, plot),
  CONSTRAINT valid_plot CHECK (plot BETWEEN 1 AND 20)
);
```

Once created, the three tables look something like this:

lab_id
A
B
C

The labs table

id	name
4291	J Simms
4319	P Taylor

The lab_techs table

lab_id	plot	current_seed_sample
A	1	AXM477
A	2	AXM478
A	3	AXM479

The plots table

While these tables may seem very simple, they will help enforce data integrity and make it simple to build an interface dynamically from the database. For example, since we'll be populating our Labs widget from the database, adding a new lab to the application is simply a matter of adding a row to the database.

The lab_checks table

The rows of the lab_checks table each represent an instance of a technician checking all the plots of a lab at a given time on a given date. We will define it using the following SQL:

```
CREATE TABLE lab_checks(
  date DATE NOT NULL, time TIME NOT NULL,
  lab_id CHAR(1) NOT NULL REFERENCES labs(id),
  lab_tech_id SMALLINT NOT NULL REFERENCES lab_techs(id),
  PRIMARY KEY(date, time, lab_id)
);
```

When created and populated, the table will look like this:

date	time	lab_id	lab_tech_id
2021-10-01	8:00	A	4291

The lab_checks table

The date, time, and lab_id columns together uniquely identify a lab check, and so we designate them collectively as the primary key. The ID of the lab technician performing the check is the lone attribute in this table, and creates a foreign key relationship to the lab_techs table.

The plot_checks table

Plot checks are the actual data records collected at individual plots. These each belong to a lab check, and so must refer back to an existing lab check using the three key values, date, time, and lab_id.

We'll begin with the primary key columns:

```
CREATE TABLE plot_checks(
  date DATE NOT NULL,
  time TIME NOT NULL,
  lab_id CHAR(1) NOT NULL REFERENCES labs(id),
  plot SMALLINT NOT NULL,
```

The `plot_checks` primary key is essentially the primary key of a `lab_check` table with the addition of a plot number; its key constraints look like this:

```
PRIMARY KEY(date, time, lab_id, plot),
FOREIGN KEY(date, time, lab_id)
  REFERENCES lab_checks(date, time, lab_id),
FOREIGN KEY(lab_id, plot) REFERENCES plots(lab_id, plot),
```

Now that we've defined the key columns, we can add the attribute columns:

```
seed_sample CHAR(6) NOT NULL,
humidity NUMERIC(4, 2) CHECK (humidity BETWEEN 0.5 AND 52.0),
light NUMERIC(5, 2) CHECK (light BETWEEN 0 AND 100),
temperature NUMERIC(4, 2) CHECK (temperature BETWEEN 4 AND 40),
equipment_fault BOOLEAN NOT NULL,
blossoms SMALLINT NOT NULL CHECK (blossoms BETWEEN 0 AND 1000),
plants SMALLINT NOT NULL CHECK (plants BETWEEN 0 AND 20),
fruit SMALLINT NOT NULL CHECK (fruit BETWEEN 0 AND 1000),
max_height NUMERIC(6, 2) NOT NULL
  CHECK (max_height BETWEEN 0 AND 1000),
min_height NUMERIC(6, 2) NOT NULL
  CHECK (min_height BETWEEN 0 AND 1000),
median_height NUMERIC(6, 2) NOT NULL
CHECK (median_height BETWEEN min_height AND max_height),
notes TEXT
);
```

When created and populated, the first several columns of the table look something like this:

date	time	lab	plot	seed_sample	humidity	light	(etc...)
2021-10-01	08:00:00	A	1	AXM477	24.19	0.97	
2021-10-01	08:00:00	A	2	AXM478	23.62	1.03	

The plot_checks table

Notice our use of data types and the `CHECK` constraint to duplicate the limits defined in the specification's data dictionary. Using these, we've leveraged the power of the database to safeguard against invalid data. This completes our table definitions for the ABQ database.

Creating a view

Before we finish our database design, we're going to create a **view** that will simplify access to our data. A view behaves like a table in most respects, but contains no actual data; it's really just a stored SELECT query. We'll create a view called data_record_view to rearrange our data for easier interaction with the GUI.

Views are created using the CREATE VIEW command, which begins like this:

```
# create_db.sql

CREATE VIEW data_record_view AS (
```

Next, inside the parentheses, we put the SELECT query that will return the table data we want in our view:

```
SELECT pc.date AS "Date", to_char(pc.time, 'FMHH24:MI') AS "Time",
    lt.name AS "Technician", pc.lab_id AS "Lab", pc.plot AS "Plot",
    pc.seed_sample AS "Seed Sample", pc.humidity AS "Humidity",
    pc.light AS "Light", pc.temperature AS "Temperature",
    pc.plants AS "Plants", pc.blossoms AS "Blossoms",
    pc.fruit AS "Fruit", pc.max_height AS "Max Height",
    pc.min_height AS "Min Height", pc.median_height AS "Med Height",
    pc.notes AS "Notes"
FROM plot_checks AS pc
    JOIN lab_checks AS lc ON pc.lab_id = lc.lab_id
    AND pc.date = lc.date AND pc.time = lc.time
    JOIN lab_techs AS lt ON lc.lab_tech_id = lt.id
    );
```

We're selecting the plot_checks table, and joining it to lab_checks and lab_techs by way of our foreign key relationships. Notice that we've aliased these tables by using the AS keyword. Short aliases like this can help make a large query more readable. We're also aliasing each field to the name used in the application's data structures. These must be enclosed in double quotes to allow for the use of spaces and to preserve casing. By making the column names match the data dictionary keys in our application, we won't need to translate field names in our application code.

The first several columns of the view look like this; compare this to the raw plot_checks table above:

Date	Time	Technician	Lab	Plot	Seed Sample	Humidity	Light
2021-10-01	8:00	J Simms	A	1	AXM477	24.19	0.97
2021-10-01	8:00	J Simms	A	2	AXM478	23.62	1.03

SQL database engines such as PostgreSQL are highly efficient at joining and transforming tabular data. Whenever possible, leverage this power and make the database do the work of formatting the data for the convenience of your application.

This completes our database creation script. Run this script in your PostgreSQL client and verify that the four tables and the view have been created. To execute the script in pgAdmin, first open the **Query Tool** from **Tools | Query Tool**, then open the file by clicking the folder icon above the **Query Editor** window. Once the file is opened, click the play button icon to execute it. To run the script at the command line, execute the following at a terminal:

```
$ cd ABQ_Data_Entry/sql
$ psql -U myuser -d abq < create_db.sql
```

Populating the lookup tables

Although the tables are all created, the lookup tables will need to be populated before we can use them; specifically:

- `labs` should have values A through C, representing the three labs.
- `lab_techs` needs the name and ID number for our four lab technicians: J Simms (4291), P Taylor (4319), Q Murphy (4478), and L Taniff (5607).
- `plots` needs all 60 of the plots, numbers 1 through 20 for each lab. The seed sample rotates between four values such as AXM477, AXM478, AXM479, and AXM480.

You can populate these tables by hand using pgAdmin, or by using the `lookup_populate.sql` script included with the example code. Execute it just as you did the `create_db.sql` script.

Now our database is ready to use with the application. Let's get the application ready to work with the database!

Connecting to PostgreSQL with psycopg2

Now that we have a nice database to work with, how do we get our application to use it? To make SQL queries from our application, we'll need to install a Python library that can talk directly to our database. In Python, each different SQL product has one or more libraries available that can be used to integrate with it.

For PostgreSQL, the most popular choice is `psycopg2`. The `psycopg2` library is not a part of the Python standard library, so you'll need to install it on any machine running your application. You can find the most current installation instructions at `http://initd.org/psycopg/docs/install.html`; however, the preferred method is to use `pip`.

For Windows, macOS, and Linux, the following command should work:

```
$ pip install --user psycopg2-binary
```

If that doesn't work, or if you'd rather install it from the source, check the requirements on the website. Take note that the `psycopg2` library is written in C, not Python, so it requires a C compiler and a few other development packages to install from source.

 Linux users can usually install `psycopg2` from their distribution's package management system.

psycopg2 basics

The essential workflow of using `psycopg2` is as follows:

1. First, we create a `Connection` object using `psycopg2.connect()`. This object represents our connection to the database engine and is used to manage our login session.
2. Next, we create a `Cursor` object from our connection using the `Connection` object's `cursor()` method. A **cursor** is our point of interaction with the database engine.
3. We can run queries by passing SQL strings to the cursor's `execute()` method.
4. If our queries return data, we can retrieve the data using the cursor's `fetchone()` or `fetchall()` methods.

The following script demonstrates the basic use of `psycopg2`:

```
# psycopg2_demo.py

import psycopg2 as pg
from getpass import getpass

cx = pg.connect(
```

```
    host='localhost',  database='abq',
    user=input('Username: '),
    password=getpass('Password: ')
)

cur = cx.cursor()

cur.execute("""
  CREATE TABLE test
  (id SERIAL PRIMARY KEY, val TEXT)
""")
cur.execute("""
  INSERT INTO test (val)
  VALUES ('Banana'), ('Orange'), ('Apple');
""")
```

We begin by importing psycopg2 and aliasing it to pg for brevity's sake; we also import getpass for prompting the user for a password. Next, we generate a connection object, cx, using the connect() function, passing in all the details required to locate the database server and authenticate to it. These details include the host name of the server, the name of the database, and the authentication credentials. The host argument can be the server name, IP address, or fully qualified domain name of the system running the PostgreSQL server. Since we're running PostgreSQL on our local system, we've used localhost here, which points back to our local system.

From the connection, we create a cursor object, cur. Finally, we've used the cursor's execute() method to execute two SQL queries.

Now let's retrieve some data from the database, like so:

```
cur.execute("SELECT * FROM test")
num_rows = cur.rowcount
data = cur.fetchall()

print(f'Got {num_rows} rows from database:')
print(data)
```

You might expect that the data retrieved from the query is found in the return value of execute(); however, that's not how it works. Instead, we execute the query, then use cursor methods and attributes to retrieve the data and the metadata about the execution. In this case, we've used fetchall() to retrieve all the rows of data at once. We have also used the rowcount attribute of the cursor to see how many rows were returned from the database.

PostgreSQL is a **transactional database**, meaning that modification operations (like our CREATE and INSERT statements) are not automatically saved to disk. To do that, we need to **commit** our transaction. We can do this in psycopg2 using the connection object's commit() method, like so:

```
cx.commit()
```

If we do not commit, the changes we make will not be saved when our connection exits. The connection will exit automatically when our application or script quits, but we can also explicitly exit using the connection's close() method, like this:

```
cx.close()
```

 You can specify autocommit=True when creating a Connection object to have psycopg2 implicitly commit the transaction after every query. This is a handy convenience, especially when working with PostgreSQL in the shell.

Parameterized queries

Quite often, we need to include runtime data, such as that entered by our users, in a SQL query. You might be tempted to do this using Python's powerful string-formatting capabilities, like this:

```
new_item = input('Enter new item: ')
cur.execute(f"INSERT INTO test (val) VALUES ('{new_item}')")

cur.execute('SELECT * FROM test')
print(cur.fetchall())
```

Never, never do this! While it initially works, it creates a vulnerability known as a **SQL injection vulnerability**. In other words, it will allow a user of the program to enter any SQL command they wish. For example, we could execute our script and add malicious data like this:

```
$ python psycopg2_demo.py
Username: alanm
Password:
Got 3 rows from database:
[(1, 'Banana'), (2, 'Orange'), (3, 'Apple')]
Enter new item: '); DROP TABLE test; SELECT ('
Traceback (most recent call last):
  File "/home/alanm/psycopg2_demo.py", line 37, in <module>
```

```
    cur.execute('SELECT * FROM test')
psycopg2.errors.UndefinedTable: relation "test" does not exist
LINE 1: SELECT * FROM test
```

In this example, we've executed the program and entered a string that closes our coded SQL statement and adds on a DROP TABLE statement. It then adds a partial SELECT statement to avoid a syntax error from the SQL engine. The result is that the test table is deleted, and we get an exception trying to query data from it!

SQL injection vulnerabilities have plagued applications for decades and been the source of many high-profile hacking disasters. Fortunately, psycopg2 gives us a way to avoid this by using **parameterized queries**. A parameterized version of the previous code looks like this:

```python
new_item = input('Enter new item: ')
cur.execute("INSERT INTO test (val) VALUES (%s)", (new_item,))

cur.execute('SELECT * FROM test')
print(cur.fetchall())
```

To parameterize a query, we use the %s string to stand in for values we want to be inserted into the query. The values themselves are passed into execute() as a second argument. For multiple values, the parameter values should be passed in as a list or tuple, and will replace the %s occurrences in order.

For complicated queries, we can also give each parameter a name, and pass in a dictionary to match up the values; for example:

```python
cur.execute(
    "INSERT INTO test (val) VALUES (%(item)s)",
    {'item': new_item}
)
```

The parameter's name is put in parentheses between the percent sign and s character. The name will then be matched to a key in the parameters value dictionary and substituted when the query is executed by the database.

> The s in this parameter string is called a **format specifier**, and derives from the original Python syntax for string substitution. It is required and should *always* be s. If your parameterized query causes an Invalid Format Specifier error, it's because you have forgotten the s or used a different character.

Parameterized queries take care of properly escaping and sanitizing our data so that SQL injection attacks are largely impossible. For example, if we try our previous hack with the parameterized code, we get the following:

```
Enter new item: '); DROP TABLE test; SELECT ('
[(1, 'Banana'), (2, 'Orange'), (3, 'Apple'), (4, "'); DROP TABLE test;
SELECT ('")]
```

Not only do parameterized queries protect us from SQL injection, but they also perform automatic conversion of certain Python types to SQL values; for example, Python `date` and `datetime` objects are automatically converted to strings that SQL will recognize as dates, and `None` is automatically converted to SQL `NULL`.

 Note that parameters only work for *data values*; there is no way to parameterize other query content like table names or commands.

Special cursor classes

By default, `Cursor.fetchall()` returns our query results as a list of tuples. This might be acceptable if we have a table of one or two columns, but for large tables like those in our ABQ database, it quickly becomes a problem remembering which tuple index corresponds to which field. Ideally, we'd like to be able to reference a field by name.

To accommodate this, `psycopg2` allows us to specify a **cursor factory** class for our connection object that allows us to use cursor objects with customized behavior. One such custom cursor class included with `psycop2` is the `DictCursor` class. We use it like so:

```python
# psycopg2_demo.py

from psycopg2.extras import DictCursor

cx = pg.connect(
    host='localhost', database='abq',
    user=input('Username: '),
    password=getpass('Password: '),
    cursor_factory=DictCursor
)
```

DictCursor is found in the psycopg2.extras module, so we have to import it separately from the main module. Once imported, we pass it to the connect() function's cursor_factory argument. Now, rows will be returned as DictRow objects, which can be treated just like dictionaries:

```
cur.execute("SELECT * FROM test")
data = cur.fetchall()
for row in data:
    print(row['val'])
```

This is much handier when dealing with a large number of columns.

 More information about the use of psycopg2 can be found in its official documentation at https://www.psycopg.org/docs/.

Integrating SQL into our application

Converting our application to a SQL backend will be no small task. The application was built around the assumption of the CSV files, and although we've taken care to separate our concerns, many things are going to need to change.

Let's break down the steps we'll need to take:

- We'll need to create a new model to interface with the SQL database.
- Our Application class will need to use the SQL model, and may need to adjust some behaviors as a result.
- The record form will need to be reordered to prioritize our key fields, use the new lookup tables, and auto-populate using information in the database.
- The record list will need to be adjusted to work with the new data model and primary keys.

Let's get started!

Creating a new model

We'll start in models.py by importing psycopg2 and DictCursor:

```
# models.py
```

```
import psycopg2 as pg
from psycopg2.extras import DictCursor
```

As you learned in the previous section, `DictCursor` will allow us to fetch results in a Python dictionary rather than the default tuples, which is easier to work with in our application.

Now, begin a new model class called `SQLModel` and copy over the `fields` property from the `CSVModel`, like so:

```
# models.py

class SQLModel:
  """Data Model for SQL data storage"""

  fields = {
    "Date": {'req': True, 'type': FT.iso_date_string},
    "Time": {'req': True, 'type': FT.string_list,
     'values': ['8:00', '12:00', '16:00', '20:00']},
    # etc. ...
```

We need to make a few changes to this dictionary, however. First, our valid Lab and Plot values are going to be pulled from the database rather than being hardcoded here, so we'll specify them as empty lists and populate them in the initializer. Also, the Technician field will become a drop-down select, also populated from the database, so we need to make it a `string_list` type with an empty list for the `values` argument.

Those three entries should look like this:

```
# models.py, in the SQLModel.fields property

    "Technician": {
      'req': True, 'type':  FT.string_list, 'values': []
    },
    "Lab": {
      'req': True, 'type': FT.short_string_list, 'values': []
    },
    "Plot": {
      'req': True, 'type': FT.string_list, 'values': []
    },
```

Before we write our initializer, let's create a method to encapsulate a lot of the boilerplate code around querying and retrieving data. We'll call this method query(); add it to the SQLModel class like so:

```
# models.py, inside SQLModel
  def query(self, query, parameters=None):
    with self.connection:
      with self.connection.cursor() as cursor:
        cursor.execute(query, parameters)

        if cursor.description is not None:
          return cursor.fetchall()
```

This method takes a query string and, optionally, a sequence of parameters. Inside the method, we begin by opening a context block using the Connection object. Using the connection this way means that psycopg2 will automatically commit the transaction if the query is successful. Next, we generate our Cursor object, also using a context manager. By using the cursor as a context manager, psycopg2 will automatically **roll back** our transaction if an exception is thrown by the execute() method. Rolling back is the opposite of committing the database: instead of saving the changes, we throw them away and start with the database as it was the last time we committed (or the beginning of the session, if we haven't called commit() yet). After rolling back, the exception will be re-raised so that we can handle it in our calling code, and, in either case, the cursor will be closed when the block exits. Essentially, it's equivalent to the following:

```
        cursor = self.connection.cursor()
        try:
          cursor.execute(query, parameters)
        except (pg.Error) as e:
          self.connection.rollback()
          raise e
        finally:
          cursor.close()
```

If we successfully execute the query and it returns data, the method will need to return that data. To determine if data was returned, we check the cursor. description property. The cursor.description property returns a list of the headers for the table returned by our query; in the event that our query returns no data (such as an INSERT query), it is set to None. It's important to realize that fetchall() will raise an exception if there is no data returned from the query, so we should check description before executing it.

Now that we have this method, we can easily retrieve results from our database like so:

```python
def some_method(self):
  return self.query('SELECT * FROM table')
```

To see how we can use the query method, let's go ahead and add an initializer method to this class:

```python
# models.py, inside SQLModel

def __init__(self, host, database, user, password):
  self.connection = pg.connect(
    host=host, database=database,
    user=user, password=password,
    cursor_factory=DictCursor
  )

  techs = self.query("SELECT name FROM lab_techs ORDER BY name")
  labs = self.query("SELECT id FROM labs ORDER BY id")
  plots = self.query(
    "SELECT DISTINCT plot FROM plots ORDER BY plot"
  )
  self.fields['Technician']['values'] = [
    x['name'] for x in techs
  ]
  self.fields['Lab']['values'] = [x['id'] for x in labs]
  self.fields['Plot']['values'] = [
    str(x['plot']) for x in plots
  ]
```

The __init__() method takes the database connection details and establishes a connection to the database using psycopg2.connect(), setting the cursor_factory to DictCursor. Then, we use our new query() method to query the database for the pertinent columns in our three lookup tables, using a list comprehension to flatten the results of each query for the respective values list.

Next, we need to write the methods that the application calls to retrieve data from the model. We'll start with get_all_records(), which looks like this:

```python
def get_all_records(self, all_dates=False):
  query = (
    'SELECT * FROM data_record_view '
    'WHERE NOT %(all_dates)s OR "Date" = CURRENT_DATE '
```

```
        'ORDER BY "Date" DESC, "Time", "Lab", "Plot"'
    )
    return self.query(query, {'all_dates': all_dates})
```

Since our users are used to working with only the current day's data, we'll only show that data by default, but add an optional flag should we ever need to retrieve all data for all time. To retrieve the current date in PostgreSQL, we can use the `CURRENT_DATE` constant, which always holds the current date according to the server. Note that we use a prepared query to pass the `all_dates` value to the query.

Next, let's create `get_record()`:

```
def get_record(self, rowkey):
    date, time, lab, plot = rowkey
    query = (
        'SELECT * FROM data_record_view '
        'WHERE "Date" = %(date)s AND "Time" = %(time)s '
        'AND "Lab" = %(lab)s AND "Plot" = %(plot)s'
    )
    result = self.query(
        query,
        {"date": date, "time": time, "lab": lab, "plot": plot}
    )
    return result[0] if result else dict()
```

This method represents a change in interface from the `CSVModel` class. We're no longer dealing in row numbers; instead, rows are identified by their primary key values. In the case of our records (that is, plot checks), we need Date, Time, Lab, and Plot to identify a record. For convenience, we'll be passing this value around as a tuple in the format (`date`, `time`, `lab`, `plot`). Thus, the first thing our method does is extract the `rowkey` tuple into those four values.

Once we have these values, we can use a prepared query to retrieve all the record data from the view we created. Keep in mind that, even when the query results are a single row, the `query()` method is going to return the results in a list. However, our application expects a single dictionary of data from `get_record()`, so our return statement extracts the first item in `result` if the list is not empty, or an empty dictionary if it is.

Retrieving a lab check record is very similar:

```
def get_lab_check(self, date, time, lab):
    query = (
        'SELECT date, time, lab_id, lab_tech_id, '
```

```
      'lt.name as lab_tech FROM lab_checks JOIN lab_techs lt '
      'ON lab_checks.lab_tech_id = lt.id WHERE '
      'lab_id = %(lab)s AND date = %(date)s AND time = %(time)s'
    )
    results = self.query(
      query, {'date': date, 'time': time, 'lab': lab}
    )
    return results[0] if results else dict()
```

In this query, we're using a join to make sure we have the technician name available and not just the ID. This method did not exist in CSVModel, because we had not yet normalized the data; but it will come in handy in our save_record() method and in our form automation methods.

Saving data

Saving data in our SQL model is a little more complex than the CSV, since each data record is represented by rows in two different tables: the lab_checks and the plot_checks tables. When we try to save a record, there are three possibilities that we need to account for:

- Neither a lab check nor a plot check record exists for the given date, time, lab, and plot. In this case, both the lab check and plot check records will need to be created.

- The lab check exists for the given date, time, and lab, but no corresponding plot check exists for the given plot. In this case, the lab check record will need to be updated (in case the user wants to correct the technician value), and the plot check record will need to be added.

- Both the lab check and plot check exist. In this case, both will need to be updated with the submitted non-primary key values.

The save_record() method we implement will need to check for these conditions and run the appropriate INSERT or UPDATE queries on each table.

We also need to consider the possibility that a user will update one of the primary key fields when editing an existing record. What should the model do in this case? Let's consider:

- From the user's point of view, each record they fill out in the application corresponds to a plot check.

- A plot check is associated with a lab check on the basis of its date, time, and lab.

- Thus, if a user alters one of those key fields, their intention is most likely to associate the plot check record with a different lab check, rather than to alter the lab check record it is already associated with.

- Since, from a GUI standpoint, the user is updating an existing record rather than adding a new one, though, it makes sense to update the plot check identified by the pre-change date, time, lab, and plot values with the newly entered values for those fields.

Therefore, when we're determining whether to run our INSERT or UPDATE queries, we should determine this based on the *entered data* for the lab check, but the *key data* for the plot check.

Let's begin implementing this logic by writing our queries, which we will store in class variables to keep our save_record() method more concise.

We'll start with the lab check queries:

```python
# models.py, in SQLModel
lc_update_query = (
  'UPDATE lab_checks SET lab_tech_id = '
  '(SELECT id FROM lab_techs WHERE name = %(Technician)s) '
  'WHERE date=%(Date)s AND time=%(Time)s AND lab=%(Lab)s'
)

lc_insert_query = (
  'INSERT INTO lab_checks VALUES (%(Date)s, %(Time)s, %(Lab)s, '
  '(SELECT id FROM lab_techs WHERE name LIKE %(Technician)s))'
)
```

These queries are fairly straightforward, though note our use of a subquery to populate lab_tech_id in each case. Our application will have no idea what a lab tech's ID is, so we'll need to look the ID up by name. Also, take note that our parameter names match the names used in our model's fields dictionary. This will save us from having to reformat the record data acquired from our form.

The plot check queries are longer but not any more complicated:

```python
pc_update_query = (
  'UPDATE plot_checks SET seed_sample = %(Seed Sample)s, '
  'humidity = %(Humidity)s, light = %(Light)s, '
  'temperature = %(Temperature)s, '
  'equipment_fault = %(Equipment Fault)s, '
  'blossoms = %(Blossoms)s, plants = %(Plants)s, '
  'fruit = %(Fruit)s, max_height = %(Max Height)s, '
```

```
    'min_height = %(Min Height)s, median_height = %(Med Height)s, '
    'notes = %(Notes)s WHERE date=%(key_date)s AND time=%(key_time)s '
    'AND lab_id=%(key_lab)s AND plot=%(key_plot)s')

 pc_insert_query = (
    'INSERT INTO plot_checks VALUES (%(Date)s, %(Time)s, %(Lab)s,'
    ' %(Plot)s, %(Seed Sample)s, %(Humidity)s, %(Light)s,'
    ' %(Temperature)s, %(Equipment Fault)s, %(Blossoms)s,'
    ' %(Plants)s, %(Fruit)s, %(Max Height)s, %(Min Height)s,'
    ' %(Med Height)s, %(Notes)s)')
```

Note that the parameter names used in the UPDATE query's WHERE clause are prefixed with key_; this will allow us to update the record identified by the date, time, lab, and plot values from the row key, as explained previously.

With the queries in place, we can start writing the save_record() method:

```
# models.py, inside SQLModel
  def save_record(self, record, rowkey):
    if rowkey:
      key_date, key_time, key_lab, key_plot = rowkey
      record.update({
        "key_date": key_date,
        "key_time": key_time,
        "key_lab": key_lab,
        "key_plot": key_plot
      })
```

The CSVModel.save_record() method took a record dictionary and an integer value, rownum, to determine which record would be updated (or None if it was a new record). In our database, we're using a compound key to identify a plot check, which we'll expect as a tuple of the date, time, lab, and plot. Therefore, if a rowkey is passed in, we'll extract its values to variables and add them to the record dictionary so that we can pass them to the queries.

Next, we need to determine what kind of query to run for the lab check table:

```
    if self.get_lab_check(
      record['Date'], record['Time'], record['Lab']
    ):
      lc_query = self.lc_update_query
    else:
      lc_query = self.lc_insert_query
```

If there is an existing lab check record with the entered date, time, and lab, we'll just update it (which will really just change the technician value to what was entered). If there is not, we'll create one.

Next, let's determine which plot check operation to do:

```
if rowkey:
  pc_query = self.pc_update_query
else:
  pc_query = self.pc_insert_query
```

This time we only need to know if a row key tuple was given to the method. If it was, this should be an existing record and we just want to update it. If not, we'll need to insert a new record.

Now, we finish off the method by just running the two queries, passing in the record dictionary as the parameter list:

```
self.query(lc_query, record)
self.query(pc_query, record)
```

Note that psycopg2 has no problem with us passing a dictionary with extra parameters that aren't referenced in the query, so we don't need to bother with filtering unneeded items from record.

Getting the current seed sample for the plot

There is one last method this model needs; since our database knows what seed sample is currently in each plot, we want our form to populate this automatically for the user. We'll need a method that takes a lab and plot_id and returns the seed sample name.

We'll call it get_current_seed_sample():

```
def get_current_seed_sample(self, lab, plot):
  result = self.query(
    'SELECT current_seed_sample FROM plots '
    'WHERE lab_id=%(lab)s AND plot=%(plot)s',
    {'lab': lab, 'plot': plot}
  )
  return result[0]['current_seed_sample'] if result else ''
```

This time, our `return` statement is not just extracting the first row of results, but the value of the `current_seed_sample` column from that first row. If there's no result, we return an empty string.

That completes our model class; now let's incorporate it into the application.

Adjusting the Application class for the SQL backend

Before it can create a `SQLModel` instance, the `Application` class will need the database connection information to pass to the model: the server name, database name, user, and password. The host and database names aren't going to change often, if at all, so we don't need to make the user enter those each time. Instead, we can just add them as settings in the `SettingsModel`:

```
# models.py, inside SettingsModel

class SettingsModel:

  fields = {
    #...
    'db_host': {'type': 'str', 'value': 'localhost'},
    'db_name': {'type': 'str', 'value': 'abq'}
  }
```

These can be saved in our JSON config file, which can be edited to switch from development to production, but the username and password used for authentication will need to be entered by the user. For that, we can use our login dialog.

Implementing SQL logins

The login dialog currently authenticates using hardcoded credentials in the `Application._simple_login()` method. This is far from ideal, so we're going to use our PostgreSQL server as a production-quality authentication backend. To start, let's create a new `Application` method called `_database_login()`, like so:

```
# application.py, inside Application

  def _database_login(self, username, password):
    db_host = self.settings['db_host'].get()
    db_name = self.settings['db_name'].get()
    try:
```

```
      self.model = m.SQLModel(
        db_host, db_name, username, password
      )
    except m.pg.OperationalError as e:
      print(e)
      return False
    return True
```

This method is analogous to our _simple_login() method, in that the
Application._show_login() method will call it to authenticate the credentials
entered by the user. Unlike _simple_login(), however, this method is an instance
method, as it needs access to the settings and needs to save the SQLModel instance
that it creates.

The method begins by pulling the database host and database name from the
settings dictionary, then attempts to create a SQLModel instance using them. A
psycopg2.OperationalError indicates a failure to connect to the database, most likely
due to failed credentials; in this case, we'll return False from the method. Otherwise,
if the connection is successful, we'll return True.

> Note that we print the error message to the console. Since other
> problems could potentially cause an OperationalError, it would
> be smart to log the exception or otherwise make it accessible for
> debugging, rather than just silencing it.

To use this login backend, we need only change a single line in the _show_login()
method:

```
# application.py, in Application

def _show_login(self):
  #...
    if self._database_login(username, password):
      return True
```

The last change we need for SQL logins is in the Application class's initializer.
We need to make sure that the settings dictionary is available *before* we show the
login dialog, since our database logins depend on the db_host and db_name settings.
Simply move the lines that load the settings to the top of __init__(), just after calling
super().__init__(), as shown here:

```
# application.py, in Application

def __init__(self, *args, **kwargs):
```

```
super().__init__(*args, **kwargs)

self.settings_model = m.SettingsModel()
self._load_settings()

self.withdraw()
if not self._show_login():
  self.destroy()
  return
self.deiconify()
```

Updating the Application._on_save() method

Since our record keys have changed from a single integer to a tuple, we need to make some small adjustments to our _on_save() method. Thanks to our efforts to keep the model object's interface intact, the core functionality of this method actually works just fine. However, when it comes to saving references to the rows that have been changed or updated, we can no longer rely on calculating the row numbers; we'll have to rely on the keys instead.

Starting in the second half of the Application._on_save() method, just after the if errors: block, change the code as follows:

```
# application,py, in Application._on_save()

data = self.recordform.get()
rowkey = self.recordform.current_record
self.model.save_record(data, rowkey)
if rowkey is not None:
  self.recordlist.add_updated_row(rowkey)
else:
  rowkey = (
    data['Date'], data['Time'], data['Lab'], data['Plot']
  )
  self.recordlist.add_inserted_row(rowkey)
# remainder of method as before
```

First, we've changed the rownum variable to rowkey to make it more descriptive of what the variable contains. Second, when we have a new record, we construct a new row key using the Date, Time, Lab, and Plot values that were passed in with the record. Note that now the contents of the RecordList widget's _updated and _inserted lists will be tuples rather than integers, so we'll need to update its code as well. We'll do that later in this chapter.

Removing file-based code

Before we move on from the Application class, we need to remove some of the file-based code that we'll no longer need. Delete or comment out the following code:

- In __init__(), remove the line that creates the CSVModel instance. We no longer want to do this.
- Also in __init__(), remove the <<FileSelect>> event from the event_callbacks dictionary.
- Remove the self._on_file_select() method definition.
- Finally, over in mainmenu.py, we can comment out calls to the _add_file_open() method in each of our menu classes.

Now the Application object is ready for SQL, let's check out our view code.

Adjusting the DataRecordForm for SQL data

Currently our DataRecordForm keeps track of its record using a row number. This is no longer going to work, since records are identified by a compound primary key. We'll need to adjust the way records are loaded, and how the record form is labeled, so that we can accurately identify the row we're working on. We also need to reorder the fields so that the key values are entered first, which will help the auto-populate to work more smoothly.

Also, our database presents us with new possibilities for auto-filling data. Once we know enough to identify a Lab Check record, we can auto-fill the Technician field, and once we know which plot we're working with, we can auto-fill the Seed Sample field.

Reordering fields

The first change we can make to DataRecordForm is the simplest. We just need to reorder the fields so that the key fields Date, Time, Lab, and Plot appear first.

The updated calls (with some arguments left out) should be ordered like so:

```
# views.py, inside DataRecordForm.__init__()
    # line 1
    w.LabelInput(
      r_info, "Date",
      #...
    ).grid(row=0, column=0)
    w.LabelInput(
```

```
    r_info, "Time",
    #...
).grid(row=0, column=1)
# swap order for chapter 12
w.LabelInput(
    r_info, "Lab",
    #...
).grid(row=0, column=2)
# Line 2
w.LabelInput(
    r_info, "Plot",
    #...
).grid(row=1, column=0)
w.LabelInput(
    r_info, "Technician",
    #...
).grid(row=1, column=1)
w.LabelInput(
    r_info, "Seed Sample",
    #...
).grid(row=1, column=2)
```

Note that you need to change the `row` and `column` arguments of the `grid()` method calls, not just the ordering of the `LabelInput` calls.

Fixing the load_record() method

The `load_record()` method only needs two adjustments. First, we'll replace the `rownum` variable with `rowkey`, to be consistent with the `Application` class. Second, we need to update the title text generated to identify the record, like so:

```
#views.py, inside DataRecordForm.load_record()

    if rowkey is None:
      self.reset()
      self.record_label.config(text='New Record')
    else:
      date, time, lab, plot = rowkey
      title = f'Record for Lab {lab}, Plot {plot} at {date} {time}'
      self.record_label.config(text=title)
```

Once again, we have extracted the `date`, `time`, `lab`, and `plot` values from the key and used them to identify which record the user is currently editing. The remainder of the method can stay the same.

Improving auto-fill

There are two auto-population callbacks we want to have for our record form. First, when the user enters a lab and plot value, we want to automatically populate the Seed Sample field with the seed value that is currently planted in that plot. Second, when the date, time, and lab values have been entered, and we have an existing lab check that matches, we should populate the name of the lab tech who did that check. Of course, if our user prefers not to have data auto-filled, we shouldn't do either of these things.

Let's start with the seed sample callback:

```python
# views.py, inside DataRecordForm

def _populate_current_seed_sample(self, *_):
    """Auto-populate the current seed sample for Lab and Plot"""
    if not self.settings['autofill sheet data'].get():
        return
    plot = self._vars['Plot'].get()
    lab = self._vars['Lab'].get()

    if plot and lab:
        seed = self.model.get_current_seed_sample(lab, plot)
        self._vars['Seed Sample'].set(seed)
```

We begin by checking whether or not the user wants data auto-filled. If not, we return from the method. If they do, we fetch the Plot and Lab values from the form's control variables dictionary. If we have both, we use them to fetch the Seed Sample value from the model and set it in the form accordingly.

We'll do something similar with the Technician value:

```python
# views.py, inside DataRecordForm

def _populate_tech_for_lab_check(self, *_):
    """Populate technician based on the current lab check"""
    if not self.settings['autofill sheet data'].get():
        return
    date = self._vars['Date'].get()
    try:
        datetime.fromisoformat(date)
    except ValueError:
        return
    time = self._vars['Time'].get()
    lab = self._vars['Lab'].get()
```

```
    if all([date, time, lab]):
      check = self.model.get_lab_check(date, time, lab)
      tech = check['lab_tech'] if check else ''
      self._vars['Technician'].set(tech)
```

This time, we use the form's date, time, and lab values to fetch the lab check record, then set the Technician value from the results (or a blank string if there are no results). Note that we've added error handling around the date value; that's because we plan to trigger these methods from a variable trace. Lab and Time are both selected from Combobox widgets, so they will only change to a complete value, but Date is a text-entry field, so it's possible we'll be getting a partially entered date. There's no point in running a SQL query (a relatively time-consuming operation) if the date string isn't valid, so we've used datetime.fromisoformat() to determine if the entered date string is valid. If it's not, we just return from the method since there's nothing more to do.

To complete this functionality, we just need to add triggers to run the methods whenever the appropriate variables are updated. Add this code to DataRecordForm.__init__():

```
# views.py, inside DataRecordForm.__init__()
    for field in ('Lab', 'Plot'):
      self._vars[field].trace_add(
        'write', self._populate_current_seed_sample
      )

    for field in ('Date', 'Time', 'Lab'):
      self._vars[field].trace_add(
        'write', self._populate_tech_for_lab_check
      )
```

Using a for loop, we've added a trace to each variable involved in determining the Seed Sample and Technician values. Now, these fields should get auto-populated whenever sufficient information is entered to determine their values.

Updating the RecordList for the SQLModel

One of our RecordList object's most important features is the ability to select a record so that the Application object can open it in the DataRecordForm view. To do this, we have to store each record's key in its respective Treeview item's IID value. This worked easily with integer row number values, but now there is a problem. Recall from *Chapter 8, Navigating Records with Treeview and Notebook*, that an IID value *must be a string*. We cannot use a tuple.

To solve this problem, we just need to come up with a consistent way to connect our row key tuple to a string value that can be used as an IID. We'll create a dictionary as an instance variable that will map row keys to IID values.

In `RecordList.__init__()`, add this line that creates our mapping:

```
# views.py, near the beginning of RecordList.__init__()
    self.iid_map = dict()
```

Now we need to update the `populate()` method to utilize the dictionary rather than integer values. First, at the beginning of the method just after deleting the existing rows, let's clear the dictionary of any current information, like so:

```
# views.py, in RecordList.populate()
    self.iid_map.clear()
```

Then, find the `for` loop in this method that populates the `Treeview` and let's edit the code as follows:

```
        for rowdata in rows:
            values = [rowdata[key] for key in cids]
            rowkey = tuple([str(v) for v in values])
            if rowkey in self._inserted:
              tag = 'inserted'
            elif rowkey in self._updated:
              tag = 'updated'
            else:
              tag = ''
            iid = self.treeview.insert(
              '', 'end', values=values, tag=tag
            )
            self.iid_map[iid] = rowkey
```

Since row numbers are no longer in the picture, we can remove the `enumerate()` call and just deal with the row data. It so happens that the four columns in the `cids` list are the same four that make up the key, and in the same order. So, we can just convert that list to a `tuple` object to create our `rowkey`. Note that we do need to convert each item in the key to a string; they come out of the database as Python objects like `date` and `int`, and we need to match them against the keys in the `_inserted` and `_updated` lists. Those values, pulled from our `DataRecordForm`, are all string values.

Once we have the key, we check if it is in one of the lists and set the `tag` value appropriately. Then, we'll save the output from `Treeview.insert()` as `iid`. When `insert()` is called without an explicit IID value, one is generated automatically and returned by the method. We then add our `rowkey` value to the mapping dictionary using the generated IID value as a key.

After the `for` loop, the last part of this method focuses the first row for keyboard users. To focus the first row before, we relied on the fact that the first IID was always `0`. Now the first IID will be an automatically generated value that we cannot predict before the data is loaded, so we'll have to retrieve the IID before we can set the selection and focus.

We can do this by using the `Treeview.identify_row()` method:

```
# views.py, in RecordList.populate()

    if len(rows) > 0:
      firstrow = self.treeview.identify_row(0)
      self.treeview.focus_set()
      self.treeview.selection_set(firstrow)
      self.treeview.focus(firstrow)
```

The `identify_row()` method takes a row number and returns the IID of that row. Once we have that, we can pass it to `selection_set()` and `focus()`.

We've taken care of mapping the row keys to our IIDs; now we need to update the `selected_id()` property method so that it returns a row key tuple. Update that method as follows:

```
# views.py, in RecordList

  @property
  def selected_id(self):
    selection = self.treeview.selection()
    return self.iid_map[selection[0]] if selection else None
```

Just as before, we're retrieving the selected IID using the `self.treeview.selection()` method. This time, though, we need to look up the row key value in the mapping dictionary before returning it.

The last change to `RecordList` needs to be done in the initializer. Currently, our first column, `Row`, displays the IID on the pretext that it is the row number. That's no longer the case, and as our updated call to `insert()` did not specify a value to display, the column is just empty. So, the best thing we can do is remove this column.

However, that's not possible. The `#0` column is required and cannot be removed. It *can*, however, be hidden. To do that, we need to set the `Treeview` widget's `show` property, like so:

```
# views.py, inside RecordList.__init__()

    self.treeview.config(show='headings')
```

The `show` property essentially determines if the `#0` column will be displayed or not. It can be set to `tree`, in which case the column will be shown, or `headings`, in which case it will be hidden. The default is `tree`, so we've changed this to `headings`. Now only our four data columns will be shown.

We're done!

Phew! That was quite a journey, but our SQL conversion is more or less complete. You should be able to launch the application, log in using your PostgreSQL credentials, and load and save records using the database. This represents a huge improvement in the application and a major shift from a simple script to append a file to a full-blown database application.

 In the real world, of course, we aren't quite done here. Unit tests and documentation would all need to be updated to reflect the new model layer and other code changes. In addition, existing data may need to be imported into the database and users would need retraining to adjust to the move away from flat files. We won't be addressing all this in the book, but keep it in mind if you're undertaking a change like this in a real production environment!

Summary

In this chapter, you learned how to work with a relational SQL database. You installed and configured PostgreSQL. You converted a flat-file dataset into relational tables by identifying the primary key fields, choosing correct data types, and normalizing the data structure to reduce the possibility of inconsistencies, redundancies, and anomalies. You learned how to install and work with the `psycopg2` library for retrieving and storing data in PostgreSQL. Finally, you went through the arduous task of building a SQL database to hold your ABQ data, building a database model class to interface with the database, and converting the application code to use the new SQL backend.

In the next chapter, we'll be reaching out to the cloud. We'll need to contact some remote servers using different networking protocols to exchange data. You'll learn about the Python standard library's module for working with HTTP, as well as third-party packages for connecting with REST services and transferring files over SFTP.

13
Connecting to the Cloud

It seems that nearly every application needs to talk to the outside world sooner or later, and your ABQ Data Entry application is no exception. You've received some new feature requests that will require some interactions with remote servers and services.

First, the quality assurance division is doing a study of how local weather conditions are impacting the environmental data in each lab; they've requested a way to download and store local weather data in the database on demand. The second request is from your manager, who is still required to upload daily CSV files to the central corporate servers. She would like this process streamlined and available at a mouse click.

In this chapter, you will learn to interface with the cloud in the following topics:

- In *HTTP using urllib*, you'll connect to web services and download data using `urllib`.
- In *RESTful HTTP using requests*, you'll learn to interact with REST services using the `requests` library.
- In *SFTP using paramiko*, you'll upload files over SSH using `paramiko`.

HTTP using urllib

Every time you open a website in your browser, you're using the Hypertext Transfer Protocol, or HTTP. HTTP was created over 30 years ago as a way for web browsers to download HTML documents, but has evolved into one of the most popular client-server communication protocols for any number of purposes.

Not only do we use it in the browser to view everything from plain text to streaming video across the internet, but applications can also use it to transfer data, initiate remote procedures, or distribute computing tasks.

HTTP transaction fundamentals

A basic HTTP transaction between a client and server goes like this:

1. First, the client creates a **request**, which it will send to the server. The request contains the following:

    *   A **URL**, which specifies the host, port, and path to which the request is being made.

    *   A **method**, also known as a verb, which tells the server what operation the client is requesting. The most common methods are GET, for retrieving data, and POST, for submitting data.

    *   A **header**, which includes metadata in key-value pairs; for example, the type of content being submitted, how the content is encoded, or authorization tokens.

    *   Finally, the request may have a **payload**, which would contain the data being submitted to a server; for example, a file being uploaded, or a set of key-value pairs from a form.

2. When the server receives the request, it returns a **response**. The response contains the following:

    *   A **header** containing metadata such as the size or content type of the response.

    *   A **payload** containing the actual content of the response, such as HTML, XML, JSON, or binary data.

In a web browser, these interactions take place in the background, but our application code will deal directly with request and response objects in order to talk to remote HTTP servers.

HTTP status codes

Every HTTP request includes a **status code** in its header, which is a 3-digit number indicating the disposition of the request. The codes, defined in the HTTP standard, are organized as follows:

*   1XX status codes are informational messages sent during the processing of the request.

- 2XX status codes indicate a successful request; for example, 200 is the most common response, indicating the request was successful.

- 3XX status codes indicate a redirection. For example, a 301 is used to redirect the client to a new URL, and 304 indicates that the content hasn't been modified since it was last downloaded (redirecting the client to its cache).

- 4XX status codes indicate an error in the client's request. For example, a 403 error indicates a forbidden request (such as a request to secure documents without authentication), while the well-known 404 error indicates that a non-existent document was requested.

- 5XX status codes indicate an error on the server's side, such as the generic 500 error issued when the server encounters a bug in the web service.

While web browser users typically only encounter the 4XX and 5XX errors, you will encounter a few different status codes as you work directly with HTTP through urllib.

Basic downloading with urllib.request

The urllib.request module is a Python module for implementing HTTP interactions. It contains a number of functions and classes for generating requests, the most basic of which is the urlopen() function. This function can create a GET or POST request, send it to a remote server, and return an object containing the server's response.

Let's explore how urllib works; open a Python shell and execute the following commands:

```
>>> from urllib.request import urlopen
>>> response = urlopen('http://python.org')
```

The urlopen() function takes, at a minimum, a URL string. By default, it makes a GET request to the URL and returns an object that wraps the response received from the server.

This response object exposes metadata or content received from the server, which we can use in our application. Much of the response's metadata is found in the header, which we can extract using its getheader() method, like so:

```
>>> response.getheader('Content-Type')
'text/html; charset=utf-8'
>>> response.getheader('Server')
'nginx'
```

The getheader() method requires a key name, and returns the value of that key if it is found in the header. If the key isn't found, it returns None.

We can also extract the status code and a text explanation of the code using the status and reason attributes, like so:

```
>>> response.status
200
>>> response.reason
'OK'
```

Remember that a 200 status means a successful request. The OK string is just a more human-readable form of the status code.

The payload of the response object can be retrieved using an interface similar to a file handle; for example:

```
>>> html = response.read()
>>> html[:15]
b'<!doctype html>'
```

Just like a file handle, the response can only be read once, using the read() method; unlike a file handle, it can't be "rewound" using seek(), so it's important to save the response data in another variable if it needs to be accessed more than once. Note that the output of response.read() is a bytes object, which should be cast or decoded into an appropriate object depending on the content downloaded.

In this case, we know from the Content-Type header that the content is a UTF-8 string, so we should convert it to str using decode(), like so:

```
>>> html.decode('utf-8')[:15]
'<!doctype html>'
```

Generating POST requests

The urlopen() function can also generate POST requests. To do this, we just need to include a data argument, as follows:

```
>>> response = urlopen('http://duckduckgo.com', data=b'q=tkinter')
```

The data value needs to be a URL-encoded bytes object. A URL-encoded data string consists of key-value pairs separated by ampersand (&) symbols, with certain reserved characters encoded to URL-safe alternatives (for example, the space character is %20, or sometimes just +).

A string like this can be created by hand, but it's easier to use the `urlencode()` function provided by the `urllib.parse` module, as demonstrated here:

```
>>> from urllib.parse import urlencode
>>> url = 'http://duckduckgo.com'
>>> data = {'q': 'tkinter, python', 'ko': '-2', 'kz': '-1'}
>>> u_data = urlencode(data)
>>> u_data
'q=tkinter%2C+python&ko=-2&kz=-1'
>>> response = urlopen(url, data=u_data.encode())
```

Note that the `data` argument must be `bytes`, not a string, so `encode()` must be called on the URL-encoded string before `urlopen()` will accept it.

Downloading weather data to ABQ Data Entry

Let's try downloading the weather data needed for our application. The site we'll be using is `http://weather.gov`, which provides weather data within the United States. The actual URL we'll be downloading is `https://w1.weather.gov/xml/current_obs/STATION.xml`, where `STATION` is replaced by the call-sign of the local weather station. In the case of ABQ, we'll be using `KBMG`, located in Bloomington, Indiana.

The QA team wants you to record the temperature (in degrees Celsius), relative humidity, air pressure (in millibars), and sky conditions (a string, like "overcast" or "fair"). They also need the date and time at which the weather was observed by the station.

Creating a weather data model

While it would be simple enough to put `urlopen()` calls in an `Application` class callback, it's more consistent with our MVC design to wrap our interactions with the weather data service in a model class. Our model class will be responsible for acquiring the weather data from the web service and translating it into a format our other components can use easily.

Open the `models.py` file and let's begin by importing `urlopen()`:

```
# models.py
from urllib.request import urlopen
```

Now, at the end of the file, let's start a new model class to wrap our data download:

```python
class WeatherDataModel:

  base_url = 'http://w1.weather.gov/xml/current_obs/{}.xml'

  def __init__(self, station):
    self.url = self.base_url.format(station)
```

Our initializer will take a `station` string as an argument and use it with the base URL value to build the download URL for the weather data. By making the `station` value a variable, we can set the station in the user's configuration file, allowing users at other ABQ facilities to use the feature as well.

Now, let's begin writing a public method for this class to retrieve the weather data:

```python
# models.py, inside WeatherDataModel

  def get_weather_data(self):
    response = urlopen(self.url)
```

We start the method by sending a GET request to the model's URL and retrieve a response. Note that this may raise an exception (for example, if the site can't be reached for some reason), which code calling this method will need to handle.

Assuming things went okay, we just need to parse out the data in this response and put it into a form that the `Application` class can pass to the SQL model. To determine how we'll handle the response, let's go back to the Python shell and examine the data there:

```python
>>> url = 'http://w1.weather.gov/xml/current_obs/KBMG.xml'
>>> response = urlopen(url)
>>> print(response.read().decode())
  <?xml version="1.0" encoding="ISO-8859-1"?>
  <?xml-stylesheet href="latest_ob.xsl" type="text/xsl"?>
  <current_observation version="1.0"
  xmlns:xsd=http://www.w3.org/2001/XMLSchema
  xmlns:xsi=http://www.w3.org/2001/XMLSchema-instance
  xsi:noNamespaceSchemaLocation=
    "http://www.weather.gov/view/current_observation.xsd">
  <credit>NOAA's National Weather Service</credit>
  <credit_URL>http://weather.gov/</credit_URL>
....
```

As the URL indicated, the payload of the response is an XML document, most of which we won't need. After some searching, though, you should be able to locate the fields we need, shown here:

```
<observation_time_rfc822>
  Tue, 29 Jun 2021 15:53:00 -0400
</observation_time_rfc822>
<weather>Mostly Cloudy</weather>
<temp_c>32.8</temp_c>
<relative_humidity>54</relative_humidity>
<pressure_mb>1020.0</pressure_mb>
```

Good, the data we need is there, so we just need to extract it from the XML string into a format our application can use. Let's take a moment to learn about parsing XML data.

Parsing the XML weather data

The Python standard library contains an xml package, which consists of several sub-modules for parsing or creating XML data. Of these, the xml.etree.ElementTree sub-module is a simple, lightweight parser that should meet our needs.

Let's import ElementTree into our models.py file as follows:

```
# models.py
from xml.etree import ElementTree
```

Now, back at the end of our get_weather_data() method, we'll parse the XML data in our response object as follows:

```
# models.py, inside WeatherDataModel.get_weather_data()

  xmlroot = ElementTree.fromstring(response.read())
```

The fromstring() method takes an XML string and returns an Element object. To get at the data we need, we'll first need to understand what an Element object represents, and how to work with it.

XML is a hierarchical representation of data; an element represents a node in this hierarchy. An element begins with a tag, which is a text string inside angle brackets. Each tag has a matching closing tag, which is just the tag with a forward-slash prefixed to the tag name.

Between the opening and closing tags, an element may have other child elements or it may have text. An element can also have attributes, which are key-value pairs placed inside the angle brackets of the opening tag, just after the tag name.

Take a look at the following example of XML:

```
<star_system starname="Sol">
  <planet>Mercury</planet>
  <planet>Venus</planet>
  <planet>Earth
    <moon>Luna</moon>
  </planet>
  <planet>Mars
    <moon>Phobos</moon>
    <moon>Deimos</moon>
  </planet>
  <dwarf_planet>Ceres</dwarf_planet>
</star_system>
```

This example is an (incomplete) XML description of the solar system. The root element has a tag of `<star_system>` with an attribute of `starname`. Under this root element, we have four `<planet>` elements and a `<dwarf_planet>` element, each of which contains a text node with the planet's name. Some of the planet nodes also have child `<moon>` nodes, each containing a text node with the moon's name.

Arguably, this data could have been structured differently; for example, planet names could have been in a child `<name>` node inside the planet elements, or listed as an attribute of the `<planet>` tag. While XML *syntax* is well-defined, the actual *structure* of an XML document is up to its creator, so fully parsing XML data requires a knowledge of the way the data is laid out in the document.

If you look at the XML weather data that we downloaded in the shell earlier, you'll notice it's a fairly shallow hierarchy. Under the `<current_observations>` node, there are a number of child elements whose tags represent specific data fields like temperature, humidity, wind chill, and so on.

To access and extract these child elements, the `Element` object offers us the following variety of methods:

Method	Returns
`iter()`	An iterator of all child nodes (recursively)
`find(tag)`	The first element matching the given tag
`findall(tag)`	A list of elements matching the given tag
`getchildren()`	A list of the immediate child nodes
`iterfind(tag)`	An iterator of all child nodes matching the given tag (recursive)

When we downloaded the XML data earlier, we identified five tags containing the data we want to extract from this document: `<observation_time_rfc822>`, `<weather>`, `<temp_c>`, `<relative_humidity>`, and `<pressure_mb>`. We'll want our function to return a Python dictionary containing each of these tags as keys.

So, inside get_weather_data(), let's create a dictionary containing the tags we want, like so:

```
weatherdata = {
  'observation_time_rfc822': None,
  'temp_c': None,
  'relative_humidity': None,
  'pressure_mb': None,
  'weather': None
}
```

Now, let's get the values from the Element object and add them to the dictionary:

```
for tag in weatherdata:
  element = xmlroot.find(tag)
  if element is not None:
    weatherdata[tag] = element.text
return weatherdata
```

For each of our tag names, we're going to use the find() method to try to locate the element with a matching tag in xmlroot. This particular XML document does not use duplicate tags (since it would make no sense for a single observation to have multiple times, temperature values, humidity values, and so on), so the first instance of any tag should be the only one. If the tag is matched, we'll get back an Element object of the matched node; if not, we get back None, so we need to make sure element is not None before trying to access its text attribute.

Once we've done that for all the tags, we can finish the function by returning the dictionary.

You can test this function in the Python shell; from a command line, navigate to the ABQ_Data_Entry directory and start a Python shell. Then enter these commands:

```
>>> from abq_data_entry.models import WeatherDataModel
>>> wdm = WeatherDataModel('KBMG')
>>> wdm.get_weather_data()
{'observation_time_rfc822': 'Mon, 09 Aug 2021 15:53:00 -0400',
'temp_c': '26.1', 'relative_humidity': '74',
'pressure_mb': '1013.7', 'weather': 'Fair'}
```

You should get back a dictionary with the current weather conditions in Bloomington, Indiana.

 You can find the station codes for other cities inside the U.S. at http://w1.weather.gov/xml/current_obs/.

Now that we have our weather data model, we just need to build the table for storing the data and the interface for triggering the operation.

Implementing weather data storage

To store our weather data, we'll start by creating a table in the ABQ database to hold the individual observation data, then build a SQLModel method to store the retrieved data in it. We don't need to worry about writing code to retrieve data back from the database, since our laboratory's QA team has their own reporting tools that they'll use to access it.

Creating the SQL table

Under the application's sql folder, open the create_db.sql file, and add a new CREATE TABLE statement as follows:

```
# create_db.sql
CREATE TABLE local_weather (
  datetime TIMESTAMP(0) WITH TIME ZONE PRIMARY KEY,
  temperature NUMERIC(5,2),
  rel_hum NUMERIC(5, 2),
  pressure NUMERIC(7,2),
  conditions VARCHAR(32)
);
```

In this table, we're using the TIMESTAMP data type on the record as a primary key; there's no point in saving the same timestamped observation twice, so this makes an adequate primary key. The (0) size after the TIMESTAMP data type indicates how many decimal places we need for the seconds measurement. Since these measurements are taken approximately hourly, and we only need one every four hours or so (when the lab checks are done), we don't need fractions of seconds in our timestamp.

Notice that we're saving the time zone; always store time zone data with timestamps when it's available! It may not seem necessary, especially when your application will be run in a workplace that will never change time zones, but there are many edge cases such as daylight savings time changes, where the lack of a time zone can create major problems.

Run this CREATE query in your database to build the table, and let's move on to creating our SQLModel method.

Implementing the SQLModel.add_weather_data() method

Over in models.py, let's add a new method to the SQLModel class called add_weather_data(), which takes a dictionary as its only argument. Start this method by creating an INSERT query as follows:

```
# models.py, inside SQLModel

def add_weather_data(self, data):
  query = (
    'INSERT INTO local_weather VALUES '
    '(%(observation_time_rfc822)s, %(temp_c)s, '
    '%(relative_humidity)s, %(pressure_mb)s, '
    '%(weather)s)'
  )
```

This is a straightforward parameterized INSERT query using variable names that match the dictionary keys which the get_local_weather() function extracts from the XML data. We should only need to pass this query and the data dictionary into our query() method.

There is one problem, however; if we get a duplicate timestamp, our query will fail due to a duplicate primary key. We could do another query to check first, but that would be slightly redundant, since PostgreSQL itself checks for duplicate keys before inserting a new row.

When it detects such an error, psycopg2 raises an IntegrityError exception, so we can just catch this exception and, if it gets raised, do nothing.

To do this, we'll wrap our query() call in the try/except block, like so:

```
    try:
      self.query(query, data)
    except pg.IntegrityError:
```

```
        # already have weather for this datetime
        pass
```

Now, our data entry staff can call this method as often as they wish, but it will only save a record when there is a fresh observation to save.

Updating the SettingsModel class

Before leaving `models.py`, we will need to add a new application setting to store the preferred weather station. Add the following new entry in the `SettingsModel.fields` dictionary:

```
# models.py, inside SettingsModel

fields = {
  # ...
  'weather_station': {'type': 'str', 'value': 'KBMG'},
}
```

We won't add a GUI to change this setting, since users won't need to update it. It'll be up to us, or the system admin at other lab sites, to make sure this is properly set on each workstation by editing the abq_settings.json file.

Adding the GUI elements for weather download

The `Application` object now needs to connect the weather download method from `WeatherDataModel` to the database method in `SQLModel` with an appropriate callback method that the main menu classes can call.

Open `application.py` and start a new method in the `Application` class called `_update_weather_data()`:

```
# application.py, inside Application

  def _update_weather_data(self, *_):
    weather_data_model = m.WeatherDataModel(
      self.settings['weather_station'].get()
    )
    try:
      weather_data = weather_data_model.get_weather_data()
```

This method begins by creating a `WeatherDataModel` instance using the `weather_station` value pulled from the `settings` dictionary. Then, it attempts to call `get_weather_data()` inside a `try` block.

Recall that in an error scenario, `urlopen()` can raise any number of exceptions, depending on what went wrong with the HTTP transaction. There isn't really anything the application can do to handle such exceptions other than informing the user and exiting the method. Therefore, we'll catch the generic `Exception` and display the text in a `messagebox` dialogbox, like so:

```python
except Exception as e:
  messagebox.showerror(
    title='Error',
    message='Problem retrieving weather data',
    detail=str(e)
  )
  self.status.set('Problem retrieving weather data')
```

In the event that `get_local_weather()` succeeds, we simply need to pass the data on to our model method. We can add this in an `else` clause:

```python
else:
  self.data_model.add_weather_data(weather_data)
  time = weather_data['observation_time_rfc822']
  self.status.set(f"Weather data recorded for {time}")
```

In addition to saving the data, we've notified the user in the status bar that the weather was updated and displayed the timestamp of the update.

With the callback method done, let's add it to our callbacks dictionary:

```python
# application.py, in Application.__init__()
  event_callbacks = {
    #...
    '<<UpdateWeatherData>>': self._update_weather_data
  }
```

Now we can add a `command` item for the callback in the main menu. In keeping with the main menu guidelines we learned in *Chapter 10*, *Maintaining Cross-Platform Compatibility*, we should consider an appropriate sub-menu for the command. On Windows, functionality like this goes in the `Tools` menu, and since neither the Gnome nor macOS guidelines seem to indicate a more appropriate location, we'll implement a `Tools` menu in the `LinuxMainMenu` and `MacOsMainMenu` classes to hold this command, just to be consistent.

Open `mainmenu.py`, and starting in the generic menu class, let's add a private method that will add the `command` item:

```
# mainmenu.py, inside GenericMainMenu

def _add_weather_download(self, menu):
    menu.add_command(
        label="Update Weather Data",
        command=self._event('<<UpdateWeatherData>>')
    )
```

Now, in each menu class's initializer, we'll create a `Tools` menu and add the command to it:

```
# mainmenu.py, inside GenericMainMenu.__init__()
    # Put between the File and Options menus
    self._menus['Tools'] = tk.Menu(self, tearoff=False)
    self._add_weather_download(self._menus['Tools'])
```

Add this same code to the macOS and Linux menu classes' initializers. In the `WindowsMainMenu` class's initializer, you only need to add the second line, since the `Tools` menu already exists. After updating the menus, you can run the application and try the new command from the `Tools` menu. If all went well, you should see an indication in the status bar as shown in the following screenshot:

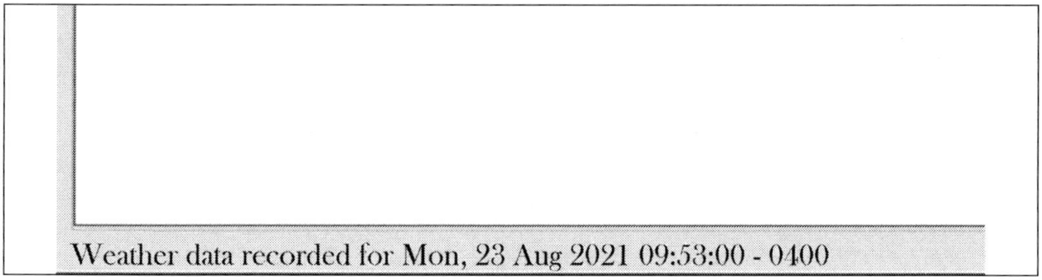

Weather data recorded for Mon, 23 Aug 2021 09:53:00 - 0400

Figure 13.1: Success downloading the weather data

You should also connect to the database with your PostgreSQL client and check that the table contains some weather data now by executing the following SQL command:

```
SELECT * FROM local_weather;
```

That SQL statement should return output similar to the following:

datetime	temperature	rel_hum	pressure	conditions
2021-08-12 18:53:00-05	26.10	74.00	1013.70	Fair

As you've seen, `urllib` is fairly simple to work with for downloading files from the web; most of the work involves parsing the downloaded file and utilizing it in the application. However, not all web transactions are as simple as a single GET or POST request. In the next section, we'll look at a more powerful tool for HTTP interactions, `requests`.

RESTful HTTP using requests

You've been asked by your manager to create a function in your program that will allow her to upload a CSV extract of the daily data to ABQ's corporate web services, which uses an authenticated REST API. **REST** stands for **REpresentational State Transfer** and refers to an approach to web services that is built around advanced HTTP semantics to provide a more code-friendly interface. Services designed around the REST concept are described as **RESTful**. Let's take a deeper look at how REST interactions work.

Understanding RESTful web services

A RESTful service is built around the idea of accessing **resources**. A resource is typically a data record or file, though it could also be something like a remote procedure or hardware interface. We access resources via **endpoints**, which are URLs that represent a particular resource.

We have seen that web servers typically allow you to fetch data using GET and submit data using POST. REST APIs, however, employ additional HTTP methods like DELETE, PUT, and PATCH to indicate different operations. Depending on which method we use when requesting an endpoint, we can perform different actions on the resource.

While implementations of REST services vary, the following table shows the generally-agreed-upon functions of HTTP methods by a typical API:

Method	Function
GET	Retrieve a resource
HEAD	Retrieve only metadata (headers) about a resource
POST	Create or update a resource based on the submitted data
PUT	Upload a resource as-is (typically for files)
PATCH	Update an existing resource with partial data (rarely implemented)
DELETE	Delete a resource

In addition to a more robust set of methods, REST services also exchange data in a way that is more code-friendly. While browser-oriented services accept data in URL-encoded strings and return HTML documents, RESTful services may accept requests and return responses in formats like JSON or XML. In some cases, clients can even request the data format to be returned.

It's critical to understand that, while some standards for RESTful services exist, the organization and behavior of REST sites (including their precise responses to different methods) vary widely. In order to interact with a REST API, you will need to consult its specific documentation.

The Python requests library

As we saw in the first section of this chapter, `urllib` is fairly simple to use for basic `GET` and `POST` requests, and being in the standard library makes it a good choice when that's all we require. However, more complex HTTP interactions involving authentication, file uploads, or additional HTTP methods can be frustrating and complicated using `urllib` alone. To get this done, we'll turn to the third-party `requests` library. This library is highly recommended by the Python community for any serious work involving HTTP. As you'll see, `requests` removes many of the rough edges and outdated assumptions left in `urllib`, providing convenient classes and wrapper functions for more modern HTTP transactions like REST. Complete documentation on `requests` can be found at `https://docs.python-requests.org`, but the next section will cover most of what you need to know to use it effectively.

Installing and using requests

The `requests` package is written in pure Python, so installing it with `pip` requires no compiling or binary downloads. Simply type `pip install --user requests` in the terminal and it will be added to your system.

Let's check out how `requests` works in the Python shell; open a shell and enter the following:

```
>>> import requests
>>> response = requests.request('GET', 'http://www.alandmoore.com')
```

The `requests.request()` function requires, at a minimum, an HTTP method and a URL. Just like `urlopen()`, it constructs the appropriate request packet, sends it to the URL, and returns an object representing the server's response. Here, we're making a GET request to this author's website.

In addition to the `request()` function, `requests` has shortcut functions that correspond to the most common HTTP methods. Thus, the same request can be made as follows:

```
>>> response = requests.get('http://www.alandmoore.com')
```

The `get()` method requires only the URL and performs a GET request. Likewise, the `post()`, `put()`, `patch()`, `delete()`, and `head()` functions send requests using the corresponding HTTP method. All of these request functions take additional optional arguments.

For example, we can send data with a POST request as follows:

```
>>> data = {'q': 'tkinter', 'ko': '-2', 'kz': '-1'}
>>> url = 'https://duckduckgo.com'
>>> response = requests.post(url, data)
```

Notice that, unlike `urlopen()`, we can use a Python dictionary directly as a `data` argument; `requests` does the job of converting it to the proper URL-encoded `bytes` object for us.

Some of the more common arguments used with request functions are as follows:

Argument	Purpose
params	Like `data`, but added to the query string rather than the payload
json	JSON data to include in the payload
headers	A dictionary of header data to use for the request
files	A dictionary of {`fieldnames: file_objects`} to send as a multipart form data request
auth	Username and password tuple to use for basic HTTP digest authentication

Note that the `auth` argument here only works to authenticate against HTTP digest authentication; this is an older method of authentication that is implemented at the web server level rather than in the actual web application, and it's rarely used on modern websites. To work with modern authentication systems, we need to understand the use of sessions.

Interacting with authenticated sites using Session

HTTP is a **stateless** protocol, meaning that each HTTP request stands on its own and is not connected to any other requests, even between the same client and server. Although it may seem like you are "connected" to your social media or banking website when you log in, in reality there is no underlying ongoing connection between you and the server, only a series of unrelated requests and responses.

How, then, do such sites manage to keep your interactions secure?

On modern sites, this is typically done using either a **session cookie** or **authentication token**. In both of these approaches, when the client authenticates to the server, the server returns a piece of data that the client can include with future requests to identify itself as the same entity that successfully authenticated. In this way, both client and server can simulate a stateful connection by associating the requests and responses between them into a session.

 The differences between session cookies and authentication tokens are immaterial for us on the client side; just know that both require us to store something from the server after authentication and provide it with each future request.

The `requests` module makes this kind of interaction simple by providing the `Session` class. A `Session` object persists settings, cookies, and tokens across multiple requests, allowing you to interact with services that require authentication or special client settings. To create a `Session` object, use the `requests.session()` factory function as follows:

```
>>> s = requests.session()
```

Now, we can call request methods like `get()`, `post()`, and others on our `Session` object, for example:

```
# Assume this is a valid authentication service that returns an auth
token
>>> s.post('http://example.com/login', data={'u': 'test', 'p': 'test'})
# Now we would have an auth token stored in s
>>> response = s.get('http://example.com/protected_content')
# Our token cookie would be listed here
>>> print(s.cookies.items())
```

Token and cookie handling like this happens in the background, without any explicit action from us. Cookies are stored in a `CookieJar` object in the `Session` object's `cookies` property.

We can also set configuration options on our `Session` object that will persist across requests; for example:

```
>>> s.headers['User-Agent'] = 'Mozilla'
>>> s.params['uid'] = 12345
# will be sent with a user-agent string of "Mozilla"
```

```
# and a parameter of "uid=12345"
>>> s.get('http://example.com')
```

In this example, we've set the user-agent string to `Mozilla`, which will then be used for all requests made from this `Session` object. We also set a default URL parameter using the `params` attribute; thus, the actual URL that was requested was `http://example.com?uid=12345`.

The requests.Response object

All the request functions and methods in `requests` return a `Response` object. These `Response` objects are not the same as those returned by `urlopen()`; they contain all the same data, but in a slightly different (and generally more convenient) form. In addition, they have some helpful methods that make quick work of translating their contents.

For example, the response headers are already translated into a Python dictionary for us, as demonstrated here:

```
>>> r = requests.get('http://python.org')
>>> r.headers
{'Connection': 'keep-alive', 'Content-Length': '49812',
'Server': 'nginx', 'Content-Type': 'text/html; charset=utf-8',
 # ... etc
```

Another difference from `urllib` is that `requests` does not automatically raise an exception on HTTP errors. However, the `.raise_for_status()` response method can be called to do so.

For example, let's make a request to a URL that will give an HTTP 404 error:

```
>>> r = requests.get('http://www.example.com/does-not-exist')
>>> r.status_code
404
>>> r.raise_for_status()
Traceback (most recent call last):
File "<stdin>", line 1, in <module>
File "/usr/lib/python3.9/site-packages/requests/models.py", line 935,
in
raise_for_status
raise HTTPError(http_error_msg, response=self)
requests.exceptions.HTTPError: 404 Client Error: Not Found for url:
http://www.example.com/does-not-exist
```

This gives us the option of dealing with HTTP errors using exception handling or more traditional flow control logic if we prefer, or to defer our exception handling to a more convenient moment.

Implementing a REST backend

To start implementing our interactions with the ABQ corporate REST server, we need to figure out what kind of requests we're going to send. We've been provided with some documentation from the corporate office that describes how to interact with the REST API.

The API documentation tells us the following things:

- Before accessing any other endpoints, we'll need to obtain an authentication token. We do this by submitting a POST request to the /auth endpoint. The payload of the POST request should include username and password as URL-encoded data. If our credentials fail, we'll get an HTTP 401 error. If we don't have a token, any other requests will fail with an HTTP 403 error.

- Once we have a token, we can work with files using the /files endpoint:

  - We can upload files using a PUT request. The file is uploaded as multipart form data specified in a parameter called file.

  - We can retrieve a file by sending a GET request in the form of /files/ FILENAME, where FILENAME is the name of the file.

  - Alternatively, we can retrieve only metadata about a file by sending a HEAD request to /files/FILENAME.

- All HTTP errors are accompanied by a JSON payload that includes the status code and a message indicating what caused the error.

 An example script, sample_rest_service.py, is included with the example code for this book that replicates the functionality of the ABQ Corporate REST services. To use it, you'll need to install the flask library using the command pip install -u flask, then run the command python sample_rest_service.py at a terminal prompt.

Once again, in keeping with our MVC design, we're going to implement a model that encapsulates all these interactions. We'll begin in models.py by importing the requests library like so:

```
# models.py

import requests
```

Now, at the end of the file, let's start a new model class, `CorporateRestModel`, for the REST site:

```
# models.py

class CorporateRestModel:

  def __init__(self, base_url):

    self.auth_url = f'{base_url}/auth'
    self.files_url = f'{base_url}/files'
    self.session = requests.session()
```

The class initializer takes a `base_url` argument defining the base URL of the REST service we want to contact. It then uses this URL to construct the endpoint URLs for upload, authentication, and file retrieval. Finally, since we're going to need to store authentication tokens, we create a session object for each method to use.

We could have just specified the `base_url` as a class attribute like we did with the `WeatherDataModel`; however, to enable us to test this class against the test service, or to accommodate the possibility of a change to the corporate servers, we'll store this value in the user's settings so it can be easily swapped out.

Before we go on, let's add a setting to our `SettingsModel` for the REST base URL:

```
# models.py, inside SettingsModel

  fields = {
    #...
    'abq_rest_url': {
      'type': 'str',
      'value': 'http://localhost:8000'
    }
  }
```

The default value of `http://localhost:8000` is the base URL of the example server provided for testing; in production, this setting can be altered by technical support for each user by editing their `abq_settings.json` file.

Now, back in our `CorporateRestModel` class, we need to implement four methods:

- An `authenticate()` method to send credentials via a `POST` request to the `/auth` endpoint.
- An `upload_file()` method to send a file via a `PUT` request to the `/files` endpoint.

- A check_file() method to retrieve only metadata from the /files endpoint.
- A get_file() method to download a file from the /files endpoint.

Let's get started!

The authenticate() method

Since we can't do anything else without an authentication token, let's start with the authenticate() method:

```
# models.py, inside CorporateRestModel

def authenticate(self, username, password):
    response = self.session.post(
        self.auth_url,
        data={'username': username, 'password': password}
    )
```

This method will take a username and password and post them to the auth_url using our model's Session object. The session will automatically store the token we receive if we're successful. Recall that the server will return an HTTP 401 error if we provide invalid credentials; we could simply check the status code of the response and return True or False from this method. However, since there are a variety of other ways that a call to a remote HTTP server can fail (for example, a problem on the server might result in a 500 error), it would be better if we could report back to the calling code some more detailed information about the failure. We could do this by calling the Response object's raise_for_status() method to send an HTTPError exception back to the calling code. That might give us an error dialog like this:

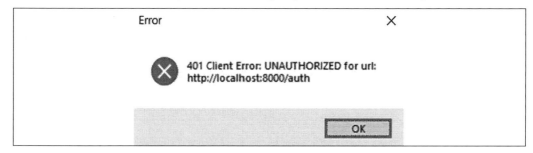

Figure 13.2: An ugly 401 error

Of course, we can, and should, do a bit better. Most users won't know what an HTTP 401 error means.

Remember from the API specification that the server also returns a JSON object with the error that contains a more meaningful message about the failure. We can write a static method for our model that will handle an `HTTPError` and convert it to an exception with a more human-friendly message. Add this method to the model:

```
@staticmethod
def _raise_for_status(response):
  try:
    response.raise_for_status()
  except requests.HTTPError:
    raise Exception(response.json().get('message'))
```

This method accepts a `Response` object, then calls its `raise_for_status()` method. If the status was a success (200), then nothing will happen and the method returns. If it raises an `HTTPError`, however, we'll extract the `message` value from the `Response` object's JSON payload and raise a new `Exception` error using that message.

Back in `authenticate()`, let's end the method by passing the response to this static method:

```
# models.py, inside CorporateRestModel.authenticate()

    self._raise_for_status(response)
```

Now a failed login looks more like this:

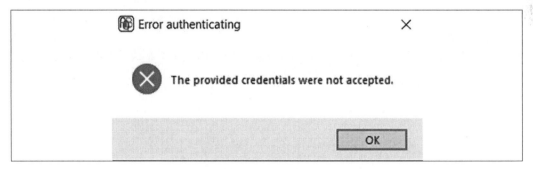

Figure 13.3: A much nicer failure message

If no exception is raised, we don't need to do anything else. The session has the token and we can proceed to other operations.

The upload_file() method

Our next method will implement actually uploading a file. Remember from the API documentation that this requires a PUT request to the /files endpoint. The method looks like this:

```
def upload_file(self, filepath):
  with open(filepath, 'rb') as fh:
    files = {'file': fh}
    response = self.session.put(
      self.files_url, files=files
    )
  self._raise_for_status(response)
```

To send a file using requests, we have to actually open it and retrieve a file handle, then place the file handle in a dictionary, which we pass to the request method's files argument. Multiple files can be sent if each one receives a different key in the dictionary; our API only allows one file at a time, however, and it must have a key of file. Once again, we finish the method by checking the response for an error code with our _raise_for_status() method.

 Notice we open the file in binary-read mode (rb). The requests documentation recommends this, as it ensures the correct Content-length value will be calculated for the request header.

The check_file() method

The next method we need is the check_file() method, which will retrieve header information about a file on the server without actually downloading it. The API documentation tells us that we can get metadata about the file by sending a HEAD request to the files/FILENAME endpoint, where FILENAME is the name of the file we want information about. HEAD requests are useful when dealing with slow connections or large files, as they allow us to find out information about the file (for example, its size or whether it exists or not) without actually downloading the entire file.

Let's implement this method like so:

```
def check_file(self, filename):
  url = f"{self.files_url}/{filename}"
  response = self.session.head(url)
  if response.status_code == 200:
    return True
```

```
    elif response.status_code == 404:
      return False
    self._raise_for_status(response)
```

For our purposes, we are mostly interested in whether files on the server exist or not, so we're going to return a Boolean value from this method depending on whether we get a status 200 (success) or 404 (file not found). Of course, other things can go wrong with the request too, so we'll also pass the response to our _raise_for_status() method if it has a different status code.

The get_file() method

The last method we'll implement is the get_file() method, for downloading file data. Add the following method to CorporateRestModel:

```
def get_file(self, filename):
  """Download a file from the server"""
  url = f"{self.files_url}/{filename}"
  response = self.session.get(url)
  self._raise_for_status(response)
  return response.text
```

Unlike other endpoints in this API, a GET request to the /files endpoint does *not* return JSON, but rather the contents of the file. We can retrieve these contents from the Response object's text attribute, which we're returning from the method. It will be up to the code that calls this method to do something suitable with the content returned from the method. We'll do this in our Application class, where we'll save the downloaded content to a file.

As our model is now complete, let's head over to the Application class to begin working on the front end.

Integrating REST upload into the application

After discussions with your manager, who is responsible for performing the REST upload, you determine that the workflow for the REST upload operation needs to go something like this:

- When a REST upload is run from the GUI, it should first check if there is any data in the database for that day, and abort if there is not. It looks bad on your manager if they upload empty files!
- If there is data, it should create a CSV extract of the day's data using the original naming format that was used before the facility went to SQL storage, since this is the filename format expected by ABQ Corporate.

- Next, it should prompt for authentication credentials for the REST API.

- After that, the program should check if a file has already been uploaded for that day's data. If not, go ahead and upload the file.

- If there is a file (sometimes she forgets and uploads twice), the program should prompt whether the file should be overwritten or not.

- In the event we're not overwriting the file, there should be an option to download the file from the server so it can be manually compared with the data in SQL.

Let's begin implementing this code!

Creating a CSV extract

Before we can upload anything, we need to implement a way to create a CSV extract of the daily data. This will be used by more than one function, so we'll implement it as a separate method.

Start a new private method in Application called _create_csv_extract(), like so:

```python
# application.py, inside Application

def _create_csv_extract(self):
    csvmodel = m.CSVModel()
    records = self.model.get_all_records()
    if not records:
        raise Exception('No records were found to build a CSV file.')
    for record in records:
        csvmodel.save_record(record)
    return csvmodel.file
```

The method begins by creating a new instance of our CSVModel class; even though we're no longer storing our data in the CSV files, we can still use the model to export a CSV file. We are not passing in any arguments, just using the default file path of the file. Next, we call the get_all_records() method of the application's SQLModel instance. Remember that our SQLModel.get_all_records() method returns a list of all records for the current day by default. Since your boss doesn't want to upload empty files, we'll raise an exception if there are no records to build a CSV with. Our calling code can catch that and display the appropriate warning. If there are records to save, the method iterates through them, saving each one to the CSV, then returns the CSVModel object's file attribute (that is, a Path object pointing to the saved file).

Creating the upload callback

Now that we have a way to create a CSV extract file, we can write the actual callback method as follows:

```
# application.py, inside Application

  def _upload_to_corporate_rest(self, *_):
    try:
      csvfile = self._create_csv_extract()
    except Exception as e:
      messagebox.showwarning(
        title='Error', message=str(e)
      )
      return
```

To begin, we attempt to create a CSV extract file; if we get any exceptions (for example, the "No records" exception we created, or perhaps a database issue) we'll display an error message and exit the method.

If we've created a CSV file successfully, our next step is to authenticate to the REST API. To do that, we need to get a username and password from the user. Fortunately, we have the perfect class for this:

```
    d = v.LoginDialog(
      self, 'Login to ABQ Corporate REST API'
    )
    if d.result is not None:
      username, password = d.result
    else:
      return
```

Our `LoginDialog` class serves us well here. Unlike with our database login, we're not going to run this in an endless loop; if the password is wrong, we will just return from the function and the user can rerun the command if need be. Recall that dialog's `result` attribute will be `None` if the user clicks `Cancel`, so we'll just exit the callback method in that case.

Now that we have credentials and a filename, we can try to authenticate to the server:

```
    rest_model = m.CorporateRestModel(
      self.settings['abq_rest_url'].get()
    )
```

```
try:
  rest_model.authenticate(username, password)
except Exception as e:
  messagebox.showerror('Error authenticating', str(e))
  return
```

We begin by creating a `CorporateRestModel` instance based on the user's `abq_rest_url` setting, then passing our credentials to its `authenticate()` method. Recall that in the event of an HTTP problem (including invalid credentials), our model will raise an `Exception` with a human-friendly message, so we can simply display that in a message box and exit the callback.

Our next step is to check if a file for today's date already exists on the server. We'll do that using our model's `check_file()` method, like so:

```
try:
  exists = rest_model.check_file(csvfile.name)
except Exception as e:
  messagebox.showerror('Error checking for file', str(e))
  return
```

Remember that `check_file()` will return a Boolean value indicating if the file exists on the server or not, or it might raise an exception if some other HTTP issue arises. As before, in the event of an error we'll just show a dialog and exit the function.

If the file already exists, we need to determine what the user wants to do about it; first, whether they want to just overwrite it, and if not, whether they want to download it. We can do that using some message boxes, like so:

```
if exists:
  overwrite = messagebox.askyesno(
    'File exists',
    f'The file {csvfile.name} already exists on the server, '
    'do you want to overwrite it?'
  )
  if not overwrite:
    download = messagebox.askyesno(
      'Download file',
      'Do you want to download the file to inspect it?'
    )
```

Remember from *Chapter 7, Creating Menus with Menu and Tkinter Dialogs*, that `askyesno()` returns a Boolean value depending on whether the user clicks **Yes** or **No**.

If the user wants to download the file, we can do that using our model, like so:

```python
if download:
    filename = filedialog.asksaveasfilename()
    if not filename:
        return
    try:
        data = rest_model.get_file(csvfile.name)
    except Exception as e:
        messagebox.showerror('Error downloading', str(e))
        return
    with open(filename, 'w', encoding='utf-8') as fh:
        fh.write(data)
    messagebox.showinfo(
        'Download Complete', 'Download Complete.'
    )
    return
```

Here, we first retrieve the filename the user wants to save the downloaded file to using a `filedialog` function. If they cancel the dialog, we'll just exit the function doing nothing. Otherwise, we attempt to download the file using our model's `get_file()` method. As before, if it fails we display the error and exit. If it succeeds, we'll open a new UTF-8 file and save the data to it. Finally, we display a success dialog once the file is written. The final `return` statement exits the method whether or not the user decides to download the file; since at this point, they've opted not to overwrite the file in either case.

If they have opted to overwrite the file, our method continues outside that `if` block as follows:

```python
try:
    rest_model.upload_file(csvfile)
except Exception as e:
    messagebox.showerror('Error uploading', str(e))
else:
    messagebox.showinfo(
        'Success',
        f'{csvfile} successfully uploaded to REST API.'
    )
```

At this point, if the method has not yet returned due to an error or user selection, we can go ahead and upload the file. This is done using our model's `upload_file()` method. We'll either get a success dialog or an error dialog depending on whether the operation succeeds or fails. In either case, our method is finished at this point.

Finishing up

The last thing we need to do is add a menu option for running the REST upload. First, add the method to the `Application` class's event callbacks as follows:

```
# application.py, inside Application.__init__()
    event_callbacks = {
      #...
      '<<UploadToCorporateREST>>': self._upload_to_corporate_rest,
    }
```

Finally, let's add the command item to our main menu. We'll start by adding a method to create the REST upload entry in the menu, as follows:

```
# mainmenu.py, inside GenericMainMenu

  def _add_rest_upload(self, menu):
    menu.add_command(
      label="Upload CSV to corporate REST",
      command=self._event('<<UploadToCorporateREST>>')
    )
```

Next, we'll need to add a call to this method in the `GenericMainMenu` class initializer and each of the platform-specific menus; in each case, it should look like this:

```
# mainmenu.py, in each menu class initializer
    # after creation of Tools menu
    self._add_rest_upload(self._menus['Tools'])
```

Now, run the application and let's try it out. To make it work, you'll need to have at least one record saved in the database, and you'll need to start up the `sample_rest_service.py` script from the example code.

If all goes well, you should get a dialog like this:

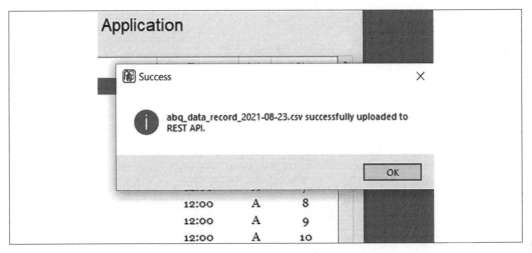

Figure 13.4: A successful upload to the REST server

Your server should also have printed some output to the terminal similar to this:

```
127.0.0.1 - - [07/Sep/2021 17:10:27] "POST /auth HTTP/1.1" 200 -
127.0.0.1 - - [07/Sep/2021 17:10:27]
   "HEAD /files/abq_data_record_2021-09-07.csv HTTP/1.1" 200 -
Uploaded abq_data_record_2021-09-07.csv
127.0.0.1 - - [07/Sep/2021 17:10:34] "PUT /files HTTP/1.1" 200 -
```

Notice the POST, HEAD, and PUT requests, as well as the filename of the CSV file in the payload of PUT.

You can also run the upload a second time, in which case you should get the dialogs asking if you want to overwrite the file, and then if you want to download it, like this:

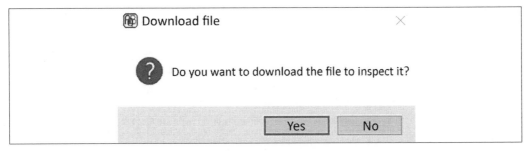

Figure 13.5: Download dialog

That completes the functionality we needed for this application. Good job!

SFTP using paramiko

While custom-written RESTful web APIs may be common with large companies and third-party services, our programs are often called upon to exchange files or data with servers using standard communication protocols. In the Linux and Unix world, the secure shell or SSH protocol has long been the de-facto standard for communication between systems. Most implementations of SSH include SFTP (**Secure File Transfer Protocol**), an encrypted replacement for the archaic FTP service.

In addition to uploading the CSV extract to the corporate REST service, your manager has to upload a second copy to a remote server using SFTP. The user workflow needs to be the same, though there is a requirement to upload the file into a particular directory on the server. You need to implement this upload in your application just as you did for the REST service.

Setting up SSH services for testing

In order to test the SFTP features we're going to code in our application, we need to have an SSH server available to us. If you don't have access to a device that runs SSH, you can easily install it on your own workstation, depending on your operating system:

- On macOS, SSH is preinstalled but needs to be enabled. You can enable it from the **Sharing** page in **System Preferences**.

- On most Linux distributions, you can find SSH in your package manager as ssh, ssh-server, or openssh if it's not already installed. Most distributions will enable the server by default after installation.

- On Windows 10 and above, you can install OpenSSH server using the **Optional Features** tool under **Settings** | **Apps** | **Apps & features**. Once installed, start the service by opening the **Services** app, selecting **OpenSSH server**, and clicking **Start the service**.

Once the service is installed and running, you can connect to your computer using an SSH client like OpenSSH Client, and log in using a local username and password. You can use your normal user account, but since our application will be creating directories and copying files under the home directory of whatever user you use to connect to SSH, you may also wish to create a test user account for login so that the application does not accidentally overwrite any of your files.

Installing and using paramiko

Although the standard library offers nothing in the way of SSH or SFTP support, the third-party paramiko library provides a full suite of tools for working with both. Install paramiko from PyPI using the following command:

```
$ pip install --user paramiko
```

paramiko is pure Python, so it should not require compilation or additional programs to be installed. You can learn more about paramiko on its website, https://www.paramiko.org.

Using paramiko

The main class we'll work with in paramiko is the SSHClient class, through which we'll connect and interact with remote servers. Open a Python shell and let's create one like so:

```
>>> import paramiko
>>> ssh_client = paramiko.SSHClient()
```

Before we can connect to any servers with the object, we need to configure its key management policy. As part of the secure design of SSH, SSH clients exchange encryption keys with the server the first time they connect; thus, when connecting to a new server for the first time with an SSH client, you'll likely see a message like this:

```
The authenticity of host 'myserver (::1)' can't be established.
ED25519 key fingerprint is
  SHA256:fwefogdhFa2Bh6wnbXSGY8WG6nl7SzOw3fxmI8Ii2oVs.
This key is not known by any other names
Are you sure you want to continue connecting (yes/no/[fingerprint])?
```

If you choose to continue, the server's key (or **fingerprint**) will be stored with the hostname in a file usually called known_hosts. When connecting to the server again, SSH consults the known hosts list to verify that we're connecting to the same server. If the keys differ, the connection will fail.

So, the first thing we need to do is load any available key store that we have; if your SSH keys are stored in a standard location, calling the load_system_host_keys() method will suffice:

```
>>> ssh_client.load_system_host_keys()
```

You can also specify a known hosts file explicitly using the `load_host_keys()` method, like so:

```
>>> ssh.load_host_keys('/home/alanm/.ssh/known_hosts2')
```

A prompt for adding an unknown host to the known hosts list may be OK for an interactive client, but within a programming library it is obviously not so practical. Instead, we need to set a policy of what the `SSHClient` object will do when we try to connect to an unknown host. By default, it will simply fail, but we can force it to automatically trust new hosts using the `set_missing_host_key_policy()`, like so:

```
>>> ssh_client.set_missing_host_key_policy(paramiko.AutoAddPolicy())
```

Here we've set the policy to an instance of `AutoAddPolicy`, which means any new host keys will automatically be trusted. `paramiko` also provides a `RejectPolicy` class (which is the default) that automatically rejects all new keys, and for advanced use cases we can define our own policy class for more nuanced behaviors. We're using `AutoAddPolicy` for convenience in this case; in a real-world, secure environment you should leave the default `RejectPolicy` setting and manage the `known_hosts` list outside the script.

You can add servers to your `known_hosts` file simply by logging into them using **OpenSSH** Client and choosing `yes` when prompted to add the key, or by retrieving the key using the `ssh-keyscan` command included with OpenSSH Client and adding them to the file manually.

Once we've settled the issue of key management, we can connect to a host. This is done using the `connect()` method, like so:

```
>>> ssh_client.connect('localhost', username='test', password='test')
```

In addition to taking a hostname or IP address as a positional argument, `connect()` accepts a number of keyword arguments, including:

Argument	Default	Description
username	Local username	Username to use for authentication.
password	None	Password for authentication. If blank, SSHClient will attempt key-based authentication.
port	22	TCP port to connect to.
pkey	None	A private key string to use for authentication.

key_file	None	A file containing private keys or certificates for authentication.
compress	False	Enable or disable compression of transmitted data.
timeout	None	A timeout in seconds before giving up on the connection.

Inspecting our connection

Once connected to a server, our code might need to get some information about the connection. This can be done by accessing the Transport object associated with the client. This object represents the connection and contains a number of methods and attributes to set or retrieve information about it.

We can retrieve the Transport object using the get_transport() method of the SSHClient, like so:

```
>>> transport = ssh_client.get_transport()
```

Now we can inspect our connection in various ways, for example:

```
# See if the connection is still active
>>> transport.is_active()
True
# See our remote username
>>> transport.get_username()
'alanm'
# See if we're authenticated
>>> transport.is_authenticated()
True
# Get the name or IP of the connected server
>>> transport.getpeername()
('::1', 22, 0, 0)
# Get the compression used by the server
>>> transport.remote_compression
'none'
```

These properties can be particularly useful in situations where the user is connecting using default values detected from the environment.

Using SFTP

Now that we've established an SSH connection to a server, we can begin using SFTP. To do this, we'll create an instance of SFTPClient using the open_sftp() method, like so:

```
>>> sftp_client = ssh_client.open_sftp()
```

We can use the methods of the SFTPClient object to execute various file management commands on the remote server over SFTP. Some of the more useful of these are shown in the following table:

Method	Arguments	Description
chdir()	path	Set the current working directory.
getcwd()	None	Return the path of the current working directory. Note that it returns None if the directory was not set with chdir().
listdir()	path (optional)	Return a list of the files and directories in path, or in the current working directory if not specified.
mkdir()	path	Create a directory on the server at path.
rmdir()	path	Remove the directory from the server described by path.
get()	remotepath, localpath	Download the file on the server at remotepath and save it to the client at localpath.
put()	localpath, remotepath	Upload the file on the client at localpath and save it on the server at remotepath.
stat()	path	Return an object containing information about the file or directory at path.
remove()	path	Remove the file from the server described by path. Does not work if path is a directory (use rmdir() instead).
close()	None	Close the SFTP connection.

For example, suppose we need to create a folder called Bananas in the Fruit directory on our server, and upload a file called cavendish.ban from /home/alanm/bananas/ to the new directory on the server. That exchange would look like this:

```
>>> sftp_client.chdir('Fruit')
>>> sftp_client.mkdir('Bananas')
>>> sftp_client.put('/home/alanm/bananas/cavendish.ban', 'Bananas/
cavendish.ban')
```

Notice that, in the destination path of the put() call, we did not include the Fruit directory. That's because it's our current working directory, so our remote paths are understood to be relative to it.

Let's see if we can use our understanding of paramiko and SFTP to implement an SFTP upload in ABQ Data Entry.

Implementing an SFTP model

As we did with our REST upload, we'll begin by encapsulating our interactions with the SFTP server in a model class.

Open `models.py` and we'll begin by importing `paramiko`:

```
# models.py

import paramiko
```

Now, let's begin our model class:

```
# models.py

class SFTPModel:

    def __init__(self, host, port=22):
        self.host = host
        self.port = port
```

Our class initializer will take a hostname for the server and optionally a port number. SSH typically runs on port 22, though it's not uncommon for system administrators to run it on another port for security reasons, so it's good to provide this as an option.

Next, we'll continue our initializer by configuring our `SSHClient` object:

```
        self._client = paramiko.SSHClient()
        self._client.set_missing_host_key_policy(
          paramiko.AutoAddPolicy()
        )
        self._client.load_system_host_keys()
```

After creating our client instance and saving it to an instance property, we're configuring it to automatically add new host keys. Finally, we load in the known hosts from the default system location.

> In a secure production environment, you may want to leave this policy at the default `RestrictPolicy` setting and manage the known hosts list outside of your application. Note, however, that the `AutoAddPolicy` only impacts connections to *new hosts*; if `SSHClient` receives an invalid fingerprint when connecting to a known host, it will still raise an exception.

That takes care of our initializer, so let's create an `authenticate()` method to establish a connection to the server:

```python
# models.py, inside SFTPModel

    def authenticate(self, username, password):
        try:
            self._client.connect(
                self.host, username=username,
                password=password, port=self.port
            )
        except paramiko.AuthenticationException:
            raise Exception(
                'The username and password were not accepted by the server.'
            )
```

This method will take a `username` and `password` and use them to establish a connection using the `connect()` method. If authentication fails, `paramiko` will raise an `AuthenticationException`. We could simply allow this to pass back to the calling code, but as we did with our REST model, we're cleaning it up a little so that our `Application` object can display a more user-friendly message.

As with our `RESTModel`, we're going to create three more methods: one to upload a file, one to download a file, and one to check if a file exists on the server. Because all of these require that we're connected and authenticated, though, it would be handy to have another method that raises an exception if we're not.

We'll create a private method for this called `_check_auth()`, like so:

```python
    def _check_auth(self):
        transport = self._client.get_transport()
        if not transport.is_active() and transport.is_authenticated():
            raise Exception('Not connected to a server.')
```

As you saw in the previous section, our connection's active and authenticated statuses can be retrieved from its `Transport` object; so, this method retrieves the transport, then raises an exception if it's not both active and authenticated.

To see how we'll use this, let's create our `get_file()` method first:

```python
    def get_file(self, remote_path, local_path):
        self._check_auth()
        sftp = self._client.open_sftp()
        sftp.get(remote_path, local_path)
```

This method will take a remote path and a local path and copy the file down from the remote path to the local one. Note that we start with a call to _check_auth() to ensure that we're properly connected to the server. Then we create our SFTP client and run the get() method. That's all there is to it!

 When creating a command or function that copies or moves data, it's a long-standing convention to put your arguments in the order (SOURCE, DESTINATION). Mixing this up may rightly earn you the extreme displeasure of your users or fellow developers.

Uploading files

Creating an upload method will be slightly more complex. Unlike the REST client, which was working with a single endpoint, the SFTP server has a filesystem structure and we have the possibility of uploading to a subdirectory on the server. If we try to upload a file to a directory that doesn't exist, paramiko will raise an exception.

So, before we upload a file, we'll need to connect to the server and make sure all the directories in the destination path are there first. If any of them are not, we'll need to create that directory.

We'll begin our method as before by checking the connection and creating an SFTPClient instance:

```
def upload_file(self, local_path, remote_path):
    self._check_auth()
    sftp = self._client.open_sftp()
```

Now, we'll check the directories:

```
remote_path = Path(remote_path)
for directory in remote_path.parent.parts:
    if directory not in sftp.listdir():
        sftp.mkdir(directory)
    sftp.chdir(directory)
```

Our remote_path will likely be a string, so the first thing we do is convert it to a pathlib.Path object for easier manipulation. remote_path.parent.parts gives us a list of all the directories that contain the file, in order from the topmost to the bottom-most. For example, if the remote_path value was Food/Fruit/Bananas/cavendish. ban, this attribute would give us the list ['Food', 'Fruit', 'Bananas'].

Once we have that list, we iterate through it, checking to see if the directory is in the contents of the current working directory. If not, we create it. Once we know that the directory exists, we change the current working directory to it and repeat with the next directory in the list.

Once the directory structure is established, we can upload the actual file:

```
sftp.put(local_path, remote_path.name)
```

The put() method takes our local path to the file and the remote path where we want to copy it. Note, however, that we're only using the name portion of the remote path; that's because the for loop that iterated over our directories has left our current working directory at the proper parent directory where the file needs to be put. Thus, we should just pass the file's name as a destination.

Checking a file's existence

The last method we need is one that checks for a file's existence on the server. For this, we'll rely on the stat() method. The stat() method of SFTPClient can be used to fetch metadata about a file on the server, such as size and modification time. We don't need that information, but one useful side effect of stat() is that it raises a FileNotFoundError if passed a path that doesn't exist.

We can use that in our method, as shown here:

```python
def check_file(self, remote_path):
  self._check_auth()
  sftp = self._client.open_sftp()
  try:
    sftp.stat(remote_path)
  except FileNotFoundError:
    return False
  return True
```

As with the other methods, this one begins by checking for authentication, then creating our SFTPClient object. Then, it attempts to stat() the file at remote_path. If a FileNotFoundError is raised, we return False. Otherwise, we return True.

This completes our SFTPModel, at least for the operation our application needs to perform; but before we leave models.py, jump up to the SettingsModel class and let's add a few SFTP-related settings:

```python
# models.py, inside SettingsModel

  fields = {
```

```
    # ...
    'abq_sftp_host': {'type': 'str', 'value': 'localhost'},
    'abq_sftp_port': {'type': 'int', 'value': 22},
    'abq_sftp_path': {'type': 'str', 'value': 'ABQ/BLTN_IN'}
}
```

These settings define the host and port of the server, as well as the subdirectory path on the server where our files will need to be uploaded. With these added, we're ready to work on the GUI side.

Using SFTPModel in our application

The SFTP upload process we need to implement is identical to the REST upload process: we need to authenticate to the server, then check to see if the file already exists. If it does, we ask the user if they want to overwrite it. If not, we offer to download the file for their inspection.

Let's begin this method in `Application`:

```
try:
    csvfile = self._create_csv_extract()
except Exception as e:
    messagebox.showwarning(
      title='Error', message=str(e)
    )
    return
```

Just as before, we begin by attempting to create a CSV file from the day's data; if we get an exception, we'll display it and exit.

Now, we'll authenticate:

```
d = v.LoginDialog(self, 'Login to ABQ Corporate SFTP')
if d.result is None:
  return
username, password = d.result

host = self.settings['abq_sftp_host'].get()
port = self.settings['abq_sftp_port'].get()
sftp_model = m.SFTPModel(host, port)
try:
```

```
    sftp_model.authenticate(username, password)
except Exception as e:
  messagebox.showerror('Error Authenticating', str(e))
  return
```

Again, just like before, we request a username and password from the user using our
`LoginDialog`, simply adjusting the label text for SFTP. Then we create our `SFTPModel`
instance using the host and port values from the `settings` object and attempt to
authenticate. Any authentication errors will be displayed in a message box.

Next, we need to check the destination path to see if it exists:

```
destination_dir = self.settings['abq_sftp_path'].get()
destination_path = f'{destination_dir}/{csvfile.name}'

try:
  exists = sftp_model.check_file(destination_path)
except Exception as e:
  messagebox.showerror(
    f'Error checking file {destination_path}',
    str(e)
  )
  return
```

This time, we need to construct a complete destination path by combining the
`abq_sftp_path` value from `settings` with the generated CSV filename. Notice that
we're building the path using string formatting rather than with a `Path` object. That's
because `Path` will join path components using the path separator character (forward-
slash or backslash) used on our *local* system. The path we're creating needs to be
compatible with the *remote* filesystem. Fortunately, `paramiko` will use forward-slashes
(Unix-style path separators) regardless of whether the remote server uses Windows
or a Unix-like system. For that reason, we're explicitly formatting our paths using
forward-slashes.

If the file exists, we need to ask the user what to do next:

```
if exists:
  overwrite = messagebox.askyesno(
    'File exists',
```

```
        f'The file {destination_path} already exists on the server,'
        ' do you want to overwrite it?'
    )
    if not overwrite:
      download = messagebox.askyesno(
        'Download file',
        'Do you want to download the file to inspect it?'
      )
      if download:
        filename = filedialog.asksaveasfilename()
        try:
          sftp_model.get_file(destination_path, filename)
        except Exception as e:
          messagebox.showerror('Error downloading', str(e))
          return
        messagebox.showinfo(
          'Download Complete', 'Download Complete.'
          )
      return
```

Once again, this is identical to our REST-based code, except that we need to remember we're dealing with paths, not just filenames. Thus, we've used destination_path where we previously used csvfile.name.

If the method has not yet returned at this point, we can go ahead and attempt to upload our file:

```
try:
  sftp_model.upload_file(csvfile, destination_path)
except Exception as e:
  messagebox.showerror('Error uploading', str(e))
else:
  messagebox.showinfo(
    'Success',
    f'{csvfile} successfully uploaded to SFTP server.'
  )
```

That finishes up our SFTP upload callback.

Some readers might wonder why our model checks its authenticated status for each call, when our callback method only runs its operations after it has successfully authenticated. First, this is a defensive programming move. We don't know how our model class may be used in the future, and the model can't always count on well-behaved views and controllers ensuring authentication before other operations. Secondly, it's because, unlike HTTP, SSH is a **stateful** protocol. That means there is an active session created when we connect which must be maintained for any operations to be done. If this session is interrupted (say, by a temporary network outage, or a laptop user switching networks) between authentication and subsequent operations, those operations would fail and we'd need to start over again. Thus, when working with stateful protocols, it's a good idea to check connection and authentication status before individual operations.

Finishing up

All that remains to do now is to add the new feature to our menu. Back in `Application.__init__()`, add the callback to our `event_callbacks` dictionary:

```python
# application.py, inside Application.__init__()

event_callbacks = {
    #...
    '<<UploadToCorporateSFTP>>': self._upload_to_corporate_sftp,
}
```

Now, head over to `mainmenu.py` and add a new private method to `GenericMainMenu`:

```python
# mainmenu.py, inside GenericMainMenu

def _add_sftp_upload(self, menu):
    menu.add_command(
        label="Upload CSV to corporate SFTP",
        command=self._event('<<UploadToCorporateSFTP>>'),
    )
```

Then, in each menu subclass, add the entry to the `Tools` menu, like so:

```python
# mainmenu.py, inside each class's _build_menu() method

    self._add_sftp_upload(self._menus['Tools'])
```

Our new upload feature is now complete! Make sure SSH is running on your system, launch ABQ Data Entry, make sure there's at least one record saved for the day, and run the upload from the **Tools** menu. You should see a success dialog like this:

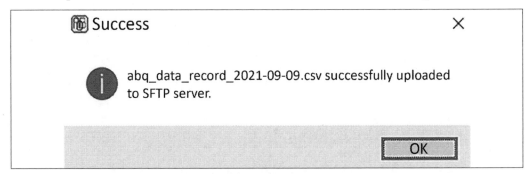

Figure 13.6: Success dialog for SFTP upload

Run the feature a second time, and you should get your warning dialog, like this:

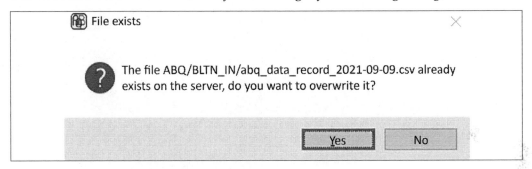

Figure 13.7: Overwrite dialog for SFTP upload

Follow through and make sure you can download the file. Excellent work!

Summary

In this chapter, we reached out to the cloud using the network protocols HTTP and SSH. You learned how to download data over HTTP using `urllib`, and how to parse XML data structures using the `ElementTree` module. You also discovered an alternative way to interact with HTTP using the `requests` library and learned the basics of interacting with a REST API. You learned to work with HTTP interactions that required authentications and session cookies, and uploaded a file. Finally, you learned how to transfer and manage remote files over SSH with SFTP services using the `paramiko` library.

In the next chapter, we'll stop long-running processes from freezing up our application and improve our application's performance by learning about asynchronous programming. We'll learn to manipulate the Tkinter event loop for better responsiveness as well as advanced asynchronous programming using Python's `threading` library.

14

Asynchronous Programming with Thread and Queue

Many times, code that works flawlessly in the simplicity of a test environment encounters problems in the real world; unfortunately, this seems to be the case for the ABQ Data Entry application. While your network functions ran instantaneously in your localhost-only test environment, the lab's slow VPN uplink has exposed some shortcomings in your programming. Users report that the application freezes or becomes unresponsive when network transactions are taking place. Although it does work, it looks unprofessional and is an annoyance to users.

To solve this problem, we're going to need to apply asynchronous programming techniques, which we'll learn about in the following topics:

- In *The Tkinter event queue*, we'll learn how to manipulate Tkinter's event processing to improve the responsiveness of the application.

- In *Running code in the background with threads*, we'll explore writing multi-threaded applications using Python's threading module.

- In *Passing messages using a queue*, you'll learn how to use Queue objects to implement inter-thread communication.

- In *Using locks to protect shared resources*, we'll utilize a Lock object to keep threads from overwriting one another.

Let's get started!

Tkinter's event queue

As we discussed in *Chapter 11, Creating Automated Tests with unittest*, many tasks in Tkinter, such as drawing and updating widgets, are done asynchronously rather than taking immediate action when called in code. More specifically, the actions you perform in Tkinter, such as clicking a button, triggering a key bind or trace, or resizing a window, place an **event** in the event queue. On each iteration of the main loop, Tkinter pulls all outstanding events from the queue and processes them one at a time. For each event, Tkinter executes any **tasks** (that is, callbacks or internal operations like redrawing widgets) bound to the event before proceeding to the next event in the queue.

Tasks are roughly prioritized by Tkinter as either **regular** or **do-when-idle** (often referred to as **idle tasks**). During event processing, regular tasks are processed first, followed by idle tasks when all the regular tasks are finished. Most drawing or widget-updating tasks are classified as idle tasks, while actions like callback functions are, by default, regular priority.

Event queue control

Most of the time, we get the behavior we need from Tkinter by relying on higher-level constructs like command callbacks and bind(). However, there are situations where we might want to directly interact with the event queue and manually control how events are processed. We've already seen some of the functionality available to do this, but let's take a deeper look at them here.

The update() methods

In *Chapter 11, Creating Automated Tests with unittest*, you learned about the update() and update_idletasks() methods. To review, these methods will cause Tkinter to execute any tasks for events currently in the queue; update() runs tasks for all events currently waiting in the queue until it's entirely clear, while update_idletasks() only runs the idle tasks.

Since idle tasks are generally smaller and safer operations, it's recommended to use update_idletasks() unless you find it doesn't do the job.

 Note that update() and update_idletasks() will cause the processing of *all* outstanding events for *all* widgets, regardless of what widget the method is called on. There is no way to only process events for a particular widget or Tkinter object.

The after() methods

In addition to allowing us to control the processing of the queue, Tkinter widgets have two methods for adding arbitrary code to the event queue on a delay: `after()` and `after_idle()`.

Basic use of `after()` looks like this:

```
# basic_after_demo.py

import tkinter as tk
root = tk.Tk()
root.after(1000, root.quit)
root.mainloop()
```

In this example, we're setting the `root.quit()` method to run after 1 second (1,000 milliseconds). What actually happens here is that an event bound to `root.quit` is added to the event queue, but with the condition that it shouldn't be executed until at least 1,000 milliseconds from the moment when `after()` is called. During that time period, any other events in the queue will be processed first. As a result, while the command will not be executed *sooner* than 1,000 milliseconds, it will very likely be executed *later*, depending on what else is being processed already in the event queue.

The `after_idle()` method also adds a task to the event queue, but rather than giving it an explicit delay it simply adds it as an idle task, ensuring that it will be run after any regular tasks.

In both methods, any additional arguments after the callback reference are simply passed to the callback as positional arguments; for example:

```
root.after(1000, print, 'hello', 'Python', 'programmers!')
```

In this example, we're passing the arguments `'hello'`, `'Python'`, and `'programmers'` to a `print()` call. This statement will schedule the statement `print('hello', 'Python', 'programmers!')` to be run as soon as possible after 1 second has elapsed.

 Note that `after()` and `after_idle()` cannot take keyword arguments for the passed callable, only positional arguments.

Code scheduled with `after()` can also be un-scheduled using the `after_cancel()` method. The method takes a task ID number, which is returned when we call `after()`.

For example, we could amend our previous example like so:

```python
# basic_after_cancel_demo.py

import tkinter as tk

root = tk.Tk()
task_id = root.after(3000, root.quit)
tk.Button(
  root,
  text='Do not quit!', command=lambda: root.after_cancel(task_id)
).pack()
root.mainloop()
```

In this script, we save the return value of `after()`, which gives us the ID of the scheduled task. Then, in the callback for our button, we call `after_cancel()`, passing in the ID value. Clicking the button before the 3 seconds is up results in the `root.quit` task being canceled and the application remaining open.

Common uses of event queue control

In *Chapter 11, Creating Automated Tests with unittest*, we made good use of queue control methods to make sure our tests ran quickly and efficiently without having to wait on human interaction. There are a few different ways we can use these methods in actual applications though, which we'll look at here.

Smoothing out display changes

In an application with dynamic GUI changes, the smoothness of these changes may suffer a bit as the windows resize in response to elements appearing and reappearing. For example, in the ABQ application, you may notice a smaller application window appearing just after login, which gets quickly resized as the GUI is built. This is not a major issue, but it detracts from the overall presentation of the application.

We can correct this by delaying the `deiconify()` call after login using `after()`. Inside `Application.__init__()`, let's alter that line as follows:

```python
# application.py, inside Application.__init__()

    self.after(250, self.deiconify)
```

Now, instead of immediately restoring the application window after login, we have delayed the restore by a quarter of a second. While barely perceptible to the user, it gives Tkinter enough time to build and redraw the GUI before displaying the window, smoothing out the operation.

 Use delayed code sparingly, and don't rely on it in situations where the delayed code's stability or security depends on some other process finishing first. This can lead to a **race condition**, in which some unforeseen circumstance like a slow disk or network connection can cause your delay to be insufficient to properly order the execution of code. In the case of our application, our delay is merely a cosmetic fix; nothing disastrous will happen if the application window is restored before it finishes drawing.

Mitigating GUI freezes

Because callback tasks are prioritized over screen-updating tasks, a callback task that blocks code execution for an extended period of time can cause the program to seem frozen or stuck at an awkward point while the redrawing tasks wait for it to complete. One way to address this is to use the `after()` and `update()` methods to control the event queue processing manually. To see how this works, we'll build a simple application that uses these methods to keep the UI responsive during a long-running task.

Start with this simple, but slow, application:

```
# after_demo.py
import tkinter as tk
from time import sleep

class App(tk.Tk):
  def __init__(self):
    super().__init__()
    self.status = tk.StringVar()
    tk.Label(self, textvariable=self.status).pack()
    tk.Button(
      self, text="Run Process",
      command=self.run_process
    ).pack()

  def run_process(self):
    self.status.set("Starting process")
```

```
        sleep(2)
        for phase in range(1, 5):
          self.status.set(f"Phase {phase}")
          self.process_phase(phase, 2)
        self.status.set('Complete')

    def process_phase(self, n, length):
      # some kind of heavy processing here
      sleep(length)


App().mainloop()
```

This application uses `time.sleep()` to simulate some heavy processing task done in multiple phases. The GUI presents the user with a button, which launches the processes, and a status indicator to show progress.

When the user clicks the button, the status indicator is *supposed* to do the following:

- Show **Starting process** for 2 seconds.
- Show **Phase 1**, **Phase 2**, through **Phase 4** for 2 seconds each.
- Finally, it should read **Complete**.

If you try it, though, you'll see it does no such thing. Instead, it freezes up the moment the button goes down and does not unfreeze until all the phases are complete and the status reads **Complete**. Why does this happen?

When the button-click event is processed by the main loop, the `run_process()` callback takes priority over any drawing tasks (since those are idle tasks) and is immediately executed, blocking the main loop until it returns. When the callback calls `self.status.set()`, the `status` variable's write events are placed in the queue (where they will eventually trigger a redraw event on the `Label` widget). However, processing of the queue is currently halted, waiting on the `run_process()` method to return. When it finally does return, all the updates to `status` that were waiting in the event queue are executed in a fraction of a second.

To make this a bit better, let's schedule `run_process()` using `after()`:

```
# after_demo2.py

  def run_process(self):
    self.status.set("Starting process")
    self.after(50, self._run_phases)

  def _run_phases(self):
```

```
    for phase in range(1, 5):
      self.status.set(f"Phase {phase}")
      self.process_phase(phase, 2)
    self.status.set('Complete')
```

This time, the loop part of run_process() is split off into a separate method called _run_phases(). The run_process() method itself just sets the starting status, then schedules _run_phases() to run 50 milliseconds later. This delay gives Tkinter time to finish up any drawing tasks and to update the status before kicking off the long blocking loop. The exact amount of time isn't critical in this case, just so long as it's sufficient for Tkinter to finish drawing operations, but short enough that users aren't likely to notice it; 50 milliseconds seems to do the job just fine.

We still aren't seeing individual phase status messages with this version, though; it goes directly from **Starting process** to **Complete** because the _run_phases() method is still blocking the event loop when it eventually runs.

To fix this, we can use update_idletasks() in the loop:

```
# after_demo_update.py

def _run_phases(self):
  for phase in range(1, 5):
    self.status.set(f"Phase {phase}")
    self.update_idletasks()
    self.process_phase(phase, 2)
  self.status.set('Complete')
```

By forcing Tkinter to run the remaining idle tasks in the queue before starting the long blocking method, our GUI kept is up to date. Unfortunately, there are some shortcomings to this approach:

- Firstly, the individual tasks still block the application while they're running. No matter how we break them up, the application will still be frozen while the individual units of the process are executing.

- Secondly, this approach is problematic for separation of concerns. In a real application, our processing phases are likely going to be running in a backend or model class of some kind. Those classes should not be manipulating GUI widgets.

While these queue control methods can be useful for managing GUI-layer processes, it's clear we need a better solution for working with slow background processes like the ABQ network upload functions. For those, we'll need to use something more powerful: threads.

Running code in the background with threads

All of the code we have written up to this point in the book can be described as **single-threaded**; that is, every statement is executed one at a time, the prior statement finishing before the next one is begun. Even asynchronous elements such as our Tkinter event queue, though they may change the order in which tasks are executed, still execute only one task at a time. This means that a long-running procedure like a slow network transaction or file read will unavoidably freeze up our application while it runs.

To see this in action, run the `sample_rest_service.py` script included with the example code for *Chapter 14* (make sure you run the *Chapter 14* version, not the *Chapter 13* version!). Now run ABQ Data Entry, make sure you've got some data in the database for today, and run the REST upload. The upload should take about 20 seconds, during which time the service script should be printing status messages like these:

```
File 0% uploaded
File 5% uploaded
File 10% uploaded
File 15% uploaded
File 20% uploaded
File 25% uploaded
```

Meanwhile, though, our GUI application is frozen. You'll find you cannot interact with any of the controls, and moving or resizing it may result in a blank gray window. Only when the upload process completes will your application become responsive again.

To truly get around this problem, we need to create a **multi-threaded** application, in which multiple pieces of code can be run concurrently without needing to wait for one another. In Python, we can do this using the `threading` module.

The threading module

Multi-threaded application programming can be quite challenging to grasp fully, but the standard library's `threading` module makes working with threads about as simple as it can be.

To demonstrate the basic use of `threading`, let's first create an intentionally slow function:

```python
# basic_threading_demo.py
from time import sleep

def print_slowly(string):
    words = string.split()
    for word in words:
        sleep(1)
        print(word)
```

This function takes a string and prints it at a rate of one word per second. This will simulate a long-running, computationally expensive process and give us some feedback that it's still running.

Let's create a Tkinter GUI frontend for this function:

```python
# basic_threading_demo.py

import tkinter as tk

# print_slowly() function goes here
# ...

class App(tk.Tk):

    def __init__(self):
        super().__init__()
        self.text = tk.StringVar()
        tk.Entry(self, textvariable=self.text).pack()
        tk.Button(
            self, text="Run unthreaded",
            command=self.print_unthreaded
        ).pack()

    def print_unthreaded(self):
        print_slowly(self.text.get())

App().mainloop()
```

This simple application has a text entry and a button; when the button is pushed, the text in the entry is sent to the `print_slowly()` function. Run this code, then enter or paste a long sentence into the `Entry` widget.

When you click the button, you'll see that the entire application freezes up as the words are printed to the console. That's because it's all running in a single execution thread.

Now let's add the threading code:

```
# basic_threading_demo.py

from threading import Thread

# at the end of App.__init__()
    tk.Button(
        self, text="Run threaded",
        command=self.print_threaded
    ).pack()

  def print_threaded(self):
    thread = Thread(
        target=print_slowly,
        args=(self.text.get(),)
    )
    thread.start()
```

This time, we've imported the `Thread` class and created a new callback called `print_threaded()`. This callback uses a `Thread` object to run `print_slowly()` in its own execution thread.

A `Thread` object takes a `target` argument that points to the callable which will be run in the new execution thread. It can also take an `args` tuple, which contains arguments to be passed into the `target` argument, and a `kwargs` dictionary, which will also be expanded in the `target` function's argument list.

To execute the `Thread` object, we call its `start()` method. This method does not block, so the `print_threaded()` callback immediately returns, allowing Tkinter to resume its event loop while `thread` executes in the background.

If you try this code, you'll see that the GUI no longer freezes while the sentence is printed. No matter how long the sentence, the GUI remains responsive the whole time.

Tkinter and thread safety

Threading introduces a great deal of complication into a code base, and not all code is written to behave properly in a multi-threaded environment.

We refer to code that is written with threading in mind as being **thread-safe**.

It's often repeated that Tkinter is not thread-safe; this isn't entirely true. Assuming your Tcl/Tk binaries have been compiled with thread support (which those included with the official Python distributions for Linux, Windows, and macOS have been), Tkinter should work fine in a multi-threaded program. However, the Python documentation warns us that there are still some edge cases where Tkinter calls across threads do not behave properly.

The best way to avoid these issues is to keep our Tkinter code within a single thread and restrict our use of threads to non-Tkinter code (such as our model classes).

More information about Tkinter and threading can be found at `https://docs.python.org/3/library/tkinter.html#threading-model`.

Converting our network functions to threaded execution

Passing a function to a `Thread` object's `target` argument is one way of running code in a thread; a more flexible and powerful approach is to subclass the `Thread` class and override its `run()` method with the code you want to execute. To demonstrate this approach, let's update the corporate REST upload feature we created for ABQ Data Entry in *Chapter 13, Connecting to the Cloud*, so that it runs the slow upload operation in a separate thread.

To begin, open up `models.py` and let's import the `Thread` class, like so:

```
# models.py, at the top

from threading import Thread
```

Rather than having a `CorporateRestModel` method execute the upload, we're going to create a class based on `Thread` whose instances will be able to execute the upload operation in a separate thread. We'll call it `ThreadedUploader`.

To execute its upload, the `ThreadedUploader` instance will need an endpoint URL and a local file path; we can simply pass those to the object in its initializer. It will also need access to an authenticated session; that presents more of a problem. We might be able to get away with passing our authenticated `Session` object to the thread, but at the time of writing there is a great deal of uncertainty as to whether `Session` objects are thread-safe, so it's best to avoid sharing them between threads.

However, we don't really need the whole `Session` object, just the authentication token or session cookie.

It turns out that when we authenticate to the REST server, a cookie called `session` is placed in our cookie jar, which we can see by inspecting the `Session.cookies` object from a terminal, like so:

```
# execute this with the sample REST server running in another terminal
>>> import requests
>>> s = requests.Session()
>>> s.post('http://localhost:8000/auth', data={'username': 'test',
'password': 'test'})
<Response [200]>
>>> dict(s.cookies)
{'session': 'eyJhdXRoZW50aWNhdGVkIjp0cnVlfQ.YTu7xA.c5ZOSuHQbckhasRFRF'}
```

The `cookies` attribute is a `requests.CookieJar` object, which behaves in many ways like a dictionary. Each cookie has a unique name, which can be used to retrieve the cookie itself. In this case, our session cookie is called `session`.

Since the cookie itself is just a string, we can safely pass it to another thread. Once there, we'll create a new `Session` object and give it the cookie, after which it can authenticate requests.

 Immutable objects, including strings, integers, and floats, are always thread-safe. Since immutable objects can't be altered after creation, we don't have to worry that two threads will try to change the object at the same time.

Let's start our new uploader class as follows:

```python
# models.py
class ThreadedUploader(Thread):

    def __init__(self, session_cookie, files_url, filepath):
        super().__init__()
        self.files_url = files_url
        self.filepath = filepath
        # Create the new session and hand it the cookie
        self.session = requests.Session()
        self.session.cookies['session'] = session_cookie
```

The initializer method starts by calling the superclass initializer to set up the `Thread` object, then assigns the passed `files_url` and `filepath` strings to instance attributes.

Next, we create a new `Session` object and add the passed cookie value to the cookie jar by assigning it to the `session` key (the same key used in the original session's cookie jar). Now we have all the information we need to execute an upload process. The actual process to be executed in the thread is implemented in its `run()` method, which we'll add next:

```python
def run(self, *args, **kwargs):
    with open(self.filepath, 'rb') as fh:
        files = {'file': fh}
        response = self.session.put(
            self.files_url, files=files
        )
        response.raise_for_status()
```

Note that this code is essentially the code from the model's `upload()` method, except that the function arguments have been changed to instance properties.

Now, let's head over to our model and see how we can use this class.

 The Python documentation recommends that you *only* override `run()` and `__init__()` when subclassing `Thread`. Other methods should be left alone for proper operation.

Using the threaded uploader

Now that we've created a threaded uploader, we just need to make `CorporateRestModel` use it. Find your model class and let's rewrite the `upload_file()` method as follows:

```python
# models.py, inside CorporateRestModel

def upload_file(self, filepath):
    """PUT a file on the server"""
    cookie = self.session.cookies.get('session')
    uploader = ThreadedUploader(
        cookie, self.files_url, filepath
    )
    uploader.start()
```

Here, we start by extracting the session cookie from our `Session` object, then pass it along with the URL and the file path to the `ThreadedUploader` initializer. Finally, we call the thread's `start()` method to begin execution of the upload.

Now, give your REST upload another try and you'll see that the application doesn't freeze up. Great job! However, it doesn't quite behave how we'd like it to yet...

 Remember, you override the run() method, but call the start() method. Mixing these up will cause your code to either do nothing or block like a normal single-threaded call.

Passing messages using a queue

We've solved the problem of the program freezing up, but now we have some new problems. The most obvious problem is that our callback immediately shows a message box claiming that we've successfully uploaded the file, even though you can see from the server output that the process is still ongoing in the background. A subtler and far worse problem is that we aren't alerted to errors. If you try terminating the test service while the upload is running (so that the callback should fail), it will still immediately claim that the upload succeeded, even though you can see on the terminal that exceptions are being raised. What's going on here?

The first problem here is that the Thread.start() method doesn't block code execution. This is what we wanted, of course, but it now means our success dialog isn't waiting until the upload process is complete before it displays. As soon as the new thread is launched, the execution of code in the main thread continues in parallel with the new thread, immediately showing the success dialog.

The second problem is that code running in its own thread cannot pass exceptions caused in the thread's run() method back to the main thread. Those exceptions are raised within the new thread, and can only be caught in the new thread. As far as our main thread is concerned, the code in the try block executed just fine. In fact, the upload operation can't communicate failures *or* successes.

In order to solve these problems, we need a way for the GUI and model threads to communicate, so that the upload thread can send error or progress messages back to the main thread to be handled appropriately. We can do this using a **queue**.

The Queue object

Python's queue.Queue class provides a **first-in first-out** (**FIFO**) data structure. Python objects can be placed into a Queue object using the put() method, and retrieved using the get() method; to see how this works, execute this in the Python shell:

```
>>> from queue import Queue
>>> q = Queue()
```

```
>>> q.put('My item')
>>> q.get()
'My item'
```

This may not seem terribly exciting; after all, you can do essentially the same thing with a list object. What makes Queue useful, though, is that it is thread-safe. One thread can place messages on the queue, and another can retrieve them and respond appropriately.

By default, the queue's get() method will block execution until an item is received. This behavior can be altered by passing False as its first argument, or using the get_nowait() method. In no-wait mode, the method will return immediately, raising an exception if the queue is empty.

To see how this works, execute the following in the shell:

```
>>> q = Queue()
>>> q.get_nowait()
Traceback (most recent call last):
  File "<stdin>", line 1, in <module>
  File "/usr/lib/python3.9/queue.py", line 199, in get_nowait
    return self.get(block=False)
  File "/usr/lib/python3.9/queue.py", line 168, in get
    raise Empty
_queue.Empty
```

We can also check whether the queue is empty using the empty() or qsize() methods; for example:

```
>>> q.empty()
True
>>> q.qsize()
0
>>> q.put(1)
>>> q.empty()
False
>>> q.qsize()
1
```

As you can see, empty() returns a Boolean indicating if the queue is empty, and qsize() returns the number of items in the queue. Queue has several other methods that are useful in more advanced multi-threading situations, but get(), put(), and empty() will be sufficient to solve our problems.

Using queues to communicate between threads

Before editing our application code, let's create a simple example application to make sure we understand how to use Queue to communicate between threads.

Start with a long-running thread:

```python
# threading_queue_demo.py

from threading import Thread
from time import sleep

class Backend(Thread):

  def __init__(self, queue, *args, **kwargs):
    super().__init__(*args, **kwargs)
    self.queue = queue

  def run(self):
    self.queue.put('ready')
    for n in range(1, 5):
      self.queue.put(f'stage {n}')
      print(f'stage {n}')
      sleep(2)
    self.queue.put('done')
```

The Backend object is a subclass of Thread that takes a Queue object as an argument and saves it as an instance property. Its run() method simulates a long-running four-phase process using print() and sleep(). At the beginning, at the end, and before each phase, we use queue.put() to place a status message into the queue module.

Now we'll create a frontend for this process in Tkinter:

```python
# threading_queue_demo.py

import tkinter as tk
from queue import Queue

class App(tk.Tk):

  def __init__(self, *args, **kwargs):
    super().__init__(*args, **kwargs)
    self.status = tk.StringVar(self, value='ready')
```

```
    tk.Label(self, textvariable=self.status).pack()
    tk.Button(self, text="Run process", command=self.go).pack()
    self.queue = Queue()
```

This simple application contains a `Label` object bound to a `status` control variable, a `Button` widget bound to a callback method, `go()`, and a `Queue` object stored as an instance variable. The idea is that, when we click the **Run process** button, the `go()` method will run our `Backend` class and the queued messages will be displayed in the label by way of the `status` control variable.

Let's create the `go()` method:

```
def go(self):
  p = Backend(self.queue)
  p.start()
```

The `go()` method creates an instance of the `Backend` class, passing in the application's `Queue` object, and starts it. Because both threads now have a reference to `queue`, we can use it to communicate between them. We've already seen how `Backend` places status messages on the queue, so how should `App()` retrieve them?

Maybe we could start a loop, like this:

```
def go(self):
  p = Backend(self.queue)
  p.start()
  while True:
    status = self.queue.get()
    self.status.set(status)
    if status == 'done':
      break
```

That won't work, of course, because the loop will block; the Tkinter event loop would be stuck executing `go()`, freezing up the GUI and defeating the purpose of using a second thread. Instead, we need a way to periodically poll the queue object for status messages and update the status whenever one is received.

We'll start by writing a method that can check the queue and respond appropriately:

```
def check_queue(self):
  msg = ''
  while not self.queue.empty():
    msg = self.queue.get()
    self.status.set(msg)
```

Using the `Queue.empty()` method, we first find out if the queue is empty or not. If it is, we don't want to do anything, because `get()` will, by default, block until it receives a message, and we don't want to block execution. If the queue object contains items, we'll want to get those items and send them to our `status` variable. We're doing this in a `while` loop so that we only leave the function when the queue is empty.

This only performs one check, of course; we want to keep polling the queue module until the thread sends a `done` message. Thus, if our status is not `done`, we need to schedule another queue check.

That can be done with a call to `after()` at the end of `check_queue()`, like this:

```
if msg != 'done':
  self.after(100, self.check_queue)
```

Now `check_queue()` will do its job, then schedule itself to run again every `100` milliseconds until the status is `done`. All that remains is to kick off the process at the end of `go()`, like so:

```
def go(self):
  p = Backend(self.queue)
  p.start()
  self.check_queue()
```

If you run this application, you'll see that we get status messages in (relatively) real time. Unlike the single-threaded application we created earlier in the chapter, there is no freezing, even while the tasks are running.

Adding a communication queue to our threaded uploader

Let's apply our knowledge of queues to fix the problems with the `ThreadedUploader` class. To begin, we'll update the initializer signature so that we can pass in a `Queue` object, then store the object as an instance attribute, like so:

```
# models.py, in ThreadedUploader
  def __init__(
    self, session_cookie, files_url, filepath, queue
  ):
  # ...
  self.queue = queue
```

Just as we did in our example application, we'll create the `Queue` object in the `CorporateRestModel` object so that both the uploader and the model have a reference to it. In addition, we'll save the queue as a public attribute of the model so that the application object can also reference it. To do that, we'll first need to import `Queue` into `models.py`, so add this import at the top:

```
# models.py, at the top

from queue import Queue
```

Now, back down in the `CorporateRestModel` initializer, create a `Queue` object:

```
# models.py, inside CorporateRestModel

def __init__(self, base_url):
    #...
    self.queue = Queue()
```

Next, we need to update the `upload_file()` method so that it passes the queue into the `ThreadedUploader` object:

```
def upload_file(self, filepath):
    cookie = self.session.cookies.get('session')
    uploader = ThreadedUploader(
        cookie, self.files_url, filepath, self.queue
    )
    uploader.start()
```

Now the GUI can access the queue from `rest_model.queue`, and we can use that connection to send messages from our upload thread back to the GUI. Before we can use that connection, however, we need to develop a communications protocol.

Creating a communications protocol

Now that we have established a channel for inter-thread communication, we have to decide how our two threads will communicate. In other words, what exactly will our uploader thread place on the queue, and how should our application thread respond to it? We could just throw anything into the queue and keep writing `if` statements on the app-side to deal with whatever shows up, but a better approach is to standardize communications by defining a simple protocol.

Our uploader thread will mainly be sending status-related information back to the application so that it can display updates about what's happening in message boxes or on the status bar. We will create a message format that we can use to determine what the thread is doing and communicate that to the user.

The message structure will look like this:

Field	Description
status	One word indicating the type of message, such as info or error
subject	A short sentence summarizing the message
body	A longer string with details about the message

We could create a structure like this using dictionary or a class, but simple collections of named fields like this are a great use-case for **named tuples**. The `collections.namedtuple()` function allows us to quickly create mini-classes that contain only named properties.

Creating a `namedtuple` class looks like this:

```
from collections import namedtuple

MyClass = namedtuple('MyClass', ['prop1', 'prop2'])
```

This is equivalent to writing:

```
class MyClass():

  def __init__(self, prop1, prop2):
    self.prop1 = prop1
    self.prop2 = prop2
```

The `namedtuple()` method is much faster to create than a class, and unlike a dictionary it enforces uniformity—that is, every `MyClass` object must have a `prop1` and a `prop2` attribute, whereas a dictionary is never required to have any particular keys.

At the top of the `models.py` file, let's import `namedtuple` and use it to define a class called `Message`:

```
# models.py, at the top
from collections import namedtuple

Message = namedtuple('Message', ['status', 'subject', 'body'])
```

Now that we've created the `Message` class, making a new `Message` object is just like making an instance of any other class:

```
message = Message(
  'info', 'Testing the class',
```

```
    'We are testing the Message class'
)
```

Let's implement the use of these `Message` objects in our queue.

Sending messages from the uploader

Now that we have established a protocol, it's time to put it to use. Locate the `ThreadedUploader` class, and let's update the `run()` method to send messages, starting with an informational message:

```
# models.py, in ThreadedUploader

def run(self, *args, **kwargs):
  self.queue.put(
    Message(
      'info', 'Upload Started',
      f'Begin upload of {self.filepath}'
    )
  )
```

Our first message is just an informational message indicating that the upload is starting. Next, we'll begin the upload and return some messages indicating the success or failure of the operation:

```
    with open(self.filepath, 'rb') as fh:
      files = {'file': fh}
      response = self.session.put(
        self.files_url, files=files
      )
    try:
      response.raise_for_status()
    except Exception as e:
      self.queue.put(Message('error', 'Upload Error', str(e)))
    else:
      self.queue.put(
        Message(
          'done',  'Upload Succeeded',
          f'Upload of {self.filepath} to REST succeeded'
        )
      )
```

As before, we begin the upload process by opening the file and making our PUT request to the web service. This time, though, we run raise_for_status() in a try block. If we catch an exception from the operation, we put a message with a status of error on the queue along with the text of the exception. If we succeed, we place a success message on the queue.

That's all that our ThreadedUploader needs to do; now we need to head over the GUI to implement a response to these messages.

Handling queue messages

Back in the Application object, we need to add some code to monitor the queue and take appropriate actions when a message is sent from the thread. As we did in our queue demo application, we'll create a method that uses the Tkinter event loop to periodically poll the queue and handle any messages sent from the model's queue object.

Start the Application._check_queue() method like so:

```
# application.py, inside Application


def _check_queue(self, queue):
  while not queue.empty():
    item = queue.get()
```

The method accepts a Queue object, and starts by checking to see whether it has any items. If so, it retrieves one. Once we have one, we need to examine it and determine what to do with it based on the status value.

First, let's handle a done status; add this code under the if block:

```
# application.py, inside Application._check_queue()


    if item.status == 'done':
      messagebox.showinfo(
        item.status,
        message=item.subject,
        detail=item.body
      )
      self.status.set(item.subject)
      return
```

When our upload finishes successfully, we want to show a message box and set the status, then return without doing anything else.

The `Message` object's `status`, `subject`, and `body` attributes map nicely to the `title`, `message`, and `detail` arguments of the message box, so we've just passed those directly to it. We also show the subject of the message in the application's status bar by setting the `status` variable.

Next, we'll handle error messages from the queue:

```python
elif item.status == 'error':
    messagebox.showerror(
        item.status,
        message=item.subject,
        detail=item.body
    )
    self.status.set(item.subject)
    return
```

Once again, we show a message box, this time using `showerror()`. We also want to exit the method, since the thread has presumably quit and we don't need to schedule the next queue check.

Finally, let's handle the `info` statuses:

```python
else:
    self.status.set(f'{item.subject}: {item.body}')
```

Informational messages don't really warrant a modal message box, so we're just sending them to the status bar.

The last thing we need to do in this method is make sure it gets called again if the thread is still going. Since done and error messages cause the method to return, if we've reached this point in the function the thread is still running and we should continue to poll it. So, we'll add a call to `after()`:

```python
self.after(100, self._check_queue, queue)
```

With `_check_queue()` written, we just need to eliminate the exception handling around `rest_model.upload_file()` at the end of `_upload_to_corporate_rest()` and call `_check_queue()` instead:

```python
# application.py, in Application._upload_to_corporate_rest()

        rest_model.upload_file(csvfile)
        self._check_queue(self.rest_queue)
```

This call doesn't need to be scheduled with `after()` since there will most likely not be a message on the first call, causing `_check_queue()` to just schedule its next call and return.

Now that we've finished that update, launch the test server and the application and try the REST upload again. Watch the status bar and you'll see the progress getting displayed, ending with a message box when the process completes. Try it with the HTTP server turned off, and you should see an error message pop up right away.

Using locks to protect shared resources

While it's great that our application no longer freezes up during slow file uploads, it raises a potential problem. Suppose a user tries to start a second REST upload while the first is ongoing? Go ahead and try this; launch the sample HTTP server and the application, and try to launch two REST uploads in quick succession, so that the second begins before the first finishes. Note the output from the REST server; depending on your timing, you may see confusing log messages with percentages going up and down as both threads upload files at the same time.

Of course, our sample REST server only simulates a slow link with `sleep()`; the actual file upload happens so fast it's unlikely to cause a problem. In a situation with a genuinely slow network, concurrent uploads could be more problematic. While it's possible that the receiving server is robust enough to sensibly handle two threads trying to upload the same file, it's best if we avoid that situation in the first place.

What we need is some kind of flag that is shared between threads which can indicate if a thread is currently uploading so that others will know not to do so. We can do this using the `threading` module's `Lock` object.

Understanding the Lock object

A lock is a very simple object with two states: **acquired** and **released**. When a `Lock` object is in the released state, any thread may call its `acquire()` method to put it in the acquired state. Once a thread has acquired the lock, the `acquire()` method will block until the lock has been released by calling its `release()` method. That means that if another thread calls `acquire()`, its execution will wait until the lock is released by the first thread.

To see how this works, look at the `basic_threading_demo.py` script we created earlier in this chapter. Run that script from a terminal prompt, enter a sentence into the `Entry` widget, and click the **Run threaded** button.

As we noted earlier, the sentence prints out at one word per second to the terminal output. But now, click the **Run threaded** button twice in quick succession. Notice that the output is a jumble of repeated words as the two threads simultaneously output text to the terminal. You can just imagine the havoc multiple threads could wreak upon a file or network session in a situation like this.

To correct this, let's create a lock. First, import Lock from the threading module and create an instance of it:

```
# basic_threading_demo_with_lock.py

from threading import Thread, Lock

print_lock = Lock()
```

Now, inside the print_slowly() function, let's add calls to acquire() and release() around the method, like so:

```
def print_slowly(string):
    print_lock.acquire()
    words = string.split()
    for word in words:
        sleep(1)
        print(word)
    print_lock.release()
```

Save this file as basic_threading_demo_with_lock.py and run it again. Now, when you click the **Run threaded** button multiple times, each run waits for the previous one to release the lock before beginning. In this way, we can force threads to wait for each other while still maintaining a responsive application.

The Lock object can also be used as a context manager so that acquire() is called on entering the block and release() upon exiting. Thus, we could rewrite the preceding example like so:

```
    with print_lock:
        words = string.split()
        for word in words:
            sleep(1)
            print(word)
```

Using a Lock object to prevent concurrent uploads

Let's apply our understanding of the Lock object to prevent concurrent uploading to the corporate REST server. To begin, we need to import Lock into models.py, like so:

```
from threading import Thread, Lock
```

Next, we'll create a Lock object as a class attribute of the ThreadedUploader class, like so:

```
class ThreadedUploader(Thread):

  rest_upload_lock = Lock()
```

Recall from *Chapter 4*, *Organizing Our Code with Classes*, that objects assigned to class attributes are shared by all instances of the class. Therefore, by creating the lock as a class attribute, any ThreadedUploader thread will have access to the lock.

Now, inside the run() method, we need to utilize our lock. The cleanest approach is to use it as a context manager, like so:

```
# models.py, inside ThreadedUploader.run()

    with self.upload_lock:
      with open(self.filepath, 'rb') as fh:
        files = {'file': fh}
        response = self.session.put(
          self.files_url, files=files
        )
        #... remainder of method in this block
```

Whether the put() call returns or raises an exception, the context manager will ensure that release() is called when the block exits so that other calls to run() can acquire the lock.

After adding this code, run the test HTTP server and the application again and try launching two REST uploads in quick succession. Now you should see that the second upload doesn't start until the first has completed.

Threading and the GIL

Whenever we discuss threading in Python, it's important to understand Python's **Global Interpreter Lock (GIL)** and how it affects threading.

The GIL is a lock mechanism that protects Python's memory management by preventing more than one thread from executing Python commands at the same time. Similar to the lock we implemented in our `ThreadedUploader` class, the GIL can be thought of like a token that can be held by only one thread at a time; whichever thread holds the token may execute Python instructions, and the rest have to wait.

It may seem like this defeats the idea of multi-threading on Python, However, there are two factors that mitigate the impact of the GIL:

- First, the GIL only limits the execution of *Python* code; many libraries execute code in other languages. For example, Tkinter executes TCL code, and `psycopg2` executes compiled C code. Non-Python code like this can run in a separate thread while Python code runs in another.

- Second, **Input/Output (I/O)** operations like disk access or network requests can run concurrently with Python code. For instance, when we make an HTTP request using `requests`, the GIL is released while waiting for the server to respond.

The only situation where the GIL really limits the utility of multi-threading is when we have computationally expensive Python code. Slow operations in typical data-oriented applications like ABQ are likely to be I/O-based operations, and for heavy-computation situations we can use non-Python libraries like `numpy`. Even so, it's good to be aware of the GIL and know that it may impact the effectiveness of a multi-threaded design.

Summary

In this chapter, you learned how to use asynchronous and multi-threaded programming techniques to remove unresponsive behavior from your program. You learned how to work with and control Tkinter's event queue using the `after()` and `update()` methods, and how to apply these methods to solve problems in your application. You also learned how to use Python's `threading` module to run processes in the background, and how to utilize `Queue` objects to communicate between threads. Finally, you learned to use the `Lock` object to prevent shared resources from getting corrupted.

In the next chapter, we're going to explore the most powerful widget in Tkinter: the Canvas. We'll learn how to draw images and animate them, and create useful and informative charts.

15
Visualizing Data Using the Canvas Widget

With months of experimental data logged in the database, it's time to begin the process of visualizing and interpreting it. Rather than exporting data into a spreadsheet to create charts and graphs, your fellow analysts have asked whether the program itself can create graphical data visualizations. Indeed it can! To implement this feature, you're going to need to learn about Tkinter's Canvas widget.

In this chapter, you'll implement data visualizations as you learn the following topics:

- In *Drawing and animation with Tkinter's Canvas*, you'll learn to use the Canvas widget for drawing and animation
- In *Creating simple graphs using Canvas*, we'll build a simple line graph using the Tkinter Canvas
- In *Advanced graphs using Matplotlib*, we'll learn to integrate the Matplotlib library for more powerful charting and graphic capabilities

Drawing and animation with Tkinter's Canvas

The Canvas widget is undoubtedly one of the most powerful widgets available in Tkinter. It can be used to build anything from custom widgets and views to complete user interfaces.

As the name implies, a Canvas widget is a blank area on which figures and images can be drawn. To understand its basic usage, let's create a small demo script.

Begin the script by creating a root window and a Canvas object:

```
# simple_canvas_demo.py
import tkinter as tk

root = tk.Tk()
canvas = tk.Canvas(
  root, background='black',
  width=1024, height=768
)
canvas.pack()
```

Creating a Canvas object is just like creating any other Tkinter widget. In addition to the parent widget and background argument, we can also specify width and height arguments to set the size of the Canvas. Setting the size of a Canvas widget is important, because it defines not only the size of the widget but also the **viewport**; that is, the area in which our drawn objects will be visible. We can actually draw anywhere on the Canvas's virtually infinite surface, but only the area inside the viewport will be visible.

We'll learn how to see the area outside the viewport below in the *Scrolling the Canvas* section.

Drawing on the Canvas

Once we have a Canvas object, we can start drawing items on it using its many create_() methods. These methods allow us to draw shapes, lines, images, and text. Let's explore these methods in more detail as we develop the simple_canvas_demo.py script.

Rectangles and squares

Rectangles or squares can be drawn on the Canvas using the create_rectangle() method, like so:

```
# simple_canvas_demo.py

canvas.create_rectangle(240, 240, 260, 260, fill='orange')
```

The first four arguments of `create_rectangle()` are the coordinates of the upper-left and lower-right corners, counted in pixels from the upper-left corner of the `Canvas`. Each `create_()` method begins with positional arguments that define the position and size of the shape. Following those, we can specify a variety of keyword arguments to describe other aspects of the shape; for example, the `fill` option used here specifies the color of the inside of the object.

 It's vital to understand that vertical coordinates on the `Canvas`, unlike coordinates on a typical chart, extend *down* from the top. For example, the coordinate (200, 100) is 100 pixels *above* (200, 200). The same is true for coordinates on all Tkinter widgets, and in many other GUI programming environments as well.

Coordinates can also be specified as tuple pairs, like so:

```
canvas.create_rectangle(
  (300, 240), (320, 260),
  fill='#FF8800'
)
```

Although this requires more characters, it improves readability considerably. The `create_rectangle()` method supports several other keyword arguments to configure the rectangle's fill and outline, including the following:

Argument	Values	Description
`dash`	Tuple of integers	Defines a dash pattern (see below) for the outline
`outline`	Color string	Specifies a color for the border
`width`	Integer	Specifies a width for the border
`stipple`	Bitmap name	Name of a bitmap pattern to use for the fill

Dashed or dotted lines can be defined on `Canvas` objects using a **dash pattern**. This is a tuple of integers that describes the number of pixels before switching between line and blank. For example, a `dash` value of (5, 1, 2, 1) would produce a repeating pattern of five pixels of line, one blank pixel, two pixels of line, and one blank.

The `stipple` value allows you to specify a bitmap to be used for filling the shape instead of a solid fill. Tkinter comes with some built-in bitmap files, such as `gray75`, `gray50`, `gray25`, and `gray12` (each of which is filled with evenly spaced pixels at the specified percentage), or you can load in a `.xbm` file of your own using the format `@filename.xbm`.

Ovals, circles, and arcs

In addition to rectangles, we can also create ovals and circles using the create_oval() method. Add an oval to the demo as follows:

```
canvas.create_oval(
  (350, 200), (450, 250), fill='blue'
)
```

As with creating a rectangle, we begin by specifying the coordinates to describe the shape; however, this time the coordinates determine the upper-left and lower-right corners of its **bounding box**. A bounding box is the smallest rectangle that will contain an item. For example, in the case of this oval, the bounding box has corners at (350, 200) and (450, 250). To make a circle, of course, we simply define an oval with a square bounding box.

create_oval() allows the same keyword arguments as create_rectangle() to configure the fill and outline of the shape.

If we want to draw only a sector of the oval, we can use the create_arc() method. This method works identically to create_oval(), but also takes extent and start keyword arguments. The start argument specifies the number of degrees from the origin at the left middle of the circle to the point where the drawing starts, and the extent argument specifies how many degrees counter-clockwise the arc will extend. For example, an extent of 90 and start of 180 will draw a quarter of the oval starting at the right side and going to the bottom, as shown here:

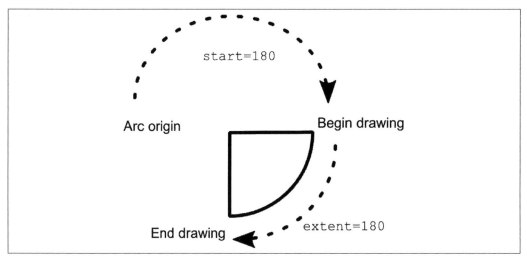

Figure 15.1: Drawing an arc

Let's add an arc to our demo:

```
canvas.create_arc(
    (100, 200), (200, 300),
    fill='yellow', extent=315, start=25
)
```

Lines

We can also draw lines on the Canvas using the create_line() method. As with rectangles, ovals, and arcs, we begin by specifying coordinates to define the line. Unlike with the shapes, the coordinates do not define a bounding box, but rather a set of points that define the line.

Let's add a line to our demo script, like so:

```
canvas.create_line(
    (0, 180), (1024, 180),
    width=5, fill='cyan'
)
```

In this example, a straight line will be drawn from the first point at (0, 180) to the second at (1024, 180). The fill argument in this case defines the color of the line, and width determines how wide it is.

The create_line() method is not limited to a single line between two points. We can specify any number of coordinate pairs as positional arguments, and Tkinter will connect them all from first to last. For example, add this to the demo:

```
canvas.create_line(
    (0, 320), (500, 320), (500, 768), (640, 768),
    (640, 320), (1024, 320),
    width=5, fill='cyan'
)
```

This time we've created a more complex line with six points.

Some of the additional arguments for `create_line()` are shown here:

Argument	Values	Description
arrow	FIRST, LAST, or BOTH	If specified, will draw arrows at the end of the line. Default is no value, indicating no arrows.
capstyle	BUTT, PROJECTING, or ROUND	Specifies the style for the end of the line. Default is BUTT.
dash	Tuple of integers	Defines the dash style for the line.
joinstyle	ROUND, BEVEL, or MITER	Specifies the style of corner joins. Default is ROUND.
smooth	Boolean	Whether to draw the line with spline curves or straight lines. Default is False (straight lines).
tags	Tuple of strings	Any number of tags to assign to the line.

Polygons

The Canvas also allows us to draw arbitrary polygons; it works in a similar fashion to lines, in which each coordinate defines a point that will be connected to draw the outline of the polygon. The difference is that the last point and the first point will also be connected to form a closed shape.

Add a polygon to our demo script like so:

```
canvas.create_polygon(
    (350, 225), (350,  300), (375, 275), (400, 300),
    (425, 275), (450, 300), (450, 225),
    fill='blue'
)
```

Note that, unlike with `create_line()`, the `fill` argument defines the color of the polygon's interior, not the color of the outline. The appearance of the polygon's outline can be configured using the same arguments that `create_rectangle()` and `create_oval()` use.

Text

In addition to simple shapes, we can also place text directly on the Canvas.

For example, let's add some text to our demo:

```
canvas.create_text(
    (500, 100), text='Insert a Quarter',
    fill='yellow', font='TkDefaultFont 64'
)
```

The single coordinate argument determines the point where the text will be anchored to the Canvas. By default, the text is attached at its own center point to the anchor point. In this case, that means that the middle of our string (somewhere around the "a") will be at x=500, y=100. However, the anchor argument can be used to specify which part of the text item is attached to the anchor point; it can be any of the cardinal direction constants (N, NW, W, and so on) or CENTER, which is the default.

The fill argument in this case determines the color of the text, and we can use font to determine the font properties of the text. Tkinter 8.6 and later also offers an angle argument that can rotate the text by the given number of degrees.

Images

Of course, we aren't limited to just drawing lines and simple shapes on the Canvas; we can also place raster images using the create_image() method. This method allows us to place a PhotoImage or BitmapImage object on the Canvas, like so:

```python
# simple_canvas_demo.py

smiley = tk.PhotoImage(file='smile.gif')
canvas.create_image((570, 250), image=smiley)
```

As with text, the image is attached to the anchor coordinate at its center by default, but the anchor argument can be used to change that to any side or corner of the image's bounding box.

Tkinter widgets

The last thing we can place on the Canvas is another Tkinter widget. Of course, since the Canvas is a widget, we can just do this using a geometry manager like pack() or grid(), but we gain a lot more control if we add it as a Canvas item using create_window().

To add a widget using create_window(), the widget need only be a child of a widget on the same parent window as the Canvas widget. We can then pass a reference to the widget to the method's window argument. We can also specify a width and height argument to determine the size of the window area to which the widget will be added; the widget will expand into that area by default.

For example, let's add a quit button to the demo:

```python
quit = tk.Button(
    root, text='Quit', bg='black', fg='cyan', font='TkFixedFont 24',
    activeforeground='black', activebackground='cyan',
```

```
    command=root.quit
)
canvas.create_window((100, 700), height=100, width=100, window=quit)
```

Just as with text and images, the widget is anchored to the given coordinate at its center by default, and the anchor argument can be used to attach it at a side or corner instead.

Canvas items and state

Note the use of the activeforeground and activebackground arguments in the code example above. Just like widgets, Canvas items can have various states set that can be used to dynamically change the appearance. The table below shows the available states for items, and what result they have:

State	Trigger	Result
normal	Default	Normal appearance
disabled	Manual setting	Disabled appearance
active	Mouse hovers over	Active appearance
hidden	Manual setting	Not shown

All drawn items (that is, not images) have state-based versions of their fill, outline, dash, width, stipple, and outlinestipple arguments, which are simply the argument with active or disabled prefixed to it. For example, activefill sets the fill value when the item is hovered over by the mouse, while disabledoutline sets the outline color when the item is set to a disabled state. Image items have disabledimage and activeimage arguments that can be set to display a different image when the item is disabled or active.

The active state is automatically set when an item is hovered over by the mouse; the disabled and hidden states can be set using the Canvas.itemconfigure() method, which is discussed below in the *Canvas object methods* section.

Canvas object methods

Canvas items are not represented by a Python object; instead, the return value of any create_() method is an integer that uniquely identifies the item in the context of the Canvas object. To manipulate Canvas items after they've been created, we need to save that identification value and pass it to various Canvas methods.

For example, we could save the ID of the image we added, then bind the image to a callback using the `Canvas.tag_bind()` method:

```python
# simple_canvas_demo.py

image_item = canvas.create_image((570, 250), image=smiley)
canvas.tag_bind(
    image_item,
    '<Button-1>',
    lambda e: canvas.delete(image_item)
)
```

Here, we've used the `tag_bind()` method to bind a left-mouse click on our image object to the `Canvas`'s `delete()` method, which (when given an item identifier) deletes the item.

The `Canvas` object has many methods that can operate on a `Canvas` item; some of the more useful ones are listed in this table:

Method	Arguments	Description
`bbox()`	Item ID	Returns a tuple describing the bounding box of the item.
`coords()`	Item ID, coordinates	If only the ID is provided, returns the coordinates of the item. Otherwise, moves the item to the given coordinates.
`delete()`	Item ID	Deletes the item from the `Canvas`.
`find_overlapping()`	Box coordinates	Returns a list of item IDs that overlap the box described by the coordinates.
`itemcget()`	Item ID, option	Returns the value of `option` for the given item.
`itemconfigure()`	Item ID, option	Sets one or more configuration options on the specified item.
`move()`	Item ID, X, Y	Moves the item on the `Canvas` relative to its current position by the given X and Y amounts.
`type()`	Item ID	Returns a string describing the type of object (rectangle, oval, arc, and so on).

Note that any of these methods that take an item ID can also take a **tag**. Recall from *Chapter 9, Improving the Look with Styles and Themes*, that a tag is just a string that can be assigned to an item when created, allowing us to refer to multiple items at once. The `Canvas` has two tags built in by default, `all` and `current`. As you might expect, `all` refers to all items on the `Canvas`, and `current` refers to the item that currently has focus.

All `create_()` methods allow the option of specifying a tuple of tag strings to attach to the object.

By the way, if you haven't yet, add `root.mainloop()` to the demo script and execute it to see what we've drawn!

Scrolling the Canvas

As mentioned earlier, the width and height of a `Canvas` widget determines the size of the viewport, but the actual drawable area on the widget stretches endlessly out in all directions. To actually see objects outside the viewport area, we need to enable scrolling.

To see how this works, let's create a scrollable starfield; open a new file called `canvas_scroll.py` and let's begin like so:

```python
# canvas_scroll.py
import tkinter as tk
from random import randint, choice

# Create root and canvas
root = tk.Tk()

width = 1024
height = 768

canvas = tk.Canvas(
    root, background='black',
    width=width, height=height,
)
canvas.grid(row=0, column=0)
```

Here, we've imported `tkinter` and some functions from `random`, then created a root window and a `Canvas` object with a viewport size of 1024x768. Finally, we've placed the `Canvas` on the root window using `grid()`.

Now, let's draw some "stars":

```python
colors = ['#FCC', '#CFC', '#CCF', '#FFC', '#FFF', '#CFF']
for _ in range(1000):
    x = randint(0, width * 2)
    y = randint(0, height * 2)
```

```
z = randint(1, 10)
c = choice(colors)
canvas.create_oval((x - z, y - z), (x + z, y + z), fill=c)
```

We begin by defining a list of color values, then start a for loop that will iterate 1000 times. Inside the loop, we'll generate random X and Y coordinates, a random size (Z), and choose one of the colors at random. We'll then have the Canvas draw a circle centered on the random point filled with the random color.

Notice that the ranges supplied for X and Y are double the size of the Canvas object. Because of this, the loop will be creating circles out to the right and down from our viewport area.

To enable scrolling of the Canvas, we first have to define a scrollregion value for it, like so:

```
canvas.configure(scrollregion=(0, 0, width * 2, height * 2))
```

The scrollregion value is a tuple of four integers that describe the bounding box of the area we want to be able to scroll. Essentially, the first two integers are the X and Y coordinates of the upper-left corner of the box, and the second two are the coordinates of the lower right.

To actually scroll the Canvas, we'll need some Scrollbar widgets. We've already encountered these in *Chapter 8, Navigating Records with Treeview and Notebook*, remember that to use them we need to create the widgets, add them to the layout, and connect the appropriate callbacks so that the scrollbars can communicate with the widget being scrolled.

Add the following code to the script:

```
xscroll = tk.Scrollbar(
    root,
    command=canvas.xview,
    orient=tk.HORIZONTAL
)
xscroll.grid(row=1, column=0, sticky='new')

yscroll = tk.Scrollbar(root, command=canvas.yview)
yscroll.grid(row=0, column=1, sticky='nsw')

canvas.configure(yscrollcommand=yscroll.set)
canvas.configure(xscrollcommand=xscroll.set)
```

Here, we've created two `Scrollbar` widgets, one for horizontal scrolling and one for vertical. We've added them to the layout just below and to the right of the `Canvas`, respectively. Then, we connect each scrollbar's `command` argument to the `Canvas`'s `xview` or `yview` method, and configure the `Canvas`'s `yscrollcommand` and `xscrollcommand` arguments to call the respective scrollbar's `set()` method.

Finish off this script with a call to `root.mainloop()` and execute it; you should see something like the picture here:

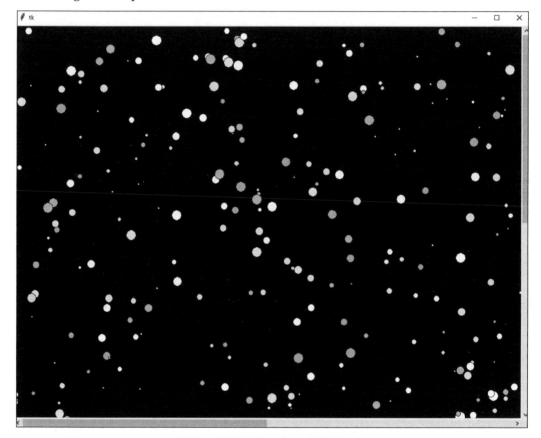

Figure 15.2: Scrolling through the stars!

 A handy trick to properly configure the scroll region after drawing runtime-defined points on the `Canvas` (for example, drawing based on user input) is to set `scrollregion` to the output of `canvas.bbox('all')` after creating the items. When passed a tag of `all`, the `bbox()` method returns a bounding box that contains the entirety of all items on the `Canvas`. You can set this value directly to `scrollregion` to make sure all your items can be viewed.

Animating Canvas objects

Tkinter's Canvas widget doesn't have a built-in animation framework, but we can still create simple animations by combining its move() method with our understanding of the event queue.

To demonstrate this, we'll create a bug race simulator, in which two bugs (represented by colored circles) will race haphazardly toward a finish line on the other side of the screen. Like real bugs, they won't have any notion that they're in a race and will move relatively randomly, the winner being whichever bug incidentally hits the finish line first.

To begin, open a new Python file and start with a basic object-oriented pattern, like so:

```python
# bug_race.py

import tkinter as tk

class App(tk.Tk):

    def __init__(self, *args, **kwargs):
        super().__init__(*args, **kwargs)
        self.canvas = tk.Canvas(self, background='black')
        self.canvas.pack(fill='both', expand=1)
        self.geometry('800x600')
App().mainloop()
```

This is just a simple OOP Tkinter boilerplate application with a Canvas object added to the root window. This will be the basic platform on which we'll build our game code.

Setting up the playing field

Now that we have the basic framework, let's set up the playing field. We want to be able to reset the playing field after each round, so rather than doing this in the initializer, we'll create a separate method called setup(), as follows:

```python
def setup(self):
    self.canvas.left = 0
    self.canvas.top = 0
    self.canvas.right = self.canvas.winfo_width()
    self.canvas.bottom = self.canvas.winfo_height()
    self.canvas.center_x = self.canvas.right // 2
```

```
        self.canvas.center_y = self.canvas.bottom // 2
        self.finish_line = self.canvas.create_rectangle(
          (self.canvas.right - 50, 0),
          (self.canvas.right, self.canvas.bottom),
          fill='yellow', stipple='gray50'
        )
```

The setup() method begins by calculating some relative locations on the Canvas object and saving them as instance properties, which will simplify the placement of objects on the Canvas object. Calculating these at runtime means we can resize the window between rounds for a longer or shorter racecourse.

The finish line is implemented as a rectangle across the right edge of the window. Note the use of the stipple argument to specify a bitmap that will overlay the solid color to give it some texture; in this case, gray50 is a built-in bitmap that alternates filled and transparent pixels. This gives us something a little more interesting than a flat color.

Add a call to setup() at the end of App.__init__() as follows:

```
# bug_race.py, in App.__init__()

        self.canvas.wait_visibility()
        self.setup()
```

Because setup() relies on the width and height values of the Canvas object, we need to make sure it isn't called until the operating system's window manager has drawn and sized the window. The simplest way of doing this is to call wait_visibility() on the Canvas object, which will block execution until the object has been drawn.

Setting our players

Now that we have the playing field, we need to create our players. We'll create a Racer class to represent a player; start it like so:

```
# bug_race.py

class Racer:

  def __init__(self, canvas, color):
    self.canvas = canvas
    self.name = f"{color.title()} player"
    size = 50
    self.id = canvas.create_oval(
```

```
        (canvas.left, canvas.center_y),
        (canvas.left + size, canvas.center_y + size),
        fill=color
    )
```

The Racer class will be created with a reference to the Canvas object and a color string, from which its color and name will be derived. We'll draw the racer initially at the middle left of the screen and make it 50 pixels in size. Finally, we save a reference to its item ID string in self.id.

Now, back in App.setup(), we'll create two racers by adding the following:

```
# bug_race.py, in App.setup()

    self.racers = [
      Racer(self.canvas, 'red'),
      Racer(self.canvas, 'green')
    ]
```

At this point, all the objects in our game are set up. Run the program and you should see a yellow-stippled finish line on the right and a green circle on the left (the red circle will be hidden under the green, since they're at the same coordinates).

Animating the racers

To animate our racers, we're going to use the Canvas.move() method. As we learned earlier, move() takes an item ID, a number of X pixels, and a number of Y pixels, and moves the item by that amount. By combining this with the random.randint() function and some simple logic, we can generate a series of moves that will send each racer on a meandering path toward the finish line.

A simple implementation may look like this:

```
from random import randint

# inside Racer
  def move_racer(self):
    x = randint(0, 100)
    y = randint(-50, 50)
    t = randint(500, 2000)
    self.canvas.after(t, self.canvas.move, self.id, x, y)
    if self.canvas.bbox(self.id)[0] < self.canvas.right:
      self.canvas.after(t, self.move_racer)
```

This method generates a random forward X movement, a random up-or-down Y movement, and a random time interval. We then use the `after()` method to schedule a call to `move()` for the generated X and Y movements after the random time interval. The `if` statement determines whether the racer's bounding box is currently at or beyond the right side of the screen; if this test evaluates to `False`, we schedule another call to `move_racer()`.

This method gets the racers to the finish line, but it isn't quite what we want. The problem is that `move()` acts instantaneously, causing the bug to jump across the screen in jerky movements rather than moving smoothly.

To make the bugs move smoothly, we're going to need to take a more complex approach:

1. First, we'll calculate a series of linear moves, each with a random delta x, delta y, and interval, that will reach the finish line
2. Then, we'll break each individual move into a number of steps determined by dividing the movement interval into a regular animation frame interval
3. Next, we'll add each step of each movement to a queue
4. Finally, we'll call a method once each animation frame interval that will pull the next step from the queue and pass it to `move()`

Let's start by defining our frame interval; in the `Racer` class, create a class attribute for this:

```
class Racer:

  FRAME_RES = 50
```

`FRAME_RES` (short for frame resolution) defines the number of milliseconds between each `Canvas.move()` call. 50 milliseconds gives us 20 frames per second and should be sufficient for smooth movements.

Next, we need to import the `Queue` class and create an instance inside the `Racer` object's initializer:

```
# bug_race.py, at top
from queue import Queue

# inside Racer.__init__()

    self.movement_queue = Queue()
```

Now, we will create the method that will plot the course to the finish line:

```
# bug_race.py, inside Racer

def plot_course(self):
    start_x = self.canvas.left
    start_y = self.canvas.center_y
    total_dx, total_dy = (0, 0)
    while start_x + total_dx < self.canvas.right:
        dx = randint(0, 100)
        dy = randint(-50, 50)
        target_y = start_y + total_dy + dy
        if not (self.canvas.top < target_y < self.canvas.bottom):
            dy = -dy
        total_dx += dx
        total_dy += dy
        time = randint(500, 2000)
        self.queue_move(dx, dy, time)
```

This method plots a course from the left center of the Canvas to a random point on the right side by generating random x and y movements until the total change in x is greater than the width of the Canvas object. The change in x will always be positive, keeping our bugs moving toward the finish line, but the change in y can be positive or negative, to allow both upward and downward movement. To keep our bugs on the screen, we constrain the total y movements by negating any change in y that would put the player outside the top or bottom bounds of the Canvas.

In addition to the random dx and dy values, we generate a random time interval for the move to take, between half a second and two seconds. Finally, the generated dx, dy, and time values are passed to a queue_move() method.

The queue_move() method will need to break the large move into individual frames of movement that describe how the racer should move in one FRAME_RES interval. To make this calculation, we will need a **partition function**, a mathematical function that will break an integer N into K approximately equal integers. For example, if we wanted to break -10 into four parts, our function should return a list like [-2, -2, -3, -3].

Let's create partition() as a static method on Racer:

```
# bug_race.py, inside Racer

@staticmethod
def partition(n, k):
    """Return a list of k integers that sum to n"""
```

```
if n == 0:
    return [0] * k
```

We start the method with the easy case: when n is 0, return a list of k zeros.

Now, we'll deal with the more complicated cases:

```
base_step = n // k
parts = [base_step] * k
for i in range(n % k):
    parts[i] += 1
return parts
```

For a non-zero n, we first calculate the base_step by dividing n by k using floor division, which rounds our result down to the nearest integer. Then, we create a list of length k that is made up of base_step values. Next, we need to distribute the remainder of n / k among this list as evenly as we can. To accomplish this, we will add 1 to the first n % k items in the parts list.

Follow the math here using our example of n = -10 and k = 4:

- The base step is calculated as -10 / 4 = -3 (remember, floor division always rounds down, so -2.5 gets rounded to -3).
- We then create a list of four base step values: [-3, -3, -3, -3].
- -10 % 4 = 2, so we add 1 to the first two items in the list.
- We arrive at an answer of [-2, -2, -3, -3]. Perfect!

Operations like this partition function are part of **discrete mathematics**, a branch of mathematics that deals with operations on whole numbers. Discrete mathematics is often used for solving spatial problems such as those encountered in drawing and animation.

Now that we have the partition method, we can write the queue_move() method:

```
def queue_move(self, dx, dy, time):
    num_steps = time // self.FRAME_RES
    steps = zip(
        self.partition(dx, num_steps),
        self.partition(dy, num_steps)
    )
    for step in steps:
        self.movement_queue.put(step)
```

We first determine the necessary number of steps in this move by dividing the time interval by FRAME_RES using floor division. We then create a list of X moves and a list of Y moves by passing dx and dy each to our partition() method. Those two lists are combined with zip() to form a single list of (dx, dy) pairs, which we iterate to add each pair to the animation queue.

To make the animation actually happen, we'll need a method to check the queue and make each move; we'll call it next_move():

```python
def next_move(self):
    if not self.movement_queue.empty():
        nextmove = self.movement_queue.get()
        self.canvas.move(self.id, *nextmove)
```

The next_move() method first checks the queue for a movement step. If there is one, canvas.move() is called with the racer's ID and the X and Y values for the step. When the game starts, this method will be called repeatedly from the App object until one of the racers has won.

Finally, we need to add a call to plot_course() to the Racer class's initializer, like so:

```python
# bug_race.py, at the end of Racer.__init__()


    self.plot_course()
```

Thus, as soon as a Racer object is created, it will plot the course to the finish line, and wait for the App class to tell it to move.

Running the game loop and detecting a win condition

To actually run the game, we need to start a game loop. Of course, we know from *Chapter 14, Asynchronous Programming with Thread and Queue,* that we can't simply use a Python for or while loop, since this would block Tkinter drawing operations and simply make the game freeze up until it was over. Instead, we need to create a method that executes a single "frame" of the game animation, then schedules itself on the Tkinter event loop to run again.

That method begins like this:

```python
# bug_race.py, inside App

def execute_frame(self):
    for racer in self.racers:
        racer.next_move()
```

It begins by iterating through the racer objects and executing their next_move() methods. After moving each racer, our next step is to determine if one of them has crossed the finish line and won.

To detect this condition, we need to check whether a racer is overlapping with the finish line item.

Collision detection between items is slightly awkward with the Tkinter Canvas widget. We have to pass a set of bounding box coordinates to find_overlapping(), which returns a tuple of item identifiers that overlap with the bounding box.

Let's create an overlapping() method for our Racer class:

```
# bug_race.py, inside Racer

@property
def overlapping(self):
    bbox = self.canvas.bbox(self.id)
    overlappers = self.canvas.find_overlapping(*bbox)
    return [x for x in overlappers if x!=self.id]
```

This method retrieves the bounding box of the Racer item using the Canvas's bbox() method. It then fetches a tuple of items overlapping this bounding box using find_overlapping(). Since this would include the ID of the Racer item itself, we'll filter that out of the tuple using a list comprehension. The result is a list of items overlapping with this Racer object's Canvas item. Since this method doesn't require any arguments and only returns a value, we've made it a property.

Back in our execute_frame() method, we'll check each racer to see if it has crossed the finish line:

```
# bug_race.py, inside App
def execute_frame(self):
    for racer in self.racers:
        racer.next_move()
        if self.finish_line in racer.overlapping:
            self.declare_winner(racer)
            return
    self.after(Racer.FRAME_RES, self.execute_frame)
```

If the finish_line ID is in the list returned by the racer's overlapping() method, the racer has hit the finish line and will be declared the winner by calling a declare_winner() method and returning from the method.

If no player was declared the winner, the `execute_frame()` method is scheduled to run again after `Racer.FRAME_RES` milliseconds. This effectively implements a game loop using the Tkinter event loop, which will run until one racer wins.

We handle a win condition in the `declare_winner()` method:

```
def declare_winner(self, racer):
  wintext = self.canvas.create_text(
    (self.canvas.center_x, self.canvas.center_y),
    text=f'{racer.name} wins!\nClick to play again.',
    fill='white',
    font='TkDefaultFont 32',
    activefill='violet'
  )
  self.canvas.tag_bind(wintext, '<Button-1>', self.reset)
```

In this method, we've just created a text item declaring `racer.name` as the winner in the center of the `Canvas`. The `activefill` argument causes the color to appear violet when the mouse is hovered over it, indicating to the user that this text is clickable.

When that text is clicked, it calls the `reset()` method:

```
def reset(self, *args):
  self.canvas.delete('all')
  self.setup()
```

The `reset()` method needs to clear off the `Canvas`, so it calls the `delete()` method with an argument of `all`. Remember that `all` is a built-in tag that applies to all items on the `Canvas`, so this line effectively deletes all `Canvas` items. Once the `Canvas` is clear, we call `setup()` to reset and restart the game.

The last thing we need to do is make sure the game starts whenever `setup()` is called. To do that, add a call to `execute_frame()` to the end of `setup()`:

```
# bug_race.py, in App.setup()
  def setup():
    # ...
    self.execute_frame()
```

The game is now complete; run the script and you should see something like this:

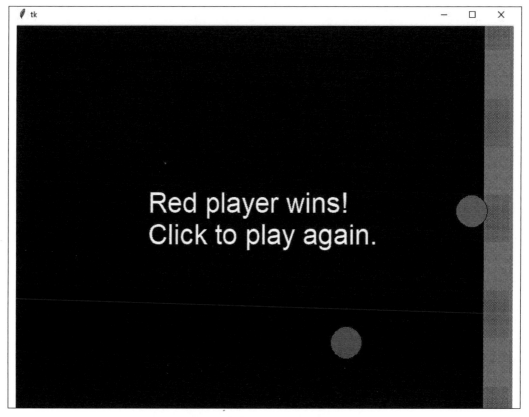

Figure 15.3: The bug race game. Red wins!

While not exactly simple, animation in Tkinter can provide smooth and satisfactory results with some careful planning and a bit of math. Enough games, though; let's get back to the lab and figure out how to use the Tkinter Canvas widget to visualize data.

Creating simple graphs using Canvas

The first graph we want to produce is a simple line graph that shows the growth of our plants over time. Each lab has varying climate conditions, and we want to see how those conditions are affecting the growth of all plants, so the chart will have one line per lab showing the average of the median height measurements for all plots in the lab over the days of the experiment.

We'll start by creating a model method to return the raw data, then create a Canvas-based line-chart view, and finally create an application callback to pull the data and send it to the chart view.

Creating the model method

Working with another data analyst at ABQ, you develop a SQL query that determines the day number of a plot check by subtracting its date from the oldest date in the plot_checks table, then pulls lab_id and the average of median_height for all plants in the given lab on the given day. The query looks like this:

```
SELECT
    date - (SELECT min(date) FROM plot_checks) AS "Day",
    lab_id,
    avg(median_height) AS "Average Height (cm)"
FROM plot_checks
GROUP BY date, lab_id
ORDER BY "Day", lab_id;
```

The query returns a table of data that looks something like this:

Day	lab_id	Average Height (cm)
0	A	1.4198750000000000
0	B	1.3320000000000000
0	C	1.5377500000000000
1	A	1.7266250000000000
1	B	1.8503750000000000
1	C	1.4633750000000000

Using this query, let's create a new SQLModel method called get_growth_by_lab() to return the needed data:

```
# models.py, inside SQLModel

def get_growth_by_lab(self):
    query = (
        'SELECT date - (SELECT min(date) FROM plot_checks) AS "Day", '
        'lab_id, avg(median_height) AS "Avg Height (cm)" '
        'FROM plot_checks '
        'GROUP BY date, lab_id ORDER BY "Day", lab_id;'
    )
    return self.query(query)
```

This is a fairly straightforward method; it just runs the query and returns the results. Recall that the SQLModel.query() method returns results as a list of dictionaries; in this case, each of the dictionaries contains three fields: Day, lab_id, and Avg Height (cm). Now we just need to develop a chart view that can visualize this data for the user.

Creating the chart view

The chart view we're going to create will need to take the data structure from our model method and use it to plot a line chart. Head over to `views.py`, where we'll create the `LineChartView` class:

```
# views.py

class LineChartView(tk.Canvas):
  """A generic view for plotting a line chart"""

  margin = 20
  colors = [
    'red', 'orange', 'yellow', 'green',
    'blue', 'purple', 'violet'
  ]
```

`LineChartView` is a subclass of `Canvas`, so we'll be able to draw items directly on it. This view will not only contain the data plots, but the axes, labels, and legend as well. It will be constructed for re-usability, so we're going to design it without any specific reference to the data we're charting in this instance. Ideally, we'd like to be able to send arbitrary datasets to it to generate line graphs. The two class attributes defined here provide a default value for the `margin` around the chart (in pixels) and a list of `colors` to use for each subsequent line plot. The growth chart we're making only has three plots (one for each lab), but the additional colors allow us to specify up to seven. You could provide additional colors in this list if you wanted to use it for charts with more than seven plots.

Now, we'll begin the initializer method:

```
# views.py, inside LineChartView

  def __init__(
    self, parent, data, plot_size,
    x_field, y_field, plot_by_field
  ):
    self.data = data
    self.x_field = x_field
    self.y_field = y_field
    self.plot_by_field = plot_by_field
```

Apart from the usual parent widget argument, we've specified these additional positional arguments:

- `data` will be our list of dictionaries containing the data from the query.
- `plot_size` will be a tuple of integers specifying the width and height of the plot area in pixels.
- `x_field` and `y_field` will be the field names to use for the X and Y values of the plot. For the growth chart this will be `Day` and `Avg Height (cm)`, respectively.
- `plot_by_field` will be the field whose value will be used to categorize the rows into individual plots. For the growth chart, this will be `lab_id`, since we want one line plot for each lab.

All these values are stored to instance variables so we can access them from our methods.

We're going to implement the plot area of this widget as a second `Canvas` placed on the `LineChartView`. The size of the `LineChartView` then will need to be the size of the chart plus the margins around the outside where the axes and labels will be drawn. We'll calculate that size, then pass it to the `LineChartView` superclass initializer, as follows:

```
self.plot_width, self.plot_height = plot_size
view_width = self.plot_width + (2 * self.margin)
view_height = self.plot_height + (2 * self.margin)

super().__init__(
  parent, width=view_width,
  height=view_height, background='lightgrey'
)
```

Note that we've saved the plot area's width and height as instance variables, as we'll need them in some of our methods.

Now that we've initialized the superclass, we can begin drawing on the main `Canvas`; to begin, let's draw the axes:

```
self.origin = (self.margin, view_height - self.margin)

# X axis
self.create_line(
  self.origin,
```

```
    (view_width - self.margin, view_height - self.margin)
  )
  # Y axis
  self.create_line(
    self.origin, (self.margin, self.margin), width=2
  )
```

Our chart's origin will be `self.margin` pixels from the bottom-left corner, and we'll draw the X and Y axes as simple black lines moving right and up from the origin to the edge of the chart. Remember that the Canvas Y coordinates count down from the top, not up from the bottom, so the Y coordinate for the origin is the height of the view area minus the margin.

Next, we'll label the axes:

```
  self.create_text(
    (view_width // 2, view_height - self.margin),
    text=x_field, anchor='n'
  )
  self.create_text(
    (self.margin, view_height // 2),
    text=y_field, angle=90, anchor='s'
  )
```

Here, we're creating the text items set to the labels for the X and Y axes, using the field names passed into the object for the text labels. Note the use of anchor to set which side of the text's bounding box is attached to the coordinates provided. In the case of the X axis, for instance, we've specified n (north), so the top of our text will be under the X-axis line. For the Y-axis label, we want the text to be sideways, so we've specified `angle=90` to rotate it. Also, note that we've used south (s) as the anchor position for the rotated text; even though it's rotated, the cardinal directions here are relative to the object *before* rotation. Thus, "south" will always be the bottom of the text as normally written, even if the object is rotated.

With the axes labeled, we need to create a second Canvas that will contain the plot area:

```
  self.plot_area = tk.Canvas(
    self, background='#555',
    width=self.plot_width, height=self.plot_height
  )
  self.create_window(
    self.origin, window=self.plot_area, anchor='sw'
  )
```

This `Canvas` object is where the actual plots will be drawn. While we could draw our plots on the `LineChartView` directly, embedding a second `Canvas` makes it easier to calculate the coordinate points for the plot, since we won't have to factor in the margin. It also allows us to use a different background color for a nicer look.

Before we can draw data on the chart, we need to create a method that can do so. Let's create a private instance method called `_plot_line()` to draw a single line plot on the chart, which begins like this:

```
def _plot_line(self, data, color):
    max_x = max([row[0] for row in data])
    max_y = max([row[1] for row in data])
    x_scale = self.plot_width / max_x
    y_scale = self.plot_height / max_y
```

This method will receive a `data` argument containing the X and Y points for the line as a list of tuples. Since our chart is a fixed number of pixels, and our data values may have any arbitrary range, the first thing we need to do is scale the data to fit just inside the size of our chart. To do this, we first find the maximum values of the X and Y fields, then create a scaling ratio for each axis by dividing the set height of the chart by the maximum value (note that this assumes the minimum value is 0. This particular chart class isn't designed to handle negative values).

Once we have the scale values, we can then transform our data points to coordinates by using a list comprehension that multiplies each data point by the scale value, as follows:

```
coords = [
    (round(x * x_scale), self.plot_height - round(y * y_scale))
    for x, y in data
]
```

Note that we are rounding the values, since we can't plot to fractional pixel values. Also, once again, since data is usually graphed with the origin in the bottom left, but coordinates on the `Canvas` measure from the top left, we'll need to flip the Y coordinates; this is done in our list comprehension as well by subtracting the new Y value from the plot height.

These coordinates can now be passed to `create_line()` along with a reasonable width and the color argument passed in by the caller, like so:

```
self.plot_area.create_line(
    *coords, width=4, fill=color, smooth=True
)
```

Note that we've also used the `smooth` argument to round out the curve a bit and make it appear more organic.

To use this method, we need to head back to the initializer and do some calculations. Since the `_plot_line()` method only handles one plot at a time, we'll need to filter out our data by the `plot_by_field` field and render the lines one at a time.

Add this code at the end of `LineChartView.__init__()`:

```python
# views.py, in LineChartView.__init__()

    plot_names = sorted(set([
      row[self.plot_by_field]
      for row in self.data
    ]))
    color_map = list(zip(plot_names, self.colors))
```

First, we get the individual plot names by retrieving the unique `plot_by_field` values from the data. These are sorted and cast to a `set` object so that we only have the unique values. Then, we create a color mapping using `zip()` to build a list of name-to-color tuples. Since `zip()` returns a generator and we're going to want to use this map more than once, it's cast to a `list` object.

Now, let's plot our lines:

```python
    for plot_name, color in color_map:
      dataxy = [
        (row[x_field], row[y_field])
        for row in data
        if row[plot_by_field] == plot_name
      ]
      self._plot_line(dataxy, color)
```

For each distinct plot name and color, we first format the data into a list of (X, Y) pairs using a list comprehension. Then we call `_plot_line()` with the data and the color. Our lines are now plotted!

One last thing we need is a legend, to tell the user what each color on the chart represents. Without that, this chart would be meaningless to the user. To create it, we'll write a `_draw_legend()` method:

```python
# views.py, inside LineChartView

  def _draw_legend(self, color_map):
    for i, (label, color) in enumerate(color_map):
      self.plot_area.create_text(
```

```
        (10, 10 + (i * 20), text=label, fill=color, anchor='w'
    )
```

Our method takes the color map list that we created in the initializer and iterates over it, using the enumerate() function to also generate an incrementing number for each iteration. For each mapping, we simply draw a text item containing the label text with the associated fill color. This is drawn starting at ten pixels from the top-left corner of the chart, with each item twenty pixels below the last.

Finally, let's call this method from the initializer:

```
# views.py, inside LineChartView.__init__()

    self._draw_legend(color_map)
```

The LineChartView is ready to go; now we just need to create the supporting code to invoke it.

Updating the application

Back in the Application class, create a new method for showing our chart:

```
# application.py, in Application

def show_growth_chart(self, *_):
    data = self.model.get_growth_by_lab()
    popup = tk.Toplevel()
    chart = v.LineChartView(
        popup, data, (800, 400),
        'Day', 'Avg Height (cm)', 'lab_id'
    )
    chart.pack(fill='both', expand=1)
```

The first order of business is to fetch the data from our get_growth_by_lab() method. Then, we build a TopLevel widget to hold our LineChartView object. On this widget, we add the LineChartView object, configuring it to be 800 by 400 pixels and specifying the fields for X (Day), Y (Avg Height (cm)), and the plot_by_field value (lab_id). This chart gets packed into the Toplevel.

The Toplevel widget creates a new, blank window outside the root window. You should use it as a base for new windows that aren't simple dialogs or message boxes.

With this method complete, add it to the `event_callbacks` dictionary in the `Application` initializer:

```
# application.py, inside Application.__init__()
    event_callbacks = {
      #...
      '<<ShowGrowthChart>>': self.show_growth_chart
    }
```

Finally, we need to add a menu item to launch the chart. Add the following method to the `GenericMainMenu` class:

```
def _add_growth_chart(self, menu):
  menu.add_command(
    label='Show Growth Chart',
    command=self._event('<<ShowGrowthChart>>')
  )
```

Then use this method in each menu class's `_build_menu()` method to add this option to the **Tools** menu. For example:

```
# mainmenu.py, in any class's _build_menu() method

    self._add_growth_chart(self._menus['Tools'])
```

When you call your function, you should see something like this:

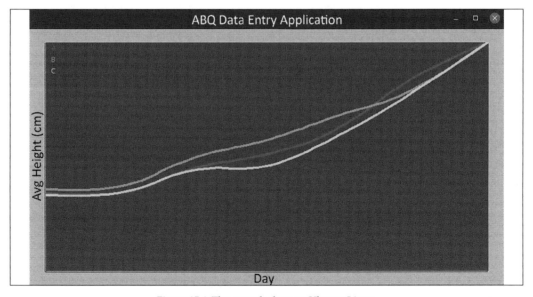

Figure 15.4: The growth chart on Ubuntu Linux

Your graph won't look like much without some sample data. Unless you just like doing data entry, there is a script for loading sample data in the `sql` directory. Run this script against your database before testing your chart.

Advanced graphs using Matplotlib

Our line graph is pretty, but it still needs considerable work to be a truly professional-looking visualization: it lacks a scale, grid lines, zoom capabilities, and other features that would make it a completely useful chart.

We could spend a lot of time making it more complete, but there's a faster way to get much more satisfactory graphs and charts in our Tkinter application: Matplotlib.

Matplotlib is a third-party Python library for generating professional-quality, interactive graphs of all types. It's a vast library with many add-ons, and we won't cover much of its actual usage, but we will look at how to integrate Matplotlib charts into a Tkinter application. To demonstrate this, we'll create a bubble chart showing the yield of each plot as it relates to humidity and temperature.

You should be able to install the `matplotlib` library using `pip` with this command:

```
$ pip install --user matplotlib
```

For complete instructions on installation, please see `https://matplotlib.org/users/installing.html`.

Data model method

Before we can make a chart, we'll need another `SQLModel` method to extract the data for the chart. Once again, you've been provided with a SQL query that returns the required data:

```
SELECT
  seed_sample,
  MAX(fruit) AS yield,
  AVG(humidity) AS avg_humidity,
  AVG(temperature) AS avg_temperature
FROM plot_checks
WHERE NOT equipment_fault
GROUP BY lab_id, plot, seed_sample
```

The purpose of this chart is to find the sweet spot of temperature and humidity for each seed sample. Therefore, we need one row per plot that includes the maximum fruit measurement, average humidity and temperature at the plot column, and the seed sample. Since we don't want any bad data, we'll filter out rows that have an Equipment Fault.

The query returns data that looks something like this:

seed_sample	yield	avg_humidity	avg_temperature
AXM480	11	27.7582142857142857	23.7485714285714286
AXM480	20	27.2146428571428571	23.8032142857142857
AXM480	15	26.2896428571428571	23.6750000000000000
AXM478	31	27.2928571428571429	23.8317857142857143
AXM477	39	27.1003571428571429	23.7360714285714286
AXM478	39	26.8550000000000000	23.7632142857142857

To provide this data to the application, let's put the query into another model method called get_yield_by_plot():

```
# models.py, in SQLModel

  def get_yield_by_plot(self):
    query = (
      'SELECT seed_sample, MAX(fruit) AS yield, '
      'AVG(humidity) AS avg_humidity, '
      'AVG(temperature) AS avg_temperature '
      'FROM plot_checks WHERE NOT equipment_fault '
      'GROUP BY lab_id, plot, seed_sample'
    )
    return self.query(query)
```

That's all the model needs, so let's move on to the views.

Creating the bubble chart view

To integrate Matplotlib into a Tkinter application, there are several module imports we need to make into views.py.

The first is matplotlib itself:

```
import matplotlib
matplotlib.use('TkAgg')
```

It may seem odd to execute methods in the import section of a script, and your code editor or IDE may even complain about it. According to Matplotlib's documentation, though, use() should be called before other modules are imported from matplotlib to tell it which rendering backend it should use. In this case, we want the TkAgg backend, which is made to integrate into Tkinter.

 Matplotlib has backends for a variety of GUI toolkits such as PyQt, wxWidgets, and Gtk3, as well as backends for non-GUI situations (for example, rendering plots directly to a file) like SVG rendering or web usage. See the documentation at https://matplotlib.org/stable/api/index_backend_api.html for more details.

Now that we've set the backend, we can import a few other items from matplotlib:

```
from matplotlib.figure import Figure
from matplotlib.backends.backend_tkagg import (
  FigureCanvasTkAgg,
  NavigationToolbar2Tk
)
```

The Figure class represents the basic drawing area on which matplotlib charts can be drawn. The FigureCanvasTkAgg class is an interface between the Figure and the Tkinter Canvas, and NavigationToolbar2Tk allows us to place a pre-made navigation toolbar for the Figure object on our GUI.

To see how these fit together, let's start our YieldChartView class in views.py:

```
# views.py
class YieldChartView(tk.Frame):

  def __init__(self, parent, x_axis, y_axis, title):
    super().__init__(parent)
    self.figure = Figure(figsize=(6, 4), dpi=100)
    self.canvas_tkagg = FigureCanvasTkAgg(self.figure, master=self)
```

After calling the superclass initializer to create the Frame object, we create a Figure object to hold our chart. Instead of a size in pixels, the Figure object takes a size in inches and a dots-per-inch (dpi) setting. In this case, our arguments of 6 by 4 inches and 100 dots per inch result in a 600-by-400-pixel Figure object. Next, we create a FigureCanvasTkAgg object that will be used to connect our Figure object with a Tkinter Canvas.

The `FigureCanvasTkAgg` object is not itself a `Canvas` object or subclass, but it contains a `Canvas` object we can place in our application. A reference to this `Canvas` object can be retrieved using the `FigureCanvasTkAgg` object's `get_tk_widget()` method. We'll go ahead and get a reference to the `Canvas` and pack it into the `YieldChartView` widget:

```
canvas = self.canvas_tkagg.get_tk_widget()
canvas.pack(fill='both', expand=True)
```

Next, we'll add the toolbar and attach it to our `FigureCanvasTkAgg` object:

```
self.toolbar = NavigationToolbar2Tk(self.canvas_tkagg, self)
```

Note that we don't need to use a geometry manager to add the toolbar; instead we just pass the `FigureCanvasTkAgg` object and the parent widget (`self`, which is our `YiedChartView` object in this case) to the toolbar's initializer, and this will attach it to our `Figure`.

The next step is to set up the axes:

```
self.axes = self.figure.add_subplot(1, 1, 1)
self.axes.set_xlabel(x_axis)
self.axes.set_ylabel(y_axis)
self.axes.set_title(title)
```

In `matplotlib`, an `Axes` object represents a single set of X and Y axes on which data can be plotted, and is created using the `Figure.add_subplot()` method. The three integers passed to `add_subplot()` establish that this is the first set of axes out of one row of one column of subplots. Our figure could conceivably contain multiple subplots arranged in a table-like format, but we only need one, thus we're passing all 1s here. After it's created, we set the labels on the `Axes` object.

To create a bubble chart, we're going to use the **scatter plot** feature of Matplotlib, using the size of each dot to indicate the fruit yield. We'll also color code the dots to indicate which seed sample the data point represents.

Let's implement a method to draw our scatter plots:

```
def draw_scatter(self, data, color, label):
    x, y, size = zip(*data)
    scaled_size = [(s ** 2)//2 for s in size]
    scatter = self.axes.scatter(
        x, y, scaled_size,
        c=color, label=label, alpha=0.5
    )
```

The data passed in should contain three columns per record, and we're breaking those out into three separate lists containing the x, y, and size values. Next, we're going to amplify the differences between the size values to make them more apparent by squaring each value then dividing it by two. This isn't strictly necessary, but it helps make the chart more readable when differences are relatively small.

Finally, we draw the data onto the axes object by calling scatter(), also passing along the color and label values for the dots, and making them semi-transparent with the alpha argument.

 zip(*data) is a Python idiom for breaking a list of n-length tuples into n lists of values, essentially the reverse of zip(x, y, s).

To draw a legend for our Axes object, we need two things: a list of our scatter objects and a list of their labels. To get these, we'll have to create a couple of blank lists in __init__() and append the appropriate values to them whenever draw_scatter() is called.

In __init__(), add some empty lists:

```
# views.py, in YieldChartView.__init__()

    self.scatters = list()
    self.scatter_labels = list()
```

Now, at the end of draw_scatter(), append the lists and update the legend() method:

```
# views.py, in YieldChartView.draw_scatter()
    self.scatters.append(scatter)
    self.scatter_labels.append(label)
    self.axes.legend(self.scatters, self.scatter_labels)
```

Note that we can call legend() repeatedly and it will simply destroy and redraw the legend each time.

Updating the Application class

Back in Application, let's create the method to show our yield data chart.

Start by creating a method to display a `Toplevel` widget with our chart view:

```
# application.py, inside Application
  def show_yield_chart(self, *_):
    popup = tk.Toplevel()
    chart = v.YieldChartView(
      popup,
      'Average plot humidity', 'Average plot temperature',
      'Yield as a product of humidity and temperature'
    )
    chart.pack(fill='both', expand=True)
```

Now let's set up the data for our scatters:

```
data = self.data_model.get_yield_by_plot()
seed_colors = {
  'AXM477': 'red', 'AXM478': 'yellow',
  'AXM479': 'green', 'AXM480': 'blue'
}
```

We've retrieved the yield data from the data model and created a dictionary that will hold the colors we want to use for each seed sample. Now we just need to iterate through the seed samples and draw the scatters:

```
for seed, color in seed_colors.items():
  seed_data = [
    (x['avg_humidity'], x['avg_temperature'], x['yield'])
    for x in data if x['seed_sample'] == seed
  ]
  chart.draw_scatter(seed_data, color, seed)
```

Once again, we're formatting and filtering down our data using a list comprehension, providing average humidity for x, average temperature for y, and yield for s.

Add the method to the callbacks dictionary and create a menu item for it just under the growth chart option.

Your bubble chart should look something like this:

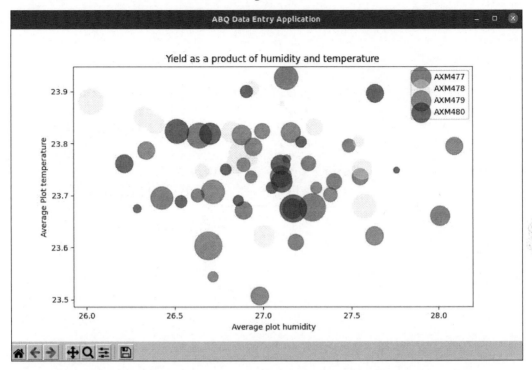

Figure 15.5: Our scatter plot showing how seed samples performed under different conditions

Take a moment to play with this chart using the navigation toolbar. Notice how you can zoom and pan, adjust the size of the chart, and save the image. These powerful tools are provided by Matplotlib automatically, and make for very professional-looking charts.

This wraps up our charting needs for the time being, but as you've seen it's quite simple to integrate Matplotlib's powerful charts and graphs into our application. And, of course, with enough effort, the sky is the limit with generating visualizations using the Canvas widget.

Summary

In this chapter, you learned about Tkinter's graphical capabilities. You learned about the Canvas widget, and how to draw shapes, lines, images, text, and widgets on it. You implemented animations on the Canvas by queuing item movements in the Tkinter event queue. You implemented a simple line chart class using a plain Canvas to provide basic data visualization for SQL query results. Finally, you learned how to integrate the powerful Matplotlib library with its wide variety of charts and graphs into your application.

In the next chapter, we'll learn how to package up our application for distribution. We'll learn how to arrange the directory for distribution as Python code, and how to use third-party tools to create executables across Windows, macOS, and Linux.

16

Packaging with setuptools and cxFreeze

Word of your application has spread throughout the ABQ corporation, and you've been asked to provide it for use at other facilities. Unfortunately, running and installing the application is not a very friendly process; you've been installing it through a tedious and error-prone copy-and-paste procedure, and users launch it from a batch or shell script you create by hand on each machine. You need to package your application in a professional way that makes it easy to install and run across Windows, macOS, and Linux.

In this chapter, you will learn the following topics:

- In *Creating distributable packages with setuptools*, you'll learn to create distributable Python source and wheel packages using the setuptools library.

- In *Creating executables with cx_Freeze*, you'll learn to create a standalone executable of your application, including specific instructions for Windows and macOS.

Creating distributable packages with setuptools

The distribution process has often been cited as a major shortcoming for Python; it is an area with a storied history of ever-evolving tools and approaches, often caught between the vestiges of the past and competing visions of the future.

That said, it works surprisingly well, as evidenced by the ease with which we have installed components using `pip` throughout this book. The aim of this section is to cut through some of the confusion and provide you with a process that respects both traditional approaches and future trends.

The standard library contains the `distutils` library, a collection of functionalities related to packaging and distributing Python code. However, both the `distutils` documentation (`https://docs.python.org/3/library/distutils.html`) and the official packaging guide recommend against using it and instead direct you to use `setuptools`.

The `setuptools` library is an extension of the `distutils` library that adds some important functionality such as dependency handling, bundling non-Python files, and generation of executables. Although `setuptools` is not part of the standard library, it is included in the official Python distributions for Windows and macOS, and is readily available from the package repositories of most Linux distributions. `setuptools` is used by the `pip` package installer, and we can use it to create packages that can be installed on any system with Python and `pip`.

 If you want to create packages that can be uploaded to PyPI, `setuptools` is what you need. For more information about preparing and uploading packages to PyPI, see the official Python packaging guide at `https://packaging.python.org`.

Preparing our package for distribution

Although the restructuring of our project directory we did in *Chapter 6, Planning for the Expansion of Our Application*, left us in fairly good shape for packaging our application, there are a few minor additions and changes we need to make for our Python package to be a good citizen as a distributed package. Let's go through what those are.

Creating a requirements.txt file

The `requirements.txt` file is a plaintext file, typically placed in the application root directory, that lists all the third-party modules that we used to develop our application. Although not used by `setuptools`, this file can be used by `pip` to install a package's dependencies.

Create a `requirements.txt` file that contains the following:

```
# requirements.txt
```

```
--index-url https://pypi.python.org/simple/

# Runtime:
Requests
Paramiko
psycopg2
matplotlib

# for testing REST:
flask
```

The first line of the file specifies the index from which we want to install packages; strictly speaking, this line isn't necessary since PyPI will be used by default. However, we can override this URL if we want to use a different package index; for example, if ABQ decided to create its own private Python package index for security reasons, we could redirect pip to that server instead.

Next, we've specified runtime requirements. Our application depends on four external libraries: requests, paramiko, psycopg2, and matplotlib, and these are simply specified one per line. Note that we can also add comments to the file by beginning a line with a # sign.

Finally, we've included flask as a requirement, which is not used by the application but was required by the test service we used for REST. It might seem odd to include these kinds of requirements, but the purpose of the requirements.txt file is to make it simple for other developers (including your future self) to reproduce the development environment for this application. You might choose to place non-runtime requirements like this in a separate file, for example, requirements.development.txt or requirements.testing.txt.

This file can then be used to direct pip to install these dependencies using the following command:

```
$ pip install -r requirements.txt
```

This command causes pip to read through the file one line at a time to install the dependencies. For each dependency, pip will first check to see if the package is already installed; if not, it will install the latest version of the package from the specified package index.

This presents a small problem, though; what if our code depends on a newer version of the package than the user has installed on their system? Or, what if an incompatible change in a newer version of a library requires that we run an older version than the latest in the index?

To address this, we can include version specifier strings in `requirements.txt`, like so:

```
# These are examples, don't include this in our requirements.txt

requests==2.26.0
paramiko>=2.6
psycopg2<3.0
matplotlib>3.2,<=3.3
```

A version specifier consists of a comparison operator followed by a version string. This will direct `pip` to ensure that the version installed matches the requirement; in this case, it would specify the following:

- `requests` would have to be *exactly* version 2.26.0

- `paramiko` would have to be at least 2.6 or higher

- `psycopg2` would have to be less than 3.0

- `matplotlib` would have to be greater than 3.2 (not including 3.2!), but 3.3 or lower

Whether you include version specifiers, and how specific you make them, depends somewhat on the needs of your project and users. In general, you shouldn't limit `pip` from installing newer versions of a library so that you don't miss out on bug fixes and security patches, but in situations where there are known bugs with newer versions, it may be essential.

The command `pip freeze` will print a list of all your installed packages with exact versions specified. Developers in mission-critical environments who want to guarantee the ability to reproduce their exact development environment often just copy this output directly to `requirements.txt`.

Creating a pyproject.toml file

Although `setuptools` is still the de facto standard for packaging Python projects, the Python community is moving toward tool-agnostic configuration to accommodate newer options as well. As part of this move, the official packaging guide recommends creating a `pyproject.toml` file in your project's root directory. Currently, this file is only used to specify your project's build system and build system requirements, but there is indication that more project settings will migrate to this file in the future.

For our project, the file should contain the following:

```
[build-system]
requires = [
    "setuptools",
    "wheel"
]
build-backend = "setuptools.build_meta"
```

This file indicates that our project requires the `setuptools` and `wheel` packages, and that we're using `setuptools.build_meta` to actually build our project. These are the recommended configurations if you wish to use `setuptools` to build your project.

Note that the requirements listed here are *build requirements*, meaning they are the packages required by the build tool used to create a distributable package. This is distinct from the requirements we listed in `requirements.txt`, which are the packages needed to *use* the package.

 TOML (Tom's Obvious, Minimal Language) is a relatively new configuration file format introduced in 2013. It extends the traditional INI-style format with new features like hierarchical structures and nested lists. It is growing in popularity particularly as a configuration format for build tools in languages like Rust, JavaScript, and of course Python. Learn more about TOML at `https://toml.io`.

Adding a license file

When you distribute code, it's important that the recipients know what they're allowed to do with that code. Unlike compiled languages such as C or Java, Python source code is necessarily included when you distribute your project using `setuptools`. To make sure that recipients use the code appropriately, we need to include a license file with our code.

When deciding on a license, there are a few concerns you need to consider.

First, if you're developing software as part of your job (such as our ABQ Data Entry program), your employer typically owns the code and you need to make sure you're specifying their preferred license for the code. Consult your employer for their policy on this issue.

Second, if you've used third-party libraries, you'll need to make sure your license is compatible with the license of those libraries. For example, if you are using a software library licensed under the **GNU Public License** (**GPL**), you may be required to release your software under the GPL or a similar, compatible license. Python and Tkinter are distributed under fairly permissive licenses; here are the licenses of our four dependencies:

Package	License	Reference
requests	Apache2	https://2.python-requests.org/projects/3/user/intro/
paramiko	LGPL 2.1	https://github.com/paramiko/paramiko (LICENSE file)
psycopg2	LGPL 2.1	https://www.psycopg.org/license
matplotlib	Matplotlib License (BSD-based)	https://matplotlib.org/stable/users/license.html

Be sure to consult these licenses before distributing your package to make sure you're complying with the requirements for software using the libraries. If neither of these situations applies, you should simply consider what license best suits the project and describes the intention you have in distributing it.

Whichever you choose, this should be included in your project root directory in a file called LICENSE.

Making our package executable

Up to this point in the project, we've been executing our application by running the abq_data_entry.py file, which we've placed in the project root directory *outside* the package. Ideally, though, we'd like all our Python code – even this trivial launcher script – to be located inside the package. We could just copy abq_data_entry.py into the package directory, right? It would seem that simple, but when we execute the script now we get an error:

```
$ python abq_data_entry/abq_data_entry.py
Traceback (most recent call last):
  File ".../abq_data_entry/abq_data_entry.py", line 1, in <module>
    from abq_data_entry.application import Application
  File ".../abq_data_entry/abq_data_entry.py", line 1, in <module>
    from abq_data_entry.application import Application
ModuleNotFoundError: No module named 'abq_data_entry.application';
  'abq_data_entry' is not a package
```

Unfortunately, the relative imports we have in the package will not work correctly when executing code inside the package. However, Python provides a solution here: we can make our *package* executable, rather than relying on a particular Python *script* for execution.

To do that, we need to create a __main__.py file inside our package. This special file inside a Python package makes the package executable; when the module is executed, Python will run the __main__.py script. However, it will run it in a slightly special way that will allow our relative imports to work.

Create a new file called abq_data_entry/__main__.py and add the following:

```
# abq_data_entry/__main__.py

from abq_data_entry.application import Application
def main():
  app = Application()
  app.mainloop()

if __name__ == '__main__':
    main()
```

The contents of __main__.py are nearly identical to abq_data_entry.py; the only difference is that we've put the creation of Application and the execution of mainloop() in a function called main(). The reason for this will be explained shortly when we start building our package.

Once we've created __main__.py, we can execute the module like so:

```
$ python -m abq_data_entry
```

The -m flag tells Python to load and execute the provided module. Note that, for the moment, this command must be executed inside the project root folder. Once we create and install our Python package, we'll be able to run it from anywhere.

Configuring a setup.py script

Now that our code is ready, we can start creating our setuptools configuration. To package our project using setuptools, we need to create a **setup script**; by convention, this is called setup.py and is created in the application's root directory.

The `setuptools` configuration can also be created as an INI-style configuration file, `setup.cfg`. Eventually, this may replace `setup.py`, but in this book we're going to stick with the Python script approach, because it allows us to execute some necessary Python code.

The basic structure of a `setup.py` file looks like this:

```
# setup.py
from setuptools import setup

setup(
  # Configuration arguments here
)
```

The vast majority of our configuration will be passed as arguments to the `setup()` function, defining the basic metadata for our package, what will be packaged, and providing some functionality after installation.

Basic metadata arguments

To begin, let's define some basic metadata about our application using these arguments in `setup.py`:

```
setup(
  name='ABQ_Data_Entry',
  version='1.0',
  author='Alan D Moore',
  author_email='alandmoore@example.com',
  description='Data entry application for ABQ AgriLabs',
  url="http://abq.example.com",
  license="ABQ corporate license",
  #...
)
```

Metadata such as this will be used in naming the package as well as providing information for PyPI. Not all of the fields are necessary if you are just packaging for personal or internal use, but if you plan to upload to PyPI, you should include all these fields as well as `long_description`, which should be a reStructuredText string that provides extended information about the program.

Often, the README.rst file can simply be used. Since this configuration script is just a Python script, we can use normal Python to read the file and use its contents for this configuration option, like so:

```
# setup.py, near the top
with open('README.rst', 'r') as fh:
  long_description = fh.read()

# inside the setup() call:
setup(
  #...
  long_description=long_description,
)
```

Packages and dependencies

Once we have specified the metadata, we need to tell setuptools which packages we're actually bundling using the packages argument. In our case, we only have the abq_data_entry package, so we'll specify it as follows:

```
setup(
  #...
  packages=[
    'abq_data_entry',
    'abq_data_entry.images',
    'abq_data_entry.test'
  ],
```

Note that we've specified both the main package and the sub-modules images and test. We need to specify all the sub-modules we want to include explicitly here, as setuptools will not automatically include them.

That could get tedious with very complex packages, so setuptools also includes the find_packages() function, which can be used instead like so:

```
from setuptools import setup, find_packages

setup(
  #...
  packages=find_packages(),
```

This will locate and include all the packages in our project directory automatically.

In addition to the modules defined in our project, our application depends on third-party modules such as psycopg2, requests, paramiko, and matplotlib. We can specify these dependencies in setup(), and, assuming they're available from PyPI, pip will install them automatically when our package is installed.

This is done using the install_requires argument as shown here:

```
setup(
    #...
    install_requires=[
        'psycopg2', 'requests', 'paramiko', 'matplotlib'
    ],
```

Note that these required packages may have their own dependencies as well; for example, matplotlib requires several other libraries including numpy and pillow. We don't have to specify all of those sub-dependencies; they will also be automatically installed by pip.

If the package requires particular versions of these modules, we can specify that as well:

```
# Just an example, do not add to your setup.py!
    install_requires=[
        'psycopg2==2.9.1', 'requests>=2.26',
        'paramiko', 'matplotlib<3.3.5'
    ]
```

This looks rather familiar, doesn't it? These are the same kind of rules we can put in requirements.txt, and the same list of runtime dependencies. Some developers take the approach of just reading in requirements.txt and sending its contents to the install_requires list; there are even tools available to help translate some of the incompatible syntax between them. Remember, though, that the intention of our requirements.txt file was to recreate our specific development environment. As such, it contains non-runtime packages, and may have very specific version specifiers for the sake of testing consistency. The install_requires list, by contrast, is meant solely for runtime requirements, and in general should be more abstract about versions and package sources. For example, while it might be helpful to specify psycopg2 version 2.9.1 for the development environment, unless we know for certain that it only works correctly with that one version, we would specify something more general here like psycopg2<3.0.

Just as we can specify package version requirements, we can also specify the version of Python required by our application using the `python_requires` argument, like so:

```
setup(
    #...
    python_requires='>= 3.6',
```

This is always a good idea to do if you're using Python features not found in earlier releases (for example, the f-strings used in our application do not work before Python 3.6), or if you want to be sure that only a specific, tested version of Python is used. If the user is not running a matching version of Python, `pip install` will abort with an error.

> The syntax for version specifiers used in `setuptools` is laid out in PEP 440, which you can find at `https://www.python.org/dev/peps/pep-0440/`.

Adding extra files

By default, `setuptools` will only copy Python files into your package. Our package contains more than that, though: we have documentation in RST, SQL scripts, and most importantly our PNG images, without which our program won't run correctly.

Non-Python files that are located *inside* our package structure can be specified using the `package_data` argument:

```
setup(
    #...
    package_data={'abq_data_entry.images': ['*.png', '*.xbm']},
)
```

The `package_data` argument takes a dictionary that matches module paths to a list of files (or globbing expressions that match a list of files) to be included in that module. Here, we're telling `setuptools` to include all the PNG and XBM files in the `images` module.

Our project also contains necessary files outside the `abq_data_entry` module; these aren't needed for the program to operate, but should nevertheless be distributed with the package. We cannot specify these in `setup()`, since it only deals with the in-package files.

To add these, we need to create a separate file in the project root directory called MANIFEST.in. For our application, the file should contain this:

```
# MANIFEST.in

include README.rst
include requirements.txt
include docs/*
include sql/*.sql
```

The MANIFEST.in file contains a series of the include directives with filenames or globbing expressions that match files we want to include. Here, we're including all files in our docs directory, all the .sql files in the sql directory, the requirements. txt file, and the README.rst file. Since setup.py relies on the README.rst and requirements.txt files for setup data, it's imperative that we include it in the package. Otherwise, our package won't be buildable on other systems.

Defining commands

Earlier, we created a __main__.py file in our package that allows our package to be run using the command python -m abq_data_entry. This is certainly cleaner than having to hunt down the right Python script to execute, but ideally we'd like our package to set up a simple command that a user can execute to launch the program.

The setuptools library offers a way to add executable commands in our package using the entry_points argument. **Entry points** are ways for external environments to access our code. One particular entry point, console_scripts, defines a list of module functions that will be mapped to external commands. When the package is installed, setuptools will create a simple, platform-appropriate executable file for each console_scripts item that, when executed, will run the function specified.

We can't point console_scripts to a Python file or package, however; it must point instead to a *function* inside the package. This is why we created the main() function in our __main__.py file earlier, so that we can specify __main__.main() as a console script entry point, like so:

```
setup(
  #...
  entry_points={
    'console_scripts': [
    'abq = abq_data_entry.__main__:main'
  ]}
)
```

Each item in the `console_scripts` list is a string in the format `{executable_name}` = `{module}.{submodule}:{function_name}`. Our code here will cause `setuptools` to create an executable called abq, which will run the `main()` function we defined in `__main__.py`. Thus, after installation, we can execute the application by just typing abq at a command line. You could define other scripts here if there were functions in the package that could run standalone.

Testing the configuration

Before we move on to creating distributable packages from our configuration, we can check it for proper syntax and content by running the following command in the project root directory:

```
$ python setup.py check
```

If all is well, this will simply return the string `running check` with no other output. If something were missing, you would get an error message. For example, if you comment out the `name` and `version` arguments to `setup()` and run the check, you'll get the following output:

```
running check
warning: check: missing required meta-data: name, version
```

While it won't find every potential problem with your `setup.py`, the check command will at least ensure you have the essential metadata specified, which is especially important if you wish to upload your package to PyPI.

Creating and using source distributions

With our configuration files all set, we can now create a **source distribution**. This kind of distribution bundles all the relevant files for building our package from source into a `.tar.gz` archive.

To create the source distribution, run `setup.py` with the `sdist` option in the project root directory:

```
$ python setup.py sdist
```

After doing this, two new directories will appear under the project root:

- `ABQ_Data_Entry.egg-info`: This directory contains the metadata files generated by `setuptools`. If you explore this directory, you'll find that all the information we passed to `setup()` is here in some form or other.

- `dist`: This directory contains the files generated for distribution; in this case, there is just a single `.tar.gz` file that contains our source package.

To install the source distribution on another computer, it first needs to be extracted. This can be done with GUI utilities or in a terminal with the `tar` command, as shown in the following example:

```
$ tar -xzf ABQ_Data_Entry-1.0.tar.gz
```

Once extracted, we can install the package by running `setup.py` inside the extracted directory using the `install` option, like so:

```
$ cd ABQ_Data_Entry/
$ python3 setup.py install
```

Testing our source distribution

If you don't have a second computer handy to test your source installer on, you can use a Python **virtual environment** instead. A virtual environment is a clean, isolated Python installation that can be activated on demand to keep installed packages from polluting your system's main Python environment.

To create one, first make sure you have the `virtualenv` package installed using `pip`:

```
$ pip install --user virtualenv
```

Next, create a directory anywhere on your system and generate a Python 3 environment in it with these commands:

```
$ mkdir testenv
$ python -m virtualenv -p python3 testenv
```

This will create a virtual environment, essentially a copy of the Python interpreter and standard library, in the `testenv` directory along with some supporting scripts and files. This environment can be modified in any way you wish without affecting your system's Python environment.

To use the new virtual environment, you need to **activate** it by executing the following code in a terminal:

```
# On Linux, macOS, and other unix-like systems:
$ source testenv/bin/activate

# On Windows
> testenv\Scripts\activate
```

Activating a virtual environment means that invocations of python will use the binaries and libraries in the virtual environment rather than your system installation. This includes Python-related commands like pip, meaning that a pip install will install packages to the environment's library rather than to your system or user Python libraries.

With your test environment active, you can now run setup.py install on your source distribution. You'll notice that Python will install psycopg2, requests, paramiko, and matplotlib, as well as their individual dependencies, even if you already have those packages on your system. That's because the virtual environment starts clean with no third-party packages, so everything must be installed again in the new environment.

If the install was successful, you should find the following things:

- You have a command called abq available in your virtual environment, which launches the ABQ Data Entry application.

- You can open a Python prompt from any directory on the system (not just in the project root) and import abq_data_entry.

- The abq_data_entry package directory can be found in testenv/lib/ python3.9/sitepackages.

When finished with your virtual environment, you can type deactivate in the terminal to go back to your system Python. If you want to remove the environment, just delete the testenv directory.

Building a wheel distribution

While a source distribution may be fine for simple software such as our application, packages with complicated build steps such as code compilation may benefit from a **built distribution**. As the name implies, a built distribution is one where any building operations (compilation or code generation, for example) has already been done. The current format used by setuptools for built distributions is the **wheel format**.

 The wheel format replaces an older distutils distribution format called egg. You will still see references to egg when using setuptools or other distutils derivatives.

A wheel (.whl) file is basically a ZIP-format archive file containing pre-built code. It comes in the following three types:

- **Universal**: This type of wheel file contains only Python code that will run on any platform with any major version of Python (2 and 3).

- **Pure Python**: This type of wheel file contains only Python code that will run on any platform, but is compatible with only one version of Python.

- **Platform**: This wheel file is limited to a particular OS, platform, or architecture, usually because it contains compiled binary code.

The default wheel file created by setuptools is a pure Python wheel, which is what our application should be (since we have no compiled code, but are compatible only with Python 3). Creating one is simply a matter of calling setup.py with the bdist_wheel option, like so:

```
$ python3 setup.py bdist_wheel
```

Like sdist, this command creates a new file in the dist directory, only this time it's a .whl file. The filename will be ABQ_Data_Entry-1.0-py3-none-any.whl, the segments of which represent the following information:

- The package name, in this case ABQ_Data_Entry.

- The version, in this case 1.0.

- Whether it's Python 3, Python 2, or universal; in this case, py3 for Python 3.

- The **Application Binary Interface** (ABI) tag, which would indicate a particular implementation of Python (for example, CPython vs. IronPython). In this case, it's none, since we have no particular ABI requirements.

- The supported platform, in this case any, since our application is not platform-specific. Note that this component can include a CPU architecture as well as an operating system.

Notice that the bdist_wheel process also creates a build directory, which is where built code is staged before it is compressed into the wheel file. You can inspect this directory to make sure that your package is being assembled correctly.

Once built, your wheel file can be installed using pip, like so:

```
$ pip install ABQ_Data_Entry-1.0-py3-none-any.whl
```

As with the source install, pip will first install any dependencies specified in the setup configuration, then install the package itself to the environment's site-packages directory. The executable abq file will also be created and copied to an executable location appropriate to your platform.

If you get an error when trying to use `bdist_wheel`, you may need to install the `wheel` module, as it's not always included with `setuptools`. This module can be installed with the command `pip install --user wheel`. Recall that we specified `wheel` as a build dependency in `pyproject.toml`, though, so this step should be taken care of by `setuptools`.

Creating executables with cx_Freeze

While source and wheel distributions are useful, they both require that Python and any third-party library dependencies be installed on the system before the program can be run. Often, it would be much handier if we could provide a file or set of files that can simply be copied and run on a system without installing anything else first. Better yet, we'd like to have platform-appropriate installation packages that set up desktop shortcuts and perform other common system configurations.

There are several ways to go about this with Python code, and several projects to choose from; in this book, we're going to look at one called `cx_Freeze`.

The basic idea of `cx_Freeze` is to bundle up all the code and shared library files for a Python project along with a Python interpreter, and then generate a small executable file that will launch the code with the bundled interpreter. This approach is commonly known as **freezing** the code (hence the package name), and it works fairly well most of the time. However, as we'll see, there are some limitations and difficulties to work around. One significant limitation is that `cx_Freeze` can only make executables for the platform that it's running on; in other words, if you want a Windows executable, you'll need to build it on Windows; if you want a Linux executable, you'll have to build it on Linux, and so on.

Complete documentation on `cx_Freeze` can be found at `https://cx-freeze.readthedocs.io`.

First steps with cx_Freeze

Install `cx_Freeze` using `pip` as shown in the following command:

```
$ pip install --user cx-Freeze
```

Linux users may also need to install the `patchelf` utility, generally available in your distribution's package manager.

Like setuptools, cx_Freeze is an extension of distutils; it shares many similarities with setuptools, but as you'll see, it takes a different approach to solving certain problems. Just like setuptools, we'll start with a script in the project directory that calls the setup() function. To distinguish this script from our setuptools script, we'll call it cxsetup.py. Open this file and enter the following:

```
# cxsetup.py

import cx_Freeze as cx

cx.setup(
    name='ABQ_Data_Entry',
    version='1.0',
    author='Alan D Moore',
    author_email='alandmoore@example.com',
    description='Data entry application for ABQ Agrilabs',
    url="http://abq.example.com",
    packages=['abq_data_entry'],
)
```

So far, this is identical to a setuptools script apart from us using the cx_Freeze. setup() function instead of the setuptools one. From here, though, things will diverge considerably.

Where setuptools uses the entry_points argument, cx_Freeze uses an executables argument. This argument takes a list of cx_Freeze.Execcutable objects, each of which describes various attributes of an executable file we want to generate. Add the following code that does this for ABQ Data Entry:

```
cx.setup(
    #...
    executables=[
      cx.Executable(
        'abq_data_entry/__main__.py',
        target_name='abq',
        icon='abq.ico'
        )
      ],
)
```

At a minimum, we need to provide a Python script that should be executed when the executable will run; we're using our abq_data_entry/__main__.py script for this purpose.

By default, the generated executable will be the script name without the `.py` extension. In this case, that would be __main__, which is not a terribly descriptive name for our application. Fortunately, we can override this default with the `target_name` argument, as we've done here. By specifying abq here, cx_Freeze will build an executable file called abq.

We can also specify an icon to use for the application using the `icon` argument. This needs to be a path to a `.ico` file, so you'll need to convert PNG or other formats to `.ico` before using them. The path to the file is relative to the project directory where the `cxsetup.py` file is, and does not need to be inside the package itself.

The build_exe options

Arguments to specific cx_Freeze operations can be passed into setup() using the `options` argument. This argument takes a dictionary in which each item is a cx_Freeze operation name paired with a dict object of operation-specific arguments. The first operation we're going to look at is build_exe, which is a universal first step for all other operations. As the name implies, this is the stage where the executable and its accompanying files are built.

Among other things, this is where we specify the package dependencies:

```
cx.setup(
    #...
    options={
        'build_exe': {
            'packages': [
                'psycopg2', 'requests',
                'matplotlib', 'numpy',
                'paramiko'
            ],
            'includes': [],
```

The packages argument is a list of the packages that need to be installed. It's similar to the install_requires argument for setuptools, with the important difference that it does not support version specifiers. Also, note that we've included some things beyond our three main dependencies. Unfortunately, because cx_Freeze doesn't always do a great job at identifying all the dependencies, it's often necessary to explicitly list sub-dependencies.

Where packages is a list of the packages that should be included, we can also specify specific *modules* to be included using the includes argument. In theory, we shouldn't need to specify anything here, but in practice cx_Freeze sometimes fails to bundle modules that our program needs.

Using the `includes` directive, we can explicitly request modules to ensure that they are included.

To figure out what should go in the list, follow a basic trial-and-error procedure:

1. Build the executable.
2. Run the executable.
3. If you get a `ModuleNotFoundError` exception stating that a module cannot be found, add the module to the `includes` list and run the build command again.
4. If you find several modules from the same package are missing, it may be more effective to add the package to the `packages` list and rebuild.

For example, suppose you build ABQ Data Entry and get the following error when running abq:

```
ModuleNotFoundError: No module named 'zlib'
```

In this situation, `zlib` would be a dependency of one of our required packages that for some reason `cx_Freeze` did not identify as necessary. To fix this, we would simply force its inclusion by updating the configuration:

```
cx.setup(
  #...
  options={
    'build_exe': {
      #...
      'includes': ['zlib'],
```

After that, a rebuilt executable should include the missing module. Generally, you don't need to do this for widely used modules, but depending on your platform and the packages you require, these issues do come up.

Including external files

As with `setuptools`, `cx_Freeze` only includes Python files by default. To get other files like images and documentation included, we can use the `include_files` argument to `build_exe`. However, there is a problem: because of the way that `cx_Freeze` bundles our Python module in a compressed archive, accessing file paths inside the module takes some extra code.

Our `images` module presents such a problem: it contains PNG files that our application accesses by calculating a relative path from its `__init__.py` file.

To address the issue, the PNG files will need to be relocated to a directory outside the package during the build process. Our code will then have to find them in the new location when it's been frozen, and in the original location when not.

To make it work, modify images/__init__.py as follows:

```
# abq_data_entry/images/__init__.py

from pathlib import Path
import sys

if getattr(sys, 'frozen', False):
  IMAGE_DIRECTORY = Path(sys.executable).parent / 'images'
else:
  IMAGE_DIRECTORY = Path(__file__).parent / 'images'
```

When running a Python script that has been frozen using cx_Freeze, the sys module has an attribute called frozen. We can test for the presence of this attribute to specify behavior that changes when the app is frozen. In this case, when our app is frozen, we're going to look for our images in an images directory located in the same directory as the executable file. The location of the executable can be found from the sys.executable variable. If the application is not frozen, we'll look for the images in the module directory as before.

Now that the script knows where to look for the images, we need to configure our cx_Freeze setup to copy the images into the location we set. To do that, we need to update our build_exe options like so:

```
# cxsetup.py

cx.setup(
  #...
  options={
    'build_exe': {
      #...
      'include_files': [('abq_data_entry/images', 'images')]
```

The include_files argument is a list of two-tuples. The first tuple member is a source path relative to the cxsetup.py script, while the second is a destination path relative to the executable file. In this case, we're telling it to copy the files in the abq_data_entry/images directory to a directory called images in the generated executable directory.

Building executables

At this point, we can build an executable by running the following command line:

```
$ python cxsetup.py build
```

The `build` command runs all steps up to `build_exe`, leaving you with the built code in a platform-specific directory under `./build` in the format `exe.(os)-(cpu_arch)-(python_version)`. For example, if you ran this command on 64-bit Linux with Python 3.9, you'd have a `build/exe.linux-x86_64-3.9` directory containing the compiled code. You can inspect this directory to make sure files are being copied over and created properly, as well as testing the generated executable binary file. In the case of our application, `cx_Freeze` should have created a binary executable file called `abq`, which will launch your application when run. It should also have created `lib` and `images` directories, and copied the `abq.ico` file.

 Note that all files in the platform-specific build directory must be present for the program to run; `cx_Freeze` does not support the creation of single-file standalone executables.

For Linux and BSD, this build directory can be zipped up and distributed as is; users on other computers should be able to just extract the directory and execute the file. For Windows and macOS, though, we're going to need to do some more work to get it ready for distribution. In fact, you may even have gotten an error running the build command or executing the binary. We'll talk about the platform-specific tweaks and configurations that need to happen in the next section.

 `cx_Freeze` supports the creation of RPM files, the package format used by certain Linux distributions such as Fedora or SUSE. If you're on an RPM-based distribution, you may want to investigate this option. Unfortunately, there is no build operation to build packages for non-RPM distributions such as Debian, Ubuntu, or Arch.

Cleaning up the build

Although we have a working executable file, you might have noticed that the distributable folder is extremely large for such a simple project as ours.

Before calling it a day, it's worth poking around inside the build directories to see what files cx_Freeze is bundling into your application and whether you really need all of it.

If you look in the platform-specific build directory under lib/python(python_version)/, you'll find all the libraries that were pulled in as dependencies of our package. You may find that some of these aren't actually necessary for running our application. For example, if you happen to have alternative GUI libraries like PyQt or PySide installed on your system, matplotlib may pull them in as dependencies.

If we do end up with extra packages like this, we can remove them using the excludes option of build_exe, like this:

```
cx.setup(
  #...
  options={
    #...
    'build_exe': {
      #...
      'excludes': [
        'PyQt4', 'PyQt5', 'PySide', 'IPython', 'jupyter_client',
        'jupyter_core', 'ipykernel','ipython_genutils'
      ],
```

After adding this change, delete your build directory and rerun the build command. You'll see that all these packages are no longer there, and the size of your build is significantly smaller.

Knowing what can be included or excluded takes research and some trial and error, but with careful pruning we can bring down the size of our distributable files and the build time for our package considerably.

Building Windows executables with cx_Freeze

To build executables on Microsoft Windows, we need to properly set the base argument to the Executable initializer. Recall from *Chapter 10*, *Maintaining Cross-Platform Compatibility*, that Windows programs launch in either console or GUI mode. For each platform, cx_Freeze has one or more base executables from which it builds the frozen executable; on Linux, BSD, and macOS the default base executable is acceptable, but on Windows the default base launches the application in console mode.

We need to specify a base that will launch our script in GUI mode instead. This can be done by passing a value of `Win32GUI` to the `base` argument. So, at the top of our `cxsetup.py` script, add this code:

```python
# cxsetup.py
import platform
base = None
target_name = 'abq'

if platform.system() == "Windows":
  base = "Win32GUI"

# Inside cx.setup()
  #...
  executables=[
    cx.Executable(
      'abq_data_entry.py',
      base=base,
      target_name=target_name,
      icon='abq.ico'
    )
  ],
```

As we learned to do in *Chapter 10*, *Maintaining Cross-Platform Compatibility*, we've used `platform.system()` to determine the operating system we're running on; if it's Windows, we'll set the base to `Win32GUI`. For other platforms, `base` should just be `None`, causing it to use the default base executable.

The application should now build successfully on Windows using `python cxsetup.py build`, and you should find `abq.exe` in the `build/exe.win-amd64-(python_version)` directory.

Building a Windows installer file

In addition to building a Windows executable, we can build a Windows installer file (`.msi`) using the `bdist_msi` operation. While our application could be distributed as is by simply zipping up the build folder and extracting it on the target system, there are a few advantages to using MSI files:

- MSI files can be more easily deployed by system administrators in a large-scale Windows environment.
- MSI files register the application with the OS when installed, making operations like upgrades, repairs, and uninstallations cleaner.

- MSI files have additional setup capabilities, such as an install wizard and desktop shortcut generation.

To get started generating an MSI file with `cx_Freeze`, we'll need to configure some aspects of our MSI by setting values in the `bdist_msi` dictionary of the `options` argument.

We'll start by specifying an **upgrade code**:

```
cx.setup(
  #...
  options = {
    #...
    'bdist_msi': {
      'upgrade_code': '{12345678-90AB-CDEF-1234-567890ABCDEF}',
```

The upgrade code is a **globally unique identifier** (GUID) value that will identify this program on the OS. By specifying this, subsequent builds of this `.msi` file will remove and replace any existing installations of the same program.

Upgrade codes consist of five segments of 8, 4, 4, 4, and 12 characters from 0 to 9 and A to F. They can be created in Microsoft Visual Studio, or using this PowerShell command:

```
[System.Guid]::NewGuid().ToString().ToUpper()
```

Once specified, you should not change the upgrade code in subsequent builds of your application.

The MSI installation process can also create application shortcuts, which will be placed on the desktop and/or programs menu when the package is installed. To do this, we'll need to define our shortcuts by creating a list of **shortcut table** tuples like these:

```
# cxsetup.py, after the imports

shortcut_data = [
  (
    'DesktopShortcut', 'DesktopFolder', 'ABQ Data Entry',
    'TARGETDIR', '[TARGETDIR]' + target_name, None,
    'Data Entry application for ABQ Agrilabs', None,
    None, None, None, 'TARGETDIR'
  ),
```

```
    (
        'MenuShortcut', 'ProgramMenuFolder', 'ABQ Data Entry',
        'TARGETDIR', '[TARGETDIR]' + target_name, None,
        'Data Entry application for ABQ Agrilabs', None,
        None, None, None, 'TARGETDIR'
    )
]
```

The preceding two tuples define a shortcut for the desktop and menu, respectively. The data contained in them matches the shortcut table layout described by Microsoft at https://msdn.microsoft.com/en-us/library/windows/desktop/aa371847.aspx.

Those fields, in order, are defined by Microsoft as follows:

- **Shortcut**: The type of shortcut to create; in our case either DesktopShortcut or MenuShortcut.

- **Directory**: A special directory key into which the shortcut will be copied. Here, DesktopFolder points to the desktop, and ProgramMenuFolder points to the programs folder in the menu.

- **Name**: The name of the shortcut; in our case, ABQ Data Entry.

- **Component**: This indicates a program whose installed or uninstalled state determines whether our shortcut should be installed or uninstalled. By specifying TARGETDIR, the install/uninstall state of our shortcuts matches the install/uninstall state of the program directory.

- **Target**: The executable file that is launched by the shortcut. This will be our target_name attribute, located inside TARGETDIR.

- **Arguments**: A string of arguments passed to the command. Whatever you specify here is simply appended to the target executable for the shortcut and available in our program from sys.argv. You might use this to, for example, create a second shortcut that launches your application in a test mode. In our case, the ABQ program expects no command-line arguments, so this is None.

- **Description**: A string used in the description field of the shortcut.

- **Icon** and **IconIndex**: These are used to locate an icon for the shortcut, if we want it to be different from the icon of the executable. These can be left as None since our executable's icon will be used by default.

- **ShowCmd**: Specifies if the program will be launched minimized, maximized, or normally. Leaving this as None will launch it normally.

- **WkDir**: Indicates the working directory to be used. We want this to be the program's directory, so we use TARGETDIR here.

Once created, these shortcut tables need to be included in the data argument of our `bdist_msi` options, like so:

```
cx.setup(
  #...
  options={
  #...
    'bdist_msi': {
      #...
      'data': {'Shortcut': shortcut_data}
```

Currently, `data` is not documented in the `cx_Freeze` documentation; `cx_Freeze` uses the standard library's `msilib` module to build the `.msi` files, and anything passed into this argument is passed along to the `add_data()` function of `msilib`. Refer to the standard library documentation for `msilib` at `https://docs.python.org/3/library/msilib.html` if you're interested in exploring this option further.

With the `bdist_msi` options specified, let's build the `.msi` file as follows:

```
$ python cxsetup.py bdist_msi
```

This command creates a new installer file in the `dist` directory, which you should be able to install on any compatible Windows system, as shown in the following screenshot:

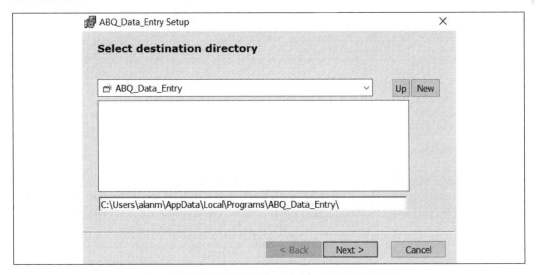

Figure 16.1: The MSI install wizard for ABQ Data Entry

Keep in mind that cx_Freeze uses Python binaries from your build environment in the application build; as a result, 64-bit Python will build a 64-bit executable, and 32-bit Python will build a 32-bit executable. Additionally, builds created on newer versions of Windows may not be compatible with older versions of Windows. For maximum compatibility, build your binaries on a 32-bit version of the oldest release of Windows you plan to support.

Building macOS executables with cx_Freeze

There are two build operations that cx_Freeze implements that are specific to macOS: bdist_mac and bdist_dmg. These operations create an **application bundle** and a **compressed disk image** file, respectively. Let's look at each operation in more detail.

Building macOS application bundles

The bdist_mac build operation creates an application bundle, a specially formatted directory with an .app extension that the Mac desktop treats as though it were an executable file. bdist_mac has several configuration options, but we're only going to use two:

```
cx.setup(
  #...
  options={
    #...
    'bdist_mac': {
      'bundle_name': 'ABQ-Data-Entry',
      'iconfile': 'abq.icns'
    }
```

Here, bundle_name sets the name of our application bundle directory, without the .app extension. Normally, this would default to the name argument passed to setup(), which in our case is ABQ_Data_Entry. We're overriding it here to use dashes instead of underscores, as it looks a little less technical for end users. Note that using spaces in this value, while technically valid, tends to create problems for cx_Freeze and is best avoided. The iconfile setting allows us to point to an ICNS file that macOS will use for the application's icon. The dimensions of this image file need to be a square number of pixels that is a power of 2 between 16 and 1,024. A compatible ABQ logo is included in the example code.

Refer to the cx_Freeze documentation for additional options here, which include code signing and explicitly specifying additional frameworks for the bundle.

Once your configuration options are added, run the `cxsetup.py` script by using the following command:

```
$ python3 cxsetup.py bdist_mac
```

When this process completes, `ABQ-Data-Entry.app` should appear in the build directory. You can double-click this directory in the macOS GUI to run it from any location, or drag it to the `/Applications` directory to install it.

It should appear something like what is shown in the following screenshot:

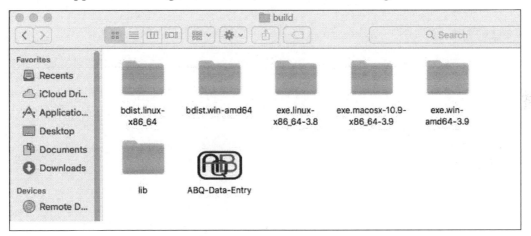

Figure 16.2: ABQ-Data-Entry bundle in the build directory

If you launch the application from this bundle, you'll see that the app menu no longer reads **Python**, as we first saw in *Chapter 10, Maintaining Cross-Platform Compatibility*; it now reads **abq**, the name of the executable file, which is what we want.

 As with Windows executables, `cx_Freeze`-generated bundles for macOS are not necessarily backward-compatible, so it's best to create them on the oldest version of macOS that you need to support.

Building macOS .dmg files

Applications on macOS are generally distributed inside a compressed disk image (`.dmg`) file. The `cx_Freeze` `build_dmg` operation allows you to build an application bundle and package it in a DMG file for easy distribution.

To do this, simply execute this command instead of the bdist_mac command:

```
$ python3 cxsetup.py bdist_dmg
```

This command first runs bdist_mac to build the application bundle and then packages it into a DMG file. The configuration options for bdist_dmg allow you to override the filename and include a shortcut to the /Applications directory for easy installation. The built file will appear in the build directory, from which you can copy it to another Macintosh to be mounted and used.

Summary

In this chapter, you learned how to prepare and package your application for distribution. You learned how to make your package executable, and how to use setuptools to create source and built distributions of it for internal use within your organization or for distribution in a public index such as PyPI. You also learned how to use cx_Freeze to convert your Python script into an executable file that can be distributed to other systems without installing Python or dependent packages, and how to make application installation packages for Windows and macOS.

Congratulations on finishing this book! Together we've taken a simple CSV file and turned it into a complex and robust graphical application. You now have the knowledge and confidence to create user-friendly GUI applications that work with files, databases, networks, and APIs across all major platforms.

As for your career with ABQ, you've just received a promotion offer to work with the corporate office as a software developer. There will be much more to learn, but with the skills you've learned so far you are ready for whatever challenges come next. Good luck!

Appendices

A

A Quick Primer on reStructuredText

When it comes to writing software documentation, software developers generally prefer to use a **lightweight markup language** over binary formats such as DOCX or other word processor files. Such languages aim to provide a standardized way of notating basic rich-text features like bullet lists, emphasized text, section headings, tables, and inline code within the limits of a plaintext file, while remaining human-readable. Documents written in lightweight markup languages can be read as-is, or compiled into other formats like PDF, DOCX, or HTML.

This approach has several advantages over the use of binary word processor files:

- The documentation can be treated like code: it can be edited with the code editor and easily managed with tools like a **Version Control System** (**VCS**).

- The documentation has universal access: it can be read from any system with a text editor, or even from a terminal prompt.

- The writing process is less distracting: as markup languages typically focus on semantic objects like headings, paragraphs, tables, and so forth rather than cosmetic concerns like colors, font faces, or text size, the developer is less distracted with appearance details and more focused on organization and correct information.

In the 1990s and earlier, developers tended to use various ASCII-art contrivances to convey rich-text features visually, such as tables made of pipes and underscores, bullet lists made with asterisks, or headings denoted with a second line of dashes. In the early 2000s, several projects worked to formalize and define these structures and develop tools that would allow developers to compile their markup into binary rich-text formats for distribution or publication.

 This book was actually written in a code editor using a markup language, and then subsequently converted by scripts to the format required by the publisher.

The reStructuredText markup language

Though several markup language options exist, the Python community tends to prefer **reStructuredText** (**RST**). The reStructuredText markup language is part of the Python Docutils project, located at `http://docutils.sourceforge.net`. The Docutils project develops the RST standard and provides utilities for converting RST to formats like PDF, ODT, HTML, and LaTeX.

Document structure

RST is geared toward the creation of structured documents; as such, the first thing we should create is a title for our document. This is denoted using a line of symbols above and below a single line of text, like so:

```
==========================
The reStructuredText saga
==========================
```

In this case, we've used the equals sign on either side of the title to denote it as our document title. We can also add a subtitle by adding another line underlined with a different symbol:

```
==========================
The reStructuredText saga
==========================
An adventure in markup languages.
---------------------------------
```

The exact symbols used here are not important; they can be any of the following:

```
! " # $ % & ' ( ) * + , - . / : ; < = > ? @ [ \ ] ^ _ ` { | } ~
```

What establishes one as a title and the other as a subtitle is the order. Whichever symbol we choose to use first in the document will become the top-level title. Whichever we use second will become a second-level title, and so on. By convention, the equals sign is typically used for level one, the hyphen for level two, the tilde for level three, and the plus symbol for level four. This is only convention, however; within a document, the hierarchy is determined by the order in which you use the symbols.

We can write titles without the top line of symbols as well, like so:

```
Chapter 1
=========
```

While not required, this style is usually preferred for section titles over the document title. The document title is denoted by creating a top-level section header with no content inside, whereas regular section headers have content.

For example, they can contain paragraphs of text. Paragraphs in RST are indicated by a blank line between blocks of text, like so:

```
Long ago the world had many markup languages, but they were ugly, and
hard to read in plain-text.

Then, one day, everything changed...
```

Note that paragraphs should not be indented. Indenting a line of text would indicate some other structure, as we'll see below.

Lists

RST is capable of denoting both bullet and number lists, both of which can contain nested lists.

Bullet lists are created by starting a line with any of *, -, or + followed by a space, as shown here:

```
Lightweight markup languages include:

- reStructuredText
- emacs org-mode
- markdown
```

To create a sub-list, simply indent two spaces, like so:

```
Lightweight markup languages include:

- reStructuredText

  - released in 2002
  - widely used in Python

- emacs org-mode

  + released in 2003
  + included with the emacs editor

- markdown

  * released in 2004
  * Several variants exist,
    including Github-flavored,
    markdown extra, and multimarkdown.
```

Note that the actual symbol used for the list doesn't have any syntactic meaning, though it can be helpful for plaintext readers to distinguish sub-lists. Also notice that we've created a multi-line bullet point (the last point under markdown) by indenting the subsequent lines to the same indent as the text in the first line of the bullet.

Note the blank lines before the first point in the list, and around each sub-list. Lists should always have a blank line before the first item in the list and after the last. Lists can optionally contain blank lines between their bullet points, which is sometimes helpful for readability.

Numbered lists are created like bullet lists, but using either digits or the # symbol, followed by a dot, as a bullet; for example:

```
Take these steps to use RST:

#. Learn RST
#. Write a document in RST
#. Install docutils:

  1. Open a terminal
```

```
   2. type pip install docutils
#. Convert your RST to another format using a command-line utility:

   * rst2pdf converts to PDF
   * rst2html converts to HTML
   * rst2odt converts to ODT
```

While the # symbol is not very helpful to plaintext readers, conversion programs will automatically generate a numbered list in this case. Note that we can nest numbered lists or bullet lists within this numbered list.

Character styles

With reStructuredText we can denote a variety of inline character styles, the most common of which are emphasis, strong emphasis, and inline literals.

This is done by surrounding the text with particular symbols, as shown in this table:

Syntax	Use for	Typical rendering
`*Single asterisks indicate emphasized text*`	Mild emphasis	Italic text
`**Double asterisks are for strongly emphasized text**`	Strong emphasis	Bold text
`` ``Double backticks are for inline literals`` ``	Literal examples, such as code	Monospace text, inline whitespace preserved

Note that there should be no space between the symbol and the text being marked up.

Blocks and quotes

When documenting code, it's quite common that we might need to include a block quote from some other source. Simple block quotes can be done in RST by indenting a paragraph with four spaces, like so:

```
In the immortal words of my late, great uncle Fred,

    Please pass the banana pudding!

Heaven rest his soul.
```

In situations where we need to preserve whitespace like indentation and line breaks, we can use a **line block**, in which each line begins with a vertical bar and a space. For example:

```
A banana haiku:

| In a skin of gold
|     To be peeled and discarded –
|     Pale treasure awaits.
```

While your documentation may contain a handful of poems or literary quotes, it's far more likely to need code blocks. A code block in RST is indicated by an indented block preceded by a paragraph containing only a double colon, like so:

```
The Fibonacci series can be calculated in
a generator function like so:

::

    def fibonacci():
        a, b = 0, 1
        while True:
            b, a = a + b, b
            yield a
```

Within a code block, whitespace will be preserved (ignoring the initial indent, of course), and no RST markup will be interpreted, just as you would expect for quoting actual code.

Tables

Tables are commonly needed in documentation, and RST provides two ways of denoting them. The simpler but more limited approach looks like this:

```
===== ============= ===========================
Fruit Variety       Description
===== ============= ===========================
Apple Gala          Sweet and flavorful
Apple Fuji          Crisp and tangy, yet sweet
Apple Red Delicious Large, bland, insipid
===== ============= ===========================
```

Using this syntax, we arrange the data in columns using spaces, and surround the table and header row with = symbols. An empty space through the whole table denotes a column break. Note that the symbols must extend as wide as the width of the longest cell. This syntax is limited in that it cannot represent multi-line cells or cells that span multiple rows or columns.

For that, we can use the more verbose table format:

```
+----------+-----------+----------------------------------+
| Fruit    | Variety   | Description                      |
+==========+===========+==================================+
| Orange   | All varieties are sweet with orange rind |
+          +-----------+----------------------------------+
|          | Navel     | Seedless, thick skin             |
+          +-----------+----------------------------------+
|          | Valencia  | Thin skin, very juicy            |
+          +-----------+----------------------------------+
|          | Blood     | Smaller, red inside              |
+----------+-----------+----------------------------------+
```

In this format, the table cells are defined using hyphens and pipes, with plus symbols at the corners of each cell. A cell can be made to span multiple rows or columns by simply omitting the border characters between them. For example, in the above table, the cell containing Orange extends to the bottom of the table, and the first row under the header spans the second and third columns. Note that table headers are denoted by using an equals symbol rather than a hyphen.

> Tables can be tedious to create in a plaintext editor, but some programming tools have plugins to generate RST tables. If you plan to make a lot of tables in an RST document, you may want to see if your editor has a tool for this.

Converting RST to other formats

If nothing else, following the reStructuredText syntax leads to a very readable and expressive plaintext file. However, the real power in using a standardized markup language is in converting it to other formats.

The docutils package, available in PyPI, comes with several command-line utilities for converting RST files. The more useful ones are listed here:

Command	Format	Format description
rst2html	Hypertext Markup Language (HTML)	Standard markup language for the web, useful for publishing to a website.
rst2html5	Hypertext Markup Language version 5 (HTML 5)	More modern version of HTML, preferred for web use.
rst2pdf	Portable Document Format (PDF)	Good for printable documents, or for distributing read-only documentation.
rst2odt	Open Document Text (ODT)	Word processing format, useful when you want to do further editing in a word processor.
rst2latex	LaTeX markup language	Very powerful markup language often used in scientific publications.
rst2man	MAN page markup	Markup used by UNIX man pages. Useful for documentation on Linux, BSD, or macOS.
rst2s5	Simple standards-based slideshow system (S5)	HTML-based slideshow format. Good for presentations.

To use any of these commands, simply call it with the name of the RST file.

Depending on the command, an output file can be specified by either an -o switch or as a second positional argument, for example:

```
# uses the -o switch
  rst2pdf README.rst -o README.pdf
# uses the positional argument
  rst2html5 README.rst README.html
```

The scripts interpret the markup in the RST file and build a nicely formatted PDF or HTML file. You can try these commands on the README.rst file included with the example code for this appendix, which is a README for the binary release of ABQ Data Entry. For example, if you render a default HTML file, it will look something like this in your browser:

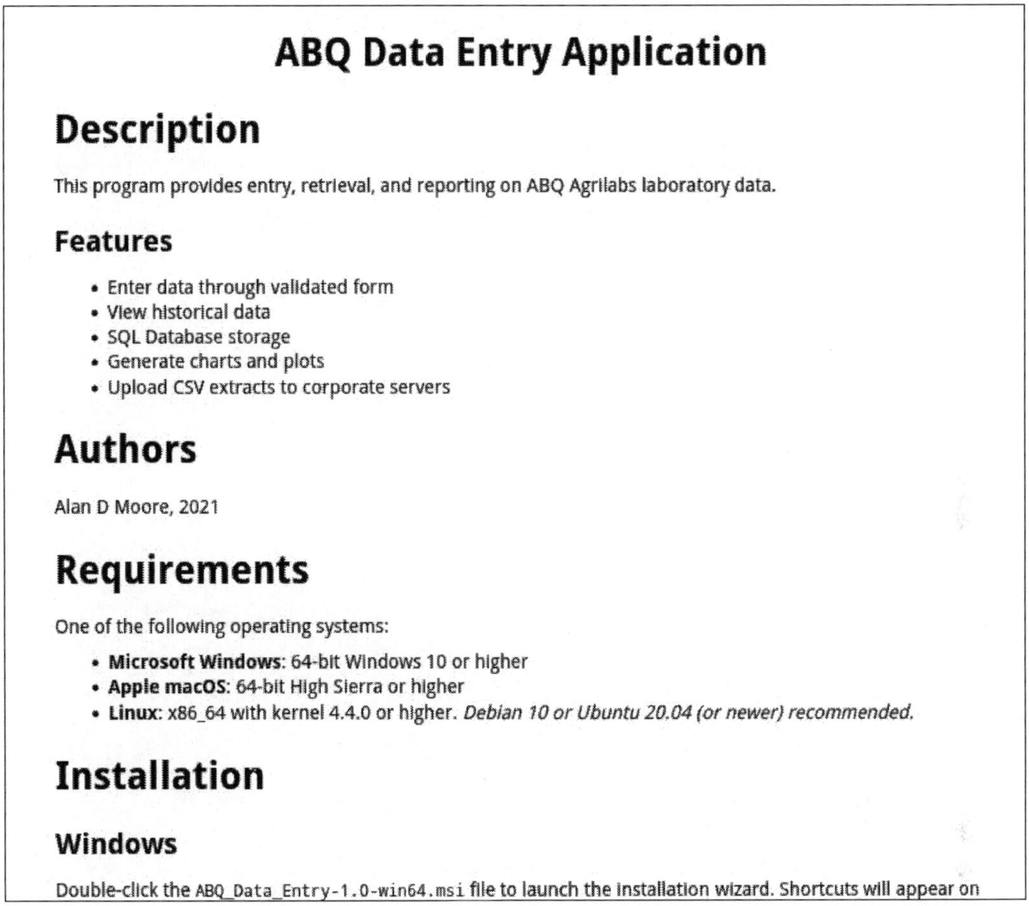

ABQ Data Entry Application

Description

This program provides entry, retrieval, and reporting on ABQ Agrilabs laboratory data.

Features

- Enter data through validated form
- View historical data
- SQL Database storage
- Generate charts and plots
- Upload CSV extracts to corporate servers

Authors

Alan D Moore, 2021

Requirements

One of the following operating systems:

- **Microsoft Windows**: 64-bit Windows 10 or higher
- **Apple macOS**: 64-bit High Sierra or higher
- **Linux**: x86_64 with kernel 4.4.0 or higher. *Debian 10 or Ubuntu 20.04 (or newer) recommended.*

Installation

Windows

Double-click the `ABQ_Data_Entry-1.0-win64.msi` file to launch the installation wizard. Shortcuts will appear on

Figure A.1: Default HTML5 rendering of README.rst

Each command has a large number of options available, which you can view by calling the command with the `--help` switch, like so:

```
$ rst2html5 --help
```

For example, the `rst2html` command allows us to specify a CSS style sheet that will be embedded into the generated HTML file. We can use that to change the look of our generated document, like so:

```
$ rst2html5 --stylesheet abq_stylesheet.css  README.rst README.abq.html
```

An `abq_stylesheet.css` file is included with the example code for this book, though you can create your own if you know CSS. If you used the bundled file, the resulting HTML looks like this in the browser:

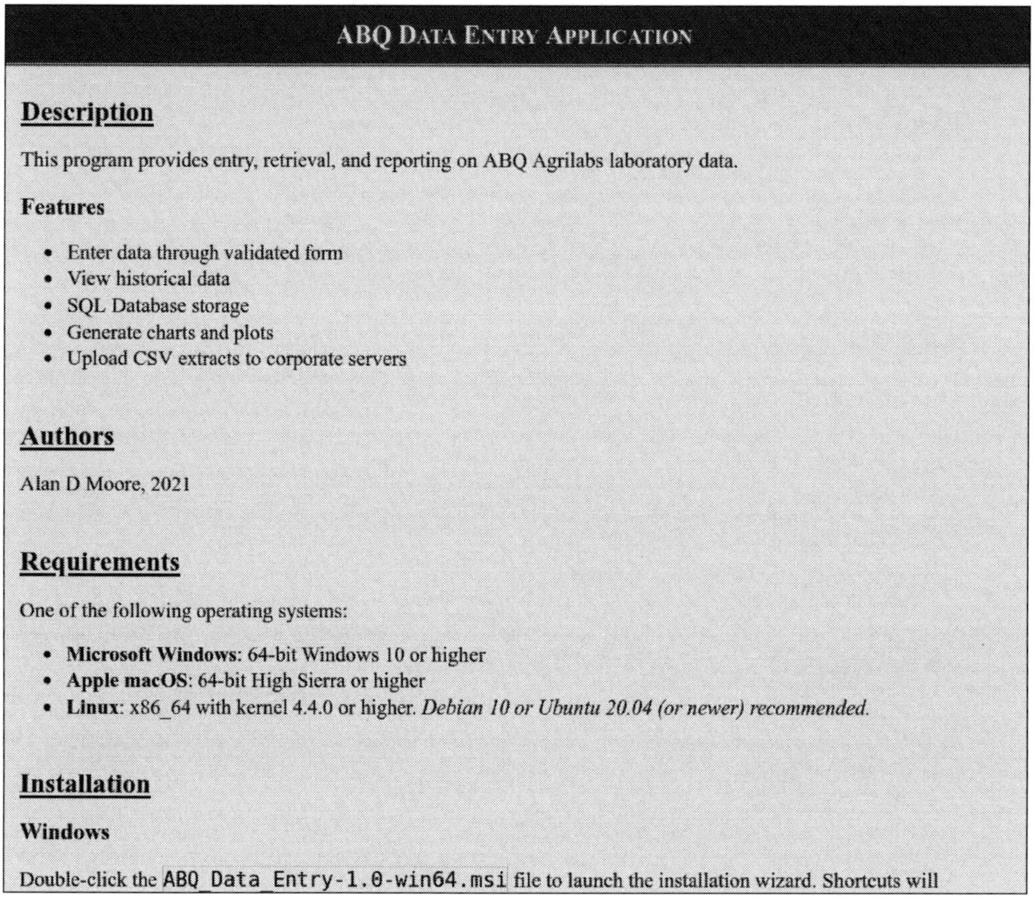

ABQ DATA ENTRY APPLICATION

Description

This program provides entry, retrieval, and reporting on ABQ Agrilabs laboratory data.

Features

- Enter data through validated form
- View historical data
- SQL Database storage
- Generate charts and plots
- Upload CSV extracts to corporate servers

Authors

Alan D Moore, 2021

Requirements

One of the following operating systems:

- **Microsoft Windows**: 64-bit Windows 10 or higher
- **Apple macOS**: 64-bit High Sierra or higher
- **Linux**: x86_64 with kernel 4.4.0 or higher. *Debian 10 or Ubuntu 20.04 (or newer) recommended.*

Installation

Windows

Double-click the `ABQ_Data_Entry-1.0-win64.msi` file to launch the installation wizard. Shortcuts will

Figure A.2: The README.rst file, but with a style sheet added

Other ways to render RST

In addition to `docutils`, there are other tools that can make use of an RST file:

- The `pandoc` utility, available from `https://pandoc.org`, can convert RST files to a wider variety of output formats with a number of additional rendering options.

- Many popular code-sharing services like GitHub, GitLab, and Bitbucket will automatically render RST files to HTML for display in their web interfaces.

- The Sphinx project, available from `https://sphinx-doc.org`, is a comprehensive documentation generator for Python projects. It can generate complete documentation for your project by rendering RST it finds in docstrings, README files, and other documentation in your code. Sphinx is widely used by Python projects, including the official Python documentation at `https://docs.python.org`.

Since RST is widely accepted as the standard for Python documentation, you can safely assume that any documentation-oriented tools for Python will expect to work with it.

 This tutorial only scratched the surface of reStructuredText syntax! For a quick syntax reference, see `https://docutils.sourceforge.io/docs/user/rst/quickref.html`. For complete documentation, see `https://docutils.sourceforge.io/rst.html`.

B

A Quick SQL Tutorial

For over three decades, relational database systems have remained a de facto standard for storing business data. They are more commonly known as SQL databases, after the **Structured Query Language (SQL)** used to interact with them. Although a full treatment of SQL warrants a book of its own, this appendix will provide a brief coverage of its basic concepts and syntax that will be adequate for following its usage in this book.

SQL concepts

SQL databases are made up of **tables**. A table is something like a CSV or spreadsheet file, in that it has rows representing individual items and columns representing data values associated with each item. A SQL table has some important differences from a spreadsheet, though:

- First, each column in the table is assigned a **data type**, which is strictly enforced. Just as Python will produce an error when you try to convert "abcd" to an int or 0.03 into a date, a SQL database will return an error if you try to insert letters into a numeric column or decimal values into a date column. SQL databases typically support basic data types like text, numbers, dates and times, Boolean values, and binary data; in addition, some implementations have specialized data types for things like IP addresses, JSON data, currency, or images.

- SQL tables can also have **constraints**, which further enforce the validity of data inserted into the table. For example, a column can be given a **unique constraint**, which prevents two rows from having the same value in that column, or a **not null** constraint, which means that every row must have a value.

SQL databases commonly contain many tables, and these can be joined together to represent much more complicated data structures. By breaking data into multiple linked tables, we can store it in a way that is much more efficient and resilient than a two-dimensional plaintext CSV file.

Syntax differences from Python

If you've only ever programmed in Python, SQL may feel odd at first, as the rules and syntax are very different. We'll be going over the individual commands and keywords, but here are some general differences from Python:

- SQL is (mostly) **case-insensitive**: Although it's conventional for readability purposes to type the SQL keywords in all caps, most SQL implementations are not case-sensitive. There are a few small exceptions here and there, but, for the most part, you can type SQL in whatever case is easiest for you.

- **Whitespace** is not significant: In Python, new lines and indentation can change the meaning of a piece of code. In SQL, whitespace is not significant and statements are terminated with a semicolon. Indents and new lines in a query are only there for readability.

- SQL is **declarative**: Python could be described as an **imperative programming language**: we tell Python what we want it to do by telling it how to do it. SQL is more of a declarative language: we *describe* what we want done, and the SQL engine figures out how to do it.

We'll encounter additional syntax differences as we look at specific SQL code examples.

SQL operations and syntax

SQL is a powerful and expressive language for doing mass manipulations of tabular data, but the basics can be grasped quickly. SQL code is executed as individual queries that either define, manipulate, or select data in the database. SQL dialects vary somewhat between different relational database products, but most of them support **ANSI/ISO-standard SQL** for core operations.

While most of the basic concepts and keywords covered here will work across SQL implementations, we'll be using PostgreSQL's dialect for the examples in this section. If you wish to try these examples on a different SQL implementation, be prepared to make some adjustments to the syntax.

To follow along with this section, connect to an empty database on your PostgreSQL database server, either using the psql command-line tool, the pgAdmin graphical tool, or another database client software of your choosing.

Defining tables and inserting data

SQL tables are created using the CREATE TABLE command, as shown in the following SQL query:

```
CREATE TABLE musicians (
  id SERIAL PRIMARY KEY,
  name TEXT NOT NULL,
  born DATE,
  died DATE CHECK(died > born)
);
```

In this example, we're creating a table called musicians. After the name, we specify a list of column definitions. Each column definition follows the format column_name data_type constraints.

Let's break down the details of these columns we've defined:

- The id column will be an arbitrary ID value for the row. Its type is SERIAL, which means it will be an auto-incrementing integer field, and its constraint is PRIMARY KEY, which means it will be used as the unique identifier for the row.

- The name field is of type TEXT, so it can hold a string of any length. Its constraint of NOT NULL means that a NULL value is not allowed in this field.

- The born and died fields are of type DATE, so they can only hold a date value.

- The born field has no constraints but died has a CHECK constraint enforcing that its value must be greater than the value of born for any given row.

Although it's not required, it's a good practice to specify a **primary key** for each table. Primary keys can be one field, or a combination of fields, but the value must be unique for any given row. For example, if we made name the primary key field, we couldn't have two musicians with the same name in our table.

To add rows of data to this table, we use the INSERT INTO command as follows:

```
INSERT INTO musicians (name, born, died)
VALUES
  ('Robert Fripp','1946-05-16', NULL),
  ('Keith Emerson', '1944-11-02', '2016-03-11'),
  ('Greg Lake', '1947-11-10', '2016-12-7'),
  ('Bill Bruford', '1949-05-17', NULL),
  ('David Gilmour', '1946-03-06', NULL);
```

The INSERT INTO command takes a table name and an optional list specifying the fields to receive data; other fields will receive their default value (NULL if not otherwise specified in the CREATE statement). The VALUES keyword indicates that a list of data values will follow, formatted as a comma-separated list of tuples. Each tuple corresponds to one table row and must match the order of the field list specified after the table name.

Note that strings are delimited by the single quote character. Unlike Python, single quotes and double quotes have different meanings in SQL: a single quote indicates a string literal, while double quotes are used for object names that include spaces or need to preserve case. For example, if we had called our table Musicians of the '70s, we would need to enclose that name in double-quotes due to the spaces, apostrophe, and capitalization.

Using double-quotes to enclose a string literal results in an error, for example:

```
INSERT INTO musicians (name, born, died)
VALUES
  ("Brian May", "1947-07-19", NULL);

-- Produces error:
ERROR:  column "Brian May" does not exist
```

To make our database more interesting, let's create and populate another table; this time, an instruments table:

```
CREATE TABLE instruments (id SERIAL PRIMARY KEY, name TEXT NOT NULL);

INSERT INTO instruments (name)
VALUES ('bass'), ('drums'), ('guitar'), ('keyboards'), ('sax');
```

Note that the VALUES lists must always use parentheses around each row, even if there's only one value per row.

To relate the musicians table to the instruments table, we'll need to add a column to it. Tables can be changed after they are created using the ALTER TABLE command. For example, we can add our new column like this:

```
ALTER TABLE musicians
    ADD COLUMN main_instrument INT REFERENCES instruments(id);
```

The ALTER TABLE command takes a table name, then a command altering some aspect of the table. In this case, we're adding a new column called main_instrument, which will be an integer.

The REFERENCES constraint we've specified is known as a **foreign key constraint**; it limits the possible values of main_instrument to existing ID numbers in the instruments table.

Retrieving data from tables

To retrieve data from tables, we can use a SELECT statement, as follows:

```
SELECT name FROM musicians;
```

The SELECT command takes a column or comma-separated list of columns followed by a FROM clause, which specifies the table or tables containing the specified columns. This query asks for the name column from the musicians table.

Its output is as follows:

name
Bill Bruford
Keith Emerson
Greg Lake
Robert Fripp
David Gilmour

Instead of a list of columns, we can also specify an asterisk, which means "all columns." For example:

```
SELECT * FROM musicians;
```

The preceding SQL query returns the following table of data:

ID	name	born	died	main_instrument
4	Bill Bruford	1949-05-17		
2	Keith Emerson	1944-11-02	2016-03-11	
3	Greg Lake	1947-11-10	2016-12-07	
1	Robert Fripp	1946-05-16		
5	David Gilmour	1946-03-06		

To filter out rows we don't want, we can specify a WHERE clause, like so:

```
SELECT name FROM musicians WHERE died IS NULL;
```

The WHERE command must be followed by a conditional expression that evaluates to True or False; rows for which the expression evaluates True are shown, while rows for which it evaluates False are left out.

In this case, we have asked for the names of musicians for which the died date is NULL. We can specify more complex conditions by combining expressions with the AND and OR operators, like so:

```
SELECT name FROM musicians WHERE born < '1945-01-01' AND died IS NULL;
```

In this case, we would only get musicians born before 1945 who don't have a died date in the database.

The SELECT command can also do operations on fields, or re-order the results by certain columns:

```
SELECT name, age(born), (died - born)/365 AS "age at death"
FROM musicians
ORDER BY born DESC;
```

In this example, we're using the age() function to determine the age of the musicians from their birth dates. We're also doing math on the died and born dates to determine the age at death for those who have passed. Notice that we're using the AS keyword to **alias**, or rename, the generated column.

When you run this query, you should get output like this:

name	age	age at death
Bill Bruford	72 years 4 mons 18 days	
Greg Lake	73 years 10 mons 24 days	69

Robert Fripp	75 years 4 mons 19 days	
David Gilmour	75 years 6 mons 29 days	
Keith Emerson	76 years 11 mons 2 days	71

Notice that age at death is NULL for those without a date of death. Mathematical or logical operations on a NULL value always return an answer of NULL.

The ORDER BY clause specifies a column or list of columns by which the results should be ordered. It also takes an argument of DESC or ASC to specify descending or ascending order, respectively.

We have ordered the output here by date of birth in descending order. Note that each data type has its own rules for sorting data, just like in Python. Dates are ordered by their calendar position, strings by alphabetical order, and numbers by their numeric value.

Updating rows, deleting rows, and more WHERE clauses

To update or delete existing rows, we use the UPDATE and DELETE FROM keywords in conjunction with a WHERE clause to select the affected rows.

Deleting is fairly simple; for example, if we wanted to delete the instrument record with an id value of 5, it would look like this:

```
DELETE FROM instruments WHERE id=5;
```

The DELETE FROM command will delete any rows that match the WHERE conditions. In this case, we match the primary key to ensure only one row is deleted. If no rows match the WHERE conditions, no rows will be deleted. Note, however, that the WHERE clause is technically optional: DELETE FROM instruments will simply delete all rows in the table.

Updating is similar, except it includes a SET clause to specify new column values, as follows:

```
UPDATE musicians SET main_instrument=3 WHERE id=1;
UPDATE musicians SET main_instrument=2 WHERE name='Bill Bruford';
```

Here, we are setting main_instrument in the musicians table to the primary key value from the instruments table that identifies the instrument we want to associate with each musician.

We can select the `musician` records we want to update using the primary key, name, or any combination of conditions. Like `DELETE`, omitting the `WHERE` clause would cause the query to affect all rows.

Any number of columns can be updated in the `SET` clause; for example:

```
UPDATE musicians
  SET main_instrument=4, name='Keith Noel Emerson'
  WHERE name LIKE 'Keith%';
```

Additional columns to be updated are just separated by commas. Note that we've also matched the record using the `LIKE` operator in tandem with the `%` wildcard character. `LIKE` can be used with text and string data types to match partial values. Standard SQL supports two wildcard characters: `%`, which matches zero or more characters, and `_`, which matches a single character.

We can also match against transformed column values:

```
UPDATE musicians SET main_instrument=1 WHERE LOWER (name) LIKE '%lake';
```

Here, we've used the `LOWER` function to match our string against the lowercase version of the column value. This doesn't permanently change the data in the table; it just temporarily changes the value for the purpose of the comparison.

 Standard SQL specifies that `LIKE` is a case-sensitive match. PostgreSQL offers an `ILIKE` operator that does case-insensitive matching, as well as a `SIMILAR TO` operator that matches using more advanced regular expression syntax.

Subqueries

Inserting data using meaningless primary key values is not very user-friendly. To make inserting these values a little more intuitive, we can use a **subquery**, as shown in the following SQL query:

```
UPDATE musicians
SET main_instrument=(
  SELECT id FROM instruments WHERE name='guitar'
)
WHERE name IN ('Robert Fripp', 'David Gilmour');
```

A subquery is a SQL query within a SQL query. If your subquery can be guaranteed to return a single value, it can be used anywhere you would use a literal value.

In this case, we're letting our database do the work of figuring out what the primary key of 'guitar' is, and inserting the returned integer for our main_instrument value.

In the WHERE clause, we've also used the IN operator to match the musician's name. Just like the Python in keyword, this SQL keyword allows us to match against a list of values. IN can be used with a subquery as well; for example:

```
SELECT name FROM musicians
WHERE main_instrument IN (
  SELECT id FROM instruments WHERE name LIKE '%r%'
)
```

In this example, we've asked the database to give us every musician whose main instrument contains the letter "r". Since IN is meant to be used with a list of values, any query that returns a single column with any number of rows is valid. In this case, our subquery returns several rows with only the id column, so it works with IN just fine.

Subqueries that return multiple rows and multiple columns can be used anywhere that a table can be used; for example, we can use a subquery in a FROM clause, like so:

```
SELECT name
FROM (
  SELECT * FROM musicians WHERE died IS NULL
) AS living_musicians;
```

In this case, SQL treats our subquery as though it were a table in the database. Note that subqueries used in a FROM clause require an alias; we've aliased this subquery as living_musicians.

Joining tables

Subqueries are one way of using multiple tables together, but a more flexible and powerful way is to use JOIN. JOIN is used in the FROM clause of a SQL statement, for example:

```
SELECT musicians.name, instruments.name as main_instrument
FROM musicians
  JOIN instruments ON musicians.main_instrument = instrument.id;
```

A JOIN statement requires an ON clause that specifies the conditions used to match rows in each table. The ON clause acts like a filter, much like the WHERE clause does; you can imagine that the JOIN creates a new table containing every possible combination of rows from both tables, then filters out the ones that don't match the ON conditions.

Tables are typically joined by matching the values in common fields, such as those specified in a foreign key constraint. In this case, our musicians.main_instrument column contains the id values from the instrument table, so we can join the two tables based on this.

Joins are used to implement four types of table relationships:

- **One-to-one joins** match exactly one row in the first table to exactly one row in the second.
- **Many-to-one joins** match multiple rows in the first table to exactly one row in the second.
- **One-to-many joins** match one row in the first table to multiple rows in the second.
- **Many-to-many joins** match multiple rows in both tables. This kind of join requires the use of an intermediary table.

The previous query shows a many-to-one join, since many musicians can have the same main instrument. Many-to-one joins are often used when a column's value should be limited to a set of options, such as fields that our GUI might represent with a Combobox widget. The table joined is often called a **lookup table**.

If we were to reverse our last query, it would be one-to-many:

```
SELECT instruments.name AS instrument, musicians.name AS musician
FROM instruments
  JOIN musicians ON musicians.main_instrument = instruments.id;
```

One-to-many joins are commonly used when a record has a list of sub-records associated with it; in this case, each instrument has a list of musicians who consider it their main instrument. The joined table is often called a **detail table**. The preceding SQL query will give you the following output:

instrument	musician
drums	Bill Bruford
keyboards	Keith Emerson
bass	Greg Lake
guitar	Robert Fripp
guitar	David Gilmour

Notice that guitar is duplicated in the instrument list. When two tables are joined, the rows of the result no longer refer to the same entity. One row in the instrument table represents an instrument.

One row in the `musician` table represents one musician. One row in *this* table represents an instrument-musician relationship.

Suppose we wanted to keep the output such that one row represented one instrument, but still include information about associated musicians in each row. To do this, we'll need to combine the matched musician rows using an **aggregate function** and a `GROUP BY` clause, as shown in the following SQL query:

```
SELECT instruments.name AS instrument,
   count(musicians.id) as musicians
FROM instruments
   JOIN musicians ON musicians.main_instrument = instruments.id
GROUP BY instruments.name;
```

The `GROUP BY` clause specifies which column or columns describe what each row in the output table represents. Output columns not in the `GROUP BY` clause must then be reduced to single values using an aggregate function.

In this case, we're using the `count()` aggregate function to count the total number of musician records associated with each instrument. Its output looks like this:

instrument	musicians
drums	1
keyboards	1
bass	1
guitar	2

Standard SQL contains several more aggregate functions, such as `min()`, `max()`, and `sum()`, and most SQL implementations extend this with their own functions as well.

Many-to-one and one-to-many joins don't quite cover every possible situation that databases need to model; quite often, a many-to-many relationship is required.

To demonstrate a many-to-many join, let's create a new table called bands, like so:

```
CREATE TABLE bands (id SERIAL PRIMARY KEY, name TEXT NOT NULL);
INSERT INTO bands(name)
VALUES ('ABWH'), ('ELP'), ('King Crimson'), ('Pink Floyd'), ('Yes');
```

A band has multiple musicians, and musicians can be part of multiple bands. How can we create a relationship between musicians and bands? If we added a band field to the `musicians` table, this would limit each musician to one band. If we added a `musician` field to the band table, this would limit each band to one musician. To make the connection, we need to create a **junction table**, in which each row represents a musician's membership in a band.

Create the `musicians_bands` table like so:

```
CREATE TABLE musicians_bands (
  musician_id INT REFERENCES musicians(id),
  band_id INT REFERENCES bands(id),
  PRIMARY KEY (musician_id, band_id)
);
INSERT INTO musicians_bands(musician_id, band_id)
VALUES (1, 3), (2, 2), (3, 2), (3, 3),
  (4, 1), (4, 2), (4, 5), (5,4);
```

The `musicians_bands` table simply contains two foreign key fields, one to point to a musician's ID and one to point to the band's ID.

Notice that instead of creating or specifying one field as the primary key, we use the combination of both fields as the primary key. It wouldn't make sense to have multiple rows with the same two values in them, so the combination makes an acceptable primary key.

To write a query that uses this relationship, our FROM clause needs to specify two JOIN statements: one from `musicians` to `musicians_bands` and one from `bands` to `musicians_bands`.

For example, let's get the names of the bands each musician has been in:

```
SELECT musicians.name, array_agg(bands.name) AS bands
FROM musicians
  JOIN musicians_bands ON musicians.id = musicians_bands.musician_id
  JOIN bands ON bands.id = musicians_bands.band_id
GROUP BY musicians.name
ORDER BY musicians.name ASC;
```

This query ties musicians to bands using the junction table, then displays musician names next to an aggregated list of the bands they've been in, and orders it by the musician's name. It gives you the following output:

name	bands
Bill Bruford	{ABWH,"King Crimson",Yes}
David Gilmour	{"Pink Floyd"}
Greg Lake	{ELP,"King Crimson"}
Keith Emerson	{ELP}
Robert Fripp	{"King Crimson"}

The array_agg() function used here aggregates string values into an array structure. This method, and the ARRAY data type, are specific to PostgreSQL.

There is no SQL standard function for aggregating string values, though most SQL implementations have a solution for it.

Managing transactions

While we can accomplish a lot of data manipulation in a single SQL query, there are times when a change requires multiple queries. Often in these cases, if one query fails, the whole set of queries must be reversed or else the data would be corrupted.

For example, suppose we want to insert 'Vocals' as a value in the instruments table, but we want it to be ID #1. To do that, we'd need to first move the other ID values in the instruments table up by one, adjust the foreign key values in the musicians table, then add the new row. The queries would look like this:

```
UPDATE instruments SET id=id+1;
UPDATE musicians SET main_instrument=main_instrument+1;
INSERT INTO instruments(id, name) VALUES (1, 'Vocals');
```

In this example, all three queries must run successfully in order to effect the change we want, and at the very least the first two must run to avoid data corruption. If only the first query ran, our data would be corrupt.

To do this safely, we need to use a **transaction**.

Using transactions in PostgreSQL involves three keywords, as shown here:

Keyword	Function
BEGIN	Start a transaction
ROLLBACK	Undo the transaction and start fresh
COMMIT	Permanently save the transaction

To put our queries in a transaction, we simply add BEGIN before the queries and COMMIT afterward, like so:

```
BEGIN;
UPDATE instruments SET id=id+1;
UPDATE musicians SET main_instrument=main_instrument+1;
INSERT INTO instruments(id, name) VALUES (1, 'Vocals');
COMMIT;
```

Now, if anything goes wrong with one of our queries, we can execute a ROLLBACK statement to revert the database to the state it was in when we called BEGIN.

> In DBAPI2-compatible modules like the psycopg2 module that we use in *Chapter 12, Improving Data Storage with SQL*, transaction management is often handled implicitly through connection settings, or explicitly through connection object methods, rather than using SQL statements.

Learning more

This has been a quick overview of SQL concepts and syntax; we've covered most of what you need to know to write a simple database application, but there's much more to learn. The PostgreSQL manual, available at https://www.postgresql.org/docs/manuals, is a great resource and reference for SQL syntax and the specific features of PostgreSQL.

packt.com

Subscribe to our online digital library for full access to over 7,000 books and videos, as well as industry leading tools to help you plan your personal development and advance your career. For more information, please visit our website.

Why subscribe?

- Spend less time learning and more time coding with practical eBooks and Videos from over 4,000 industry professionals
- Improve your learning with Skill Plans built especially for you
- Get a free eBook or video every month
- Fully searchable for easy access to vital information
- Copy and paste, print, and bookmark content

At www.packt.com, you can also read a collection of free technical articles, sign up for a range of free newsletters, and receive exclusive discounts and offers on Packt books and eBooks.

Other Books You May Enjoy

If you enjoyed this book, you may be interested in these other books by Packt:

Expert Python Programming - Fourth Edition

Michal Jaworski

Tarek Ziade

ISBN: 9781801071109

- Explore modern ways of setting up repeatable and consistent Python development environments
- Effectively package Python code for community and production use

- Learn modern syntax elements of Python programming, such as f-strings, enums, and lambda functions
- Demystify metaprogramming in Python with metaclasses
- Write concurrent code in Python
- Extend and integrate Python with code written in C and C++

Python Object-Oriented Programming - Fourth Edition

Steven F. Lott

Dusty Phillips

ISBN: 9781801077262

- Implement objects in Python by creating classes and defining methods
- Extend class functionality using inheritance
- Use exceptions to handle unusual situations cleanly
- Understand when to use object-oriented features, and more importantly, when not to use them
- Discover several widely used design patterns and how they are implemented in Python
- Uncover the simplicity of unit and integration testing and understand why they are so important
- Learn to statically type check your dynamic code
- Understand concurrency with asyncio and how it speeds up programs

Learn Python Programming - Third Edition

Fabrizio Romano

Heinrich Kruger

ISBN: 9781801815093

- Get Python up and running on Windows, Mac, and Linux
- Write elegant, reusable, and efficient code in any situation
- Avoid common pitfalls like duplication, complicated design, and over-engineering
- Understand when to use the functional or object-oriented approach to programming
- Build a simple API with FastAPI and program GUI applications with Tkinter
- Get an initial overview of more complex topics such as data persistence and cryptography
- Fetch, clean, and manipulate data, making efficient use of Python's built-in data structures

Packt is searching for authors like you

If you're interested in becoming an author for Packt, please visit authors.packtpub.com and apply today. We have worked with thousands of developers and tech professionals, just like you, to help them share their insight with the global tech community. You can make a general application, apply for a specific hot topic that we are recruiting an author for, or submit your own idea.

Share Your Thoughts

Now you've finished *Python GUI Programming with Tkinter, Second Edition*, we'd love to hear your thoughts! Scan the QR code below to go straight to the Amazon review page for this book and share your feedback or leave a review on the site that you purchased it from.

https://packt.link/r/1801815925

Your review is important to us and the tech community and will help us make sure we're delivering excellent quality content.

Index

A

ABQ AgriLabs
  data, recording 31-33
  problem, analyzing 29, 30
  problem, assessing 30
  problem, information gathering 30, 31
ABQ AgriLabs, data analyzing 33
  from application user 35, 36
  from data consumer 37
  from data originators 34
  from technical support 36
ABQ application menu
  File menu, adding 217-220
  Help menu, adding 216
  implementing 215, 216
  main menu, viewing 223
  settings menu, adding 220-222
ABQ database
  creating 415
  lookup tables, populating 420
  tables, creating 415
  view, creating 419, 420
ABQ Data Entry
  color, adding to 313-316
  company logo, adding to 278
  error dialogs, displaying 199, 200
  image path problem, dealing with 278-280
  users font options, providing 302-305
  weather data, downloading to 451
ABQ Data Entry application
  callback functions, writing 73
  cross-platform compatibility, improving 349
  data record form, building 66
  designing 42
  encoding, specifying for CSV file 351
  fields, grouping 44, 45

  form, laying out 46
  implementing 64
  input widgets 42-44
  laying out 47, 48
  platform-appropriate menus, creating 351
  preferences, storing 349, 350
  Python modules, importing 65
  rewriting, with classes 100
  starting 65
  testing 78
**ABQ Data Entry application, rewriting
    with classes**
  application class, creating 112-114
  form class, creating 106-111
  LabelInput class, creating 103-106
  StringVar, adding to Text widget 100, 101
ABQ data entry program specification
  writing 39-42
abq_data_entry.py file 168
accelerator keys 347
accelerators
  adding 355, 356
after() methods 495, 496
aggregate function 613
ANSI/ISO-standard SQL 604
API documentation 466
Apple human interface guidelines
  reference link 346
application
  problems, solving 194
  record list, adding to 254
  REST upload, integrating into 471
  running 188
  SFTPModel, using 487-489
  splitting, into multiple files 172
  testing 268

GUI freezes, mitigating 497-499
update() methods 494
uses 496
event sequence
examples 380
specifying 379
event type 379
executables
build, cleaning up 580
building 580
creating, with cx_Freeze 575

F

file browser
building 239
Treeview, configuring 240-242
Treeview, creating 240-242
Treeview, populating with data 242, 243
Treeview records, sorting 244-246
Treeview virtual events, using 247
filedialog 201
using 201-204
File menu 211
adding 217, 218
file reading
testing, in get_all_records() 383, 384
file saving
testing, in save_record() 385-387
filesystems 328
case sensitivity 331, 332
locations, identifying on OS 328
path separators and drives 328
path variables 333, 334
symbolic link 332, 333
fingerprint 479
first-in first-out (FIFO) data structure 506
first normal form 409, 410
fixtures 370, 374
floating-point error 141
focus 380
font options
providing, in ABQ Data Entry 302-305
foreign key 406
foreign key constraint 607

form class
creating 106-111
form GUI
updating, with validated widgets 146-148
form widgets
styles, adding to 316-318
validation interaction, implementing
between 149
freezing 575

G

geometry manager methods 8
grid() 14
pack() 14
place() 15
widgets, arranging with 14-18
get_all_records()
file reading, testing in 383, 384
implementing 233-235
get_file() method 471
get_record()
implementing 235, 236
Git
download link 190
using 189
Git repository
configuring 190
initializing 190
Global Interpreter Lock (GIL) 518, 519
globally unique identifier (GUID) 408, 583
global namespace 7
Gnome HIG 347
GNU Public License (GPL) 564
grab focus 380
graphs
creating, with Canvas 542
with Matplotlib 551
GUI
building, with Tkinter widgets 10-13
validated widgets, implementing 129
GUI elements
adding, for weather download 458-460
GUI mode 337, 338
GUI utility
used, for configuring PostgreSQL 405